OS X
Mountain Lion

the missing manual®

The book that should have been in the box®

"Here's to the crazy ones.
The rebels. The troublemakers. The ones who see things differently.
While some may see them as the crazy ones,
we see genius."

Dedicated to the memory of Steve Jobs

OS X
Mountain Lion

the missing manual®

The book that should have been in the box®

David Pogue

O'REILLY®

Beijing | Cambridge | Farnham | Köln | Sebastopol | Tokyo

OS X Mountain Lion: The Missing Manual

by David Pogue

Copyright © 2012 David Pogue. All rights reserved.
Printed in the United States of America.

Published by O'Reilly Media, Inc.,
1005 Gravenstein Highway North, Sebastopol, CA 95472.

O'Reilly Media books may be purchased for educational, business, or sales promotional use. Online editions are also available for most titles: *safari@oreilly. com*. For more information, contact our corporate/institutional sales department: 800-998-9938 or *corporate@oreilly.com*.

July 2012:	First Edition.
August 2012:	Second Printing.
September 2012:	Third Printing.
May 2013:	Fourth Printing.

ISBN: 978-1-4493-33027-9
[LSI] [05/13]

Table of Contents

Part Three: The Components of OS X

Part Six: Appendixes

TABLE OF CONTENTS

The Missing Credits

About the Author

 David Pogue (author) is the weekly tech columnist for *The New York Times*, host of several *NOVA* miniseries on PBS, an Emmy-winning correspondent for *CBS News Sunday Morning*, and the creator of the Missing Manual series. He's the author or coauthor of 60 books, including 25 in this series, six in the "For Dummies" line (including *Macs, Magic, Opera,* and *Classical Music*), two novels, and *The World According to Twitter*. In his other life, David is a former Broadway show conductor, a piano player, and a magician. He lives in Connecticut with his three awesome children.

Links to his columns and weekly videos await at *www.davidpogue.com*. He welcomes feedback about his books by email at *david@pogueman.com*.

About the Creative Team

Julie Van Keuren (copy editor) quit her newspaper job in 2006 to move to Montana and live the freelancing dream. She and her husband, M.H. (who is living the novel-writing dream), have two sons, Dexter and Michael. *Email:* little_media@yahoo.com.

Kirill Voronin (technical editor) is the head of an IT consulting company, aptly called Shortcut, based in Moscow, Russia. He has worked with Macs since the '90s, and he's an Apple Certified System Administrator and Apple Certified Trainer for IT courses. He lives with his wife, Maria, and son, Nil. In his spare time, he enjoys backpacking. Email: *kirill.voronin@shortcut.ru*.

Phil Simpson (design and layout) runs his graphic design business from Southbury, Connecticut. His work includes corporate branding, publication design, communications support, and advertising. In his free time, he is a homebrewer, ice cream maker, wannabe woodworker, and is on a few tasting panels. He lives with his wife and four great felines. Email: *phil.simpson@pmsgraphics.com*.

Brian Jepson (technical consultant) is an O'Reilly editor and hacker, and co-organizer of Providence Geeks and the Rhode Island Mini Maker Faire. He's also been involved in various ways over the years with AS220, a nonprofit arts center in Providence, Rhode Island. Email: *bjepson@oreilly.com*.

Acknowledgments

Over the years, over the eight editions of this book, many friends and colleagues have contributed enthusiasm, expertise, and even prose to this book's editions. They include Zachary Brass, Dan Pourhadi, Rich Koster, J.D. Biersdorfer, Teresa Noelle Roberts, and Lesa Snider.

In addition to the dream team members identified above, I owe debts of thanks to O'Reilly's Missing Manuals editor-in-chief, Brian Sawyer; Apple's Monica Sarkar for going beyond the call of duty to chase down tweaky tech answers; Ben Waldie, who did a beautiful job updating the Automator/AppleScript material in Chapter 7; Philip Michaels, who wrote about Game Center for this book; my crack team of eleventh-hour proofreaders, Diana D'Abruzzo, Kellee Katagi, and Judy Le; the PBS NOVA crew, who gracefully accommodated my nutty book schedule during our shoots; my assistant Jan Carpenter, who fixed hundreds of captions and generally helped me survive; Brian Jepson, who wrote up OS X Server; and the most spectacular screenshotter/index-marathoner ever, my beautiful Nicki.

I've never met, or even spoken to, Kirill Voronin; he lives in Moscow. But he submitted so many corrections to the previous edition's Errata page online that I wound up hiring him to be the tech editor for this book—and he knocked it out of the park.

I also wish I could send out an "I Made the Book Better!" T-shirt to every reader who ever took the time to write with corrections, suggestions, tips, and tricks. And thanks, as always, to David Rogelberg for believing in the idea.

Above all, this book owes its existence to the patience and affection of Kelly, Tia, and Jeffrey. They make these books—and everything else—possible.

—David Pogue

The Missing Manual Series

Missing Manuals are witty, superbly written guides to computer products that don't come with printed manuals (which is just about all of them). Each book features a handcrafted index; cross-references to specific page numbers (not just "see Chapter 14"); and an ironclad promise never to put an apostrophe in the possessive pronoun *its*.

Here's a list of current and upcoming titles:

For the Mac

- *AppleScript: The Missing Manual* by Adam Goldstein

- *FileMaker Pro 12: The Missing Manual* by Susan Prosser and Stuart Gripman

- *iMovie '11 & iDVD: The Missing Manual* by David Pogue and Aaron Miller

- *iPhoto '11: The Missing Manual* by David Pogue and Lesa Snider

- *iWork '09: The Missing Manual* by Josh Clark

- *Office 2011: The Missing Manual* by Chris Grover

- *Switching to the Mac: The Missing Manual, Mountain Lion Edition* by David Pogue

- *Photoshop CS6: The Missing Manual* by Lesa Snider

For Windows

- *Windows 7: The Missing Manual by* David Pogue
- *Windows 8: The Missing Manual* by David Pogue
- *Access 2010: The Missing Manual* by Matthew MacDonald
- *Excel 2010: The Missing Manual* by Matthew MacDonald
- *Microsoft Project 2010: The Missing Manual* by Bonnie Biafore
- *Office 2010: The Missing Manual* by Chris Grover, Matthew MacDonald, and E. A. Vander Veer
- *QuickBooks 2012: The Missing Manual* by Bonnie Biafore
- *Photoshop CS6: The Missing Manual* by Lesa Snider
- *Photoshop Elements 10: The Missing Manual* by Barbara Brundage

Electronics

- *David Pogue's Digital Photography: The Missing Manual* by David Pogue
- *iPhone: The Missing Manual,* Fifth Edition by David Pogue
- *iPhone App Development: The Missing Manual* by Craig Hockenberry
- *iPad: The Missing Manual, Fourth Edition* by J.D. Biersdorfer
- *iPod: The Missing Manual, Tenth Edition* by J.D. Biersdorfer
- *Kindle Fire: The Missing Manual* by Peter Meyers
- *Motorola Xoom: The Missing Manual* by Preston Gralla
- *Netbooks: The Missing Manual* by J.D. Biersdorfer
- *NOOK Tablet: The Missing Manual* by Preston Gralla
- *Droid X: The Missing Manual* by Preston Gralla
- *Droid X2: The Missing Manual* by Preston Gralla
- *Galaxy S II: The Missing Manual* by Preston Gralla
- *Galaxy Tab: The Missing Manual* by Preston Gralla

Web Technologies

- *Adobe Edge Preview 7: The Missing Manual,* Third Edition by Chris Grover
- *Creating a Web Site: The Missing Manual,* Third Edition by Matthew MacDonald
- *CSS: The Missing Manual,* Second Edition, by David Sawyer McFarland
- *Dreamweaver CS6: The Missing Manual* by David Sawyer McFarland
- *Flash CS6: The Missing Manual* by E. A. Vander Veer and Chris Grover

- *Google+: The Missing Manual* by Kevin Purdy
- *HTML5: The Missing Manual* by Matthew MacDonald
- *JavaScript & jQuery: The Missing Manual*, Second Edition by David Sawyer McFarland
- *PHP & MySQL: The Missing Manual* by Brett McLaughlin

Life
- *Personal Investing: The Missing Manual* by Bonnie Biafore
- *Your Brain: The Missing Manual* by Matthew MacDonald
- *Your Body: The Missing Manual* by Matthew MacDonald
- *Your Money: The Missing Manual* by J.D. Roth

Introduction

OS X is an impressive technical achievement; many experts call it the best personal-computer operating system on earth. But beware its name.

The X is meant to be a Roman numeral, pronounced "ten." Don't say "oh ess ex." You'll get funny looks in public.

In any case, OS X Mountain Lion is the ninth major version of Apple's Unix-based operating system. It's got very little in common with the original Mac operating system, the one that saw Apple through the 1980s and 1990s. Apple dumped that in 2001, when CEO Steve Jobs decided it was time for a change. Apple had just spent too many years piling new features onto a software foundation originally poured in 1984. Programmers and customers complained of the "spaghetti code" the Mac OS had become.

On the other hand, underneath OS X's classy, translucent desktop is Unix, the industrial-strength, rock-solid OS that drives many a Web site and university. It's not new by any means; in fact, it's decades old and has been polished by generations of programmers.

Note: Apple no longer refers to its computer operating system as Mac OS X. Now it's just "OS X," without the "Mac." Why? Apple says it's to match up better with iOS, its operating system for the iPhone and iPad.

The Mac Becomes an iPad

If you could choose only one word to describe Apple's overarching design goal in Lion and Mountain Lion, there's no doubt about what it would be: *iPad*. That's right.

In this software, Apple has gone about as far as it could go in trying to turn the Mac into an iPad.

Two things made the iPad the fastest-selling electronic gadget in history. First, it's so simple. No overlapping windows; every app runs full screen. No Save command; everything is autosaved. No files or folders. No menus. All your apps are in one place, the Home screen. To beginners, technophobes, and even old-timers, the iPad's software represents a refreshing decluttering of the modern computer.

The second huge iPad sales point is that multitouch screen. You operate the whole thing by touching or dragging your fingers on the glass. For example, you cycle through screens by swiping. You zoom out on a map, photo, or Web page by pinching two fingers. You rotate a photo by twisting two fingers, and so on.

So Apple thought, if simplicity and touch gestures made the iPad a megahit, why can't we do the same for the Mac?

And it set out to bring as many of the iPad's features and as much of its personality to your Mac as possible. Today's OS X features like Full Screen mode, Auto Save, and Launchpad are total iPad rip-offs; if Apple hadn't stolen these features from itself, it would surely be suing for copyright infringement. In Mountain Lion, even the app names are the same as what's on iOS: Reminders, Notes, Notification Center, Game Center, and so on.

UP TO SPEED

What's Missing

There are 200 new features in Mountain Lion, by Apple's count. A lot of it is welcome new features. (Check out "what's new in Mountain Lion" in this book's index.)

But some of the changes aren't additions; they're subtractions. A few traditional features didn't make the cut. Here's a list of the most notable excisions.

Some disappeared back in Lion: Front Row, the feature that turned your Mac into a living-room multimedia player; faxing; iSync; and FTP services, no doubt because FTP is not a very secure protocol.

The Sidebar icons in the Finder are no longer in color; they're all sort of washed out and monochrome, a trend in the Mac OS these days. And the tiny list-view icon of an open folder no longer looks like a tiny open folder.

Some changes are really tiny. The Digital Color Meter utility no longer converts hex colors and can no longer copy color data to the Clipboard. Image Capture has lost its ability to function as a remote-controlled Webcam or nannycam. iPhoto no longer has its own Time Machine mode for recovering lost photos. There's no more To Do list in Mail. You can no longer zoom into a Quick Look preview.

In Mountain Lion, Web Sharing is gone. The ability to read RSS feeds in Mail and Safari is gone, too. All shreds of Notes and To Dos are gone from Mail (because you now get dedicated Notes and Reminders apps). Techies might mourn the loss of the X11 app and Xgrid support.

Lots of things have been renamed, too, so that they match the iPhone/iPad better: iCal, Address Book, and iChat are now Calendar, Contacts, and Messages.

Some of those losses might sting a little. But in the big Mountain Lion picture, you gain a lot more than you lose.

Apple even brought over the whole multitouch thing to the Mac. No, you don't touch the screen; you'd get screaming arm pain if you had to spend the day with your arm outstretched, manipulating tiny controls on a vertical surface three feet away. (The resulting ache actually has a name in the computer biz: gorilla arm.)

Instead, you use all those same iPad gestures and more, right on the surface of your laptop trackpad, Apple Magic Trackpad, or (if you have Apple's Magic Mouse) the top surface of the mouse.

All of Mountain Lion's big-ticket features are intended to work together. For example, suppose you're looking at a document in full-screen view (feature #1). How are you supposed to switch to the next app? By swiping across the trackpad in the "next app" gesture (feature #2). Then you might pinch four fingers together (feature #3) to open Launchpad so you can open another program.

It's a new way to work, for sure. And it's optional. If it doesn't float your boat, you can ignore all of it (full-screen, gestures, Launchpad, Auto Save). But you should at least make an informed decision—and this book, especially Chapter 0, should come in handy that way.

Note: Truth is, Mountain Lion represents only a gentle continuation of the iPadization that began with OS X 10.7, known as Lion. Often in this book, you'll read references to "Lion/Mountain Lion," because they're fundamentally the same software. Even so, there are enough nips, tucks, and improvements to justify the 20 bucks you just shelled out.

About This Book

You can't get Mountain Lion on a disc or flash drive; it's a download-only operating system. In other words, you don't get a single page of printed instructions.

To find your way around, you're expected to use Apple's online help system. And as you'll quickly discover, these help pages are tersely written, offer very little technical depth, lack useful examples, and provide no tutorials whatsoever. You can't even mark your place, underline, or read them in the bathroom.

The purpose of this book, then, is to serve as the manual that should have accompanied OS X—version 10.8 in particular.

OS X Mountain Lion: The Missing Manual is designed to accommodate readers at every technical level. The primary discussions are written for advanced-beginner or intermediate Mac fans. But if you're a Mac first-timer, miniature sidebar articles called Up To Speed provide the introductory information you need to understand the topic at hand. If you're a Mac veteran, on the other hand, keep your eye out for similar shaded boxes called Power Users' Clinic. They offer more technical tips, tricks, and shortcuts.

When you write a book like this, you do a lot of soul-searching about how much stuff to cover. Of course, a thinner book, or at least a thinner-looking one, is always preferable; plenty of readers are intimidated by a book that dwarfs the Tokyo White Pages.

On the other hand, Apple keeps adding features and rarely takes them away. So this book isn't getting any thinner.

Even so, some chapters come with free downloadable appendixes—PDF documents, available on this book's "Missing CD" page at *www.missingmanuals.com*—that go into further detail on some of the tweakiest features. (You'll see references to them sprinkled throughout the book.)

Maybe this idea will save a few trees—and a few back muscles when you try to pick this book up.

About the Outline

OS X Mountain Lion: The Missing Manual is divided into six parts, each containing several chapters:

- **Part One: The OS X Desktop** covers everything you see on the screen when you turn on an OS X computer: the Dock, the Sidebar, Spotlight, Dashboard, Spaces, Mission Control, Launchpad, Time Machine, icons, windows, menus, scroll bars, the Trash, aliases, the menu, and so on.

- **Part Two: Programs in OS X** is dedicated to the proposition that an operating system is little more than a launchpad for *programs*—the actual applications you use in your everyday work, such as email programs, Web browsers, word processors, graphics suites, and so on. These chapters describe how to work with applications in OS X—how to open them, switch among them, swap data between them, use them to create and open files, and control them using the AppleScript and Automator automation tools.

- **Part Three: The Components of OS X** is an item-by-item discussion of the individual software nuggets that make up this operating system—the 29 panels of System Preferences, and the 50-some programs in your Applications and Utilities folders.

- **Part Four: The Technologies of OS X** treads in more advanced territory. Networking, file sharing, and screen sharing are, of course, tasks OS X was born to do. These chapters cover all of the above, plus the prodigious visual talents of OS X (fonts, printing, graphics, handwriting recognition), and its multimedia gifts (sound, speech, movies).

- **Part Five: OS X Online** covers all the Internet features of OS X, including the Mail email program and the Safari Web browser; Messages for instant messaging and audio or video chats; Internet sharing; Apple's free, online iCloud services; and connecting to, and controlling, your Mac from across the wires—FTP, SSH, VPN, and so on.

- **Part Six: Appendixes.** This book's appendixes include guidance on installing this operating system; a troubleshooting handbook; a Windows-to-Mac dictionary (to help Windows refugees find the new locations of familiar features in OS X); and a thorough master list of all the keyboard shortcuts and trackpad/mouse gestures in Mountain Lion.

About→These→Arrows

Throughout this book, and throughout the *Missing Manual* series, you'll find sentences like this one: "Open the System folder→Libraries→Fonts folder." That's shorthand for a much longer instruction that directs you to open three nested folders in sequence, like this: "On your hard drive, you'll find a folder called System. Open that. Inside the System folder window is a folder called Libraries; double-click to open it. Inside *that* folder is yet another one called Fonts. Double-click to open it, too."

Similarly, this kind of arrow shorthand helps to simplify the business of choosing commands in menus, such as →Dock→Position on Left.

About MissingManuals.com

To get the most out of this book, visit *www.missingmanuals.com*. Click the "Missing CD-ROM" link—and then this book's title—to reveal a neat, organized, chapter-by-chapter list of the shareware and freeware mentioned in this book.

The Web site also offers corrections and updates to the book. (To see them, click the book's title, and then click View/Submit Errata.) In fact, please submit such corrections and updates yourself! In an effort to keep the book as up to date and accurate as possible, each time O'Reilly prints more copies of this book, I'll make any confirmed corrections you've suggested. I'll also note such changes on the Web site so that you can mark important corrections into your own copy of the book, if you like. And I'll keep the book current as Apple releases more Mac OS 10.8 updates.

The Very Basics

To use this book, and indeed to use a Macintosh computer, you need to know a few basics. This book assumes you're familiar with a few terms and concepts:

- **Clicking.** To *click* means to point the arrow cursor at something on the screen and then—without moving the cursor—press and release the clicker button on the mouse or trackpad. To *double-click,* of course, means to click twice in rapid succession, again without moving the cursor at all. And to *drag* means to move the cursor while holding down the button.

 When you're told to ⌘-*click* something, you click while pressing the ⌘ key (which is next to the space bar). *Shift-clicking, Option-clicking,* and *Control-clicking* work the same way—just click while pressing the corresponding key.

 (There's also *right-clicking.* That important topic is described in depth on page 237.)

- **Menus.** The *menus* are the words at the top of your screen: , File, Edit, and so on. Click one to make a list of commands appear.

 Some people click and release to open a menu and then, after reading the choices, click again on the one they want. Other people like to press the mouse button continuously after the initial click on the menu title, drag down the list to the desired command, and only then release the mouse button. Either method works fine.

- **Keyboard shortcuts.** If you're typing along in a burst of creative energy, it's disruptive to have to grab the mouse to use a menu. That's why many Mac fans prefer to trigger menu commands by pressing key combinations. For example, in word processors, you can press ⌘-B to produce a boldface word. When you read an instruction like "press ⌘-B," start by pressing the ⌘ key, and then, while it's down, type the letter B, and finally release both keys.

Tip: You know what's really nice? The keystroke to open the Preferences dialog box in every Apple program—Mail, Safari, iMovie, iPhoto, TextEdit, Preview, and on and on—is always the same: ⌘-comma. Better yet, that standard is catching on in other apps, too, like Word, Excel, and PowerPoint.

- **Gestures.** A *gesture* is a swipe across your trackpad (on your laptop, or on an external Apple trackpad) or across the top surface of the Apple Magic Mouse. Gestures have been given huge importance in Mountain Lion. Page 833 contains a handy list of these gestures, or you can get a tutorial of life with gestures in Chapter 0.

- **Icons.** The colorful inch-tall pictures that appear in your various desktop folders are the graphic symbols that represent each program, disk, and document on your computer. If you click an icon one time, it darkens, indicating that you've just *highlighted* or *selected* it. Now you're ready to manipulate it by using, for example, a menu command.

- **Dialog boxes.** See Figure I-1 for a tour of the onscreen elements you'll frequently be asked to use, like checkboxes, radio buttons, tabs, and so on.

A few more tips on mastering the Mac keyboard appear at the beginning of Chapter 6. Otherwise, if you've mastered this much information, you have all the technical background you need to enjoy *OS X Mountain Lion: The Missing Manual*.

Figure I-1:
Knowing what you're doing on the Mac often requires knowing what things are called. Here are some of the most common onscreen elements. They include checkboxes (turn on as many as you like) and radio buttons (only one can be turned on in each grouping).

Pressing Return is usually the same as clicking the default button—the lower-right button that almost always means "OK, I'm done here."

Part One:
The OS X Desktop

1

The Mountain Lion Landscape

As noted in the Introduction, Apple's overarching design philosophy in creating its operating system lately has been "Make it more like an iPad." But what does that mean? Do all the new iPaddish features really add up to a single, flowing, new way of working?

The following pages are a tutorial. They walk you through a typical Mountain-ized working session the way Apple intended you to work. If you follow along, you'll wind up with a good sense of how much you like (or don't like) the iPaddified Mac.

Note: In this book, you'll see touch gestures provided separately for *trackpads* (either the one on your laptop, or Apple's external Magic Trackpad) and the *Magic Mouse* (Apple's latest mouse, whose surface is touch sensitive).

Why aren't the gestures identical? Because the Magic Mouse requires at least two fingers to *hold,* so some of the more multi-fingered gestures aren't practical. And remember, on the trackpad you need a finger just to move the cursor—and on the Magic Mouse, *moving the mouse* moves the cursor.

Launchpad

All right. It's Monday morning. Yawn, stretch, fluff your hair (if any).

You want to start with a quick Web check. And for that, you'll need Safari, the Mac's Web browser.

1. **Put four fingers on the trackpad (thumb and three fingers), and pinch them inward toward the center.**

 If you have a Magic Mouse, just click Launchpad on the Dock.

Your screen goes dark and fills up with what looks like the Home screen on the iPhone or iPad. You've just opened the Launchpad. Here are the icons of all your Mac's programs, evenly spaced, arrayed (if there are lots of them) on multiple "pages." Figure 0-1 shows the idea.

Note: The four-finger pinch gesture opens Launchpad only on trackpads. If you don't have one, click the Launchpad icon on the Dock instead. It looks like a rocket ship (⊘).

Figure 0-1:
Launchpad displays all of your programs' icons at once, neatly spaced and ready to open with a single click. To see more pages full of icons, swipe left or right with two fingers on your trackpad (or with one finger on your Magic Mouse).

New in Mountain Lion: The search bar at top.

Suppose, for the sake of this exercise, that you can't find the Safari icon. It's on a different page.

2. **With two fingers on the trackpad, swipe left or right to change "pages." Stop when you spot Safari.**

 If you have a Magic Mouse, swipe left or right with *one* finger.

Tip: This same gesture—swiping left or right—also works as Back or Forward in Safari.

You could, if you like, customize Launchpad just as you would on an iPhone or an iPad. You can drag the icons around, put them on different pages, combine them into folders, or delete them (see page 164). For now, you just want to open the Web browser.

3. **Click the Safari icon once.**

 That's one difference between opening a program in Launchpad (one click) and in your Applications folder (two clicks).

Full-Screen Mode, Safari

Once Safari opens, you're ready for your first full-screen experience.

1. Click the ⬈ icon in the upper-right corner of the Safari window.

With a smooth animation, your Mac hides the menu bar and the bookmarks bar. The only thing remaining is the address bar. The window's edges expand all the way to the edges of the screen (Figure 0-2).

Tip: You may as well learn the keyboard shortcut to enter full-screen mode: Control-⌘-F. The same keystroke *leaves* full-screen mode, but you can also tap the Esc key for that purpose.

Figure 0-2:
This, ladies and gentlemen, is full-screen mode, one of the flagship features of Mountain Lion. The idea is to fight back against the forces of window clutter that have been encroaching on your document windows for years now. Your actual work, your photo or Web page, fills every pixel of that giant screen you paid so much money for.

You don't have to panic, though. The menu bar is still available: Move the pointer to the top of the screen to make the menus reappear.

Tip: Wouldn't it be nice if there were a keyboard shortcut for bringing the menu bar back—if nothing else, so that you can check your battery level and the time of day? There is—but not one that Apple intended. Just press ⌘-space bar. That's the keystroke for Spotlight, the Mac's master search bar—but it also makes the menu bar appear. Press the same keystroke to hide the menu bar again.

For the next demonstration, call up an actual Web page, preferably one with a lot of text on it—*www.nytimes.com*, for example. Now suppose you want to scroll down the page.

2. With two fingers on the trackpad, drag upward.

If you have a Magic Mouse, drag up with *one* finger.

If you just tried this, you're no doubt frowning right now. You just scrolled *down* the page by moving your fingers *up*. That's backward, isn't it?

For your entire computing career so far, you've always dragged the scroll bar *down* to move the contents of the page *up*—and now, in Lion/Mountain Lion, Apple has swapped the directions. Why would Apple throw such a monkey wrench into your life?

The main reason is (what else?) to make the Mac match the iPad/iPhone, where you drag your finger *up* to move the page *up*.

Anyway, you have two choices: You can spend a couple of days getting used to the new arrangement—or you can put things back the way they've always been. (To do that, open System Preferences. *For a trackpad:* Click Trackpad, click Scroll & Zoom, and then turn off "Scroll direction: natural." *For a Magic Mouse:* Click Mouse, click Point & Click, and then turn off "Scroll direction: natural.")

Note: If you have a non-Apple mouse that has a scroll wheel, then the Mouse preference pane doesn't offer this scroll-direction option. You can still reverse the scroll-direction logic, though, if you're handy in Terminal (page 469).

Just open Terminal and type *defaults write ~/Library/Preferences/.GlobalPreferences com.apple.swipescroll-direction -bool false.* When you press Return and log out, you'll find that the time-honored scroll directions have been restored.

3. **Find a photo or a block of text. With two fingers, lightly double-tap the trackpad.**

 These are *taps*, not full clicks. On the Magic Mouse, double-tap with *one* finger.

 Safari neatly magnifies the photo or text block to fill the screen, just as on an iPhone or an iPad. Neat, huh?

4. **Repeat the double-tap to restore the original size. Click a link to visit a different page.**

 For this demonstration, it doesn't make any difference what other Web page you visit. The point is for you to see how cool it is when you swipe your trackpad instead of clicking the Back button.

5. **Go back to the first page by swiping leftward with two fingers on the trackpad.**

 On a Magic Mouse, use *one* finger.

 The previous page slides back into view as though it's a tile sliding back into place. You can swipe the other way, too—to the right—to go forward a page.

Full-Screen Apps, Mission Control

You're still in Safari, right? And it's still full screen, right?

But if Safari is full screen, how are you supposed to get to other open programs? That's what you'll find out in this exercise. You'll get to see what it's like to run multiple full-screen apps.

1. **Pinch your trackpad with your thumb and three fingers.**

 Launchpad appears, at your service. (As you may recall, this doesn't work on the Magic Mouse, so if you're trackpadless, you'll have to exit full-screen mode and then click Launchpad on the Dock.)

2. **Find Calendar.**

 You may have to change Launchpad "pages" to find it. Swipe horizontally with two fingers (trackpad) or one finger (Magic Mouse) to change pages.

3. **Click to open Calendar. Make the new window full screen by clicking the ⬀ in the upper-right corner.**

 In theory, you now have *two* apps running at full screen: Safari and Calendar. Now comes the fun part.

4. **With three fingers on the trackpad, swipe left or right.**

 (On the Magic Mouse, use *two* fingers.)

 The full-screen apps slide into or out of view. If you keep three-finger swiping to the right, you'll see that Dashboard is all the way at the left end of the "channels" that you're changing. (If it doesn't work, somebody might have changed the setting to require *four* fingers in System Preferences.)

 You'll also discover that any *other* programs—the ones that aren't full screen—are gathered onto a *single* screen, as they have been for years. Each full-screen app is one "screen," and the Finder and all your other apps huddle on another one. But it doesn't have to be that way.

5. **With three fingers on the trackpad, swipe upward.**

 If you have a Magic Mouse, double-tap (don't fully click) with two fingers.

 You now enter Mission Control, a special screen full of miniatures of all your *other* screens; see Figure 0-3. (Again, if three fingers doesn't work, someone might have changed your trackpad preferences to require four fingers.)

 Mission Control has all kinds of cool features. It lets you jump to one window in a haystack. It lets you set up multiple virtual screens. It lets you reorganize the full-screen app screens you already have. For the full rundown, jump to page 173.

In this miniature crash course, you've had a glimpse at the future that awaits you: a future of trackpad (or Magic Mouse) finger gestures, full-screen apps, and the new centralized organizing features like Launchpad and Mission Control.

If any of this seems intimidating (or unnecessary), here's the point to remember: *It's all optional.* If you think the Mac works just fine without them, you can ignore the

new features and forget about them completely; all the techniques you already know still work just fine.

But if you think you could get efficiency and pleasure out of adopting a couple of these features, then Mountain Lion is ready for you. Full speed ahead!

Figure 0-3:
Here in Mission Control, each full-screen app gets its own "screen," as indicated by the map at top. But every running program appears here in the main screen area, in miniature. You can click one to jump there, or point and then press the space bar to get a full-size Quick Look.

Folders & Windows

Getting into OS X

When you first turn on a Mac running OS X 10.8, an Apple logo greets you, soon followed by an animated, rotating "Please wait" gear cursor—and then you're in. No progress bar, no red tape.

Logging In

What happens next depends on whether you're the Mac's sole proprietor or have to share it with other people in an office, school, or household.

- **If it's your own Mac,** and you've already been through the setup process described in Appendix A, no big deal. You arrive at the OS X desktop.

- **If it's a shared Mac,** you may encounter the newly redesigned login screen, shown in Figure 1-1. It's like a portrait gallery, set against a handsome piece of dark gray linen. Click your icon.

 If the Mac asks for your password, type it and then click Log In (or press Return). You arrive at the desktop.

Note: The *very* first time you run Mountain Lion, you get a huge Scrolling in Mountain Lion warning window. Apple wants to draw your attention to the new drag-up-to-scroll-up behavior of a fresh Mountain Lion installation, which freaks out a lot of baffled customers. For details on this whole reversed-scrolling business (and how to turn it off), see page 12.

Chapter 13 offers much more on this business of user accounts and logging in.

Note: In certain especially paranoid workplaces, you may not see the rogue's gallery shown in Figure 1-1. You may just get two text boxes, where you're supposed to type in your name and password. Without even the icons of known account holders, an evil hacker's job is that much more difficult.

Figure 1-1:
On Macs used by multiple people, this is one of the first things you see upon turning on the computer. Click your name. (If the list is long, you may have to swipe the trackpad to find your name—or just type its first few letters.)

Inset: At this point, you're asked to type in your password. Type it, and then click Log In (or press Return). If you type the wrong password, the box vibrates, in effect shaking its little dialog-box head, suggesting that you guess again.

The Elements of the OS X Desktop

The desktop is the shimmering, three-dimensional OS X landscape shown in Figure 1-2. On a new Mac, it's covered by a photo of a spectacular spiral galaxy; if you lean forward and squint, you might just be able to make out Apple's headquarters. (If you upgraded from an earlier version of OS X, you keep whatever desktop picture you had before.)

If you've ever used a computer before, most of the objects on your screen are nothing more than updated versions of familiar elements. Here's a quick tour.

Note: If your desktop looks even emptier than this—no menus, no icons, almost nothing on the Dock—then somebody in charge of your Mac has turned on *Simple Finder mode* for you. Details on page 512.

The Dock

This row of translucent, almost photographic icons is a launcher for the programs, files, folders, and disks you use often—and an indicator to let you know which programs are already open. They appear to rest on a sheet of transparent smoked glass.

In principle, the Dock is very simple:

- **Programs go on the left side.** Everything else goes on the right, including documents, folders, and disks. (Figure 1-2 shows the dividing line.)

- **You can add a new icon to the Dock by dragging it there.** Rearrange Dock icons by dragging them. Remove a Dock icon by dragging it away from the Dock—and enjoy the animated puff of smoke that appears when you release the mouse button. (You can't, however, remove the icon of a program that's currently open.)

Figure 1-2:
The OS X landscape looks like a more futuristic version of the operating systems you know and love. This is just a starting point, however. You can dress it up with a different background picture, adjust your windows in a million ways, and, of course, fill the Dock with only the programs, disks, folders, and files you need.

- **Click something once to open it.** When you click a program's icon, a tiny, bright, micro-spotlight dot appears under it to let you know it's open.

 When you click a folder's icon, you get a *stack*—an arcing row of icons, or a grid of them, that indicates what's inside. See page 134 for more on stacks.

- **Each Dock icon sprouts a pop-up menu.** To see the menu, hold the mouse button down on a Dock icon—or Control-click it, or right-click it. A shortcut menu of useful commands pops right out.

- **If you have a trackpad, you can view miniatures of all open windows in a program by pointing to its Dock icon and then swiping down with three fingers.** Details on how to turn on this feature are on page 199.

Because the Dock is such a critical component of OS X, Apple has decked it out with enough customization controls to keep you busy experimenting for months. You can

change its size, move it to the sides of your screen, hide it entirely, and so on. Chapter 4 contains complete instructions for using and understanding the Dock.

The menu

The menu houses important Mac-wide commands like Sleep, Restart, and Shut Down. They're always available, no matter which program you're using.

The menu bar

Every popular operating system saves space by concealing its most important commands in menus that drop down. OS X's menus are especially refined:

- **They stay down.** OS X menus stay open until you click the mouse, trigger a command from the keyboard, or buy a new computer, whichever comes first.

Tip: Actually, menus are even smarter than that. If you give the menu name a quick click, the menu opens and stays open. If you click the menu name and hold the mouse button down for a moment, the menu opens but closes again when you release the button. Apple figures that, in that case, you're just exploring, reading, or hunting for a certain command.

- **They're logically arranged.** The first menu in every program, which appears in bold lettering, tells you at a glance what program you're in (Safari, Microsoft Word, whatever). The commands in this Application menu include About (which indicates what version of the program you're using), Preferences, Quit, and commands like Hide Others and Show All (which help control window clutter, as described on page 204).

 In short, all the Application menu's commands actually pertain to the application you're using.

 The File and Edit menus come next. The File menu contains commands for opening, saving, and closing files. (See the logic?) The Edit menu contains the Cut, Copy, and Paste commands.

 The last menu is almost always Help. It opens a miniature Web browser that lets you search the online Mac help files for explanatory text.

- **You can operate them from the keyboard.** Once you've clicked open a menu, you can highlight any command in it just by typing the first letter (*g* for Get Info, for example). (It's especially great for "Your country" pop-up menus on Web sites, where "United States" is about 200 countries down in the list. You can type *united s* to jump right to it.)

 You can also press Tab to open the next menu, Shift-Tab to open the previous one, and Return or Enter to "click" the highlighted command.

Note: The menu bar is partly see-through, for no apparent reason. You can turn that off if you want; open System Preferences→Desktop & Screen Saver→Desktop, and then turn off "Translucent menu bar."

Disk icons on the desktop

For years, Apple has encouraged its flock to keep a clean desktop, to get rid of all the icons that many of us leave strewn around. Especially the hard drive icon, which had appeared in the upper-right corner of the screen since the original 1984 Mac.

Today, the Macintosh HD icon doesn't appear on the screen. "Look," Apple seems to be saying, "if you want access to your files and folders, just open them directly—from the Dock or from your Home folder (page 71). Most of the stuff on the hard drive is system files of no interest to you, so let's just hide that icon, shall we?"

Note: If you'd prefer that the disk icons return to your desktop where they used to be, Mountain Lion can accommodate you. Choose Finder→Preferences, click General, and turn on the checkboxes of the disks whose icons you want on the desktop: hard disks, external disks, CDs, and so on.

Windows and How to Work Them

In designing OS X, one of Apple's key goals was to address the window-proliferation problem. As you create more files, stash them in more folders, and launch more programs, it's easy to wind up paralyzed before a screen awash with overlapping rectangles.

That's the problem admirably addressed by Mission Control, described in detail on page 173. Some handy clutter and navigation controls are built into the windows themselves, too. For example:

The Sidebar

The Sidebar (Figure 1-3) is the pane at the left side of every Finder window, unless you've hidden it. (It's also at the left side of every Open dialog box and every full-sized Save dialog box.)

The Sidebar has as many as three sections, each preceded by a collapsible heading.

Note: The little flippy triangles that could collapse (hide) each Sidebar heading are gone. Instead, if you point to a heading without clicking, a tiny Hide or Show button appears. Click it to collapse or expand that heading's contents.

Here are the headings you'll soon know and love. (New in Mountain Lion: You can drag these headings up and down in the Sidebar to rearrange them.)

- **Favorites.** This primary section of the Sidebar is the place to stash things for easy access. You can stock this list with the icons of disks, files, programs, folders, and the virtual, self-updating folders called *saved searches*.

 Each icon is a shortcut. For example, click the Applications icon to view the contents of your Applications folder in the main part of the window. And if you click the icon of a file or a program, it opens.

Here, too, you'll find the icons for two recent Mac features: All My Files (see the box on the facing page) and AirDrop, the instant-file-sharing feature described on page 553.

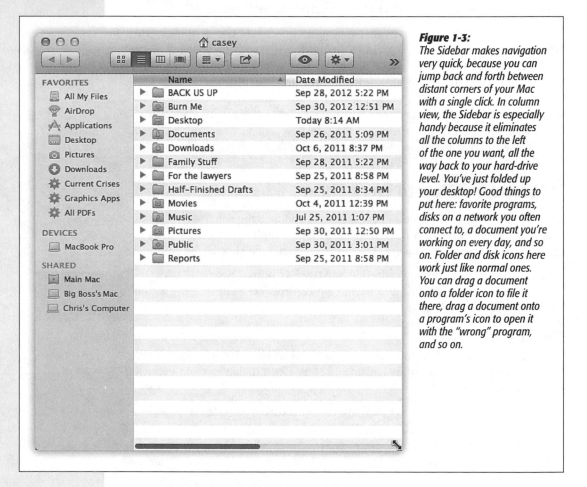

Figure 1-3:
The Sidebar makes navigation very quick, because you can jump back and forth between distant corners of your Mac with a single click. In column view, the Sidebar is especially handy because it eliminates all the columns to the left of the one you want, all the way back to your hard-drive level. You've just folded up your desktop! Good things to put here: favorite programs, disks on a network you often connect to, a document you're working on every day, and so on. Folder and disk icons here work just like normal ones. You can drag a document onto a folder icon to file it there, drag a document onto a program's icon to open it with the "wrong" program, and so on.

- **Shared.** Here's a complete list of the other computers on your network whose owners have turned on File Sharing, ready for access (see Chapter 14 for details). Back to My Mac (page 584) is also listed here.

- **Devices.** This section lists every storage device connected to, or installed inside, your Mac: hard drives, iPhones, iPads, iPods, CDs, DVDs, memory cards, USB flash drives, and so on. (Your main hard drive doesn't usually appear here, but you can drag it here.) The removable ones (like CDs, DVDs, i-gadgets) bear a little gray ⏏ logo, which you can click to eject that disk.

Note: If you remove everything listed under one of these headings, the heading itself disappears to save space. The heading reappears the next time you put something in its category back into the Sidebar.

Fine-tuning the Sidebar

The beauty of this parking lot for containers is that it's so easy to set up with your favorite places. For example:

- **Remove an icon** by ⌘-dragging it out of the Sidebar entirely. It vanishes with a puff of smoke (and even a little whoof sound effect). You haven't actually removed anything from your Mac; you've just unhitched its alias from the Sidebar.

All My Files

There it is, staring you in the face at the top of the Sidebar in every window: an icon called All My Files. What is this, some kind of geeked-out soap opera?

Nope. It's a new Lion/Mountain Lion feature that Apple thought you might find handy: a massive, searchable, sortable list, all in a single window, of every human-useful file on the computer. That is, pictures, movies, music, documents—no system files, preference files, or other detritus. No matter what folders they're actually in, they appear here in a single window. You can summon it whenever you want, just by clicking the All My Files icon in the Sidebar.

When you first open All My Files, it has your files grouped by type: Contacts, Events & To Dos, Images, PDF Documents, Music, Movies, Presentations, Spreadsheets, Developer (which lists HTML Web-site files and Xcode programming files), and Documents (meaning, "everything else"). In icon view—the factory setting—each class of icons appears in a single scrolling row. Use a two-finger scroll (trackpad) or one-

finger slide (Magic Mouse) to move through the horizontal list. (If you'd rather not have to scroll, click the tiny Show All button that appears at the right end of each row. Now you're seeing *all* of the icons of this type; click Show Less to return to the single-row effect.)

You can see how this sorting method—which is the new Arrange By command at work (page 43)—might be useful. Suppose you're looking for a certain PowerPoint or Keynote presentation, but you can't remember what you called it or where you filed it. Open All My Files, make sure it's arranged by Kind, and presto: You're looking at a list of every presentation file on your Mac. Using Quick Look (page 59), you can breeze through them, inspecting them one at a time, until you find the one you want.

Apple thinks you'll like All My Files as a starting point for standard file-fussing operations so much that All My Files is the window that appears automatically when you choose File→New Finder Window (or press ⌘-N). (Of course, you can change that in Finder→Preferences.)

Tip: You can't drag items out of the Shared list. Also, if you drag a Devices item out of the list, you'll have to choose Finder→Preferences→Sidebar and then turn on the appropriate checkbox to put it back in.

Note that the requirement to press the ⌘ key is relatively new. Evidently Apple tech support got one phone call too many from hapless customers who'd dragged stuff off of the Sidebar by accident.

- **Rearrange the icons** by dragging them up or down in the list. For example, in Mountain Lion, hard drives don't appear at the top of the Sidebar anymore, but you're free to drag them back into those coveted spots. (You're not allowed to rearrange the computers listed in the Shared section, though.)

- **Rearrange the sections** by dragging *them* up or down—a new Mountain Lion feature. For example, you can drag Favorites to the bottom but promote the Shared category.

- **Install a new icon** by dragging it off your desktop (or out of a window) into any spot in the Favorites list of the Sidebar. Press the ⌘ key after beginning the drag. You can't drag icons into any section of the Sidebar—just Favorites.

Tip: You can also highlight an icon wherever it happens to be and then choose File→Add to Sidebar, or just press ⌘-T.

- **Adjust the width** of the Sidebar by dragging its right edge—either the skinny divider line or the extreme right edge of the vertical scroll bar, if there is one. You "feel" a snap at the point when the line covers up about half of each icon's name. Any covered-up names sprout ellipses (…) to let you know there's more (as in "Secret Salaries Spreadsh…").

- **Hide the Sidebar** by pressing ⌘-Option-S, which is the shortcut for the View→Hide Sidebar command. Bring the Sidebar back into view by pressing the same key combination (or by using the Show Sidebar command).

UP TO SPEED

Fixing the Sidebar

Anything you drag out of the Sidebar can be dragged back in again, including the big-ticket items like Applications and Pictures. That's good to know if you drag something important out of the Sidebar and then change your mind.

Even so, there's a quicker way to restore the Sidebar to its factory settings.

If you choose Finder→Preferences and then click the Sidebar button, you discover

the checkboxes shown here. They let you put back the Apple-installed icons that you may have removed in haste. Just turn on a checkbox to restore its icon to your Sidebar. So if something you expect to see in your Sidebar isn't there, check back here.

On the other hand, you may as well stream-line your computing life by turning *off* the checkboxes of icons you *never* want to see filling your Sidebar.

Tip: You can hide and show the Sidebar manually, too: To hide it, drag its right edge all the way to the left edge of the window. Unhide it by dragging the left edge of the window to the right again.

Then again, why would you ever want to hide the Sidebar? It's one of the handiest navigation aids since the invention of the steering wheel. For example:

- **It takes a lot of pressure off the Dock.** Instead of filling up your Dock with folder icons (all of which are frustratingly alike and unlabeled anyway), use the Sidebar to store them. You leave the Dock that much more room for programs and documents.

- **It's better than the Dock.** In some ways, the Sidebar is a lot like the Dock, in that you can stash favorite icons of any sort there. But the Sidebar reveals the names of these icons, and the Dock doesn't until you use the mouse to point there.

- **It makes ejecting easy.** Just click the ⏏ button next to any removable disk to make it pop out. (Other ways to eject disks are described in Chapter 12.)

- **It makes burning easy.** When you've inserted a blank CD or DVD and loaded it up with stuff you want to copy, click the ☢ button next to its name to begin burning that disc. (Details on burning discs are in Chapter 12.)

- **You can drag onto its folders and disks.** That is, you can drag icons onto Sidebar icons, exactly as though they were the real disks, folders, and programs they represent.

- **It simplifies connecting to networked disks.** Park your other computers' shared folder and disk icons here, as described in Chapter 14, to shave several steps off the usual connecting-via-network ritual.

Title Bar

The title bar (Figure 1-4) has several functions. First, when several windows are open, the darkened title bar, window name, mini-icon, and colored left-corner buttons tell you which window is active (in front); in background windows, these elements appear dimmed and colorless. Second, the title bar acts as a handle that lets you move the window around on the screen.

You can also move a window by dragging the solid gray strip on the bottom, if there is one, like the Status bar that you can turn on in the Finder or the Safari Web browser.

Tip: Here's a nifty keyboard shortcut: You can cycle through the different open windows in one program without using the mouse. Just press ⌘-~ (that is, the tilde key, to the left of the number 1 key on U.S. keyboards). With each press, you bring a different window forward within the current program. It works both in the Finder and in your everyday programs, and it beats the pants off using the mouse to choose a name from the Window menu. (Note the difference from ⌘-Tab, which cycles through different open *programs*.)

After you've opened one folder that's inside another, the title bar's secret folder hierarchy menu is an efficient way to backtrack—to return to the enclosing window. Get

in the habit of right-clicking (or Control-clicking, or ⌘-clicking) the name of the window to access the menu shown in Figure 1-5. (You can release the Control or ⌘ key immediately after clicking.)

Close button
Minimize button
Zoom button Toolbar Folder proxy icon Title bar Search box

Sidebar Status bar Icon-size slider

Figure 1-4:
When Steve Jobs unveiled Mac OS X at Macworld Expo in 2000, he said his goal was to oversee the creation of an interface so attractive, "you just want to lick it." Desktop windows, with their juicy, fruit-flavored controls, are a good starting point.

By choosing the name of a folder from this menu, you open the corresponding window. When browsing the contents of the Users folder, for example, you can return to the main hard drive window by Control-clicking the folder name Users and then choosing Macintosh HD from the menu.

Tip: Keyboard lovers, take note. Instead of using the title bar menu, you can also jump to the enclosing window by pressing ⌘-↑ (up arrow), which is the shortcut for the Go→Enclosing Folder command.

Pressing ⌘-↓ (down arrow) takes you back into the folder you started in, assuming that it's still highlighted. (This makes more sense when you try it than when you read it.)

Once you've mastered dragging, you're ready for these terrific title bar tips:

- **Pressing the ⌘ key** lets you drag the title bar of an inactive window—one that's partly covered by a window in front—without bringing it to the front. (Drag any empty part of the title bar—not the title itself.)

By the way, you can close, minimize, or zoom a background window without the help of the ⌘ key. Just click one of those three corresponding title-bar buttons normally, even if the window you're working on is in front.

Figure 1-5:
Control-click (or right-click, or ⌘-click) a Finder window's title bar to summon the hidden folder hierarchy menu. This trick also works in most other OS X programs. For example, you can ⌘-click a document window's title to find out where the document is actually saved on your hard drive.

- **By double-clicking the title bar,** you minimize the window, making it collapse into the Dock exactly as though you had clicked the Minimize button (assuming you haven't turned off this feature in System Preferences→Dock, of course).

- **The Option key** means, "Apply this action to all windows in the current program." For example, Option-double-clicking any title bar minimizes all desktop windows, sending them flying to the Dock.

- **Click the ▼ button in the title bar,** if you see one, to open a menu full of commands that let you rewind a document to a previous state. This is part of the new Auto Save feature, and it works only in certain programs; see page 220.

Close Button

As the tip of your cursor crosses the three buttons at the upper-left corner of a window, tiny symbols appear inside them: ✕, —, and ✚. Ignore the gossip that these symbols were added to help color-blind people who can't distinguish the colors red, yellow, and green. Color-blind people are perfectly capable of distinguishing the buttons by their positions, just as they do with traffic lights.

But for people who aren't paying attention to button position, these cues distinguish the buttons when all three are identical shades of gray, as they are when you use Graphite mode (page 150). They also signal when it's time to click. For example, as described in the previous section, you can use these three buttons even when the

POWER USERS' CLINIC

The Go to Folder Command

Sometimes a Unix tentacle pokes through the friendly OS X interface and you find a place where you can use Unix shortcuts instead of the mouse.

One classic example is the Go→Go to Folder command (Shift-⌘-G). It brings up a box like the one shown here.

The purpose of this box is to let you jump directly to a certain folder on your Mac by typing its Unix *folder path*. Depending on your point of view, this special box is either a shortcut or a detour.

For example, if you want to see what's in the Documents folder of your Home folder, you could choose Go→Go to Folder and type this:

/Users/chris/Documents

Then click Go or press Return. (In this example, of course, *chris* is your short account name.)

In other words, you're telling the Mac to open the Users folder in your main hard drive window, then your Home folder inside that, and then the Documents folder inside that. Each slash means, "and then open." (You can leave off the name of your hard drive; that's implied by the opening slash.) When you press Return, the folder you specified pops open immediately.

Of course, if you really wanted to jump to your Documents folder, you'd be wasting your time by typing all that. Unix (and therefore OS X) offers a handy shortcut that means "home folder." It's the tilde character (~) at the upper-left corner of the U.S. keyboard.

To see what's in your Home folder, then, you could type just that ~ symbol into the Go to Folder box and then press

Return. Or you could add some slashes to it to specify a folder inside your Home folder, like this:

~/Documents

You can even jump to someone *else's* Home folder by typing a name after the symbol, like this:

~ chris

If you get into this sort of thing, here's another shortcut worth noting: If you type nothing but a slash (/) and then press Return, you jump immediately to the main hard drive window.

Note, too, that you don't have to type out the full path—only the part that drills down from the *window you're in*. If your Home folder window is already open, for example, then you can open the Pictures folder just by typing *Pictures*.

But the Go to Folder trick really turns into a high-octane timesaver if you use *autocompletion*. Here's how it works: After each slash, you can type only enough letters of a folder's name to give OS X the idea—*de* instead of *desktop*, for example—and then wait a fraction of a second (or, if you're late for a plane, press the Tab key). OS X instantly and automatically fills in the rest of the folder's name. It even auto-capitalizes the folder names for you. (In Unix, capitalization matters.)

For example, instead of typing */Applications/Microsoft Office/clipart/standard*, you could type nothing more than */ap/mi/cl/st*, remembering to press Tab after each pair of letters. Now *that's* a way to feel like a Unix programmer.

window is not at the front. You know the buttons are ripe for the clicking when you see the little symbols appear under your cursor.

The most important window gadget is the Close button, the red, droplet-like button in the upper-left corner (Figure 1-4). Clicking it closes the window, which collapses back into the icon from which it came.

Tip: If, while working on a document, you see a tiny dot in the center of the Close button, OS X is trying to tell you that you haven't yet saved your work. (It doesn't appear in Autosave programs like TextEdit.) The dot goes away when you save the document.

The universal keyboard equivalent of the Close button is ⌘-W (for window)—a keystroke well worth memorizing. If you get into the habit of dismissing windows with that deft flick of your left hand, you'll find it far easier to close several windows in a row, because you won't have to aim for successive Close buttons.

In many programs, something special happens if you're pressing the Option key when using the Close button or its ⌘-W equivalent: You close all open windows. This trick is especially useful in the Finder, where a quest for a particular document may have left your screen plastered with open windows for which you have no further use. Option-clicking the Close button of any one window (or pressing Option-⌘-W) closes all of them.

On the other hand, the Option-key trick doesn't close all windows in every program—only those in the current program. Option-closing a Microsoft Word document closes all Word windows, but your Finder windows remain open.

Moreover, Option-closing doesn't work in all programs.

Minimize Button

Click this yellow drop of gel to minimize any Mac window, sending it shrinking, with a genie-like animated effect, into the right end of the Dock, where it then appears as an icon. The window isn't gone. It's just out of your way for the moment, as though you've set it on a shelf. To bring it back, click the newly created Dock icon; see Figure 1-6. Chapter 4 has more on the Dock.

Minimizing is a great window-management tool. In the Finder, minimizing a window lets you see whatever icons were hiding behind it. In a Web browser, minimizing lets you hide a window that has to remain open (because you're waiting for some task to finish) so you can read something else in the meantime.

And now, some Minimize button micro-goodies:

• If you enjoy the ability to roll up your windows in this way, remember that you actually have a bigger target than the tiny Minimize button. The entire title bar becomes a giant Minimize button when you double-click anywhere on it. (That's an option in the General panel of System Preferences, described in Chapter 9.)

Better yet, you can also minimize the frontmost window of almost any program (including the Finder) from the keyboard by pressing ⌘-M. That's a keystroke worth memorizing on Day One.

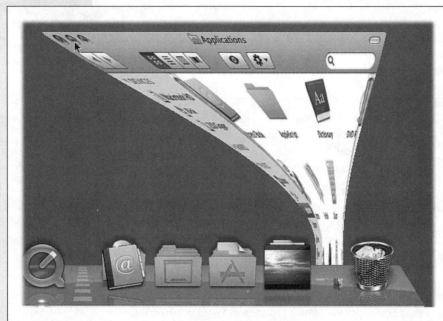

Figure 1-6:
*Clicking the Mini-
mize button sends
a window scurrying
down to the Dock,
collapsing in on itself
as though being
forced through a
tiny, invisible funnel.
A little icon appears
on the lower-
right corner of its
minimized image to
identify the program
it's running in.*

- Option-clicking one minimized window on the Dock un-minimizes all a program's windows—at least for Cocoa programs (page 227). But if it's a Carbon program, like old versions of Word, then you have to click the windows one at a time on the Dock to bring them back.

Tip: OS X can change menu commands as you press modifier keys. For example, open a couple of Finder windows and then click the Window menu. Focus your eyes on the Minimize Window command. Now press Option and watch both the wording and the listed keyboard equivalent change instantly to Minimize All (Option-⌘-M).

The Option key works wonders on the File menu, too.

- In the bad old days (up to late 2009), minimizing a bunch of documents could get really messy. Each one flew onto the Dock, putting a new icon there, creating a tighter and tighter squeeze, shrinking the Dock's icons until they were the size of Tic Tacs.

 In Mountain Lion, you can have your document windows minimize themselves into their program's Dock icon, rather than creating new Dock icons for themselves. That way, your Dock doesn't get any more crowded, and the icons on it don't keep shrinking away to atoms.

To turn on this feature, choose ⌘→System Preferences→Dock. Turn on "Minimize windows into application icon."

So how do you get those windows back out of the Dock icon? You use Dock Exposé, which is described on page 199.

Zoom Button

A click on this green geltab (see Figure 1-4) makes a desktop window just large enough to reveal all the icons inside it (or, in programs, large enough to reveal all the text, graphics, or music). If your monitor isn't big enough to show all the icons in a window, then Zoom resizes the window to show as many as possible.

In either case, a second click on the Zoom button restores the window to its previous size. (The Window→Zoom command does the same thing.)

The Folder Proxy Icon

In the Finder, there's a tiny icon next to the window's name (Figure 1-7). It's a stand-in—a proxy—for that window's folder itself.

By dragging this tiny icon, you can move or copy the folder into a different folder or disk, into the Sidebar, into the Trash, or into the Dock without having to first close the window.

POWER USERS' CLINIC

Adjusting the Genie Speed

Apple has a name for the animation you see when you minimize, open, or close a window: the *genie effect*, because it so closely resembles the way Barbara Eden, Robin Williams, and other TV and movie genies entered and exited their magic lamps and bottles.

But you don't have to watch the "genie" animation in precisely the same way, day in and day out. You can slow it down or speed it up, like this:

Slow it down. When Steve Jobs first demoed Mac OS X, one of his favorite bits was slowing down the animation so we could see it in graceful slow motion. How did he do that?

If you Shift-click a window's Minimize button, it collapses into the Dock at about one-tenth its usual speed—an effect sure to produce gasps from onlookers. The Shift key also slows the un-minimizing animation, the one you see when you click a window icon in the Dock to restore it to full size. (Shift-clicking a button to slow down its animation is a

running theme in OS X. You'll find it mentioned in several spots in this book.)

Speed it up. There's no keystroke for making the animation go faster. You can, however, substitute a faster *style* of minimizing animation.

To do so, choose ⌘→Dock→Dock Preferences. From the "Minimize windows using" pop-up menu, choose Scale Effect, and then close the window. Now, instead of collapsing through an invisible funnel, minimized windows simply shrink as they fly down to the Dock, remaining rectangular. The time you save isn't exactly going to get you home an hour earlier each day, but at least you have the illusion of greater speed.

(Actually, there's a third animation style, too, but there's a trick to unleashing it: You need the free utility called Tinker-Tool. It's available from this book's "Missing CD" page at *www.missingmanuals.com.*)

Tip: You have to hold down the mouse button on the folder proxy icon until the icon darkens before dragging. (It darkens in a fraction of a second.)

Figure 1-7:
When you find yourself confronting a Finder window that contains useful stuff, consider dragging its proxy icon to the Dock. That will install its folder or disk icon there for future use. It's not the same as minimizing the window, which puts the window icon into the Dock only temporarily. (Note: Most document windows also offer a proxy-icon feature, but it usually produces only an alias when you drag the proxy to a different folder or disk.)

When you drag this proxy icon to a different place on the same disk, the usual folder-dragging rules apply: Hold down the Option key if you want to copy the original disk or folder; ignore the Option key to move the original folder. (You'll find details on moving and copying icons in the next chapter.)

Many programs, including Microsoft Word, Preview, TextEdit, and others, offer the same mini-icon in open document windows. Once again, you can use it as a handle to drag a document into a new folder or onto a new disk. Sometimes, doing that really does move the document—but more often, you just get an alias of it in the new location.

The Finder Toolbar

Chapter 4 describes this fascinating desktop-window element in great detail.

Two Clicks, One Window

Double-clicking a folder in a window doesn't leave you with two open windows. Instead, double-clicking a folder makes the contents of the original window disappear (Figure 1-8).

Tip: If you Option-double-click a folder, you don't simply replace the contents of a fixed window that remains onscreen; you actually switch windows, as evidenced by their changing sizes and shapes.

Figure 1-8:
To help you avoid window clutter, Apple has designed OS X windows so that double-clicking a folder in a window (top) doesn't actually open another window (bottom). Every time you double-click a folder in an open window (except in column view), its contents replace whatever was previously in the window. If you double-click three folders in succession, you still wind up with just one open window.

So what if you've now opened inner folder B, and you want to backtrack to outer folder A? In that case, just click the tiny ◄ button—the Back button—in the upper-left corner of the window, or use one of these alternatives:

- Choose Go→Back.

- Press ⌘-[(left bracket).

- Press ⌘-↑ (up arrow).

- Choose Go→Enclosing Folder.

None of that helps you, however, if you want to move a file from one folder into the other, or to compare the contents of the two windows. In that case, you probably want to see both windows open at the same time.

You can open a second window using any of these techniques:

- Choose File→New Finder Window (⌘-N).

Tip: What folder contents fill the "new" window that appears when you use this command? Usually, it's the All My Files folder, showing your entire universe of files.

But you can choose any window you want. To make the change, choose Finder→Preferences. Click the General icon. Change the "New Finder windows show" pop-up menu to whatever folder you'd like to use as the starting point for your computing life. "All My Files" is a good choice; so is your Home folder. But you're also free to choose your Documents folder, your iDisk, or any folder at all. Now every new Finder window shows you that specified folder, which is a much more useful arrangement.

- ⌘-double-click a disk or folder icon.

- Double-click a folder or disk icon on your desktop.

- Choose Finder→Preferences and turn on "Always open folders in a new window." Now when double-clicked, all folders open into new windows. (This is the option for veteran Mac fans who don't care for the new behavior.)

Old Finder Mode

The upper-right corner of every Finder window used to contain a little button that looked like a half-inch squirt of Crest toothpaste. Clicking it entered Old Finder Mode.

"Old Finder Mode" (not the technical Apple term) was designed for people who come to OS X from an earlier version, like Mac OS 9, and lose half their hair when they discover how different things are in OS X.

GEM IN THE ROUGH

Multiple Views, Same Folder

If you've read this section carefully, you may have discovered a peculiar quirk of the OS X Finder: By choosing File→New Finder Window (or ⌘-double-clicking a disk or folder icon), you open a second, completely independent Finder window. Therefore, if you stop to think about it, there's nothing to stop you from opening a third, fourth, or fifth copy of *the same folder window.* Once they're open, you can even switch them into different views.

Try this, for example: Choose Go→Applications. Choose File→New Finder Window (⌘-N), and then choose Go→Applications *again.* Using the View menu or the con-

trols in the toolbar, put one of these windows into list view and the other into icon view.

This ability has its advantages. For example, you might decide to open the same window twice while doing some hard drive housekeeping. By keeping a list view open, you can check the Size column as you move your files into different folders (so you can make sure the folders fit onto a blank CD, for example). By keeping a *column* view open, on the other hand, you gain quicker navigational access to the stuff on your drive.

In this mode, two of the biggest behavioral differences between OS X and its predecessors disappear:

- The Sidebar and the toolbar blink out of sight.

- Double-clicking a folder now works like it did back in 2000. Every time you double-click a folder, you open a new window for it.

The Old Finder Mode button no longer appears, but the mode itself is still available. Press Option-⌘-T, the equivalent for the View→Hide Toolbar command. (Repeat that keystroke or command to turn Old Finder Mode off again.)

Scroll Bars

Here's one of the biggest changes in Lion/Mountain Lion: Scroll bars don't appear nearly as often as they used to (see Figure 1-8).

A scroll bar, of course, is the traditional window-edge slider that lets you move through a document that's too big for the window. Without scroll bars, for example, you'd never be able to write a letter that's taller than your screen.

On the very first Macs, scroll bars were a necessary evil; those computers were too slow and underpowered to manage visibly moving the contents of the window. That's why scroll bars were invented in the first place: to give you some feedback about how

Figure 1-9:
In Mountain Lion, scroll bars don't appear at all while you're working (bottom); you have that much more screen area dedicated to your work. If you begin to scroll by sliding your fingers across the trackpad or Magic Mouse, only the scroll-bar handle appears, so you know where you are (middle).

New in Mountain Lion: If you point to the scroll bar, it fattens up so you can operate it more easily (top).

far you were moving into a document, because the window itself went pure white when you dragged the handle.

Today, though, you can manipulate the contents of a window and see where you are at all times. Nobody questions the absence of scroll bars on an iPad, right? Because you just push the contents of a window around with your fingers to scroll.

In Mountain Lion, you scroll by pushing two fingers up the trackpad (or one finger up the Magic Mouse) or by turning your mouse's scroll wheel. You almost never use the antiquated method of dragging the scroll bar's handle manually, with the mouse.

Tip: More reasons nobody uses the mouse on the scroll bar: You can scroll using the keyboard. Your Page Up and Page Down keys let you scroll up and down, one screen at a time, without having to take your hands off the keyboard. The Home and End keys are generally useful for jumping directly to the top or bottom of your document (or Finder window). And if you've bought a mouse that has a scroll wheel on the top, you can use it to scroll windows, without pressing any keys at all.

That's a long-winded way of explaining why, in most Mountain Lion programs, the scroll bars are hidden. See Figure 1-9 for details.

Note: If the missing scroll bars leave you jittery and disoriented, you can bring them back. Open System Preferences→General and then turn on "Show scroll bars: Always."

Resizable Edges

For the first 28 years of its existence, the Mac offered only one way to make a window bigger or smaller: Drag the ribbed-looking lower-right corner.

In Mountain Lion, you can drag *any* edge of a window to change its shape. Just move the pointer carefully to the exact top, bottom, left, or right edge; once its shape changes to a double-headed arrow, you can drag to move that window's edge in or out.

NOSTALGIA CORNER

How the Scroll Bar Used to Work

If you are that rare, special individual who still operates the scroll bar by clicking it with the mouse, the old-style controls are still around.

For example: Ordinarily, when you click in the scroll bar track above or below the dark gray handle bar, the window scrolls by one screenful. But another option awaits when you choose →System Preferences→General and turn on "Jump to the spot that's clicked." Now when you click the scroll-bar track, the Mac considers the entire scroll bar

a proportional map of the document and jumps precisely to the spot you clicked. That is, if you click at the very bottom of the scroll-bar track, you see the very last page.

No matter which scrolling option you choose in the Appearance panel, you can always override your decision on a case-by-case basis by *Option*-clicking the scroll-bar track. In other words, if you've selected the "Jump to the spot that's clicked" option, you can produce a "Jump to the next page" scroll by Option-clicking in the scroll-bar track.

Tip: There are a few cool, totally undocumented variations on the window-edge-dragging business. First, if you press the Option key while dragging, you resize the *opposite edge* simultaneously. For example, if you Option-drag the bottom edge upward, the top edge simultaneously collapses downward.

If you press Shift as you drag, you resize the *entire* window, retaining its proportions.

And if you Shift-Option drag, you resize the window around its center, rather than from its edges.

Path Bar

This little item appears when you choose View→Show Path Bar. It's a tiny map at the bottom of the window that shows where you are in the folder hierarchy. If it says Casey→Pictures→Picnic, well, then, by golly, you're looking at the contents of the Picnic folder, which is inside Pictures, which is inside your Home folder (assuming your name is Casey).

Tip: Each tiny folder icon in this display is fully operational. You can double-click it to open it, Control-click (right-click) it to open a shortcut menu, or even drag things into it.

Status Bar

Out of the box, OS X hides yet another information strip at the bottom of a window: the status bar, which tells you how many icons are in the window ("14 items," for example) and the amount of free space remaining on the disk. To make it appear, choose View→Show Status Bar.

Tip: The status bar shows you disk-space information for the entire disk, but not how much disk space *this particular window's* contents occupy.

To find out *that* piece of information, make sure no icon in the window is highlighted. Then choose File→Get Info (or press ⌘-I). The resulting Info window, which is described at the end of the next chapter, shows the size of the folder or disk whose window you're browsing, along with other useful statistics.

The Four Window Views

You can view the files and folders in a desktop window in any of four ways: as icons; as a single, tidy list; in a series of neat columns; or in Cover Flow view, where you can flip through giant document icons like they're CDs in a music-store bin. Figure 1-10 shows the four views.

Every window remembers its view settings independently. You might prefer to look over your Applications folder in list view (because it's crammed with files and folders) but view the Pictures folder in icon or Cover Flow view, where the larger icons serve as previews of the photos.

To switch a window from one view to another, just click one of the four corresponding icons in the window's toolbar (Figure 1-10).

You can also switch views by choosing View→as Icons (or View→as Columns, or View→as List, or View→as Cover Flow), which can be handy if you've hidden the toolbar. Or, for less mousing and more hard-bodied efficiency, press ⌘-1 for icon view, ⌘-2 for list view, ⌘-3 for column view, or ⌘-4 for Cover Flow view.

The following pages cover each of these views in greater detail.

Figure 1-10:
From the top: the same window in icon view, list view, column view, and Cover Flow view. Very full folders are best navigated in list or column views, but you may prefer to view emptier folders in icon or Cover Flow views, because larger icons are easier to preview and click. Remember that in any view (icon, list, column, or Cover Flow), you can highlight an icon by typing the first few letters of its name. In icon, list, or Cover Flow views, you can also press Tab to highlight the next icon (in alphabetical order), or Shift-Tab to highlight the previous one.

Note: One common thread in the following discussions is the availability of the View Options palette, which lets you set up the sorting, text size, icon size, and other features of each view, either one window at a time or for all windows.

Apple gives you a million different ways to open View Options. You can choose View→Show View Options, or press ⌘-J, or choose Show View Options from the ✿ menu at the top of every window.

Icon View

In icon view, every file, folder, and disk is represented by a small picture—an icon. This humble image, a visual representation of electronic bits and bytes, is the cornerstone of the entire Macintosh religion. (Maybe that's why it's called an icon.)

Icon Size

OS X draws those little icons using sophisticated graphics software. As a result, you can scale them to almost any size without losing quality or clarity. If you choose View→Status Bar so that the bottom-edge strip shown in Figure 1-11 appears, you get a size slider that you can drag to the right or left to make that window's icons larger or smaller. (For added fun, make little cartoon sounds with your mouth.)

Figure 1-11:
Once you make the status bar appear, you can choose an icon size to suit your personality. For picture folders, it can often be very handy to pick a jumbo size, in effect creating a slide-sorter "light table" effect. Icons can be an almost ridiculously large 512 pixels square.

Icon Previews

The Mac expands the notion of "an icon is a representation of its contents" to an impressive extreme. As you can see in Figure 1-12, each icon actually looks like a miniature of the first page of the real document.

Because you can make icons so enormous, you can actually watch movies, or read PDF and text documents, right on their icons.

To check out this feature, point to an icon without clicking. A Play button (▶) appears on any movie or sound file; as shown in Figure 1-12, ⊕ and ⊛ page buttons appear on a multipage document (like PDF, Pages, or even presentation documents like PowerPoint and Keynote). You can actually page through one of these documents right there on its icon without having to open the program!

Tip: If you Option-click the little ⊕ and ⊛ buttons on a PDF, PowerPoint, or Keynote icon preview, you jump to the first or last page or slide in the document.

Figure 1-12:
You can page through PDF and presentation icons, or play movies and sounds, right on their icons. (Movie icons even display a circular progress bar so you know how far you are into the video.)

THE HALF STEP.pdf

Kelly Balloons.mov

Icon-View Options

OS X offers a number of useful icon-view options, all of which are worth exploring. Start by opening any icon-view window, and then choose View→Show View Options (⌘-J). The dialog box shown in Figure 1-13 appears.

Always open in icon view

It's easy—almost scarily easy—to set up your preferred look for all folder windows on your entire system. With one click on the "Use as Defaults" button (described below), you can change the window view of 20,000 folders at once—to icon view, list view, or whatever you like.

The "Always open in icon view" option lets you override that master setting, just for this window.

For example, you might generally prefer a neat list view with large text. But for your Pictures folder, it probably makes more sense to set up icon view, so you can see a thumbnail of each photo without having to open it.

That's the idea here. Open Pictures, change it to icon view, and then turn on "Always open in icon view." Now every folder on your Mac is in list view except Pictures.

Note: The wording of this item in the View Options dialog box changes according to the view you're in at the moment. In a list-view window, for example, it says, "Always open in list view." In a Cover Flow–view window, it says, "Always open in Cover Flow." And so on. But the function is the same: to override the default (master) setting.

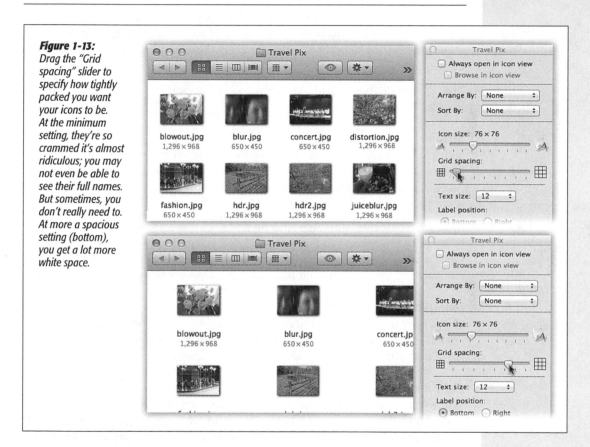

Figure 1-13:
Drag the "Grid spacing" slider to specify how tightly packed you want your icons to be. At the minimum setting, they're so crammed it's almost ridiculous; you may not even be able to see their full names. But sometimes, you don't really need to. At more a spacious setting (bottom), you get a lot more white space.

Browse in icon view

This option makes sure that any folders inside the current window open up into icon view, too, even if you'd previously set them to open into some other view. So if you're looking at your Pictures folder in icon view and you open the Grand Canyon Jaw-Droppers folder inside it, that folder also will be in icon view.

Arrange By, Sort By

For a discussion of these pop-up menus, see "Arrange By and Sort By" on page 43.

Icon size

It's super easy to make all your icons bigger or smaller; just drag the Icon Size slider in the lower-right corner of the window.

But for the benefit of old-timers who expect to find that slider here, in the View Options window, well, there's an identical slider here.

Grid spacing

Listen up, you young whippersnappers! When I was your age, back when computers used Mac OS 9, you could control how closely spaced icons were in a window. Why, if I wanted to see a lot of them without making the window bigger, I could pack 'em in like sardines!

That feature disappeared—for seven years. But back in Mac OS X 10.5, it finally returned. Figure 1-13 shows all.

Text size

Your choices range only from 10 to 16 points, and you still can't choose a different font for your icons' names. But using this pop-up menu, you can adjust the type size. And for people with especially big or especially small screens—or for people with aging retinas—this feature is much better than nothing.

In fact, you can actually specify a different type size for every window on your machine. (Why would you want to adjust the point size independently in different windows? Well, because you might want smaller type to fit more into a crammed list view without scrolling, while you can afford larger type in less densely populated windows.)

Label position

Click either Bottom or Right to indicate where you want an icon's name to appear, relative to its icon. As shown in Figure 1-14 at bottom, this option lets you create, in effect, a multiple-column list view in a single window.

Show item info

While you've got the View Options palette open, try turning on "Show item info." Suddenly you get a new line of information (in tiny blue type) for certain icons, saving you the effort of opening up the folder or file to find out what's in it. For example:

- **Folders.** The info line lets you know how many icons are inside each without having to open it up. Now you can spot empties at a glance.

- **Graphics files.** Certain other kinds of files may show a helpful info line, too. For example, graphics files display their dimensions in pixels.

- **Sounds and QuickTime movies.** The light-blue bonus line tells you how long the sound or movie takes to play. For example, an MP3 file might say "03' 08"," which means 3 minutes, 8 seconds.

- **.zip files.** On compressed archives like .zip files, you get to see the archive's total size on disk (like "48.9 MB").

You can see the effect illustrated in Figure 1-13.

Show icon preview

This option is what makes icons display their contents, as shown in Figures 1-11 and 1-12. If you turn it off, then icons no longer look like miniature versions of their contents (tiny photos, tiny PDF files, and so on). Everything takes on generic icons.

You might prefer this arrangement when, for example, you want to be able to pick out all the PDF files in a window full of mixed document types. Thanks to the matching icons, it's easy now.

Background

Here's a luxury that other operating systems can only dream about: You can fill the background of any icon-view window on your Mac with a certain color—or even a photo.

Color coordinating or "wallpapering" certain windows is more than just a gimmick. In fact, it can serve as a timesaving visual cue. Once you've gotten used to the fact that your main Documents folder has a sky-blue background, you can look at a screen

Figure 1-14:
The View Options dialog box for an icon view window offers the chance to create colored backgrounds for certain windows or even to use photos as window wallpaper (bottom). Using a photo may have a soothing, comic, or annoying effect—like making the icon names completely unreadable. (Note, by the way, how the icons' names have been set to appear beside the icons, rather than underneath, in the lower illustration. You now have all the handy, freely draggable convenience of an icon view, along with the more compact vertical spacing of a list view.)

filled with open windows and pick it out like a sharpshooter. Color-coded Finder windows are also especially easy to distinguish at a glance when you've minimized them to the Dock.

Note: Background colors and pictures show up only in icon view.

Once a window is open, choose View→View Options (⌘-J). The bottom of the resulting dialog box offers three choices, whose results are shown in Figure 1-14.

- **White.** This is the standard option (not shown).

- **Color.** When you click this button, you see a small rectangular button beside the word Color. Click it to open the Color Picker, which you can use to choose a new background color for the window. (Unless it's April Fools' Day, pick a light color. If you choose a dark one—like black—you won't be able to make out the lettering of the icons' names.)

- **Picture.** If you choose this option, a "Drag image here" square appears. Now find a graphics file—one of Apple's in the Desktop Pictures folder, or one of your own, whatever—and drag it into that "well."

 When you click Select, you see that OS X has superimposed the window's icons on the photo. As you can see in Figure 1-14, low-contrast or light-background photos work best for legibility.

 Incidentally, the Mac has no idea what sizes and shapes your window may assume in its lifetime. Therefore, OS X makes no attempt to scale down a selected photo to fit neatly into the window. If you have a high-res digital camera, therefore, you may see only the upper-left corner of your photo in the window. For better results, use a graphics program to scale the picture down to something smaller than your screen resolution.

Use as Defaults

This harmless-looking button can actually wreak havoc on your kingdom—or restore order to it—with a single click. It applies the changes you've just made in the View Options dialog box to all icon-view windows on your Mac (instead of only the frontmost window).

If you set up the frontmost window with a colored background, big icons, small text, and a tight grid, and then you click Use as Defaults, you'll see that look in every disk or folder window you open.

You've been warned.

Fortunately, there are two auxiliary controls that can give you a break from all the sameness.

First, you can set up individual windows to be weirdo exceptions to the rule; see "Always open in icon view" on page 38.

Second, you can remove any departures from the default window view—after a round of disappointing experimentation on a particular window, for example—using a secret button. Choose View→Show View Options to open the View Options dialog box. Now hold down the Option key. The Use as Defaults button magically changes to say Restore to Defaults, which means, "Abandon all the changes I've foolishly made to the look of this window."

Arrange By and Sort By

In OS X Lion, Apple completely replaced the old, complex system for organizing and sorting icons.

Now you can wield two different kinds of control over the files in a Finder window: arranging and sorting.

Tip: You can perform all these obsessive reorganizations in *any view:* icon view, list view, column view, or Cover Flow view. That's a big change from the pre-Lion days.

Arranging

Arranging files means, "Put my files into related clumps, separated by headings that identify them." You can arrange files in any of the views—icon, list, column, Cover Flow—and there are some incredibly useful options here.

For example, you can arrange your documents into Application groups (meaning, which program opens each one); now you can see at a glance which files will open in, say, iTunes when you double-click them. Or you can organize your Pictures folder into Date Added groups, with headings like "Today," "Last 7 Days," and "Earlier."

Figure 1-15 shows a few examples.

Tip: In icon view, the icons under each heading appear in a *single row*, scrolling off endlessly to the right. Use the usual sideways-scrolling gesture to flip through a row. (That is, swipe to the left on a trackpad with two fingers, or with one finger on a Magic Mouse.)

If you're not into gestures, or if you don't have a swipeable input device, click the tiny Show All button at the right end of a row. Now you've turned off that one-row-per-heading thing, and all the icons under that heading appear in the usual rows and columns; scroll down to see them all.

Apple wants to make extra, extra sure you're aware of the new Arrange commands. It gives you four different ways to find them:

- **Choose View→Arrange By.** Choose one of the criteria from the submenu. Your options are Name (alphabetically); Kind (type of file, like Images, Movies, and Documents); Application (which program opens which documents); Date (Last Opened, Added [to the window], Modified, or Created); Size; or Label (Finder label colors, described on page 89). Marvel as the Finder puts your files into tidy categorized groups.

Note: When you're looking at the Applications folder, you get a special choice: Application Category. It clumps your programs by what they do: Productivity, Social Networking, Music, Video, Board Games, Entertainment, Utilities, Reference, Photography, and so on. Pretty cool, actually.

Figure 1-15:
You can view your Finder-window files in neat little groups, separated by headings.
Top left: the Applications window, in icon view, arranged by Application Category.

Middle: the Documents folder, in list view, arranged by Application (meaning "which program opens this document").

Bottom: the Desktop folder, in column view, arranged by Date Added.

- **Choose from the** ▦▾ **icon.** This icon appears in the toolbar of every Finder window. It contains the same options listed in the previous paragraph.

- **Control-click (or right-click) an empty spot in an icon-view window; choose from the Arrange By shortcut menu.** Yep, it's those same commands yet again.

- **In the View Options palette (seen in Figure 1-13), use the Arrange By pop-up menu.** Yes, it's a fourth place to find the same six options.

Note: In each case, you can choose None to turn off the grouping altogether.

Remember, arranging (clumping) is not sorting. You can, in fact, sort the icons differently within each arranged group; read on.

Sorting

Sorting means just what it says (except that it used to be called "arranging"): You can sort your files alphabetically (by Name), chronologically (by Date), in order of hugeness (by Size), and so on. See Figure 1-16.

Figure 1-16:
Use either the View menu or the View Options window (right) to turn on permanent cleanliness mode. You've told the Mac to keep these icons on the invisible grid, sorted the way you requested. Just don't get frustrated when you try to drag an icon and then discover that it won't budge.

You can sort a window whether or not you've also arranged (grouped) it. You can even sort by different criteria. For example, you might have the programs in your Applications folder arranged by Application Category, but sorted alphabetically within each category.

Once again, Apple gives you four ways to sort:

- **While pressing the Option key, choose View→Sort By.** (Pressing Option turns the Arrange By submenu into the Sort By submenu.) Choose one of the criteria: Name, Size, and so on.

- **While pressing the Option key, click the ✿ icon.** Once again, the Option key turns the Arrange By options into Sort By options.

- **Control-click (or right-click) an empty spot in an icon-view window. Press the Option key.** And again, Option turns the Arrange By options into Sort By options.

- **In the View Options palette, use the Sort By pop-up menu.** Hey, guess what? You didn't have to press the Option key this time.

Tip: In icon view, you get an additional option: Snap to Grid. It means, "Let me drag these icons into any sequence I want, using the trackpad or mouse." When you release each drag, the icon jumps into the nearest position on the underlying spacing grid (unless you press the ⌘ key, which gives you full manual control of the icon's position).

This option appears only if Arrange By is set to None. After all, if you've asked the Mac to arrange your icons into groups, then you've relinquished control of their grid spacing.

Free dragging—and grid spacing

Whenever you've applied an Arrange or a Sort to an icon view, the icons remain rooted to an invisible underlying rows-and-columns grid. You can't budge them.

Tip: You can, however, control how tight or loose that grid is, using the "Grid spacing" slider described above.

But there are two situations when you're allowed to drag icons freely into any order you want:

- **Icons never snap to the grid.** If both Arrange By and Sort By are set to None, then you can go nuts, freely dragging icons into sloppy, off-the-grid positions.

 If, later, you become overwhelmed by shame at your untidiness, you can choose View→Clean Up (if nothing is selected) or View→Clean Up Selection (if some icons are highlighted). Now all icons in the window, or those you've selected, jump to the closest positions on the invisible underlying grid.

 These same commands appear in the shortcut menu when you Control-click or right-click anywhere inside an icon-view window, which is handier if you have a huge monitor.

 (There's even a Clean Up By submenu in the View menu and the shortcut menu. These commands don't just put icons back onto the closest grid positions; they put the icons into their proper sorted positions among the other icons—by name, size, date, and so on.)

Tip: If you press Option, then the Mac swaps the wording of the command. Clean Up changes to Clean Up Selection, and vice versa.

- **Icons always snap to the grid.** If Arrange By is set to None but Sort By is set to Snap to Grid, then you can drag icons into any order you like (that is, not in any particular sorted order)—but they'll snap to the grid when you let go of the mouse button.

Tip: If you press the ⌘ key as you release the drag, you can reverse the snapping logic. That is, the icons *will* snap to the grid if Sort By is set to None, but you can drag them freely if it's set to Snap to Grid. (Don't press the key until after you've begun to drag.)

Although it doesn't occur to most Mac fans, you can also apply any of the commands described in this section—Clean Up, Arrange, Sort—to icons lying loose on your

desktop. Even though they don't seem to be in any window at all, you can specify small or large icons, automatic alphabetical arrangement, and so on. Just click the desktop before using the View menu or the View Options dialog box.

Note: There's only one View Options dialog box. Once it's open, you can adjust the icon sizes or arrangement options of other windows just by clicking them. Each time you click inside a window, the View Options dialog box remains in front, changing to reflect the settings of the window you just clicked.

Incidentally, you can get rid of the View Options box the same way you summoned it: by pressing ⌘-J.

List View

In windows that contain a lot of icons, list view is a powerful weapon in the battle against chaos. It shows you a tidy table of your files' names, dates, sizes, and so on (Figure 1-17). Very faint alternating blue and white background stripes help you read across the columns.

Figure 1-17:
You control the sorting order of a list view by clicking the column headings (top). Click a second time to reverse the sorting order (bottom). You'll find the ▲ or ▼ triangles—indicating the identical information—in email programs, iTunes, and anywhere else where reversing the sorting order of a list can be useful.

You get to decide how wide your columns should be, which of them should appear, and in what order (except that Name is always the first column). Here's how to master these columns.

Sorting the List

Most of the world's list-view fans like their files listed alphabetically. It's occasionally useful, however, to view the newest files first, largest ones first, or whatever.

When a desktop window displays its icons in list view, a convenient new strip of column headings appears. These headings aren't just signposts; they're buttons, too. Click Name for alphabetical order, Date Modified to view the newest first, Size to view the largest files at the top, and so on.

Don't miss the tiny ▼ or ▲ that appears in the column you've most recently clicked. It shows you which way the list is being sorted. When it's ▲, then the oldest files, smallest files, or files beginning with numbers (or the letter A) appear at the top of the list, depending on which sorting criterion you have selected.

Tip: It may help you to remember that when the smallest portion of the triangle is at the top (▲), the smallest files are listed first when viewed in size order.

To reverse the sorting order, click the column heading a second time. Now the ▼ shows you that the newest files, largest files, or files beginning with the letter Z appear at the top of the list.

Note: You can also change the sorting order using the Sort By command described earlier (in the View menu, the [▦▾] pop-up menu, or the View Options dialog box). But, honestly, clicking the column headings is much faster.

Arranging the List

You can arrange your list view into groups by name, date, kind, and so on, with tidy headings that help you make sense of it all. This unsung feature is described under "Arrange and Sort By" on page 43.

Flippy Triangles

One of the Mac's most attractive features is the tiny triangle that appears to the left of a folder's name in a list view. In its official documents, Apple calls these buttons *disclosure triangles;* internally, the programmers call them *flippy triangles.*

When you click one, the list view turns into an outline, showing the contents of the folder in an indented list, as shown in Figure 1-18. Click the triangle again to collapse the folder listing. You're saved the trouble and clutter of opening a new window just to view the folder's contents.

By selectively clicking flippy triangles, you can in effect peer inside two or more folders simultaneously, all within a single list-view window. You can move files around by dragging them onto the tiny folder icons.

Tip: Once you've expanded a folder by clicking its flippy triangle, you can even drag a file icon out of the folder so that it's loose in the list-view window. To do so, drag it directly upward onto the column headings area (where it says Name, for example). When you release the mouse, you see that the file is no longer inside the expanded folder.

Figure 1-18:
Click a "flippy triangle" (left) to see the list of the folders and files inside that folder (right). Or press the equivalent keystrokes: → (to open) and ← (to close).

Flippy Triangle Keystrokes

The keystrokes that let you open and close flippy triangles in a list view are worth committing to memory.

First, pressing the Option key when you click a flippy triangle lets you view a folder's contents *and* the contents of any folders inside it. The result, in other words, is a longer list that may involve several levels of indentation.

If you prefer to use the keyboard, then substitute → (to expand a selected folder's flippy triangle) or ← (to collapse the folder listing again). Here again, adding the Option key expands or collapses *all* levels of folders within the selected one.

Suppose, for example, that you want to find out how many files are in your Pictures folder. The trouble is, you've organized your graphics files within that folder in several category folders. And you realize that the "how many items" statistic in the status bar shows only how many icons are

visible in the window. In other words, you won't know your total photo count until you've expanded all the folders within the Pictures folder.

You could perform the entire routine from the keyboard like this: Get to your Home folder by pressing Shift-⌘-H. Select the Pictures folder by typing the letter P. Open it by pressing ⌘-O (the shortcut for File→Open) or ⌘-↓. Switch to list view, if necessary, with a quick ⌘-2. Highlight the entire contents by pressing ⌘-A (short for Edit→Select All).

Now that all folders are highlighted, press Option-→. You may have to wait a moment for the Mac to open every subfolder of every subfolder. But eventually, the massive list appears, complete with many levels of indentation. At last, the "items" statistic in the status bar gives you a complete, updated tally of how many files and folders, combined, are in the window.

Your Choice of Columns

Choose View→Show View Options. In the dialog box that appears, you're offered on/off checkboxes for the different columns of information OS X can show you, as illustrated in Figure 1-19.

Figure 1-19:
The checkboxes you turn on in the View Options dialog box determine which columns of information appear in a list-view window. Many people live full and satisfying lives with only the three default columns—Date Modified, Kind, and Size—turned on. But the other columns can be helpful in special circumstances; the trick is knowing what information appears there.

- **Date Modified.** This date-and-time stamp indicates when a document was last saved. Its accuracy, of course, depends on the accuracy of your Mac's built-in clock.

Note: Many an up-to-date file has been lost because someone spotted a very old date on a folder and assumed that the files inside were equally old. That's because the modification date shown for a folder doesn't reflect the age of its contents. Instead, the date on a folder indicates only when items were last moved into or out of that folder. The actual files inside may be much older, or much more recent.

- **Date Created.** This date-and-time stamp shows when a document was *first* saved.

- **Date Added.** This option shows when a file was added to this folder or window.

- **Size.** With a glance, you can tell from this column how much disk space each of your files and folders is taking up in kilobytes, megabytes, gigabytes, or terabytes— whichever the Mac thinks you'll find most helpful.

Tip: For disks and folders, you see only a dash—at first. You can, however, instruct the Mac to reveal their sizes, as described on page 52.

- **Kind.** In this column, you can read what kind of file each icon represents. You may see, for example, Folder, JPEG Image, Application, and so on.

- **Version.** This column displays the version numbers of your programs. For folders and documents, you just see a dash.

- **Comments.** This rarely seen column can actually be among the most useful. Suppose you're a person who uses the Comments feature (highlight an icon, choose File→Get Info, type notes about that item into the Spotlight Comments box). This column displays the first line of those comments about each icon, which comes in handy when tracking multiple versions of your documents, as shown in Figure 1-20.

- **Label.** Labels are colors and identifying phrases that you can slap onto icons, wherever they appear, to help you categorize and group them. For details, see page 89.

Figure 1-20:
If your monitor is big enough, you can expand the Comments column to show several paragraphs, all in a single line—enough to reveal the full life history of each icon. (To enter some comments about an icon, type into the Spotlight Comments box in its Get Info, as shown here at bottom.)

Even with this column turned off, you can still see an icon's color, of course. But only by turning on this column do you get to see the text phrase you've associated with each label.

Other View Options

The View Options for a list view include several other useful settings; choose View→Show View Options or press ⌘-J.

- **Always open in list view.** Turn on this option to override your system-wide preference setting for all windows. See "Always open in icon view" on page 38 for details.

- **Browse in list view.** Ensures that any folder inside this one will also open up in list view, even if its regularly scheduled view is something else.

- **Icon size.** These two buttons offer you a choice of icon sizes for the current window: either standard or tiny. Unlike icon view, list view doesn't give you a size slider.

Fortunately, even the tiny icons aren't so small that they show up blank. You still get a general idea of what they're supposed to look like.

- **Text size.** You can change the type size for your icon labels, either globally or one window at a time.

- **Show columns.** Turn on the columns you'd like to appear in the current window's list view, as described in the previous section.

- **Use relative dates.** In a list view, the Date Modified, Date Added, and Date Created columns generally display information in a format like this: "Tuesday, March 5, 2013." (The Mac uses shorter date formats as the column gets narrower.) But when the "Use relative dates" option is turned on, the Mac substitutes the words "Yesterday" or "Today" where appropriate, making recent files easier to spot.

- **Calculate all sizes.** See the box below.

- **Show icon preview.** Exactly as in icon view, this option turns the icons of graphics files into miniatures of the photos or images within.

FREQUENTLY ASKED QUESTION

Calculate All Sizes

When I sort my list view by size, I see only dashes for folder sizes. What am I doing wrong?

Nothing at all; that's normal. When viewing a Finder window, you see a Size statistic for each file. For folders and disks, however, you're shown only an uninformative dash.

Most Mac fans study this anomaly momentarily, scratch their chins, and then get back to their work. Former Windows people don't even scratch their chins; Windows PCs *never* show folder-size or disk-size information in list views.

Here's what's going on: It can take a computer a long time to add up the sizes of all files inside a folder. Your System→Library folder alone, for example, contains over 100,000 files. Instead of making you wait while the Mac does all the addition, OS X simply shows you a dash in the folder's Size column.

On occasion, however, you really do want to see how big your folders are. In such cases, choose View→Show View Options and turn on "Calculate all sizes." You see the folder sizes slowly begin to pop onto the screen, from the top of the window down, as the Mac crunches the numbers on the files within. (You'll know that the crunching is still in progress,

because you'll see the size statistics for some icons appear in light gray. That's the Mac's way of saying, "I'm not totally sure about this folder's size yet.")

In fact, you can even turn on the "Calculate all sizes" option *globally*—that is, for all windows. In the Mac operating systems of days gone by, this act would have caused a massive slowdown of the entire computer. But remember that OS X is multithreaded; it has the opposite of a one-track mind. It's perfectly capable of devoting all its attention to calculating your folder sizes *and* to whatever work you're doing in the foreground.

Now consider this anomaly: Suppose you've opted to sort a particular window by folder size—in other words, you've clicked Size at the top of the column. Turning on "Calculate all sizes" bewilders the unprepared, as folders arbitrarily begin leaping out of order, forcing the list to rearrange itself a couple of times per second.

What's happening, of course, is that all folders begin at the bottom of the list, showing only dashes in the Size column. Then, as the Mac computes the size of your folders' contents, they jump into their correct sorted order at what may seem to be random intervals.

• **Use as Defaults.** Click to make your changes in the View Options box apply to all windows on your Mac. (Option-click this button to restore a wayward window back to your defaults.)

Rearranging Columns

You're stuck with the Name column at the far left of a window. However, you can rearrange the other columns just by dragging their gray column headers horizontally. If the Mac thinks you intend to drop a column to, say, the left of the column it overlaps, you'll actually see an animated movement—indicating a column reshuffling—even before you release the mouse button.

Adjusting Column Widths

If you place your cursor carefully on the dividing line between two column headings, you'll find that you can drag the divider line horizontally. Doing so makes the column to the left of your cursor wider or narrower.

What's delightful about this activity is watching OS X scramble to rewrite its information to fit the space you give it. For example, as you make the Date Modified (or Created) column narrower, "Saturday, March 9, 2013, 2:22 PM" shrinks first to "Sat, Mar 9, 2013, 2:22 PM," then to "3/9/13, 2:22 PM," and finally to a terse "3/9/13."

If you make a column too narrow, OS X shortens the file names by removing text from the middle. An ellipsis (…) appears to show you where the missing text would have appeared. (Apple reasoned that truncating the ends of file names, as in some other operating systems, would hide useful information, like the numbers at the end of "Letter to Marge 1," "Letter to Marge 2," and so on. It would also hide the three-letter extensions, such as Thesis.doc, that may appear on file names in OS X.)

For example, suppose you've named a Word document "Justin Bieber—A Major Force for Humanization and Cure for Depression, Acne, and Migraine Headache." (Yes, file names can really be that long.) If the Name column is too narrow, you might see only "Justin Bieber—A Major…Migraine Headache."

Tip: You don't have to make the column mega-wide just to read the full text of a file whose name has been shortened. Just point to the icon's name without clicking. After a moment, a yellow, floating balloon appears—something like a tooltip in Microsoft programs—to identify the full name.

In fact, now you can move your mouse up or down a list over truncated file names and their tooltip balloons appear instantaneously. (This trick works in list, column, or Cover Flow views—and in Save and Open dialog boxes, for that matter.)

Column View

The goal of column view is simple: to let you burrow down through nested folders without leaving a trail of messy, overlapping windows in your wake.

The solution is shown in Figure 1-21. It's a list view that's divided into several verti-cal panes. The first pane (not counting the Sidebar) shows whatever disk or folder you first opened.

Figure 1-21:
If the rightmost folder contains pictures, sounds, Office documents, or movies, you can look at them or play them, right there in the Finder. You can drag this jumbo preview icon anywhere— into another folder or to the Trash, for example.

When you click a disk or folder in this list (once), the second pane shows a list of everything in it. Each time you click a folder in one pane, the pane to its right shows what's inside. The other panes slide to the left, sometimes out of view. (Use the hori-zontal scroll bar to bring them back.) You can keep clicking until you're looking at the file icons inside the most deeply nested folder.

If you discover that your hunt for a particular file has taken you down a blind alley, it's not a big deal to backtrack, since the trail of folders you've followed to get here is still sitting before you on the screen. As soon as you click a different folder in one of the earlier panes, the panes to its right suddenly change, so that you can burrow down a different rabbit hole.

The beauty of column view is that, first of all, it keeps your screen tidy. It effectively shows you several simultaneous folder levels but contains them within a single window. With a quick ⌘-W, you can close the entire window, panes and all. Second, column view provides an excellent sense of where you are. Because your trail is visible at all times, it's much harder to get lost—wondering what folder you're in and how you got there—than in any other window view.

Column View by Keyboard

Efficiency fans can operate this entire process by keyboard alone. For example:

- You can jump from one column to the next by pressing the ← or → keys. Each press highlights the first icon in the next or previous column.

- You can use any of the commands in the Go menu, or their keyboard equivalents, or the icons in the Sidebar, to fill your columns with the contents of the corresponding folder—Home, Favorites, Applications, and so on.

- The Back command (clicking the ◂ button on the toolbar, pressing ⌘-[, or choosing Go→Back) works as it does in a Web browser: It retraces your steps backward. You can repeat this command until you return to the column setup that first appeared when you switched to column view. Once you've gone back, in fact, you can then go forward again; choose Go→Forward, or press ⌘-].

- Within a highlighted column, press the ↑ or ↓ keys to highlight successive icons in the list. Or type the first couple of letters of an icon's name to jump directly to it.

- When you finally highlight the icon you've been looking for, press ⌘-O or ⌘-↓ to open it (or double-click it, of course). You can open anything in any column; you don't have to wait until you've reached the rightmost column.

Manipulating the Columns

The number of columns you can see without scrolling depends on the width of the window. That's not to say, however, that you're limited to four columns (or whatever fits on your monitor). You can make the columns wider or narrower—either individually or all at once—to suit the situation, according to this scheme:

- **To make a single column wider or narrower,** drag the fine vertical line that separates it from the column to its right (see Figure 1-22).

- **To make *all* the columns wider or narrower simultaneously,** hold down the Option key as you drag one of the divider lines.

- **To make a column precisely as wide as necessary** to reveal all the names of its contents, double-click the divider line on its right side.

POWER USERS' CLINIC

The Fine Points of the Column-View Triangle

This is really tweaky and geeky, but take a look: There's a tiny triangle (▸) to the right of every folder's name in column view. It can be either solid dark or hollow.

If you *click* a folder, that triangle is dark. But if you highlight a folder by typing a few letters of its name, or by pressing the ↑ or ↓ keys, the triangle remains hollow. (At that point, pressing Tab makes it darken.)

Who cares? Well, it actually makes a difference here and

there. When the triangle is dark, the Mac is trying to tell you that the *next column to the right* is actually selected. Pressing ⌘-A (Select All) at this point, for example, highlights all the icons in that *next* column. If you press the ↑ or ↓ keys, you walk up and down the list in that *next* column.

But when the triangle is hollow, you haven't left the *original* column. Pressing the arrow keys walks up and down *this* list, and ⌘-A highlights everything in *this* list.

It's subtle. But cool.

- To make *all* columns as wide as required—when you absolutely, positively don't want any names truncated—Option-double-click a column's right-side divider line.

Tip: If you're having trouble remembering all of those key and click combinations, you're not alone. Fortunately, you can use a new right-click trick instead.

If you Control-click (or right-click) the divider line at the right side of a column, you get a shortcut menu that offers these commands: Right Size This Column (make it exactly as wide as necessary), Right Size All Columns Individually (make *every* column exactly as wide as necessary), and Right Size All Columns Equally (make all columns *the same width*, based on whatever width is necessary to see all the names in the *narrowest* one).

Figure 1-22:
When you move your cursor close to one of the vertical dividing lines between columns, the cursor becomes a double-headed arrow. That's a sign that you can now drag that line to adjust the column width.

Grouping the Column Contents

Yes, the Arrange commands are available to column view, too; you can add those gray category headings to the clumps of files in each window. And, once again, you can also use the Sort By commands to change the sequence of files within each grouping. It all works exactly as described on pages 43–47.

View Options

Just as in icon and list view, you can choose View→Show View Options to open a dialog box—a Spartan one, in this case—offering additional control over your column views.

- **Always open in column view.** Once again, this option lets you override your system-wide preference setting for all windows. See "Always open in icon view" on page 38 for details.

- **Browse in column view.** Ensures that any folder inside this one will open up in column view when double-clicked.

- **Arrange By, Sort By.** You can put column-view icons into arranged groups—and sort them within those groups—just as described on pages 43–47.

- **Text size.** Whatever point size you choose here affects the type used for icons in all column views.

- **Show icons.** For maximum speed, turn off this option. Now you see only file names—not the tiny icons next to them—in all column views. Weird!

- **Show icon preview.** Turn off this option if you don't want the tiny icons in column view to display their actual contents—photos showing their images, Word and PDF documents showing their first pages, and so on. You get generic, identical icons for each file type (text, photo, or whatever).

- **Show preview column.** The far-right Preview column can be handy when you're browsing graphics, sounds, or movie files. Feel free to enlarge this final column when you want a better view of the picture or movie; you can make it really big.

The rest of the time, though, the Preview column can get in the way, slightly slowing down the works and pushing other, more useful columns off to the left side of the window. If you turn off this checkbox, the Preview column doesn't appear.

Tip: No matter what view you're in, remember this: If you ever start dragging an icon and then change your mind, just press the Esc key or ⌘-period, even while the mouse button is still down. The icon flies back to its precise starting place. Or, if you've already dragged something to a new window and now you regret it, press ⌘-Z (for Undo). Too bad real life doesn't have a similar feature.

Cover Flow View

Cover Flow is a visual display that Apple stole from its own iTunes software, where Cover Flow simulates the flipping "pages" of a jukebox, or the albums in a record-

NOSTALGIA CORNER

Everything Old Is New Again

To many observers, OS X's column view was one of the most radical new features of the operating system. The truth, however, is that it's not new at all.

In fact, column view's most recent ancestor appeared in the NeXT operating system, which Apple bought (along with Steve Jobs, its CEO) in 1997. But column view is even older than that.

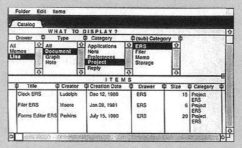

As you can see in this sketch from May 1980, the idea of a single-window, multiple-column view had been kicking around at Apple long before the Macintosh debuted.

In the end, this view was deemed too complex for the original Mac, which finally appeared (with only list and icon views) in 1984. Column view took 17 more years to find its way into the standard Mac OS.

store bin (Figure 1-23). There you can flip through your music collection, marveling as the CD covers flip over in 3-D space while you browse.

The idea is the same in OS X, except that now it's not album covers you're flipping; it's gigantic file and folder icons.

Figure 1-23:
The top half of a Cover Flow window is an interactive, scrolling "record bin" full of your own stuff. It's especially useful for photos, PDF files, Office documents, and text documents. When a PDF or presentation document comes up in this virtual data jukebox, you can click the arrow buttons to page through it; for a movie, click the little ▶ button to play the video, right in place.

To fire up Cover Flow, open a window. Then click the Cover Flow ▥ button in the toolbar. Or choose View→as Cover Flow, or press ⌘-4.

Now the window splits. On the bottom: a traditional list view, complete with sortable, arrangeable columns, exactly as described above.

On the top: the gleaming, reflective-black Cover Flow display. Your primary interest here is the scroll bar. As you drag it left or right, you see your files and folders float by and flip in 3-D space. Fun for the whole family!

The effect is spectacular, sure. It's probably not something you'd want to set up for every folder, though, because browsing is a pretty inefficient way to find something. But in folders containing photos or movies (that aren't filled with hundreds of files), Cover Flow can be a handy and satisfying way to browse.

And now, notes on Cover Flow:

- **You can adjust the size of the Cover Flow display** (relative to the list-view half) by dragging up or down on the grip-strip area just beneath the Cover Flow scroll bar.

- **Multipage documents, presentation files, movies, and sounds are special.** When you point to one, you get either the ▶ button (to play a movie or sound) or ◀ and ➡ arrow buttons (to flip through a PDF, Pages, PowerPoint, or Keynote document), exactly as you can with icons in icon view.

- **You can navigate with the keyboard, too.** Any icon that's highlighted in the list view (bottom half of the window) is also front and center in the Cover Flow view. Therefore, you can use all the usual list-view shortcuts to navigate both at once. Use the ↓ and ↑ keys, type the first few letters of an icon's name, press Tab or Shift-Tab to highlight the next or previous icon alphabetically, and so on.

- **Cover Flow shows whatever the list view shows.** If you expand a flippy triangle to reveal an indented list of what's in a folder, then the contents of that folder become part of the Cover Flow.

- **The previews are actual icons.** When you're looking at a Cover Flow minidocument, you can drag it with your mouse—you've got the world's biggest target—anywhere you'd like to drag it: another folder, the Trash, wherever.

- **You can use the Arrange and Sort commands.** Yes, you can put the list-view portion of the window into tidy groupings—and sort within those groupings—just as described on pages 43–47.

Quick Look

As the preceding several thousand pages make clear, there are lots of ways to view and manage the seething mass of files and folders on a typical hard drive. Some of them actually let you see what's in a document without having to open it—the Preview column in column view, the giant icons in Cover Flow, and so on.

Quick Look takes this idea to another level. It lets you open and browse a document at nearly full size—without switching window views or opening any new programs. You highlight an icon (or several) and then do one of these things:

- **Press the space bar.** This is by far the best technique to learn. After all, unless you're editing a file's name, what's the space bar ever done for you in the Finder? Nothing. But in OS X, you can highlight any icon and then tap the space bar for an instant preview.

- **Tap with three fingers.** Here's a bonus for laptops, and it's new in Mountain Lion. Tap an icon with three fingers on the trackpad (don't fully click down) to open its preview.

- **Press ⌘-Y.** Another keystroke for the same function. The space bar is still better, though.

- **Click the ◉ icon at the top of the window.** But who uses the mouse anymore?

- **Choose File→Quick Look.**

- **Choose Quick Look from the Action menu (✿) at the top of every Finder window.**

• Control-click (or right-click) an icon; from the shortcut menu, choose Quick Look.

You exit Quick Look in any one of these same ways.

Note: Whenever Quick Look appears in a menu or a shortcut menu, its wording changes to reflect the name of the icon. For example, it might say, "Quick Look 'Secret Diary.doc.' "

Figure 1-24:
Once the Quick Look window is open, you can play a file (movies and sounds), study it in more detail (most kinds of graphics files), or even read it (PDF, Word, and Excel documents). You can also click another icon, and another, and another, without ever closing the preview; the contents of the window simply change to reflect whatever you've just clicked. Supertip: Quick Look even works on icons in the Trash, so you can figure out what something is before you nuke it forever.

In any case, the Quick Look window now opens, showing a gigantic preview of the document (Figure 1-24). Rather nice, eh?

The idea here is that you can check out a document without having to wait for it to open in the traditional way—at full size. For example, you can read the fine text in a Word or PowerPoint document without actually having to open Word or PowerPoint, which saves you about 45 minutes.

Tip: You can use the usual "next page" gesture (two-finger swipe on a trackpad, one-finger swipe on the Magic Mouse) to page through PDF or iWork documents, or to move among photos if you've highlighted a whole bunch.

It's astonishing how few Mac fans are aware of this incredibly useful feature. Learn it!

What Quick Look Knows

You might wonder: How, exactly, is Quick Look able to display the contents of a document without opening it? Wouldn't it have to somehow understand the internal file format of that document type?

Exactly. And that's why Quick Look doesn't recognize all documents. If you try to preview, for example, a Final Cut Pro video project, a sheet-music file, a .zip archive, or a database file, all you'll see is a six-inch-tall version of its generic icon. You won't see what's inside.

Over time, people will write plug-ins for those nonrecognized programs. Already, plug-ins that let you see what's inside folders and .zip files await at *www.qlplugins.com* and *www.quicklookplugins.com*. In the meantime, here's what Quick Look recognizes right out of the box:

- **Graphics files and photos.** This is where Quick Look can really shine, because it's often useful to get a quick look at a photo without having to haul iPhoto or Photoshop out of bed. Quick Look recognizes all common graphics formats, including TIFF, JPEG, GIF, PNG, RAW, and Photoshop documents.

- **PDF and text files.** Using the scroll bar, you can page through multipage documents, right there in the Quick Look window.

- **Audio and movie files.** These begin to play instantly when you open them into the Quick Look window. Most popular formats are recognized (MP3, AIFF, AAC, MPEG-4, H.264, and so on). A scroll bar appears so that you can jump around in the movie or song.

- **Pages, Numbers, Keynote, and TextEdit documents.** Naturally, since these are Apple programs, Quick Look understands the document formats.

- **Microsoft Word, Excel, and PowerPoint documents.** Because these formats are so common, OS X comes with a Quick Look plug-in to recognize them. Move through the pages using the vertical scroll bar; switch to a different Excel spreadsheet page using the Sheet tabs at the bottom.

- **Fonts.** Totally cool. When you open a font file in Quick Look, you get a crystal-clear, huge sampler that shows every letter of the alphabet in that typeface.

- **vCards.** A vCard is an address-book entry that people can send one another by email to save time in updating their Rolodexes. When you drag a name out of Apple's or Microsoft's address books and onto the desktop, for example, it turns into a vCard document. In Quick Look, the vCard opens up as a handsomely formatted index card that displays all the person's contact information.

- **HTML (Web pages) and Safari archived pages.** If you've saved some Web pages to your hard drive, here's a great way to inspect them without firing up your Web browser.

In fact, Quick Look has started seeping even faster into other programs—not just the Finder. For example, you can preview any of the following:

- **A link in a Mail message.** In Mail, there's a tiny ▾ next to each Web link. Click it to view the actual Web page it leads to, right there in a pop-up bubble!

- **An address in Mail or Safari.** If you ever see a street address in an email message or on a Web page, click the tiny ▾ next to it. You're offered the options to add this person to your address book, or to see a map of that address in Safari, courtesy of Google Maps.

- **An address in Contacts.** In the Contacts program, click the label for an address (like "Work" or "Home"); from the shortcut menu, choose Map This Address. You get to see, once again, an aerial photo of that spot in Safari, thanks to Google.

- **Anything in the Spotlight menu.** When you use the Spotlight search feature described in Chapter 3, point to anything in the results menu without clicking. In a moment, a big Quick Look bubble pops out to the left, showing what's actually in that document or file.

- **Anything in Mission Control, or a Dock menu.** You can also tap the space bar to get a Quick Look preview of anything in the Mission Control view (page 173) or the stack, list, or grid of a Dock folder (page 134).

And you were alive to see the day!

Fun with Quick Look

Here are some stunts that make Quick Look even more interesting:

- **Full screen.** When you click the Full Screen button (⬈), the Quick Look window expands to fill your screen. Keep this trick in mind when you're trying to read Word, Excel, or PDF documents, since the text is usually too small to read otherwise. (When you're finished with the closeup, click the Full Screen button again to restore the original Quick Look window, or the ⊗ button to exit Quick Look altogether.)

Tip: How's this for an undocumented shortcut? If you press Option-space bar, or Option-click the eyeball icon in any Finder window, you go straight into Full Screen mode without having to open the smaller Quick Look window first. Kewl.

(OK, this is actually part of the slideshow feature described below, but it's also good for super-enlarging a single icon.)

- **Share it.** Click the ⬆ button in the title bar to open the new Share pop-up menu—a quick way to send this document onto somebody or post it online.

- **Open with [Program Name].** This button shows up at the top-right corner of your Quick Look window. It might say, for example, "Open with Preview."

 Handy, really. It says: "Oh, so you've been Quick-Looking to find a particular document, and this is the one you wanted? Click me to jump directly into the program that opens it, so you can get to work reading or editing. I've just saved you having to close the window and double-click the icon."

Tip: Actually, you have a much bigger target than the "Open with" button in the corner. You can double-click *anywhere in the Quick Look window* to open the document (in whatever program is named on the "Open with" button).

Better yet: If you click and hold your cursor on that "Open with" button, you get a secret pop-up menu of other programs that could open the file you're looking at.

- **Keep it going.** Once you've opened Quick Look for one icon, you don't have to close it before inspecting another icon. Just keep clicking different icons (or pressing the arrow keys to walk through them); the Quick Look window changes instantly with each click to reflect the new document.

The Quick Look Slideshow

OS X is supposed to be all about graphics and other visual delights. No wonder, then, that it offers a built-in, full-screen slideshow feature.

It works like this: Highlight a bunch of icons, and then open Quick Look. Click the ⬚ (Full Screen) button in the top right corner. The screen goes black, and the documents begin their slideshow. Each image appears on the screen for about 3 seconds before the next one appears. (Press the Esc key or ⌘-period to end the show.) It plays all documents it recognizes, not just graphics.

It's a useful feature when you've just downloaded or imported a bunch of photos or Office documents and want a quick look through them. Use the control bar shown in Figure 1-25 to manage the playback.

Figure 1-25:
Once the slideshow is under way, you can use this control bar. It lets you pause the slideshow, move forward or backward manually, enlarge the current "slide" to fill the screen, or end the show. (The iPhoto button appears only when displaying photos.) The Index view is especially handy. (You can press ⌘-Return to "click" the Index View button.) It displays an array of labeled miniatures, all at once—a sort of Exposé for Quick Look. Click a thumbnail to jump directly to the Quick Look document you want to inspect.

Previous Pause Next Index View Add to iPhoto Exit Full Screen Exit Quick Look

Note: This same slideshow mechanism is available for graphics in Preview and Mail; Preview even offers crossfades between pictures.

Logging Out, Shutting Down

If you're the only person who uses your Mac, finishing up a work session is simple. You can either turn off the machine or simply let it go to sleep, in any of several ways.

Sleep Mode

If you're still shutting down your Mac after each use, you may be doing a lot more waiting than necessary. Sleep mode consumes very little power, keeps everything you were doing open and available, and wakes up almost immediately when you press a key or click the mouse.

To make your machine sleep, do one of the following:

- **Close the lid.** (Hint: This tip works primarily on laptops.)

- **Choose ** → **Sleep.** Or press Option-⌘-⏏.

- **Press Control-⏏.** In the dialog box shown in Figure 1-26, click Sleep (or type S).

Figure 1-26:
Once the Shut Down dialog box appears, you can press the S key instead of clicking Sleep, R for Restart, Esc for Cancel, or Return for Shut Down.

- **Press the power button (⏻) on your machine.** On desktop models, doing so makes it sleep immediately; on laptops, you get the dialog box shown in Figure 1-26.

- **Hold down the Play/Pause button on your remote for 3 seconds.** Many Mac models used to come with Apple's tiny white remote control.

- **Just walk away,** confident that the Energy Saver setting in System Preferences will send the machine off to dreamland automatically at the specified time.

Tip: Ordinarily, closing your MacBook's lid means putting it to sleep. And, ordinarily, putting it to sleep means cutting it off from the world. In Mountain Lion, though, a new feature called Power Nap lets your Mac stay connected to your network and to the Internet, even while it's otherwise sleeping. It can download email, back up your stuff, download software updates, and so on. For details, see page 358.

Restart

You shouldn't have to restart the Mac very often—only in times of severe trouble-shooting mystification, in fact. Here are a few ways to do it:

- **Choose →Restart.** A confirmation dialog box appears; click Restart (or press Return).

Tip: If you press Option as you release the mouse on the →Restart command, you won't be bothered by an "Are you sure?" confirmation box.

- **Press Control-⌘-⏏.**

- **Press Control-⏏** to summon the dialog box shown in Figure 1-26; click Restart (or type R).

Shut Down

To shut down your machine completely (when you don't plan to use it for more than a couple of days, when you plan to transport it, and so on), do one of the following:

- **Choose →Shut Down.** A simple confirmation dialog box appears; click Shut Down (or press Return).

Tip: Once again, if you press Option as you release the mouse, no confirmation box appears.

- **Press Control-Option-⌘-⏏.** (It's not as complex as it looks—the first three keys are all in a tidy row to the left of the space bar.)

- **Press Control-⏏** to summon the dialog box shown in Figure 1-26. Click Shut Down (or press Return).

- **Wait.** If you've set up the Energy Saver preferences (page 355) to shut down the Mac automatically at a specified time, then you don't have to do anything.

The "Reopen windows" option

In the Shut Down dialog box illustrated in Figure 1-26, you'll notice one of Lion/Mountain Lion's most-hyped new features: a checkbox called "Reopen windows when logging back in." That simple box does something very useful: The next time you start up your Mac, every running program, and every open window, will reopen exactly as they were at the moment you used the Restart or Shut Down command. The new option gives the Mac something like the old Hibernate feature in Windows—and saves you a lot of reopening the next time you sit down to work.

If you turn off that checkbox when you click Restart or Shut Down, then your next startup will take you to the desktop, with no programs running, as though this were still some year between 1984 and 2010. And if you want the Mac to stop asking—if you never want your programs and windows to reopen—open →System Preferences→General, and turn on "Close windows when quitting an application."

Log Out

If you share your Mac, then you should log out when you're done. Doing so ensures that your stuff is safe from the evil and the clueless even when you're out of the room. To do it, choose →Log Out Casey (or whatever your name is). Or, if you're in a hurry, press Shift-⌘-Q.

When the confirmation dialog box appears, click Log Out (or press Return) or just wait for 1 minute (a message performs the countdown for you). The Mac hides your world from view and displays the Log In dialog box, ready for its next victim.

Tip: Last time: If you press Option as you release the mouse on the →Log Out command, you squelch the "Are you sure?" box.

Logging out is described in much more detail in Chapter 13.

Getting Help in OS X

It's a good thing you've got a book about OS X in your hands, because the only user manual you get with it is the Help menu, a browser-like program that reads a set of help files that reside in your System→Library folder.

Tip: In fact, you may not even be that lucky. The general-information help page about each topic is on your Mac, but thousands of the more technical pages reside online and require an Internet connection to read.

You're expected to find the topic you want in one of these three ways:

- **Use the search box.** When you click the Help menu, a tiny search box appears just beneath your cursor (Figure 1-27). You can type a few words here to specify what you want help with: "setting up printer," "disk space," whatever.

Tip: You can also hit ⌘-Shift-/ (that is, ⌘-?) to open the help search box. And you can change that keystroke, if you like, in System Preferences→Keyboard.

Figure 1-27:
You don't have to open the Help program to begin a search. No matter what program you're in, typing a search phrase into the box shown here produces an instantaneous list of help topics, ready to read.

After a moment (sometimes several moments), the menu becomes a list of Apple help topics pertaining to your search. Click one to open the Help browser described next; you've just saved some time and a couple of steps.

Tip: The results menu does not, however, show all of Help's results—only the ones Apple thinks are most relevant. If you choose Show All Help Topics at the bottom of the menu, the Help browser opens (described below). It shows a more complete list of Help search results.

- **Drill down.** Alternatively, you can begin your quest for assistance the old-fashioned way: by opening the Help browser first. To do that, choose Help→Help Center. (That's the wording in the Finder. In other programs, it might say, for example, "Mail Help." Either way, this command appears only when nothing is typed in the search box. To empty the search box, click the ⊗ button at the right end.)

After a moment, you arrive at the Help browser program shown at top in Figure 1-28. The starting screen offers several "quick click" topics that may interest you—presumably the ones that trigger the most help-hotline calls to Apple. If so, keep clicking text headings until you find a topic you want to read.

GEM IN THE ROUGH

Menu Help in the Help Menu

OS X contains a weird, wonderful little enhancement to its online help system. It helps you find menu commands you can't find.

You're floundering in some program. You're *sure* there's a page numbering command in those menus somewhere. But there are 11 menus, and 143 submenus hiding in those menus, and you haven't got time for the pain.

That's when you should think of using the Help menu. When you type *page number* (or whatever) into its search box, the results menu lists, at the top, the names of any menu commands in that pro-

gram that contain the words you typed. Better still, it actually *opens that menu* for you, and displays a big, blue, animated, floating arrow pointing to the command you wanted. You'd have to have your eyes closed to miss it.

Simply slide your cursor over, click the menu command

you wanted, and get on with your life.

Supertip: This feature is especially helpful in Web browsers like Safari and Firefox, because it even finds entries in your Bookmarks and History menus!

In Safari, for example, you can pluck a recently visited site out of the hundreds in the daily History submenus, like the "Wednesday, January 4" submenu. You've just saved yourself a *lot* of poking around menus, trying to find the name of a site you know you've seen recently.

Ultratip: If you think about it, this feature also means you have complete keyboard power over every menu in every program in the world. Hit ⌘-Shift-/ (that is, ⌘-?) to open the Help search box, type a bit of the command's name, and then use the arrow keys to walk down the results. Hit Return to trigger the command you want.

You can backtrack by clicking the ◄ button at the top of the window. And you can always return to the starting screen by clicking the little ⌂ icon at the top.

Tip: Annoyingly, the help window still insists on floating in front of all other windows; you can't send it to the back like any normal program. Therefore, consider making the window tall and skinny, so you can put it beside the program you're working in. Drag any edge of the box to change the window's shape.

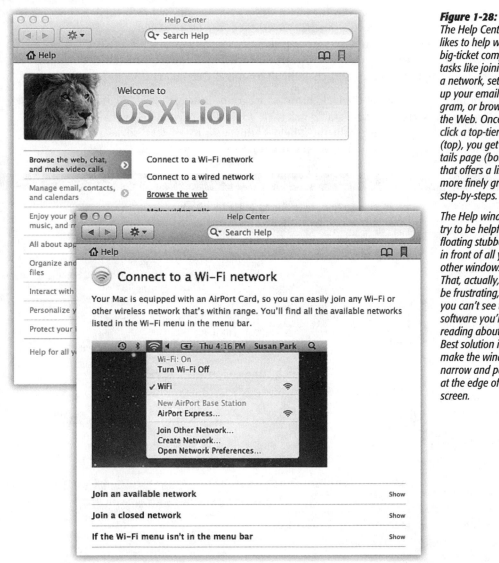

Figure 1-28:
The Help Center likes to help with big-ticket computer tasks like joining a network, setting up your email program, or browsing the Web. Once you click a top-tier topic (top), you get a details page (bottom) that offers a list of more finely grained step-by-steps.

The Help windows try to be helpful by floating stubbornly in front of all your other windows. That, actually, can be frustrating, since you can't see the software you're reading about. Best solution is to make the window narrow and park it at the edge of your screen.

- **Use the "Search Help" blank.** Type the phrase you want, like *printing* or *switching applications,* into the search box at the top of the window, and then press Return. As you type, a list of proposed matches drops down from the Search box. When you click the closest match, you're shown a list of help-screen topics that may pertain to what you need; see Figure 1-28 for details.

Note: Actually, there's one more place where Help crops up: in System Preferences dialog boxes. Click the circled question-mark button (⑦) in the lower-right corner of most System Preferences panels to open a help page that identifies each control.

Along the way, keep in mind that you can always bookmark useful Help pages for quick reference later, saving you the trouble of searching or burrowing the next time (Figure 1-29).

Figure 1-29:
Click the new Add Bookmark icon (▤) to flag a page for quick finding later (left). When that later time comes, click the Bookmarks icon (▥) to see a list of all your saved bookmarks; double-click one to jump to its page.

OS X: THE MISSING MANUAL

Organizing Your Stuff

The OS X Folder Structure

For the first 20 years of the Mac's existence, you began your workday by double-clicking the Macintosh HD icon in the upper-right corner of the screen. That's where you kept your files.

These days, though, you'd be disappointed if you did that. All you'll find in the Macintosh HD window is a set of folders called Applications, Library, Users, and so on—folders *you* didn't put there.

Most of these folders aren't very useful to you, the Mac's human companion. They're there for OS X's own use—which is why, today, the Macintosh HD icon doesn't even appear on the screen. (At least not at first; you can choose Finder→Preferences and turn the "Hard disks" checkbox back on, if you really want to.)

Think of your main hard drive window as storage for the operating system itself, which you'll access only for occasional administrative purposes.

Your Home Folder

So where is your nest of files, folders, and so on? All of it, everything of yours on this computer, lives in the *Home folder.* That's a folder bearing your name (or whatever name you typed in when you installed OS X).

OS X is rife with shortcuts for opening this all-important folder:

- Choose Go→Home, or press Shift-⌘-H.
- In the Sidebar (page 19), click the ⌂ icon.

You might also consider adding your Home folder to the Dock (page 131) or making it the window that appears when you press ⌘-N or choose File→New Finder Window (see page 32).

All these steps open your Home folder directly.

If you're the compulsive sort, you can also navigate to it the long way: Double-click the Users folder, and then double-click the folder inside it that bears your name and looks like a house (see Figure 2-1).

What's in the
hard drive window

A Home folder for
each account holder

What's in your
Home folder

Figure 2-1:
*This is it: the folder
structure of OS X.
For the most part,
what you care
about are the
Applications folder
in the main hard
drive window and
your own Home
folder. If you have
an administrator
account, you can
save your docu-
ments and park
your icons almost
anywhere.*

So why has Apple demoted your files to a folder three levels deep? The answer may send you through the five stages of grief—denial, anger, bargaining, depression, and, finally, acceptance—but if you're willing to go through it, much of the mystery surrounding OS X will fade away.

OS X has been designed from the ground up for *computer sharing*. It's ideal for any situation where different family members, students, or workers share the same Mac.

Each person who uses the computer will turn on the machine to find his own separate desktop picture, set of files, Web bookmarks, font collection, and preference settings. (You'll find much more about user accounts in Chapter 13.)

Like it or not, OS X considers you one of these people. If you're the only one who uses this Mac, fine—simply ignore the sharing features. (You can also ignore all that business at the beginning of Chapter 1 about logging in.) But in its little software head, OS X still considers you an account holder and stands ready to accommodate any others who should come along.

In any case, now you should see the importance of the Users folder in the main hard drive window. Inside are folders—the Home folders—named for the different people

who use this Mac. In general, nobody is allowed to touch what's inside anybody else's folder.

If you're the sole proprietor of the machine, of course, there's only one Home folder in the Users folder—named for you. (The Shared folder doesn't count; it's described on page 526.)

Yes, OS X imposes a fairly rigid folder structure. But by keeping such tight control over which files go where, OS X keeps itself pure—and very, very stable. Furthermore, keeping all your stuff in a single folder makes it very easy for you to back up your work. It also makes life easier when you try to connect to your machine from elsewhere in the office (over the network) or elsewhere in the world (over the Internet), as described in Chapter 21.

What's on Your Hard Drive

If you *did* want to explore the entirety of OS X, to examine the contents of your hard drive (choose Go→Computer and double-click "Macintosh HD"), you'd find the following folders in the main hard drive window:

- **Applications.** This folder contains the complete collection of OS X programs on your Mac (not counting the invisible Unix ones). Even so, you'll rarely open programs by opening this folder; the Dock is a far more efficient launcher, as described in Chapter 4.

- **Library.** This folder bears more than a passing resemblance to the System Folder subfolders of Macs gone by, or the Windows folder on PCs. It stores components for the operating system and your programs (sounds, fonts, preferences, help files, printer drivers, modem scripts, and so on).

UP TO SPEED

The Computer Window

In your explorations of the Finder's Go menu, you may have wondered about the command called Computer (Shift-⌘-C). ("Go to Computer? Jeez, I thought I was already *at* my computer!")

As in Microsoft Windows, the Computer window holds the icons for all the disks connected to your machine—the hard drive, a CD that you've inserted, an iPod, another external hard drive, and so on—as well as an icon called Network. (The Network icon appears even if you're not, in fact, on a network.) This is the topmost level of your Mac. This is the stuff that can't be put into any folder at all.

So what's it for? In some ways, the Computer window is redundant. After all, OS X displays your disk icons on the desktop *and* in the Sidebar.

But some people, particularly Windows refugees, don't care for that icons-on-the-desktop feature. In the interest of creating a neater, cleaner desktop, they turn it off (by choosing Finder→Preferences and turning off the three checkboxes under "Show these items on the Desktop"). Furthermore, in the interest of creating neater windows, some people also *hide* the Sidebar.

In that case, the Computer window still provides access to all your disks.

Otherwise, the Computer window really doesn't serve much purpose except as a familiar landmark to Windows veterans and Mac fans who grew used to it in the era before the Sidebar came along.

- **System.** This is Unix, baby. These are the actual files that turn on your Mac and control its operations. You'll rarely have any business messing with this folder.

- **User Information.** Here's a link to a folder that contains random Getting Started guides from Apple, including a user guide for your particular Mac.

- **Users.** As noted earlier, this folder stores the Home folders for everyone who uses this machine.

- **Your old junk.** If you upgraded your Mac from an earlier Mac operating system, then your main hard drive window also lists whatever folders you kept there.

What's in Your Home Folder

Within the folder that bears your name, you'll find another set of standard Mac folders. (The Mac considers them holy: they have special logos on their folder icons, and you can't rename them.) OS X creates these folders solely as a convenience:

- **Desktop.** When you drag an icon out of a window and onto your OS X desktop, it may *appear* to show up on the desktop. But that's just an optical illusion, a visual convenience. In truth, nothing in OS X is really on the desktop. It's actually in this Desktop folder, and mirrored on the desktop area.

 The reason is simple enough: Everyone who shares your machine will, upon logging in, see his own stuff sitting on the desktop. Now you know how OS X does it: There's a separate Desktop folder in every person's Home folder.

Tip: The fact that the desktop is actually a folder is handy, because it gives you a sneaky way to jump to your Home folder from anywhere. Simply click the desktop background and then press ⌘-↑ (which is the keystroke for Go→Enclosing Folder). Because that keystroke means "open whatever folder contains the one I'm examining," it instantly opens your Home folder. (Your Home folder is, of course, the "parent" of your Desktop folder.)

The Wacky Keystrokes of OS X

OS X offers a glorious assortment of predefined keystrokes for jumping to the most important locations on your Mac: your Home folder, the Applications folder, the Utilities folder, the Computer window, your iDisk, the Network window, and so on.

Better yet, the keystrokes are incredibly simple to memorize: Just press Shift-⌘ and the first letter of the location you want. Shift-⌘-H opens your Home folder, Shift-⌘-A opens the Applications folder, and so on. You learn one,

you've learned 'em all. The point here is that Shift-⌘ means *places*.

The other system-wide key combo, Option-⌘, means *functions*. For example, Option-⌘-D hides or shows the Dock, Option-⌘-H is the Hide Others command, Option-⌘-+ magnifies the screen (if you've turned on this feature), Option-⌘-Esc brings up the Force Quit dialog box, and so on. Consistency is always nice.

- **Documents.** Apple suggests that you keep your actual work files in this folder. Sure enough, whenever you save a new document (when you're working in Keynote or Word, for example), the Save As box proposes storing the new file in this folder, as described in Chapter 5.

 Your programs may also create folders of their own here. For example, you may find a Microsoft User Data folder for your Outlook/Entourage email, a Virtual Machines folder for use with VMware Fusion, and so on.

- **Library.** As noted earlier, the *main* Library folder (the one in your main hard drive window) contains folders for fonts, preferences, help files, and so on.

 You have your own Library folder, too, in your Home folder. It stores the same kinds of things—but they're *your* fonts, *your* preferences.

Note: In Mountain Lion, your own Library folder is invisible. But as you'll soon learn as you peruse this book, having access to it is frequently useful. That's why Apple gave you a sneaky way to open it *even* when it's invisible: Press Option as you open the Go menu in the Finder; choose Library (which doesn't appear in the menu until you press Option).

Once again, this setup may seem redundant if you're the only person who uses your Mac. But it makes perfect sense in the context of families, schools, or offices where numerous people share a single machine. Because you have your own Library folder, you can have a font collection that's "installed" on the Mac only when *you're* using it. Each person's program preference files (the files that determine where Photoshop's palettes appear, and so on) are stored independently, too. And each person, of course, sees her own email when launching OS X's Mail program—because mail, too, is generally stored in your personal Library folder.

Other Library folders store your Bookmarks, Web browser plug-ins and cached Web pages, keyboard layouts, sound files, and so on.

FREQUENTLY ASKED QUESTION

Printing a Window—or a List of Files

In Mac OS 9, I could print a Finder window. I'd get a neat list of the files, which I could use as a label for a CD I was going to burn, or whatever. How do I print a Finder window in OS X? (The File→Print command prints a selected document, not the list of files in a window.)

It's easy enough to make a list of files for printing. Once the window is open on your screen, choose Edit→Select All. Choose Edit→Copy. Now switch to a word processor and paste. (If you're using TextEdit, use Edit→Paste and Match Style instead.) You get a tidy list of all the files in that window, ready to format and print.

This simple file name list isn't the same as printing a window; you don't get the status bar showing how many items are on the disk and how full the disk is. For that purpose, you can always make a screenshot of the window (page 611) and print that. Of course, that technique is no good if the list of files is taller than the window itself.

Really, what you want is Print Window, a handy shareware program dedicated to printing out your Finder windows, without these workarounds and limitations. You can download it from this book's "Missing CD" page at *www. missingmanuals.com.*

• **Movies, Music, Pictures.** The various OS X programs that deal with movies, music, and pictures will propose these specialized folders as storage locations. For example, when you plug a digital camera into a Mac, the iPhoto program automatically begins to download the photos on it—and stores them in the Pictures folder. Similarly, iMovie is programmed to look for the Movies folder when saving its files, and iTunes stores its audio files in the Music folder.

• **Public.** If you're on a network, or if others use the same Mac when you're not around, this folder can be handy: It's the "Any of you guys can look at these files" folder. Other people on your network, as well as other people who sit down at this machine, are allowed to see whatever you've put in here, even if they don't have your password. Details on sharing the Mac are in Chapter 13, and those on networking are in Chapter 14.

• **Sites.** OS X used to have a built-in *Web server,* software that turns your Mac into a Web site that people on your network—or, via the Internet, all over the world—can connect to. This OS X feature relied on a program called the Apache Web server, which is so highly regarded in the Unix community that programmers lower their voices when they mention it.

The Web server is gone in Mountain Lion, as described in Chapter 21. If you have a Sites folder, it's where you put the actual Web pages you wanted to make available to the Internet at large—in a previous version of OS X.

Icon Names

Every document, program, folder, and disk on your Mac is represented by an *icon:* a colorful little picture that you can move, copy, or double-click to open. In OS X, icons look more like photos than cartoons, and you can scale them to practically any size.

An OS X icon's name can have up to 255 letters and spaces. If you're accustomed to the 31-character or even eight-character limits of older computers, that's quite a luxurious ceiling.

If you're used to Windows, you may be delighted to discover that in OS X, you can name your files using letters, numbers, punctuation—in fact, any symbol except the colon (:), which the Mac uses behind the scenes for its own folder-hierarchy designation purposes. And you can't use a period to *begin* a file's name.

To rename a file, click its name or icon (to highlight it) and then press Return. (Or, if you have time to kill, click once on the name, wait a moment, and then click a second time.)

In any case, a rectangle appears around the name (Figure 2-2). At this point, the existing name is highlighted; just begin typing to replace it. If you type a very long name, the rectangle grows vertically to accommodate new lines of text.

Tip: If you simply want to add letters to the beginning or end of the file's existing name, press the ← or →
key after pressing Return. The insertion point jumps to the beginning or end of the file name.

Figure 2-2:
Click an icon's name (top left) to produce the renaming rectangle (top right), in which you can edit the file's name. OS X is kind enough to highlight only the existing name, and not the suffix (like .jpg or .doc).

Now begin typing to replace the existing name (bottom left). When you're finished typing, press Return, Enter, or Tab to seal the deal, or just click somewhere else.

You can give more than one file or folder the same name, as long as they're not in
the same folder. For example, you can have as many files named "Chocolate Cake
Recipe" as you like, provided each is in a different folder. And, of course, files called
Recipe.doc and Recipe.xls can coexist in a folder, too.

As you edit a file's name, remember that you can use the Cut, Copy, and Paste com-
mands in the Edit menu to move selected bits of text around, just as though you
were word processing. The Paste command can be useful when, for instance, you're
renaming many icons in sequence (Quarterly Estimate 1, Quarterly Estimate 2…).

And now, a few tips about renaming icons:

- When the Finder sorts files, a space is considered alphabetically *before* the letter A.
 To force a particular file or folder to appear at the top of a list view window, insert
 a space (or an underscore) before its name.

- Older operating systems sort files so that the numbers 10 and 100 come before 2,
 the numbers 30 and 300 come before 4, and so on. You wind up with alphabeti-
 cally sorted files like this: "1. Big Day," "10. Long Song," "2. Floppy Hat," "20. Dog
 Bone," "3. Weird Sort," and so on. Generations of computer users have learned to
 put zeros in front of their single-digit numbers just to make the sorting look right.

 In OS X, though, you get exactly the numerical list you'd hope for: "1. Big Day," "2.
 Floppy Hat," "3. Weird Sort," "10. Long Song," and "20. Dog Bone."

- In addition to letters and numbers, OS X also assigns punctuation marks an "alpha-
 betical order," which is this: ` (the accent mark above the Tab key), ^, _, -, space, –,
 —, comma, semicolon, !, ?, ', ", (,), [,], {, }, @, *, /, &, #, %, +, <, =, ≠, >, |, ~, and $.

Numbers come after punctuation; letters come next; and bringing up the rear are these characters: μ (Option-M); π (Option-P); Ω (Option-Z), and (Shift-Option-K).

- When it comes time to rename files en masse, add-on shareware can help you. A Better Finder Rename, for example, lets you manipulate file names in a batch—numbering them, correcting a spelling in dozens of files at once, deleting a certain phrase from their names, and so on. You can download this shareware from this book's "Missing CD" page at *www.missingmanuals.com*.

Selecting Icons

To highlight a single icon in preparation for printing, opening, duplicating, or deleting, click the icon once. (In a list or column view, as described in Chapter 1, you can also click on any visible piece of information about that file—its size, kind, date modified, and so on.) Both the icon and the name darken in a uniquely OS Xish way.

Tip: You can change the color of the oval highlighting that appears around the name of a selected icon. Choose →System Preferences, click General, and use the Highlight Color pop-up menu.

That much may seem obvious. But most first-time Mac users have no idea how to manipulate *more* than one icon at a time—an essential survival skill in a graphic interface like the Mac's.

Figure 2-3:
You can highlight several icons simultaneously by dragging a box around them. To do so, drag from outside the target icons diagonally across them, creating a translucent gray rectangle as you go. Any icons or icon names touched by this rectangle are selected when you release the mouse. If you press the Shift or ⌘ key as you do this, then any previously highlighted icons remain selected.

Selecting by Clicking

To highlight multiple files in preparation for moving or copying, use one of these techniques:

- **Highlight all the icons.** To select all the icons in a window, press ⌘-A (the equivalent of the Edit→Select All command).

- **Highlight several icons by dragging.** You can drag diagonally to highlight a group of nearby icons, as shown in Figure 2-3. In a list view, in fact, you don't even have to drag over the icons themselves—your cursor can touch any part of a file's row, like its modification date or file size.

Tip: If you include a particular icon in your diagonally dragged group by mistake, ⌘-click it to remove it from the selected cluster.

- **To highlight consecutive icons in a list.** If you're looking at the contents of a window in list view or column view, you can drag vertically over the file and folder names to highlight a group of consecutive icons, as described above. (Begin the drag in a blank spot.)

There's a faster way to do the same thing: Click the first icon you want to highlight, and then Shift-click the last file. All the files in between are automatically selected, along with the two icons you clicked. Figure 2-4 illustrates the idea.

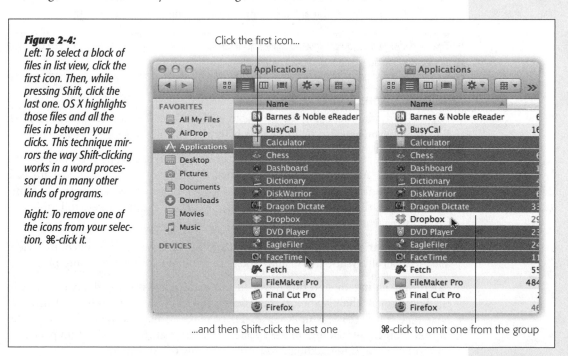

Figure 2-4:
Left: To select a block of files in list view, click the first icon. Then, while pressing Shift, click the last one. OS X highlights those files and all the files in between your clicks. This technique mirrors the way Shift-clicking works in a word processor and in many other kinds of programs.

Right: To remove one of the icons from your selection, ⌘-click it.

Click the first icon...

...and then Shift-click the last one

⌘-click to omit one from the group

- **To highlight random icons.** If you want to highlight only the first, third, and seventh icons in a window, for example, start by clicking icon No. 1. Then ⌘-click each of the others (or ⌘-drag new rectangles around them). Each icon darkens to show that you've selected it.

If you're highlighting a long string of icons and click one by mistake, you don't have to start over. Instead, just ⌘-click it again so the dark highlighting disappears. (If you do want to start over, you can deselect all selected icons by clicking any empty part of the window—or by pressing the Esc key.) The ⌘ key trick is especially handy if you want to select almost all the icons in a window. Press ⌘-A to select everything in the folder, then ⌘-click any unwanted icons to deselect them.

> *Tip:* In icon view, you can either Shift-click *or* ⌘-click to select multiple individual icons. But you may as well just learn to use the ⌘ key when selecting individual icons. That way you won't have to use a different key in each view.

Once you've highlighted multiple icons, you can manipulate them all at once. For example, you can drag them en masse to another folder or disk by dragging any *one* of the highlighted icons. All other highlighted icons go along for the ride. This technique is especially useful when you want to back up a bunch of files by dragging them onto a different disk, delete them all by dragging them to the Trash, and so on.

When multiple icons are selected, the commands in the File and Edit menus—like Duplicate, Open, and Make Alias—apply to all of them simultaneously.

> *Tip:* Don't forget that you can instantly highlight all the files in a window (or on the desktop) by choosing Edit→Select All (⌘-A)—no icon-clicking required.

Selecting Icons from the Keyboard

For the speed fanatic, using the mouse to click an icon is a hopeless waste of time. Fortunately, you can also select an icon by typing the first few letters of its name.

When looking at your Home window, for example, you can type *M* to highlight the Movies folder. And if you actually intended to highlight the Music folder instead, then press the Tab key to highlight the next icon in the window alphabetically. Shift-Tab highlights the previous icon alphabetically. Or use the arrow keys to highlight a neighboring icon.

(The Tab-key trick works only in icon, list, and Cover Flow views—not column view, alas. You can always use the ← and → keys to highlight adjacent columns, however.)

After highlighting an icon this way, you can manipulate it using the commands in the File menu or their keyboard equivalents: Open (⌘-O), put it into the Trash (⌘-Delete), Get Info (⌘-I), Duplicate (⌘-D), or make an alias (⌘-L), as described later in this chapter. By turning on the special disability features described on page 336, you can even *move* the highlighted icon using only the keyboard.

If you're a first-time Mac user, you may find it excessively nerdy to memorize key-

strokes for jobs the mouse can do. If you make your living using the Mac, however, memorizing these keystrokes will reward you immeasurably with speed and efficiency.

Moving and Copying Icons

In OS X, there are two ways to move or copy icons from one place to another: by dragging them and by using the Copy and Paste commands.

Copying by Dragging

You can drag icons from one folder to another, from one drive to another, from a drive to a folder on another drive, and so on. (When you've selected several icons, drag any *one* of them; the others tag along.) As you drag, you see the ghostly images of *all* the selected icons moving with your cursor. And the cursor itself sprouts a circled number that reminds you how many files you're moving.

Tip: You can tell that the copying is under way even if the progress bar is hidden. In Mountain Lion, a tiny progress bar appears right on the icon of the copied material in its new home. You can cancel the process either by pressing ⌘-period or by clicking the ⊗ in the progress window.

GEM IN THE ROUGH

Smart Handling of Identically Named Icons

What if you're dragging a file or folder into some window—and there's already a file or folder there with the same name?

In operating systems in days of yore, a warning message appeared. It let you Stop (the whole operation) or Replace (the existing items with the ones you were moving).

Mountain Lion is just a little bit smarter. It offers a third option: Keep Both.

For example, if you drag or paste *files* of the same name, you're offered a button called Keep Both Files. If you click it, OS X adds the number 2 (or 3, or 4…) to the end of the incoming file's name, so you can tell it apart from the existing one in the destination.

Tip: If you're dragging *several* files whose names match existing files in the destination folder, then OS X asks you individually about each one (Stop, Replace, Keep Both Files?). If you intend to answer the same way for every single file, save yourself the insanity by turning on the "Apply to all" checkbox before answering the question.

There's another, related new feature that comes into play when you paste a *folder* into a spot where there's another folder with the same name. In this case, the Mac offers to *merge the contents* of the two folders.

It might say, for example: "An item named 'Notes' already exists in this location. Do you want to replace it with the one you're moving? Each folder has unique items such as 'Salary Projections' and 'Stealth Projects.doc.' " And your choices are Stop, Keep Both, or Replace All. (These options appear only when you're *pasting* a folder into a new window—not dragging it. They also appear when you Option-drag a folder into a new window to copy it there, or when you drag it to a different disk.)

If you click Keep Both, the Finder *combines the contents* of the two folders. The folder you're pasting disappears, but its contents join the contents of the other folder (the one in the destination window) in blissful harmony.

Understanding when the Mac *copies* a dragged icon and when it *moves* it bewilders many a beginner. However, the scheme is fairly simple when you consider the following:

- On a single disk, dragging from one folder to another *moves* the icon.

- Dragging from one disk (or disk partition) to another *copies* the folder or file. (You can drag icons either into an open window or directly onto a disk or folder icon.)

- If you press the Option key as you release an icon you've dragged, you *copy* the icon instead of moving it. Doing so within a single folder produces a duplicate of the file called "[Whatever its name was] copy."

- If you press the ⌘ key as you release an icon you've dragged from one disk to another, you *move* the file or folder, in the process deleting it from the original disk.

Note: This business of pressing Option or ⌘ *after* you begin dragging is a tad awkward, but it has its charms. For example, it means you can change your mind about the purpose of your drag in mid-movement, without having to drag back and start over.

And if it turns out you just dragged something into the wrong window or folder, a quick ⌘-Z (the shortcut for Edit→Undo) puts it right back where it came from.

Copying or Moving with Copy and Paste

Dragging icons to copy or move them probably feels good because it's so direct: You actually see your arrow cursor pushing the icons into the new location.

But you pay a price for this satisfying illusion. You may have to spend a moment or two fiddling with your windows to create a clear "line of drag" between the icon to be moved and the destination folder. (A background window will courteously pop to the foreground to accept your drag. But if it wasn't even open to begin with, you're out of luck.)

There's a better way. Use Copy and Paste to move icons from one window into another.

The routine goes like this:

1. **Highlight the icon or icons you want to move.**

 Use any of the techniques described starting on page 79.

FREQUENTLY ASKED QUESTION

Dragging to Copy a Disk

Help! I'm trying to copy a CD onto my hard drive. When I drag it onto the hard drive icon, I get only an alias—not a copy of the CD.

Sure enough, dragging a disk onto a disk creates an alias.

But producing a copy of the dragged icon is easy enough:

Just press Option or ⌘ as you drag.

Honestly, though: Why are you trying to copy a CD this way? Using Disk Utility (page 456) saves space, lets you assign a password, and usually fools whatever software was on the CD into thinking that it's still *on* the original CD.

2. **Choose Edit→Copy.**

 Or press the keyboard shortcut: ⌘-C.

Tip: You can combine steps 1 and 2 by Control-clicking (or right-clicking) an icon and choosing the Copy command from the shortcut menu that appears—or by using the ⚙ menu. If you've selected several icons, say five, then the command says, "Copy 5 items."

3. **Open the window where you want to put the icons. Choose Edit→Paste.**

 Once again, you may prefer to use the keyboard equivalent: ⌘-V. And once again, you can also Control-click (right-click) inside the window and then choose Paste from the shortcut menu that appears, or you can use the ⚙ menu.

 If you add the Option key—press Option-⌘-V—you *move* the icons to the new window instead of copying them. That is, the originals disappear after they appear in the new location. (This might make more sense if you use the menu way: If you open the Edit menu and press Option, you'll see the Paste Items command change to say Move Items Here.) It took 27 years, but you can finally *cut* and paste icons, just as in Windows.

 You can press ⌘-period to interrupt the process. When the progress bar goes away, it means you've successfully transferred the icons, which now appear fully fleshed in the new window.

Dragging from the Title Bar

You may remember from Chapter 1 that the title bar of every Finder window harbors a secret pop-up menu. When you ⌘-click it, you're shown a little folder ladder that delineates your current position in the folder hierarchy. You may also remember that the tiny icon just to the left of the window's name is actually a handle that you can drag to move a folder into a different window.

In many programs, you get the same features in *document* windows, as shown in Figure 2-5. For example, by dragging the tiny document icon next to the document's name, you can perform these three interesting stunts:

GEM IN THE ROUGH

Icon's Progress: The Least-Marketed Feature in Mountain Lion

Here's an unsung little Mountain Lion feature: When you're copying a file or a folder, a tiny progress bar appears right on the icons as they sit in their new location. Animated and everything!

Doesn't matter if it's list view, icon view, or what—you'll see the progress bar.

You'll also see the little ⊗ button at the top left corner. That, of course, means "click me to cancel this copying job, since you obviously don't know about the ⌘-period keystroke."

Think of it as a little bit of mistake-recovery insurance, finally on the Mac after almost 30 years.

• **Create an alias on the desktop or the Dock.** By dragging this icon to the desktop or onto a folder or disk icon, you create an instant alias of the document you're working on. (If you drag into the right end of the Dock, you can park the document's icon there, too.) Before Lion's Resume Windows feature came along, this was a useful feature when, for example, you were about to knock off for the night, and you wanted easy access to the file you'd been working on when you returned the next day.

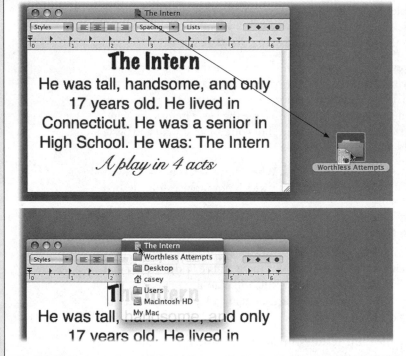

Figure 2-5:
Top: By dragging the document-window proxy icon, you can create an alias of your document on the desktop or anywhere else. (Make sure the icon has darkened before you begin to drag.)

Bottom: If you ⌘-click the name of the document in its title bar, you get to see exactly where this document sits on your hard drive. (Choosing the name of one of these folders opens that folder and switches you to the Finder.)

• **Attach a file to an email message.** You can drag a document (using its proxy icon as a handle) onto the icon of an email program like Mail or Outlook. That process creates a new, outgoing message with the file you dragged already attached. (If an outgoing message is already open in that program, you can drag the file directly into its window, too.) In either case, use the ⌘-Tab switcher (page 172) in mid-drag to switch programs.

• **Launch from a Dock icon.** By dragging this title-bar icon onto another program's *Dock icon,* you open your document in that other program. For example, if you're in TextEdit working on a memo and you decide that you'll need the full strength of Microsoft Word to dress it up, you can drag its title-bar icon directly onto the Word icon in the Dock. Word then launches and opens up the TextEdit document, ready for editing.

Note to struggling writers: Unfortunately, you can't drag an open document directly into the Trash.

Spring-Loaded Folders: Dragging Icons into Closed Folders

Here's a common dilemma: You want to drag an icon not just into a folder, but into a folder nested *inside* that folder. This awkward challenge would ordinarily require you to open the folder, open the inner folder, drag the icon in, and then close both windows. As you can imagine, the process is even messier if you want to drag an icon into a sub-subfolder or a *sub*-sub-subfolder.

Instead of fiddling around with all those windows, you can instead use the *spring-loaded folders* feature (Figure 2-6).

It works like this: With a single drag, drag the icon onto the first folder—but keep your mouse button pressed. After a few seconds, the folder window opens automatically, centered on your cursor. **In icon and Cover Flow views,** the new window instantly

Figure 2-6:
Top: To make spring-loaded folders work, start by dragging an icon onto a folder or disk icon. Don't release the mouse button. Wait for the window to open automatically around your cursor.

Bottom: Now you can either let go of the mouse button to release the file in its new window or drag it onto yet another, inner folder. It, too, will open. As long as you don't release the mouse button, you can continue until you've reached your folder-within-a-folder destination.

replaces the original. **In column view,** you get a new column that shows the target folder's contents. **In list view,** a second window appears.

Still keeping the button down, drag onto the inner folder; its window opens, too. Now drag onto the *inner* inner folder—and so on. (If the inner folder you intend to open isn't visible in the window, you can scroll by dragging your cursor close to any edge of the window.)

Tip: You can even drag icons onto disks or folders whose icons appear in the Sidebar (Chapter 1). When you do so, the main part of the window flashes to reveal the contents of the disk or folder you've dragged onto. When you let go of the mouse, the main window changes back to reveal the contents of the disk or folder where you *started* dragging.

In short, Sidebar and spring-loaded folders make a terrific drag-and-drop way to file an icon from anywhere to anywhere—without having to open or close any windows at all.

When you finally release the mouse, you're left facing the final window. All the previous windows closed along the way. You've placed the icon into the depths of the nested folders.

Making Spring-Loaded Folders Work

That spring-loaded folder technique sounds good in theory, but it can be disconcerting in practice. For most people, the long wait before the first folder opens is almost enough wasted time to negate the value of the feature altogether. Furthermore, when the first window finally does open, you're often caught by surprise. Suddenly your cursor—mouse button still down—is inside a window, sometimes directly on top of another folder you never intended to open.

Fortunately, you can regain control of spring-loaded folders using these tricks:

- Choose Finder→Preferences. On the General pane, adjust the "Spring-loaded folders and windows" delay slider to a setting that drives you less crazy. For example, if the first folder takes too long to open, then drag the slider toward the Short setting.

- You can turn off this feature entirely by choosing Finder→Preferences and turning off the "Spring-loaded folders and windows" checkbox.

- Tap the space bar to make the folder spring open at your command. That is, even with the Finder→Preferences slider set to the Long delay setting, you can force each folder to spring open when *you* are ready by tapping the space bar as you hold down the mouse button. True, you need two hands to master this one, but the control you regain is immeasurable.

Tip: The space bar trick works even when the "Spring-loaded folders and windows" checkbox (in Finder→Preferences) is turned off. That's a handy arrangement, because it means folder windows never pop open accidentally.

- Whenever a folder springs open into a window, twitch your mouse up to the newly opened window's title bar or down to its information strip. Doing so ensures that your cursor won't wind up hovering on, and accidentally opening, an inner folder. With the cursor parked on the gradient gray, you can take your time to survey the newly opened window's contents, and plunge into an inner folder only after gaining your bearings.

Tip: Email programs like Outlook and Mail have spring-loaded folders, too. You can drag a message out of the list and into one of your filing folders, wait for the folder to spring open and reveal its subfolders, and then drag it directly into one of them.

Aliases: Icons in Two Places at Once

Highlighting an icon and then choosing File→Make Alias (or pressing ⌘-L) generates an *alias,* a specially branded duplicate of the original icon (Figure 2-7). It's not a duplicate of the *file*—just of the *icon;* therefore it requires negligible storage space. When you double-click the alias, the original file opens. (A Macintosh alias is essentially the same as a Windows *shortcut.*)

Figure 2-7:
Top: You can identify an alias by the tiny arrow badge on the lower-left corner. (Longtime Mac fans should note that the name no longer appears in italics.)

Bottom: If the alias can't find the original file, you're offered the chance to hook it up to a different file.

You can create as many aliases as you want of a single file; therefore, in effect, aliases let you stash that file in many different folder locations simultaneously. Double-click any one of them and you open the original file, wherever it may be on your system.

Tip: You can also create an alias of an icon by Option-⌘-dragging it out of its window. (Aliases you create this way lack the word *alias* on the file name—a delight to those who find the suffix redundant and annoying.) You can also create an alias by Control-clicking (or right-clicking) a normal icon and choosing Make Alias from the shortcut menu that appears, or by highlighting an icon and then choosing Make Alias from the ✿ menu.

What's Good about Aliases

An alias takes up very little disk space, even if the original file is enormous. Aliases are smart, too: Even if you rename the alias, rename the original file, move the alias, and move the original around on the disk, double-clicking the alias still opens the original file.

And that's just the beginning of alias intelligence. Suppose you make an alias of a file that's on a removable disc, like a DVD. When you double-click the alias on your hard drive, the Mac requests that particular disc by name. And if you double-click the alias of a file on a different machine on the network, your Mac attempts to connect to the appropriate machine, prompting you for a password—even if the other machine is thousands of miles away and your Mac must go online to connect.

Here are a couple of ways you can put aliases to work:

- You can file a document you're working on in several different folders, or place a particular folder in several different locations, for convenience.

- You can use the alias feature to save you some of the steps required to access another hard drive on the network. (Details on this trick are in Chapter 14.)

Tip: OS X makes it easy to find the file an alias "points to" without actually having to open it. Just highlight the alias and then choose File→Show Original (⌘-R), or choose Show Original from the ✿ menu. OS X immediately displays the actual, original file, sitting patiently in its folder, wherever that may be.

POWER USERS' CLINIC

Designing Your Own Icons

You don't have to be content with the icons provided by Microsoft, Apple, or whoever else wrote your software. You can paste new icons onto your file, disk, and folder icons to help you pick them out at a glance.

The easiest way to replace an icon is to copy it from *another* icon. To do so, highlight the icon you want to copy, hold down the Option key, and choose File→Show Inspector. In the resulting window, click the icon, and then choose Edit→Copy.

Next, click the icon to which you want to transfer the copied picture. Its icon now appears in the Info dialog box that's still open on the screen. Click the icon in the dialog box, and this time choose Edit→Paste.

If you'd rather introduce all-new icons, you're welcome to steal some of the beautifully designed ones waiting at *www. iconfactory.com* and the icon sites linked to it. Once you've

downloaded these special icon files, you can copy their images from the Get Info window as you would any icon.

To design an OS X icon from scratch, use a graphics program like Photoshop or a shareware app like Pixelmator or GraphicConverter.

Once you've saved your icon file, select it, and then copy and paste its icon using the Show Inspector method described above.

Note that you can't change certain folder icons that OS X considers important, like Applications or System. You're also not allowed to change icons that belong to other people who share your Mac and sign in under a different name (Chapter 13).

You can, however, change the special OS X folder icons in your Home folder—Pictures, Documents, and so on—and your hard drive icon.

Broken Aliases

An alias doesn't contain any of the information you've typed or composed in the original file. Don't email an alias to the Tokyo office and then depart for the airport, hoping to give the presentation upon your arrival in Japan. When you double-click the alias, now separated from its original, you'll be shown the dialog box at the bottom of Figure 2-7.

If you find yourself 3,000 miles away from the hard drive on which the original file resides, click Delete Alias (to delete the orphan alias) or OK (to do nothing, leaving it where it is).

In certain circumstances, however, the third button—Fix Alias—is the most useful. Click it to summon the Fix Alias dialog box, which you can use to navigate the folders on your Mac. When you click a new icon and then click Choose, you associate the orphaned alias with a different file.

Such techniques become handy when, for example, you click your book manuscript's alias on the desktop, forgetting that you recently saved it under a new name and deleted the older draft. Instead of simply showing you an error message that says " 'Enron Corporate Ethics Handbook' can't be found," the Mac displays the box that contains the Fix Alias button. By reassociating the alias with the new document, you can save yourself the trouble of creating a new alias. From now on, double-clicking your manuscript's alias on the desktop opens the new draft.

Tip: You don't have to wait until the original file no longer exists before choosing a new original for an alias. You can perform alias reassignment surgery anytime you like. Just highlight the alias icon and then choose File→Get Info. In the Get Info dialog box, click Select New Original. In the resulting window, find and double-click the file you'd now like to open whenever you double-click the alias.

Color Labels

You can tag selected icons with one of seven different labels, each of which has both a text label and a color associated with it.

To do so, highlight the icons. Open the File menu (or the ✿ menu, or the shortcut menu that appears when you Control-click/right-click the icons). There, under the heading Label, you'll see seven colored dots, which represent the seven labels you can use. Figure 2-8 shows the routine.

Tip: If you use labels a lot, Control-click (or right-click) a Finder-window toolbar; choose Customize Toolbar; and drag the Label pop-up menu up to your toolbar. The advantage here is that once you've selected a label from this pop-up menu, you can reapply it to subsequent icons with one click–you don't have to open the menu the next time.

What Labels Are Good For

After you've applied labels to icons, you can perform some unique file-management tasks—in some cases on all of them simultaneously, even if they're scattered across multiple hard drives. For example:

- **Round up files with Find.** Using the Find command described in Chapter 3, you can round up all the icons with a particular label. Thereafter, moving these icons at once is a piece of cake—choose Edit→Select All, and then drag any one of the highlighted icons out of the results window and into the target folder or disk.

 Using labels in conjunction with Find like this is one of the most useful and inexpensive backup schemes ever devised: Whenever you finish working on a document that you'd like to back up, Control-click it and apply a label called, for example, Backup. At the end of each day, use the Find command to round up all the files with the Backup label—and then drag them as a group onto your backup disk.

Figure 2-8:
Use the File menu, ⚙ menu, or shortcut menu to apply label tags to highlighted icons. You can even apply a label within an icon's Get Info dialog box.

Instantly, the icon's name takes on the selected shade. In a list or column view, the entire row takes on that shade, as shown in Figure 2-9. (If you choose the little X, you remove any labels you may have applied.)

- **Sort a list view by label.** No other Mac sorting method lets you create an arbitrary order for the icons in a window. When you sort by label, the Mac creates alphabetical clusters *within* each label grouping, visible in Figure 2-9.

This technique might be useful when, for example, your job is to process several different folders of documents; for each folder, you're supposed to convert graphics files, throw out old files, or whatever. As soon as you finish working your way through one folder, flag it with a label called Done. The folder jumps to the top (or bottom) of the window, safely marked for your reference pleasure, leaving the next unprocessed folder at your fingertips, ready to go.

Tip: In a list view, the quickest way to sort by label is to first make the label column visible. Do so by choosing View→Show View Options and then turning on the Label checkbox.

Figure 2-9:
Top left: In the Labels tab of the Preferences dialog box, you can change the predefined label text. Each label can be as long as you could possibly want it.

Bottom right: Now your list and column views reveal meaningful text tags instead of color names.

- **Track progress.** Use different-colored labels to track the status of files in a certain project. For example, the first drafts have no labels at all. Once they've been edited and approved, make them blue. Once they've been sent to the home office, make them purple.

 (Heck, you could have all kinds of fun with this: Money-losing projects get red tints; profitable ones get green; things that make you sad are blue. Or not.)

Changing Labels

When you install OS X, the seven labels in the File menu are named for the colors they show: Red, Orange, Yellow, and so on. Clearly, the label feature would be much more useful if you could rewrite these labels, tailoring them to your purposes.

Doing so is easy. Choose Finder→Preferences. Click Labels. Now you see the dialog box shown in Figure 2-9, where you can edit the text of each label.

The Trash

No single element of the Macintosh interface is as recognizable or famous as the Trash icon, which appears at the end of the Dock. (It's actually a wastebasket, not a can, but let's not quibble.)

You can discard almost any icon by dragging it into the Trash can. When the tip of your arrow cursor touches the Trash icon, the little wastebasket turns black. When you release the mouse, you're well on your way to discarding whatever it was you dragged. As a convenience, OS X even replaces the empty-wastebasket icon with a wastebasket-filled-with-crumpled-up-papers icon, to let you know there's something in there.

It's worth learning the keyboard alternative to dragging something into the Trash: Highlight the icon, and then press ⌘-Delete (which corresponds to the File→Move to Trash command). This technique is not only far faster than dragging, but it also requires far less precision, especially if you have a large screen. OS X does all the Trash-targeting for you.

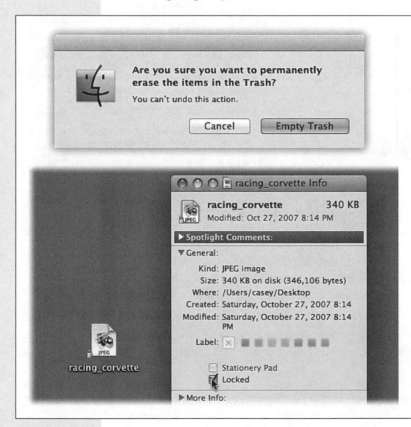

Figure 2-10:
Top: Your last warning. OS X doesn't tell you how many items are in the Trash or how much disk space they take up.

Bottom: The Get Info window for a locked file. Locking a file in this way isn't military-level security by any stretch—any passing evildoer can unlock the file in the same way. But it does trigger a warning when you try to put it into the Trash, providing at least one layer of protection against losing or deleting it.

Note: If a file is locked, a message appears to let you know; it offers you the chance to fling it into the Trash anyway. That's a better solution than in older versions of OS X, when you were forced to unlock the file before you could trash it.

Rescuing Files and Folders from the Trash

File and folder icons sit in the Trash forever—or until you choose Finder→Empty Trash, whichever comes first.

If you haven't yet emptied the Trash, you can open its window by clicking the waste-basket icon once. Now you can review its contents: icons that you've placed on the waiting list for extinction. If you change your mind, you can rescue any of these items in any of these ways:

- **Use the Put Back command.** This feature flings the trashed item back into whatever folder it came from, even if that was weeks ago.

 You'll find the Put Back command wherever fine shortcut menus are sold. For example, it appears when you Control-click the icon, right-click it, or click the icon and then open the ✿ menu.

Tip: The same keystroke you use to hurl something *into* the trash—⌘-Delete—also works to hurl it back *out* again. That is, you can highlight something in the Trash and press ⌘-Delete to put it back where it once belonged.

- **Hit Undo.** If dragging something to the Trash was something you just did, you can press ⌘-Z—the keyboard shortcut for the Edit→Undo command. (The Finder offers a five-level Undo, meaning that you can retrace your last five actions.)

 Undo not only removes a file from the Trash, but also returns it to the folder from which it came. This trick works even if the Trash window isn't open.

GEM IN THE ROUGH

Opening Things in the Trash

Now and then, it's very useful to see what some document in the Trash *is* before committing it to oblivion—and the only way to do that is to open it.

Trouble is, you can't open it by double-clicking; you'll get nothing but an error message.

Or at least that's what Apple *wants* you to think.

First of all, you can use Quick Look (page 59) to inspect something in the Trash.

But if Quick Look can't open the file—or if you want to *edit* it instead of just reading it—drag the document onto the icon of a program that can open it. That is, if a file called Don't Read Me.txt is in the Trash, you can drag it onto, say, the Word or TextEdit icon in your Dock.

The document dutifully pops open on the screen. Inspect, close, and *then* empty the Trash (or rescue the document).

• **Drag it manually.** Of course, you can also drag any icon out of the Trash with the mouse, which gives you the option of putting it somewhere new (as opposed to back in the folder it started from).

Emptying the Trash I: Quick and Easy

If you're confident that the items in the Trash window are worth deleting, use any of these three options:

• Choose Finder→Empty Trash.

• Press Shift-⌘-Delete. Or, if you'd just as soon not bother with the "Are you sure?" message, then throw the Option key in there, too.

• Control-click the wastebasket icon (or right-click it, or just click it and hold the mouse button down for a moment); choose Empty Trash from the shortcut menu.

The Mac asks you to confirm your decision. (Figure 2-10 shows this message.) If you click Empty Trash (or press Return), OS X deletes those files from your hard drive.

Tip: If you'd rather not be interrupted for confirmation every time you empty the Trash, you can suppress this message permanently. To do that, choose Finder→Preferences, click Advanced, and then turn off "Show warning before emptying the Trash."

Emptying the Trash II: Secure and Forever

When you empty the Trash as described above, each trashed icon sure looks like it disappears. The truth is, though, the data *in* each file is still on the hard drive. Yes, the space occupied by the dearly departed is now marked with an internal "This space available" message, and in time, new files may overwrite that spot. But in the meantime, some future eBay buyer of your Mac—or, more imminently, a savvy family member or office mate—could use a program like Data Rescue or FileSalvage to resurrect those deleted files. (In more dire cases, companies like DriveSavers.com can use sophisticated clean-room techniques to recover crucial information—for several hundred dollars, of course.)

That notion doesn't sit well with certain groups, like government agencies, international spies, and the paranoid. As far as they're concerned, deleting a file should *really, really* delete it, irrevocably, irretrievably, and forever.

OS X's *Secure* Empty Trash command to the rescue! When you choose this command from the Finder menu, the Mac doesn't just obliterate the parking spaces around the dead file. It actually records *new* information over the old—random 0's and 1's. Pure static gibberish.

The process takes longer than the normal Empty Trash command, of course. But when it absolutely, positively has to be gone from this earth for good (and you're absolutely, positively sure you'll never need that file again), Secure Empty Trash is secure indeed.

Tip: You can also direct the Mac to use this secure method *all the time.* To do that, choose Finder→Preferences, click Advanced, and turn on "Empty Trash securely."

Locked Files: The Next Generation

By highlighting a file or folder, choosing File→Get Info, and turning on the Locked checkbox, you protect that file or folder from accidental deletion (see Figure 2-10 at bottom). A little 🔒 icon appears on the corner of the full-size icon, also shown in Figure 2-10.

Locked files these days behave quite differently than they did in early OS X versions:

- Dragging the file into another folder makes a copy; the original stays put.

- Putting the icon into the Trash produces a warning message: "Item 'Shopping List' is locked. Do you want to move it to the Trash anyway?" If so, click Continue.

- Once a locked file is in the Trash, you don't get any more warnings. When you empty the Trash, that item gets erased right along with everything else.

You can unlock files easily enough. Press Option-⌘-I (or press Option as you choose File→Show Inspector). Turn off the Locked checkbox in the resulting Info window. (Yes, you can lock or unlock a mass of files at once.)

Get Info

By clicking an icon and then choosing File→Get Info, you open an important window like the one shown in Figure 2-11. It's a collapsible, multipanel screen that provides a wealth of information about a highlighted icon.

For example:

- For a document icon, you see when it was created and modified, and what programs it "belongs" to.

- For an alias, you learn the location of the actual icon it refers to.

- For a program, you see whether or not it's been updated to run on Intel-based Macs. If so, the Get Info window says either "Kind: Intel" (requires an Intel Mac) or "Kind: Universal" (runs on Intel and older Macs). If it says "Kind: PowerPC," then it can't run in Mountain Lion.

- For a disk icon, you get statistics about its capacity and how much of it is full.

- If you open the Get Info window when *nothing* is selected, you get information about the desktop itself (or the open window), including the amount of disk space consumed by everything sitting on or in it.

- If you highlight so many icons simultaneously that their Get Info windows would overwhelm your screen, OS X thoughtfully tallies up their information into a single summary window. It shows you how many icons you highlighted, breaks them down by type ("23 documents, 3 folders," for example), and adds up the total of their file sizes. That's a great opportunity to change certain file characteristics on numerous files simultaneously, such as locking or unlocking them, hiding or

showing their file name suffixes, changing their ownership or permissions (page 558), and so on.

How many icons do you have to highlight to trigger this Multiple Item Info box? That depends on the size of your screen; bigger monitors can hold more Get Info boxes. If you highlight fewer than that magic number of icons, OS X opens up individual Get Info windows for each one.

Tip: You can force the Multiple Item Info dialog box to appear, though, even if you've highlighted only a couple of icons. Just press Control-⌘-I. (The Option-⌘-I trick described next works for this purpose, too.)

Figure 2-11:
Top: The Get Info window can be as small as this, with all its information panes collapsed.

Bottom: Or, if you click each flippy triangle to open its corresponding panel of information, it can be as huge as this—shown here split in two because the book isn't tall enough to show the whole thing. The resulting dialog box can easily grow taller than your screen, which is a good argument for either (a) closing the panels you don't need at any given moment or (b) running out to buy a really gigantic monitor.

And as long as you're taking the trouble to read this caption, here's a tasty bonus: There's a secret command called Get Summary Info. Highlight a group of icons, press Control-⌘-I, and marvel at the special Get Info box that tallies up their sizes and other characteristics.

Uniwindow vs. Multiwindow

Ordinarily, when you click an icon and then choose File→Get Info, a new dialog box appears for each icon (unless you've highlighted a lot of icons, as described above).

But there's a useful variation on the Get Info dialog box called the Inspector. It's a single Get Info window that *changes,* even though it remains open on the screen, as you click different icons. It's a clutter-free way to explore different files, icons, and disks.

To open the Inspector, highlight an icon and then press Option-⌘-I (or hold down Option and choose File→Show Inspector). The Get Info Inspector window that appears looks slightly different (it has a smaller title bar and a dimmed Minimize button), and it changes to reflect whatever icons you now click.

The Get Info Panels

Apple built the Get Info window out of a series of collapsed "flippy triangles," as shown in Figure 2-11. Click a triangle to expand a corresponding information panel.

Tip: The title-bar hierarchical menu described on page 25 works in the Get Info dialog box, too. That is, ⌘-click the Get Info window's title bar to reveal where this icon is in your folder hierarchy.

Depending on whether you clicked a document, program, disk, alias, or whatever, the various panels may include the following:

- **Spotlight Comments.** Here you can type in comments for your own reference. Later, you can view these remarks in any list view if you display the Comments column—and you can find them when you conduct Spotlight searches (Chapter 3).

- **General.** Here's where you can view the name of the icon and also see its size, creation date, most recent change date, locked status, and so on.

 If you click a disk, this info window shows you its capacity and how full it is. If you click the Trash, you see how much stuff is in it. If you click an alias, this panel shows you a Select New Original button and reveals where the original file is. The General panel always opens the first time you summon the Get Info window.

- **More Info.** Just as the name implies, here you'll find more info, most often the dimensions and color format (graphics only) and when the icon was last opened. These morsels are also easily Spotlight-searchable.

- **Name & Extension.** On this panel, you can read and edit the name of the icon in question. The "Hide extension" checkbox refers to the suffix on OS X file names (the last three letters of Letter to Congress.doc, for example).

 Many OS X documents, behind the scenes, have file name extensions of this kind—but OS X comes factory-set to hide them. By turning off this checkbox, you can make the suffix reappear for an individual file. (Conversely, if you've elected to have OS X *show* all file name suffixes, then this checkbox lets you hide the extensions on individual icons.)

- **Open with.** This section is available for documents only. Use the controls on this screen to specify which program will open when you double-click this document, or any document of its type.

- **Preview.** When you're examining pictures, text files, PDF files, Microsoft Office files, sounds, clippings, and movies, you see a magnified thumbnail version of what's actually *in* that document. This preview is like a tiny version of Quick Look (Chapter 1). A controller lets you play sounds and movies, where appropriate.

- **Sharing & Permissions.** This panel is available for all kinds of icons. If other people have access to your Mac (either from across the network or when logging in, in person), this panel lets you specify who is allowed to open or change this particular icon. See Chapter 13 for a complete discussion of this hairy topic.

Shortcut Menus, Action Menus

It's part of the Mac's user-friendly heritage: You can do practically everything using only the mouse. Everything is out front, unhidden, and clickable, whether it's an icon, button, or menu.

But as in rival operating systems, you can shave seconds and steps off your workload if you master *shortcut menus:* short menus that sprout out of things you click, offering commands that the software thinks you might want to invoke at the moment, as shown in Figure 2-12.

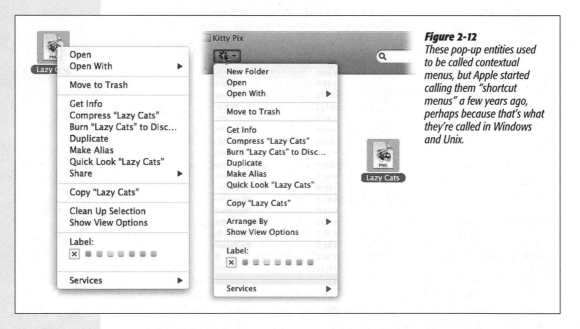

Figure 2-12
These pop-up entities used to be called contextual menus, but Apple started calling them "shortcut menus" a few years ago, perhaps because that's what they're called in Windows and Unix.

To summon one, just right-click or Control-click something—an icon, the desktop, a window, a link in Safari, text in a word processor, whatever. You can also trigger

these shortcut menus with special clicks on your trackpad or Magic Mouse; see page 237 for additional options.

In any case, a menu drops down listing relevant commands: Get Info, Move to Trash, Copy, and so on. You can click the command you want, or type the first couple of letters of it and then tap the space bar.

These menus become more useful the more you get to know them. The trouble is, millions of Mac fans never even knew they existed.

That's why there's a second way to access them. At the top of every Finder window, you'll find a ✿ pop-up menu that's technically called the *Action menu* (shown in Figure 2-12).

It lists the same sorts of commands you'd find in the shortcut menus, but it's *visible*, so novices stand a better chance of stumbling onto it.

The Finder shortcut menus offer some of the most useful Mac features ever. Don't miss these two in particular:

New Folder with Selection

Imagine this: You've got a bunch of scattered icons on your desktop, or a mass of related files in a window. You can now highlight all of them; right-click any one of them; and from the shortcut menu, choose "New Folder with Selection (12 items)" (or whatever the number of icons is).

With a cool animation, the Finder visibly throws the selected icons into a brand-new folder. It's initially named New Folder With Items (duh), but the hard part is over. All you have to do is rename it—and be grateful that you were spared the 736 steps it would have taken you to do the same job manually.

Share ☝

Here's one of Mountain Lion's headliner new features: a handy pop-up menu filled with ways to send whatever's highlighted to somebody else. In the case of selected

UP TO SPEED

Compressing, Zipping, and Archiving

OS X comes with a built-in command that compresses a file or folder down to a single, smaller icon—an archive—suitable for storing or emailing. It creates .zip files, the same compression format used in Windows. That means you can now send .zip files back and forth to PC owners without worrying that they won't be able to open them.

To compress something, Control-click (or right-click) a file or folder and choose "Compress [the icon's name]" from the shortcut menu. (Of course, you can use the File menu or ✿ menu instead.)

OS X thoughtfully creates a .zip archive, but it leaves the original behind so you can continue working with it.

Opening a .zip file somebody sends you is equally easy: Just double-click it. Zip!—it opens.

Finder icons, you can zip it away to someone using any of these three methods (see Figure 2-13):

- **Email.** Yes, it's the long-awaited "email this file right off the desktop" command. It whips open Mail and creates a new, outgoing message with the selected file (or files) already attached. Address and send, and make a sacrifice to the right-clicky gods.

- **Message.** This command lets you send a file—a photo or video clip, for example—to somebody's iPhone. Type a little message and then click Send. Off it goes, just as though you'd sent an iMessage from the Messages app described in Chapter 20.

- **AirDrop.** AirDrop is a slick, simple way to shoot a file from one Mac to another without involving any setup, network settings, or user accounts. Until Mountain Lion, you had to use the AirDrop *window* for this, as described on page 553.

 But in Mountain Lion, you don't have to budge from your current window. Click the file(s) you want to send, click Share→AirDrop, click the name of the nearby destination Mac, and click Send. Off it goes!

 This menu may also offer to send your file to Twitter, Facebook, or (if it's a photo or video (Flickr or Vimeo).

 For details on these and other Share-menu options, see page 268.

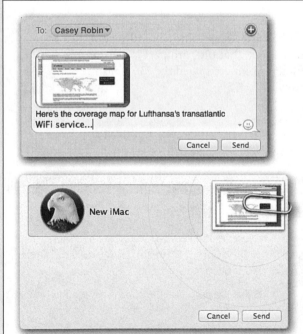

Figure 2-13:
The new Share menu in every Finder window offers direct access to three ways of transmitting a selected file icon to somebody else.

Top: For example, you can send a file to somebody's cellphone or iMessages account. Just specify the lucky winner's name here—and add a smiley face, if the mood strikes you (use the pop-up menu in the lower right).

Bottom: Alternatively, you can send a file to a nearby Mac (running Lion or later) without having to fiddle with network or sharing settings. Just type the name of the Mac you want and then click Send.

Spotlight

Every computer offers a way to find files. And every system offers several different ways to open them. But Spotlight, a star feature of OS X, combines these two functions in a way that's so fast, so efficient, so spectacular, it reduces much of what you've read in the previous chapters to irrelevance.

That may sound like breathless hype, but wait till you try it. You'll see.

The Spotlight Menu

See the little magnifying-glass icon (Q) in your menu bar? That's the mouse-driven way to open the Spotlight search box.

The other way is to press ⌘-space bar. If you can memorize only one keystroke on your Mac, that's the one to learn. It works both at the desktop and in other programs.

In any case, the Spotlight text box appears just below your menu bar (Figure 3-1).

Begin typing to identify what you want to find and open. For example, if you're trying to find a file called *Pokémon Fantasy League.doc,* typing just *pok* or *leag* would probably suffice. (The search box doesn't find text in the *middles* of words, though; it searches from the beginnings of words.)

A menu immediately appears below the search box, listing everything Spotlight can find containing what you've typed so far. (This is a live, interactive search; that is, Spotlight modifies the menu of search results *as you type.)* The menu lists every file, folder, program, email message, Contacts entry, calendar appointment, picture, movie, PDF document, music file, Web bookmark, Microsoft Office document (Word, PowerPoint, Excel, Entourage), System Preferences panel, To Do item, chat transcript,

Web site in your History list, and even font that contains what you typed, regardless of its name or folder location.

Note: Apple keeps enhancing Spotlight's file-finding skills with each new version of OS X. In Snow Leopard, Spotlight starting finding photos according to *who is in them* (using iPhoto's Faces feature) or where they were taken (using iPhoto's Places feature). If you use Messages (Chapter 20), Spotlight also finds the lucky members of your Buddy lists.

Now, in Lion/Mountain Lion, Spotlight also finds things according to their file types (type *.doc* to find Word files), download source (type *cnet.com* to find programs you downloaded from that site), sender (a name or email address), and Finder label.

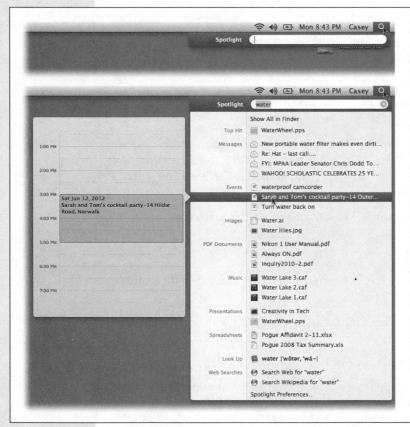

Figure 3-1:
Top: Press ⌘-space bar, or click the magnifying-glass icon, to make the search box appear.

Bottom: As you type, Spotlight builds the list of every match it can find, neatly organized by type: programs, documents, folders, images, PDF documents, and so on. But don't miss what may be one of the most useful tweaks ever: If you're not sure what something is, point to it without clicking—or pause on it as you walk down the list with the arrow keys. A Quick Look preview pops out to the left. It shows exactly what's in that movie, picture, document, or whatever. If your search has found an appointment from your calendar, you actually see a slice of that day's calendar, showing the appointment in context!

How to Handle Your Results

If you see the icon you were hoping to dig up, just click it to open it. Or use the arrow keys to walk down the menu, and then press Return to open the one you want.

You can use the new Quick Look preview to see what something is before you take the time to open it, as shown in Figures 3-1 and 3-2. Or check out Figure 3-2 to see how to find out *where something is*.

If you click an application, it opens. If you select a System Preferences panel, System Preferences opens and presents that panel. If you choose an appointment, the Calendar program opens, already set to the appropriate day and time. Selecting an email message opens that message in Mail or Outlook. And so on.

Spotlight is so fast, it eliminates a lot of the folders-in-folders business that's a side effect of modern computing. Why burrow around in folders when you can open any file or program with a couple of keystrokes?

Tip: You can drag icons right out of the results list. For example, you can drag one onto the Desktop to park it there; into a window or a folder to move it; into the Trash to delete it; onto the AirDrop icon (in the Sidebar) to hand it over to a colleague; to another disk icon to back it up; and so on.

Figure 3-2:
If you press ⌘-Option as you point to one of the results, you get a line of text beneath the image that identifies the file's location.

Spotlight-Menu Tips

It should be no surprise that a feature as important as Spotlight comes loaded with options, tips, and tricks. Here it is—the official, unexpurgated Spotlight Tip-O-Rama:

- If the very first item—labeled Top Hit—is the icon you were looking for, just press Return to open it. This is a huge deal, because it means that in most cases, you can perform the entire operation without ever taking your hands off the keyboard.

 To open Safari in a hurry, for example, press ⌘-space bar (to open the Spotlight search box), type *safa*, and hit Return, all in rapid-fire sequence, without even looking. Presto: Safari is before you.

 And what, exactly, is the Top Hit? OS X chooses it based on its *relevance* (the importance of your search term inside that item) and timeliness (when you last opened it).

Tip: Spotlight makes a spectacular application launcher. That's because Job One for Spotlight is to display the names of matching programs in the results menu. Their names appear in the list nearly instantly—long before Spotlight has built the rest of the menu of search results.

If some program on your hard drive doesn't have a Dock icon, for example—or even if it does—there's no faster way to open it than to use Spotlight.

- To jump to (highlight) a search result's Finder icon instead of opening it, ⌘-click its name. Or arrow-key your way to the result's name and then press ⌘-Return.

- Spotlight's menu shows you only 20 of the most likely suspects, evenly divided among the categories (Documents, Applications, and so on). The downside: To see the complete list, you have to open the Spotlight *window* (page 112).

The upside: It's fairly easy to open something in this menu from the keyboard. Just press ⌘-↑ (or ⌘-↓) to jump from category to category. Once you've highlighted the first result in a category, you can walk through the remaining four by press-

GEM IN THE ROUGH

Sweet Spotlight Serendipity: Equations and Definitions

Spotlight has two secret features that turn it into a different beast altogether.

First, it's a tiny pocket calculator, always at the ready. Click in the search box (or press ⌘-space bar), type or paste *38*48.2-7+55*, and marvel at the first result in the Spotlight menu: *1879.6.* There's your answer—and you didn't even have to fire up the Calculator.

(For shorter equations— only a few characters long—the first result in the Spotlight menu shows the *entire* equation, like *.15*234=35.1.)*

And it's not just a four-function calculator, either. It works with square roots: Type *sqrt(25)*, and you'll get the answer 5. It also works with functions like *log(x), exp(x), sin(x), sinh(x)*, and *e*. You can even type *pi* to represent, you know, pi.

You can copy the result to the Clipboard, or even drag it out of the Spotlight bar into another program.

(Sadly, not all of the math functions from previous OS X versions work in Mountain Lion. The *pow(x,y)* command, for example, is gone.)

Second, the Spotlight menu is now a full-blown English dictionary. Or, more specifically, it's wired directly into OS X's *own* dictionary, which sits in your Applications folder.

So if you type a word— say, *myrmecophile*—into the search box, you'll see the Dictionary definition near the bottom of the results. Point to it without clicking to read the full-blown entry, thanks to the pop-out Quick Look preview. (In this example, that would be: "n: an invertebrate or plant that has a symbiotic relationship with ants.")

ing the arrow key by itself. Then, once you've highlighted what you want, press Return to open it.

In other words, you can get to anything in the Spotlight menu with only a few keystrokes.

- The Esc key (top-left corner of your keyboard) offers a two-stage "back out of this" method. Tap it once to close the Spotlight menu and erase what you've typed, so that you're all ready to type in something different. Tap Esc a *second* time to close the Spotlight text box entirely, having given up on the whole idea of searching.

- Think of Spotlight as your little black book. When you need to look up a number in Contacts, don't bother opening Contacts; it's faster to use Spotlight. You can type somebody's name or even part of someone's phone number.

- If you're searching for just one word, you'll see a "Look Up" category near the bottom of the results menu. Click it to open up that word's definition in the Dictionary program.

- The bottom of Spotlight always lists commands for "Search Web for [your phrase]" and "Search Wikipedia for [your phrase]." They take you straight to the Google search or the Wikipedia (online encyclopedia) results for whatever you typed.

- Among a million other things, Spotlight tracks the keywords, descriptions, faces, and places you've applied to your pictures in iPhoto. As a result, you can find, open, or insert any iPhoto photo at any time, no matter what program you're using, just by using the Spotlight box at the top of every Open File dialog box! This is a great way to insert a photo into an outgoing email message, a presentation, or a Web page you're designing. iPhoto doesn't even have to be running.

- Spotlight is also a quick way to adjust one of your Mac's preference settings. Instead of opening the System Preferences program, type the first few letters of, say, *volume* or *network* or *clock* into Spotlight. The Spotlight menu lists the appropriate System Preferences panel, so you can jump directly to it.

- As shown in Figure 3-2, you get a preview of what's inside a file listed in the Spotlight menu when you point to it without clicking. But if you add the ⌘ key, you see a tiny line of text below the preview. It tells you the item's actual name—which is useful if Spotlight listed something because of text that appears *inside* the file, not its name—and if you wait a moment, you also see its folder path (that is, where it is on your hard drive).

Tip: If you're in a hurry, just press ⌘-Option as you point. That makes the folder path appear immediately.

- While you're pointing to something in the results list, you can press ⌘-I to open the Get Info window for it.

- The Spotlight menu lists 20 found items. In the following pages, you'll learn about how to see the rest of the stuff. But for now, note that you can eliminate some of the categories that show up here (like PDF documents or Bookmarks), and even

rearrange them, to permit more of the *other* kinds of things to enjoy those 20 seats of honor. Details on page 126.

- Spotlight shows you only the matches from *your account* and the public areas of the Mac (like the System, Application, and Developer folders)—but not what's in anyone else's Home folder. If you were hoping to search your spouse's email for phrases like "meet you at midnight," forget it.

- If Spotlight finds a different version of something on each of two hard drives, it lets you know by displaying a faint gray hard drive name after each such item in the menu.

- Spotlight works by storing an *index*, a private, multimegabyte Dewey Decimal System, on each hard drive, disk partition, or USB flash (memory) drive. If you have some oddball type of disk, like a hard drive that's been formatted for Windows, Spotlight doesn't ordinarily index it—but you can turn on indexing by using the File→Get Info command on that drive's icon.

What Spotlight Knows

The beauty of Spotlight is that it doesn't just find files whose names match what you've typed. That would be *so* 2004!

No, Spotlight actually looks *inside* the files. It can actually read and search the contents of text files, RTF and PDF documents, documents from iWork, Keynote, Pages, Photoshop, Microsoft Office (Word, Excel, Entourage, and PowerPoint), and so on.

Over time, software companies can release bits of add-on software—plug-ins—that will make their documents searchable by Spotlight, too. Check periodically by Googling, for example, *spotlight plug-in* and the kind of software you use. For example, free Spotlight plug-ins are available for OmniGraffle, OmniOutliner, TypeIt4Me, MacDraft, REALbasic, Painter, Wolfram Notebook, and many others.

But that's only the beginning. Spotlight searches files not only for the text inside them, but also for over 125 other bits of text—a staggering collection of information tidbits including the names of the layers in a Photoshop document, the tempo of an MP3 file, the shutter speed of a digital-camera photo, a movie's copyright holder, a document's page size,

and on and on.

Technically, this sort of secondary information is called *metadata*. It's usually invisible, although a lot of it shows up in the Get Info dialog box described in Chapter 2.

You might think that typing something into the Spotlight search box triggers a search. But to be technically correct, Spotlight has already done its searching. In the first 15 to 30 minutes after you install Mountain Lion—or in the minutes after you attach a new hard drive—Spotlight invisibly collects information about everything on your hard drive. Like a kid cramming for an exam, it reads, takes notes on, and memorizes the contents of all your files. (During this time, if you click the Q icon on the menu bar, you'll be told that Spotlight is indexing the drives.) Once it has indexed your hard drive in this way, Spotlight can produce search results in seconds.

After that initial indexing process, Spotlight continues to monitor what's on your hard drive, indexing new and changed files in the background, in the microseconds between your keystrokes and clicks in other programs.

Tip: Spotlight can even find words inside files on other computers on your network—as long as they're also Macs running Mac OS X Leopard (10.5) or later. If not, Spotlight can search only for the names of files on other networked computers.

Advanced Menu Searches

Most people just type the words they're looking for into the Spotlight box. But if that's all you type, you're missing a lot of the fun.

Use quotes

If you type more than one word, Spotlight works just the way Google does. That is, it finds things that contain both words *somewhere* inside.

But if you're searching for a phrase where the words really belong together, put quotes around them. You'll save yourself from having to wade through hundreds of results where the words appear *separately*.

For example, searching for *military intelligence* rounds up documents that contain those two words, but not necessarily side by side. Searching for *"military intelligence"* finds documents that contain that exact phrase. (Insert your own political joke here.)

Limit by kind

You can confine your search to certain categories using a simple code. For example, to find all photos, type *kind:image*. If you're looking for a presentation document but you're not sure whether you used Keynote, iWork, or PowerPoint to create it, type *kind:presentation* into the box. And so on.

Here's the complete list of kinds. Remember to precede each keyword type with *kind* and a colon.

To find this:	Use one of these keywords:
A program	app, application, applications
Someone in your address book	contact, contacts
A folder or disk	folder, folders
A message in Mail	email, emails, mail message, mail messages
A Calendar appointment	event, events
A Calendar task	to do, to dos, todo, todos
A graphic	image, images
A movie	movie, movies
A music file	music
An audio file	audio
A PDF file	pdf, pdfs
A System Preferences control	preferences, system preferences
A Safari bookmark	bookmark, bookmarks
A font	font, fonts
A presentation (PowerPoint, iWork)	presentation, presentations

You can combine these codes with the text you're seeking, too. For example, if you're pretty sure you had a photo called "Naked Mole-Rat," you could cut directly to it by typing *mole kind:images* or *kind:images mole* (the order doesn't matter).

Limit by recent date

You can use a similar code to restrict the search by chronology. If you type *date:yesterday*, then Spotlight limits its hunt to items you last opened yesterday.

Here's the complete list of date keywords you can use: *this year, this month, this week, yesterday, today, tomorrow, next week, next month, next year.* (The last four items are useful only for finding upcoming Calendar appointments. Even Spotlight can't show you files you haven't created yet.)

Limit by metadata

If your brain is already on the verge of exploding, now might be a good time to take a break.

These days, you can limit Spotlight searches by *any* of the 125 different info-morsels that may be stored as part of the files on your Mac: author, audio bit rate, city, composer, camera model, pixel width, and so on. Page 120 has a complete discussion of these so-called *metadata* types. (Metadata means "data about the data"—that is, descriptive info-bites about the files themselves.) Here are a few examples:

• *author:casey.* Finds all documents with "casey" in the Author field. (This presumes that you've actually *entered* the name Casey into the document's Author box. Microsoft Word, for example, has a place to store this information.)

• *width:800.* Finds all graphics that are 800 pixels wide.

• *flash:1.* Finds all photos that were taken with the camera's flash on. (To find photos with the flash *off*, you'd type *flash:0*. A number of the yes/no criteria work this way: Use 1 for yes, 0 for no.)

• *modified:3/7/12-3/10/12.* Finds all documents modified between March 7 and March 10, 2012. You can also type *created:6/1/12* to find all the files you created on June 1, 2012. Type *modified:<=3/9/12* to find all documents you edited *on or before* March 9, 2012.

As you can see, three range-finding symbols are available for your queries: <, >, and - (hyphen). The < means "before" or "less than"; the > means "after" or "greater than"; and the hyphen indicates a range (of dates, sizes, or whatever you're looking for).

Tip: Here again, you can string words together. To find all PDFs you opened today, use date:today kind:PDF. And if you're looking for a PDF document that you created on July 4, 2012, containing the word wombat, you can type created:7/4/12 kind:pdf wombat—although at this point, you're not saving all that much time.

Now, those examples are just a few representative searches out of the dozens that OS X makes available.

It turns out that the search criteria codes you can type into the Spotlight box (*author:casey, width:800,* and so on) correspond to the master list that appears when you choose Other in the Spotlight *window,* as described on page 121. In other words, there are *125 different* search criteria.

There's only one confusing part: In the Other list, lots of metadata types have spaces in their names—*pixel width, musical genre, phone number,* and so on.

Yet you're allowed to use only *one* word before the colon when you type a search into the Spotlight box. For example, even though *pixel width* is a metadata type, you have to use *width:* or *pixelwidth:* in your search.

So it would probably be helpful to have a master list of the *one-word* codes that Spotlight recognizes—the shorthand versions of the criteria described on page 121.

Here it is, a Missing Manual exclusive, deep from within the bowels of Apple's Spotlight department: the master list of one-word codes. (Note that some search criteria have several alternate one-word names.)

Real Search Attribute	One-Word Name(s)
Keywords	keyword
Title	title
Subject	subject, title
Theme	theme
Authors	author, from, with, by
Editors	editor
Projects	project
Where from	wherefrom
Comment	comment
Copyright	copyright
Producer	producer
Used dates	used, date
Last opened	lastused, date
Content created	contentcreated, created, date
Content modified	contentmodified, modified, date
Duration	duration, time
Item creation	itemcreated, created, date
Contact keywords	contactkeyword, keyword
Version	version
Pixel height	pixelheight, height
Pixel width	pixelwidth, width
Page height	pageheight, height
Page width	pagewidth, width
Color space	colorspace
Bits per sample	bitspersample, bps
Flash	flash
Focal length	focallength
Alpha channel	alpha
Device make (camera brand)	make
Device model (camera model)	model
ISO speed	iso
Orientation	orientation
Layers	layer
White balance	whitebalance
Aperture	aperture, fstop
Profile name	profile

Resolution width	widthdpi, dpi
Resolution height	heightdpi, dpi
Exposure mode	exposuremode
Exposure time	exposuretime, time
EXIF version	exifversion
Codecs	codec
Media types	mediatype
Streamable	streamable
Total bit rate	totalbitrate, bitrate
Video bit rate	videobitrate, bitrate
Audio bit rate	audiobitrate, bitrate
Delivery type	delivery
Altitude	altitude
Latitude	latitude
Longitude	longitude
Text content	intext
Display name	displayname, name
Red eye	redeye
Metering mode	meteringmode
Max aperture	maxaperture
F-number	fnumber, fstop
Exposure program	exposureprogram
Exposure time	exposuretime, time
Headline	headline, title
Instructions	instructions
City	city
State or province	state, province
Country	country
Album	album, title
Sample rate	audiosamplerate, samplerate
Channel count	channels
Tempo	tempo
Key signature	keysignature, key
Time signature	timesignature
Audio encoding application	audioencodingapplication
Composer	composer, author, by
Lyricist	lyricist, author, by
Track number	tracknumber
Recording date	recordingdate, date
Musical genre	musicalgenre, genre
General MIDI sequence	ismidi
Recipients	recipient, to, with
Year recorded	yearrecorded, year
Organizations	organization
Languages	language
Rights	rights
Publishers	publisher
Contributors	contributor, by, author, with
Coverage	coverage
Description	description, comment
Identifier	id
Audiences	audience, to
Pages	pages
Security method	securitymethod
Content Creator	creator
Due date	duedate, date
Encoding software	encodingapplication
Rating	starrating

```
Phone number. . . . . . . . . . . . . . . . . . . . . . . . . . . . . . . . . phonenumber
Email addresses . . . . . . . . . . . . . . . . . . . . . . . . . . . . . email
Instant message addresses . . . . . . . . . . . . . . . . . . . . . imname
Kind. . . . . . . . . . . . . . . . . . . . . . . . . . . . . . . . . . . . . . . . kind
URL. . . . . . . . . . . . . . . . . . . . . . . . . . . . . . . . . . . . . . . . url
Recipient email addresses . . . . . . . . . . . . . . . . . . . . . email
Email addresses . . . . . . . . . . . . . . . . . . . . . . . . . . . . . email
Filename. . . . . . . . . . . . . . . . . . . . . . . . . . . . . . . . . . . . filename
File pathname. . . . . . . . . . . . . . . . . . . . . . . . . . . . . . . path
Size . . . . . . . . . . . . . . . . . . . . . . . . . . . . . . . . . . . . . . . size
Created . . . . . . . . . . . . . . . . . . . . . . . . . . . . . . . . . . . . created
Modified . . . . . . . . . . . . . . . . . . . . . . . . . . . . . . . . . . . modified
Owner. . . . . . . . . . . . . . . . . . . . . . . . . . . . . . . . . . . . . . owner
Group . . . . . . . . . . . . . . . . . . . . . . . . . . . . . . . . . . . . . . group
Stationery . . . . . . . . . . . . . . . . . . . . . . . . . . . . . . . . . . stationery
File invisible . . . . . . . . . . . . . . . . . . . . . . . . . . . . . . . . invisible
File label . . . . . . . . . . . . . . . . . . . . . . . . . . . . . . . . . . . label
Spotlight comments. . . . . . . . . . . . . . . . . . . . . . . . . . spotlightcomment, comment
Fonts . . . . . . . . . . . . . . . . . . . . . . . . . . . . . . . . . . . . . . font
Instrument category. . . . . . . . . . . . . . . . . . . . . . . . . . instrumentcategory
Instrument name . . . . . . . . . . . . . . . . . . . . . . . . . . . . instrumentname
```

Boolean searches

What comp sci professors call *Boolean* searches are terms that round up results containing *either* of two search terms, *both* search terms, or one term but *not* another.

To go Boolean, you're supposed to incorporate terms like AND, OR, or NOT into your search queries.

For example, you can round up a list of files that match *two* terms by typing, say, *vacation AND kids.* (That's also how you'd find documents coauthored by two people—you and a pal, for example. You'd search for *author:Casey AND author:Chris.* Yes, you have to type Boolean terms in all capitals.)

Tip: You can use parentheses instead of AND, if you like. That is, typing (vacation kids) finds documents that contain both words, not necessarily together. But the truth is, Spotlight runs an AND search whenever you type two terms, like vacation kids—neither parentheses nor AND is required.

If you use OR, you can find items that match *either* of two search criteria. Typing *kind:jpeg OR kind:pdf* turns up photos and PDF files in a single list.

The minus sign (hyphen) works, too. If you did a search for *dolphins,* hoping to turn up sea-mammal documents, but instead find your results contaminated by football-team listings, by all means repeat the search with *dolphins -miami.* OS X eliminates all documents containing "Miami."

Tip: The word NOT works the same way. You could type dolphins NOT miami to achieve the same effect. But the hyphen is faster to type.

The Spotlight Window

As you may have noticed, the Spotlight menu doesn't list *every* match on your hard drive. Unless you own one of those extremely rare 60-inch Apple Skyscraper Displays, there just isn't room.

Instead, Spotlight uses some fancy behind-the-scenes analysis to calculate and display the *20 most likely* matches for what you typed. But at the top of the menu, you usually see that there are many other possible matches; it says, "Show All in Finder," meaning that there are other candidates. (OS X no longer tells you how *many* other results there are.)

There is, however, a second, more powerful way into the Spotlight labyrinth. And that's to use the Spotlight *window*, shown in Figure 3-3. It had an extreme makeover in Lion.

You can open the Spotlight window in either of two ways:

From Spotlight Menu

If the Spotlight menu—its Most Likely to Succeed list—doesn't include what you're looking for, then click Show All in Finder. You've just opened the Spotlight window.

Now you have access to the *complete* list of matches, neatly listed in what appears to be a standard Finder window.

From the Finder

When you're in the Finder, you can also open the Spotlight window *directly*, without using the Spotlight menu as a trigger. Actually, there are three ways to get there:

- ⌘-F (for *Find*, get it?). When you choose File→Find (⌘-F), you get an *empty* Spotlight window, ready to fill in for your search (Figure 3-3, top).

Tip: When the Find window opens, what folder does it intend to search?

That's up to you. Choose Finder→Preferences→Advanced. From the "When performing a search" pop-up menu, you can choose Search This Mac, Search the Current Folder (usually what you want), or Use the Previous Search Scope (that is, either "the whole Mac" or "the current folder," whichever you set up last time).

- **Option-⌘-space bar.** This keystroke opens the same window. But it always comes set to search everything on your Mac (except other people's Home folders, of course), regardless of the setting you made in Preferences (as described in the Tip above).

- **Open any desktop window, and type something into the search box at upper right.** Presto—the mild-mannered folder window turns into the Spotlight window, complete with search results.

Tip: You can change the Find keystrokes to just about anything you like. See page 127.

The Basic Search

When the Searching window opens, you can start typing whatever you're looking for into the search box at the top.

As you type, the window fills with a list of the files and folders whose names contain what you typed. It's just like the Spotlight menu, but without the 20-item limit (Figure 3-3, middle).

Figure 3-3:
Top: The Spotlight window stands ready to search the currently open window.

Middle: When you begin to type your search term, OS X presents a pop-up menu of suggestions. For example, when you type apple, it's asking: "Would you like me to limit the search results to files with the word 'apple' in their names?" If you ignore the suggestions, the window shows you all matches—including files with the word "apple" inside them.

Bottom: But if you click one of those suggestions— "Filename contains apple," in this case—the results window changes. Now you're seeing only icons that contain the word "apple."

Where to look

The three phrases at the top of the window—This Mac, [Folder Name], and Shared—are buttons. Click one to tell Spotlight where to search:

- **This Mac** means your *entire* computer, including secondary disks attached to it (or installed inside)—minus other people's files, of course.

- **"Letters to Congress"** (or whatever the current window is) limits the search to whatever window was open. So if you want to search your Pictures folder, open it first and *then* hit ⌘-F. You'll see the "Pictures" button at the top of the window, and you can click it to restrict the search to that folder.

- **Shared.** Click this button to expand the search to your *entire network* and all the computers on it. (This assumes, of course, that you've brought their icons to your screen as described in Chapter 14.)

 If the other computers are Macs running Leopard (Mac OS X 10.5) or later, Spotlight can search their files just the way it does on your own Mac—finding words inside the files, for example. If they're any other kind of computer, Spotlight can search for files only by name.

Tip: If the object of your quest doesn't show up, you can adjust the scope of the search with one quick click on another button at the top of the window, like This Mac or Shared. Spotlight updates the results list.

Then again, if you always prefer one of those options, don't forget that you can save yourself a click by choosing it to be the new factory setting. Specify your favorite "where to look" option by visiting Finder→Preferences→Advanced and using the "When performing a search" pop-up menu. Your choices are Search This Mac, Search the Current Folder, or Use the Previous Search Scope (that is, "whatever I chose last time").

The suggestions list

Until Lion came along, the Find window offered two other important buttons at the top: **Contents,** meaning, "Search for the words inside your files, along with all the metadata attached to them," and **File Name,** for when it's faster to search for characters in the file's name, just as people did before Spotlight came along.

In Mountain Lion, those buttons are gone. Instead, OS X tries to *figure out* what you're looking for—file names or words inside files. It may show you both in the same results list.

But more important, it offers a new suggestions pop-up menu, shown in Figure 3-4. Its purpose is to help you narrow down the results list with one quick click. Whatever you click here is instantly immortalized as a search token, described below.

You may see any of these headings in the suggestions list:

- **Filenames.** The top option is always "Filenames"; click it to search by the files' names only. If you type *chris* into the box, you want files whose *names* contain that word.

- **Sent by.** If you type *chris,* the Mac wants to know if, by chance, you're looking for email messages and other documents from somebody *named* Chris (or Christina, or Christopher…).

- **Kinds.** If you type *image,* the Kinds option here offers you choices like *image* (any kind), *JPEG image, Disk image,* or *Portable Network Graphics Image.* If you type *document,* you get options like *Word document* and *PDF document.* If you search for *photo,* the menu lets you pinpoint files whose *file type* contains "photo"—like iPhoto Libraries or Adobe Photoshop files. And so on.

- **Downloaded From.** You see this option when what you type is a Web address. If you type *Macworld* into the search box, then "Downloaded From Macworld.com" appears in the results list—a handy way to round up all the files you've downloaded from a specific site.

Figure 3-4:
If you find these suggestions helpful, click one (or press the ↓ key to walk down the list, and then press Enter to select the one you want). If you're fine with the search results as they've already popped up—no further refining necessary—tap the Esc key to close the drop-down list.

- **Dates.** If you type a month (*august, aug,* or *august 2013)* or a year into the search box, the suggestions pop-up menu says, "Dates: August 2013" (or whatever). Clicking it lets you do a quick roundup of all files you created, modified, last opened, or added during that period.

- **Labels.** Here's yet another way to use the file labels described on page 89. When you type a search term that matches one of your labels (for example, *green*), the suggestions menu includes "Labels: green."

In each case, the suggestions in this menu reflect only files that actually *exist* on your Mac. If you search for "green," but green isn't one of your Finder labels, then the Labels suggestion doesn't appear. If you haven't downloaded anything from Macworld.com, then that option doesn't appear. And so on.

Once you learn to actually start *using* these suggestions—once you get a hang of the kinds of things they offer—you can get a lot of mileage out of them.

If, on the other hand, you just find them confusing, no big deal. Tap the Esc key to close the suggestions list and reveal the existing Searching window.

Power Searches with Tokens

The real beauty of the Searching window is that it can hunt down icons via more specific searches than you could do using the Spotlight menu. For example, a Lion/Mountain Lion feature called *tokens* let you combine criteria, so you find only *music* files sent to you by *Casey*. (A token, in Apple's usage, means "a visual representation of a search criterion.")

Here, for example, is how you might search for pictures of Chris that were last opened in December.

1. **In the Finder, press ⌘-F.**

 The Spotlight window opens.

2. **In the search box, type *image*.**

 Sure enough: The window now shows everything on your Mac that *is* an image or *contains* the word "image" in its name, or even contains the word "*image*" within the file. But the list of suggestions (Figure 3-4) wants to know: which do you really want? Files that are images? Or files with the word "image" in their names?

3. **In the suggestions menu, under Kinds, click *Image*.**

 You've just pared down the list of results. Now it shows only the files that *are* photos.

 Note, too, that the first *token* has appeared. Each time you click a refinement criterion, as you did in this step, OS X enshrines it in the search box as a shaded bubble. In this case, it created a token that says "Kind: Image." (You can see it in Figure 3-5.)

Note: See the tiny ▾ next to the search token's name? You can click it to see a very short pop-up menu of options: the criterion you selected (like "Kind:" or "Date:"), and another command that says "Everything." Choosing it undoes the filtering effect of the suggestion, so that this token searches for *any* attribute of your file (like the words inside it).

Why do you need an "Everything" option here? If you'd wanted to search all attributes on your Mac, you could have just typed directly into the search box without even using the suggestions menu.

Three reasons. First, you might want to expand the scope (from "Kind" to "Everything," for example) without having to retype the search term. Second, because you might want to make this token part of a smart folder—a saved search—described at the end of this chapter. Finally, you might want to go on to add another search criterion—another search token—that builds on this search for "Everything."

 Now you need to narrow the quest to files containing the word Chris.

4. **Continue typing in the search box. This time, type *chris*.**

 The suggestions appear again, offering options for file names and, probably, a Sent By list that lists everyone named Chris who's ever sent you messages or files. What you want is images whose names contain the *word* "Chris."

5. **Click *Filename*.**

The list of files is much smaller now. It shows only image files with "Chris" in their names.

For your final stunt, you'll screen out all but the December images.

6. **Continue typing in the search box. This time, type** *dec.*

This time, the suggestions list offers dates like *December 2011* and *December 2012.* You can see the result so far in Figure 3-5.

Figure 3-5:
Each time you add a criterion by clicking the drop-down list shown in Figure 3-4, the Mac adds a new token (criterion bubble) to the search box.

7. **Click the month you want.**

And voilà: The results list shows you only the December photos of Chris.

To delete a token, click it and then press the Delete key, or backspace over it. You can also edit one: Double-click the right side of the token bubble; now you can retype the search term.

Note: This same feature is also in Mail, where it's even more useful; you have search options like Subject, From, To, and so on.

Power Searching the Old Way

Search tokens are supposed to make multi-criteria searches easier than they used to be. But they're not as powerful as the Old Way, which is still around.

Using the Old Way of power searching, you can set up a search that finds a document whose name begins with the letters *Cro,* is over a megabyte in size, was created after 10/1/12 but before the end of the year, was changed within the past week, has the file name suffix *.doc,* and contains the phrase "attitude adjustment." (Of course, if you knew *that* much about a file, you'd probably know where it is, too. But you get the picture.)

In all, the Old Way lets you specify over 125 different search criteria: date modified, file size, the "last opened" date, color label, copyright holder's name, shutter speed (of a digital photo), tempo (of a music file), and so on. Figure 3-6 illustrates how detailed this kind of search can be.

To set up a complex search like this, use the second row of controls at the top of the window.

And third, and fourth, and fifth. Each time you click one of the **+** buttons at the right end of the window, a new criterion row appears; use its pop-up menus to specify *what* date, *what* file size, and so on.

Tip: If you press Option, the **+** button changes into a "…" button. When you click it, you get sub-rows of parameters for a single criterion. A pop-up menu lets you choose Any, All, or None, so that you can build what are called exclusionary searches.

The idea here is that you can set up a search for documents created between November 1 and 7 or documents created between November 10 and 14. Or files named Complaint that are also either Word or InDesign files.

The mind boggles.

Figure 3-6:
*By repeatedly clicking the **+** button, you can turn on as many criteria as you'd like; each additional row further narrows the search. To delete a row, click the **−** button at its right end.*

Here's a rundown of the ways you can restrict your search, according to the options in the first pop-up menu of a row. Note that after you choose from that first pop-up menu (Last Opened, for example), you're supposed to use the additional pop-up menus to narrow the choice ("within last," "2," and "weeks," for example), as you'll read below.

Note: It may surprise you that choosing something from the Kind pop-up menu triggers the search instantly. As soon as you choose Applications, for example, the window fills with a list of every program on your hard drive. Want a quick list of every folder on your entire machine? Choose Folders. (Want to see which folders you've opened in the past couple of days? Add another row.)

If you also type something into the search box at the very top of the window—before or after you've used one of these pop-up menus—the list pares itself down to items that match what you've typed.

Kind

When the first pop-up menu says Kind, you can use the second pop-up menu to indicate what kind of file you're looking for: Applications, Documents, Executables (programs and Dashboard widgets), Folders, Images, Movies, Music, PDF files, Presentations, Text files, or Other.

For example, when you're trying to free up some space on your drive, you could round up all your movie files, which tend to be huge. Choosing one of these file types makes the window begin to fill with matches automatically and instantly.

And what if the item you're looking for isn't among those 10 canned choices? What if it's an alias, or a Photoshop plug-in, or some other type?

That's what the Other option is all about. Here you can type in almost anything that specifies a kind of file: *Word, Excel, TIFF, JPEG, AAC, final cut, imovie, alias, zip, html,* or whatever.

Last opened date/Last modified date/Created date

When you choose one of these options from the first pop-up menu, the second pop-up menu lets you isolate files, programs, and folders according to the last time you opened them, the last time you changed them, or when they were created.

- **Today, yesterday, this week, this month, this year.** This second pop-up menu offers quick, canned time-limiting options.

- **Within last, exactly, before, after.** These let you be more precise. If you choose "before," "after," or "exactly," then your criterion row sprouts a month/day/year control that lets you round up items that you last opened or changed before, after, or on a specific day, like 5/27/13. If you choose "within last," then you can limit the search to things you've opened or changed within a specified number of days, weeks, months, or years.

 These are awesomely useful controls, because they let you specify a chronological window for whatever you're looking for.

Tip: You're allowed to add two Date rows—a great trick that lets you round up files that you created or edited between two dates. Set up the first Date row to say "is after" and the second one to say "is before."

In fact, if it doesn't hurt your brain to think about it, how about this? You can even have more than two Date rows. Use one pair to specify a range of dates for the file's creation date and two other rows to limit when it was modified.

Science!

Name

Spotlight likes to find text *anywhere* inside your files, no matter what their *names* are. But when you want to search for an icon by the text that's in only its *name,* this is your ticket. (Capitalization doesn't matter.)

Wouldn't it be faster just to click Filename in the suggestions pop-up menu (Figure 3-4)? Yes—but using the Searching window offers you far more control, thanks to the second pop-up menu that offers you these options:

- **Matches.** You'll see files whose names contain entire words you're looking for. For example, if you search for peas, you'll find files called "Peas & Crackers" and "Snow Peas"—but not "Appeasement."

- **Contains.** The position of the letters you type doesn't matter. If you type *then,* you find files with names like "Then and Now," "Authentic Cajun Recipes," and "Lovable Heathen."

- **Starts with.** The Find program finds only files beginning with the letters you type. If you type *then,* you find "Then and Now," but not "Authentic Cajun Recipes" or "Lovable Heathen."

- **Ends with.** If you type *then,* you find "Lovable Heathen," but not files called "Then and Now" or "Authentic Cajun Recipes."

- **Is.** This option finds only files named *precisely* what you type (except that capitalization still doesn't matter). Typing *then* won't find any of the file names in the previous examples. It would unearth only a file called simply "Then." In fact, a file with a file name suffix, like "Then.doc," doesn't even qualify.

 (If this happens to you, though, here's a workaround: From the first pop-up menu, choose Other; in the dialog box, pick Filename. The Filename criterion ignores extensions; it would find "Then.doc" even if you searched for "then.")

Contents

You can think of this option as the opposite of Name. It finds *only* the text that's inside your files, and completely ignores their icon names.

That's a handy function when, for example, a document's name doesn't match its contents. Maybe a marauding toddler playing Kid Pix renamed your doctoral thesis "xggrjpO#$5%////." Or maybe you just can't remember what you called something.

Other

If this were a math equation, it might look like this: *options × options = overwhelming.*

WORKAROUND WORKSHOP

Feeding the Barren Pop-up Menus

The first little pop-up menu in the Spotlight window lists these handy search starting points: Kind, Last opened date, Name, and so on.

But it's actually *less* fully stocked than it was in the OS X of days gone by. Apple streamlined the options a bit.

For example, you used to be able to search by *label*. You could therefore easily round up all files pertaining to a certain project for backing up, deleting, or burning to a CD

en masse. That's off the menu as you first see it.

Fortunately, you can restore these options to the criterion pop-up menu easily enough. The trick is to use the Other option, as already described. In the dialog box shown in Figure 3-4, search for *label* (or whatever the missing criterion is). When you find the criterion you want, turn on the "In menu" checkbox and click OK.

Presto: You've got your menu back.

Choosing Other from the first pop-up menu opens a special dialog box containing at least 125 *other* criteria. Not just the big kahunas like Name, Size, and Kind, but far more targeted (and obscure) criteria like "Bits per sample" (so you can round up MP3 music files of a certain quality), "Device make" (so you can round up all digital photos taken with, say, a Canon Rebel camera), "Key signature" (so you can find all the GarageBand songs you wrote in the key of F sharp), "Pages" (so you can find all Word documents that are really long), and so on. As you can see in Figure 3-7, each one comes with a short description.

Figure 3-7:
Here's the master list of search criteria. Turn on the In Menu checkboxes of the ones you'll want to reuse often, as described in the box on the facing page. Once you've added some of these search criteria to the menu, you'll get an appropriate set of "find what?" controls ("Greater than" and "Less than" pop-up menus, for example).

You may think Spotlight is offering you a staggering array of file-type criteria. In fact, though, big bunches of information categories (technically called *metadata)* are all hooks for a relatively small number of document types. For example:

- **Digital photos and other graphics files** account for the metadata types alpha channel, aperture, color space, device make, device model, EXIF version, exposure mode, exposure program, exposure time, flash, f-number, focal length, ISO speed, max aperture, metering mode, orientation, pixel height, pixel width, red eye, resolution height, resolution width, and white balance.

- **Digital music files** have searchable metadata categories like album, audio bit rate, bits per sample, channel count, composer, duration, General MIDI sequence, key signature, lyricist, musical genre, recording date, sample rate, tempo, time signature, track number, and year recorded. There's even a special set of parameters for

The Raw Power of the Raw Query

You may have just slogged through 20 pages of Spotlight details—but if you can believe it, there are another 40 or 60 someone could write. It turns out that the Spotlight most people see is only a subset of the true power awaiting in OS X.

For example, what if you wanted to see all the files you've opened in the past 24 hours *except* email messages and Contacts entries? Or what if you want to round up all PDF documents *and* PostScript files you've opened in the past week? Using the Spotlight tools that most people see, you wouldn't be able to set up searches or smart folders that are quite that smart.

Fortunately for the true Mac geek, Spotlight also understands a *query language*—a programming-like syntax that lets you establish far more specific and nuanced searches. You can use it to pull off stunts that would be impossible using the Spotlight menu or window alone.

To read about the basics of the query language, start at *http://developer.apple.com/macosx/spotlight. html;* it will lead you to a number of Web pages that explain the full scope of Spotlight's internal lingo.

You may also get a kick out of studying how Spotlight uses the query language itself. To do that, create a smart folder, and then Get Info on it. (Control-click or right-click it and, from the shortcut menu, choose Get Info.) On the General panel, inspect the string of query text that Spotlight generated behind the scenes (as shown here).

What you'll learn is that the basic search command always includes the command kMDItem. To search for something by its file type, your query should begin with *kMDItemContentType*; for when you last opened it, use *kMDItemLastUsedDate* and so on.

For example, here's how to type a query that rounds up all files that contain the keyword "kumquat": *kMDItemKeywords* == *"*kumquat*"*. (The double equals symbol just means "equals." You can also use <, >, <=, and so on. The asterisks are wildcards that mean, "There may be other text here, or not; it's still a good match.")

To signify "and," use two ampersands, like this: &&. For "or," use two vertical bars, like this: ||.

Once you've read more about this query language, you can build much more complicated searches. This one, for example, finds all audio and video files whose author is either Kevin or Steve that were modified in the past week:

```
((kMDItemAuthors == "Kevin"wc ||
    kMDItemAuthors == "Steve"wc)
    && (kMDItemContentType ==
        "audio"wc || kMDItemCon-
        tentType == "video"wc))
    && (kMDItemFSCon-
    tentChangeDate == $time.
    this_week)
```

And here's how you'd find all PDF documents and PostScript files with a single search:

```
((kMDItemContentType-
    Tree == 'com.adobe.pdf')
|| (kMDItemKind == 'PostScript
document'))
```

(Most of this stuff actually stands for useful things: *MD* for metadata, *wc* for "word-based, case-insensitive," and so on.)

And where, you may ask, are you supposed to type all these queries? You have two options.

In the Finder, when you choose File→Find to produce the Spotlight window, choose Other from the Kind pop-up menu. In the list of 6 gazillion search parameters, choose Raw Query. You can type your elaborate search string into the text box that appears.

Second, you can open Terminal (page 469) and use Spotlight's Unix equivalent. The main command you want to learn about is *mdfind*. For example, at the Terminal prompt, you could type *mdfind "kMDItemAcquisitionModel == 'Canon PowerShot S95'"* (and then press Return) to see a list of all photos you took with that particular camera model.

Spotlight: The Missing Manual? Hmm. Has a nice ring to it, doesn't it?

GarageBand and Soundtrack documents, including instrument category, instrument name, loop descriptors, loop file type, loop original key, and loop scale type.

- **Microsoft Office documents** can contain info bits like *authors, contributors, fonts, languages, pages, publishers,* and contact information (*name, phone number,* and so on).

This massive list also harbors a few criteria you may use more often, like Size, File Label, and Visibility (which lets you see all the invisible files on your hard drive). See the box on page 120.

Now, you could argue that in the time it takes you to set up a search for such a specific kind of data, you could have just rooted through your files and found what you wanted manually. But hey—you never know. Someday, you may remember *nothing* about a photo you're looking for except that you used the flash and an f-stop of 1.8.

Tip: Don't miss the search box in this dialog box. It makes it super-easy to pluck one useful criterion needle—Size, say—out of the haystack. Also don't forget about the In Menu checkbox in the right column. It lets you add one of these criteria to the main pop-up menu, so you don't have to go burrowing into Other again the next time.

What to Do with Search Results

The results window is a regular old Finder window, with all the familiar views and controls (Figure 3-8).

Figure 3-8:
Click a result once to see where it sits on your hard drive (bottom). If the window is too narrow to reveal the full folder path, run your cursor over the folders without clicking. As your mouse moves from one folder to another, the Mac briefly reveals its name, compressing other folders as necessary to make room. (Sub-Tip: You can drag icons into these folders, too.)

You can work with anything in the results window exactly as though it were in a regular Finder window: Drag something to the Trash, rename something, press the space bar for a Quick Look at it, drag something to the desktop to move it there, drag something onto a Dock icon to open it with a certain program, Option-⌘-drag it to the desktop to create an alias, and so on.

You can move up or down the list by pressing the arrow keys, scroll a "page" at a time with the Page Up and Page Down keys, and so on. You can also highlight multiple icons simultaneously, the same way you would in a Finder list view: Highlight all of them by choosing Edit→Select All, highlight individual items by ⌘-clicking them, drag diagonally to enclose a cluster of found items, and so on.

Or you can proceed in any of these ways:

- **Change the view (list, column, etc.)** by clicking one of the View icons or choosing from the View menu (see Chapter 1). Actually, Cover Flow is a *great* view for search results; since this list is culled from folders all over the computer, you otherwise have very little sense of context as you examine the file names.

- **Sort the results** by clicking the column headings (in list and Cover Flow views).

- **Arrange the results** by using the Arrange pop-up menu button (⊞▾). That way, you group the results as described on page 43. It can be especially useful to clump them by Kind, so that similar file types are clustered together (Documents, Images, Messages, and so on), or to sort by Last Opened, so that the list is chronological.

- **Change the view options.** Press ⌘-J (or choose View→Show View Options) to open the View Options panel for the results window. Here you can add a couple of additional columns (Date Modified, Date Created); change the icon size or text size; or turn on the "always" checkbox at the top, so that future results windows will have the look you've set up here.

- **Get more information** about a result by selecting it and then choosing File→Get Info (⌘-I). The normal Get Info window appears, complete with date, size, and location information.

- **Find out where it is.** It's nice to see all the search results in one list, but you're not actually seeing them in their native habitats: the Finder folder windows where they physically reside.

 If you click once on an icon in the results, the bottom edge of the window becomes a folder map that shows you where that item is.

 For example, in Figure 3-8, the notation in the Path strip means: "The Kids at Russian Academy.JPG icon you found is in the St. Pete Photos folder, which is in the Pictures folder, which is in d's Home folder."

 To get your hands on the actual icon, choose File→Open Enclosing Folder (⌘-R). OS X highlights the icon in question, sitting there in its window wherever it happens to be on your hard drive.

- **Open the file (or open one of the folders it's in).** If one of the found files is the one you were looking for, double-click it to open it (or highlight it and press either ⌘-O or ⌘-↓). In many cases, you don't know or care where the file was—you just want to get into it.

Tip: You can also double-click to open any of the folders in the folder map at the bottom of the window. For example, in Figure 3-8, you could double-click the selected JPEG icon to open it, or the St Pete Photos folder to open it, and so on.

- **Move or delete the file.** You can drag an item directly out of the found-files list and into a different folder, window, or disk—or straight to the Dock or the Trash. If you click something else and then re-click the dragged item in the results list, the folder map at the bottom of the window updates itself to reflect the file's new location.

- **Start over.** If you'd like to repeat the search using a different search phrase, just edit the text in the search box. (Press ⌘-F to empty the search box and the Spotlight window.)

- **Give up.** If none of these avenues suits your fancy, you can close the window as you would any other (⌘-W).

Customizing Spotlight

You've just read about how Spotlight works fresh out of the box. But you can tailor its behavior, both for security reasons and to fit it to the kinds of work you do.

Here are three ways to open the Spotlight preferences center:

- **Choose Spotlight Preferences** at the bottom of the Spotlight menu just after you've performed a search.

- **Use Spotlight itself.** Hit ⌘-space bar, type *spotl*, and press Return.

POWER USERS' CLINIC

All Roads Lead to Spotlight

As you know, you can open the Spotlight window using a keystroke or from the Spotlight menu after performing a search. But those methods are only the beginning.

Try this: Highlight a phrase in any program (except Microsoft ones and a few other weirdos). Control-click (or right-click) the highlighted phrase, and then choose Search in Spotlight from the shortcut menu. Boom: The Spotlight window opens, already stocked with the search results that match your highlighted phrase.

Remember, too, that Spotlight has its claws in all kinds of individual OS X programs. You'll find a Spotlight search box in System Preferences (so that you can pull up the correct panel), in Mail (to find a certain message), in Automator (to search for components for your software robots), and so on. As software companies get around to it, they're also welcome to incorporate pieces of the Spotlight technology into their own programs.

• Choose →System Preferences. Click Spotlight.

In any case, you wind up face to face with the dialog box shown in Figure 3-9.

You can tweak Spotlight in three ways here, all very useful:

• **Turn off categories.** The list of checkboxes identifies what Spotlight tracks. If you find that Spotlight uses up valuable menu space listing, say, Web bookmarks or fonts—stuff you don't need to find very often—then turn off their checkboxes. Now the Spotlight menu's 20 precious slots are allotted to icon types you care more about.

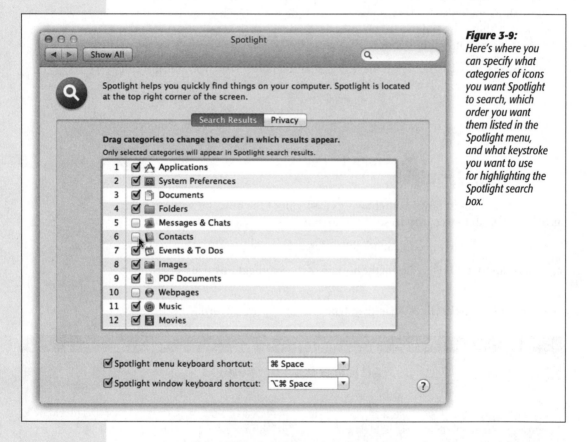

Figure 3-9:
Here's where you can specify what categories of icons you want Spotlight to search, which order you want them listed in the Spotlight menu, and what keystroke you want to use for highlighting the Spotlight search box.

• **Prioritize the categories.** This dialog box also lets you change the *order* of the category results; just drag a list item up or down to change where it appears in the Spotlight menu.

The factory setting is for Applications to appear first in the results. That makes a lot of sense if you use Spotlight as a quick program launcher (which is a great idea). But if you're a party planner who spends all day on the phone, and the most important Spotlight function for you is its ability to look up someone in your ad-

dress book, then drag Contacts to the top of the list. You'll need fewer arrow-key presses once the results menu appears.

• **Change the keystroke.** Ordinarily, pressing ⌘-space bar highlights the Spotlight search box in your menu bar, and Option-⌘-space bar opens the Searching window. If these keystrokes clash with some other key assignment in your software, though, you can reassign them to almost any other keystroke you like.

Most people notice only the pop-up menu that lets you select one of your F-keys (the function keys at the top of your keyboard). But you can also click inside the white box that lists the keystroke and then press *any* key combination—Control-S, for example—to choose something different.

Apple assumes no responsibility for your choosing a keystroke that messes up some other function on your Mac. ⌘-S, for example, would not be a good choice.

On the other hand, if you choose a Spotlight keystroke that OS X uses for some other function, a little yellow alert icon appears in the Spotlight pane. This icon is actually a button; clicking it brings you to the Keyboard & Mouse pane, where you can see exactly which keystroke is in dispute and change it.

Privacy Settings

Ordinarily, Spotlight looks for matches wherever it can, except in other people's Home folders. (That is, you can't search through other people's stuff).

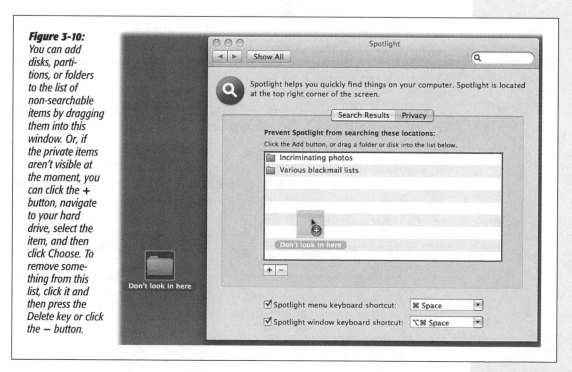

Figure 3-10:
You can add disks, partitions, or folders to the list of non-searchable items by dragging them into this window. Or, if the private items aren't visible at the moment, you can click the + button, navigate to your hard drive, select the item, and then click Choose. To remove something from this list, click it and then press the Delete key or click the − button.

But even within your own Mac world, you can hide certain folders from Spotlight searches. Maybe you have privacy concerns—for example, you don't want your spouse Spotlighting your stuff while you're away from your desk. Maybe you just want to create more focused Spotlight searches, removing a lot of old, extraneous junk from its database.

Either way, the steps are simple. Open the Spotlight panel of System Preferences, as described previously. Click the Privacy tab. Figure 3-10 explains the remaining steps.

Tip: When you mark a disk or folder as non-searchable, Spotlight actually deletes its entire *index* (its invisible card-catalog filing system) from that disk. If Spotlight ever seems to be acting wackily, you can use this function to make it rebuild its own index file on the problem disk. Just drag the disk into the Privacy list and then remove it again. Spotlight deletes, and then rebuilds, the index for that disk.

(Don't forget the part about "remove it again," though. If you add a disk to the Privacy list, Spotlight is no longer able to find *anything* on it, even if you can see it right in front of you.)

Once you've built up the list of private disks and folders, close System Preferences. Spotlight now pretends the private items don't even exist.

Smart Folders

A *smart folder* is a self-updating folder that, in essence, performs a continual, 24/7 search for the criteria you specify. (Smart folders are a lot like smart albums in iPhoto and iTunes, smart mailboxes in Mail, and so on.)

Note: In truth, the smart folder performs a search for the specified criteria *at the moment you open it.* But because it's so fast, it feels as though it's been quietly searching all along.

The key to creating one, as it turns out, is the little Save button in the upper-right corner of the Spotlight window when you've built a search request (either using tokens or using individual criteria rows).

Here's a common example—one that you can't replicate in any other operating system. You choose File→Find. You set up the pop-up menus to say "last opened date" and "this week." You click Save. You name the smart folder something like Current Crises, and you turn on Add to Sidebar (Figure 3-11).

Tip: Behind the scenes, smart folders you create are actually special files that are stored in your Home→Library→Saved Searches folder.

From now on, whenever you click that smart folder, it reveals all the files you've worked on in the past week or so. The great part is that these items' *real* locations may be all over the map, scattered around your Mac and your network. But through the magic of the smart folder, they appear as though they're all in one neat folder.

Tip: If you decide your original search criteria need a little fine-tuning, click the smart folder. From the ✿ menu, choose Show Search Criteria. You're back on the original setting-up-the-search window. Use the pop-up menus and other controls to tweak your search setup, and then click the Save button once again.

To delete a smart folder, just drag its icon out of the Sidebar. (Or if it's anywhere else, like on your desktop, drag it to the Trash like any other folder.)

Figure 3-11:
OS X can preserve your search as a smart folder listed in the Sidebar (lower left)—at least, it does as long as Add to Sidebar is turned on. You can stash a smart folder in your Dock, too, although it doesn't display a stack of its contents, as normal folders do.

OS X: THE MISSING MANUAL

Dock, Desktop & Toolbars

Y ou can't help reacting, one way or another, to the futuristic, sleek looks of OS X the first time you arrive at its desktop. There's the Dock, looking photorealistic and shiny on its 3-D mirrored shelf. There are those Finder windows, slick and textureless with their gentle gradient-gray title bars. And then there's the shimmering backdrop of the desktop itself.

This chapter shows you how to use and control these most dramatic elements of Mountain Lion.

The Dock

For years, most operating systems maintained two lists of programs. One listed unopened programs until you needed them, like the Start menu (Windows) or the Launcher (Mac OS 9). The other kept track of which programs were open at the moment for easy switching, like the taskbar (Windows) or the Application menu (Mac OS 9).

In OS X, Apple combined both functions into a single strip of icons called the Dock.

Apple's thinking goes like this: Why must you know whether or not a program is already running? That's the computer's problem, not yours. In an ideal world, this distinction should be irrelevant. A program should appear when you click its icon, whether it's open or not—just as on an iPhone or iPad.

"Which programs are open" already approaches unimportance in OS X, where sophisticated memory-management features make it hard to run out of memory. You can have dozens of programs open at once.

And that's why the Dock combines the launcher and status functions of a modern operating system. Only a tiny white reflective dot beneath a program's icon tells you that it's open—and you can even hide that, if you want. (Choose →Dock→Dock Preferences, and turn off "Show indicator lights for open applications.")

Apple has made it as easy as possible to learn to like the Dock. You can customize the thing to within an inch of its life, use it to control and manipulate windows in elaborate ways, or even get rid of it completely. This section explains everything you need to know.

Setting Up the Dock

Apple starts the Dock off with a few icons it doesn't want you to miss: Finder, Launchpad, Mission Control, App Store, Mail, the Safari Web browser, and so on. But using your Mac without putting your own favorite icons in the Dock is like buying an expensive suit and turning down the free alteration service. At the first opportunity, you should make the Dock your own.

The concept of the Dock is simple: Any icon you drag onto it (Figure 4-1) is installed there as a button. You can even drag an open window onto the Dock—a Microsoft Word document you're editing, say—using its proxy icon (page 30) as a handle.

Tip: New in Mountain Lion: If you right-click a folder, or any other icon, in the *Sidebar* (page 19), you get an Add to Dock command for that icon. Bet you can't guess what it does..

A single click, not a double-click, opens the corresponding icon. In other words, the Dock is an ideal parking lot for the icons of disks, folders, documents, programs, and Internet bookmarks that you access frequently.

Divider
← Programs side Everything else →

Open programs Minimized document windows

Figure 4-1:
To add an icon to the Dock, simply drag it there. You haven't moved the original file; when you release the mouse, it remains where it was. You've just installed a pointer–like a Macintosh alias or a Windows shortcut.

You can even install batches of icons onto the Dock all at once—just drag them as a group. That's something you can't do with the other parking places for favorite icons, like the Sidebar and the Finder toolbar.

Here are a few aspects of the Dock that may throw you at first:

- **It has two sides.** See the grayish dotted line running down the Dock? That's the divider (Figure 4-1). Everything on the left side is an application—a program. Everything else goes on the right side: files, documents, folders, disks, and minimized windows.

 Remember this division. If you try to drag an application to the right of the line, for example, the Mac teasingly refuses to accept it. (Even aliases observe that distinction. Aliases of applications can go only on the left side, and vice versa.)

- **Its icon names are hidden.** To see the name of a Dock icon, point to it without clicking. You'll see the name appear above the icon.

 When you're trying to find a certain icon in the Dock, run your cursor slowly across the icons without clicking; the icon labels appear as you go. You can often identify a document just by looking at its icon.

- **Folders and disks sprout stacks.** If you click a folder or a disk icon on the right side of the Dock, a list of its contents sprouts from the icon. It's like X-ray vision without the awkward moral consequences. Turn to page 134 for details on stacks.

Tip: If you press Shift as you click, the stack opens in slow motion. Amaze your friends.

- **Programs appear there unsolicited.** Nobody but you (and Apple) can put icons on the right side of the Dock. But program icons appear on the left side of the Dock automatically whenever you open one, even one that's not listed in the Dock. Its icon remains there for as long as it's running.

Organizing and Removing Dock Icons

You can move the tiles of the Dock around by dragging them horizontally. As you drag, the other icons scoot aside to make room. When you're satisfied with its new position, drop the icon you've just dragged.

GEM IN THE ROUGH

Living Icons

OS X brings to life a terrific idea, a new concept in mainstream operating systems: icons that *tell* you something. If the Dock is big enough, you can often tell documents apart just by looking at their icons.

Some program icons even change over time. The Mail icon, for example (Chapter 18) bears a live counter that indicates how many new email messages are waiting for you. (After all, why should you switch into the Mail program if you'll only be disappointed?) The Messages icon lets you

know how many chat responses are waiting. You can make your Activity Monitor graph show up right on its icon. Toast illustrates the progress of a disc you're burning.

Think of the possibilities. One day the Safari icon could change to let you know when interesting new Web pages have appeared, the Quicken icon could display your current bank balance, and the Microsoft Word icon could change every time Microsoft posts a bug fix.

To remove a Dock icon, just drag it away. (You can't remove the icons of the Finder, the Trash, or any minimized document window.) Once your cursor has cleared the Dock, release the mouse button. The icon disappears in a charming little puff of animated smoke. The other Dock icons slide together to close the gap.

Something weird happens if you drag away a Dock program's icon while that program is running. You don't see any change immediately, because the program is still open. But when you quit the program, its previously installed icon disappears from the Dock.

Pop-up Dock Folders ("Stacks")

When you click a disk or folder icon on the Dock, you'll witness the effect shown in Figure 4-2. In essence, OS X is fanning out the folder's contents so you can see all of them. If it could talk, it would be saying, "Pick a card, any card."

Tip: You can change how the icons in a particular stack are sorted: alphabetically, chronologically, or whatever. Use the "Sort by" section of the shortcut menu (Figure 4-2, top left).

In principle, of course, pop-up folders are a great idea, because they save you time and clicking. Click a folder to see what's in it; click the icon you want inside; and you're off and running, without having had to open, manage, and close a window.

Anyway, here's how to operate pop-up Dock folders.

Fan vs. grid vs. list

When you click a disk or folder icon on the Dock, what happens? You see its contents, arrayed in your choice of three displays:

- **Fan.** The fan is a single, gently curved column of icons that pops out of the disk or folder icon. It's ideal for folders that contain very few icons, because there's room for only a handful of items in a fan (the exact number depends on your screen size). After the first few, you see only a "31 more in Finder" button, which you can click to see everything in that folder—but now you've wasted time, not saved it.

Note: When your Dock is positioned on a side of the screen instead of the bottom, the fan option isn't available.

- **Grid.** If you've set a folder to open as a grid, you get to see many more icons in a big rectangular window. File names often get abbreviated because there's not enough horizontal room, but you get to see many more icons this way. Actually, thanks to the scroll bar, you get to see all the icons this way. (You can also type the beginning of an icon's name to select it.)

Tip: A cool white-ghostly-highlighting effect is available, which makes it easier to see which icon you're pointing to as you move your mouse around in a grid or a fan. To make it appear, click-and-hold a folder on the Dock—and then, without releasing the mouse, slide onto the grid or fan. The highlighting follows your cursor.

Alternatively, as soon as the grid or fan appears, press the arrow keys on your keyboard to move from icon to icon—complete with ghostly selection square.

- **List.** You can also opt for a simple list of the folder's contents, like a pop-up menu; in Mountain Lion, you actually see little tiny icons for the files and folders within. The list appears much faster than a fan or a grid does.

There's no scroll bar, but you can scroll the list nonetheless just by pointing to the top or bottom of it with your mouse. And, of course, you can type-select.

Tip: The List view also displays a little ▸ to the right of each folder within the Dock folder. That is, it's a hierarchical list, meaning that you can burrow into folders within folders, all from the original Dock icon, and all without opening a single new window. You can stick your entire Home folder, or even your whole hard drive icon, onto the Dock; now you have complete menu access to everything inside, right from the Dock.

Figure 4-2:
What happens when you click a folder in the Dock? You see its contents in one of three views. Here's how you choose the file you're looking for in each:

Top left: In List view, the folder contents appear as a menu; you can "drill down" into subfolders, and you open something by choosing its name.

Top right: In Fan view, click an icon to open it.

Bottom: In Grid view, many more icons appear than can fit in Fan view.

In any of the views, you can get a quick look at a document's contents by using Quick Look. That is, highlight the icon (point without clicking, or use the keyboard to type-select), and the press the space bar. A window sprouts, showing the actual document contents.

- **Automatic.** There's a fourth option in the shortcut menu for a Dock folder, too: Automatic. If you turn this on, then OS X chooses either Fan or Grid view, depending on how many icons are in the folder.

So how do you choose which display you want? Control-click (or right-click) the Dock folder's icon, and make a selection from the shortcut menu. Each disk or folder icon remembers its own fan/grid/list setting.

The Finer Points of Pop-up Dock Folders

Those were the basics of pop-up Dock folders. Here's the advanced course:

- **Ever-Changing Folder-Icon Syndrome (ECFIS).** When you add a folder or disk icon to the Dock, you might notice something wildly disorienting: Its icon keeps changing to resemble whatever you most recently put into it. Your Downloads folder might look like an Excel spreadsheet icon today, a PDF icon tonight, and a photo tomorrow—but never a folder. The annoying part is that you can't get to know a folder by its icon.

 Fortunately, this problem is easy to fix. Control-click (or right-click) the Dock folder. From the shortcut menu, in the "Display as" section, you can choose either Folder (which looks like a folder forever) or Stack (which changes to reflect its contents.)

- **Ready-made pop-up folders.** When you install OS X, you get a couple of starter Dock folders, just to get you psyched. One is Downloads; the other is Documents. (Both of these folders are physically inside your Home folder. But you may well do most of your interacting with them on the Dock.)

 The Downloads folder collects all kinds of online arrivals: files you download from the Web using Safari, files you receive in a Messages file-transfer session, file attachments you get via Mail, files sent to you using AirDrop (Chapter 14), and so on. Unless you intervene, they're sorted by the date you downloaded them.

 It's handy to know where to find your downloads, and nice not to have them all cluttering your desktop.

Tip: Once you've opened a stack's fan or grid, you can drag any of the icons right out of the fan or grid. Just drag your chosen icon onto the desktop or into any visible disk or folder. In other words, what lands in the Downloads folder doesn't have to stay there. (You can't drag out of a list, however.)

- **Hierarchical folders.** The fans and grids are hierarchical—that is, you can drill down from their folders into their folders. Figure 4-3 makes this concept clearer.

Tip: Figure 4-3 shows you how to open a folder in a grid or a list using the mouse—but you can do it all from the keyboard, too. Once a folder is selected, press Return, ⌘-O, or ⌘-↓ to see what's inside it; press ⌘-↑ to backtrack to the original display. When a folder is highlighted, you can press ⌘-Return to open it in a Finder window; add the Option key to open that Finder window without closing the grid or fan.

- **Type selecting.** Once a list, fan, or grid is on the screen, you can highlight any icon in it by typing the first few letters of its name. For example, once you've popped open your Applications folder, you can highlight Safari by typing *sa*. (Press Return to open the highlighted icon.)

Tip: Alternatively, you can "walk" through the fan, grid, or list by pressing the arrow keys. A highlighting effect makes it crystal clear which icon you're selecting. Once an icon is selected, press Return to open it.

Figure 4-3:
If you spot a folder inside a list or a grid (left), click it once. You're now looking at a fan or grid of its contents (right). You can go on burrowing like this as deeply as your folders go. You can also "back out" again by clicking the Back button in the upper-left corner.

- **Two ways to bypass the pop-up.** If you just want to see what's in a folder, without all the graphic overkill of the fan or the grid, then Control-click (or right-click) the Dock folder's icon and choose the first command—Open "Applications" (or whatever the folder's name is—from the shortcut menu. You go straight to the corresponding window.

Actually, if you *really* value your time, you'll learn the shortcut: Option-⌘-click the Dock folder's icon. That accomplishes the same thing.

Tip: Alternatively, you can ⌘-click a folder on the Dock—or, indeed, any icon on the Dock—to jump to the window that contains that folder's icon. (Bonus: This same trick—⌘-clicking—also works in the menu of Spotlight search results.)

Three Ways to Get the Dock Out of Your Hair

The bottom of the screen isn't necessarily the ideal location for the Dock. All Mac screens are wider than they are tall, so the Dock eats into your limited vertical screen space. You have three ways out: Hide the Dock, shrink it, or rotate it 90 degrees.

Auto-hiding the Dock

To turn on the Dock's auto-hiding feature, choose →Dock→Turn Hiding On (or press Option-⌘-D).

Tip: You also find this on/off switch when you choose →Dock→Dock Preferences (Figure 4-4), or when you click the System Preferences icon in the Dock, and then the Dock icon. (Chapter 9 contains much more about the System Preferences program.)

When the Dock is hidden, it doesn't slide into view until you move the cursor to the Dock's edge of the screen. When you move the cursor back to the middle of the screen, the Dock slithers out of view once again. (Individual Dock icons may occasionally shoot upward into Desktop territory when a program needs your attention—cute, very cute—but otherwise, the Dock lies low until you call for it.)

On paper, an auto-hiding Dock is ideal; it's there only when you summon it. In practice, however, you may find that the extra half-second the Dock takes to appear and disappear makes this feature slightly less appealing.

Many Mac fans prefer to hide and show the Dock at will by pressing the hide/show keystroke, Option-⌘-D. This method makes the Dock pop on and off the screen without requiring you to move the cursor.

Shrinking and enlarging the Dock

Depending on your screen's size, you may prefer smaller or larger Dock buttons. The official way to resize them is shown in Figure 4-4.

There's a much faster way to resize the Dock, though: Just position your cursor carefully on the Dock's divider line so that it turns into a double-headed arrow (shown in Figure 4-5). Now drag up or down to shrink or enlarge the Dock.

Tip: If you press Option as you drag, the Dock snaps to certain canned icon sizes—those that the programmer actually drew. (You won't see the in-between sizes that OS X generally calculates on the fly.)

As noted in Figure 4-5, you may not be able to enlarge the Dock, especially if it contains a lot of icons. But you can make it almost infinitely smaller. This may make you wonder: How can you distinguish among icons if they're the size of molecules?

The answer lies in the →Dock→Turn Magnification On command. What you've just done is trigger the swelling effect shown in Figure 4-4. Now your Dock icons balloon to a much larger size as your cursor passes over them. It's a weird, magnetic, rippling, animated effect that takes some getting used to. But it can actually come in handy when you find your icons shrinking away to nothing.

Tip: You can get Dock magnification à la carte, too. If you press Shift-Control as your cursor approaches the Dock, the icons swell into magnification mode even if magnification is turned off in the →Dock menu. (The icons swell to whatever maximum size you specified in System Preferences (Figure 4-4).

Moving the Dock to the sides of the screen

Yet another approach to getting the Dock out of your way is to rotate it, so that it sits vertically against a side of your screen. You can rotate it in either of two ways:

- **The menu way.** From the →Dock submenu, choose Position on Left, Position on Right, or Position on Bottom, as you see fit.

- **The mouse way.** While pressing Shift, drag the Dock's divider line, like a handle, to the side of the screen you want.

Figure 4-4:
To make your Dock icons bigger or smaller, choose →Dock→Dock Preferences. Leave the Dock Preferences window open on the screen, as shown here. After each adjustment of the Dock size slider, try out the Dock (which still works when the Dock Preferences window is open) to test your new settings.

Figure 4-5:
Look closely—you can see the secret cursor that resizes the Dock. If you don't see any change in the Dock size as you drag upward, then you've reached the size limit. The Dock's edges are already approaching your screen's edges.

You'll probably find that the right side of your screen works better than the left. Most OS X programs put their document windows against the left edge of the screen, where the Dock and its labels might get in the way.

Note: When you position your Dock vertically, the "right" side of the Dock becomes the bottom of the vertical Dock. In other words, the Trash now appears at the bottom of the vertical Dock. So as you read references to the Dock in this book, mentally substitute the phrase "bottom part of the Dock" when you read references to the "right side of the Dock."

Using the Dock

Most of the time, you'll use the Dock as either a launcher (you click an icon once to open the corresponding program, file, folder, or disk) or as a status indicator (the tiny, shiny reflective spots identified in Figure 4-1 indicate which programs are running).

But the Dock has more tricks than that up its sleeve. You can use it, for example, to pull off any of the following stunts.

Switch Applications

The Dock isn't just a launcher; it's also a switcher. Here are some of the tricks it lets you do:

- Jump among your open programs by clicking their icons.
- Drag a document (such as a text file) onto a Dock application (such as the Microsoft Word icon) to open the former with the latter. (If the program balks at opening the document, yet you're sure the program should be able to open the document, then add the ⌘ and Option keys as you drag.)
- Hide all windows of the program you're in by Option-clicking another Dock icon.
- Hide all other programs' windows by Option-⌘-clicking the Dock icon of the program you do want (even if it's already in front).
- Switch windows in one program by pointing to that program's Dock icon without clicking, and then doing a three-finger downward swipe on your trackpad. (This feature, called App Exposé, doesn't work until you turn it on in System Preferences→Trackpad→More Gestures.)

Tip: This trick—the three-finger downswipe—works even on the Dock icons of programs that aren't running. In those situations, you get the effect shown on page 199. For some Apple programs, at least, it's a quick way to get to the icons of recently opened documents.

This is just a quick summary of the Dock's application-management functions; you'll find the full details in Chapter 5.

Operate the Dock by Keyboard Control

If you turn on keyboard navigation, you can operate the Dock entirely from the keyboard; see page 210.

Secret Menus

If you Control-click a Dock icon, or right-click it, or click-and-hold on it, you see its very useful shortcut menu (Figure 4-6).

Figure 4-6:
Left: Control-click a Dock icon to open the secret menu. In Mountain Lion–aware programs, the top half of the menu lists recently opened documents, followed by currently open ones.

Right: Control-click the divider bar to open a different hidden menu. This one lists a bunch of useful Dock commands, including the ones listed in the ■*→Dock submenu.*

If you've clicked a minimized window icon, this shortcut menu says only Open (unless it's a minimized Finder window, in which case it also says Close).

But if you've clicked any other kind of icon, you get some very useful hidden commands. For example:

- **[Window names].** The secret Dock menu of a running program usually lists one or more tiny, neatly labeled window icons, like those shown in Figure 4-6. This useful feature means you can jump directly not only to a certain program, but also to a certain open window in that program.

 For example, suppose you've been using Word to edit three different chapters. You can use Word's Dock icon as a Window menu to pull forward one particular chapter, or (if it's been minimized) to pull it up—even if a different program is in front of Word. (The checkmark indicates the *frontmost* window, even if the entire program is in the background. A diamond symbol means that the window is minimized and therefore not visible on the screen at the moment.)

 In Mountain Lion–aware programs like TextEdit and the iWork programs, there are actually two lists of documents, separated by a horizontal line. (You can see the effect in Figure 4-6.) The top group lists files you've recently opened in that program; the next batch lists currently open documents.

Tip: The Finder tile that's always at the beginning of the Dock is, in effect, its own Window menu. Its shortcut menu lists all open desktop windows. The Window menu at the top of the Finder screen does the same thing, but the Dock is available no matter what program you're using.

- **Show All Windows/Show Recents.** When a program on the Dock is open, this command says Show All Windows; when it's not running, it says Show Recents. Either way, it takes you to the screen shown in Figure 4-6, where the icons of recently opened documents appear for easy clicking and reopening. (OK, they may appear. Apple programs like TextEdit and Pages show these recent icons, but non-Apple programs have to be Mountain Lion–updated before they'll show you the recent-document icons.)

 To exit the Recents screen, press Esc or ⌘-period.

- **Options.** This submenu contains a bunch of miscellaneous commands:

 Options→Keep In Dock. Whenever you open a program, OS X puts its icon in the Dock—marked with a shiny, white spot—even if you don't normally keep its icon there. As soon as you quit the program, its icon disappears again from the Dock.

Tip: You can get rid of that shiny, white "running program" indicator dot, if you like. Open System Preferences→Dock and turn off "Show indicator lights for open applications."

If you understand that much, then the Keep In Dock command makes a lot of sense. It means, "Hello, I'm this program's icon. I know you don't normally keep me in your Dock, but I *could* stay here even after you quit my program. Just say the word." If you find you've been using, for example, Terminal a lot more often than you thought you would, this command may be the ticket.

Tip: Actually, there's a faster way to tell a running application to remain in the Dock from now on. Just drag its icon off the Dock and then right back onto it—yes, while the program is running. You have to try it to believe it.

If you don't want a program's icon to appear on the Dock when it's not running, choose this command again so that the checkmark disappears.

Note: If the program is already running, turning off Keep In Dock doesn't *immediately* remove its icon from the Dock. That's because a program always appears in the Dock when it's open. What you're doing here is saying, "Disappear from the Dock when you're *not* running"—and you'll see the proof as soon as you quit that program.

Options→Open at Login. This command lets you specify that you want this icon to open itself automatically each time you log into your account. It's a great way to make sure your email Inbox, your calendar, or the Microsoft Word thesis you've been working on is fired up and waiting on the screen when you sit down to work.

To make this item *stop* auto-opening, choose this command again so that the checkmark no longer appears.

Options→Show In Finder. This command highlights the actual icon (in whatever folder window it happens to sit) of the application, alias, folder, or document you've clicked. You might want to do this when, for example, you're using a program that you can't quite figure out, and you want to jump to its desktop folder in hopes of finding a Read Me file there.

Tip: Once again, there's a much faster way to reveal a Dock icon in its enclosing window: ⌘-click its Dock icon.

• **Hide/Show.** You can hide all traces of the program you're using by choosing Hide from its Dock icon. (You could accomplish the same thing in many other ways, of course; see page 203.)

What's cool here is that (a) you can even hide the Finder and all *its* windows, and (b) if you press Option, the command changes to say Hide Others. This, in its way, is a much more powerful command. It tells all the programs you're *not* using—the ones in the background—to get out of your face. They hide themselves instantly.

Note: Once you've hidden a program's windows, this command changes to say Show, which is how you make them reappear.

• **Quit.** You can quit any program directly from its Dock shortcut menu. (Finder, Launchpad, and Mission Control are exceptions.) The beauty of this feature is that you don't have to switch into a program to get to its Quit command.

(If you get nothing but a beep when you use this Quit command, it's because you've hidden the windows of that program, and one of them has unsaved changes. Click the program's icon, save your document, and then try to quit again.)

Tip: If you hold down the Option key—even after you've opened the pop-up menu—the Quit command changes to say Force Quit. That's your emergency hatch for jettisoning a locked-up program.

• **Miscellaneous.** You might find other commands in Dock shortcut menus; software companies are free to add specialty options to their own programs.

For example, the Finder icon's shortcut menu offers direct access to commands like Find, Connect to Server, and New Finder Window. Microsoft Office programs (Word, Excel, and so on) come with an Open Recent command, with a list of documents you've opened recently. The Mail icon offers Get New Mail and Compose New Message commands. The Safari icon has a New Window command. The System Preferences icon sprouts a complete list of the preference panes (Sound, Keyboard, Trackpad, and so on). You get the idea.

Tip: If you Control-⌘-click a program's Dock icon, you get an abbreviated shortcut menu. It lists *only* the Options, Hide, and Quit commands and maybe some recent documents—not the full list of commands. If all you want to do is quit a program or something, this abbreviated menu is faster and easier to comprehend.

Conduct Speed Tests

When you click an application icon in the Dock, its icon jumps up and down a few times as the program launches, as though with excitement at having been selected. The longer a program takes to start up, the more bounces you see. This has given birth to a hilarious phenomenon: counting these bounces as a casual speed benchmark for application-launching times. "InDesign took 12 bouncemarks to open in Mac OS X 10.7," you might read online, "but only three bouncemarks in 10.8."

Tip: If you find the icon-bouncing a bit over the top, try this: Choose →Dock→Dock Preferences. In the Dock preference pane (shown in Figure 4-4), turn off "Animate opening applications." From now on, your icons won't actually bounce—instead, the little shiny spot underneath it will simply *pulse* as the application opens.

Drag and Drop

Dock icons are spring-loaded. That is, if you drag any icon onto a Dock folder or disk icon and pause—or, if you're in a hurry, tap the space bar—the Dock icon opens to receive the dragged file.

Note: It opens, that is, *if* the spring-loaded folder feature is turned on in Finder→Preferences→General.

This technique is most useful in these situations:

• Drag a document icon onto a Dock folder icon. The folder's Finder window pops open so you can continue the drag into a subfolder.

• Drag a document into an application. The classic example is dragging a photo onto the iPhoto icon. When you tap the space bar, iPhoto opens automatically. Since your mouse button is still down, and you're technically still in mid-drag, you can now drop the photo directly into the appropriate iPhoto album or Event.

You can drag an MP3 file into iTunes or an attachment into Mail or Outlook in the same way.

Do Your Filing

Once you've tried stashing a few important folders on the right side of your Dock, there's no going back. You can mostly forget all the other navigation tricks you've learned in OS X. The folders you care about are always there, ready for opening with a single click.

Better yet, they're easily accessible for putting away files; you can drag files directly into the Dock's folder icons as though they were regular folders.

In fact, you can even drag a file into a subfolder in a Dock folder. That's because, again, Dock folders are spring-loaded. When you drag an icon onto a Dock folder and pause, the folder's window appears around your cursor, so you can continue the drag into an inner folder (and even an inner inner folder, and so on). Page 202 has the details on spring-loaded folders.

Tip: When you try to drag something into a folder on the Dock, the Dock icons scoot out of the way; the Dock assumes you're trying to put that something *onto* the Dock. But if you press the ⌘ key as you drag an icon to the Dock, the existing icons freeze in place. Without the ⌘ key, you wind up playing a frustrating game of chase-the-folder.

Great Things to Put in Your Dock

Now that you know what the Dock is about, it's time to set up shop, installing the programs, folders, and disks you'll be using most often.

They can be whatever you want, of course, but don't miss these opportunities:

- **Your Home folder.** Many people immediately drag their hard drive icons—or, perhaps more practically, their Home folders—onto the right side of the Dock. Now they have quick access to every file in every folder they ever use.

- **The Applications folder.** Here's a no-brainer: Stash the Applications folder here so you'll have quick pop-up menu access to any program on your machine.

- **Your Applications folder.** As an even more efficient corollary, create a new folder of your own. Fill it with the aliases of just the programs you use most often and park it in the Dock. Now you've got an even more useful Applications folder that opens as a stack.

- **The Shared folder.** If you're using the Mac's accounts feature (Chapter 13), this is your wormhole to all the accounts—the one place you can put files where everybody can access them (page 526).

The Finder Toolbar

At the top of every Finder window is a small set of function icons, all in a gradient-gray row (Figure 4-7). The first time you run Mountain Lion, you'll find only these icons on the toolbar:

- **Back (◄), Forward (►).** The Finder works something like a Web browser. Only a single window remains open as you navigate the various folders on your hard drive.

 The Back button (◄) returns you to whichever folder you were just looking at. (Instead of clicking ◄, you can also press ⌘-[, or choose Go→Back—particularly handy if the toolbar is *hidden*, as described below.)

 The Forward button (►) springs to life only after you've used the Back button. Clicking it (or pressing ⌘-]) returns you to the window you just backed out of.

- **View controls.** The four tiny buttons next to the ◄ button switch the current window into icon, list, column, or Cover Flow view, respectively. And remember, if the toolbar is hidden, you can get by with the equivalent commands in the View menu at the top of the screen—or by pressing ⌘-1 for icon view, ⌘-2 for list view, ⌘-3 for column view, or ⌘-4 for Cover Flow view.

- **Arrange.** This pop-up menu lets you group the files in a window by date, name, or other criteria; see page 43.

- **Quick Look.** The ◉ icon opens the Quick Look preview for a highlighted icon (or group of them); see page 59.

Figure 4-7:
If you Control-click (or right-click) a blank spot on the toolbar, you get a pop-up menu that offers you a choice of looks for the buttons here: Icon Only, Text Only, or Icon and Text. In Text Only mode (bottom), the four View buttons are replaced by a little pop-up menu called View. Furthermore, the search box turns into a one-word button called Search. Clicking it brings up the Searching window.

- **Action (✿).** You can read about this context-sensitive pop-up menu on page 99.

- **Search box.** This little round-ended text box is yet another entry point for the Spotlight feature described in Chapter 3. It's a handy way to search your Mac for some file, folder, disk, or program.

Hiding or Shrinking the Toolbar

With the toolbar, the Dock, the Sidebar, and the large icons of OS X, it almost seems like there's an Apple conspiracy to sell big screens.

Fortunately, the toolbar doesn't have to contribute to that impression. You can hide it by choosing View→Hide Toolbar or by pressing Option-⌘-T. (The same keystroke, or choosing View→Show Toolbar, brings it back.)

Of course, you can also just make it smaller by hiding the labels (or the icons), as shown in Figure 4-7.

Customizing the Icons on the Toolbar

OS X offers a collection of beautifully designed icons for alternate (or additional) toolbar buttons. But you can also add anything to the toolbar, turning it into a supplementary Dock or Sidebar. This is great news for people who've run out of space for stashing favorite icons in the Dock or the Sidebar. (Of course, if that's your problem, you need a bigger monitor.)

Apple's toolbar-icon collection

The first step in tweaking the toolbar is choosing View→Customize Toolbar. The window shown in Figure 4-8 appears.

Figure 4-8:
While this window is open, you can add icons to the toolbar by dragging them into place from the gallery before you. You can also remove icons from the toolbar by dragging them up or down off the toolbar. Rearrange the icons by dragging them horizontally.

This is your chance to rearrange the existing toolbar icons or to delete the ones you don't use. You can also add any of Apple's buttons to the toolbar by dragging them from the "gallery" onto the toolbar itself. The existing icons scoot out of your cursor's way, if necessary.

Most of the options in the gallery duplicate the functions of menu commands. Here are a few that don't appear on the standard toolbar:

- **Path.** Most of the gallery elements are buttons, but this one creates a pop-up menu on the toolbar. When clicked, it reveals (and lets you navigate) the hierarchy— the path—of folders you open to reach whichever window is open. (Equivalent: ⌘-clicking a window's title.)

- **Eject (⏏).** This button ejects whichever disk or disk image is currently high-lighted. (Equivalent: the File→Eject command, or holding down the ⏏ key on your keyboard.)

- **Burn.** This button burns a blank CD or DVD with the folders and files you've dragged onto it. (Equivalent: the File→Burn [Thing Name] to Disc command.)

- **Space.** By dragging this mysterious-looking item into the toolbar, you add a gap between it and whatever icon is to its left. The gap is about as wide as one icon. (The fine, dark, rectangular outline that appears when you drag it doesn't actually show up once you click Done.)

- **Flexible Space.** This icon, too, creates a gap between the toolbar buttons. But this one expands as you make the window wider. Now you know how Apple got the search box to appear off to the right of the standard toolbar, a long way from its clustered comrades to the left.

- **New Folder.** Clicking this button creates a new folder in whichever window you're viewing. (Equivalent: the File→New Folder command, or the Shift-⌘-N keystroke.)

- **Delete.** This option puts the highlighted file or folder icons into the Trash. (Equivalent: the File→Move to Trash command, or the ⌘-Delete keystroke.)

Tip: Weirdly enough, if you highlight an icon in the Trash and then click this Delete button, you trigger the Put Back function—flinging the icon back into the folder it came from. That is, clicking Delete in this case actually *un*deletes.

- **Connect.** If you're on a home or office network, this opens the Connect to Server dialog box so you can tap into another computer. (Equivalent: the Go→Connect to Server command, or ⌘-K.)

- **Labels.** This item is a pop-up menu—a quick way to apply Finder color labels to your icons. Often, you don't even have to open the menu; just *click* the pop-up menu to apply the most recent color again.

- **Get Info.** This button opens the Get Info window for whatever's selected.

- **Search.** This item represents the Spotlight search box described in Chapter 3.

- **Drag the default set.** If you've made a mess of your toolbar, you can always reinstate its original Apple arrangement by dragging this rectangular strip directly upward onto your toolbar.

If the window ever gets too narrow to show all the icons you've added to the toolbar, the right end of the toolbar sprouts a ≫ symbol. Click it for a pop-up menu that names whichever icons don't fit at the moment. (You'll find this toolbar behavior in many OS X programs, not just the Finder: Safari, Mail, and so on.)

Note: Two of the toolbar options disappeared in the Lion version. There's no longer a Separator line to help group your toolbar items, probably because Apple is going for a cleaner, purer look. And the iDisk icon is gone, because the iDisk itself went away when the MobileMe service became the iCloud service.

Adding your own stuff

Millions of Mac fans will probably trudge forward through life using the toolbar to hold the suggested Apple function buttons and the Sidebar to hold the icons of favorite folders, files, and programs. They may never realize that you can drag any icons at all onto the toolbar—files, folders, disks, programs, or whatever—to turn them into one-click buttons.

In short, you can think of the Finder toolbar as yet another Dock or Sidebar (Figure 4-9).

Figure 4-9:
You don't need to choose View→ Customize Toolbar to add your own icons to the toolbar. Just drag them from the desktop or any folder window directly onto the toolbar at any time. Pause with your cursor on the toolbar for a moment before releasing the icon.

Rearranging or Removing Toolbar Icons

You can drag toolbar icons around, rearranging them horizontally, by pressing ⌘ as you drag. Taking an icon off the toolbar is equally easy. While pressing the ⌘ key, just drag the icon clear away from the toolbar. It vanishes in a puff of cartoon smoke. (If the Customize Toolbar sheet is open, you can perform either step without the ⌘ key. You can also get rid of a toolbar icon by right-clicking it and choosing Remove Item from the shortcut menu.)

Designing Your Desktop

In some ways, just buying a Macintosh was already a renegade act of self-expression. But that's only the beginning. Now it's time to fashion the computer screen itself according to your personal sense of design and fashion.

System Preferences

Cosmetically speaking, OS X offers two dramatic full-screen features: desktop backgrounds and screen savers. For details, see Chapter 9.

Graphic Designers' Corner: The Gray Look

One of the earliest objections to the lively, brightly colored look of OS X came from Apple's core constituency: artists and graphic designers. Some complained that OS X's bright blues (of scroll-bar handles, progress bars, the menu, pulsing OK buttons, and highlighted menu names and commands), along with the red, green, and yellow window-corner buttons, threw off their color judgment.

Apple has been de-colorizing OS X ever since. The pulsing effects are subtler, the three-dimensional effects are less drastic, and the button colors are less intense. In Snow Leopard, both the menu and the Spotlight menu went from colorful to black, and in Lion, the Sidebar lost its color.

Tip: The Highlight Color pop-up menu lets you choose a different accent color for your Mac world. This is the background color of highlighted text, the colored oval that appears around highlighted icon names, and a window's "lining" as you drag an icon into it.

But in case the color scheme still bothers artists, Apple created what it calls the Graphite look for OS X, which turns all those interface elements gray instead of blue. To try out this look, choose →System Preferences; click General, and then choose Graphite from the Appearance pop-up menu.

Desktop Sounds

Desktop sounds are the tiny sound effects that accompany certain mouse drags. And we're talking tiny—they're so subdued that you might not have noticed them. You hear a little plink/crunch when you drop an icon onto the Trash, a boingy thud when you drag something into a folder, a *whoof!* when you drag something off the Dock and into oblivion, and so on. The little thud you hear at the end of a file-copying job is actually useful, because it alerts you that the task is complete.

If all that racket is keeping you awake, however, it's easy enough to turn it off. Open System Preferences, click the Sound icon, and then turn off "Play user interface sound effects."

And if you decide to leave them turned on, please—use discretion when working in a library, church, or neurosurgical operating room.

FREQUENTLY ASKED QUESTION

Desktop Fonts

How do I change the fonts used by the OS X Finder?

In Mac OS versions gone by, you could choose any font you liked for your icon labels. You even had a choice of fonts for use in your menus.

Nowadays, that flexibility is gone. You get Lucida Grande in your menus and as icon labels—love it or leave it.

For now, Apple intends to remain conservative with the look of OS X—both for "branding" reasons (to make OS X instantly recognizable) and for technical ones (to make sure it doesn't open a Pandora's box of interface hacks that wind up destabilizing the machine).

Menulets: The Missing Manual

See the menu-bar icons in Figure 4-10? Apple calls them Menu Extras, but Mac fans on the Internet have named them menulets. Each menulet is both an indicator and a menu that provides direct access to certain settings in System Preferences. One lets you adjust your Mac's speaker volume; another lets you change the screen resolution; yet another shows you the remaining power in your laptop battery; and so on.

Figure 4-10:
These little guys are the cousins of the controls found on the Windows system tray.

Macintosh HD

To make the various menulets appear, you generally visit a certain pane of System Preferences (Chapter 9) and turn on a checkbox called, for example, "Show volume in menu bar." Here's a rundown of the various Apple menulets you may encounter, complete with instructions on where to find the magic on/off checkbox for each.

Along the way, you'll discover that secondary, hidden features lurk in many of these menulets, if you happen to know the secret: Press the Option key.

Tip: The following descriptions indicate the official, authorized steps for installing a menulet. There is, however, a folder on your hard drive that contains *24 of them* in a single window, so you can install one with a quick double-click. To find them, open your hard drive→System→Library→CoreServices→Menu Extras folder.

- **AirPlay,** new in Mountain Lion, lets you send the Mac's screen image to a TV, provided you have an Apple TV (details on page 494). This menulet turns blue when you're projecting, and its menu lets you turn AirPlay on or off. *To find the Show checkbox:* Open System Preferences→Displays→Display tab.

- **AirPort** lets you turn your WiFi (wireless networking) circuitry on or off, join existing wireless networks, and create your own private ones. *To find the Show checkbox:* Open System Preferences→Network. Click Wi-Fi.

Tip: Once you've installed this menulet, you can *Option-click* it to produce a secret menu full of details about the wireless network you're on right now. You see its channel number, password-security method (WEP, WPA, None, whatever), speed, and such geeky details as the MCS Index and RSSI.

• **Battery** shows how much power remains in your laptop's battery, how much time is left to charge it, whether it's plugged in, and more. When you click the icon to open the menu, you see how many actual hours and minutes are left on the charge. You can also choose Show Percentage to add a percentage-remaining readout (43%) to the menu bar. (Sadly, Mountain Lion no longer lets you put the time-remaining display right in the menu bar.) *To find the Show checkbox:* Open System Preferences→Energy Saver.

Note: You may see a new item at the top of the Battery menulet that conveys the battery's health. It might say, for example, "Service Battery," "Replace Soon," "Replace Now," or "Check Battery." Of course, we all know laptop batteries don't last forever; they begin to hold less of a charge as they approach 500 or 1,000 recharges, depending on the model.

Is Apple looking out for you, or just trying to goose the sale of replacement batteries? You decide.

• **Bluetooth** connects to Bluetooth devices, "pairs" your Mac with a cellphone, lets you send or receive files wirelessly (without the hassle of setting up a wireless network), and so on. *To find the Show checkbox:* Open System Preferences→Bluetooth.

Tip: You can Option-click this menulet to see three additional lines of nerdy details about your Bluetooth setup: the Bluetooth software version you're using, the name of your Mac (which is helpful when you're trying to make it show up on another Bluetooth gadget), and its Bluetooth MAC [hardware] address.

• **Clock** is the menu-bar clock that's been sitting at the upper-right corner of your screen from Day One. Click it to open a menu where you can check today's date, convert the menu-bar display to a tiny analog clock, and so on. *To find the Show checkbox:* Open System Preferences→Date & Time. On the Clock tab, turn on "Show date and time in menu bar."

• **Displays** adjusts screen resolution. On Macs with a projector or second monitor attached, it lets you turn *screen mirroring* on or off—a tremendous convenience to anyone who gives PowerPoint or Keynote presentations. *To find the Show checkbox:* Open System Preferences→Displays→Display tab.

• ⏏ is the oddball: There's no checkbox in System Preferences to make this menulet appear. The fact that it even exists is something of a secret.

To make it appear, open your System→Library→CoreServices→Menu Extras folder as described above, and then double-click the Eject menu icon. That's it! The ⏏ menulet appears.

You'll discover that its wording changes—"Open Combo Drive," "Close DVD-ROM Drive," "Eject [Name of Disc]," or whatever—to reflect your particular drive type and what's in it at the moment.

• **Messages** is a quick way to let the world know, via the Messages application (Chapter 20) and the Internet, that you're away from your keyboard, or available and ready to chat. Via the New Message command, it's also a quick way to open Messages

itself. *To find the Show checkbox:* Open Messages; it's in your Applications folder. Choose Messages→Preferences→General.

- **Remote Desktop** is a program, sold separately, that lets teachers or system administrators tap into your Mac from across a network. In fact, they can actually see what's on your screen, move the cursor around, and so on. The menulet lets you do things like send a message to the administrator. *To find the Show checkbox:* Open System Preferences→Sharing, and then click Remote Management.

- **Script Menu** lists a variety of useful, ready-to-run AppleScript programs. *To find the Show checkbox:* Open the AppleScript Editor program (in your Applications Utilities folder). Choose AppleScript Editor→Preferences→General.

- **Text Input** switches among different text input modes. For example, if your language uses a different alphabet, like Russian, or thousands of characters, like Chinese, this menulet summons and dismisses the alternative keyboards and input methods you need. Details on page 253. *To find the Show checkbox:* Open System Preferences→Language & Text→Input Sources.

- **Time Machine** lets you start and stop Time Machine backups (see Chapter 6). *To find the Show checkbox:* Open System Preferences→Time Machine.

- **Universal Access** offers simple on/off status indicators for features that are designed to help with visual, hearing, and muscle impairments. Chapter 9 has a rundown of what they do. *To find the Show checkbox:* Open System Preferences→Universal Access.

- **User** identifies the account holder (Chapter 13) who's logged in at the moment. To make this menulet appear (in bold, at the far-right end of the menu bar), turn on *fast user switching,* which is described on page 527.

- **Volume,** of course, adjusts your Mac's speaker or headphone volume. *To find the Show checkbox:* Open System Preferences→Sound.

- **VPN** stands for virtual private networking, which allows you to tap into a corporation's network so you can, for example, check your work email from home. You can use the menulet to connect and disconnect, for example. *To find the Show checkbox:* Open System Preferences→Network. Click the name of your VPN.

- **WWAN** is useful only if you've equipped your Mac with one of those glorious *cellular modems,* sold by Verizon, Sprint, AT&T, and T-Mobile. These little USB sticks get you onto the Internet wirelessly at near-cable-modem speeds (in big cities, anyway)—no WiFi required—for $60 a month. And this menulet lets you start and stop that connection. *To find the Show checkbox:* Open System Preferences→Network. Click the name of your cellular modem.

Note: A few other items lurk in the Menu Extras folder: PPPoE, Ink, IrDA, ExpressCard, and so on. They're relics of an earlier age, when laptops had card slots and infrared lenses.

To remove a menulet, ⌘-drag it off your menu bar, or turn off the corresponding checkbox in System Preferences. You can also rearrange menulets by ⌘-dragging them horizontally.

These little guys are useful, good-looking, and respectful of your screen space. The world could use more inventions like menulets.

Part Two:
Programs in OS X

2

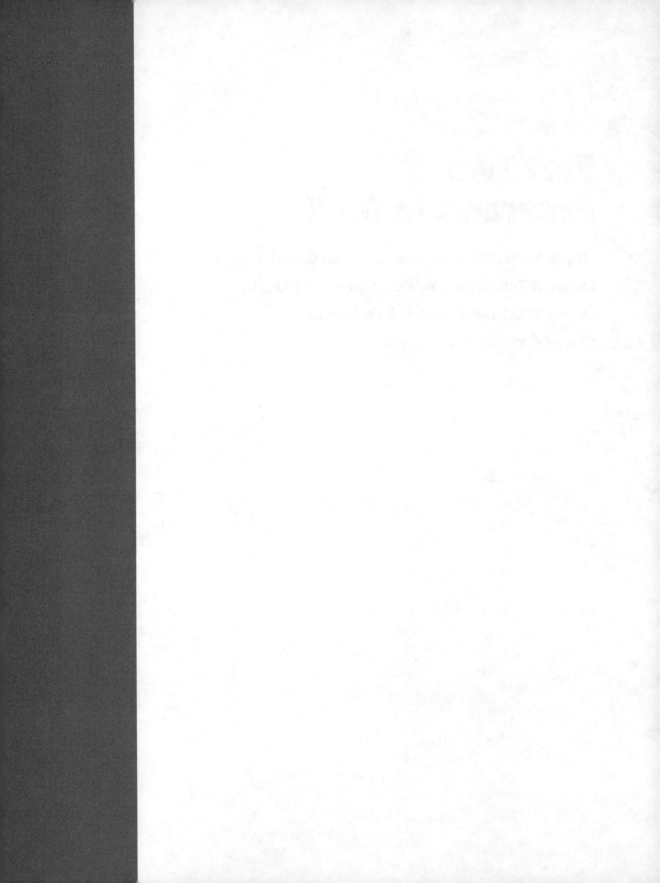

Documents, Programs & Mission Control

The whole point of owning a computer, of course, is to run *programs*—or, as Apple likes to call them, apps. And in Mountain Lion, Apple wants programs to look and work like they do on the iPad: simply. As full-screen, autosaving worlds. You're supposed to open them from a simple Home screen arrayed with app icons, and you're supposed to switch among them by swiping with your fingers on your trackpad or mouse.

This radical new vision of running programs is actually possible in Mountain Lion—sort of. The hitch is that a lot of the iPaddy features, including full-screen mode and autosaving, don't work in pre-Lion programs. Software companies have to update their apps to add these features.

Most of them will do that, but in the meantime, you'll go through a weird period of mixed metaphors, where some programs can do those tricks and others can't.

In any case, this chapter covers Apple's New Way of Running Programs, and all of its Capitalized Elements: the Mac App Store, Launchpad, Mission Control, Full Screen, Auto Save, Versions, and more.

The Mac App Store

For years, people installed software onto their computers by buying disks: floppies, CDs, and, later, DVDs.

But starting with the iPhone, people installed software onto their *phones* by downloading it directly from the Internet. Once everybody saw how convenient (and profitable) that system was, it didn't take Apple long to realize it could bring the same convenience to the Mac.

So now there's the Mac App Store—or, as the program is called in your Applications folder, just App Store. It's an online catalog of software from huge software companies, tiny one-person software companies, and everything in between. You can read about the programs, check out customer reviews, and, finally, download them directly to your Mac. (As you probably know, Mountain Lion itself is an App Store purchase.)

There are some huge advantages to this system. Since there's no box, disc, registration card, shipping, or stocking, the software can cost a lot less; Apple's own programs certainly reflect this price advantage. Plenty of programs on the App Store are actually free.

Furthermore, Apple controls the transaction on both ends—it knows who you are—so there are no serial numbers to type in. The installation no longer interrupts you with warnings like "Please enter your password to install this software" or "This software appears to have been downloaded from the Internet"; once you click Buy, the software downloads and installs itself *automatically*, without any interaction from you at all.

And there are no discs to store and hunt down later. If you ever need to reinstall a program from the App Store, or if you ever get a new Mac, you just re-download it from the Purchases tab; the App Store remembers that you're a legitimate owner. Better yet, you'll be downloading the latest version of that program; you won't have to install all the ".01" patches that have come along since.

UP TO SPEED

Classic and Rosetta, RIP

There are two chief kinds of OS X–compatible programs, known by the geeks as *Carbon* and *Cocoa* programs. These terms refer to the programming tools that were used to create them, which also have a small effect on how well they run in OS X. Page 227 covers them in more detail, but the point is that this chapter describes how to use Carbon and Cocoa programs–true OS X programs.

Now, until Leopard (Mac OS X 10.5) came along, there was a third software category. Older Macs (pre-Intel Macs) could also run the very old, pre-2001 operating system known as Mac OS 9 and all of its programs. Mac OS X came with a built-in Mac OS 9 *simulator* called Classic. But Classic disappeared in Mac OS X 10.6. The bottom line: Today's Macs can't run those ancient Mac OS 9 programs.

When Apple switched all of its Macs over to Intel processors in 2006, it had to write *another* simulator. This time, it was an invisible translation program, Rosetta, that permitted the existing library of OS X programs–Photoshop, Word, and so on–to run, unmodified, on Intel Macs.

Unfortunately, Rosetta-needing apps didn't run especially fast. To make their programs perform at full speed on Intel-based Macs, programmers had to update their wares. It took a couple of years, but eventually all the major and minor software companies still in the Mac business did indeed convert their programs into *universal binaries*–programs that ran equally well on PowerPC- *and* Intel-based Macs with a double-click on the very same Finder icon. These days, all Mac programs are either universal or Intel only.

In Mountain Lion, Rosetta is gone. The number of affected programs is small–programs whose software companies never updated them for Intel chips–but some of them are beloved by Mac fans: Canvas, and AppleWorks, for example. (Fortunately, Pages and Number can convert most Apple-Works documents.)

Mountain Lion is all modern, all the time, making life simpler for Apple–and a little more complicated for anyone who used to rely on those older programs.

Tip: To hide an app you've bought so it no longer appears in Purchases, right-click its name and choose Hide Purchase. (To unhide it later, click the Account link on the main page of the App Store; under the iTunes in the Cloud heading, choose View Hidden Purchases.)

And speaking of updates: Since Apple knows what programs you have, it can let you know when new versions are available. The Notification Center can notify you about new versions of any programs you own. The updates are small files, so they download fast; the App Store delivers only the pieces that have actually changed.

One final advantage: If you decide to use Launchpad, described in the following pages, anything you've bought from the App Store is easy to delete with a single click.

The only people bemoaning the App Store Era are people with slow Internet connections (or whose Internet services are limited to a certain amount of data each month).

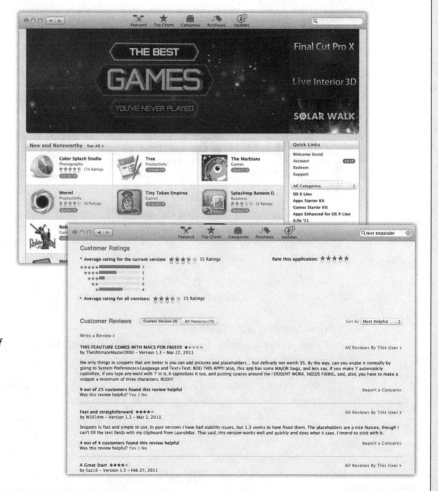

Figure 5-1:
Top: Mastering the App Store won't take you much time; just about everything you need is in the toolbar at the top, including a search box and buttons like Featured, Top Charts, and Categories, which are meant to help you dive into the enormous catalog of Mac software. The remaining tab, Purchases, shows everything you've ever bought using your Apple account. If you visit this page using a different Mac, you can re-download anything you've bought—no charge.

Bottom: As with the iPhone/iPad app store, you can read reviews of each piece of software, written by other people who've tried it.

Apple cheerfully invites them to take their Macs to an Apple Store, where there's a free, high-speed, in-store WiFi network.

To use the Mac App Store, open the App Store program in your Applications folder (or on your Launchpad).

In general, the App Store here works exactly like the iPhone/iPad App Store. Click a program's icon to open its details page. Here you'll find reviews and ratings from other people, a description, pictures (screenshots) of the program, and much more information to help you make a good buying decision. See Figure 5-1 for more details.

When you buy an app, Launchpad opens automatically, so you can see where it went.

Other Ways to Get Mac Software

In general, new programs arrive on your Mac via one of two avenues: as an Internet download (whether from the App Store or not), or on a CD or DVD.

Downloading Compressed Files

Programs you download from the Web (not the App Store) generally arrive in a specially encoded, compressed form. And unless you've changed the settings, they arrive in the Downloads folder on your Dock.

The downloaded file's name usually has one of these file name extensions:

- **.zip** is the standard compression file format for Windows and Mac files. In fact, OS X has a built-in Compress command right in the File menu.

- **.sit** indicates a *StuffIt* file, the standard Macintosh file-compression format of years gone by.

- **.dmg** is a disk image, described below.

You may occasionally run into .tar files (*tape archive,* an ancient Unix utility), .gz (*gzip,* a standard Unix compression format), or combo formats like .tar.gz or .tgz.

Fortunately, you generally don't have to worry about any of this; most Web browsers, including Safari, automatically unzip and unstuff downloads of all types.

Disk images (.dmg files)

Once you've downloaded a program, it often takes the form of a *disk image* file, whose name ends with the letters *.dmg* (second from the top in Figure 5-2).

Disk images are extremely common in OS X. All you have to do is double-click the .dmg icon. After a moment, it magically turns into a disk icon on your desktop, which you can work with just as though it were a real disk (third from the top in Figure 5-2). For example:

- Double-click it to open it. The software you downloaded is inside.

- Remove it from your desktop by dragging it to the Trash (whose icon turns into a big silver ⏏ key as you drag), highlighting it and pressing ⌘-E (the shortcut

for File→Eject), clicking its ⏏ button in the Sidebar, or Control-clicking (right-clicking) it and then choosing Eject from the shortcut menu.

You've still got the original .dmg file you downloaded, so you're not really saying goodbye to the disk image forever.

When you've finished unzipping or unstuffing a downloaded file, you may have several icons on your desktop or in the Downloads folder. Some are useful; some you're free to trash:

- **The original compressed file.** It's safe to throw away the .sit, .tar, .gz, or .tgz file you originally downloaded (after it's decompressed, of course).

- **The .dmg file.** Once you've turned it into an actual disk-drive icon, installed the software from it, and "ejected" the disk-drive icon, you can delete the .dmg file. Keep it only if you think you might need to reinstall the software someday.

Figure 5-2:
Downloading a new program may strew your desktop or Downloads folder with icons. A: These are the downloaded files. Delete them after they're de-compressed. B: The compressed file turns into this .dmg file. Double-click it to "mount" the disk im-age (if it didn't ap-pear automatically). C: And now, the disk image itself. Double-click it to open the software installer window. (Dismiss the warning that the software came from the Internet.) "Eject" it after the instal-lation is complete. D: Here's the actual software installer window. After the installation, you can delete all this stuff (except maybe the .dmg file, if you think you might want to install the software again later).

Note: If you try to trash the .dmg file before removing the disk-drive icon from the screen, you'll get a "file in use" error message when you try to empty the Trash.

- **The disk image itself.** This final icon, the one that contains the actual software or its installer (third from the top in Figure 5-2), doesn't exist as a file on your hard drive. It's a phantom drive, held in memory, that will go away by itself when you log out. So after installing its software, feel free to drag it to the Trash (or highlight it and press ⌘-E to "eject" it).

Performing the installation

Once you've got a disk icon on your desktop—either a pseudo-disk from a disk image or a CD or DVD you've inserted—you're ready to install the software. You can install many OS X programs just by dragging their icons or folders to your hard drive (usually the Applications folder). Others offer a traditional installer program that requires you to double-click, read and accept a license agreement, and so on.

Uninstalling Software

If you got a program from the App Store, it's easy to delete from the Launchpad (page 168).

If you got it from some other source, well, there's generally no Uninstall program. To uninstall a program, you just drag it (or its folder) to the Trash.

FREQUENTLY ASKED QUESTION

Submit to Apple

What the—I was working along in Safari, and all of a sudden it just vanished! Poof! And all I got was this lousy dialog box about "submitting to Apple." What's going on?

Apple is trying to assimilate you.

Or, more accurately, it's trying to enlist your help in ferreting out all the little glitches that make modern computing so much fun. If you're willing to click the Submit Report button and type a few comments ("I was running Word, minding my own business, and when I clicked the Print button, the whole thing just crashed"), then Apple will add your report to the thousands flowing in from everyone else.

The idea is that when its programmers get a moment, they'll study these reports, track down the patterns ("Hmm, we've received 50,000 reports about that Print button in Word"), and then chase down the software company responsible—and, presumably, get a fix under way.

The report you submit is full of technical info that helps the programmers figure out what was happening at the time of the crash, but no personal information goes along for the ride. So if you feel like doing some good for your fellow Mac fans, by all means submit the report (via the Internet) whenever you're offered the chance.

Some programs leave harmless scraps of themselves behind; to check for them, look for preference files or folders bearing the dearly departed program's name in your Library folders (especially in Application Support) and in your Home→Library→Preferences folder.

Opening OS X Programs

You can launch (open) an application in any of several ways:

- Single-click an icon on the Launchpad, described on the following pages.

- Single-click a program's icon on the Dock, the Sidebar, or the Finder toolbar.

- Use Spotlight. Hit ⌘-space bar, type the first letters of the program's name, and then press Return.

- Double-click an app's icon in the Finder.

- If you've added the Applications folder to your Dock, click the Dock icon to open the pop-up fan, grid, or list of icons. Then click the program you want (or even type the first few letters of its name and then press Return).

- Highlight an application icon and then press ⌘-O (short for File→Open) or ⌘-down arrow.

- Use the submenus of the menu's Recent Items→Applications command.

Note: OS X stores a list of your recently used programs in a text file called com.apple.recentitems.plist, located in your Home folder→Library→Preferences folder. And with about a dollar, that information will buy you a cup of coffee in most restaurants.

FREQUENTLY ASKED QUESTION

What's with the Big "Duh"?

So I've just installed Mountain Lion, I'm all excited, and I double-click an Excel document. And now the Mac asks me: "You are opening Microsoft Excel for the first time. Do you want to continue?" Well, HELLO! I double-clicked the icon, didn't I? Does Apple think I'm some kind of idiot?

It's not you Apple is worried about. It's the silent parade of evil hackers, lurking out there in Internet Land, waiting for the right moment to bring down the Mac.

See, spyware authors have to be sneaky about how they install their stuff on your computer. You wouldn't be so stupid as to double-click an application called Spyware Installer™, of course. So the spyware tricks you into running its installer.

In the Windows world, it commandeers a certain document type (like MP3 or JPEG), reassigning it to its installer. You innocently double-click some document, but an unanticipated program opens—and you've just opened Pandora's box.

In OS X, that can't happen. When double-clicking some document opens a program for the first time, this dialog box appears, just to let you know what's about to happen. If the program that's about to open isn't the one you were expecting, well, you've got a chance to back out of it.

And if it *is* the program you were expecting, click Continue. You won't be asked again about this version of this particular program.

• Open a *document* icon in any of these ways, or drag a document onto the icon of a program that can open it (whether in the Dock, the Finder toolbar, the Sidebar, or a folder window).

Tip: If you press Option as you open an application (or anything else) in the Finder, you automatically close the window that contains its icon. Later, when you return to the Finder, you find a neat, clean desktop—no loitering windows.

Launchpad

The Launchpad app presents a dark background with evenly spaced icons that represent all your programs (Figure 5-3). You can open one with a single click.

Figure 5-3:
You can open Launchpad by clicking its Dock icon (it's the very next one after the Finder icon), or by using a four-finger pinching gesture on your trackpad. Launchpad covers your entire main monitor, hiding everything else.

Use the arrow keys to navigate a page; press ⌘-arrow to move between pages; press Option to make the start wiggling, ready for deletion.

Why did Apple feel the need to create yet *another* way to open programs?

First, because Launchpad fits right into the general theme of Mountain Lion: making the Mac look and work more like the iPad. Launchpad is a dead ringer for the Home screens of an iPad, iPhone, or iPod Touch.

Second, it's a much less intimidating place for technophobes to learn to love than, say, the Applications folder.

And third, it's a lot quicker to get to than the Applications folder. You can summon it instantly, using any of these methods:

- **Put four fingers on your trackpad and pinch them together.** The Launchpad appears instantly, no matter what program you were in; you don't have to duck back into the Finder, navigate to the Applications folder, and so on.

- **Press the Launchpad key.** Recent Macs have a special Launchpad icon painted right on the F4 key (⊞).

- **Click its icon on the Dock.** It's the second one, resembling a rocket (🚀).

- **Press a keyboard shortcut of your choice.** To set that up, choose →System Preferences→Keyboard. Click the Keyboard Shortcuts tab, and then click Launchpad & Dock in the left-side list. On the right, make sure Show Launchpad is turned on—and then double-click in the blank space to the right of it and press the key combination you want.

- **Move the cursor into one of the screen's four corners.** To set up these options, open →System Preferences→Mission Control. Click Hot Corners to choose a corner of the screen for Launchpad.

- **Open it as you would any other program.** It's in your Applications folder.

One thing's for sure: Sooner or later, you'll wind up in Launchpad.

Only three visual elements appear there:

- **Icons.** Each icon represents one of your programs. Apple's programs are listed first, in alphabetical order: App Store, Automator, Calculator, and so on. Then come all your other programs, again in A-to-Z order. Click one to open that program.

Note: The only program icon that *doesn't* appear in Launchpad…is Launchpad's. That's a good thing. You wouldn't want to wind up in an infinite loop, would you?

- **Search box.** This box at the top of the screen, new in Mountain Lion, lets you pluck one needle from your haystack of apps, no matter what page it's on. You don't have to click there first—just start typing when Launchpad is before you. With each letter you type, Launchpad hides everything but the matching app icons.

- **Home-page dots.** As you install more and more programs, Launchpad makes room for them by creating additional screens. You can spread your new programs' icons across an unlimited number of launch screens.

 The little white dots are your map. Each represents one Launchpad screen. If the third one is "lit up," then you're on the third screen.

 To move among the screens, press ⌘-arrow keys, or swipe horizontally with two fingers on the trackpad. (Magic Mouse: one finger.) Or tap directly on one of the little dots to jump to the corresponding screen.

Tip: To exit Launchpad without opening anything, click a blank spot, tap the Esc key, or—most fun of all—*spread* the same four fingers on the trackpad.

Redesigning the Launchpad Screens

If you use Launchpad a lot, it's worth taking a moment to arrange its icons into logical categories or a sensible sequence. As it turns out, you can freely drag them into new spots; the other icons scoot aside to make room.

Tip: You can even drag an icon directly to the Dock to install it there for quicker access.

When Programs are Actually Folders

OS X programs don't seem to have 50,000 support files strewn across your hard drive. Most programs just sit there, naked and shivering, in your Applications folder—seemingly unaccompanied by libraries, dictionaries, foreign language components, and other support files and folders.

The question is: Where did all those support files go?

OS X features *packages* or *bundles*, which are folders that behave like single files. Every properly written OS X program looks like a single, double-clickable application icon. Yet to the Mac, it's actually a folder that contains both the actual application icon and all its hidden support files. (Even documents can be packages, including iDVD project files, Keynote files, and some TextEdit documents.)

If you'd like to prove this to yourself, try this experiment. Choose Go→Applications. See the Calculator program? Control-click it or right-click it. From the shortcut menu, choose Show Package Contents. You're asking OS X to show you what's inside the Calculator's "application icon" folder.

The Calculator package window opens, revealing a Contents folder you've never seen before. If you open this folder, you'll find a handful of strange-looking, Unix-named folders and files that are, behind the scenes, pieces of the Calculator program itself.

The application-as-folder trick is convenient for you, of course, because it means you're generally free to move the application to a different window—or uninstall the program by dragging this single icon to the Trash—without worrying that you're leaving behind its entourage of support files. It's also convenient for programmers, because they can update certain aspects of their applications just by replacing one of these component files, without having to rewrite the entire program.

You can even try out this programmery benefit for yourself. In the case of the Calculator and many other OS X programs, the Resources folder contains individual graphics files—PDF or TIFF files—that serve as the graphic elements you see when using the program. For example, the file lcd.tiff in the Calculator's Resources folder contains the image of the calculator's screen (where the numbers appear as you punch the calculator buttons).

Using a graphics program, you can change the background of this light-yellow calculator screen to, say, light blue. The next time you double-click Calculator—which you now realize is actually a folder behind the scenes—you'll see your modified calculator design.

(P.S. There are still hundreds or thousands of support files that aren't embedded within their programs' icons. They're sitting in your Library→Application Support folder, organized by software company.)

You can create additional screens, too. To do that, drag an icon to the right edge of the screen; keep your mouse button down. The first screen slides off to the left, leaving you on a new, blank one, where you can deposit the icon.

You can organize your icons on these Home pages by category, frequency of use, color, or whatever tickles your fancy.

Tip: Launchpad's backdrop is a softly blurred version of your current Desktop picture. If the icons are still hard to read against it, press ⌘-B. With each press, you cycle through another version of that wallpaper: your original Desktop picture, the blurry version, a black-and-white version, and a blurry black-and-white version. One of those should do the trick.

Folders

The Launchpad just wouldn't be like the iPad if it didn't also let you organize your apps into *folders*. Folders let you organize your apps, de-emphasize the ones you don't use often, and restore order to that horribly flat, multipage display of icons.

To create a folder, drag one app's icon *on top of another*. Mountain Lion puts both of them into a single new folder (Figure 5-4). If they're the same kind of app, it even tries to figure out what category they both belong to—and names the new folder accordingly ("Music," "Photos," "Games," or whatever). This new name is only a proposal; an editing window also appears so that you can type a custom name you prefer.

Take an app out of a folder by dragging its icon anywhere else on the screen. The other icons scoot aside to make room. If you remove all but one app from a folder, the folder disappears.

Move a folder around by dragging, as you would any other icon.

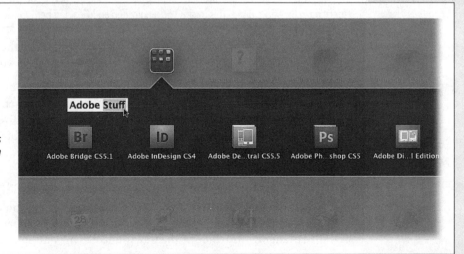

Figure 5-4:
Open a folder by clicking once, or by pressing ⌘-↓. A special black panel sprouts from the folder icon, revealing its contents; the rest of the screen goes dim. Now you can drag the icons around inside it. You can also edit the folder's name (click it first).

Deleting Mac Store Apps

If you've downloaded some apps from the App Store, you'll find a bonus feature here in Launchpad: They're especially fun to delete.

Start by holding the mouse down on any icon until, after about a second, all the icons begin to—what's the correct term?—*wiggle*. (If you have an iPhone, iPad, or iPod Touch, this should look familiar.)

Tip: You can also just press the Option key to trigger the wiggling. Sometimes, every second counts.

At this point, you may notice that some of them have sprouted little red X's. Those are the ones you downloaded from the App Store.

To delete an App Store program you don't need anymore, click that X to make it say bye-bye—instantly and for good. It doesn't even have a layover in the Trash.

Note: You can't delete non–App Store apps this way, so no X appears on those icons. Why not? Because this deletion method is so fast and permanent. It's not much of a risk for App Store apps, because you can always download them again—but that would not be true of other apps.

Windows that Auto-Reopen

When you open a program, the Mac reads its computer code, which lies on your hard drive's surface, and feeds it quickly into RAM (memory). During this brief interval, the icon of the opening program jumps up and down eagerly in your Dock.

Tip: You don't have to wait for the application to finish bouncing—you're wasting perfectly good computing time. Just switch to another program and get back to work; the newly opened program keeps right on launching in the background. This means you, Photoshop and Final Cut nerds.

For decades, opening a program on the Mac presented exactly the same thing every time: a blank screen, or maybe a welcome screen. It was up to you to specify what *document* you then wanted to work on.

In Mountain Lion, though, whatever documents were open when you last quit that program magically *re*open, ready for you to get back to work. Everything is *exactly* as it was, including your window and palette positions. Incredibly, any text that was highlighted when you last quit the program is still highlighted, and the insertion point is just where you left it.

This is all extremely handy if you tend to work on the same documents day after day; the auto-reopened document serves as a nice refresher on what you were in the middle of doing. You can skip fussing with the Open command, remembering what you were doing, rearranging the windows the way you like them, and so on.

Then again, maybe you can't stand this feature.

Fortunately, it's easy to turn it off, either globally, on a per-program basis, or on a per-Quit basis.

- **Turn off auto-reopen for good.** Open System Preferences→General, and turn off "Restore windows when quitting and re-opening apps."

- **Prevent your current setup from being memorized.** You can also prevent just *one particular* program from reopening its documents the next time—at the time you're quitting it. To do that, press Option while you quit the program (for example, when you choose Safari→Quit or press ⌘-Q). The Quit command magically changes to say, "Quit and Discard Windows." The next time you open the program, it will have forgotten all about your window setup.

 (On the other hand, if you've turned *off* the "Restore windows" feature in System Preferences, pressing the Option key makes the Quit command say, "Quit and *Keep* Windows.")

- **Make a program forget its window setup as you reopen it.** If it's too late for the tip in the previous paragraph, you can force a program to start up in its empty, virginal state by pressing the Shift key as it opens. That forces the program to forget the previous window setup.

POWER USERS' CLINIC

Shutting Down One Program's Window Memorizing

Mountain Lion stashes information about your window setup in a "saved state" folder for each program. This data is in your Home→Library→Saved Application State folder.

The thing is, your Library folder is ordinarily invisible, which makes it a little tough to see the Saved Application State folder inside. Fortunately, you can jump directly to its contents by pressing Option as you choose Go→Library. Then open the Saved Application State folder within.

You get something like the window shown here: a folder for each program you use. You can delete one of these folders manually, but of course the Mac will recreate it the next time you run that program.

So if you want the Mac to stop memorizing a program's setup for good, find its Saved State folder. For Safari, for example, it's called *com.apple. Safari.savedState*.

Open the folder and empty it out; you've just made it forget the most recent settings. Now close the folder again.

With the folder still highlighted, choose File→Get Info and, in the Get Info box, turn on the Locked checkbox. From now on, the Mac won't be able to record that program's window setup. (Later, you can turn off the Locked checkbox to undo your surgery.)

• **Turn off auto-open for one program.** Suppose you like the auto-window-reopening feature in *most* programs. But there's one particular program that you *never* want to memorize your window setup—maybe for security reasons, or maybe because you use that app for something different every day.

Before long, some shareware program will crop up to make that easy. For now, though, you can do the job manually. It's a quick, one-time step, but it does involve mucking around with one of the Mac's invisible folders. See the box on page 169.

The Application Menu

In every app, the very first menu (to the right of the menu) appears with bold lettering and identifies the program you're using. It might say iTunes, or Microsoft Word, or Stickies.

This Application menu (Figure 5-5) offers a number of commands pertaining to the entire program and its windows, including About, Quit, and Hide.

Figure 5-5:
The first menu in every program lets you know, at a glance, which program you're actually in. It also offers overall program commands like Quit and Hide.

Quitting Programs

You quit a program by pressing ⌘-Q, the keyboard equivalent of the Quit command. (The Quit command is always at the bottom of the Application menu.)

But OS X offers two much more fun ways to quit a program:

• Control-click or right-click a program's Dock icon to make its shortcut menu appear. Then choose Quit. (Or, if you do the *click-and-hold* thing on a program's Dock icon, a Quit button appears just above your cursor.)

• When you've pressed ⌘-Tab to summon the "heads-up display" of open programs, type the letter Q without releasing the ⌘ key. The highlighted program quits without further ado.

Force Quitting Programs

OS X is a rock-solid operating system, but that doesn't mean that *programs* never screw up. Individual programs are as likely as ever to freeze—or, rather, to *hang* (lock up and display the "spinning beach ball of death" cursor). In such cases, you have no choice but to *force quit* the program—the computer equivalent of terminating it with a blunt instrument.

Doing so doesn't destabilize your Mac; you don't have to restart it. In fact, you can usually reopen the very same program and get on with your life.

You can force quit a stuck program in any of several ways:

- Click-and-hold on the program's Dock icon, or Control-click it, or right-click it. A Quit button appears just above your cursor. Press the Option key to make the button say Force Quit (Figure 5-6, left). Click it. Bingo—that program is outta here.

- Press Option-⌘-Esc, the traditional Mac force-quit keystroke, or choose →Force Quit. Either way, proceed as shown in Figure 5-6 at bottom.

Figure 5-6:
Top: You can force quit a program from the Dock—by pressing Option as you click-and-hold (or after you've Control-clicked). Or, if the Mac knows that the program has frozen, this command says Force Quit without your needing the Option key.

Bottom: When you press Option-⌘-Esc or choose Force Quit from the menu, a tidy box listing all open programs appears. Just click the one you want to abort, click Force Quit, and click Force Quit again in the confirmation box. (Using more technical tools like the Unix kill command, there are other ways to jettison programs. But this is often the most convenient.)

The only downside to force quitting a program is that you lose any unsaved changes to your open documents, along with any preference settings you may have changed while the program was open.

The "Heads-Up" Program Switcher

Only one program can be in front, or active, at a time.

To switch to a different program, you could click or double-click its icon (in the Dock, the Applications folder, Launchpad, or wherever). But the fastest method is often to use the ⌘-Tab keystroke (Figure 5-7).

Figure 5-7:
Apple calls this row of open program icons a "heads-up display," named after the projected data screen on a Navy jet windshield that lets pilots avoid having to look down at their instruments.

You can use this feature in three different ways, which are well worth learning:

• If you keep the ⌘ key pressed, each press of the Tab key highlights the Dock icon of another program, in left-to-right Dock order. Release both keys when you reach the one you want. OS X brings the corresponding program to the front. (To move *backward* through the open programs, press *Shift-*⌘*-Tab.*)

• If you leave the ⌘ key pressed, you can choose a program by clicking its icon with your mouse, or by pressing the ← or → keys.

• A single press of ⌘-Tab takes you to the program you used most recently, and another, separate ⌘-Tab bounces back to the program you started in.

Imagine, for example, that you're doing a lot of switching between two programs, like your Web browser and your email program. If you have five other programs open, you don't want to waste your time ⌘-Tabbing your way through all the open programs just to get back to your Web browser.

Tip: Here's a related keystroke, equally awesome. If you press ⌘-tilde (the ~ key next to the number 1), you switch to the next window in the *same* program.

Mission Control: Death to Window Clutter

In its day, the concept of overlapping windows on the screen was brilliant, innovative, and extremely effective. (Apple borrowed this idea—well, bought it in a stock swap—from a research lab called Xerox PARC.) In that era before digital cameras, MP3 files, and the Web, managing windows was easy this way; after all, you had only about three of them.

These days, however, managing all the open windows in all the open programs can be like herding cats. Off you go, burrowing through the microscopic pop-up menus of your Dock, trying to find the window you want. And heaven help you if you need to duck back to the desktop—to find a newly downloaded file, for example, or to eject a disk. You'll have to fight your way through 50,000 other windows on your way to the bottom of the "deck."

Mission Control tackles this problem in a fresh way. The concept is delicious: With one mouse click, keystroke, or finger gesture, you shrink all windows in all programs to a size that fits on the screen (Figure 5-8), like index cards on a bulletin board, clumped by open program. Now you feel like an air-traffic controller, with all your screens arrayed before you. You click the window or program you want, and you're there. It's fast, efficient, animated, and a lot of fun.

Now, if you've used earlier versions of OS X, you may remember three other window-management features: Exposé, which also served to shrink windows so you could find them; Spaces, which provided virtual side-by-side monitors; and Dashboard, which presented a gaggle of tiny, single-purpose apps on a single screen.

Mission Control combines all three of those features—Exposé, Spaces, and Dashboard—into one.

Starting and Stopping Mission Control

Mission Control is a program, just like any other. So you can open it with a click on its Dock icon, from Launchpad, from the Applications folder, and so on.

But it's really meant to be opened quickly, fluidly, naturally, whenever the mood seizes you—with a *gesture*. On the trackpad, that's a swipe upward with three fingers. (On the Magic Mouse, it's a double-tap with *two* fingers—taps, not clicks.)

Note: You can change this gesture so that it requires an additional finger, if you like, in System Preferences→Trackpad (or Mouse)→More Gestures→Mission Control. Use the pop-up menu.

Or you can press the dedicated ▦ key (formerly the Exposé key), if you have one, on the top row of your keyboard. Substitute the F9 key if you don't.

And even that's just the beginning of the ways you can open Mission Control; read on.

Note: To *exit* Mission Control without clicking any of your windows or virtual screens, swipe *down* with three fingers. Or tap the Esc key.

Figure 5-8:

Top: Quick! Where's System Preferences in all this mess?

Bottom: With a three-finger upward swipe on the trackpad, you can spot that window, shrunken but not overlapped. Each program's thumbnail cluster offers an icon and a label to help you identify it. These aren't static snapshots of the windows at the moment you Mission Controlled them. They're live, still-updating windows, as you'll discover if one of them contains a playing QuickTime movie or a Web page that's still loading.

Mission Control keystrokes

You can reassign the Mission Control functions to a huge range of other keys, with or without modifiers like Shift, Control, and Option. To view your options, choose →System Preferences and then click the Mission Control icon (Figure 5-9).

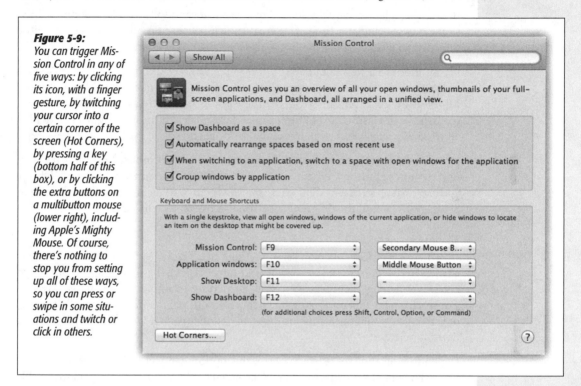

Figure 5-9:
You can trigger Mission Control in any of five ways: by clicking its icon, with a finger gesture, by twitching your cursor into a certain corner of the screen (Hot Corners), by pressing a key (bottom half of this box), or by clicking the extra buttons on a multibutton mouse (lower right), including Apple's Mighty Mouse. Of course, there's nothing to stop you from setting up all of these ways, so you can press or swipe in some situations and twitch or click in others.

Here you'll find four pop-up menus. The first, Mission Control, lets you specify how you want to open Mission Control. The other three—"Application windows," "Show Desktop," and "Show Dashboard"—correspond to the three functions of the older Exposé and Dashboard features, described later in this chapter.

Within each pop-up menu, for example, you'll discover that all your F-keys—F1, F2, F3, and so on—are available as triggers. If, while the pop-up menu is open, you press one or more of your modifier keys (Shift, Option, Control, or ⌘), all these F-key choices *change* to reflect the key you're pressing; now the pop-up menu says Shift-F1, Shift-F2, Shift-F3, and so on. That's how you can make *Shift*-F1 trigger Mission Control, for example.

These pop-up menus also contain choices like Left Shift, which refers to the Shift key on the left side of your keyboard. That is, instead of pressing F9 to open Mission Control, you could simply tap the Shift key.

Note: This is only an example. Repeat: This is only an example. *Actually* using the Shift key to open Mission Control is a terrible, terrible idea, as you'll quickly discover the next time you try to type a capital letter. This feature is intended exclusively for hunt-and-peck typists who never use the Shift key on one side.

If you have a laptop, you'll also find out that you can tap the Fn key alone for Mission Control—and this time, it's a great choice, because Fn otherwise has very little direction in life.

If your mouse has more than one button, you see a second column of pop-up menus in System Preferences. Each pop-up menu offers choices like Right Mouse Button, Middle Mouse Button, and so on. Use these pop-up menus to assign Mission Control (or Exposé, or Dashboard) to the various clickers on your mouse: right-click to hide all windows, left-side click to reveal the desktop, and so on.

Note, by the way, that on a laptop, the wording isn't "right mouse button"—it's "secondary mouse button." Which means "right-click." Which means that on a laptop, you can set it up so that a "right-click" *trackpad gesture* triggers one of these functions. See page 237 for all the different ways you can trigger a right-click.

Screen corners

If you click Hot Corners, you see something like Figure 9-10 (page 352). The four corners here represent the corners of your screen. Using these menus, you can assign a window-management feature to each corner; for example, if you choose Mission Control from the first pop-up menu, then when your pointer hits the upper-left corner of the screen, you'll open Mission Control. (Launchpad and Notification Center are options here, too.)

Depending on the size of your screen, this option can feel awkward at first. But if you've run out of keystrokes that aren't assigned to other functions, be glad that Apple offers you this alternative.

Note: In previous versions of OS X, whipping the pointer into a corner was one good way to turn on your *screen saver.* Apple hasn't forgotten about that, which is why you'll also find commands called Start Screen Saver and Disable Screen Saver in the pop-up menus. Apple wants to make sure you don't get confused and assign two different functions to the same corner.

Managing Windows in Mission Control

Once you open Mission Control, you see two major elements: your *Spaces* (virtual screens) at the top, and the actual window thumbnails below that.

You can click anything here to jump to it: Jump to a different Space (desktop) by clicking its thumbnail, switch to a different program by clicking its icon, or click one of the window miniatures.

Tip: Try holding down the Shift key as you do it. You'll enjoy watching all your windows shift around with OS X's patented slow-motion animation, which can be quite a sight.

Or, if you decide to abandon ship and return to whatever you were doing, swipe *down* with three fingers on the trackpad (two on the Magic Mouse), or press the Esc key.

The trouble with miniaturized windows is that, well, they're miniaturized. The more windows you have open, the smaller they are, and the harder it is to see what's in them.

If you need a little help identifying a window miniature, you have three options:

- Point to the cluster of windows in one app, and do a two-finger swipe up on the trackpad. Mountain Lion helpfully spreads the window thumbnails out and enlarges them a little bit, so it's easier to tell them apart and click the one you want.

- Point to a window thumbnail without clicking. OS X puts a colored border on it to show that it's highlighted; now press the space bar. That, of course, is the Quick Look keystroke, and it works here, too. It magnifies the window you're pointing to, making it full size—big enough for you to read its contents and identify it.

- Press ⌘-~. That keystroke takes you into Application Exposé, described later in this chapter.

Spaces in Mission Control

Mission Control's other star feature, Spaces, gives you up to 16 *full-size monitors.* Ordinarily, of course, attaching so many screens to a single computer would be a massively expensive proposition, not to mention detrimental to your living space and personal relationships.

Fortunately, Spaces monitors are *virtual.* They exist only in the Mac's little head. You see only one at a time; you switch using Mission Control or a gesture.

But just because the Spaces screens are simulated doesn't mean they're not useful. You can dedicate each one to a different program or *kind* of program. Screen 1 might contain your email and chat windows, arranged just the way you like them. Screen 2 can hold Photoshop, with an open document and the palettes carefully arrayed. On Screen 3: your Web browser in full-screen mode.

You can also have the *same* program running on multiple screens—but with different documents or projects open on each one.

These desktops are also essential to Mountain Lion's *full-screen apps* feature, because each full-screen app gets its own Spaces desktop.

Now, virtual screens aren't a new idea—this sort of software has been available for years. But until the Mac came along, it had never been a standard feature of a consumer operating system, and rarely has it been executed with such finesse.

Creating a Desktop

Mission Control starts you off with two Spaces (or desktops, as they're labeled). One of them shows the Dashboard, described later in this chapter; the other shows your regular Mac world. If you've clicked the ⬒ button in an app to make it full screen, it fills an additional desktop unto itself.

To create another desktop, enter Mission Control. You can now proceed in either of two ways:

- **The long way.** Point to the upper-right corner of the screen; a big **+** button slides into view (Figure 5-10). Click it to create a new mini desktop in the top row.

 Now it's time to park some windows onto the new desktop. Either drag a window thumbnail onto the blank desktop—or, to move *all* of one program's windows there, drag the application icon. All the windows go along for the ride.

Note: If you've positioned your Dock against the right side of the screen, the **+** button appears when you point to the upper-*left* corner. And to create a new screen by dragging a window's or program's icon (see "The short way," next), drag to the upper-left corner of the screen.

Figure 5-10:
Create a new blank Space by clicking the big + button. Or save time and energy by dragging a window, or a whole program's icon, into the empty space at the right end of the Spaces thumbnails. You've just created a Space and loaded it up with windows in one fell swoop.

- **The short way.** Drag one window thumbnail into a blank spot at the upper-right corner of the screen—or, to move *all* of one program's windows there, drag the application icon. Again, all the windows go along for the ride.

Tip: There are two ways to move a window to a different Space without opening Mission Control first. First, you can drag a window (using its title bar as a handle) all the way to the edge of the screen. Stay there with the mouse button still down. After about a second, you'll see the adjacent screen slide into view; you've just moved the window.

Second, switch to the new Space. Hold your mouse down on the app's icon; from the shortcut menu, choose Options→Assign To→This Desktop. The Mac whisks that app's windows from whatever *other* screen they're on to *this* screen.

Switching Spaces

Once you've got Spaces set up and turned on, the fun begins. Start by moving to the virtual screen you want; it's like changing the channel. Here are some ways to do that:

- Swipe horizontally on your trackpad with three fingers. (On the Magic Mouse, it's two fingers.) If you have a trackpad or a Magic Mouse, this is definitely the method to learn; it's fast, fluid, and happy.

 You can change this gesture so that it requires an additional finger, if you like, in System Preferences→Trackpad (or Mouse)→More Gestures.

Tip: If you perform this swipe *slowly,* you can drag the next Space only *partway* onto the screen. That's sometimes handy when you want to get your bearings, or to just *peek* into the next screen.

- Enter Mission Control. Click the desktop you want.

- Press Control-← or Control-→ to rotate to the previous or next desktop.

- While pressing the Control key, type the number of the desktop you want. For example, hit Control-3 to jump to your third screen. (You have to turn on this feature first, though. See Figure 5-11.)

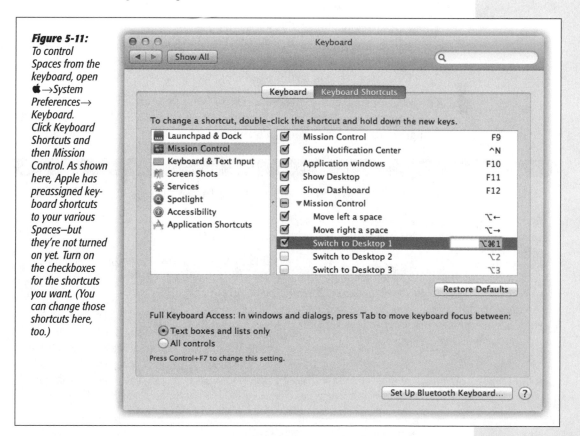

Figure 5-11:
To control Spaces from the keyboard, open ➔*System Preferences*➔ *Keyboard. Click Keyboard Shortcuts and then Mission Control. As shown here, Apple has preassigned key-board shortcuts to your various Spaces—but they're not turned on yet. Turn on the checkboxes for the shortcuts you want. (You can change those shortcuts here, too.)*

As you'll quickly discover, the Mac thinks your desktops are arranged *horizontally*—not in a grid, as in Snow Leopard. You can't rearrange them, either.

When you make a switch, you see a flash of animation as one screen flies away and another appears. Now that you're "on" the screen you want, open programs and arrange windows onto it as usual.

Tip: What if you're using Spaces, and you want to drag something from one screen (like a photo in iPhoto) into a window that's on a different screen (like an outgoing email message)?

Two ways; take your pick. First, you can start dragging whatever it is—and then, in mid-drag, press the keystroke for Mission Control (usually Fn-F9); complete the drag directly onto the other Space, and even into the relevant window *in* that Space.

Another approach: Start dragging. With the mouse button still down, press ⌘-Tab to open the application switcher. Continue the drag onto the *icon* of the receiving program, and still keep the mouse button down. OS X switches to the appropriate virtual screen automatically.

Two Eccentric Spaces Settings

Deep in System Preferences→Mission Control, two settings govern the way Spaces works.

- **Automatically rearrange spaces based on most recent use.** If this option is turned on, then Mountain Lion will constantly rearrange your virtual desktops so that the most recently used ones are first. (The most recent one becomes Desktop #2, since Desktop #1 is always your main desktop.)

 The point, of course, is to make it quick and easy to return to whatever you were doing most recently. But if you find it disorienting to have your desktops constantly changing their sequence, you can turn this option off.

GEM IN THE ROUGH

Pinning One App to One Space—or to All Spaces

Usually, you slap each app (or each window) onto only one Spaces desktop. Your Web browser on Space 1. Email on Space 2. iTunes on Space 3. And so on.

Sometimes, though, you might find it useful to keep an app's windows on *all* your desktops—perhaps because you use it so often, you want it always with you. The Finder and System Preferences are great examples. Or maybe your calendar app, your browser, or your email program.

To do that, make sure the program's icon is in your Dock (either because you've put it there or because the program is running). Hold the mouse button down on the program's

icon until the shortcut menu appears. From this menu, choose Options.

You'll see two useful options. One, Assign To→All Desktops, puts this program's windows on all your desktops. Wherever you go, there you are.

The other one, Assign To→This Desktop, gives you yet another quick way to *move* an app's windows—from whatever desktop they're on now to the one you're using at the moment. You've just "pinned" that app to that Space, and that's where it will stay. That's a convenience for neat freaks who like to know exactly where each app will live.

- **When switching to an application, switch to a space with open windows for the application.** There must be some clearer way to write this checkbox.

 In any case, it means that when you click the Dock icon for a running program, Mountain Lion jumps to the Space that contains that program's open windows already, instead of leaving you on the current Space.

 For example, suppose you're working in your browser on Desktop #3. Then you click the Mail icon on the Dock. If this option is turned on, you jump to Desktop #2 (or wherever you've been already working in Mail). If it's not turned on, Mail jumps to the foreground, but you won't see any windows—they're stranded back on Desktop #2.

Pictures for Every Desktop

Unless you intervene, Mountain Lion uses your main desktop's background picture for all additional Spaces.

Coolly enough, though, you can set a different wallpaper photo (desktop background) to each Space. You might find it easier to get your bearings that way. When you restart the computer, Mountain Lion will remember not just which Spaces you had open and what was on them, but also what pictures lay behind them.

You can go about assigning desktop pictures in two ways. First, switch to the Space whose picture you want to change. Then:

- Open System Preferences→Desktop & Screen Saver→Desktop.
- Control-click (or right-click) a blank spot on the existing desktop background. From the shortcut menu, choose Change Desktop Background.

Note: In both cases, you may have to move the System Preferences window onto your current Space. You can do that by popping into Mission Control.

Either way, you wind up in the Preferences panel for choosing desktop wallpaper. Click the backdrop you want for this screen. Then switch to the next Space and repeat.

Deleting a Desktop

To delete a desktop, enter Mission Control. Point to one of the screen thumbnails without clicking until a ⊗ appears in its corner; click it. The desktop disappears, and whatever windows were on it get shoved onto Desktop #1, your main desktop.

Tip: If you don't have the 1½ seconds to wait for the – to appear, then press Option as you point. The Close button appears instantly.

By the way, this trick doesn't work for apps running in full-screen mode. You can't get rid of their desktops unless you first switch to them and get out of full-screen mode.

Dashboard

As you know, the essence of using a computer is running *programs*, which often produce *documents*. In OS X, however, there's a third category: a set of weird, hybrid entities that Apple calls *widgets*. They appear, all at once, on a virtual desktop—the leftmost of the ones in Mission Control.

Note: Apple thought that parking the Dashboard widgets on their own little virtual screen was a convenient place to keep them. They do, after all, feel like they constitute a separate little software world.

But if you prefer the old Way of the Dashboard, where widgets appeared *in front* of whatever window you have open, open **⟐→System Preferences. Click Mission Control, and then turn off "Show Dashboard as a space." From now on, Dashboard widgets appear as a constellation of little app windows on top of whatever else you were doing, just as they did in the pre-Lion days.

Here, for example, is how you can find them:

- If your F4 key bears the Dashboard logo (◉), press it.

Note: On the very newest Macs, F4 bears a Launchpad icon (▦) instead. On the very oldest Mountain Lion–capable Macs, the Dashboard keystroke is usually F12. Or, on laptops where F12 is the ◉ key, you have to hold down the Fn key (lower-left corner).

In all of these cases, you can change the Dashboard keystroke to whatever you like, as described below.

Figure 5-12:
When you summon the Dashboard, you get a fleet of miniprograms that convey or convert all kinds of useful information, on a Spaces screen all their own. You get rid of Dashboard either by pressing the same key again (F4 or whatever), by swiping three fingers to the right on your trackpad, or by clicking anywhere except on a widget.

- Swipe with three fingers on your trackpad, repeatedly, if necessary, until you reach the far left "desktop." (On the Magic Mouse, swipe with two fingers.)

- Open Mission Control; click the Dashboard thumbnail at the top left of the screen.

- Dashboard is an actual program, with an icon of its own in your Applications folder. You can open it with a double-click, or by using any of the usual program-opening tricks.

In any case, you now see the display shown in Figure 5-12. Welcome to the Dashboard.

What are these weird, hybrid entities, anyway? They're not really programs, because they don't create documents or have Dock icons (although Dashboard itself has a Dock icon). They're certainly not documents, because you can't name or save them. What they most resemble, actually, is little Web pages. They're meant to display information, much of it from the Internet, and they're written using Web programming languages like HTML and JavaScript.

Mastering the basics of Dashboard won't take you long at all:

- **To move a widget,** drag it around the screen. (Click anywhere except on a button or a control.)

- **To close a widget,** press the Option key as you move the mouse across the widget's face. You'll see the ⊗ button appear at the widget's top-left corner; click it.

- **To open a closed widget,** click the big ⊕ button at the bottom of the screen. Now Mountain Lion's new Widget browser appears (Figure 5-13), as described in the following section. Open the widget you want by clicking its icon.

Figure 5-13:
You'll probably have to scroll the Widget bar, by clicking the arrows at either end, to see all the widgets. When you're finished opening new widgets, close the Widget bar by clicking anywhere on the background.

• **To hide one of Apple's widgets,** or to delete one you've installed yourself, use the Widget browser described next.

The Widget Browser

The new Widget browser screen appears when you click the big ❂ button at the bottom of Dashboard. As shown in Figure 5-13, it's simply a master collection of every widget on your Mac, even the ones that you haven't dragged onto the main Dashboard screen. Its goal in life: Managing all your *other* widgets.

This browser works exactly like the Launchpad. For example, you can move widget icons around by dragging them. Drag one widget's icon on top of another to create a folder. Search them using the box at the top of the screen. Start them wiggling, for ease of mass deletion, by holding your cursor down on any icon, or you clicking the big — button. For details, read pages 164–167 again, taking care to mentally substitute the word "widget" for "app."

Note: Even in wiggling-icon mode, you're not allowed to delete Apple's widgets—only ones you've downloaded and installed yourself.

But what you'll do here most often is simply *click* a widget's icon to install it onto the main Dashboard screen.

(To close the browser without pulling a new icon out of it, click anywhere on the background.)

The Widget browser also harbors the godlike power of the More Widgets button, described later in these pages.

Dashboard Tips

Dashboard is crawling with cool tips and tricks. Here are a few of the biggies:

• To refresh a certain widget—for example, to update its information from the Internet—click it and press ⌘-R. The widget instantly *twist-scrambles* itself into a sort of ice-cream swirl (you've got to see it to believe it) and then untwists to reveal the new data.

• You can open more than one copy of the same widget. Just click its icon more than once in the Widget browser. You wind up with multiple copies of it on your screen: three World Clocks, two Stock Trackers, or whatever. That's a useful trick when, for example, you want to track the time or weather in more than one city, or when you maintain two different stock portfolios.

• If you keep the Shift key pressed when you click the big ❂ button, the Widget browser fades in in gorgeous *slow motion.* Aren't you just glad to be alive?

Dashboard Preferences

To change the Dashboard keystroke to something other than F4 or F12, choose →System Preferences, and then click Mission Control.

Here you'll discover that you can choose almost any other keyboard combination to summon and dismiss the Dashboard, or even choose a screen corner that, when your mouse lands there, acts as the Dashboard trigger. This works exactly as described on page 175.

Note: Yes, yes, you can also change the Dashboard keystroke on the Keyboard→Keyboard Shortcuts pane of System Preferences. But if you use the Mission Control pane instead, then you can set up a screen corner or a mouse button to trigger Dashboard—not just a keyboard combo.

Widget Catalog

Here's a rundown of the 16 standard widgets that come preinstalled. True, they look awfully simple, but some of them harbor a few secrets.

Calculator

Here's your basic four-function pocket calculator, with one-number memory storage. Begin by clicking it to make active; once it is, any typing you do on the number keys gets intercepted by this little calculator. (Using the keyboard is much faster than clicking the onscreen numbers.)

There's not a lot to this calculator. If you need scientific and hexadecimal features, or even square root functions, use the regular Calculator described on page 390.

Calendar

Sure, you can always find out today's date by clicking the clock on your menu bar. But this one is so much nicer looking. And besides, you can use this calendar to look ahead or back, or to check your schedule for the day. As you click this widget, it cycles through three degrees of expansion; see Figure 5-14.

Tip: Press Shift as you click to see the panels expanding or collapsing in slow motion.

Figure 5-14:
Click the "today's date" panel to expand the second panel, which shows the month. (Click ◄ and ► to move a month at a time.) Click a third time to reveal whatever's on the calendar for the remainder of the day today, as recorded in Calendar.

Contacts

The concept is to give you faster access to your own address book. (Trudging off to the actual Contacts program takes way too long when you just want to look up a number.) It's filled with clickable shortcuts. For example:

- **Search box.** Type a few letters of somebody's name here. As you type, the widget fills with matching names from the Contacts program.

Tip: Actually, it shows you entries with text that match any part of each person's "card," not just names. For example, you could type *212* to find everyone with that area code, or *cherr* to find someone whose name you've forgotten—but you know she lives on Cherrystone Avenue.

When you spot the name of the person you're looking for, click it to open that person's full Rolodex card.

- **Phone number.** Click it to fill your screen with the phone number, big enough to see from outer space. Or at least from across the room as you dial the number on your desk phone.

- **Email address.** Click to fire up your email program, complete with a fresh outgoing message already addressed to this person. All you have to do is type your message and click Send.

- **Mailing address.** Clicking the mailing address fires up your Web browser and takes you to MapQuest.com, already opened up to a map that reveals the pinpoint location of the specified address. Very, very slick.

Dictionary

Apple has provided about 65,000 different ways to access its built-in dictionary/thesaurus (like the Dictionary app or the Spotlight menu), and here's another one. Just type the word you want and press Return. Instantly, a handy definitions panel

FREQUENTLY ASKED QUESTION

Unchained Widgets

I love the widgets, but I wish they weren't locked away in their own OS X "layer." I'd like to work with the Calculator widget, for example, while I'm doing an Excel spreadsheet, without having to send the spreadsheet to the background.

No problem—if you're sneaky and not afraid to type one line into Terminal (page 469).

First, turn off "Show Dashboard as a space" (in System Preferences→Mission Control). Now open the Terminal program (it's in your Applications→Utilities folder).

Type this line carefully, and then press Enter:

```
defaults write com.apple.
dashboard demode YES
```

Open Dashboard again. Find the widget you'd like to move out of Dashboard-land. Start dragging it; without releasing the mouse button, press F4 again to close Dashboard. Incredibly, your widget stays with your cursor! You can keep dragging until the widget, freed of its Dashboard captivity, lands anywhere on the screen you want it to.

drops down. Use the ▲ and ▼ buttons in the upper-left corner to walk through your most recent lookups and the pop-up menu to specify whether you want to search the dictionary, the thesaurus, or the Apple terminology glossary.

Tip: Once you've looked up a word, you can look up new words by typing only the first few letters. (You don't even have to press Return.) The Dictionary or Thesaurus automatically displays the definition for the first matching word. If you click the ❶ button in the lower-left corner, the panel spins around to reveal, in addition to a font-size control, the Oxford American Dictionaries logo. Someday when you're feeling curious, click it. (It fires up the Oxford University Press Web page.)

Tip: See how the first letter of your word appears in a special rounded tab at the left edge of the panel? If you click that letter, you get to see the word you looked up in its alphabetical context among all the other words in the dictionary. It's a neat way to check for additional word forms, to see if perhaps you've misspelled the word, or to scrabble your way out of a tight situation when you're playing the word game ghost with someone.

ESPN

This widget shows the current or final scores of college and professional sports games. (If the game hasn't started yet, you see the start time.) Click the ❶ button to choose the sport you want to track. Click the News button to see headlines—and click a headline to visit ESPN's full article online.

Flight Tracker

This handy widget (Figure 5-15) lets you find out which flights fly between which cities—and if the flight is already en route, it shows you where it is on the map, how high it's flying, how fast, and whether or not it's going to be on time.

This may look like a small window, but there's a lot going on here:

- **Flight Finder.** If you're planning a trip, the widget can show you a list of flights that match your itinerary. Use the pop-up menus to specify the arrival and departure cities, and which airline you want to study, if any. (Actually, it's usually faster to *type* the name of the city into the box, if you know how to spell it, or, better yet, its three-letter airport code.) Then click Find Flights, or press Return.

 After a moment, the right side of the screen becomes a scrolling list of flights that match your query. You can see the flight number, the departure and arrival time, and the name of the airline.

 This is a great tool when a friend or relative is flying in and you're unsure of the flight number, airline, or arrival time.

- **Flight Tracker.** Most of the time, the status column of the results says "Scheduled," meaning that you're looking at some future flight. Every now and then, however, you get lucky, and it says "Enroute." This is where things get really fun: Double-click

that row of results to see the plane's actual position on a national or international map (Figure 5-15, bottom).

Tip: If you click the little ❶ button before performing a flight search, the panel flips around to reveal the logo of the company that supplies the flight data. Click the logo to open its Web page.

Figure 5-15:
Top: Most of the time, Flight Tracker is like a teeny, tiny travel agent, capable of showing you which flights connect to which cities. But if one of the flights is marked "Enroute," double-click it.

Bottom: You see an actual map of its progress, as shown here. You also get to see its speed and estimated arrival status (early, late, or on time), and even which terminal it will use upon landing. If you click the plane, you can zoom in on it.

Movies

Look up the local movie-theater listings for any day this week—without having to endure the hassle of the newspaper, the hellish touchtone labyrinth of a phone system, or the flashing ads of a Web site.

When you open this widget, you see a miniature movie poster that changes to a different current movie every 3 seconds. At any point, you can click the poster itself to see what's on the back of the widget (Figure 5-16).

In the left column, you get a scrolling list of movies in your area. The one whose poster you clicked is highlighted, but you can click any one of them to see, at bottom, all the details: release date, rating, length, cast, genre, a plot synopsis, and a link to the preview (trailer). (After you've watched the trailer, click the left-pointing arrow button at the lower-left corner of the widget.)

The center column lists the theaters near you where the selected movie is playing. Click a theater to see the movie showtimes in the right column.

Tip: So how does the widget know what's "near you"? Because you've told it. You've clicked the **❶** button to flip the widget around to the back, where you can input your Zip code or your city and state.

(And yes, it's true: You've now seen *three faces* of this two-dimensional widget. It's got a front, a back, and a *back* of the back.)

Figure 5-16:
The Movies widget starts out with a slideshow of movie posters.

But on the back, shown here, you can read about current movies in theaters, find out which theaters they're in, and see today's showtimes. The pop-up menu at upper right lets you see the schedule for Today, Tomorrow, and the following four days.

Incidentally, you're not stuck with this "Choose a movie, and we'll show you the theaters" view. See at the top left, where the title "Movies Theaters" appears? Click Theaters to reverse the logic. Now you're in "Choose a theater, and we'll show you what movies are playing there" mode. This view is much better when, for example, there's only one theater nearby, and you want to know what your options are there.

Tip: To return to the original cycling movie-poster display, click an empty part of the title bar.

Stickies

Stickies is a virtual Post-it note that lets you type out random scraps of text—a phone number, a Web address, a grocery list, or whatever.

Of course, OS X already comes with a Stickies program. So why did Apple duplicate it in Dashboard? Simple—because you can call this one up with press of your Dashboard keystroke, making it faster to open.

On the other hand, the Stickies widget isn't quite as flexible as the Stickies application. For example, you can't resize the page. And to add a second or a third note, you have to open the Widget browser, and then click the Stickies icon for each new page.

On the *other* other hand, this Stickies isn't quite as bare bones as you might think. If you click the little ❶ button at the bottom-right corner, the note spins around to reveal, on the back, a choice of paper colors, fonts, and font sizes.

Stocks

Hey, day traders, this one's for you. This widget lets you build a stock portfolio and watch it rise and fall throughout the day (Figure 5-17).

Figure 5-17:
More of Apple's built-in widgets. Clockwise from top left: Translation, Stocks, Tile Game (showing a penguin photo dragged in to replace the original picture), and Weather.

To set up your portfolio, click the little ❶ button at the bottom of the window. The widget flips around, revealing the configuration page on the back:

- **Add a stock to your list** by typing its name or stock abbreviation into the box at the top; then click the **+** button or press Return. If there's only one possible match—Microsoft, for example—the widget adds it to the list instantly. If there's some question about what you typed, or several possible matches, you'll see a pop-up menu listing the alternatives, so you can click the one you want.

- **Remove a stock from the list** by clicking its name and then clicking Remove.

Tip: Ordinarily, the widget displays the ups and downs of each stock as a dollar amount ("+.92" means up 92 cents, for example). But if you turn on "Show change as a percentage," then you see these changes represented as percentages of their previous values.

But why bother? Once you're looking at the actual stock statistics, you can switch between dollar and percentage values just by clicking any one of the red or green up/down status buttons.

Click Done to return to the original stock display. Here's your list of stocks, their current prices (well, current as of 20 minutes ago), and the amount they've changed—green if they're up, red if they're down. Click a stock's name to see its chart displayed at the bottom. (You control the time scale by clicking one of the little buttons above the graph: "1d" means one day, "3m" means three months, "1y" means one year, and so on.)

Finally, if you double-click the name of the stock, you fly into your Web browser to view a much more detailed stock-analysis page for that stock, courtesy of Quote.com (Lycos Finance).

Tile Game

For generations, Microsoft Windows has had its Solitaire game—and for generations, the Mac has had the Tile Game. The idea, of course, is to click the squares of the puzzle, using logic to rearrange them back into the original sequence, so that the put-together photograph reappears.

Tip: The widget starts you out with a handsome photo of a big cat. But you can substitute any photo you like.

To pull this off, begin by exiting the Dashboard. Go find the photo you prefer (on the desktop or in iPhoto, for example). Now begin dragging it in any direction. While the mouse is still down, press F4 (or whatever your Dashboard keystroke is)—and drop the dragged graphic directly on the Tile Game puzzle. You've just replaced the existing graphic with your new one. (Figure 5-17 shows an example.)

The first time you use the Tile Game, click inside it to trigger the animated tile-scrambling process. Click a second time to stop the scrambling; in other words, Apple leaves it up to you to decide just how difficult (how scrambled) the puzzle is.

And what should you do if you get frustrated and give up, or you miss the old photo? Just open the Widget bar and open a fresh copy of the Tile Game.

Translation

The next time you travel, go somewhere that has wireless Internet access wherever you go (yeah, right). You'll be able to use this module to translate your utterances—or those of the natives—to and from 13 languages.

Just choose the language direction you want from the "from" and "to" pop-up menus, and then type a word, sentence, or paragraph into the Translate From box. In a flash, the bottom of the window shows the translation, as shown at top left in Figure 5-17. (Don't click the curvy double-headed arrow button to perform the translation; that button means "Swap the 'to' and 'from' languages.")

Of course, these translations are performed by automated software robots on the Web. As a result, they're not nearly as accurate as what you'd get from a paid professional. On the other hand, when you're standing in the middle of a strange city and you don't know the language—and you desperately need to express yourself—what Dashboard provides may just be good enough.

Tip: Your first instinct may be to assume that this module is designed for translating things you want to say into the local language. However, you may find it even more useful for translating foreign-language paragraphs—from email or Web pages, for example—into your own language so that you can read them.

Unit Converter

No matter what units you're trying to convert—meters, grams, inches, miles per hour—the Unit Converter widget is ready.

From the upper pop-up menu, choose the kind of conversion you want: Temperature, Area, Weight, or whatever. (Take a moment to enjoy the clever graphic at the top of the window that helps identify the measurement you've selected.)

Use the lower pair of pop-up menus to specify which units you want to convert to and from, like Celsius to Fahrenheit. Then type in either the starting or ending measurement. To convert 48 degrees Celsius to Fahrenheit, for example, type *48* into the Celsius box. You don't have to click anything or press any key; the conversion is performed for you instantly and automatically as you type.

Never let it be said that technology isn't marching forward.

Tip: Unit Converter is especially amazing when it comes to currency conversions—from pesos to American dollars, for example—because it actually does its homework. It goes online to download up-to-the-minute currency rates to ensure that the conversion is accurate.

Weather

This famous Dashboard module shows a handy current-conditions display for your city (or any other city) and, if you choose, even offers a six-day forecast (Figure 5-17, lower left).

Before you get started, the most important step is to click the ❶ button at the lower-right corner. The widget flips around, and on the back panel, you'll see where you can specify your city and state or Zip code. You can also specify whether you prefer degrees Celsius or degrees Fahrenheit, and whether you want the six-day forecast to show both highs and lows. (It ordinarily shows only the highs.) Click Done.

Now the front of the widget displays the name of your town, today's predicted high and low, the current temperature, and a graphic representation of the sky conditions (sunny, cloudy, rainy, and so on). Click anywhere to reveal the six-day forecast.

Tip: Evidently, the Weather widget team members at Apple were really proud of their artwork. Lest you miss out on seeing all the beautiful weather graphics, they've given you a secret keystroke that reveals all 19 of the gorgeous and witty sky-weather graphics.

All you have to do is hold down ⌘ and Option as you click repeatedly on the widget. You'll see that, for the town of Nowhere, the weather changes every time you click.

Web Clip

Web Clip lets you make your *own* widgets with one click. This particular widget, however, is nothing more than a little ad for the Web Clips feature—and a reminder that you must start your Web Clip adventure in Safari, not Dashboard. See "Web Clips" on the next page.

World Clock

Sure, this clock shows the current time, but your menu bar does that. The neat part is that you can open up several of these clocks—click World Clock in the Widget bar repeatedly—and set each one to show the time in a different city. The result looks like the row of clocks in a hotel lobby, making you look Swiss and precise.

To specify which city's time appears on the clock, click the ❶ button at the lower-right corner. The widget flips around, revealing the pop-up menus that let you choose a continent and city.

More Widgets

The best part of the Dashboard is that it's expandable. *Thousands* of new widgets, written by other people, are available on the Web: games, chat and email notifiers, gas-price reporters, calculators and translators, news and sports updaters, finance and health trackers, and on and on.

Note: That's lucky, because some really good widgets have disappeared. For some reason, Apple deleted the old widgets called iTunes, Ski Report, and the two for looking up phone numbers—People Finder, Business (a White Pages and Yellow Pages). It's up to independent programmers to fill in the gaps.

To see Apple's current list of goodies, use one of these tactics:

- **The short way.** Control-click (or right-click) the Dashboard icon in the Dock. From the shortcut menu, choose More Widgets.

- **The long way.** In Dashboard, open the Widgets browser; click More Widgets.

Either way, you go to the Apple Dashboard downloads page. Some of the most intriguing widget offerings include the Yahoo Local Traffic widget (gives you the traffic conditions in your area), Air Traffic Control (identifies wireless AirPort base stations within range of your laptop), and TV Tracker (shows what you could be watching on TV right now instead of working). There are also FedEx package trackers, joke-of-the-day widgets, comic-strip-of-the-day widgets, and many other varieties. (See Figure 5-18.)

Installing a widget

When you download a widget, OS X asks if you're sure you want to install it; if you confirm, OS X downloads it and then displays it proudly in the Widget browser. Click it to open. (Behind the scenes, it's been copied into your Home→Library→Widgets folder. Only you will see that Dashboard widget, because it's been copied into the Widgets folder of *your account*. Anyone else who has an account on this Mac won't see it.)

Figure 5-18:
Not all good things come from Apple. Here's a representative sample of widgets written by other people. Clockwise from top left: Facebook Alert, Dashboard Aquarium, Scenario Poker, and Dancing Gingerbread Man.

Web Clips: Make Your Own Widgets

You don't have to be satisfied with Apple's widgets *or* the several thousand that other people have written. You can make a Dashboard widget of your own—in about three clicks.

Web Clips exploit an inescapable characteristic of widgets: An awful lot of them exist to deliver real-time information from the Web: weather widget, stocks, flights, and so on.

But what if your interest isn't snowstorms, stocks, or sports? What if it's *The New York Times* front page? Or the bestselling children's books on Amazon? Or the most-viewed video on YouTube? Or some cool Flash game?

That's the beauty of Web Clips, a joint venture of Dashboard and the Safari Web browser. They let you turn *any section of any Web page* into a Dashboard widget that updates itself every time you open it. It's like having a real-time keyhole peek at all your favorite Web sites at once.

Creating a Web Clips Widget

Here's how you go about creating a do-it-yourself widget:

1. **In Safari, go to the Web page that contains the information you want to snip. Choose File→Open in Dashboard.**

 The screen goes dark, with only a small window of white. As you move your cursor around the page, the white rectangle conveniently snaps to fit the various rectangular sections of the page (Figure 5-19).

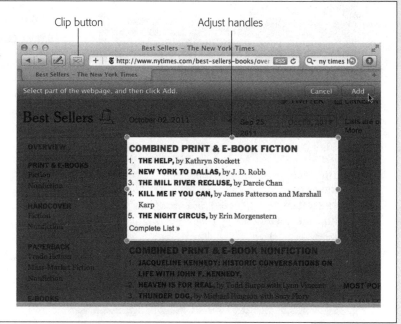

Figure 5-19:
Drag the little round handles to make the white box just big enough to surround the part of the page you want to enshrine. Or drag inside the box to move the whole thing.

Clip button Adjust handles

Your job is to make a frame around the part of the page that usually shows the information you want. If the Web site ever redesigns its pages, it'll wreck your widget—but what the heck. It takes only 5 seconds to make it again.

2. **Adjust the corner or side handles to enclose the piece of page you want. When you're finished, click Add or press Return.**

 Now Dashboard's Widget browser opens automatically. But wait—what's this? There's a new widget here that wasn't here before.

 At this point, you can dress up your widget, adding a little polish to this raw clipping you've ripped out of a Web page. Click the ❶ button that appears when you move your mouse to the lower-right corner. The widget flips around to reveal the controls shown in Figure 5-20.

 Here you can click one of the frame styles to give your widget a better-looking border.

If you click Edit, the widget flips around to face you again, and here's where it gets weird: You can reposition your widget's contents as though they were a window on a Web page that's visible behind it. Drag the widget contents in any direction within the frame, or resize the frame using the lower-right resize handle. Click Done.

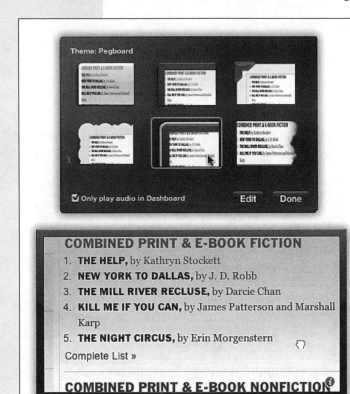

Figure 5-20:
Top: Click a frame style to give your widget better-looking edges. If the widget plays sound, it keeps playing sound when you close the Dashboard unless you turn on "Only play audio in Dashboard."

Bottom: Click Edit to return to the front of the widget, where you can adjust its position on the underlying Web page.

You can make as many Web Clips widgets as you want.

But here's a big screaming caution: If you close one of these homemade widgets, it's gone forever (or at least until you recreate it). Web Clips are never represented as icons on the Widget bar, as ordinary widgets are. Ah, well—easy come, easy go, right?

Note: If you're of the programmer persuasion—if you're handy in JavaScript and HTML, for example—it's much easier to write custom widgets than ever before. (Not just Web Clips widgets, *real* widgets.)

All you need is Dashcode, an easy-to-use widget-assembly environment. It's part of Apple's Xcode software programming toolkit, which is a free download from the Mac App Store. You'll find tutorials and examples by typing *dashcode tutorial* into Google.

Exposé

Before Mission Control, there was Exposé. It was flexible, it was novel, it was a little confusing. In Lion, Apple incorporated the main functions of Exposé into Mission Control—but Apple didn't want to break all those Exposé fans' hearts. So Exposé is still there, for the benefit of old-timers who don't like change.

Well, it's *mostly* there. There used to be three different Exposé modes. One showed you miniatures of *all* windows in *all* programs; one showed you miniatures of all windows in *just one program;* and one hid *all windows in all programs* so you could see the desktop.

In Mountain Lion, only the second and third Exposé functions still exist. (The first one—showing *all* windows in *all* programs—is what Mission Control is for.)

Both of these modes can be triggered using different combinations of the mouse and keyboard. The following pages will cover all of them, but of course you're not expected to learn all that. Just find the *one* trigger that seems most convenient, and stick with it.

One-App Exposé

When you trigger Mission Control, you see the thumbnails of *all* windows in *all* apps.

But sometimes it's useful to see only the windows of *one* app arrayed before you—the app you're *using.*

TROUBLESHOOTING MOMENT

A Tedious Side Note about the Aluminum Apple Keyboards

In the beginning, you could trigger the three Exposé modes described on these pages with three simple keystrokes: F9, F10, and F11.

Then Apple's aluminum keyboards and laptops came along. On these, Apple devoted the F3 key to Exposé functions—and reassigned the F9, F10, and F11 keys to speaker-volume control!

You *can* make them operate as in the days of yore—by adding the Fn key. That is: Fn-F9 for Mission Control, Fn-F10 for one-app Exposé, and Fn-F11 for desktop Exposé. (Details on the Fn key appear on page 237.)

So here's the point: On modern Macs, you have a choice

of two Exposé keystroke suites: the F3 key (by itself, with Control, and with ⌘)—or the Fn key plus F9, F10, and F11.

Actually, it's even more complicated than that. If you find yourself using *Exposé* more than you use the volume keys, you can get rid of the requirement to press Fn. Open System Preferences→Keyboard→Keyboard. Here you'll find a checkbox that reverses this logic. It's called "Use all F1, F2, etc. keys as standard function keys."

If that checkbox is *on,* then you can use F9, F10, and F11 to trigger Mission Control and Exposé. Now you need the Fn key only when you want those keys to adjust the *volume.*

That's great when you're Web browsing or word processing. This Exposé function makes the program's windows spread out, and shrink if necessary, so you can click the one you want (Figure 5-21, top).

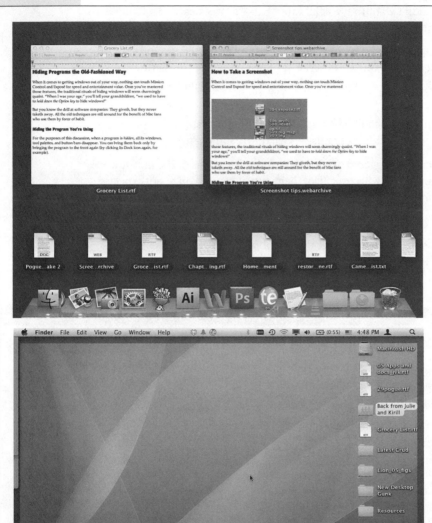

Figure 5-21:
Top: When you trigger one-app Exposé, you get a clear shot at any window in the current program (TextEdit, in this example). In the meantime, the rest of your screen attractively dims. In model Apple apps, like TextEdit and Preview, you even get a little row of icons at the bottom. They represent recently opened files, ready for clicking.

Bottom: Trigger desktop Exposé when you need to duck back to the desktop for a quick administrative chore. Here's your chance to find a file, throw something away, eject a disk, or whatever, without having to disturb your application windows.

In either case, tap the same function key again to turn off Exposé. Or click one of the window edges, which you can see peeking out from all four edges of the screen.

Here's how Apple intends for most people to trigger this option:

- **Swipe down on your trackpad with three fingers.** You're shown the miniatures of your current app's windows. If you point to an icon *on the Dock* before you swipe, you trigger Exposé for that app instead. (There's no equivalent on the Magic Mouse—although if you install the free BetterTouchTool, you can dream up a gesture of your own.)

Note: You have to turn this feature on in System Preferences→Trackpad→More Gestures. Once you've done that, you can change this gesture to four fingers on the trackpad using the pop-up menu—handy if you find yourself triggering the function by accident.

- **Press Control-F3 (⊞).** That's the keystroke on aluminum keyboards. (If you have a plastic keyboard, press F10 or Fn-F10, whichever works.)

Tip: As noted in the box on page 197, you can also press Fn-F10, or with some tweaking, F10 alone. Or you can change the keystroke altogether as described on page 213.

- **Enter Exposé from the heads-up display.** The heads-up display is the OS X application switcher—the row of "these are your open programs" icons—which appears when you press ⌘-Tab.

 The cool thing is that once you've got that heads-up display open, you can press ↑ or ↓ to enter Exposé for whatever program's icon is highlighted! From there, release the keys and hit Tab to cycle through your open apps.

- **Use Dock Exposé.** Click the program's Dock icon and hold the button down for half a second. (Or, for faster service, Control-click or right-click the program's Dock icon.)

 This feature has one chief advantage over the keystroke method: You can Exposé-ize *any* program's windows, not just the one you're using at the moment.

- **Shove your mouse into whatever corner of the screen you've chosen.** See page 352 for instructions.

Once you've triggered Exposé, you're not quite finished yet. As shown in Figure 5-21, beneath the window thumbnails, you get to see the icons of documents you've worked on recently in this app (at least in enlightened Apple programs like TextEdit).

Furthermore, here's the Exposé tip of the year: *Press the Tab key.* With each tap, you cycle through the open apps, each getting the Exposé treatment in turn. It's an informative way to inspect what's happening in each open program without losing your way. (Pressing ⌘-~ does the same thing.)

Desktop Exposé

The other flavor of Exposé is surprisingly handy. It sends *all* windows in *all* programs cowering to the edges of your screen, revealing the desktop beneath in all its uncluttered splendor (Figure 5-21, bottom).

Here's the keystroke scheme:

- **Current keyboards: Press ⌘-F3 (▣).** That's the trigger for current aluminum keyboards and laptops.

Note: Once again, you can also press Fn-11, or (if you set it up) F11 by itself. See the box on page 197.

- **Plastic keyboards: Press F11.**

The windows fly off to the edges of the screen, where they remain—forever, or until you tap the keystroke again, click a visible window edge, double-click an icon, or take some other window-selection step.

This is a spectacular opportunity to save headache and hassle in situations like these:

- **You're writing an email message, and you want to attach a file.** Tap the desktop Exposé keystroke, and then root around in the Finder until you locate the file you want. Begin to drag it, and then, without releasing the mouse button, tap the desktop Exposé keystroke again to bring back your email window. (Or drag the attachment directly onto your email program's icon on the Dock and pause until its window thumbnails appear.)

 Move your cursor, with the file in mid-drag, directly over the outgoing message window; release the cursor to create the attachment. You've just added an attachment from the desktop in one smooth motion.

Tip: You can apply the same life-changing shortcut to dragging a graphic into a page-layout program, a folder of photos into iPhoto, a sound or graphic into iMovie, and so on.

- **You want to open a different document.** For many people, having access to the entire Finder beats the pants off having to use the Open dialog box. Double-clicking the icon you want automatically opens it and turns off Exposé.

- **You're on the Web, and you want to see if some file has finished downloading.** Trigger desktop Exposé to survey the situation on your desktop.

If the layer of open programs is the atmosphere, the Finder is the earth below—and the ability to teleport back and forth is a huge timesaver.

Tip: You can switch between the two Exposé modes (one-app or desktop), even after you've triggered one. For example, if you three-finger downswipe to shrink only that program's windows, you can then press ⌘-F3 to see the desktop. In fact, you can also get to one-app Exposé from within Mission Control—just press ⌘-~.

Exposé Tip-O-Rama

Just having your world o' windows spread out like index cards is magic enough. But these windows are *live*. You can work with them. Let us count the ways.

- **Tab through Exposé'd apps.** Once you've started one-app Exposé and a program's windows are arrayed before you, tap the Tab key to switch to the *next* running program. All *its* windows spring to the fore. Tab, Tab, Tab through all your open programs. (Shift-Tab, as usual, cycles through the programs in the opposite direction.)

Tip: You can also switch to another app's micro-windows by clicking its Dock icon.

- **Change Exposé'd apps using the heads-up display.** Here's another way to change programs once you're in one-app Exposé: Press ⌘-Tab to bring up the heads-up display (yes, even while your windows are shrunken). Tab your way through the program icons (Figure 5-21) until the one you want is selected, and then release the keys. That program's windows spring to the front, still miniaturized and arrayed for your selection pleasure.

- **Hold down instead of two presses.** Most of the time, you'll probably use Exposé in two steps. You'll tap the keystroke once to get the windows out of the way, and

GEM IN THE ROUGH

Using the Dock or Sidebar for Drag-and-Drop

The Mac is smart about the relationship between documents and applications. If you double-click a TextEdit document icon, for example, TextEdit opens automatically and shows you the document.

But it's occasionally useful to open a document using a program other than the one that created it. Perhaps, as is often the case with downloaded Internet graphics, you don't *have* the program that created it, or you don't know which one was used. This technique is also useful if you want to open a ReadMe file into your word processor, such as Word, instead of the usual TextEdit program.

In such cases, the Dock is handy: Just drag the mystery document onto one of the Dock's tiles, as shown here. Doing so forces the program to open the document—if it can.

(Dragging onto a program's icon in the Sidebar or even the Finder toolbar works just as well.)

Incidentally, in general only the Dock icons of programs that can, in fact, open the file you're dragging become highlighted. The others just shrug indifferently or even scoot aside, thinking you're trying to drag the file *into* the Dock.

Pressing Option-⌘ as you drag forces Dock icons to be more tolerant. Now all of them "light up" as your document touches them, indicating that they'll *try* to open your file. Even so, a "could not be opened" error message may result. As they say in Cupertino, sometimes what a can really needs is a can opener.

tap it again to bring them back (if, indeed, you haven't *clicked* a window to bring them back).

In some cases, though, you may find it easier to *hold down* the relevant key. For example, hold down ⌘-F3 (Show Desktop) to see if a file is finished copying to the desktop, and then release the keys to bring back all the windows. (Actually, you can let go of the ⌘ key as soon as you've entered Exposé.) For quick window-clearing situations, that method saves you the step of having to press the keystroke a second time to turn off Exposé.

- **Use the spring-loaded Dock.** This trick is great when you want to drop a file from one program into a particular window belonging to another.

 The most common example: You want to add an attachment to an outgoing email message. In the Finder, locate the file's icon. Drag it directly onto your email program's Dock icon—and *pause* with your finger still on the button. After a half second, Exposé happens, showing all your email program's open windows. Now continue your drag onto the miniaturized window of the outgoing message so it's highlighted, tap the space bar to open it, and then release. Presto! The file is attached.

NOSTALGIA CORNER

Window Layering

OS X takes a layered approach to your programs' windows. They're not all in front or all in back; it's entirely possible to wind up with the windows of different programs sandwiched and layered, front to back.

Suppose, for example, you have Microsoft Excel in the foreground but Word in the background. If you click within a visible portion of a background window, you bring only that window of Word to the front.

The remedy for this situation, if it bothers you, is the Window→Bring All to Front command, which appears in the Finder and many other programs. It brings all a program's windows to the front. (You can do the same thing by simply clicking the program's Dock icon, or using the ⌘-Tab "heads-up" display.)

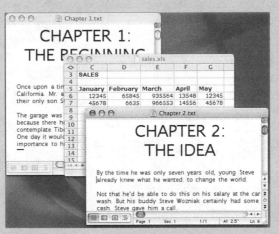

Layered windows shine when you're comparing two documents in two different programs, because they free you of the window clutter of other open documents. But the time will come when you're ready to bring all a background program's windows to the front. Get into the habit of clicking its Dock icon, or pressing ⌘-Tab to select its icon, rather than clicking inside one window. When you do that, all open windows in that application come forward, from wherever they may be.

This trick also works great when you want to drop a photo into a newsletter, for example, or a text clipping into a word-processing document.

- **Dip into Quick Look.** Once you've got shrunken windows on the screen, tap your arrow keys to highlight a window (or point with your mouse at them without clicking). A bright-blue border moves from window to window.

At any point, you can press the space bar to make that one window return to life size. You haven't really activated it—you can't edit it—but at least you can see it at full size.

And here's the very cool part: Once you've triggered Quick Look like this, you can press the arrow keys to zap *other* miniwindows back to full size, without having to exit Quick Look. Or, again, point to other windows without clicking. Each zooms in to 100 percent size. (All of this is much easier to do than to imagine.)

You can keep examining your windows at full size until you spot the one you're after; now tap Return (or click the mouse in the window) to exit Quick Look *and* Exposé. You've just opened that window, and you're ready to roll.

Tip: Keep in mind that you can change all of these Exposé triggers—keyboard shortcuts, hot corners, and so on. See page 175.

Hiding Programs the Old-Fashioned Way

When it comes to getting windows out of your way, nothing can touch Mission Control and Exposé for speed and entertainment value. Once you've mastered those features, the traditional rituals of hiding windows will seem charmingly quaint. "When I was your age," you'll tell your grandchildren, "we used to have to *hold down the Option key* to hide windows!"

But you know the drill at software companies: They giveth, but they never taketh away. All the old techniques are still around for the benefit of Mac fans who use them by force of habit.

Hiding the Program You're Using

For the purposes of this discussion, when a program is *hidden,* all its windows, tool palettes, and button bars disappear. You can bring them back only by bringing the program to the front again (by clicking its Dock icon again, for example).

If your aim is to hide only the frontmost program, OS X offers a whole raft of approaches. Many of them involve the Option key, as listed here:

- **Option-click any visible portion of the desktop.** The program you were in vanishes, along with all its windows.

- **Option-click any other program's icon on the Dock.** You open that program (or bring all its windows to the front) *and* hide all the windows of the one you were using.

- **Option-click any visible portion of another program's windows.** Once again, you switch programs, hiding the one you were using at the time.

- **From the Application menu, choose Hide iPhoto (or whatever the program is).** The Application menu is the boldfaced menu that bears the program's name.

- **From the program's Dock icon shortcut menu, choose Hide.** You open the shortcut menu, of course, by Control-clicking (or right-clicking). You also get a Hide button if you click-and-hold on the Dock icon for half a second.

- **When you've highlighted a program's icon by pressing ⌘-Tab to rotate through the running programs, press the letter H key.** The program hides itself instantly. Leave the ⌘ key down the whole time, and after pressing the H, press Tab again to move on to the next program. If you release the keys while "stopped" on the program instead, you'll bring it forward rather than hiding it.

- **Press ⌘-H.** This may be the easiest and most useful trick of all (although it doesn't work in a few oddball programs). Doing so hides the program you're in; you then "fall down" into the next running program.

Tip: Consider this radical timesaving proposal: Never quit the programs you use frequently. Instead, simply hit ⌘-H whenever you're finished working in a program. That way, the next time you need it, the program launches with zero wait time.

There's a limit to this principle; if you have only 2 gigabytes of memory and you keep 20 programs open, and one of them is Photoshop, you'll incur a speed penalty. In more moderate situations, though, OS X's virtual-memory scheme is so good that there's almost no downside to leaving your programs open all the time.

To unhide a program and its windows, click its Dock icon again, choose the Show All command in the Application menu, or press ⌘-Tab to summon the heads-up application display.

Tip: The Dock continues to display the icons of all running programs without any indication that you've hidden them. Fortunately, that's easy enough to fix. All you need is the free program TinkerTool, which is available on this book's "Missing CD" page at *www.missingmanuals.com.* It offers a simple checkbox that makes hidden programs appear with transparent Dock icons.

Hiding All Other Programs

Choosing Hide Others from your program's Application menu means, of course, "Hide the windows of every program but this one." It even hides your Finder (desktop) windows, although desktop icons remain visible.

Better yet, there's a keystroke for this command: Option-⌘-H. That's one small step for keystrokes, one giant leap for productivity geeks.

Tip: If you Control-click or right-click a program's Dock icon, you get its shortcut menu, including a Hide command. If you press Option, it changes to say Hide Others. It's a lot more work than the methods described above, but, you know. One strives for thoroughness.

If this trick interests you, you might also enjoy its corollary, described next.

The Bring-Forward, Hide-All-Others Trick

Here's a terrific technique that lets you bring one program to the front (along with all its open windows), and hide all other windows of all *other* open programs—all with one click.

You might think of it as Hero mode, or Front-and-Center mode, or Clear My Calendar mode.

In any case, the trick is to Option-⌘-click the lucky program's icon on the Dock. As it jumps to the fore, all other windows on your Mac are instantly hidden. (You can bring them back, of course, by clicking the appropriate Dock icons.)

Hiding (Minimizing) Individual Windows

You can also hide or show *individual windows* of a single program. In fact, Apple must believe that hiding a window will become one of your favorite activities, because it offers at least four ways to do so:

- Choose Window→Minimize Window, if your program offers such a command, or press ⌘-M.

- Click the Minimize button on the window's title bar.

- Double-click the window's title bar. (If this doesn't work, choose →System Preferences→Appearance. Make sure "Double-click a window's title bar to minimize" is turned on.)

In any case, the affected window shrinks down until it becomes a new icon on the right side of the Dock. Click that icon to bring the window back.

How Documents Know Their Parents

Every operating system needs a mechanism to associate documents with the applications that created them. When you double-click a Microsoft Word document icon, for example, it's clear that you want Microsoft Word to launch and open the document.

So how does OS X know how to find a document's mommy?

It actually has two different mechanisms.

- **File name extensions.** A *file name extension* is a suffix following a period in the file's name, as in *Letter to Mom.doc.* (It's usually three letters long, but it doesn't have to be.) These play a role in determining which documents open into which programs.

That's how Windows identifies its documents, too. If you double-click something called *memo.doc,* it opens in Microsoft Word. If you double-click *memo.wri,* it opens in Microsoft Write, and so on.

Note: OS X comes set to hide most file name extensions, on the premise that they make the operating system look more technical and threatening. If you'd like to see them, however, choose Finder→Preferences, click the Advanced button, and then turn on "Show all filename extensions." Now examine a few of your documents; you'll see that their names display the previously hidden suffixes.

You can hide or show these suffixes on an icon-at-a-time basis, too (or a clump-at-a-time basis). Just highlight the icon or icons you want to affect, and then choose File→Get Info. In the resulting Info window, proceed as shown in Figure 5-22.

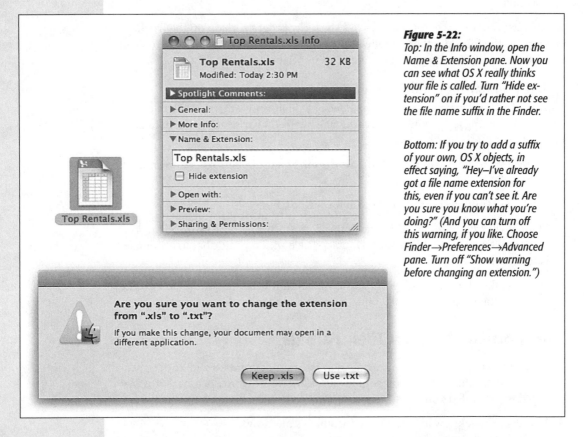

Figure 5-22:
Top: In the Info window, open the Name & Extension pane. Now you can see what OS X really thinks your file is called. Turn "Hide extension" on if you'd rather not see the file name suffix in the Finder.

Bottom: If you try to add a suffix of your own, OS X objects, in effect saying, "Hey—I've already got a file name extension for this, even if you can't see it. Are you sure you know what you're doing?" (And you can turn off this warning, if you like. Choose Finder→Preferences→Advanced pane. Turn off "Show warning before changing an extension.")

- **Your preferences.** If you've used the Always Open With command to *specify* which program opens your document, that's the one that opens; this preference overrides the file name extension system. OS X memorizes that new pairing.

Note: Apple is moving away from using the invisible, four-letter *Type and Creator codes* that had been a mainstay of program-document relationships since the first days of the Mac. The Creator code identified the program; the Type code specified the document's file format: GIF, JPEG, TIFF, and so on. (Apple used to monitor and track these codes, in conjunction with the various Mac software companies, so that no two Creator codes were alike.) Apparently Apple thought that two different parent-document systems were plenty.

It's possible to live a long and happy life without knowing anything about these suffixes and relationships. Indeed, the vast majority of Mac fans may never even encounter them. But if you're prepared for a little bit of technical bushwhacking, you may discover that understanding document-program relationships can be useful in troubleshooting, keeping your files private, and appreciating how OS X works.

Reassigning Documents to Programs

Unfortunately, file name extensions aren't always especially specific. Suppose you've downloaded a graphic called Sunset.jpg. Well, almost any program these days can open a JPEG graphic—Photoshop, Pages, Word, Preview, Safari, and so on. How does OS X know which of these programs to open when you double-click the file?

Fortunately, *you* can decide. You can *reassign* a document (or all documents of its kind) to a specific program. Here's the rundown.

Reassigning a certain document—just once

Double-clicking a graphics file generally opens it in Preview, the graphics viewer included with OS X. Most of the time, that's a perfectly good arrangement. But Preview has only limited editing powers. What if you decide to edit a graphics file more substantially? You'd want it to open, just this once, into a different program—Photoshop Elements, for example.

To do so, you must access the Open With command. You can find it in three places:

- Highlight the icon, and then choose File→Open With.

- Highlight the icon, and then open the ✿ menu. In the menu, choose Open With.

- Control-click (or right-click) the file's icon. From the shortcut menu, choose Open With.

Study the submenu for a moment (Figure 5-23, top). The program whose name says "(default)" indicates which program *usually* opens this kind of document. From this pop-up menu, choose the name of the program you'd *rather* open this particular file, right now, just this once.

Reassigning a certain document—permanently

After opening a TIFF file in, say, Photoshop Elements for editing, you haven't really made any changes in the fabric of your Mac universe. The next time you double-click that file, it opens once again in Preview.

If you wish this particular file would *always* open in Photoshop Elements, the steps are slightly different. In fact, there are three different ways:

• In the Choose an Application dialog box (the one that appears when you double-click a document whose "parent" program isn't clear), turn on Always Open With (shown at bottom in Figure 5-23).

Figure 5-23:
Top: The shortcut menu offers a list of programs capable of opening an icon. If you were to press the Option key right now, the words Open With would suddenly change to say Always Open With.

Bottom: If you choose Other, you're prompted to choose a different program. Turn on Always Open With if you'll always want this document to open in the new parent program. Otherwise, this is a one-time reassignment.

- Start out with one of the previously described techniques (for example, File→Open With, or right-click the file's icon and choose Open With)—but after you see the menu, press the Option key, too. Before your very eyes, the Open With command changes to say *Always* Open With.

- Highlight the icon, and then choose File→Get Info. Open the "Open with" panel. Choose a new "parent" program's name from the pop-up menu. You'll see that the word "(default)" changes position, now tacking itself onto the name of the program you've chosen.

Tip: You can use a similar trick to reassign the parenthood of a whole *flock* of selected icons at once. Once you've selected them, keep the Option key pressed as you choose File→Show Inspector. In the Open With section of this specialized Get Info window, choose a new program from the pop-up menu. The message at the top of the window—"22 items," for example—reminds you that you're changing the whole batch at once.

Reassigning all documents of one type

So much for reassigning one document (or a group of documents) at a time. What if you're writing, say, a book about OS X, and you've been taking a lot of screenshots? OS X saves each captured screen illustration as a graphics file in something called PNG format. That's all fine, except that every time you double-click one of thesc, it opens into Preview, where you can't paint out unwanted details.

You could reassign all these files, one at a time, to a different program, but your grand-children would have grandchildren by the time you finished. In this case, you want to tell OS X, "For heaven's sake, make *all* PNG files open in Photoshop from now on!"

To make it happen, start by highlighting *any* PNG file. Choose File→Get Info. (The shortcut menus won't help you in this case.) Open the "Open with" panel.

From its pop-up menu, choose the program you want to open this kind of document from now on.

Tip: If the one you prefer isn't listed, use the Other option, which opens the Choose an Application dialog box so you can navigate to the one you want, as shown in Figure 5-23 at bottom . Find and double-click the program.

Or, instead of choosing Other, you can also choose App Store. It's Apple's way of saying, "Hey—if you don't have a program that can open this document, maybe you should just *go buy one right now!*"

This time, follow up by clicking Change All beneath the pop-up menu. (This button is dimmed until you've actually selected a different program from the pop-up menu.) Confirm by clicking Continue or pressing Return.

From now on, double-clicking any similar kind of document opens it in the newly selected program.

Keyboard Control

Mountain Lion offers a fantastic feature for anyone who believes life is too short: keyboard-controllable menus, dialog boxes, pop-up menus, and even Dock pop-up menus. You can operate every menu in every program without the mouse.

In fact, you can operate every control in every dialog box from the keyboard, including pop-up menus and checkboxes. And you can even redefine many of the built-in OS X keystrokes, like Shift-⌘-3 to capture the screen as a graphic.

In fact, you can even add or change *any menu command in any program*. If you're a keyboard-shortcut lover, your cup runneth over.

Here are some of the ways you can control your Mac mouselessly. In the following descriptions, you'll encounter the factory settings for the keystrokes that do the magic—but as you'll see in a moment, you can change these key combos to anything you like. (The System Preferences→Keyboard→Keyboard Shortcuts tab contains the on/off switches for these features.)

Note: On modern-day aluminum keyboards, the keystrokes described below may not work unless you also press the Fn key simultaneously.

If that seems just a tad clumsy, you can eliminate the Fn-key requirement either by using the "Use all F1, F2, etc. keys as standard function keys" option described in the box on page 197—or by choosing a different keystroke altogether (page 213).

Control the Menus

When you press Control-F2, the menu is highlighted. At this point, you can "walk" to another menu by pressing the ← or → keys (or Tab and Shift-Tab). When you reach the menu you want, open it by pressing ↓, space, Return, or Enter.

Walk down the commands in the menu by pressing ↑ or ↓, or jump directly to a command in the menu by typing the first couple of letters of its name. Finally, "click" a menu command by pressing Enter, Return, or the space bar.

You can also close the menu without making a selection by pressing Esc or ⌘-period.

Control the Dock

Once you've pressed Control-F3, you can highlight *any* icon on the Dock by pressing the appropriate arrow keys (or, once again, Tab and Shift-Tab).

Then, once you've highlighted a Dock icon, you "click" it by pressing Return or the space bar. Again, if you change your mind, press Esc or ⌘-period.

Tip: Once you've highlighted a disk or folder icon, you can press the ↑ or ↓ keys to make its shortcut menu appear. (If you've positioned the Dock vertically, use ← or → instead.)

Cycle Through Your Windows

Every time you press Control-F4, you bring the next window forward, eventually cycling through *every window in every open program*. Add the Shift key to cycle through them in the opposite order.

You may remember that OS X offers a different keystroke for cycling through the different windows in your *current* program (it's ⌘-~, the tilde symbol at the upper left on your keyboard). Control-F4, on the other hand, tours all windows in *all* programs. Both keystrokes are useful in different situations.

Control the Toolbar

This one is on the unpredictable side, but it more or less works in most programs that display an OS X–style toolbar: the Finder, System Preferences, and so on.

When you press Control-F5, you highlight the first button on that toolbar. Move the "focus" by pressing the arrow keys or Tab and Shift-Tab. Then tap Return or the space bar to "click" the highlighted button.

Control Tool Palettes

In a few programs that feature floating tool palettes, you can highlight the frontmost palette by pressing Control-F6. At this point, use the arrow keys to highlight the various buttons on the palette. You can see the effect when, for example, you're editing text

Figure 5-24:
If you choose All Applications from the top pop-up menu, you can change the keyboard combo for a certain command wherever it appears. You could, for example, change the keystroke for Page Setup in every program at once. (Beware the tiny yellow triangles; they let you know if a chosen keystroke conflicts with another OS X keystroke.)

in TextEdit and you've also opened the Font palette. Pressing Control-F6 highlights the Font palette, taking the "focus" off your document.

Control Menulets

Here's a gem you may not have heard about: You can operate *menulets*—those menu-bar status indicators for your speaker volume, wireless networks, and so on—from the keyboard, too.

This time, the trick is to hit Control-F8. That highlights the leftmost Apple menulet. Now you can use your ← and → arrow keys to move around the menu bar; when you've highlighted the one you want, press Return or the space bar to "click" that menu and open it.

Control Dialog Boxes

You can also navigate and manipulate any *dialog box* from the keyboard.

See the dialog box shown in Figure 5-24? If you turn on "All controls" at the bottom, then pressing the Tab key highlights the next control of any type, whatever it may be—radio button, pop-up menu, and so on. Press the space bar to "click" a button or to open a pop-up menu. Once a menu is open, use the arrow keys (or type letter keys) to highlight commands on it, and use the space bar to "click" your choice.

Changing a Menu Keyboard Shortcut

Suppose you love iPhoto (and who doesn't?). But one thing drives you crazy: The Revert to Original command, which discards all the changes you've ever made since taking the photo, has no keyboard shortcut. You must trek up to the menu bar every time you need that command.

This is why OS X lets you add keyboard shortcuts to menu commands that lack them—or change the commands in programs whose key assignments break with tradition. (It works in any program that uses the standard OS X menu software, which rules out older versions of Microsoft Office.) Here's the routine:

1. **Choose →System Preferences→Keyboard. Click the Keyboard Shortcuts tab, and then click Application Shortcuts in the left-side list.**

 You're shown a list of any keyboard assignments you've created so far.

2. **Click the + button just beneath the list.**

 The dialog box shown in Figure 5-24 appears.

3. **Indicate which program needs behavior modification.**

 In this example, you'd choose iPhoto from the Application pop-up menu. (If the program's name doesn't appear in the pop-up menu, then choose Other; navigate to, and double-click, the program you want.)

4. **Carefully type in the name of the menu command whose keyboard shortcut you want to change or add.**

Type it *exactly* as it appears in the menu, complete with capitalization and the little ellipsis (…) that may follow it. (You make the ellipsis character by pressing Option-semicolon.)

5. **Click in the Keyboard Shortcut box. Press the new or revised key combo you want.**

For example, press Control-R for iPhoto's Revert to Original command. You'll see the Mac's notation of your keystroke appear in the Keyboard Shortcut box—unless, of course, the combo you selected is already in use within that program. In that case, you hear only an error sound that means, "Try again."

6. **Click Add.**

The dialog box closes. By scrolling down in your Keyboard Shortcuts list, you see that the keystroke you selected has now been written down for posterity under the appropriate program's flippy triangle. (To get rid of it, click its name and then click the − button beneath the list.)

The next time you open the program you edited, you'll see that the new keystroke is in place.

Tip: To delete or change one of your custom menu shortcuts, open System Preferences→Keyboard→Keyboard Shortcuts. Click Application Shortcuts in the list at left. Click the command you'd like to edit. Press Delete to get rid of it; or, to try a different key combo, click where the existing keyboard shortcut appears and then press a new one.

Redefining a Keystroke

As you've no doubt become painfully aware, there are *hundreds* of keyboard combinations for the various OS X functions and settings. That's good, because keyboard shortcuts are efficient and quicker than using the mouse. But that's also bad, because there's no *way* you'll be able to remember all of them—and some of the most useful shortcuts are ridiculous, multikey affairs that you'll never remember at all.

In the keyboard-shortcut center, shown in Figure 5-25, you can look over all the common OS X hidden keyboard functions—for Mission Control, Exposé, Spotlight, Dashboard, the Dock, and many others—and *change them.*

Here's how it goes:

1. **Choose →System Preferences. Click Keyboard. Click the Keyboard Shortcuts tab.**

You arrive at the dialog box shown in Figure 5-25.

2. **In the left-side list, click the category or function you want.**

Your choices include Launchpad & Dock, Mission Control, Keyboard & Text Input, and so on. When you click a category name, you see the available keyboard shortcuts.

Tip: You don't have to be content with *changing* one of these keyboard shortcuts. You can also *turn it off* by clicking the corresponding checkbox. That's great if one of Apple's predefined keystrokes—for a function you don't even use—is interfering with one in a program you like.

3. **Click the command you want to change. Then click the current keyboard combination.**

 Suppose, for example, that you wish the Show Desktop Exposé keystroke were something easier to remember, like Control-D. So in step 2, you'd click Mission Control. In this step, you'd click Show Desktop. Then you'd click where it currently says "F11."

Figure 5-25:
The keyboard-shortcut center lets you redefine the keystrokes that trigger many basic OS X features, menu commands in your programs, and software you've built yourself using Automator (Chapter 7).

4. **Press a new key combination.**

 In this example, you'd press Control-D.

 Be careful, though. OS X keystrokes take precedence over *all others*. So if you choose a keystroke like ⌘-P for something, well, by golly, you'll no longer be able to use ⌘-P to print anything in any of your programs. Think before you assign. Run a couple of tests afterward.

The Save and Open Dialog Boxes

When you choose File→Save, you're asked where you want the new document stored on your hard drive. The resulting dialog box is a miniature Finder. All the skills you've picked up working at the desktop come into play here.

To give it a try, launch any program that has a Save or Export command—TextEdit, for example. Type a couple of words, and then choose File→Save. The Save sheet appears (Figure 5-26).

Tip: In most programs, a quick glance at the Close button in the upper-left corner of a document window tells you whether it's been saved. When a small dot appears in the red button, it means you've made changes to the document that you haven't saved yet. (Time to press ⌘-S!) The dot disappears as soon as you save your work.

In programs that offer the Auto Save and Versions features described later in this chapter, like TextEdit, the red-dot convention has been retired. Instead, when you've made changes to a document since saving it, you see the light gray word *Edited* in the title bar.

Figure 5-26:
Top: The Save dialog box, or sheet, often appears in its compact form.

Right (inset): If you open the Where pop-up menu, you'll find that OS X lists all the places it thinks you might want to save your new document: on the hard drive, in a folder you've put into your Sidebar, or into a folder you've recently opened.

Bottom: If you want to choose a different folder or create a new folder, click the ▼ button indicated by the cursor above to expand the dialog box. Here, you see the equivalent of the Finder—with a choice of icon, list, or column view. Even the Sidebar is here, complete with access to other disks on the network.

Tip: In most programs, you can enlarge the Save or Open dialog box by dragging one of its edges. You can also adjust the width of the Sidebar by dragging its right edge.

Sheets

In the days of operating systems gone by, the Save dialog box appeared dead center on the screen, where it commandeered your entire operation. Moreover, because it seemed stuck to your *screen* rather than to a particular *document,* you couldn't actually tell which document you were saving—a real problem when you quit out of a program that had three unsaved documents open.

In most Mac programs, there's no mystery regarding which document you're saving, because a little Save dialog box called a *sheet* slides directly out of the document's title bar.

Better still, this little Save box is a sticky note attached *to the document.* It stays there, neatly attached and waiting, even if you switch to another program, another document, the desktop, or wherever. When you finally return to the document, the Save sheet is still there, waiting for you to type a file name and save the document.

The Mini Finder

Of course *you,* O savvy reader, have probably never saved a document into some deeply nested folder by accident, never to see it again. But millions of novices (and even a few experts) have fallen into this trap.

When the Save sheet appears, a pop-up menu shows you precisely where the Mac proposes to put your newly created document: usually in the Documents folder of your own Home folder. For many people, this is an excellent suggestion. If you keep everything in your Documents folder, it will be extremely easy to find, and you'll be able to back up your work just by dragging that single folder to a backup disk.

As shown at top in Figure 5-26, the Where pop-up menu gives you direct access to some other places you might want to save a newly created file. (The keystrokes for the most important folders work here, too—Shift-⌘-H for your Home folder, for example.)

In any case, when you save a file, the options in the Where pop-up menu have you covered 90 percent of the time. Most people work with a limited set of folders for active documents.

But when you want to save a new document into a new folder, or when you want to navigate to a folder that isn't listed in the Where pop-up menu, all is not lost. Click the ▾ button identified in Figure 5-26. The Save sheet expands into a very familiar sight: a miniature version of the Finder.

Tip: You can switch back and forth between the compact and expanded versions of this dialog box by pressing the undocumented shortcut ⌘-=.

There's your Sidebar, complete with access to the other computers on your network. There are the ◄/► buttons. There are your little buttons for icon, list, column, and (in most programs) even Cover Flow views.

Tip: In column view, your first instinct should be to widen this window, making more columns available. Do so by carefully dragging either edge of the dialog box. The Mac remembers the size for this Save sheet independently in each program.

And in list view, how's this for a tip? If you Control-click (or right-click) one of the column headings, like Name or Date Modified, you get a secret pop-up menu of column names: Last Opened, Size, Kind, Label, and so on. That's right: You can customize the list view within an Open or Save dialog box. You can sort, too, by clicking one of the column headings, just as at the desktop.

Most of the familiar Finder navigation shortcuts work here, too. For example, press the ← and → keys to navigate the columns, or the ↑ and ↓ keys to highlight the disk and folder names *within* a column. Once you've highlighted a column, you can also type to select the first letters of disk or folder names.

In fact, you can use Quick Look (page 59) in the Open and Save dialog box, too. Highlight any file or folder in the list and tap the space bar to view it in a full-size window.

Tip: Even in the Save or Open dialog box, you can highlight an icon (or several) and then press ⌘-I. You switch back to the Finder, where the Get Info box is waiting with the date, size, and other details about the selected icons.

When you're finished playing around, open the folder where you want to save your newly created document, and then click Save to store it there.

Tip: Here's one of the weirdest tricks in Mountain Lion. When the Open or Save dialog box is open before you, you can press Shift-⌘-period (.) to make all your Mac's *hidden* files appear. (As a Unix-based outfit, OS X is crawling with these invisible files, which are of primary interest to technical types.) Press that keystroke again to hide the hidden files once again. Fun for geeks!

If you use a non-American number-formatting system (where one thousand is 1.000, for example), use Shift-⌘-comma instead.

Alternatively, click New Folder (or press the usual New Folder keystroke, Shift-⌘-N) to create a new folder *inside* the folder you're looking at.

You'll be asked to type the new name for the folder. After you've done so, click Create (or press Return). The new folder appears and opens before you, empty. You can now proceed with saving your new document into it, if you like.

The next time you save a new document, the Save sheet reappears in whatever condition you left it. That is, if you used column view the last time, it's still in column view. At any time, you can collapse it into simplified view, shown at top in Figure 5-26, by clicking the ▲ button to the right of the Where pop-up menu.

Tip: For years, there's been a keyboard shortcut for the Don't Save button that appears when you close a new document without saving it: ⌘-D. In Mountain Lion, however, modern Apple programs like TextEdit, Preview, Grab, Pages, and Keynote present a Delete button instead of a Don't Save button. In that case, you can press ⌘-Delete to "click" it instead of using the mouse.

Spotlight

The search box at the top of the Open and Save dialog box is a clone of the Finder's search box (Chapter 3). Press ⌘-F to make your insertion point jump there. Type a few letters of the name of the file or folder you're looking for, and up it pops, regardless of its actual hard-disk location.

Your savings: 5 minutes of burrowing through folders to find it, and several pages of reading about how to navigate the Save and Open boxes.

Insta-Jumping to a Folder Location

Whether you're using the mini-sheet or the expanded view, you can save yourself some folder-burrowing time by following the tip shown in Figure 5-27. This feature is totally undocumented—but well worth learning.

Tip: If, when the Save box is in its expanded condition, you click the name of an existing file, OS X thoughtfully copies the name of the clicked file into the Save As: text box (which otherwise said "Untitled" or was blank).

This trick can save you time when you're saving a second document with a slightly modified name ("Oprah and Me: The Inside Story, Chapter 1" and then "Oprah and Me: The Inside Story, Chapter 2"). It's also useful if you want to replace the original file with the new one you're saving. Instead of having to type out the entire name of the file, you can just click it.

Figure 5-27:
The quickest way to specify a folder location is to drag the icon of any folder or disk from your desktop directly into the Save or Open sheet. OS X instantly displays the contents of that folder or disk.

The File Format Pop-up Menu

The Save dialog box in many programs offers a pop-up menu of file formats below the Save As box. Use this menu when preparing a document for use by somebody else—somebody whose computer doesn't have the same software. For example, if you've used a graphics program to prepare a photograph for use on the Web, this menu is where you specify JPEG format (the standard Web format for photos).

The Open File Dialog Box

The dialog box that appears when you choose File→Open is almost identical to the expanded Save File sheet. Because you encounter it only when you're opening an existing file, this dialog box lacks a Save button, file name field, and so on.

Note: Furthermore, the Open dialog box gives you access only to disks, folders, and documents that you can actually open at this moment. For example, when you're using GarageBand, picture files show up dimmed.

But the Open box adds a special Sidebar category called Media (see Figure 5-28), which gives you direct access to all your photos, music, and movies. Apple figures you might want to import these items *into* a document you're working on.

Figure 5-28:
The Media Browser is built right into the Open dialog box. That is, you get miniature listings of your iTunes, iPhoto, and movie files right in the Sidebar, for convenience in importing them into (for example) Keynote, PowerPoint, or a Web design program.

Most of the other Save File dialog box controls are equally useful here. That handy Spotlight search bar is still there, only a ⌘-F away. Once again, you can begin your navigation by seeing what's on the desktop (press ⌘-D) or in your Home folder (Shift-⌘-H). Once again, you can find a folder or a disk by beginning your quest with the Sidebar, and then navigate using icon, list, or column view. And once again, you can drag a folder, disk, or file icon off your desktop directly into the dialog box to specify where you want to look. (If you drag a *file* icon, you're shown the folder that contains it.)

When you've finally located the file you want to open, double-click it or highlight it (which you can do from the keyboard), and then press Return, Enter, or ⌘-O.

In general, most people don't encounter the Open File dialog box nearly as often as the Save File dialog box. That's because the Mac offers many more convenient ways to *open* a file—double-clicking its icon in the Finder, choosing its name from →Recent Items, and so on—but only a single way to *save* a new file.

Note: Certain anointed apps, like TextEdit and Pages, present a new twist to the Open dialog box: the iCloud button, for saving your documents online. Details begin on page 225.

Auto Save and Versions

In the beginning, Jobs created the Save command—because computers were slow.

Every time you saved, your work was interrupted for a few seconds (or a lot of seconds) as the very slow program on your very slow computer saved your work onto a very slow floppy disk.

And *that,* ladies and gentlemen, is why most programs still don't autosave: because the interruptions were just too annoying.

Apple figured it's high time the world revisit that scenario. Computers now have plenty of horsepower. They could be saving your work *continuously,* and you'd never even know it. Why shouldn't *all* programs save your work as you go, automatically and invisibly? As long as you also have the option to rewind and take your document in a different direction, what could possibly be the harm?

And so it is that, in Lion, Auto Save was one of the key new features. And in Mountain Lion, it's been made a lot less confusing.

Unfortunately, it's available in only a few programs, at least at the outset. You'll find it in Apple's showcase programs like Pages, Keynote, Numbers, Preview, and TextEdit.

In these programs, your document is saved every time there's even the tiniest pause in your typing or working—in the background. No progress bar, no interruption. If you quit or close the document without remembering to save, no problem: your work will be there when you open the document again later.

Note: "But wait a minute," cry the masses—"I *like* being able to close a document without saving changes! Sometimes all I wanted to do was fool around, play 'what-if' games—and then close it without saving changes!"

Just for you, in Mountain Lion, Apple put a pair of sneaky little checkboxes into System Preferences→General. First, "Ask to keep changes when closing documents." If that's turned on, then when you close a document with unsaved changes, the Mac asks if you want to keep the edits, just as it does in all other programs.

But if you *quit* the program without saving, your changes *are* auto-preserved; Auto Save apps autosave your documents when you quit their programs, so you can pick up where you left off the next time. You can override that, too, if you like; turn on "Close windows when quitting an application," also in System Preferences→General. Now you'll get the "Save changes?" box when you quit the app with unsaved changes.

Versions

In those enlightened programs that work with Auto Save, there's a more complicated but more powerful feature at work: Versions. It's an invisible paper trail of every in-progress condition of your document—and you can return to any earlier version at any time. You can even return to an earlier version and copy just a *chunk* of it into the current version, which is great when one paragraph of your previous draft was gold, but the rest was junk.

The Versions world of document management is quite a bit different from the old setup. Here's what you need to know:

- **All the version information is stored in the same original document file.** (It's not like there's a rat's nest of icons for each thing you're working on.) But when you send the document to somebody else (by email or network, for example), the Mac is smart enough to send only the current version, stripping out all the history. Nobody will ever know how much you labored over your work (or how little).

Note: Behind the scenes, the various versions of each document are saved in an invisible folder on your hard drive called *.DocumentRevisions-V100*. But you probably guessed that.

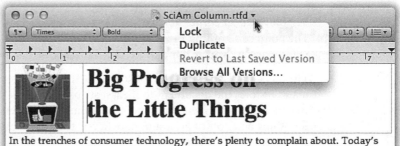

Figure 5-29:
Point to the title of your document to see this secret menu. It contains the full list of commands that pertain to Versions.

- **OS X creates a new snapshot of your document once an hour.** You can also create new snapshots manually at even shorter intervals—by using the File→Save command (⌘-S), as you always have.

These snapshots, or *versions,* represent rewind points that you can return to later, even months or years after you first created the document. Thoughtfully enough, the Mac records, invisibly, only what's *changed* between versions, so your files don't get all big and bloated.

Note: All right, you don't have *total* time-rewinding control. Mountain Lion stores hourly versions for a day, daily versions for a month, and weekly versions for all previous months.

- **The Save As command is hidden in these programs.** It appears in the File menu only when you hold down the Option key.

Apple's hoping that you'll learn to use the new way. When you want to spin off a different version of a document—to experiment with taking it into a radical new direction, for example—choose File→Duplicate. (Or choose Duplicate from the title-bar menu shown in Figure 5-29.)

Before your very eyes, a copy of the open window springs into existence. If the original was called "Kumquat Tarts," then the new one is called "Kumquat Tarts copy"—but that name is highlighted, selected, right in the title bar.

To leave your duplicated document in the same folder as the original, just type a new name and press Return. To file it in a different folder, choose File→Save. You get the standard Save dialog box, where you can choose a name and a folder for it.

Tip: You can also choose to move a document to a different folder later right there in the program—a first in the Mac operating system. Just choose File→Move To, and choose a new storage bin for it. (You can even store it in iCloud at this point; see page 226.)

- **There's a secret Versions menu in the title bar.** Point to the name of your document. In Auto Save–compatible files, a little ▾ appears in the title bar (Figure 5-29).

Rewinding to an earlier version

The point of all of this, of course, is to make it easy to go back in time—to undo the mediocre work you've done, or to resurrect some genius work that you later deleted.

The quick way is to choose File→Revert to→Last Saved (or Last Opened). That command restores the document to the last snapshot version (or to the way it was when you most recently opened it, if no new versions have been created). That, of course, is nothing new; lots of programs have Revert to Saved commands that work similarly.

What's new is that you can revert your document to *any* snapshot, even an ancient one from weeks or months ago.

To do that, choose File→Revert to→Browse All Versions. (Or open the Versions menu shown in Figure 5-29, and from the pop-up menu, choose Browse All Versions.)

After a moment, you see the stunning display shown in Figure 5-30. On the left, you see your document in its current condition. On the right, you see a stack of windows that represent all the different snapshots of your document, going back in time. (And behind it all, you see another sort of version: Apple's animated, starry version of the galaxy.)

Figure 5-30:
If you've ever used OS X's Time Machine feature, this display should look familiar. It's your chance to go back in time to recover an earlier, better version of your document (or just a part of it).

You can have all kinds of productive fun in this version browser:

- **Compare the current version (on the left) with the next-most-recent one (on the right).** These are live documents, so you can scroll through them as necessary. If you decide to stick with the latest edition on the left, just click Done. You leave the starry version-history world and go back to editing.

- **Zoom back in time to inspect older versions (snapshots) of your document.** On the right side of the screen, you see earlier versions of the document—maybe even dozens of them, stretching back in time.

 You can click individual windows' title bars to see what's in them. You can also click or drag your cursor through the notches at the right side. It's like a time ruler that flies through the windows into the past. (As you go, the time/date stamp below the right-side window identifies where you are in time—that is, which version you're examining.)

• **Restore an earlier version.** If you finally find the incarnation of the document you consider superior to your current one, click Restore. You leave Starry Versionland and return to your document, which has now been rewound to its earlier condition.

If you later decide you should not have gone back to that earlier version, no problem. Your later version—the one you started out with—is still in the version browser, too. So you can fast-forward back to it, if necessary.

Tip: If you press Option, the Restore button changes to say Restore a Copy. In other words, you'll create a previous-version duplicate of the document, without disturbing the current condition of the one you've just been working on.

• **Restore *part* of an earlier version.** Often, the current version of your work is *generally* good, but you really wish you could recover *one* magical sentence or paragraph or section—something you've since edited or deleted.

You can do that in Starry Versionland, too, because Copy and Paste work here!

Use the time ruler to find the earlier edition of your document, the one containing the good stuff. Then drag through the desired text or graphics in the window on the right, as shown in Figure 5-30. Now copy the highlighted material (either press ⌘-C, or move your mouse to the top of the screen so that the menu bar appears, and choose Edit→Copy). Click in the *current* version of the document, the one

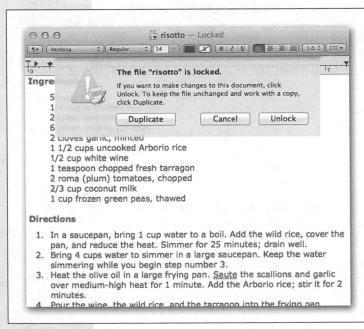

Figure 5-31:
If you try to make changes to a document, the Mac gives you two choices. You can unlock the document or click Duplicate, which spins off an unlocked perfect copy.

at left, and now paste (⌘-V, or use the menu bar). Click Done to complete this astonishing act of salvation.

- **Delete a version.** There are all kinds of reasons why you might want to delete one of your older snapshots. Maybe you wrote it in a fit of pique (or exhaustion), and you want to make sure nobody ever, ever reads that awful prose. Maybe you know there's nothing valuable in it, and you'd rather not dedicate hard drive space to it.

 In any case, deleting a version is easy to do. Once you're in Starry Versionland, point to the ▾ in the title bar of the version (on the right side). You'll discover that the menu now contains only one command: Delete This Version. Click Delete in the confirmation box. Any questions?

Tip: If you press Option, the command says Delete *Old* Versions. Once you confirm your decision, you'll be left with only the most recent edition, without any way to rewind.

Revert

Here's another important Mountain Lion fix: the File→Revert To command is back.

In fact, you can revert to the Last Opened or Last Saved version of the file. Yes, even though Auto Save is constantly backing up your document, it also remembers how the file looked the moment you opened it. And you want to know what's crazy? It can revert to that condition even if you've been manually saving your work all along! That's better than the old Revert command ever was.

Locking documents

If all this version recording is making you dizzy, you can call a halt. You can freeze a document in its current condition so that nobody can make any further changes to it. You might lock a contract document before you send it to someone, for example, or just freeze your novel into what you hope is its final form.

To do that, click the ▾ in the title bar; from the shortcut menu, choose Lock.

Now the title bar says "Locked." If you try to edit the document, you're offered the dialog box shown in Figure 5-31.

(Fortunately, OS X no longer locks every document two weeks after you last made changes to it, as it did in Lion.)

Documents in the Cloud

Truth is, "cloud" is an annoying buzzword. Most of the time, when people say "in the cloud," they mean "online" or "on the Internet"—terms that have served us perfectly well for years.

In any case, one of Mountain Lion's headline new features is "documents in the cloud"— which means, of course, saving your files online, into an iCloud storage locker. The advantage here is that your file is now available for opening or editing from any computer you use, including iPhones, iPads, and iPod Touches.

Your programs have to be Mountain Lionized before they offer this option—and at the outset, only Pages, Keynote, Numbers, Preview, and TextEdit have the documents-in-the-cloud treatment.

Tip: *If you'd rather not see the* ☁ *iCloud buttons shown in Figure 5-32, open System Preferences→iCloud and turn off Documents and Data. That makes the iCloud option disappear from the Save and Open boxes.*

Saving, Opening, and Moving Files

Using this feature couldn't be simpler:

- **Save a document to iCloud** by choosing File→Save in the usual way. When the Save box appears, choose iCloud from the Where pop-up menu (Figure 5-32, top), if it's not already selected. Or choose an iCloud folder's name, if you've made one.

- **Open a document later from iCloud** by choosing File→Open in the usual way. The usual Open dialog box has a new button that wasn't there before: iCloud. Click it to see the list of documents you've saved online (Figure 5-32, bottom).

Tip: *You can also add documents to your iCloud storage locker by dragging their icons into the Open dialog box shown in Figure 5-32, right off the desktop in the Finder.*

Figure 5-32:
Top: iCloud-aware programs like TextEdit propose saving new documents online.

Bottom: When you click the iCloud button in the top left corner of the Open box, you see all of the documents you've saved online, from newest to oldest. You can switch between list and icon views (lower left). You can create folders by dragging one icon onto another. You can even send these documents on to others, using the ↪ button.

- **Move a document between your Mac and iCloud** by choosing File→Move To. You get a tiny version of the Save sheet, where you can choose either iCloud or any folder on your Mac. When you click Move, that file physically moves—from iCloud to your Mac, or vice versa.

Tip: The dialog box shown in Figure 5-32 shows your iCloud-saved documents, and lets you open them, even when you're offline. How? Tursn out your Mac stores a secret "local" copy. The changes you mtake won't update the online copy, until you're online again, but at least you're never cut off from your own files.

All of this hints at a crazy new conception of file storage. You can't start at the desktop. You have to open the program you want *first*, and then open up the document you want from within it.

The Open and Save dialog boxes for iCloud-stored files have *some* traditional features—list view and icon view, for example, a Search bar, and the ability to put things folders (see Figure 5-32)—but not very many. iCloud's "desktop" for your files is about where the Mac was in 1989.

Documents Across Devices

Some programs are available for more than one machine—including Apple's own iWork suite (Numbers, Pages, Keynote). Those programs are available for Mac, iPhone/iPod Touch, and iPad.

In that delicious situation, you can create or edit a document on *one* kind of machine, and marvel as iCloud automatically syncs it with all your *other* devices. You can edit a Pages file on the Mac, jump on a train, and continue editing it on your iPad; any changes you make are saved back to the online copy.

All you have to do is open System Preferences→iCloud and turn on Documents & Data. (Caution: When you open an iWork file on the iPad, you may lose some of the features that it had on the Mac, like footnotes. That's because the iPad version doesn't offer the complete features list.)

From now on, any documents you save to iCloud, as described above, are available on other Macs, iPhones, iPads, and iPod Touches.

Cocoa and Carbon

OS X was supposed to make life simpler. It was supposed to eliminate the confusion and complexity that the old Mac OS had accumulated over the years—and replace it with a smooth, simple, solid system.

Someday, that's exactly what OS X will be. For the moment, however, you're stuck with running two different kinds of programs, each with different characteristics: *Cocoa and Carbon.*

The explanation involves a little bit of history and a little bit of logic. To take full advantage of Mac OS X's considerable technical benefits, software companies had to write new programs for it from scratch. So what should Apple have done—sent out

an email to the authors of the 18,000 existing Mac programs, suggesting that they throw out their programs and rewrite them from the bottom up?

At most big software companies, that suggestion would wind up on the Joke of the Week bulletin board.

Instead, Apple gave software companies a break. It wrote Mac OS X to let programmers and software companies choose precisely how much work they wanted to put into compatibility with the new system. There are two levels:

- **Update the existing programs (Carbon).** If programmers were willing to put *some* effort into getting with the Mac OS X program, they could simply adapt, or update, their existing software.

 The resulting software looks and feels almost like a true OS X program—you get the crash protection, the good looks, the cool-looking graphics, the Save sheets, and so on—but behind the scenes, the bulk of the computer programming is the same as it was in Mac OS 9. These are what Apple calls *Carbonized* programs, named for the technology (Carbon) that permits them to run on OS X.

 For years, many famous Mac programs were simply Carbonized: Photoshop versions before CS3, FileMaker before version 11, Microsoft Office before version 2011, and so on. Believe it or not, the Finder itself was a Carbon program until Snow Leopard (Mac OS X 10.6) came along. After six years, Apple finally rewrote the Finder from scratch as a true-blue Cocoa program.

 Most Carbonized programs don't offer all the features available to OS X, however. In the following pages, you'll discover which OS X goodies you sacrifice when using programs adapted this way.

 On the other hand, such software offers a feature that software companies like *a lot:* A Carbon program is a lot easier to write concurrently with a Windows version of the same software. A Cocoa program, by contrast, is almost certainly locked into Macintosh-Only Land.

FREQUENTLY ASKED QUESTION

The Return of Classic?

Are you kidding me? Classic is gone? No more Mac OS 9 at all? But I need to run a couple of old programs!

Yes, the Classic mode—which, until Mac OS X 10.5, let you run older Mac OS 9 programs in a sort of simulation mode—is gone. You can run only OS X programs in OS X.

Or at least that's what Apple wants you to think. Truth is, there's a sneaky way to run Mac OS 9 programs, even in

Mountain Lion: a little something called SheepShaver. It's an open-source Classic Mac emulator, meaning that it's been written by volunteer collaborators across the Internet.

SheepShaver is difficult to install and isn't what you'd call rock solid. But it's good to know that, someday, when you absolutely, positively have to run that old program, you're not entirely out of luck.

- **Write new programs from scratch (Cocoa).** As OS X became more popular, more software companies created programs exclusively for it. The geeks call such programs *Cocoa* applications. Although they look exactly like Carbonized programs, they feel a little bit more smooth and solid. And they offer a number of special features that Carbonized programs don't offer.

 These days, almost every name-brand program is a true Cocoa application, including Photoshop, Microsoft Office, FileMaker, iMovie, iPhoto, iDVD, Safari, Messages, TextEdit, Stickies, Mail, Contacts, and so on.

The Cocoa Difference

Here are some of the advantages Cocoa programs offer. May it clear up any confusion you have about why certain features seem to be present only occasionally.

Note: The following features appear in almost all Cocoa programs. That's not to say that you'll never see these features in *Carbonized* programs; the occasional Carbon program may offer one of these features or another. That's because programmers have to do quite a bit of work to bring them into Carbon applications—and almost none to include them in Cocoa ones.

The Font panel

The Mac has always been the designer's preferred computer, and OS X only strengthens its position. For one thing, OS X comes with over 200 beautiful fonts that Apple licensed from commercial type companies.

When you use a Carbon program, you usually access these fonts the same way as always: using a Font menu. But when you use a Cocoa program, you get the Font *panel,* which makes it far easier to organize, search, and use your font collection. Chapter 15 describes fonts, and the Font panel, in more detail.

Retina friendliness

In general, Cocoa programs automatically sharpen up their text when you view it on a Retina display—Apple's name for super-high-resolution screens like the one on the 2012 MacBook Pro. Text in Carbonized programs, on the other hand, looks blotchy and awful until their software companies make the effort to make them Retina-friendly.

Title-bar tricks

You may remember from Chapter 2 that the title bar of every Finder window harbors a secret pop-up menu. When you Control-click it (or right-click it, or ⌘-click it), you're shown a little folder ladder that delineates your current position in your folder hierarchy. You may also remember that the tiny icon just to the left of the window's name is actually a handle you can drag to move a folder into a different window.

In Cocoa programs, you get the same features in *document* windows, as shown back in Figure 2-5 (page 84). By dragging the tiny document icon next to the document's name, you can perform stunts—like dragging that little icon to the desktop, or to the Dock icon of a different program for opening—right from your document's title bar.

Secret keyboard shortcuts

For the most part, it's possible to ignore the Unix that beats within the heart of OS X. But every now and then, a refreshing reminder pokes its head up through the fields of gradient gray—and here's one of them.

Although you'll never see it mentioned in the instruction manuals for Cocoa applications (if there even were such things as instruction manuals anymore), most of

The Color Picker

Here and there—in System Preferences, iMovie, TextEdit, Microsoft Office, and many other programs—OS X offers you the opportunity to choose a *color* for some element: for your desktop background, a window, and so on.

The dialog box that appears offers a miniature color lab that lets you dial in any color in the Mac's rainbow—several color labs, actually, arrayed across the top, each designed to make color choosing easier in certain circumstances:

Color wheel. Drag the scroll bar vertically to adjust the brightness, and then drag your cursor around the ball to pick the shade.

Color sliders. From the pop-up menu, choose the color-mixing method you prefer. CMYK stands for cyan, magenta, yellow, and black. People in the printing industry will feel immediately at home, because these four colors are the component inks for color printing. (These people may also be able to explain why K stands for black.)

RGB is how a TV or computer monitor thinks of colors: as proportions of red, green, and blue light. Gray Scale means shades of gray, like a black-and-white TV. And HSB stands for Hue, Saturation, and Brightness—a favorite color-specifying scheme in scientific circles.

In each case, just drag the sliders to mix up the color you want, or type in the percentages of each component.

Color palettes. This option presents canned sets of color swatches. They're primarily for programmers who want quick access to the standard colors in OS X. The Web Safe

Colors list is useful for Web designers, too; they can use it to ensure that the color they choose will display properly on other computers.

Image palettes. Here's the visible rainbow arrayed yet another way: in cloudy, color-arranged streaks. (Cool tip: If you drag a graphics file directly into the dialog box, it appears in the spectrum's place. That's a handy trick if you're trying to identify the color of a certain spot of an image, for example. And don't miss the pop-up button at the bottom of the dialog box, which offers a few other stunts.)

Crayons. Now this is a good user interface. You can click each crayon to see its color name: Mocha, Fern, Cayenne, and so on. (Some interior decorator in Cupertino had a field day naming these crayons.)

In any of these color pickers, you can also "sample" a color that's outside the dialog box—a color you found on a Web page, for example. Just click the magnifying-glass icon and then move your cursor around the screen. You'll see the sliders and numbers change inside the dialog box automatically when you click.

Finally, note that you can store frequently used (or frequently admired) colors in the tiny palette squares at the bottom. To do that, drag the big rectangular color swatch (next to the magnifying glass) directly down into one of the little squares, where it will stay fresh for weeks.

If you don't have space for all the colors you want at the bottom of the window, you can drag the small circular dot down to make room for more.

them respond to certain keystrokes left over from the NeXT operating system, which was OS X's ancestor. If you're a card-carrying number of KIAFTMA (the Keyboard Is Always Faster Than the Mouse Association), you'll love these additional keyboard navigation strokes:

- **Control-A.** Moves your insertion point to the beginning of the paragraph. (*Mnemonic:* A = beginning of the Alphabet.)

- **Control-E.** Deposits your insertion point at the end of the paragraph. (*Mnemonic:* E = End.)

- **Control-D.** Forward delete (deletes the letter to the *right* of the insertion point).

- **Control-K.** Instantly deletes all text from the insertion point to the right end of the line. (*Mnemonic:* K = Kills the rest of the line.)

- **Control-O.** Inserts a paragraph break, much like Return, but leaves the insertion point where it was, above the break. This is the ideal trick for breaking a paragraph in half when you've just thought of a better ending for the first part.

- **Control-T.** Moves the insertion point one letter to the right—and along with it, drags whichever letter was to its left. (*Mnemonic:* T = Transpose letters.)

- **Option-Delete.** Deletes the entire word to the left of the insertion point. When you're typing along in a hurry and you discover that you've just made a typo, this is the keystroke you want. It's much faster to nuke the previous word and retype it than to fiddle around with the mouse and the insertion point just to fix one letter.

Figure 5-33:
The beauty of being able to select multiple blobs of text is that you can format all of them simultaneously (making them bold, for example) with one click. You can also copy the selected portions; when you paste them into a different document, you get a tidy excerpt containing only the parts you wanted, all run together.

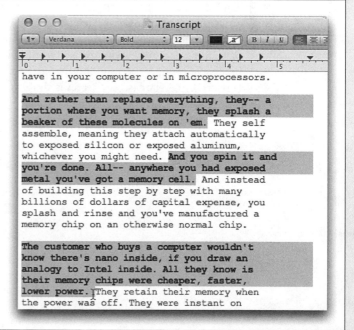

Four additional keystrokes duplicate the functions of the arrow keys. Still, as long as you've got your pinky on that Control key…

- **Control-B, Control-F.** Move the insertion point one character to the left or right, just like the left and right arrow keys. (*Mnemonic:* **Back, Forward**).

- **Control-N, Control-P.** Move the insertion point one row down or up, like the down and up arrow keys. (*Mnemonic:* **Next, Previous**).

Cool text-selection tricks

By holding down certain keys while dragging through text in a Cocoa program, you gain some wild and wacky text-selection powers (especially useful in, for example, TextEdit and Pages):

- **Highlight only one column** out of several by Option-dragging. Instead of highlighting all the text, margin to margin, you get only the text within your selection rectangle.

- **Highlight several passages simultaneously** by ⌘-dragging. Each time you ⌘-drag, you highlight another block of text, even though the earlier blocks are still selected (see Figure 5-33).

Tip: In most Cocoa programs, you can combine these two tricks. That is, you can select multiple, arbitrary (not full-page-width) blocks of text by pressing both Option and ⌘ as you drag.

Background window control

The ⌘ key unlocks a slick trick in Cocoa programs: It lets you operate the buttons and controls of an inactive background window without bringing it to the front. You can operate a background window's resize box, buttons, pop-up menus, and scroll bars, all while another window is in front of it. In fact, you can even *drag through text* in a background window—and then drag and drop it into the foreground window. (Freaky!) In every case, the secret is simply to keep ⌘ pressed as you click or drag.

Data: Typing, Dictating, Sharing & Backing Up

The original 1984 Mac didn't make jaws drop because of its speed, price, or sleek looks. What amazed people was the simplicity and elegance of the user interface. At some point in every Apple demo, the presenter copied a graphic drawn in a painting program (MacPaint) and pasted it directly into a word processor (MacWrite), where it appeared neatly nestled between typed paragraphs of text.

We take these examples of data input and data exchange for granted today. But in those days, that little stunt struck people like a thunderbolt. After all, if this little computer let you copy and paste between different programs, it could probably do anything.

Today, the Mac is even more adept at helping you enter, move, and share your hard-won data. OS X offers several ways to move information within a single document, between documents, between programs, and even between the Mac and Windows computers. This chapter leads you through this broad cycle of data: from entering it with the mouse and keyboard, to moving it around, to backing it up.

The Macintosh Keyboard

All through this book, you'll find references to certain keys on Apple's keyboards. "Hold down the ⏏ key," you might read, or "Press Control-F2." If you're coming from Mac OS 9, from Windows, or even from a typewriter, you might be a bit befuddled. (The reader email generated by previous editions of this book made that quite clear. "The alphabet has 26 letters," one went. "Why do I need 101 keys?")

To make any attempt at an explanation even more complicated, Apple's keyboards keep changing. The one you're using right now is probably one of these models:

- **The current keyboards,** where the keys are flat little jobbers that poke up through square holes in the aluminum (Figure 6-1). That's what you get on current laptops, wired keyboards, and Bluetooth wireless keyboards.

Figure 6-1:
On the top row of aluminum Mac keyboards, the F-keys have dual functions. Ordinarily, the F1 through F4 keys correspond to Screen Dimmer (☀), Screen Brighter (☀), Mission Control (▦), and either Dashboard (◉) or Launchpad (⊞⊞⊞). Pressing the Fn key in the corner changes their personality.

- **The older, plastic desktop keyboards,** or the white or black plastic laptop ones.

Here, then, is a guided tour of the non-typewriter keys on the modern Mac keyboard:

Tip: To see closeups of Apple's current wired and wireless keyboards, visit *www.apple.com/keyboard*.

- **Fn.** How are you supposed to pronounce Fn? Not "function," certainly; after all, the F-keys on the top row are already known as function keys. And not "fun"; goodness knows, the Fn key isn't particularly hilarious to press.

 What it *does*, though, is quite clear: It changes the purpose of certain keys. That's a big deal on laptops, which don't have nearly as many keys as desktop keyboards. So for some of the less commonly used functions, you're supposed to press Fn and a regular key. (For example, Fn turns the ↑ key into a Page Up key, which scrolls upward by one screenful.)

Note: On most Mac keyboards, the Fn key is in the lower-left corner. The exception is the full-size Apple desktop keyboard (the one with a numeric keypad); there, the Fn key is in the little block of keys between the letter keys and the number pad.

You'll find many more Fn examples in the following paragraphs.

- **Numeric keypad.** The number-pad keys do exactly the same thing as the numbers at the top of the keyboard. But with practice, typing things like phone numbers and prices is much faster with the number pad, since you don't have to look down at what you're doing.

 Apple has been quietly eliminating the numeric keypad from most of its keyboards, but you can still find it on some keyboard models. And on some old Mac laptops, the numbers 0 through 9 have been painted onto a block of *letter* keys near the

right side. (1, 2, and 3 are J, K, and L, for example.) You can turn those letter keys into their numeric alter egos by pressing the Fn key with your left hand.

Eventually, Apple eliminated this embedded-keyboard effect from its laptops, having discovered that almost nobody was using it.

- ☼, ☀ (**F1, F2**). These keys control the brightness of your screen. Usually, you can tone it down a bit when you're in a dark room or when you want to save laptop battery power; you'll want to crank it up in the sun.

Tip: If you hold down the Shift and Option keys, then tapping the brightness keys adjusts the brightness by just a little bit—a fraction of one of the larger brightness steps. Control freaks, rejoice.

- ▦ (**F3**). This one fires up Mission Control, the handy window-management feature described in Chapter 5.

- ☉ or ▦ (**F4**). Tap the ☉ key to open Dashboard, the archipelago of tiny, single-purpose widgets like Weather, Stocks, and Movies. Chapter 5 describes Dashboard in detail.

 On recent Macs, the F4 key bears a ▦ logo instead. Tapping it opens (what else?) Launchpad, which is described on page 164.

- ☼, ☀ (**F5, F6**). Most recent Mac laptops have light-up *keys,* which is very handy indeed when you're typing in the dark. The key lights are supposed to come on automatically when it's dark, but you can also control the illumination yourself by tapping these keys. (On most other Macs, the F5 and F6 keys aren't assigned to anything. They're free for you to use as you see fit.)

- ◄◄, ►ıı, and ►► (**F7, F8, F9**). These keys work in the programs you'd expect: iTunes, QuickTime Player, DVD Player, and other programs where it's handy to have Rewind, Play/Pause, and Fast Forward buttons.

Tip: Tap either ◄◄ or ►► to skip to the previous or next track or chapter. Hold one down to rewind or fast-forward.

- ◄, ◄), ◄)) (**F10, F11, F12**). These three keys control your speaker volume. The ◄ key means Mute; tap it once to cut off the sound completely and again to restore its previous level. Tap the ◄) repeatedly to make the sound level lower, the ◄)) key to make it louder.

 With each tap, you see a big white version of each key's symbol on your screen, your Mac's little nod to let you know it understands your efforts.

Tip: If you hold down the Shift and Option keys, then tapping the volume keys adjusts the volume by smaller increments, just as with the brightness keys.

- ⏏. This is the Eject key. When there's a CD or DVD in your Mac, tap this key to make the computer spit it out.

- **Home, End.** The Home key jumps to the top of a window, the End key to the bottom. If you're looking at a list of files, the Home and End keys jump to the top or bottom of the list. In iPhoto, they jump to the first or last photo in your collection. In iMovie, the Home key rewinds your movie to the very beginning. In Safari, it's the top or bottom of the Web page.

 (In Word, they jump to the beginning or end of the line. But then again, Microsoft has always had its own ways of doing things.)

 On keyboards without a dedicated block of number keys, you get these functions by holding down Fn as you tap the ← and → keys.

- **Pg Up, Pg Down.** These keys scroll up or down by one screenful. The idea is to let you scroll through word-processing documents, Web pages, and lists without having to use the mouse.

 On keyboards without a numeric keypad, you get these functions by pressing Fn plus the ↑ and ↓ keys.

- **Clear.** Clear (on the old full-size keyboards only) gets rid of whatever you've highlighted, but without putting a copy on the invisible Clipboard, as the Cut command would do.

- **Esc.** Esc stands for Escape, and it means "cancel." It's fantastically useful. It closes dialog boxes, dismisses menus, and exits special modes like Quick Look, slideshows, screen savers, and so on. Get to know it.

- **Delete.** The backspace key.

- **⌦.** Many a Mac fan goes for years without discovering the handiness of this delightful little key: the Forward Delete key. Whereas Delete backspaces over whatever letter is just to the *left* of the insertion point, this one (labeled Del on older keyboards) deletes whatever is just to the *right* of the insertion point. It comes in handy when, for example, you've clicked into some text to make an edit—but wound up planting your cursor in just the wrong place.

 The old full-size Apple keyboard has a dedicated key for this. On all other keyboards, you get this function by holding down Fn as you tap the regular Delete key.

- **Return and Enter.** In almost all programs, these keys do the same thing: Wrap your typing to the next line. When a dialog box is on the screen, tapping the Return or Enter key is the same as clicking the confirmation button (like OK or Done). Very few programs treat these keys as different, although Microsoft Excel is one of them.

- **⌘.** This key triggers keyboard shortcuts for menu items.

- **Control.** The Control key triggers shortcut menus, described on the following pages.

- **Option.** The Option key (labeled Alt on keyboards in some countries) is sort of a "miscellaneous" key. It's the equivalent of the Alt key in Windows. It lets you access secret features—you'll find them described all through this book—and type special

symbols. For example, you press Option-4 to get the ¢ symbol, and Option-Y to get the ¥ (yen) symbol.

- **Help.** In the Finder, Microsoft programs, and a few other places, this key opens up the electronic help screens. But you'd guessed that.

The Complicated Story of the Function Keys

As the previous section makes clear, the F-keys at the top of modern Mac keyboards come with predefined functions. They control screen brightness, keyboard brightness, speaker volume, music playback, and so on.

But they didn't always. Before Apple gave F9, F10, and F11 to the fast-forward and speaker-volume functions, those keys controlled the Exposé window-management function described in Chapter 5.

So the question is: What if you don't *want* to trigger the hardware features of these keys? What if you want pressing F1 to mean "F1" (which opens the Help window in some programs)? What if you want F9, F10, and F11 to control Exposé's three modes, as they once did?

For that purpose, you're supposed to press the Fn key. The Fn key (lower left on small keyboards, center block of keys on the big one) switches the function of the function keys. In other words, pressing Fn *and* F10 triggers an Exposé feature, even though the key has a Mute symbol (◄) painted on it.

But here's the thing: What if you use those F-keys for software features (like Cut, Copy, Paste, and Exposé) *more often* than the hardware features (like brightness and volume)?

In that case, you can reverse the logic, so that pressing the F-keys *alone* triggers software functions, and governs brightness and audio only when you're pressing Fn. To do that, choose →System Preferences→Keyboard. Turn on the cryptically worded checkbox "Use F1, F2, etc. as standard function keys."

And that's it. From now on, you press the Fn key to get the functions painted on the keys (◄◄, ►ıı, ►►, ◄, ◄), ◄))), ⋮⋅⋅, ⋰⋅⋅⋅, and so on).

Notes on Right-Clicking

Apple isn't too proud to steal good ideas from Microsoft; goodness knows, Microsoft has stolen enough from Apple. In OS X, *shortcut menus* are more important than ever (Figure 6-2).

They're so important, in fact, that it's worth this ink and this paper to explain the different ways you can trigger a "right-click" (or a *secondary click,* as Apple calls it, because not all of these methods actually involve a second mouse button, and it doesn't *have* to be the right one):

- **Control-click.** For years, you could open the shortcut menu of something on the Mac screen by Control-clicking it—and you still can. That is, while pressing the Control key (bottom row), click the mouse on your target.

• **Right-click.** Experienced computer fans have always preferred the one-handed method: right-clicking. That is, clicking something by pressing the *right* mouse button on a two-button mouse.

Figure 6-2:
A shortcut menu is one that pops out of something you're clicking—an icon, a button, a folder. The beauty of a shortcut menu is that its commands are contextual. They bring up useful commands in exactly the spots where they're most useful, in menus that are relevant only to what you're clicking.

"Ah, but that's what's always driven me nuts about Apple," goes the common refrain. "Their refusal to get rid of their stupid one-button mouse!"

Well, not so fast.

First of all, you can attach any old $6 USB two-button mouse to the Mac, and it'll work flawlessly. Recycle the one from your old PC, if you like.

Furthermore, if you've bought a desktop Mac since late 2005, you probably already *have* a two-button mouse—but you might not realize it. Take a look: Is it a white, shiny plastic capsule with a tiny, gray scrolling track-pea on the far end? Then you have a Mighty Mouse. Is it a cordless, flattened capsule instead? Then it's a Magic Mouse. Each has a *secret* right mouse button. It doesn't work until you ask for it.

To do that, choose →System Preferences. Click Mouse. There, in all its splendor, is a diagram of the Mighty or Magic Mouse.

Your job is to choose Secondary Button from the pop-up menu that identifies the right side of the mouse. (The reason it's not called a "right button" is because left-handers might prefer to reverse the right and left functions.)

From now on, even though there aren't two visible mouse buttons, your Mighty Mouse does, in fact, register a left-click or a right-click depending on which side of the mouse you push down. It works a lot more easily than it sounds like it would.

• **Use the trackpad.** If you have a trackpad (a laptop, for example), you can trigger a right-click in all kinds of ways.

Out of the box, you do it by clicking the trackpad with *two* fingers. The shortcut menu pops right up.

Or you can use the pre-Lion method, which still works: Point to whatever you want to click. Rest two fingers on the trackpad—and then click with your thumb.

Figure 6-3:
The Trackpad pane of System Preferences looks different depending on your laptop model. But this one shows the three ways to get a "right-click."

But even those aren't the end of your options. In System Preferences→Trackpad, you can also turn on even more right-click methods (and watch little videos on how to do them; see Figure 6-3). For example, you can "right-click" by clicking either the lower-right or lower-left corner of the trackpad—one finger only.

Power Typing

Something strange has been quietly taking place at Apple: *Typing* has been getting a lot of attention.

It began when Apple created *system-wide* spelling and grammar checkers. For the first time in computer history, the *operating system* took over typos and grammos. You didn't have to maintain a separate spelling checker for each program you used. Now there's just one, and it works in most programs: TextEdit, Stickies, Messages, Mail,

Calendar, Safari, Pages, iPhoto, iMovie, and so on. Add a word to the dictionary in one program, and it's available to all the others.

Today, there's much more. There's text substitution, where you type *addr* and the system types out "Irwina P. McGillicuddy, 1293 Eastport Lane, Harborvilletown, MA, 02552." (The same system autocorrects common typos like *teh* instead of *the.*) There's also a case-flipping feature that can change selected text to ALL CAPS, all lowercase, or First Letter Capped. Both of these new features are available in most Apple programs and in any other programs that tap into OS X's built-in text-processing circuitry (although not, alas, Microsoft programs).

GEM IN THE ROUGH

Instant Accented Characters, Courtesy of the iPhone

It's been a problem since the dawn of computing: How do you produce accented characters—líké thêsë—on a keyboard with only 26 letter keys?

For most of computing history, the answer has been: You bring up some special palette on the screen, or you memorize key combinations. And yes, those options are still available in OS X.

But today, there's a new option, which Apple stole from its own iPhone software: Hold down the letter you want accented—*e*, for example. After a moment, you get a pop-up panel of possible accented versions. You can click the one you want, or, if you'd rather not lift your hands off the keyboard, you can type the corresponding number that appears in light gray beneath each letter.

This feature works in almost all programs, although there may be some where it doesn't…pop up.

Now, if you're the kind of person who needs accents from time to time, you're probably delighted with this new, clever way to get them. But if holding down a key produces an accented character, that means holding down a key no longer *repeats* the key, right? It means you can no longer

type, "You go, grrrrrrrrrl!" or "rated XXXXXXXX" or "I love you SOOOOOOOOOOO much!" Right?

Right. A few characters that people routinely type lines of, like ***** and ……. and ____, still repeat when you hold them down. But none of the 26 letter ketys repeat anymore.

There are, fortunately, a couple of quick and easy ways to restore the old key-repeating behavior, if you're a "SOOOOO much" kind of person.

The non-intimidating way is to download the free program Lion Tweaks. It's available on this book's "Missing CD" page at *www.missingmanuals.com*. Open it up, and where it says, "Enable repeating keys," click Yes. Ta-da!

The non-downloading way is to open up Terminal (page 469). Type this one line, exactly as it appears here:

```
defaults write -g ApplePressAnd-
HoldEnabled -bool false
```

…and then press Enter. Log out and back in.

Either way, you've just flipped off the switch for the new Lion accent picker. Now every key repeats, just as it always used to.

The OS X Spelling and Grammar Checker

Your Mac can give you live, interactive spelling and grammar checking, just as in Microsoft Word and other word processors. That is, misspelled words or badly written sentences or fragments get flagged with a dashed red underline (for grammar problems, a green underline) the moment you type them. Here's the crash course:

- **Check the spelling of one word:** Highlight the word. Choose Edit→Spelling and Grammar→Show Spelling and Grammar. The spell-check dialog box opens, with the proposed corrections visible.

- **Check spelling as you type.** Choose Edit→Spelling and Grammar→Check Spelling While Typing. (If Check Grammar With Spelling is turned on in the same submenu, you'll get a grammar check, too.)

 Now, as you type, you'll see those red and green underlines on words the Mac thinks represent spelling or grammar mistakes. To fix one, Control-click (right-click) the underlined word, and proceed as shown in Figure 6-4.

Tip: In TextEdit, the factory setting for error-underlining is On. To turn it off for all new documents, choose TextEdit→Preferences, click New Document, and then turn off "Check spelling as you type."

- **Check spelling after the document is finished.** Choose Edit→Spelling and Grammar→Show Spelling and Grammar (or press ⌘-:). The Spelling dialog box appears.

Figure 6-4:
Top: You're never more than a Control-click (or right-click) away from more accurate spelling. Once you Control-click a questionable word, the suggestions of Apple's built-in dictionary appear right in the shortcut menu, along with the Learn Spelling and Ignore Spelling commands.

Bottom: If you've opted for autocorrected spelling, you get the little iPhoney suggestion bubble when you pause after typing a word. Ignore it to accept the suggestion; click the X in the bubble to keep what you typed.

The first error it spots appears in the top box, with the proposed corrections in the bottom one.

If you like one of Apple's proposals, click it and then click Change. If the word was correct already (for example, the guy's last name really is Teh), then click Find Next ("Leave the word as I typed it"), Ignore ("It's OK everywhere in this document"), or Learn ("Never flag this word again").

Handily enough, you can also click Define to look up a highlighted word (one of the spelling suggestions, for example) in the Mac's built-in Dictionary app. Also handily enough, the spelling checker is smart enough to maintain different spelling checkers (dictionaries) for different languages—and to recognize, within a single document, which language you're using!

• **Fix spelling as you type.** Note the difference. *Checking* your spelling just means "finding the misspelled words." *Fixing* means autocorrecting the errors as they occur, as you type. You might not even notice that it's happening!

This most tantalizing option is found in Edit→Spelling and Grammar→Correct Spelling Automatically. And sure enough, when this option is turned on, common typos like *teh* and *frmo* and *dont* get fixed as you type; you don't have to do anything to make it happen.

Note: If you're typing slowly enough, you might see the suggestion bubble illustrated in Figure 6-4. That, of course, is a feature Apple brought to the Mac from the iPhone/iPad. It's saying, "Here's the word I *think* you meant—and if you just keep on typing, I'll go ahead and make the change I'm proposing. If you disagree, click on the X in the word bubble to make me shut up and leave what you typed, just as you typed it."

It's not perfect. It doesn't correct all errors (or even most of them). It occasionally even corrects a word you didn't mean to have corrected. (When it makes a mistake, hit ⌘-Z, the Undo command, to restore what you typed.) And sometimes it doesn't make the change until you're halfway through the sentence.

Still, though. Kind of cool.

Text Substitution (Abbreviation Expansion)

This useful feature autoreplaces *one* thing you type with something else. Why? Because it can do any of these things.

Insert the proper typographical symbols

For example, the Mac can insert attractive "curly quotes" automatically as you type "straight ones," or em dashes—like this—when you type two hyphens (--like that). It can also insert properly typeset fractions (like ½) when you type "1/2."

You can see the list of built-in substitutions—and create your own—in the System Preferences→Language & Text→Text tab, as shown in Figure 6-5.

Apple doesn't want to drive you nuts, though, so it makes sure *you're* sure you really want these swappings to take place. So you have to turn on each of these features

manually, in each program. (These commands are available anywhere you do a *lot* of typing, like TextEdit, Mail, and Stickies.)

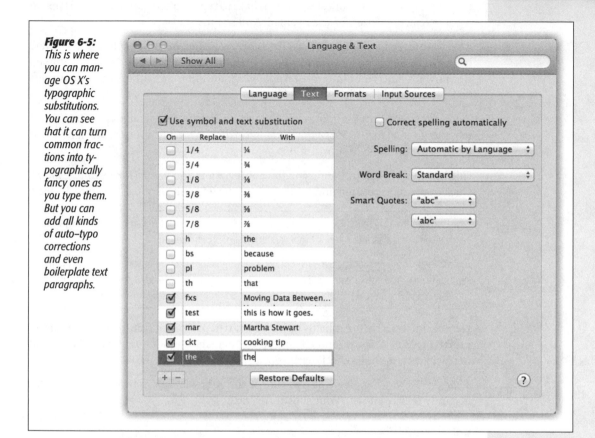

Figure 6-5:
This is where you can manage OS X's typographic substitutions. You can see that it can turn common fractions into typographically fancy ones as you type them. But you can add all kinds of auto–typo corrections and even boilerplate text paragraphs.

- **Auto-quotes.** To make the quotes curlify themselves, choose Edit→Substitutions→ Smart Quotes, so that a checkmark appears.

Note: In the System Preferences→Language & Text→Text tab, you can specify which kind of fancy quotation mark you prefer: «this kind,» „this kind," or whatever. You international thing, you!

- **Auto-dashes.** To turn double hyphens into these (—) long dashes, choose Edit→ Substitutions→Smart Dashes, so that a checkmark appears.

- **Smart links.** There's also an option to create smart links, where any Web address you type turns into a blue, underlined, *clickable* link to a Web page. Turn on Edit→ Substitutions→Smart Links.

Tip: You can also choose Edit→Substitutions→Show Substitutions to make a floating panel appear, complete with on/off checkboxes for all these features.

Replace abbreviations with much longer phrases

You can program *addr* to type your entire return address. Create two-letter abbreviations for big legal or technical words you have to type a lot. Set up *goaway* to type out a polite rejection letter for use in email. And so on.

This feature has been in Microsoft Office forever (called AutoCorrect), and it's always been available as a shareware add-on (TypeIt4Me and TextExpander, for example). But now it's built right into most Apple programs, plus any others that use Apple's text-input plumbing.

You build your list of abbreviations in the System Preferences→Language & Text→Text tab, shown in Figure 6-5. See the list at left? Click the **+** button to create a new row in the scrolling table of substitutions.

Click in the left column and type the abbreviation you want (for example, *addr*). Click in the right column and type, or paste, the text you want OS X to type instead.

Tip: Don't be shy—you're not limited to short snippets. The replacement text can be pages long, which is handy if you're a lawyer and you build your contracts out of boilerplate chunks of canned text.

You can even create multiple paragraphs—but not by hitting Return when you want a new line; no, hitting Return means, "I'm finished entering this text" and closes up the box. Instead, press Option-Return when you want a paragraph break.

Here again, you have to explicitly *turn on* the text-replacement feature in each program (TextEdit, Mail, Stickies, and so on). To do that, choose Edit→Substitutions→Text Replacement, so that a checkmark appears.

That's it! Now, whenever you type one of the abbreviations you've set up, the Mac instantly replaces it with your substituted text.

Case Swapping

The final chunk in OS X's text-massaging tool chest is case swapping—that is, changing text you've already typed (or pasted) from ALL CAPS to lowercase or Just First Letters Capitalized.

FREQUENTLY ASKED QUESTION

Smart Copy and Paste

Hey, I saw one more auto-fix feature in the Edit→Substitutions submenu: "Smart Copy/Paste." What's that about?

It's about spaces.

Ordinarily, when you cut or copy a word out of a sentence and then paste it into a new one, you have some cleanup to do. You leave an extra space behind, and you have to add a

space after the word when you paste.

Smart Copy/Paste simply cleans up these spaces for you. If you cut a word out of a sentence, only *one* space gets left between the words where it used to be. And when you paste text, a space is added on either side automatically—but only one.

This one's simple: Select the text you want to change, and then choose from the Edit→ Transformations submenu. Your options are Make Upper Case (all caps), Make Lower Case (no caps), and Capitalize (first letters, like a movie title).

Keep that in mind the next time some raving lunatic SENDS YOU AN EMAIL THAT WAS TYPED ENTIRELY WITH THE CAPS LOCK KEY DOWN.

Tip: Here's a sneaky one: You can double-tap a word with three fingers on your trackpad to get a pop-up dictionary and thesaurus definition. (That's a light double-*tap,* not a full double-*click.*) This trick doesn't work in all programs, and it requires you to turn it on in System Preferences→Trackpad→Point & Click. And it's a tad bit finicky.

But once you have it working, check it out: It also works in text documents you're examining in Quick Look!

Dictation

For the first time in Mac history, dictation is built into the Mac, just as it is on the latest iPhones and iPads. You can now speak to type.

In fact, Mountain Lion's dictation feature is identical to the iPhone/iPad's. It lets you speak to enter text anywhere, into any program, just by speaking. (Behind the scenes, it's using the same Nuance recognition technology that powers Dragon Dictate.) You can blather away into an email, fire off a text message, or draft a memo without ever looking at the screen.

GEM IN THE ROUGH

The Least-Known Typing Feature

This may come as a shock if you think you know your Mac pretty well, but here goes: OS X actually offers system-wide autocomplete of big words, just like the iPhone.

We're not talking about the spelling checker, and we're not talking about text substitution. We're talking, you start typing a word and the Mac finishes it for you. It's ideal when you're in a hurry, when you're not sure how to finish a word (is it independance or independence?), or when you're trying to solve a crossword puzzle. It works in all the standard Mac programs (TextEdit, Mail, Safari, Pages, and so on).

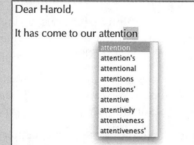

Once you've begun typing a word, press either F5 or Option-Esc to produce the list of possible word completions shown here. If the Mac correctly anticipates the rest of the word, great; press Tab, Return, or the space bar to accept the suggestion, and then keep right on typing. If it guesses wrong, you can either select a different word in the list (using the mouse or the arrow keys), or tap Esc to ignore the suggestions and continue typing.

Now, before you get all excited, here are the necessary footnotes:

- Voice typing works only when you have an Internet connection. (The audio of each utterance is transferred to servers online, which convert it into text and send it back to your screen.)

- Voice typing works best if there's not a lot of background noise. It works even better on Macs that have dual microphones, like the 15-inch MacBook Pro with Retina display; those two mikes create a "beam array"—a directional alignment that helps them differentiate your voice from the background noise.

- Voice typing isn't always practical, since everybody around you can hear what you're doing.

- Voice typing isn't 100 percent accurate. Very often, you'll have to correct an error or two.

All right—expectations set? Then here's how to type by speaking.

Dictation Step by Step

First, fire up some program where you can type. TextEdit, Mail, Word, whatever. Dictation works in any program.

Now tap the Fn key twice. (You can also choose the Start Dictation command, which magically appears in almost every program's Edit menu. Or you can choose a different keystroke, as described below.)

Note: The first time you trigger dictation, the Mac asks for confirmation that you do, indeed, want to turn on dictation. It warns you that proceeding means that the Mac will send the names in your Contacts app to Apple, so that you'll be able to say things like "Dear Mr. Szvredyk" and get a correct transcription. If that prospect unnerves you—if you think that it means that some Apple or Nuance employee will wind up reading the list of names in your personal Rolodex—then you shouldn't proceed.

See the tiny microphone button that appears next to the insertion point (Figure 6-6, top)? When it appears, you hear a single xylophone note. Say what you have to say. You don't have to speak slowly, loudly, or weirdly; speak normally.

You have to speak your own punctuation, like this: "Dear Dad (colon): Please send money (dash)—as much as you can (comma), please (period)." The table at the end of this section describes all the punctuation symbols you can dictate.

After you finish speaking, click Done or press Enter.

Tip: Here's a shortcut. You can also *hold down the Fn key* on the second tap; do your speaking; and then release the key when you're done. In other words, you can use it like a push-to-talk button on a walkie-talkie. That saves you the final press of the Enter key.

The Mac plays another xylophone note—higher, this time—and transmits the audio data to distant computers. They analyze your speech and transmit the resulting typed-out text back to your screen. (During this time, three blinking purple dots occupy the text area where you dictated. You can click Cancel if you're getting impatient.) The transcribed text appears all at once, in a big blob.

If the transcription contains errors, you can click to edit them, exactly as you would fix an error in something you typed. Better yet, if the Mac *knows* it made errors, it underlines them, and you can often fix them with a quick click (Figure 6-6, bottom). Or, if the whole thing is a mess, you can press ⌘-Z, the universal keystroke for Undo.

Usually, you'll find the accuracy pretty darned good, considering you didn't have to train the software to recognize your voice. You'll also find that the accuracy is better when you dictate complete sentences, and long words fare better than short ones.

Figure 6-6:
For the first time, the Mac has a built-in "speak to type" feature.

Top: When you double-press the Fn key, the Mac goes into listening mode. The bouncing glow of the microphone icon is your level meter. It lets you know that the Mac hears you.

If you haven't released the Fn key or clicked Done (or pressed Enter) after 30 seconds, the Mac stops listening on its own. 30 seconds is the maximum talking time per blurt.

Bottom: If you see the dashed underline, Control-click or right-click it. You get a pop-up menu that includes alternative transcriptions.

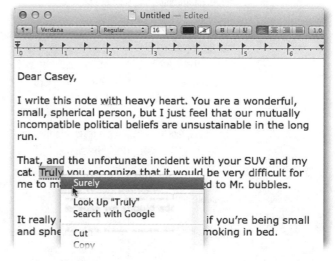

Punctuation

Here's a handy table that shows you what punctuation you can say, and how to say it.

Say this:	To get this:	For example, saying this:	Types this:
"period" or "full stop"	. [space and capital letter afterward]	"Best (period) date (period) ever (period)"	Best. Date. Ever.
"dot" or "point"	. [no space afterward]	"My email is frank (dot) smith (at sign) gmail (dot) com"	My email is frank. smith@gmail.com
"comma," "semicolon," "colon"	, ; :	"Mom (comma) hear me (colon) I'm dizzy (semicolon) tired"	Mom, hear me: I'm dizzy; tired
"question mark," "exclamation point"	? ! [space and capital letter afterward]	"Ellen (question mark) Hi (exclamation point)"	Ellen? Hi!
"inverted question mark," "inverted exclamation point"	¿ ¡	"(inverted question mark) Que paso (question mark) "	¿Que paso?
"ellipsis" or "dot dot dot"	…	"Just one (ellipsis) more (ellipsis) step (ellipsis)"	Just one… more… step…
"space bar"	[a space, especially when a hyphen would normally appear]	"He rode the merry (space bar) go (space bar) round"	He rode the merry go round
"open paren" then "close paren" (or "open bracket/close bracket," or "open brace/close brace")	() or [] or { }	"Then she (open paren) the doctor (close paren) gasped"	Then she (the doctor) gasped
"new line"	[a press of the Return key]	"milk (new line) bread (new line) Cheez Whiz"	milk bread Cheez Whiz
"new paragraph"	[two presses of the Return key]	"autumn leaves (new paragraph) softly falling"	autumn leaves softly falling
"quote," then "unquote"	" "	Her perfume screamed (quote) available (unquote)	Her perfume screamed "available"
"numeral"	[writes the following number as a digit instead spelling it out]	"Next week she turns (numeral) eight"	Next week she turns 8

Say this:	To get this:	For example, saying this:	Types this:
"asterisk," "plus sign," "minus sign," "equals sign"	*, +, –	"numeral eight (asterisk) two (plus sign) one (minus sign) three (equals sign) fourteen"	8*2+1–3=14
"ampersand," "dash"	&, –	"Barry (ampersand) David (dash) the best (exclamation point)"	Barry & David–the best!
"hyphen"	- [without spaces]	"Don't give me that holier (hyphen) than (hyphen) thou attitude"	Don't give me that holier-than-thou attitude
"backquote"	'	"Back in (backquote) (numeral) fifty-two"	back in '52
"smiley," "frowny," "winky" (or "smiley face," "frowny face," "winky face")	:-) :-(;-)	"I think you know where I'm going with this (winky face)."	I think you know where I'm going with this ;-)

You can also say "percent sign" (%), "at sign" (@), "dollar sign" ($), "cent sign") (¢), "euro sign" (€), "yen sign" (¥), "pounds sterling sign" (£), "section sign" (§), "copyright sign" (©), "registered sign" (®), "trademark sign" (™), "greater-than sign" or "less-than sign" (> or <), "degree sign" (°), "caret" (^), "tilde" (~), "vertical bar" (l), and "pound sign" (#).

The software automatically capitalizes the first new word after a period, question mark, or exclamation point. But you can also force it to capitalize words you're dictating by saying "cap" right before the word, like this: "Dear (cap) Mom, I've run away to join (cap) The (cap) Circus (comma), a nonprofit cooperative for runaway jugglers."

Here's another table—this one shows the other commands for capitalization, plus spacing and spelling commands.

Say this:	To get this:	For example, saying this:	Types this:
"cap" or "capital"	Capitalize the next word	"Give me the (cap) works"	Give me the Works
"caps on," then "caps off"	Capitalize the first letter of every word	"Next week, (caps on) the new england chicken cooperative (caps off) will hire me"	Next week, The New England Chicken Cooperative will hire me

Say this:	To get this:	For example, saying this:	Types this:
"all caps," then "all caps off"	Capitalize everything	"So (all caps on) please please (all caps off) don't tell anyone"	So PLEASE PLEASE don't tell anyone
"all caps"	Type just the next word in all caps	"We (all caps) really don't belong here"	We REALLY don't belong here
"no caps"	Type the next word in lowercase	"see you in (no caps) Texas"	see you in texas
"no caps on," then "no caps off"	Prevents any capital letters	"I'll ask (no caps on) Santa Claus (no caps off)"	I'll ask santa claus
"no space"	Runs the next two words together	"Try new mega (no space) berry flavor"	Try new megaberry flavor
"no space on," then "no space off"	Eliminates all spaces	"(No space on) I can't believe you ate all that (no space off) (comma) she said excitedly"	Ican'tbelieveyou ateallthat, she said excitedly
[alphabet letters]	Types the letters out, though usually not very accurately.	"The stock symbol is A P P L"	The stock symbol is APPL

You don't always have to dictate these formatting commands, by the way. The Mac automatically inserts hyphens into phone numbers (you say, "2125561000," and it types "212-556-1000"); formats two-line street addresses without your having to say "New line" before the city; handles prices automatically ("six dollars and thirty-two cents" becomes "$6.32"). It formats dates and Web addresses well, too; you can even use the nerdy shortcut "dub-dub-dub" when you want the "www" part of a Web address.

The Mac recognizes email addresses, too, as long as you remember to say "at sign" at the right spot. You'd say, "harold (underscore) beanfield (at sign) gmail (dot) com" to get harold_beanfield@gmail.com.

Speech Settings

In System Preferences→Speech→Dictation & Speech, you can fiddle with several settings:

- **On/Off.** If you turn Dictation off, you can no longer dictate to type; the little microphone button won't appear.

- **Shortcut.** Here's where you specify what key you want to double-tap in order to dictate. From this pop-up menu, you can choose the Fn key (on laptops) or the right or left ⌘ key—or you can choose Customize to make up any keystroke you want. The Shortcut box goes empty; press a key combination you prefer (Control-S, for example).

- **Language.** What language and accent do you have? The options here include English in three accents—American, British, and Australian—plus German, Japanese, and French. Apple says it will add more languages over time.

- **About Dictation and Privacy.** Here, you can read more about that business of your utterances and address-book names being transmitted to Apple.

Note: You can also issue spoken commands to your Mac—"Open Safari," for example. In Mountain Lion, Apple has moved this PlainTalk feature to System Preferences→Accessibility. For details, see this chapter's free online PDF appendix, "PlainTalk," on this book's "Missing CD" page at *www.missingmanuals.com*.

The Many Languages of OS X Text

Apple has always taken pride in its language-friendliness. You can shift from language to language on the fly, as you type, even in midsentence—without reinstalling the operating system or even restarting the computer.

Mountain Lion's facility with language, though, goes the extra overseas mile. It lets you type vertical Japanese and Chinese text; includes fonts for 20 more non-Roman alphabets (including the ones you need for five Indian languages); offers "filtering by tones, ordering and filtering by radical or stroke count, and improved pinyin-han conversion accuracy" (you have to be a Chinese speaker to appreciate those tweaks); and much more.

First, tell your Mac which languages you'd like to have available. Open System Preferences→Language & Text. On the Language tab, you see a listing of the languages the Mac can switch into, in the corresponding languages—Français, Español, and so on. Just drag one of the languages to the top of the list to select it as the target language, as shown in Figure 6-7.

Note: You can mix English with right-to-left languages like Hebrew and Arabic. There's even a split-cursor option that makes the pointer flip directions at the boundary between right-to-left and left-to-right text.

Now launch Safari, TextEdit, Mail, or Stickies. Every menu, button, and dialog box is now in the new language you selected! If you log out and back in (or restart) at this point, the entire Finder will be in the new language, too.

Note: Programs differ widely in their "language awareness." If you use a language beyond the 30 in the list, adding it (with the Edit List button) ensures that its relevant features will be available in all programs. (You may still have to add additional language software to make your menus and dialog boxes change.)

Formats Tab

Of course, if you're *really* French (for example), you'll also want to make these changes:

- On the Formats tab, choose your French-speaking country from the Region pop-up menu, so that time and date formats, number punctuation, and currency symbols also conform to your local customs. (Turn on "Show all regions" if necessary.)

For example, the decimal and thousands separator characters for displaying large numbers differ from country to country. (The number 25,600.99, for example, would be written as "25 600,99" in France, and as "25.600,99" in Spain.) And what

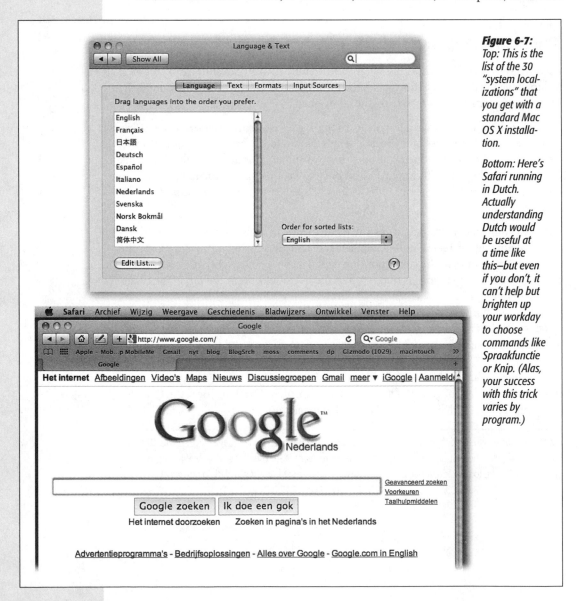

Figure 6-7:
Top: This is the list of the 30 "system local-izations" that you get with a standard Mac OS X installa-tion.

Bottom: Here's Safari running in Dutch. Actually understanding Dutch would be useful at a time like this—but even if you don't, it can't help but brighten up your workday to choose commands like Spraakfunctie or Knip. (Alas, your success with this trick varies by program.)

appears to an American to be July 4 (the notation "7/4"), to a European indicates April 7.

If, for some reason, Apple's preprogrammed settings aren't right for your region, you'll see Customize buttons that let you override them.

- Choose the French *keyboard layout* from the Input Sources tab, as explained next.

Input Sources Tab

While the Mac can display many different languages, *typing* in those languages is another matter. The symbols you use when you're typing in Swedish aren't the same as when you're typing in English. Apple solved this problem by creating different *keyboard layouts,* one for each language. Each rearranges the letters that appear when you press the keys. For example, when you use the Swedish layout and press the semicolon key, you don't get a semicolon (;)—you get an ö.

Apple even includes the famous Dvorak layout and the not-very-famous Colemak layout. Both are scientific rearrangements of the standard layout that put the most

GEM IN THE ROUGH

Draw Those Chinese Characters

In Mountain Lion, Apple makes a huge push to appeal to Chinese Mac fans. There's a new Chinese dictionary and improved text input; eight new Chinese fonts; compatibility with popular Chinese mail services like QQ, 163, and 126; built-in Safari searching using Baidu (like a Chinese Google); and Share-button posting directly to Youku and Tudou (like YouTube) and Sina Weibo (a microblogging service).

If you want to write in Chinese, you can draw the characters you want, right on your laptop's trackpad. (This trick requires a recent Mac laptop, one of the multitouch models.)

To set this up, turn on Chinese–Simplified or Chinese–Traditional, choose the Chinese writing system you prefer, and then turn on Trackpad Handwriting in the System Preferences→Language & Text→Input Sources pane.

Then, when you're actually writing, use the flag (Input) menulet to choose Pinyin–Simplified (or whichever system you like). Now press Shift-Control-space bar to make the writing panel appear, as shown here.

The trick is to understand that the panel is a full map of your trackpad. Draw your character by dragging across the trackpad; white lines appear as you go.

On both sides of the on-screen panel, you see the Mac's interpretations of your character; to choose one, tap the corresponding spot on the outside edges of your actual trackpad. (Or, to backspace–delete your most recent line–tap the upper-left corner of your trackpad.) The Mac drops the character into your document.

Press Shift-Control-space bar again to hide the panel, and shake your head in wonder.

common letters directly under your fingertips on the home row. Fans of the Dvorak layout, and the more modern Colemak layout, claim greater accuracy, better speed, and less fatigue.

Use the list in the Input Sources pane to indicate which keyboard layout you want. If you select anything in the list, then "Show input menu in menu bar" turns on automatically. That option puts a tiny flag icon in your menu bar—a keyboard *menulet* that lets you switch from one layout to another just by choosing its name. (To preview a certain keyboard arrangement, launch the Keyboard Viewer program described next.)

Tip: The icon of the Input menulet changes. It becomes a colorful flag to show the currently selected language.

The Character Viewer

There you are, two-thirds of the way through your local matchmaker newsletter, when it hits you that you need a heart symbol. Right now.

You can't help wishing there were an easy way to find those special symbols that hide among your fonts—fancy brackets, math symbols, special stars and asterisks, and so on.

The Keyboard Viewer, described next, can generate a few of them. But to see the full range of symbols available, you need the Character Viewer. To make it appear, choose Edit→Special Characters.

Most programs have this command. If yours doesn't, here's the long way: Open System Preferences, click Language & Text, click the Input Sources tab, and then turn on the Keyboard & Character Viewer checkbox. You've just installed the Keyboard menulet.

Then, next time you're word processing or doing page layout, choose Show Character Viewer from this menu. The resulting window (Figure 6-8, top) rounds up all symbols from all your fonts at once. To find a particular symbol, click the "by Category" tab, and then click the various category headings: Arrows, Bullets/Stars, Math Symbols, and so on.

When you find the symbol you want, double-click it. The correct symbol pops into your document. (If not, you may get the correct character in the wrong font. In that

GEM IN THE ROUGH

Styled Text

When you copy text from, for example, Microsoft Word, and then paste it into another program, such as Mail, you may be pleasantly surprised to note that the formatting of that text—bold, italic, font (size, color, and so on)—appears intact in Mail. You're witnessing one of the Mac's most useful but underpublicized features: its handling of styled text on the Clipboard.

Almost all Mac programs transfer the formatting along with the copied text. Every time you paste formatted text copied from one of these programs, the pasted material appears with the same typographical characteristics it had in the original program. Over time, this tiny timesaver spares us years' worth of cumulative reformatting effort—yet another tiny favor the noble Macintosh does mankind.

case, change the font of the inserted character manually. To find out what font it came from, click the symbol in the Font Variation panel to see the font name.)

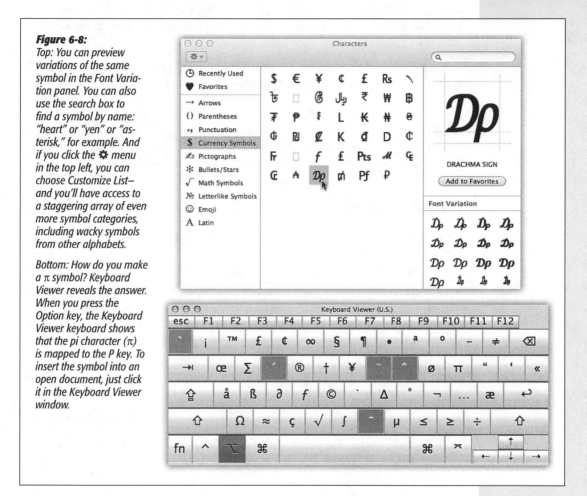

Figure 6-8:
Top: You can preview variations of the same symbol in the Font Variation panel. You can also use the search box to find a symbol by name: "heart" or "yen" or "asterisk," for example. And if you click the ⚙ menu in the top left, you can choose Customize List—and you'll have access to a staggering array of even more symbol categories, including wacky symbols from other alphabets.

Bottom: How do you make a π symbol? Keyboard Viewer reveals the answer. When you press the Option key, the Keyboard Viewer keyboard shows that the pi character (π) is mapped to the P key. To insert the symbol into an open document, just click it in the Keyboard Viewer window.

Keyboard Viewer

Keyboard Viewer, which is descended from the Key Caps program of old, consists of a single window containing a tiny onscreen keyboard (Figure 6-8, bottom). When you hold down any of the modifier keys on your keyboard (like ⌘, Option, Shift, or Control), you can see exactly which keys produce which characters. The point, of course, is to help you learn which keys to press when you need special symbols or non-English characters, such as © or ñ, in each keyboard layout.

Note: Keyboard Viewer shows only the symbols you can produce by typing keystrokes. A font may contain thousands of other characters that can't actually be typed; the Character Viewer is the only way to access these other symbols.

It's a great tool—if you can find it.

Here's how. Open System Preferences→Language & Text, click Input Sources, and then turn on Keyboard & Character Viewer at the top of the list. The Input menu-let—usually a tiny flag—appears at the top of the screen. You can open the Keyboard Viewer by choosing its name from this menulet.

To see the effect of pressing the modifier keys, either click the onscreen keys or press them on your actual keyboard. The corresponding keys on the onscreen keyboard light up as they're pressed.

Tip: You're not stuck viewing the characters in a 12-point font size—a good thing, because some of them are hard to read when displayed that small. You can make the Keyboard Viewer window nearly fill the screen by clicking its Zoom button. That will magnify the Keyboard Viewer window and its font size.

Data Detectors

Here's a cool step-saver, something no other operating system offers—a little something Apple likes to call *data detectors*.

In short, Mac programs like Mail and TextEdit can recognize commonly used bits of information that may appear in your text: a physical address, a phone number, a date and time, and so on. With one quick click, you can send that information into the appropriate program, like Calendar, Contacts, or your Web browser (for looking up an address on a map).

Here's how it works: When you spot a name, address, date, or time, point to it without clicking. A dotted rectangle appears around it. Control-click inside the rectangle, or right-click, or click the ▾ at the right side.

A shortcut menu appears. Its contents vary depending on what you're pointing to:

- **A mailing address.** You can choose Show Address in Google Maps from the shortcut menu; your Web browser opens automatically and shows you that address on a Google map.

 Alternatively, you can choose Create New Contact (to add a Contacts entry for this address) or Add to Existing Contact (if the *person* is in your address book—just not the *address*). Like magic, a little editing box sprouts out of the data-detected rectangle, prefilled with the information from the message, so that you can approve it.

- **A date and time.** When you click the ▾, you get the amazing pop-up menu shown in Figure 6-9. It shows you the actual Calendar day view where Mountain Lion is proposing adding the appointment. The logic of this feature is overwhelming; after all, when someone emails you to ask if you're free for drinks next Thursday at 10, what's the first thing you usually want to do? Check your calendar, of course.

Tip: If, while working in Calendar, you ever forget where this event came from, double-click it. In the Info balloon, you'll see a link that takes you right back to the original Mail message that started it all.

- **A phone number.** As with mailing addresses, the shortcut menu here offers you things like Create New Contact and Add to Existing Contact. The third one, Large Type, is great when you want to call this person right now—it displays the phone number in *huge* type, filling your screen, so you can see it from across your mansion.

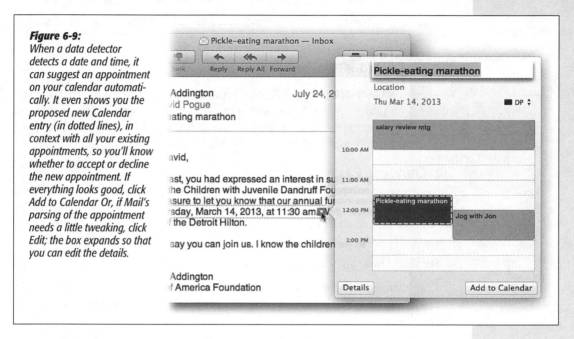

Figure 6-9:
When a data detector detects a date and time, it can suggest an appointment on your calendar automatically. It even shows you the proposed new Calendar entry (in dotted lines), in context with all your existing appointments, so you'll know whether to accept or decline the new appointment. If everything looks good, click Add to Calendar Or, if Mail's parsing of the appointment needs a little tweaking, click Edit; the box expands so that you can edit the details.

- **A flight number.** When you highlight flight information (for example, "AA 152"), the data detector offers a Show Flight Information command. It opens the Flights widget of Dashboard so you can see the flight's departure time, arrival time, and other details. It works only if the airline is represented as a two-letter code.

- **A Web address.** When you click the ▾ next to a URL (like *www.nytimes.com)*, you get a pop-up balloon that contains the *actual Web page!* You get a quick look, without even having to leave your email message.

- **A package tracking number.** When you send a package using a service like FedEx, UPS, or the U.S. Postal Service, you usually get a confirmation email. A data detector can recognize such numbers and, when you click the ▾, offer you a Track Shipment command. Choosing it displays a pop-up window right there at your cursor, showing the courier company's tracking page for that package, and thereby letting you know exactly where your package is right now.

Tip: In the unlikely event that you don't actually care for data detectors and would rather not see those dotted lines and ▾ buttons, you can shut down the whole feature. To do that, open Terminal (page 469). Carefully type this command, and then press Enter:

```
defaults write com.apple.mail DisableDataDetectors YES
```

You can always turn them back on again by repeating that step—and substituting *NO* for the final word.

Moving Data Between Documents

You can't paste a picture into your Web browser, and you can't paste MIDI music information into your word processor. But you can put graphics into your word processor, paste movies into your database, insert text into Photoshop, and combine a surprising variety of seemingly dissimilar kinds of data.

Cut, Copy, and Paste

The original copy-and-paste procedure of 1984—putting a graphic into a word processor—has come a long way. Most experienced Mac fans have learned to trigger the Cut, Copy, and Paste commands from the keyboard, quickly and without even thinking. Here's how the process works:

1. **Highlight some material in a document.**

 Drag through some text in a word processor, for example, or highlight graphic, music, movie, database, or spreadsheet information, depending on the program you're using.

2. **Use the Edit→Cut or Edit→Copy command.**

 Or press the keyboard shortcuts ⌘-X (for Cut—think of the X as a pair of scissors) or ⌘-C (for Copy). The Macintosh memorizes the highlighted material, socking it away on an invisible storage pad called the Clipboard. If you chose Copy, nothing visible happens. If you chose Cut, the highlighted material disappears from the original document.

 At this point, most Mac fans take it on faith that the Cut or Copy command actually worked. But if you're in doubt, switch to the Finder (by clicking its Dock icon, for example), and then choose Edit→Show Clipboard. The Clipboard window appears, showing whatever you've copied.

3. **Click to indicate where you want the material to reappear.**

 This may entail switching to a different program, a different document, or simply a different place in the same document.

4. **Choose the Edit→Paste command (⌘-V).**

 The copy of the material you had originally highlighted now appears at your insertion point—*if* you're pasting into a program that can accept that kind of information. (You won't have much luck pasting, say, a block of spreadsheet numbers into World of Warcraft.)

The most recently cut or copied material remains on your Clipboard even after you paste, making it possible to paste the same blob repeatedly. Such a trick can be useful when, for example, you've designed a business card in your drawing program and want to duplicate it enough times to fill a letter-sized printout. On the other hand, whenever you next copy or cut something, whatever was already on the Clipboard is lost forever.

Drag-and-Drop

As useful and popular as it is, the Copy/Paste routine doesn't win any awards for speed. After all, it requires four steps. In many cases, you can replace that routine with the far more direct (and enjoyable) drag-and-drop method. Figure 6-10 illustrates how this works.

Note: Most Cocoa programs (page 227) require you to press the mouse button for a split second before beginning to drag.

Virtually every Apple program works with the drag-and-drop technique, including TextEdit, Stickies, Mail, QuickTime Player, Preview, iMovie, iPhoto, and System Information, not to mention other popular programs like Microsoft applications, Web browsers, and so on.

When to use drag-and-drop

As shown in Figure 6-10, drag-and-drop is ideal for transferring material between windows or between programs—from a Web page into Photoshop, for example. It's especially useful when you've already copied something valuable to your Clipboard, since drag-and-drop doesn't involve (and doesn't erase) the Clipboard.

Figure 6-10:
To use drag-and-drop, highlight some material. Click anywhere in the highlighted area and press the mouse button for about half a second. Now, with the button still pressed, drag to another place in the document, into a different window, or into a different application. As your cursor enters the target window, a shaded outline appears inside the window's boundaries—the Mac's way of letting you know it understands your intention. When you release the mouse, the highlighted material appears instantly in its new location.

ELEMENTS OF LIBRARY TALK

A brief history of science
Transition into quantum theory
Surprise Ralph Nader appearance
Pros/cons of Quark research
Lunch break
Group discussion

FINAL AGENDA

Surprise Ralph Nader appearance
A brief history of science
Transition into quantum theory
Pros/cons of Quark research

Lunch break

Group discussion

Its most popular use, however, is rearranging text within a single document. In Word or Pages, for example, you can rearrange entire sections, paragraphs, sentences, or even individual letters, just by dragging them—a wonderfully efficient editing technique.

Tip: When you use drag-and-drop to move text within a document, the Mac moves the highlighted text, deleting the highlighted material from its original location. If you press Option as you drag, however, you make a copy of the highlighted text.

Drag-and-drop to the desktop

You can also use drag-and-drop in the one program you use every single day: the Finder itself. As shown in Figure 6-11, you can drag text, graphics, sounds, and even movie clips out of your document windows and directly onto the desktop. Graphics and movies generally turn into ordinary graphic or movie files; text becomes an icon called a *clipping file*.

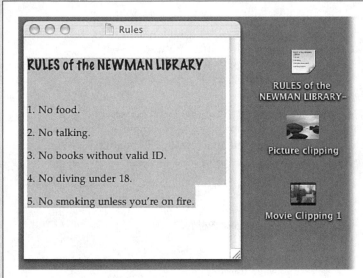

Figure 6-11:
When you drag material out of the document window and onto the desktop, you get a clipping file. Its icon depends on the kind of material contained within: (from top) text clipping, picture clipping, or movie clipping. (For easy identification, Mac OS X conveniently titles text clippings by the first line of the text contained inside.) You can view a clipping just by double-clicking it, so that it opens into its own window (left).

Later, you can examine a clipping's contents using Quick Look—just select its icon and then tap the space bar. Or you can double-click a clipping file and then select a portion of the text to copy.

When you drag a clipping from your desktop *back* into an application window, the material in that clipping reappears. Drag-and-drop, in other words, lets you treat your desktop itself as a giant, computer-wide pasteboard—an area where you can temporarily stash pieces of text or graphics as you work.

Tip: When the material you drag to the desktop contains nothing but an Internet address, such as an email address or a Web page URL, it gets a special icon and a special function: an Internet location file. You can stash it in a folder, double-click it for quick access, and so on.

Export/Import

When it comes to transferring large chunks of information—especially address books, spreadsheet cells, and database records—from one program to another, none of the data-transfer methods described so far in this chapter does the trick. For these purposes, use the Export and Import commands found in the File menu of almost every database, spreadsheet, email, and address-book program. (In some programs, the Save As command serves this function.)

These Export/Import commands aren't part of OS X, so the manuals (if any) of the applications in question should be your source for instructions. For now, however, the power and convenience of this feature are worth noting—it means that your four years' worth of collected addresses in, say, some old email program can find their way into a newer program, like Contacts, in a matter of minutes.

Exchanging Data with Other Macs

Considering how many ways there are to move files back and forth between Macs, it seems almost comical that anybody complained when Apple discontinued built-in floppy disk drives. Here's a catalog of the different ways you can move your files from one computer to another, including some that might not have occurred to you.

By Network

You can shoot a file to another Lion/Mountain Lion Mac with a single drag-and-drop operation, thanks to AirDrop (page 553) or another file-sharing method. You can open files from the other drives, copy stuff back and forth—anything you would do with your own disk. Step-by-step instructions are in Chapter 14.

Best for files of any size, when the computers are in the same building.

Tip: And for $0, you can create an *ad hoc* network, meaning a tiny wireless network between just two computers (or a handful). Great when you're in the car somewhere, or in the airport waiting lounge, or a hotel lobby, and someone says, "Hey, can I have a copy of that?" Details are on page 550.

By Email

Best for small files. High on convenience; computers can be in different countries.

Tip: Of course, the problem with email is that it generally can't handle file attachments larger than 5 or 10 megabytes. You can easily get around that limitation using a free Web site like Sendthisfile.com, which can handle enormous files by sending the recipient only a link to them by email.

Using Dropbox

Dropbox is a free service, almost universally adored, that lets you create synchronized folders on multiple computers. Add a file to, say, your New Projects folder on your home Mac, and it appears instantly in the matching folder on your Windows folder at work.

You can use Dropbox to share folders with other people, too. Just drag a new file into a shared folder, and marvel as your associates get an auto-generated email message letting them know that you've posted a new document. They open the shared folder on their *own* desktops, and there are your files, waiting. (Details are at *www.dropbox. com/help/19.*)

The great thing about services like Dropbox is that you don't have to worry about the small file-size limits imposed by email. (There's a 2-gigabyte storage limit on Dropbox's free accounts, but you can upgrade to larger storage capacities for a fee; you also get more storage granted when you refer a friend to Dropbox.)

By CD or DVD

You can always burn your files onto a blank CD or DVD and then carry or mail it to the recipient. Awfully slow and clumsy, but it does result in a safety copy of whatever you're transferring.

FireWire Disk Mode/Thunderbolt Disk Mode (Target Disk Mode)

FireWire Disk Mode/Thunderbolt Disk Mode is a brilliant but little-known Macintosh-only feature that lets you turn one Mac into an external hard drive for another. This is by far the fastest method yet for transferring a lot of data—even faster than copying files over a network. It's extremely useful in any of these situations:

- **You're traveling with a laptop.** You want to copy your life onto it from your main Mac, including your entire 5 GB email folder and project files, before taking it on a trip, and then unload it when you return.

- **You have a new Mac.** You want to copy everything off the old one, without having to wait all night.

- **One Mac won't start up.** You want to repair it, using another Mac as a "front end."

Unfortunately, not all Macs have a FireWire or Thunderbolt jack. If you're among the lucky, though, you can use the following trick. (In the following steps, suppose your main Mac is an iMac and you want to use a MacBook as an external hard drive for it.)

1. **Connect the FireWire (Thunderbolt) jacks of both computers with a cable.**

 If you have an older Mac with a FireWire 400 jack, you need a *6-pin* FireWire cable—*not* the one that connects a camcorder to a Mac. The one you need has the same large connector on both ends.

 Modern Macs have Apple's FireWire 800 jacks, which require a 9-pin FireWire cable (and give you much greater speed). If only one Mac has a FireWire 800 jack, then use that computer's traditional FireWire 400 connector instead. Otherwise,

you need either a special FireWire 800–to–FireWire 400 cable, or the 400-to-800 adapter that came with your Mac.

2. **On the MacBook, choose ****→System Preferences. Click Startup Disk.**

 The Startup Disk panel opens.

3. **Click Target Disk Mode. In the confirmation box, click Restart.**

 The MacBook turns off, then on again. A giant gray FireWire icon (✯) or Thunderbolt icon (⚡) bounces around the laptop screen.

 Now take a look at the iMac's screen: Sure enough, there's the MacBook's hard drive icon on the desktop. You're ready to copy files onto or off of it, at extremely high speeds, and go on with your life.

4. **When you're finished working with the MacBook, eject it from the iMac's screen as you would any disk. Then turn off the laptop by pressing the power button.**

The next time you turn on the MacBook, it'll start up from its own copy of OS X, even if the cable is still attached. (You can disconnect the cable whenever you please.)

Note: The steps above describe the Lion/ Mountain Lion method of setting up Target Disk Mode. But the old way still works, too. Leave the iMac turned on, but shut down the MacBook. (Make sure it's plugged in. You wouldn't want the battery to die in the middle of this process.) Now turn the MacBook on again, but hold down the T key immediately after the chime. After a moment, you see the big Y-shaped FireWire icon (✯) on the laptop screen, and the laptop's hard drive shows up on the iMac's desktop. Continue from step 4 above.

This method is arguably quicker, because you don't have to open up System Preferences. And this method works when the Mac is too sick even to start up.

Via the iPod

An iPod is an extremely fine music player with enormous capacity. That's because it contains an actual hard drive (or a bunch of memory) that stores the songs.

But because the modern iPod has a USB connector, most models make dandy portable hard drives for everyday files, too—not just music.

To set the iPod up for data transfer, proceed like this:

1. **Connect the iPod to your Mac with its white USB cable. Open iTunes. Click the iPod icon in the left-side Source list.**

 The iPod Summary screen appears.

2. **Turn on "Enable disk use."**

 A dialog box warns you that even when you're just syncing up your music collection (and not using the iPod as a hard drive for files), you have to manually eject the iPod after each use.

3. **Click OK, and then OK again.**

After a moment, you see the iPod's icon appear on your desktop.

Now you've got yourself a multigigabyte external hard drive. Just drag your files onto or off the iPod icon, exactly as though it's a disk (which it is). The iPod automatically keeps your data files separate from your music files; your other files won't be touched when you update your music collection from iTunes.

Whenever you're finished using the iPod as a hard drive, eject it in any of the usual ways. For example, in the Finder, drag its icon to the Trash, or Control-click it and choose Eject from the shortcut menu.

Via Flash Drive

A flash drive, also called a thumb drive, is one of those keychain-like doodads that plug into your USB jack. Inside is a big chunk of memory that acts like a miniature hard drive. When the flash drive is plugged into your Mac, its icon shows up on the desktop as a disk. Use it as a tiny, 8-gigabyte hard drive (or whatever size you've bought).

The beauty of a flash drive is that it works instantly and automatically with any Mac *or* any Windows machine, without software installation or configuration. It's small and light enough to carry around on your keychain…and it's *so darned cool*. If you regularly transfer documents between Macs or between Macs and PCs, a flash drive will change your life.

Via Bluetooth

Bluetooth is a cable-elimination technology. It's designed to let Bluetooth-equipped gadgets communicate within about 30 feet, using radio signals.

Bluetooth comes built into most computers and cellphones, plus the occasional printer, pocket organizer, even camera or camcorder.

Bluetooth is built into all recent Macs. It's ready, therefore, to connect with Apple's wireless keyboard and mouse; to get on the Internet using a Bluetooth cellphone as a cordless modem; to listen to music through wireless headphones or speakers; and to transfer files through the air to similarly equipped gear.

Bluetooth is pretty slow. (You get transfer speeds of 30 to 150 K per second, depending on the distance.) But when you consider the time you'd have taken for wiring, passwords, and configuration using any other connection method, you may find that Bluetooth wins, at least in casual, spur-of-the-moment, airport-seat situations.

And Bluetooth works no matter what the gadget—Mac, Windows, cellphone—so it's great as a universal file-exchange translator, too.

Note: For more details on configuring your Mac for Bluetooth connections, see page 340.

Sending a file

To shoot a file or two across the airwaves to a fellow Bluetooth-equipped Mac fan, first *pair* your Mac with the other Bluetooth machine, as described on page 340. In System Preferences→Bluetooth, make sure your Mac is Discoverable. *Discoverable*

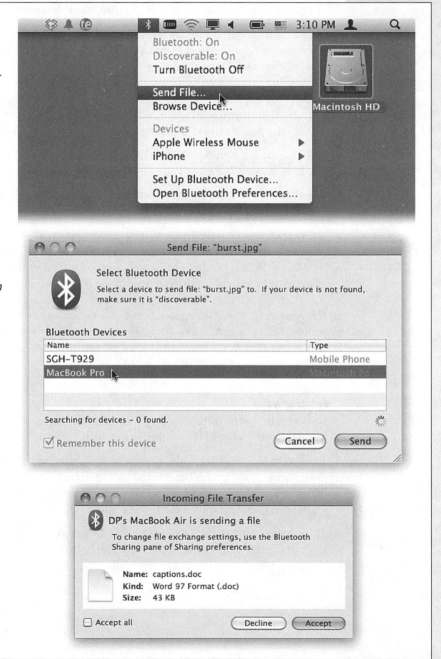

Figure 6-12:

Top: Once your Mac is paired with the other gadget, it's super-easy to shoot a file to it wirelessly. In this example, you'll start by choosing Send File. (But you could save the second step by choosing the gadget's name from this menulet and then Send File from the submenu.)

Middle: OK. The Mac is saying: "Send this file to what gadget?" Click the one you want. (If the device isn't in Discoverable mode, then no other Bluetooth gizmos can see it.)

Bottom: This is the view from the receiving machine (a Mac, in this case). "Someone's sending you a file. Do you want it?"

means, "Other Bluetooth gadgets can see me." (Check the receiving gadget, too, to make sure *it's* in Discoverable mode.) Then you're ready to send:

1. **From the Bluetooth ✳ menulet (Figure 6-12, top), choose Send File.**

 If you don't *have* the Bluetooth menulet on your menu bar, then open System Preferences. Click Bluetooth, and turn on "Show Bluetooth status in the menu bar."

 After a moment, the Select File to Send dialog box appears. (You've actually succeeded in opening a program called Bluetooth File Exchange, which sits in your Applications→Utilities folder.)

2. **Navigate to, and select, the files you want to send.**

 If you're trying to send a bunch of them, you may find it easier to drag their icons onto the Bluetooth File Exchange icon in your Applications→Utilities folder.

 Either way, a new Send File dialog box appears, showing the list of Bluetooth machines within range (Figure 6-12, middle).

3. **In the list of found machines, click the name of the one you want to send your files to, and then click Send.**

 What happens now depends on how the receiving machine has been set up. In most cases, a dialog box tells the receiver that files are arriving (Figure 6-12, bottom); if he clicks Accept, then the download proceeds. He's then offered the chance to either (a) open each transferred file or (b) reveal its highlighted icon in the Finder.

Tip: In System Preferences→Sharing→Bluetooth Sharing, you can control what happens when someone sends you files via Bluetooth. Usually, you'll want your Mac to ask whether or not to accept these files. (That's what the option "Ask What to Do" means.) You can also specify where you want received files to wind up—for example, in your Downloads folder.

Fetching a file

You can also perform this entire procedure in reverse. That is, you can go fishing through your buddy's files without her explicitly having to send anything.

To make a Mac invadable, the person to be invaded must open System Preferences→Sharing and turn on Bluetooth Sharing. Here's also where she can specify what folder is available to you for examination (the Mac proposes her Home→Public folder), and what kind of security she wants to set up.

Then all you have to do is choose Browse Device from your own menulet (you can see it in Figure 6-12)—and let the rummaging begin!

Exchanging Data with Windows PCs

Documents can take one of several roads between your Mac and a Windows machine: via disk (such as a CD), flash drive, network, email, Bluetooth, iPod, Web page, FTP download, and so on.

Preparing the Document for Transfer

The Mac is more Windows-compatible than ever. Still, before sending a document to a colleague who uses Windows, you must be able to answer "yes" to both of the questions below.

Is the document in a file format Windows understands?

Most popular programs are sold in both Mac and Windows flavors, and the documents they create are freely interchangeable. For example, documents created by recent versions of Word, Excel, PowerPoint, FileMaker, Illustrator, Photoshop, Dreamweaver, and many other Mac programs don't need any conversion. The corresponding Windows versions of those programs open such documents with nary a hiccup.

Files in standard exchange formats don't need conversion, either. These formats include JPEG and PNG (digital photos), GIF (cartoon/logo graphics on Web pages), HTML (raw Web page documents), Rich Text Format (a word-processor exchange format that maintains bold, italic, and other formatting), plain text (no formatting at all), MP3 and AAC files (for audio), MIDI files (for music synthesizers), and so on.

But what about documents made by Mac programs that don't exist on the typical Windows PC hard drive, like Keynote or Pages? You certainly can't count on your recipient having the application.

Do your recipients the favor of first saving such documents into one of those exchange formats. In Pages, for example, choose File→Export; in the resulting dialog box, click Word. Click Next. Now name this special version of the document (complete with the *.doc* suffix), and then click Save.

Does the file have the correct file name suffix?

Every document on your hard drive has some kind of tag to tell the computer what program is supposed to open it: either a pair of invisible four-letter codes or a file name suffix like *.doc.*

Microsoft Windows uses *only* the latter system for identifying documents. Here are some of the most common such codes:

Kind of document	Suffix	Example
Microsoft Word (old)	.doc	Letter to Mom.doc
Microsoft Word (latest)	.docx	Letter to Mom.docx
Excel	.xls or .xlsx	Profit Projection.xls

PowerPoint	.ppt	Slide Show.ppt
JPEG photo	.jpg	Baby Portrait.jpg
GIF graphic	.gif	Logo.gif
Web page	.htm	index.htm

The beauty of OS X is that its programs add these file name suffixes automatically and invisibly, every time you save a new document. You and your Windows comrades can freely exchange documents without ever worrying about this former snag in the Macintosh/Windows relationship.

Notes on Disk Swapping

Once you've created a document destined for a Windows machine, your next challenge is to get it *onto* that machine. One way is to put the file on a disk—a CD you've burned, for example—which you then hand to the Windows owner.

Macs and PCs format *hard drives* differently. The Mac can read Windows disks and flash drives (which use unappetizingly named formatting schemes like FAT32 and NTFS), but Windows can't read Mac hard drives or flash drives.

CDs and DVDs use the same format on both kinds of computers, though, so you should have very little problem moving these between machines. Chapter 12 has details on disc burning.

Network Notes

OS X can "see" shared disks and folders on Windows PCs that are on the same network. Complete instructions are in Chapter 14.

Via the Internet

Chapter 21 offers details on FTP and Web sharing, two ways to make your Mac available to other computers—Windows PCs or not—on the Internet. And, of course, you can always email files between Macs and PCs.

The Mountain Lion Share Button

In its never-ending efforts to bring the best of the iPad to the Mac, Apple has built the Share button into many spots in Mountain Lion. It's a quick, one-click way to send something (text, link, photo, video) to somebody else (by email, Twitter, Facebook,text message, AirDrop).

If you've seen an iPhone or iPad, then you've seen this Share icon: ↱. On the Mac, this button, or a command that just says Share, pops up in all kinds of programs: the Finder's shortcut menus. Quick Look panels. The Open File dialog box in Apple programs. OS X programs like Contacts, Notes, Preview, Safari, Photo Booth, TextEdit, iPhoto, and so on. Other companies can add it to their programs, too, or install new commands into the Share menu for transmitting stuff to new channels.

To use this feature, select or open some text, a photo, a video, a file icon, a Web link, or something else that you want to send to friends. When you click this button or command, you're offered various ways to share the selected item. The choices vary according to the program you're using, but here are some examples:

- **Email.** Mountain Lion copies the selected material into a new, outgoing email message, or attaches the selected file to an outgoing message. Just add a few explanatory notes, address the message, and send.

- **Twitter.** Opens up the Twitter "share sheet" pictured in Figure 6-13, middle. A counter helps you keep your message under the legal limit of 140 characters. Explain what your linked item is about, and then click Send.

Figure 6-13:
Top: Here's how you might tweet a link to a page from Safari. Choose Twitter from the ⬆ button; type a comment; click Send.

Bottom: Other share sheets you might encounter. Lower left: posting a photo to Flickr. Lower right: sending a file using AirDrop.

Very bottom: Posting a photo to Facebook. Note the tiny pop-up menus. One lets you control who sees this post; the other specifies where it goes (which album, for example).

Keyboard fans: For Twitter or Facebook, press Shift-⌘-D to "click" the Send or Post button.

• **Facebook.** Attaches the selected photo, video, or text to the Facebook "sheet" shown at bottom in Figure 6-13. This tiny box offers two pop-up menus. The one at top left lets you specify who gets to see this post: Only Me, Friends, Friends and Networks, Everyone, or one of your Facebook lists, if you've set them up. If you're posting a photo or video, a second pop-up menu one at top right lets you indicate what album you want this item to land in—your Wall or an existing photo album.

Note: The Facebook features of Mountain Lion aren't available in the original release; Apple added them in the fall of 2012.

• **Messages.** Puts the selected material into an outgoing message, ready to send as a text message or an iMessage (Chapter 20). Just address and send.

Tip: In the Finder, the Share command offers a brilliantly simple way to send a file to somebody. Just Control-click (or right-click) a file icon, choose Share→Message, and then enter the person's phone number (to send to an iPhone) or Apple ID (to send by iMessage). Click Send—off it goes!

• **AirDrop.** As you can read on page 553, AirDrop lets you shoot Finder files to nearby Macs, wirelessly, without having to fuss with passwords, file sharing, mounting disks, and so on. And now, thanks to the Share button, it's even easier to use.

In the Finder, Control-click (or right-click) the file icon (or icons) that you want to send to another Mac. From the shortcut menu, choose AirDrop. In a flash, you get the AirDrop "share sheet" shown in Figure 6-13, lower right. It lists every nearby Mac whose AirDrop window is open. Click the one you want, and then click Send; if the other guy clicks Accept, then the file is on its way to his Mac.

• **Vimeo.** When you select a video (in the Finder, for example), you have the option of posting it to Vimeo, which is a lot like YouTube but smaller and with a more mature tone. You're asked for a name, description, and tags (keywords) for your video, and you're given the option to keep it private (rather than public). When you click Send, the movie goes on its way. After the upload, a tiny status box appears, showing you the link that takes you to the newly posted video; click the ✎ to jump to it in your Web browser.

• **Flickr.** Flickr is the most popular photo-sharing site. Now you can post a photo from your Mac directly to that Web site, even from the Finder. You're asked to provide a title and description for the photos, and then off it goes to your online Flickr account. After the upload, the tiny status box shows you the link.

All the online services mentioned here—Twitter, Facebook, Flickr, Vimeo—require free accounts. And using the Share button assumes that you've entered your account name and password in System Preferences→Mail, Contacts & Calendars. Once you've recorded your account info there, it's stored; you can use the corresponding Share options in any program without having to log in again.

This list of options in the Share pop-up menu isn't complete; you may find other oddball options in the Share menus of certain programs. For example, in Photo

Booth, you get the usual choices like Twitter, Flickr, Email, and Message. But you also get choices like Add to iPhoto, Set Buddy Picture, Set Account Picture, or Change Twitter Profile Picture—all handy things to do with a picture you've just taken with your Mac's built-in camera.

Time Machine

There are two kinds of people in the world: those who have a regular backup system—and those who *will.*

You'll get that grisly joke immediately if you've ever known the pain that comes with deleting the wrong folder by accident, or making changes that you regret, or worst of all, having your hard drive die. All those photos, all that music you've bought online, all your email—gone.

Yet the odds are overwhelming that at this moment, you do not have a complete, current, automated backup of your Mac. Despite about a thousand warnings, articles, and cautionary tales a year, guess how many do? About *four percent.* Everybody else is flying without a net.

If you don't have much to back up—you don't have much in the way of photos, music, or movies—you can get by with burning copies of stuff onto blank CDs or DVDs (Chapter 12) or using a free online backup system like Dropbox, CrashPlan, or IDrive. But those methods leave most of your Mac unprotected: all your programs and settings.

What you really want, of course, is a backup that's rock-solid, complete, and *automatic.* You don't want to have to remember to do a backup, to insert a disc, and so on. You just want to know you're safe.

That's the idea behind Time Machine, a marquee feature of OS X. It's a silent, set-it-and-forget-it piece of peace of mind. You sleep easy, knowing there's a safety copy of your *entire* system: your system files, programs, settings, music, pictures, videos, document files—*everything.* If your luck runs out, you'll be *so* happy you set up Time Machine.

Setting Up Time Machine

Here's the bad news: Time Machine requires a second hard drive. That's the only way to create a completely safe, automatic backup of your *entire* main hard drive.

That second hard drive can take any of these forms:

- An external USB, FireWire, or Thunderbolt hard drive.
- An Apple Time Capsule. That's an AirPort wireless base station/network backup hard drive in one; it's available in gigantic capacities.
- Another internal hard drive.
- A partition of any one of those drives.

- An iPod, if you've turned on "Enable disk use" (in iTunes) or if it's a flash-memory one like the Nano.

- The hard drive of another Mac on the network (Mac OS X 10.5 or later) that you've mounted on your screen.

Tip: *It's perfectly OK to back up several Macs onto the same external hard drive, as long as it's got enough room. You can also back up onto a hard drive that has other stuff on it, although of course that means you'll have less room for Time Machine backups.*

In all cases, the backup disk must be bigger than the drive you're backing up (preferably *much* bigger).

Here's what you *can't* use as the backup disk: a CD or your startup drive.

Note: *The backup drive must be a standard Mac-formatted hard drive—yet many new drives bought by Mac fans come preformatted as Windows disks. Fortunately, Time Machine automatically reformats them to the Mac OS Extended (Journaled) scheme, which it requires. Thoughtful, really.*

Sure, it sounds like an Apple plot to sell more hard drives. But you'd be surprised at how cheap hard drives are. At this writing, you can buy a 1-*terabyte* hard drive (1,000 gigabytes) for $60, for goodness' sake—and hard drive prices-per-gigabyte go only down.

The first time the Mac sees your second hard drive, it invites you to use it as Time Machine's backup drive (Figure 6-14). That could be the moment you connect an external drive, or the first time you turn on the Mac after installing an internal drive.

Figure 6-14:
The Mac has just encountered a second hard drive. Time Machine still works if there's other stuff on the drive, but life is simpler if you don't use that drive for anything but Time Machine.

If you click Use as Backup Disk, you're taken immediately to the Time Machine pane of System Preferences (Figure 6-15). It shows that Time Machine is now on, your backup disk has been selected, and the copying process has begun. The Mac starts copying *everything* on your hard drive, including OS X itself, all your programs, and everyone's Home folders. You know that because you see both a progress message and the ♺ symbol that appears next to the backup drive's name in your Sidebar.

And that, ladies and gentlemen, is the easiest setup for a backup program in history.

Note: Unless you turn on encryption (see the box on page 274), Time Machine doesn't use any compression or encoding; it's copying your files exactly as they sit on your hard drive, for maximum safety and recoverability. On the other hand, it does save some space on the backup drive, because it doesn't bother copying cache files, temporary files, and other files you'll never need to restore.

Figure 6-15:
Use the big On/Off switch to shut off all Time Machine activity, although it would be hard to imagine why you'd want to risk it. You can click Select Disk to choose a different hard drive to represent the mirror of your main drive (after the first one is full, for example).

FREQUENTLY ASKED QUESTION

The End of Time

What happens when my backup drive gets full?

Good question. The whole idea of Time Machine is that it preserves multiple backups, so that you can rewind a window or a drive not just to *a* backup, but to *any* date in the past. The bigger the hard drive, the farther back those monthly backups are preserved.

Eventually, of course, your backup drive runs out of space. At that point, Time Machine notifies you and offers you a choice: "Your backup disk is now full. The oldest remaining backup disk is..." (and then the date.)

You can keep using that drive; Time Machine will begin deleting the oldest backups to make room for newer ones.

Or you can install a new Time Machine backup drive. New backups will go on that one; your older backups will still be available on the original drive.

If you ever need to retrieve files or folders from the older disk, Control-click (right-click) the Time Machine icon in the Dock; from the shortcut menu, choose Browse Other Time Machine Disks. In the list of disks, choose the older one. Then click the Time Machine icon on the Dock to enter the Restore mode.

Now go away and let the Mac do its thing. The first backup can take hours as the Mac duplicates your entire internal hard drive onto the second drive. The Mac may feel drugged during this time.

Tip: New in Mountain Lion: You can create multiple backups on different disks—a great feature if you have a laptop that you carry between work and home. You can have a backup drive at both places; Time Machine will seamlessly switch between them. To set this up, just choose another backup disk in System Preferences→ Time Machine. Time Machine will automatically back up to that drive, too.

How the Backups Work

From now on, Time Machine quietly and automatically checks your Mac once an hour. If any file, folder, or setting has changed, it gets backed up at the end of the hour. These follow-up backups are quick; Time Machine backs up only what's changed.

So, should disaster strike, the only files you can lose are those you've changed within the past 59 minutes.

Tip: And even then, you can force more frequent backups if you want to. Just choose Back Up Now from the Time Machine menulet. Or choose Back Up Now from the shortcut menu of the Dock's Time Machine icon.

You can pause the backup the same way—if you need to use the backup drive for another quick task, for example. Open System Preferences→Time Machine and turn the big switch Off. Don't forget to turn the backing-up on again when you're finished.

POWER USERS' CLINIC

Encrypted Time Machine Backups

Time Machine can encrypt your backups.

Without encryption, an evildoer could theoretically bust into your house, steal your backup disk, and have full, unfettered access to all your backed-up files. It's never happened yet, but—you know. It could.

If you're interested in encrypting your backups, there are some prerequisites. The hard drive must use HFS (Journaled) formatting—a Mac hard drive, in other words. The drive has to be physically, directly connected to your Mac using USB, FireWire, or Thunderbolt—or else a wireless Apple Time Capsule (that's new in Mountain Lion).

To turn this feature on, open System Preferences→Time Machine. Click Select Disk. Turn on "Encrypt backup disk." You're asked for a password. Type it in, and whatever you do, don't forget it! Without that password, you won't be able

to recover your files if something goes wrong. Keep that password somewhere safe—on the bottom of the backup drive, for example. (Joke! That's a joke.)

Once you click OK, the encryption begins. It takes a long time. Go away for the weekend.

Once it's done, you won't notice any difference—until the day comes when you need to recover your files. At that point, you'll be asked for your password when you enter Time Machine.

If something serious ever happens to your Mac, you can connect the encrypted Time Machine drive to any other Mac that's running Lion or Mountain Lion. You'll be able to enter your password there and recover your files onto that different Mac.

By the end of the day, you'll have 24 hourly backups on that second disk, all taking up space. So at day's end, Time Machine replaces that huge stash with a single *daily* backup. You can no longer rewind your system to 3:00 p.m. last Monday, but you can rewind to the way it was at the *end* of that day.

Similarly, after a month, Time Machine replaces those 30 dailies (for example) with four weekly backups. Now you may not be able to rewind to October 14, but you can rewind to November 1. (Apple assumes it won't take you a whole week to notice that your hard drive has crashed.)

Tip: You can see these backups, if you want. Open your backup drive, open the *Backups.backupdb* folder, and then open the folder named for your computer. Inside, you'll find a huge list of backup folders, bearing names like 2013-03-22-155831. That's the backup from March 22, 2013, at 15:58 (that is, 3:58 p.m.) and 31 seconds.

Declaring Stuff Off-Limits to Time Machine

The whole point of Time Machine is to have a backup of your entire hard drive. That's how most people use it.

It's conceivable, though, that you might want to exclude some files or folders from the Time Machine treatment. There are two reasons.

First, you might not want certain, ahem, private materials to be part of your incriminating data trail.

Second, you might want to save space on the backup drive, either because it's not as big as your main drive or because you'd rather dedicate its space to more backups of the essential stuff. For example, you might decide not to back up your collection of downloaded TV shows, since video files are enormous. Or maybe you use an online photo-sharing Web site as a backup for all your photos, so you don't think it's necessary to include those in the Time Machine backup.

To eliminate certain icons from the backup, open the Time Machine pane of System Preferences. Click Options.

In the resulting list, click the **+** button; navigate to your hard drive, and then select the files or folders you don't want backed up. Or just find their actual icons in the Finder and drag them into the list here. (Use the **−** button to remove items from the list, thereby excluding them from the excluded list.)

If you're strapped for disk space, one logical candidate to exclude is the System folder on your main hard drive—that is, OS X itself. After all, if you lose your hard drive, you already have a copy of OS X: the original App Store installer.

When you add the System folder to the exclusion list, Time Machine makes another space-saving offer: "Would you like to also exclude other files installed with Mac OS X, such as system applications and UNIX tools?"

Agreeing (by clicking Exclude All System Files) saves you another several gigabytes of backup space.

The point is that Time Machine doesn't just keep *one* copy of your stuff. It keeps *multiple* backups. It remembers how things were in every folder—not just yesterday, but last week, last month, and so on. It keeps on making new snapshots of your hard drive until the backup drive is full.

At that point, the oldest ones get deleted to make room for new ones.

Tip: Ordinarily, Time Machine alerts you when it has to start deleting old backups. If you'd rather have it just do it without bothering you, then open System Preferences, click Time Machine, click Options, and then turn off "Notify after old backups are deleted."

By the way, if a backup is interrupted—if you shut down the Mac, put it to sleep, or take your laptop on the road—no big deal. Time Machine resumes automatically the next time you're home and connected.

Local Snapshots

If you're among the 75 percent of Mac fans with a laptop, Time Machine used to be something of a bust in one regard: Whenever you were away from your backup disk (at home or the office, for example), you lost the benefits of Time Machine.

In Mountain Lion, crazy as this may sound, Time Machine keeps on working even on a laptop that's far from home. Thanks to a feature called local snapshots, Time Machine works as usual by making its backups right on the laptop's own hard drive.

Of course, this system won't help you if your hard drive dies; your backup is on the same drive, so you'll lose the originals and the backups simultaneously. But what local snapshots do provide is a safety net—a way to recover a file that you deleted or changed during this time away. Better yet, once you're home again, when your laptop rejoins the network, the local snapshots are intelligently merged with the master Time Machine backups, as though you'd never been away.

If Time Machine is turned on on your laptop, it makes local snapshots automatically—once an hour, as usual. As time goes on, Time Machine condenses those backups to daily or weekly snapshots to save disk space.

Note: If your laptop gets really low on disk space, Time Machine stops making new snapshots and may even delete old ones so that you can keep using your Mac. When you make more space, snapshots resume automatically.

If you need to recover a file, enter Time Machine as usual. Your local snapshots show up on the same timeline as backups made on your regular, external backup disk, but they're color-coded: pink tick marks for external backups, gray for local ones. If the pink bars are dimmed, it's because you're not hooked up to your external Time Machine backup drive.

Tip: To see how much disk space your local snapshots are eating up, choose →About This Mac. Click More Info. Click the Storage tab. The color-coded graph clearly indicates the space being used for backups.

Changing Time Machine Settings

Time Machine has four faces. There's the application itself, which sits in your Applications folder; open it only when you want to enter Restore mode. There's its Dock icon, which also enters Restore mode, but which has a shortcut menu containing useful commands like Back Up Now (and Stop Backing Up).

There's the Time Machine menulet, which may be the handiest of all. It identifies the time and date of the most recent backup; offers Back Up Now/Stop Backing Up commands; and has direct access to Time Machine's restore mode and preferences pane.

Tip: If you Option-click the Time Machine menulet, you get two secret new commands: Verify Backups (just in case you're a little nervous about your backups' integrity) and Browse Other Backup Disks. Yes, it's perfectly possible to back up onto multiple hard drives–to keep one offsite so you won't be hosed in case of fire, flood, or burglary, for example–and this is how. (Control-clicking the Time Machine icon on the Dock is another way to get this command.)

Finally, then there's its System Preferences pane, where you adjust its settings (Figure 6-15). To see it, choose →System Preferences→Time Machine. Or choose Time Machine Preferences from Time Machine's Dock icon or menulet.

Recovering Lost or Changed Files

All right, you've got Time Machine on the job. You sleep easy at night, confident that your life is in order—and your stuff is backed up.

Then, one day, it happens: Your hard drive crashes. Or you can't find a file or folder you know you had. Or you save a document in some non–Auto Save program and then wish you could go back to an earlier draft. Some kind of disaster—sunspots, clueless spouse, overtired self—has befallen your files. This is Time Machine's big moment.

Start by pinpointing what you're looking for, in one of these two ways:

- Open the disk or folder window where the missing or changed item was.

- Type what you're looking for into the search box at the top of any Finder window. Click the location button that makes the most sense: "This Mac" or the name of the window you're in.

 In the case of deleted files or folders, the search will probably come up empty; that's totally OK.

Now click the Time Machine icon on the Dock, or choose Enter Time Machine from the menulet (Figure 6-16, top). Don't look away; you'll miss the show.

Your desktop *slides down the screen* like a curtain that's been dropped from above. And it reveals…outer space. This is it, the ultimate Apple eye candy: an animated starry universe, with bits of stardust and meteors occasionally flying outward from the massive nebula at the center.

Front and center is your Finder window—or, rather, dozens of them, stretching back in time (Figure 6-16, bottom). Each is a snapshot of that window at the time of a Time Machine backup.

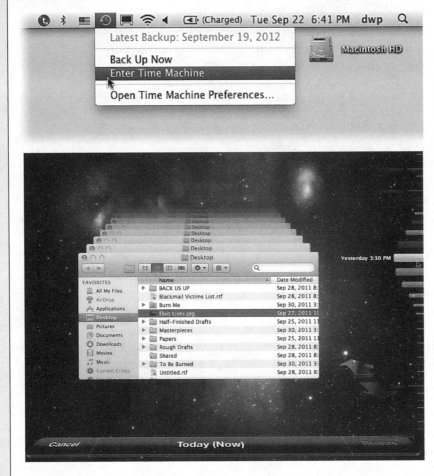

Figure 6-16:
Top: Choose Enter Time Machine from the menulet. (If you don't see this menulet, turn on "Show Time Machine status in the menu bar," shown in Figure 6-15.)

Bottom: This is the big payoff for all your efforts. The familiar desktop slides down, dropping away like a curtain. For the first time, you get to see what's been behind the desktop all this time. Turns out it's outer space. Time Machine shows you dozens of copies of the Finder window, representing its condition at each backup, stretching back to the past. If the "ruler tick marks" are both pink and gray, you're seeing backups on both your laptop's own hard drive and the usual external drive, as described earlier in this chapter.

You have four ways to peruse your backup universe:

- **Click individual windows to see what's in them.**

- **Drag your cursor through the timeline at the right side.** It's like a master dial that flies through the windows into the past.

- **Click one of the two big, flat perspective arrows.** The one pointing into the past means, "Jump directly to the most recent window version that's *different* from the way it is right now."

In other words, it's often a waste of time to go flipping through the windows one at a time, because your missing or changed file might have been missing or changed for the last 25 backups (or whatever). What you want to know is the last time the contents of this window *changed*. And that's what the big flat arrows do. They jump from one *changed* version of this window to another. (Or, if you began with a search, the arrow takes you to the most recent backup with a matching result.)

- **Use the search box in the corner of the window.** You can search for whatever you're missing in the current backup.

As you go, the very bottom of the screen identifies where you are in time—that is, which backup you're examining.

Tip: OK, it's all very dazzling and all. But if you're technically inclined, you don't have to sit still for the big show. Just open the backup disk itself, whose icon appears on your desktop. Inside, you'll find nested folders, neatly representing every computer, every backup, every day, and every hour—which you can rummage through by hand.

In many ways, the recovery mode is just like the Finder. You can't actually open, edit, rename, or reorganize anything here. But you can use Quick Look to inspect the documents to make sure you've got the right version. And you can use icon, list, column, or Cover Flow views to sort through the files you're seeing.

If you're trying to recover an older *version* of a file or folder, highlight it and then click the flat arrow button that's pointing away from you; Time Machine skips back to the most recent version that's *different* from the current one.

If you're trying to restore a deleted file or folder that you've now located, highlight it and then click Restore (lower right). The OS X desktop rises again from the bottom of the screen, there's a moment of copying, and then presto: The lost file or folder is back in the window where it belonged.

Note: Time Machine prides itself not just on recovering files and folders, but also on putting them back where they belong.

If you recover a different version of something that's still there, OS X asks if you want to replace it with the recovered version—or to keep both versions.

And if you're recovering a document whose original folder no longer exists, Time Machine automatically recreates the folder so that the recovered item feels at home.

Recovering from Contacts and Mail

The Finder isn't the only program that's hooked into Time Machine's magic. Contacts and Mail work with Time Machine, too. Other software companies can also revise their own applications to work with it.

In other words, if you want to recover certain addresses or email messages that have been deleted, you don't start in the Finder; you start in Contacts or Mail.

Then click the Time Machine icon on the Dock. Once again, you enter the starry recovery mode—but this time, you're facing a strange, disembodied, stripped-down copy of Contacts or Mail (Figure 6-17).

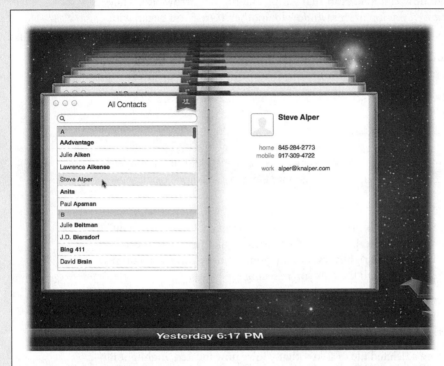

Figure 6-17:
The Time Machine version of Contacts is a weird, simplified, viewing-only version. You can't do much here besides browse your backups—but when you're in dire straits, that's enough.

You're ready to find your missing data. Click the Jump Back arrow to open the most recent version of your address book file or email stash that's different from what you've got now. (You can also use the timeline on the right if you remember the date when things went wrong.)

Tip: If you're looking for something particular, specify that before you start clicking. For example, type a name into the Contacts search box first.

At this point, you can select individual Contacts entries or email messages to restore; just click the Restore button.

Often, though, you'd rather reinstate the *entire* Contacts file or email collection from the backup. That's what the Restore All button is for.

If you click it, the experience is slightly different. Contacts may discover a lot of duplicate name-and-address entries and invite you to step through them, deciding which ones "win" (the old or the new).

Note: When you finish restoring in Mail, you'll find the restored messages in the On My Mac→Time Machine→Recovered folder at the left side of the window.

Recovering the entire hard drive

Every hard drive will die at some point. You just hope it won't happen while *you* own the computer.

But if it does, you, as a Time Machine aficionado, won't care. You'll just repair or replace the hard drive, and then proceed as follows.

1. **Connect the Time Machine backup disk to the Mac. Start the recovery mode.**

 There are actually three ways to recover a dead Mac or a dead hard drive, none of which require an actual DVD, as in the days of yore. If the hard drive is fine but it just can't start up your Mac, hold down ⌘-R during startup. If the hard drive is empty, you can restart from the Internet itself (if it's a Mac released since Lion came out). And if all else fails, you can always use the Recovery Disk Assistant that you wisely made long in advance of your horror-story dead-disk day.

 Appendix B covers all three of these recovery modes in more detail.

 The point is, however, that all three of them present "Restore from a Time Machine backup" as one of the options.

2. **Choose "Restore from a Time Machine backup." Click Continue.**

 Now you're shown a list of Time Machine backup disks. You probably have only one.

3. **Click your Time Machine backup disk. In the list of backups, click the most recent one.**

 The installer goes about copying *everything* from the backup disk onto your new, empty hard drive. When it's all over, you'll have a perfect working system, just the way it was before your series of unfortunate events.

Beware, however: Restoring your earlier version also *erases any files* you've created or changed since you installed the update. Back them up manually before you proceed!

Then follow the steps; when you're asked to choose a backup to restore, choose the most recent one. When it's all over, copy the latest files (the ones that you manually backed up) back onto the hard drive.

Recovering to another Mac

Weirdly enough, you can also use Time Machine as a glorified data bucket that carries your world from one computer to another. You can bring over some or part of any Time Machine backup to a totally different Mac.

On the new machine, connect your backup disk. In the Applications→Utilities folder, open the program called Migration Assistant. On the first screen, click "From another Mac, PC, Time Machine backup, or other disk." The subsequent screens invite you to

choose which backup, which Home folder, and which elements (applications, settings, files) you want to bring over.

Frequently Asked Questions

Time Machine is a very different kind of backup program, and a real departure for longtime Mac addicts. A few questions, therefore, are bound to come up—like these:

- **Can I back up more than one Mac onto the same disk?** Yes. Each Mac's backup is stored in a separate folder on that disk.

- **Does the backup disk have to be dedicated to Time Machine?** No. It can have other files and folders on it. Keep in mind, though, that the more space that's available, the further back your backup trail can go.

- **Can I use more than one backup disk—like one at the office and one at home?** Yes. Just use the Time Machine panel of System Preferences (or the Time Machine Dock icon's shortcut menu) to select the new backup drive each time you switch.

- **Can I delete something for good, from all the backups at once?** Yes. Click the Time Machine icon on the Dock to enter the Restore (outer-space) mode. Find and select the file or folder you want to obliterate. From the ✿ menu, choose Delete All Backups of [the Thing's Name]. (Sneaky, huh? That command is never in the ✿ menu *except* when you're in Time Machine restoring mode.)

- **Can Time Machine back up other hard drives besides the main internal one?** Yes. Open System Preferences→Time Machine. Click Options. Your secondary drives are listed here on the excluded-items list. If you want them backed up, too, *remove* them from the list (click the drive name and then click the − button.)

Note: For many generations of OS X, iSync was an attractive, simple program designed to keep the calendars and phone lists on your various computers, Palm organizer, cellphone, and even your iPod in perfect synchronization.

But over the years, Apple began stripping away iSync features, and in Mountain Lion, it's gone entirely. That doesn't mean that syncing is gone; au contraire! Syncing today is far more complete and ambitious than it ever was before, thanks to iCloud (Chapter 17).

Automator, AppleScript & Services

Apple's specialty has always been taking complex, expensive technologies and somehow making them simple, attractive, and magical. It's done it with video editing, digital photos, DVD authoring, WiFi, Web design, music production, podcasting—you name it.

Popularizing one particular task, however, has continued to elude Apple: *programming*.

Through the years, Apple has introduced various new technologies for helping novices automate their Macs:

- **AppleScript** (born in 1993) was the first Apple tool for automating your Mac. You type out English-like commands in a text file called a *script*, one command per line, and then click Run to have your Mac carry out the result (Figure 7-1, bottom).

 AppleScript is a power user's dream come true, but it's still a programming language. If you want to automate even a simple custom job like converting music files to MP3s, you have to get your hands dirty hunting for the AppleScript command that does exactly what you want—and that can be a real pain.

- **Automator** (born in Mac OS 10.4, Tiger) is a newer program that lets you create your own programs by assembling a series of visual building blocks called *actions*. Drag actions into the right order, click a big Run button, and your Mac faithfully runs through the list of steps you've given it (Figure 7-1, top).

 You have a list of preprogrammed actions at your fingertips, so you never have to do any coding or learn any programming language. Creating the little software robots (called *workflows)* is exceptionally easy.

On the other hand, your selection of building blocks is limited to what other programmers have already written, so Automator workflows are limited in what they can do. You can't automate a complex newspaper layout using Automator alone,

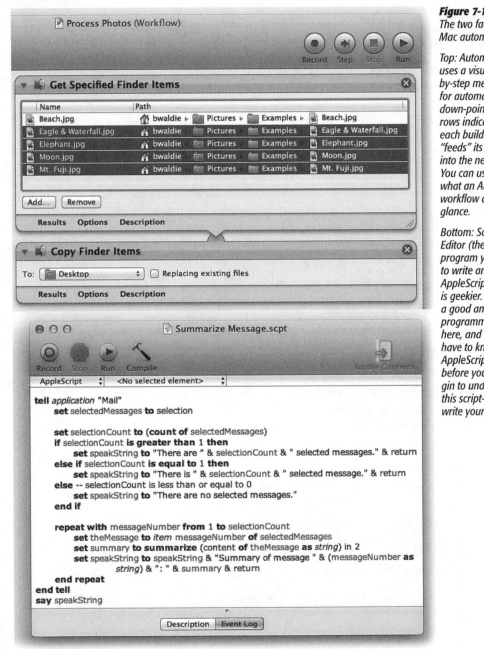

Figure 7-1:
The two faces of Mac automation.

Top: Automator uses a visual, step-by-step metaphor for automation; the down-pointing arrows indicate how each building block "feeds" its result into the next action. You can usually tell what an Automator workflow does at a glance.

Bottom: Script Editor (the program you use to write and edit AppleScript code) is geekier. There's a good amount of programmerese here, and you have to know basic AppleScript syntax before you can begin to understand this script—let alone write your own.

for example, because nobody has written the building-block actions necessary to control all the stages of newspaper production.

For novices, the most exciting feature might be Watch Me Do mode. It lets you just *do* what you want Automator to learn, as Automator watches and memorizes each keystroke, mouse click, and menu selection. Later, Automator can replay those steps faithfully, like a true-blue macro program.

- **Services** are smart, handy commands, available in most Mac programs and in shortcut menus in the Finder. They're a place to *list* the Automator programs you've created as Services, making them available everywhere—along with a couple of dozen ready-made ones from Apple.

This chapter covers these three build-your-own-software technologies: Services, Automator, and AppleScript. True, the latter two require some technical ability. But even if you consider yourself a technophobe, at least read the section about Services. Some real gems await you, and you don't have to do anything but click them.

Services

Apple has always dreamed of a software architecture that would let you mix and match features from different programs—the Mac's spell checker in Microsoft Word, the drawing tools of PowerPoint in your email, and so on. (Remember Apple's OpenDoc software project? Neither does anybody else.)

For several generations of Mac OS X, a menu called Services sat in every single program's Application menu, listing such interchangeable functions. And for all those years, most people pretty much ignored them.

That's because the Services menu was *baffling*. It listed all kinds of weird commands. Most of them, most of the time, were dimmed and unavailable. None of them were described or explained anywhere. They sort of felt like a mistake.

But things changed with Snow Leopard, when Apple gave Services an extreme makeover, in hopes of making them useful again. Today, they continue to make forward strides (though they're still a *little* baffling).

Services commands are contextual, meaning that they show up only when relevant; when a photo is selected, the text-related commands don't appear. Services can filter out unnecessary material automatically. Run a command on a phone number, for example, and Services are smart enough to ignore any other inadvertently selected text.

It's a snap to install Services. As with Dashboard Widgets and Safari plug-ins, you just double-click a Service's icon (you can download tons of them). The Mac asks if you want to install it (Figure 7-2).

Note: Mountain Lion can also auto-install Automator actions. Just double-click one, and it gets routed to the place it needs to go for Automator to see it. (In case you're wondering, that place is Home→Library→Automator.)

Once installed, Services appear in a number of places:

- The Services submenu, which is in the Application menu of every single program.

- The shortcut menu that appears when you Control-click (or right-click) a Finder icon.

Figure 7-2:
Double-click an Automator Service workflow file, and it automagically gets installed in your Home→Library→Services folder. Before Lion, you had to install Services manually. Since your Library folder is now hidden, this auto-installation is a useful thing.

- The shortcut menu that appears when you Control-click (or right-click) highlighted text in a Services-compatible program.

- The ✿ menu at the top of a Finder window.

Figure 7-3 shows what the Services menu looks like when you've highlighted some text in TextEdit.

Figure 7-3:
In the Services menu, each command has a tiny icon to help you distinguish it, and the commands are grouped by function. Any keyboard shortcuts you've established appear right in the menu. Services are also available from the shortcut menus and from the Finder ✿ menu.

You can turn off Services you never use (in System Preferences), thereby hiding them, and you can even assign your own keystrokes to the Services you do use. Finally, you can very easily create your *own* Services menu items, using Automator.

Now, Services *still* aren't first-class Mac citizens. They show up in the shortcut menus of most of the everyday Apple programs (Safari, Mail, TextEdit, Messages, Stickies, Terminal, and so on). But weirdly enough, they're not available in any of the shortcut menus of commercial Apple programs, like iLife (iPhoto, iMovie, GarageBand), iWork (Pages, Keynote, Numbers), or the professional apps like Aperture and Final Cut. You can still get to some of them from the Application→Services menu in these programs, though, so all is not lost.

Six Services that Come in Handy

If you visit System Preferences→Keyboard→Keyboard Shortcuts, you see that OS X comes with a big set of starter Services (Figure 7-5). A lot of them are turned off at the outset (see the checkboxes?). That's because a lot of them are fairly obscure or technical, like "Open man Page in Terminal" and "New Terminal at Folder" Services. Unless you're a Unix pro, you won't find these especially useful.

Here are some examples of what you can do using the built-in Services. These examples also illustrate some of the different ways you can trigger these commands.

Drop in screenshots as you type

You're trying to explain to your mom, or your teacher, or your boss, how to connect to another Mac on the network. What you *really* need to create is an illustrated step-by-step guide.

So you open TextEdit and type up the first step. When it comes time to pop in an illustration, you Control-click (or right-click) the spot on the page; from the shortcut menu, you choose Capture Selection from Screen.

A message appears: "Drag over the portion of the screen you want to capture." You do so, and *snap!*—a picture of the screen area you selected appears right in your document. You continue on that way, typing and illustrating as you go.

One-click desktop picture

Someone just sent you the most *wicked* cool digital photo. It's sitting on your desktop.

Control-click (or right-click) it. From the shortcut menu, choose Set Desktop Picture. *Bam!*—that picture is now your desktop wallpaper, saving you a clunky trip to System Preferences.

Note: In the shortcut menus, Services commands appear at the bottom. If there are more than four of them, they get grouped into a *submenu* called Services.

Text to email, in one step

You're reading on the Web, and you find an article that *totally* settles the argument you've been having with your buddy. Select the text. From the Safari→Services menu, choose New Email With Selection.

Bing! Your Mac opens the Mail program and pastes the highlighted text into the body of a new outgoing email message. You're saved the trouble of copying, launching Mail, creating a new message, and pasting.

Text to a spoken iTunes track

You like to read *The New York Times'* main stories in the morning, but there's never time before work. Or you're supposed to read some document before school. It hits you: Too bad you couldn't *listen* to these documents, read to you on your iPod or iPhone, as you exercise or commute.

Now you can. In Safari, TextEdit, Mail, or wherever, select the text you want converted to audio. Control-click (or right-click) it. From the shortcut menu, choose Add to

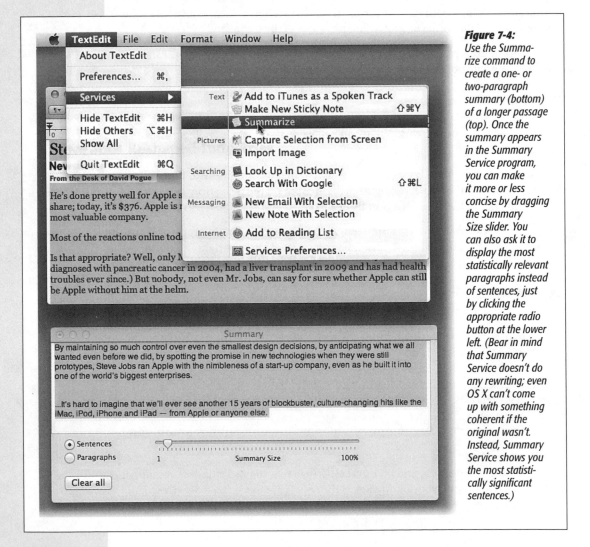

Figure 7-4:
Use the Summarize command to create a one- or two-paragraph summary (bottom) of a longer passage (top). Once the summary appears in the Summary Service program, you can make it more or less concise by dragging the Summary Size slider. You can also ask it to display the most statistically relevant paragraphs instead of sentences, just by clicking the appropriate radio button at the lower left. (Bear in mind that Summary Service doesn't do any rewriting; even OS X can't come up with something coherent if the original wasn't. Instead, Summary Service shows you the most statistically significant sentences.)

iTunes as a Spoken Track. In the dialog box that appears, enter a name for the track and choose one of the Mac's built-in digital voices, like Alex, to read it.

Zap! In a flash, you'll find a new file in your iTunes library, ready to sync to your iPod or iPhone. It's an *audio file* of the chosen voice, reading the article aloud.

Make a new sticky note

You find a phone number, address, Web address, sage proverb, whatever, in an email message, a TextEdit document, or on the Web. Highlight it and then press Shift-⌘-Y. *Pow!*—it's now pasted into a new yellow sticky note in Stickies.

(Shift-⌘-Y, it turns out, is the keyboard shortcut for the Make New Sticky Note command in Services. Any Services command can have a keystroke, and you can change them at will—including this one. See page 213.)

Shorten a long-winded writer

Someone has sent you a speech, proposal, or breakup letter. You haven't got time for the pain. "Just gimme the executive summary," you mutter to yourself.

Highlight all the text, Control-click (or right-click) it, and choose Summarize. (If you don't see Summarize—or another one of the Services mentioned here—go to System Preferences→Keyboard→Keyboard Shortcuts, scroll down, and turn on the checkbox to the left of the missing Service.)

Bing! Your Mac analyzes the sentences you've highlighted and, after a moment, launches Summary Service. This little program, which you probably never even knew you had, displays a greatly shortened version of the original text. Figure 7-4 offers details.

Note: Lots of add-on Mac programs stock the Services menu with commands of their own. OmniFocus, for example, adds an option to send selected text to your to-do inbox. OmniOutliner, QuickSilver, TextWrangler, Twitter, and many other programs add to the Services menu, too.

More Great Examples from Downloadable Services

The preceding pages describe the best of the *built-in* Services. But there are hundreds more available on the Web.

Consider visiting *www.macosxautomation.com*, for example. That's the Web site maintained by Apple's Services/Automator/AppleScript team. Here, when you click Services, you can find a Download page filled with useful, ready-made Services. A few examples:

- **Disk Item • New Disk Image with Selection.** Highlight a folder or a group of icons. Choose this command from the ✿ menu, and *presto!*—a new disk image file (.dmg) containing the selected Finder items.

- **Mail • New Message with Video Snapshot.** You open the Mail program and select this command from the Services menu. Your iSight camera comes to life, takes a photo of your mug, and inserts it into a new outgoing message. For added flair,

apply a stationery template to the new message before sending. ("Happy birthday, honey—here's a snazzy picture of me!")

- **Image • Change File Type.** Highlight some photo files in a Finder window. From the ✿ menu, choose this command. It auto-converts them to the new graphics file format of your choice.

- **PDF • Encrypt File.** Highlight a PDF document in the Finder, and then choose this command from the ✿ menu or the file's shortcut menu. You get a duplicate of the PDF file, encrypted with a password you supply, with the word "(encrypted)" appended to its name.

Clearly, there's all kinds of fun (and utility) to be found in Services.

Turning Them On and Off—and Adding Keyboard Shortcuts

The Services command center is in the System Preferences→Keyboard→Keyboard Shortcuts pane. (You can also get there by choosing Services→Services Preferences from any program's Application menu.)

Here, turn the checkboxes on or off to choose which Services you want available (Figure 7-5).

Figure 7-5:
Here's the Services command center. You can purge your shortcut menus and Services menus of the useless Services by turning off their checkboxes. You can also assign (or change) keyboard shortcuts. Click a Service's name and then press Return to open the Keyboard Shortcut box; then press the desired keystroke on your keyboard.

Handier still, you can double-click to the right of a Service's name and then press a keyboard combination. That will become its new keyboard shortcut, available system-wide. (The usual caveats apply: Any keystroke you make up *here* overrides the same keystrokes that your programs may use for themselves, so be careful.)

Automator

Automator is the OS X program that lets you create your *own* little programs—and your own Services, if you like. Like most programs on your Mac, it sits waiting in your Launchpad (in a folder called Other). Click its icon to open it. (Automator's robot icon is supposedly named Otto. Get it? Otto Matic? Stop, you're killing us!)

Note: Like many other updated Lion/Mountain Lion programs, Automator now offers Autosave and Versions (page 220). Those are especially useful in a programming app like this; often, you'll get things working just fine, and then make some change that causes everything to break. No problem; now you can just revert back to the working version.

In Lion/Mountain Lion, Automator also includes a handful of new and useful actions, like the Website Popup action described later in this chapter. Another converts text files to ePub (a popular eBook format), and another one converts a word or phrase to an image. Now you can quickly prepare that family cookbook for publishing in the iBookstore, or add a phrase to your blog using some strange and obscure font.

Seven Startup Templates

As you'll soon discover, building an Automator workflow is a satisfying intellectual exercise and a delicious talent to acquire. But if the point of all the effort is to create

GEM IN THE ROUGH

Open Any Program with a Keystroke

It's a feature that's been achingly missing from the Mac since Day One: assigning keyboard shortcuts to *opening programs.* You couldn't set up Control-W to bring up Microsoft Word, Control-S to open Safari, and so on. (At least not without the help of add-on shareware.)

With Services, now you can.

First, use Automator to build a simple, one-step workflow. The first and only action should be Launch Application. Use its pop-up menu to specify *which* program you want to open from the keyboard.

At the very top of the workflow pane, change the pop-up menus so that they read, "Service receives no input in any

application" (where the underlined phrases are pop-up menus). That "any application" part is important; otherwise, your keystroke will work in only one program.

Save the result and name it "Open Word," or "Open Contacts," or whatever you like.

Finally, open System Preferences→Keyboard→Keyboard Shortcuts. Click Services. Find your new Service and give it a keystroke as described on page 213.

And that's it! You've just created a keystroke that can open the desired program—using only OS X's built-in tools. Hurrah!

a timesaving, step-saving software robot, you'll need some way to *trigger* it—to run it, just the way you run an email program or a Web browser.

Fortunately, you can save a workflow as a regular, double-clickable application, if you like, or turn it into a Service, as described above, or embed it in shortcut menus all over your Mac. In fact, when you fire up Automator, the first thing it wants to know is: What *is* the desired destination for this workflow?

You're offered seven options in the template screen shown in Figure 7-6:

- **Workflow.** An Automator Workflow file (with file name extension *.workflow*) is what you create if you want to study and refine your project. It's not the best format for *using* your homemade app, though, because to run it, you have to open Automator and click the Run button.

- **Application.** A workflow saved as an application has all the benefits associated with normal OS X programs. You can double-click its Finder icon to launch it, drag it to the Dock for one-click launching, or just leave it in your Applications folder, nestled among all the "professional" programs, so you can run it from your Launchpad.

Figure 7-6:
Automator has seven choices for the final form of your workflow. If you're not sure which format you'll want to use for a particular workflow, choose Workflow for now. You can always save the result into a different format (or multiple formats).

So why wouldn't you just save your workflows as applications *all* the time? First, workflow applications are *much* larger than workflow documents—as much as 20 times larger. That's worth remembering if you plan to distribute your workflows online or via email.

Also, when a workflow application runs, it doesn't give you access to the Workflow *log*—a big downside if you want to monitor the progress of your workflow in minute detail. Instead, you get a dinky action indicator in the menu bar, as shown in Figure 7-7.

Figure 7-7:
The menu-bar indicator tells you that the workflow application is, in fact, running (the spinning ✿). When you click it, a menu tells you which action is running and how far along the workflow is (the little pie chart). If you want to cancel the workflow halfway through, click the ✖ button.

Finally, it's a pain to edit a workflow application if something goes wrong; you have to open the whole thing in Automator and resave it.

- **Service.** Ahhh, now we're talking. Yes, that's right: You can now build your own Services, as described above, and give them all the privileges of Apple's own Services. One sample benefit: You can assign your own keyboard shortcuts to them, as described on page 213. The beauty of Automator-created Services is that they show up *instantly* in all the places where Services show up: in the Services menu, in the shortcut menu that appears when you right-click a Finder icon or selected text, and in the Finder's ✿ menu—all ready to use. In other words, enhancing and debugging your workflow is incredibly easy, because the Services you create are immediately ready to try out in the "real world" of your Mac.

- **Folder Action.** Folder Actions are workflows that run automatically when you add files to a *folder* in the Finder. Folder Actions are extremely powerful for image processing, network backup jobs, and much more, but they're also extremely complicated. For an explanation of the ins and outs, read this chapter's bonus Apple-Script appendix (on this book's "Missing CD" page at *www.missingmanuals.com*).

- **Print Plugin.** Print workflows show up as menu items inside the Print dialog box's PDF menu (page 598). If you save a workflow as a Print workflow plug-in, you can easily run the workflow on a document you're about to print—applying a ColorSync filter to the document to compensate for slight discolorations, for example.

- **Calendar Alarm.** This powerful plug-in format lets you schedule workflows to run at specific times. When you save a workflow in this format, Calendar opens and creates a new event named after your plug-in; you're supposed to drag and edit this event to whatever time and day you want the workflow to run. (You can

even use Calendar's "repeat" pop-up menu to have the workflow run every day, week, and so on.)

This is a fantastic tool. If you have a workflow that plays an iTunes song, for example, you can easily build an alarm clock using nothing more than Calendar alarms.

- **Image Capture Plugin.** Image Capture is a program for importing photos from a camera or scanner. If you save a workflow as an Image Capture plug-in, you can choose to run the workflow whenever you import new photos with this program— so you can easily shrink the new images to a smaller size, for example.

You can click these icons one at a time to read capsule descriptions. You don't have to make a choice now, though; you can start by just saving a Workflow file and then change it to something else later, when you decide what you really want to do with it.

Now, go forth and automate!

Tip: You can find extra Automator resources, including useful workflows and actions, at sites like *http:// macscripter.net* and *www.macosxautomation.com.*

Automator Tour

Once you've chosen a finished format for the workflow you're about to create, you wind up in Automator itself. A tour may be in order:

Toolbar

At the top of the Automator window, the toolbar offers six fairly self-explanatory buttons. From left to right (Figure 7-8):

- **Hide Library.** This button hides the entire left Library pane of Automator, where all the prefab building-block steps are listed. You wind up with one big Workflow pane.

- **Media.** Click to open the standard Media Browser box that pops up all over OS X. You can drag your music, photos, or movies from the Media Browser directly into the Workflow pane, *or* into an action itself (one with a matching data type, of course) to use that media in your workflow.

Tip: Media from the Media Browser aren't all you can add to Automator. You can also drag files—text documents, media, folders, and so on—straight from the Finder into your workflow, saving you the hassle of having to *search* for them in Automator. You can even drag text from an open TextEdit document or Safari window.

- **Record.** Click to enter Watch Me Do mode, where Automator memorizes the steps that you perform manually (page 310).

- **Step, Stop, Run.** These buttons control playback of the workflow you're building. Run and Stop are obvious. Step lets you run through the workflow at your leisure, one action at a time; you tell it when to advance.

Tip: To save screen space, you can hide the entire Automator toolbar by choosing View→Hide Toolbar. (You can bring it back by choosing View→Show Toolbar.)

While the toolbar is hidden (and even when it's visible), you can still start and stop playback by choosing Workflow→Run (⌘-R) and Workflow→Stop (⌘-period).

Figure 7-8:
Automator's screen design comes in big slices: a Library list at left, indi- vidual Actions in the middle, and the actual workflow-build- ing area at the right.

Library list Actions/Variables list Workflow pane

Description Hide/Show the Logs

Library pane

The Library pane is the entire left section of the Automator window. It includes the search box, Library list, Description field, and the list of Actions or Variables. These are described on the following pages.

Tip: You can resize either of Automator's left-side columns (Library and Actions) by dragging the vertical divider lines between them.

Search box

Like OS X's other search boxes, this one works in real time—it displays matching actions or variables as you type.

If you start by selecting a category in the Library list at left, you're telling Automator, "Search only within this category of actions or variables." If you want to search for actions that can process files in the Finder, for example, click Files & Folders in the Library list, and then type *file* in the search box.

Tip: You can tell Automator to group actions by application, instead of category, if you prefer. Choose View→Arrange Actions by→Application. (To switch it back, choose View→Arrange Actions by→Category).

Or, to search *all* Automator's categories, click Library at the top of the Library list before searching. (That's the best way to find an action or variable if you're not sure what category it's in.)

Your search results appear in the Actions/Variables list, sorted alphabetically. You can begin dragging actions directly into the Workflow pane at the right side to build a workflow, as described shortly.

Click the ✪ button in the search box to return to the complete list of actions or variables.

Library

Above the Library list, two buttons appear that govern what's displayed in the Library pane:

- **Actions.** When you click Actions, the Library lists all the features and data that Automator actions can control: Files & Folders, Music, Photos, Text, and so on. (Or, if they're arranged by application: Contacts, Finder, Calendar, Mail, and others.) When you click a category, the Actions list on the right shows every action related to that type of data. For example, when you click Photos in the left-side list, the right-side list of actions offers steps like Flip Images, Crop Images, and so on.

 When you find an action you want to use in your workflow, drag it to the right into the large Workflow pane.

- **Variables.** *Variables* are memorized info chunks that you can reuse in an Automator workflow, exactly as in real programming languages. The Variables list is divided into categories like Date & Time (today's date, today's month, and so on), Locations (the paths to various folders on your Mac), and User (your name, phone number, and other information).

 Later in this chapter, you'll see how it's useful to incorporate these information tidbits into your workflows.

Note: Variables whose icons look like a boxed V are variables that you can *change*, once you've added them to a workflow. For example, you can change the formatting of the "Current time" variable by double-clicking it in the variables log area at the bottom of the Workflow pane.

Variables with ✿ icons are predefined and unchangeable.

Description field

When you click an action or variable in the list, the Description box provides some terse, superficial information on how to use it. You might see what the action does, what kind of data it expects to receive from the previous action (*input*), and what the action sends on to the following action (*result*).

If the variable is editable (it has a V icon), you get to see what parts of it you can change.

Tip: To save space, you can hide the Description field by clicking the ▾ button on the bottom-left edge of the window. Click it again to bring the Description field back.

✿ button

The ✿ button in the lower-left corner of the window is a pop-up menu. Its four commands let you create and delete customizable collections called *groups* and *smart groups*. They behave exactly like playlists and smart playlists in iTunes. For example, you can create a group that holds the actions you use most often, so you don't have to keep hunting for them.

Smart groups are constantly updated with actions that match the criteria you set for that smart group. (They're available only for actions, not variables.) For example, you can create a smart group that lists only actions that work with iPhoto, or actions with input types that contain the word "image." Add more criteria by clicking the **+** button.

Note: Automator's Library list comes with two factory-installed smart groups: Most Used, which displays the actions you've used the most in your workflows; and Recently Added, which displays actions added by newly installed applications, for example, or actions you downloaded and added yourself.

Workflow pane

The Workflow pane is Automator's kitchen. It's where you put your actions in whatever order you want, set any action-specific preferences, and fry them all up in a pan.

The Workflow pane also shows how the information from one action gets piped into another, creating a stream of information. That's how the Workflow pane differentiates Automator from the dozens of nonvisual, programming-based automation tools out there. Figure 7-9 shows what a piece of a workflow (an action) might look like in the Workflow pane.

Figure 7-9:
Anatomy of an Automator action. You can drag the action by its title bar to move it to an earlier or later position in your workflow.

When you drag an action out of the Actions list into the Workflow pane, any surrounding actions scoot aside to make room.

Tip: If you double-click an action in the Actions list, Automator inserts it at the *bottom* of the Workflow pane. (Pressing Return when an action is highlighted does the same thing.)

Log viewer

Under the Workflow pane on the left are two tiny buttons, identified in Figure 7-8. They hide and show two useful pop-up panels that contain *logs* (mini reports): the Workflow log, which shows which actions ran successfully, which failed (if any), what each action did, and so on; and the Variables list (Figure 7-10), which shows all the variables used in your workflow.

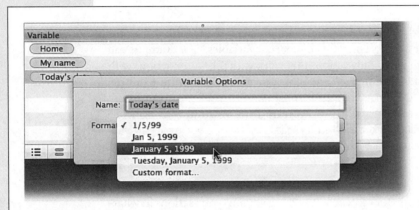

Figure 7-10:
The Variables list shows all the variables you're using in your workflow. The light blue variables are editable; double-click one to modify the variable's name and its settings (in this case, the format for "Today's date").

Opening Existing Workflows

Automator comes with three prebuilt workflows that show off its capabilities. Find them by clicking Help→Open Examples Folder; open one of these workflows for inspection by dragging it to your desktop and double-clicking it. (If you don't drag it to your desktop, thus making a copy of it, before opening it, Automator will start barking that you don't have access to modify the workflow.)

Tip: You don't actually have to *open* an Automator document to see how it's set up. Simply select a workflow in the Finder and hit the space bar to activate Quick Look (page 59), which gives you a preview of the entire workflow—actions and all.

Note, though, that this works only with workflows saved with Automator in Snow Leopard or later. Since Apple's own example workflows were created in the older 10.4 version and never updated, Quick Look won't properly display them until they're opened and *resaved*.

Sadly, the included workflows aren't especially useful. In fact, two of them don't work consistently. Here's a rundown:

- **Process Images** applies special visual effects to whatever photos you specify in the workflow. This is the most useful of these examples. No, people haven't exactly been clamoring for an automated way to create mirror-image camera shots, but

this workflow does show you the basics of batch-processing photos. You can use it as a template for building your own "Convert to JPEG" or "Scale to 640 × 480 pixels" workflow, for example. Later in this chapter, you'll find a complete walk-through of how it works.

- **Import MobileMe Photo Album into iPhoto** didn't work even when the MobileMe service was still around. You can, however, use this workflow on other Web sites that include linked images, such as NASA's Astronomy Picture of the Day (*http://apod.nasa.gov/apod/*). The concept of the workflow is simple: It slurps linked photos from a Web page and copies them into iPhoto. From there, you can view a full-screen slideshow of the images, or even edit them.

Tip: You can download a *working* version of this workflow (renamed to Import NASA Picture of the Day into iPhoto) from this book's "Missing CD" page at *www.missingmanuals.com.*

- **Display Trailers in Safari** is intended to show you how you can create workflows that work with Web addresses. This one sneaks out to Apple's popular movie-previews Web site, rounds up the list of the latest movie ads, and opens each in a new Web-browser tab.

Tip: Apple provides more Automator examples at its Automator Web site, *www.macosxautomation.com.* "Welcome to the Party!" for example, cleverly demos two complex features of Automator—variables and the Loop action—by showing you how to create a workflow that takes photos of your friends and turns them into a cool, party-ready screen saver. The instructions are a little outdated, but if you can manage to follow along, this one still works like a charm in Mountain Lion.

Understanding a Workflow

Before you build your own workflows, it's a good idea to understand how actions work together to process information. Here's a step-by-step analysis of the Process Images workflow described above (and in Figure 7-11), which will give you deeper insight into building your *own* workflows.

1. **Ask for Confirmation.**

 This common action, available in the Utilities category (in the Library list), produces a dialog box that tells the innocent bystander what's about to happen (Figure 7-12). It's often smart to begin each of your *own* workflows with a box like this, to remind yourself (or your minimum-wage minions) what the workflow actually does.

 In this case, the message informs your audience that the workflow is about to take some of your desktop pictures, apply some wacko effects to them, and then open them up in Preview to display the results.

Tip: If you want the dialog box to appear with a bright warning sign—to inform you, for example, that you're about to erase your entire hard drive—click the robot icon in the upper-left corner of the Ask for Confirmation action. Automator swaps in a robot-with-yellow-triangle icon.

Keep in mind, too, that the entire Ask for Confirmation action is 100 percent customizable. Not only can you change the text that appears in the dialog box—you can even change the names of the Cancel and OK buttons.

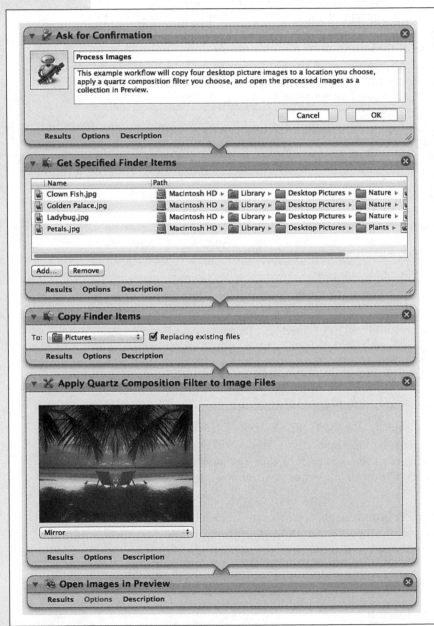

Figure 7-11:
The Process Images workflow consists of only five actions. (The first action, which just displays an explanatory dialog box, shouldn't even count.) Still, this simple action does in 10 seconds what would take most humans at least 5 minutes: applying the same photo effect to several images.

2. Get Specified Finder Items.

The next step in the Process Images workflow comes from the Files & Folders Library category. Here's where you specify which files you want your workflow to operate on. Apple has set it to use some of your desktop pictures, but you can use the Add and Remove buttons to edit the list—to add your own images to be mirrored, for example—or you can drag files straight from the Finder into this list.

When this action is finished, it passes on a list of files and/or folders to the next action, ready for further processing.

Tip: This example workflow always operates on the same set of files. But if you were to substitute the Files & Folders→Ask for Finder Items action instead, Automator would *ask* which files to process *each time* you ran the workflow, which is a heck of a lot more useful.

Figure 7-12:
A dialog box created by the Ask for Confirmation action. Feel free to edit the action with your own text; the stuff Apple provides is pretty dry.

3. Copy Finder Items.

This is a very important Files & Folders action: It makes a *copy* of the specified files and folders (in this case, the ones you identified in step 2) so you don't gum up the originals. You can change where you want the copies stored by editing the To pop-up menu in the action. The menu lists obvious locations like Pictures and Desktop, or you can choose Other to select any folder you like.

Note: The "Replacing existing files" checkbox tells Automator that, if there are old files in the Pictures folder with the same names as your new files, you want to delete the old files automatically.

If you click Options in the action, you see that the "Show this action when the workflow runs" checkbox is turned on. That way, when your workflow runs, Automator will ask where to store the copies so that the destination can be different each time. Otherwise, the files will automatically be copied to whatever folder you select in the pop-up menu right now.

4. Apply Quartz Composition Filter to Image Files.

This action (which came from the Photos category) processes the newly duplicated images from step 3; in this case, it applies a mirror filter to them. The action then

passes the newly mirrored images on to step 5. If you prefer, you can choose a different filter from the pop-up menu—to make the image look like a comic-book drawing, for example, instead of applying the mirror filter.

Note: The Quartz Composition Filter, a piece of OS X's Quartz display technology, can modify images and photos in real time. Photo Booth uses this technology, which is why many of Photo Booth's effects are also in the action's Filter pop-up menu. (See *http://developer.apple.com/technologies/mac/graphics-and-animation.html* for the incredibly nerdy details on Quartz.)

Since "Show this action when the workflow runs" under Options is turned on, you'll have the chance to choose a different filter each time this workflow runs.

(By the way, the image of the beach is intended to demonstrate the filter's effect; it's not actually one of your photos.)

Note: The big box on the right side of the action isn't there because Apple had nothing to fill the space. Certain filters have settings you can modify, which appear in that box. The Glow filter, for example, lets you specify *how much* glow you want applied to the image(s).

5. **Open Images in Preview.**

This final action, which also comes from the Photos category, takes the post-filter images from step 4 and opens them in Preview. From there, you can flip, resize, or resave the images.

Try running the workflow by clicking Run. The bottom of the Workflow pane tells you which step of the workflow is running at the moment. As each action finishes, a green checkmark appears in its lower-left corner.

Note: If something goes wrong while your workflow is running (or if you click Cancel in a dialog box), your workflow stops in its tracks. To identify the offending step, look for the red X in an action's lower-left corner, or check the Log.

Unfortunately, if your workflow shuts down in the middle, you can't restart it from there. When you click Run the next time, the workflow plays from the beginning.

Building Your Own Workflow

You could spend all day playing with the workflows Apple gives you, making minor tweaks and seeing how they affect the workflow's progress. You could even download more preassembled workflows from *http://macscripter.net* or *www.macosxautomation.com*, if you were so inclined.

Still, those options don't give you the kind of hands-on experience you need to automate your Mac on your own. That's why the following pages walk you through building two different Automator workflows from scratch. Along the way, you'll learn several tricks that you'll find handy when you start building your own workflows.

Tip: If you're feeling lazy, you can download the completed workflow projects from this book's "Missing CD" page at *www.missingmanuals.com.*

Build Your Own Web Browser

Quick Look is great for previewing Mail attachments and files in the Finder without opening them. Wouldn't it be cool if you could do the same for a Web address you find in a document? Who wants to go through all the trouble of opening up Safari for something you might not even care about? Well, with the Website Popup Automator action in Mountain Lion, you can create your own Quick Look URL Service.

Note: In Mountain Lion, Mail offers Quick Look for Web addresses—but the following steps let you add that feature to any other program, too.

1. **In Automator, choose File→New (or press ⌘-N).**

 The templates dialog box appears (shown back in Figure 7-6).

2. **Double-click Service.**

 You want this puppy to be available from the shortcut menu in programs like Stickies and TextEdit—and that's the beauty of the Service.

 You wind up with a new panel at the top of the workflow, bearing the peculiar legend, "Service receives selected text in any application" (where the underlined phrases are pop-up menus).

 Remember, Services are contextual; they're smart enough to know when to show up in your menus. That's the purpose of these pop-up menus: to let you specify when your new Service should appear. In this case, you want the Service to appear only if you've selected a URL.

3. **From the first pop-up menu, choose "URLs." Leave the second set to "any application." From the third, choose "only URLs" (Figure 7-13).**

Figure 7-13:
You want this Service to appear in your shortcut menus only when you've right-clicked a URL in a program. You can set the Website Popup action to display a preview of the URL at the size of your choice: Large, Medium, iPhone, iPad, and so forth.

The third pop-up menu becomes enabled when you choose "URLs" from the first pop-up menu.

OK: You've now established what kind of information the Service will work on, and in which programs (in this case, any program). Now you have to tell Automator what you want to *do* with the URL: Display it in a Quick Look window.

4. In the Library list at left, click the Internet category.

(Make sure the Actions button is clicked above the list.) You've just narrowed down the list of available actions to those that pertain to Safari and other Internet-related activities.

5. From the Actions column, drag the action called Website Popup into the Workflow pane.

Use the search box at the top if you don't feel like reading through the list of actions.

6. In the Website Popup action, in the Workflow pane, select Medium from the Site Size pop-up menu.

This makes sure that, when you run the Service, the Quick Look window doesn't obscure everything on screen.

If you look at the description for this action, you'll see that the Input accepts "(URLs)." It explains that if a URL is passed from the previous action, it will be opened.

Tip: You can also set the pop-up to appear centered or wherever your mouse pointer may be located.

Even cooler, you can actually choose the user agent (the kind of browser) the window uses. You can set it to Safari, iPhone, or even iPad. With iPhone, for example, you'll see the mobile version of the Web site (if available) in a little iPhone-size window, just as it would appear on your actual iPhone.

7. Choose File→Save. In the dialog box, name your new Service command. Click Save.

You can call it "Preview Webpage," or "Quick Look URL," or "Show Me What This Will Look Like on My iPhone." Whatever you like.

That's actually all there is to it. Now for the testing. Switch to TextEdit and create a new document. Type in a full URL, such as *http://www.apple.com*. Select the URL you just typed, Control-click (or right-click) it (Figure 7-14, top). From the shortcut menu, choose Preview Webpage (or whatever you called your Service).

Note: If there are more than four Services at the bottom of the shortcut menu, your new command will be added to a submenu called Services. If you'd rather avoid this extra step—preferring a longer list of Services right there in the shortcut menu—then download the free Services Menu Items Utility from this book's "Missing CD" page at *www.missingmanuals.com*. It lets you stack up to 25 Services in the shortcut menu without segregating them into a Services submenu.

Instantly, a Quick Look–like window appears and shows you a preview of the URL you just typed—no Safari involved (Figure 7-14, bottom). Super cool!

Figure 7-14:
Top: Once you've saved your Service, your Preview Webpage command is ready to go! Control-click (or right-click) any selected URL in Mail or TextEdit.

Bottom: When you run the workflow, a preview of the selected URL pops up in its own self-contained browser window.

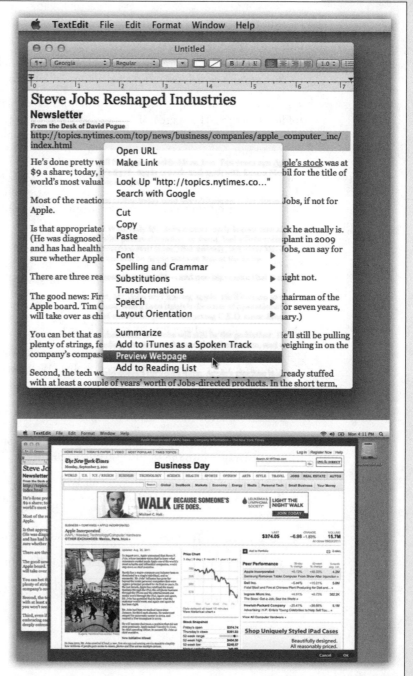

Tip: Want to change the type of a workflow, for example, from an Application program to a Service? Just open the workflow in Automator, choose File→Duplicate To, and select a new type from the templates dialog box. An exact replica of the workflow is created, ready for you to save in the new format. Before, changing a workflow's type was a manual process that took about 100 steps.

Burn an iPhoto Picture CD

iPhoto is a fantastic program for organizing digital photos. It even has its own photo-backup feature, which burns selected albums' photos to a blank CD or DVD.

However, those backup discs maintain iPhoto's complex and user-hostile Library folder structure. That's great if you expect one day to restore the backup *to iPhoto,* because the backup maintains all your keywords, ratings, albums, comments, and other iPhoto data.

But it's not so great if you want to hand the CD or DVD to someone who *doesn't* use iPhoto (like an Adobe Lightroom fan or a Windows person), because they'll have a devil of a time figuring out where the photos *are* in the convoluted Library folder structure.

If you build an Automator workflow to back up your photos instead, you can (a) burn a disc containing *only* the photos in one simple folder; (b) have more control over which photos are backed up; and (c) learn even more tricks for automating sophisticated operations. Figure 7-15 shows what the final workflow looks like.

Here's how to put it together:

1. **Create a new Automator workflow (⌘-N).**

 The templates appear. In this example, you'll create a standalone, double-clickable program. You're a programmer now, baby! (Well, sort of.)

2. **Double-click Application.**

 You arrive at the main workflow-construction area.

3. **Click the Photos category. In the list of available actions, find Get Specified iPhoto Items. Drag it into the empty Workflow pane.**

 As shown in Figure 7-15, you've so far told Automator to get some pictures from iPhoto. But when this program *runs,* you'll want it to let you choose *which* pictures. So:

4. **Click Options. Turn on "Show this action when the workflow runs."**

 Your newly hatched workflow, when it runs, will begin by asking you which photos you want to back up.

Tip: What you really want is to round up only the latest batch of photos–since your last backup, for example. Fortunately, one of the actions in the Photos folder is called Find iPhoto Items, and it lets you specify a time period like "Within the last 2 weeks." It would be perfect for this workflow–if it weren't so buggy. (For example, when searching for photos that were photographed in the past two weeks, the result doesn't include photos from today.)

For best results, then, create a Smart Album in iPhoto that lets you filter photos based on certain criteria–all your photos taken in the past two months, for example. When you run the workflow, you can choose that album to back up, so that you get only the most recent shots.

Figure 7-15:
Top: The first action presents a dialog box telling you what this workflow does.

Middle: The second action lets you select from your iPhoto Library the images you want to back up.

Bottom: The last action, in a single step, burns those images onto a CD or DVD. It works regardless of whether your Mac has an internal or external burner. Try that simplicity on a PC!

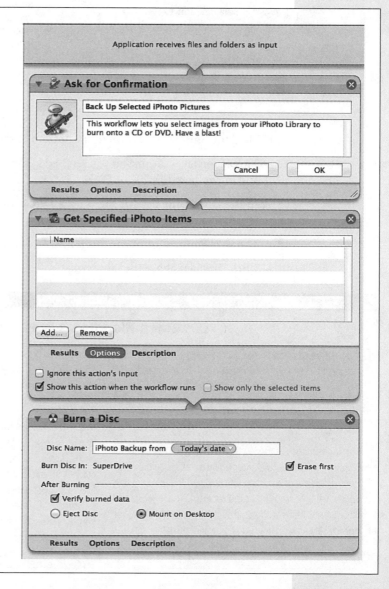

5. In the Library list, click the Utilities folder. Drag the Ask for Confirmation action into the Workflow pane, above the Get Specified iPhoto Items action. Fill in the text as shown at the top of Figure 7-15.

Be sure to drag it *above* the Get Specified iPhoto Items action so it's the first thing that happens when you run your workflow. Now you've just directed Automator to begin its work by displaying a dialog box (Figure 7-16).

Figure 7-16:
The explanatory dialog box from the iPhoto Backup workflow. Making the dialog box appear is optional, but it's helpful if you come back to your workflow in a few months and forget what it's supposed to do.

Back Up Selected iPhoto Pictures

This workflow lets you select images from your iPhoto Library to burn onto a CD or DVD. Have a blast!

Cancel OK

6. Drag the Burn a Disc action to the bottom of the Workflow pane.

This action takes the images you selected in the Get Specified iPhoto Items action and burns them to a CD or DVD.

7. In the Disc Name field of the Burn a Disc action, type "iPhoto Backup from " (that's a space after "from").

The workflow will complete this phrase later.

8. Click Variables above the Library list.

FREQUENTLY ASKED QUESTION

Checking a Workflow's Progress

Some of these actions take their sweet time. Is there some progress bar that will tell me how far along my workflow is?

Actually, Automator provides two ways to check on the status of your workflow: the simple way (call it "the Indicator") and the Workflow log.

The Indicator lies in the lower-left corner of the Automator window, next to the Log buttons. When your workflow is running, a little status message appears here to tell you exactly which action is running at the moment. You can use that information, along with some common sense, to figure out how close your workflow is to being finished. If the workflow has run its course, the Indicator says, "Workflow completed."

(You can also identify whatever action is running at this moment, thanks to the spinning-sprocket indicator in its lower-left corner.)

The Workflow log is even more powerful. Activate it by clicking the list-like button in the bottom-left corner of the Workflow pane (or by hitting Option-⌘-L). It tells you when each action begins and ends, and it also displays geeky data-conversion information (like when OS X is turning "image files" into plain-vanilla "Finder files"). And unlike the Indicator, the Workflow log keeps its information around even after your workflow is finished—so you can see how long your entire workflow took to run, for example.

Those variables are about to come in handy. You're going to complete the phrase "iPhoto Backup from " with whatever the date of the backup is.

9. **Click the Date & Time category in the Library list. Drag the "Today's date" variable into the Disc Name field after "from."**

The CD or DVD's name will be something like "iPhoto Backup from 4/9/12," making it easy for you to see *when* you made the backup disc. The date automatically changes whenever you run the workflow.

10. **Choose File→Save. Type a name for your new program (like "Back Up This Month's iPhoto Pix to CD"), and save it wherever you like (on the desktop, for example).**

Now try it out. Double-click your newly forged program; your workflow springs into action, asking you to specify the photos you want, asking for a blank disc, and then burning it.

Tip: To make sure the workflow doesn't get hung up while waiting for a disc, it's a good idea to get your disc ready first, and insert it into your drive, so it's ready to go.

Doing More with Automator

Automator is not a static, this-or-nothing program: It's a versatile, *expandable* tool with ever-increasing potential. There are two especially good ways to increase Automator's power beyond using the factory-installed actions: adding more actions yourself, and using the new Watch Me Do feature.

Getting More Action(s)

Automator comes with dozens of actions, but you're bound—eventually—to find yourself wishing there were a few more. Perhaps you'd like some Automator actions to control non-Apple programs like Photoshop, or you'd just like to have a few extra actions to control OS X itself.

Fortunately, Automator can handle actions written by non-Apple programmers, too. Just visit any of the Web sites devoted to Automator actions (like *http://macscripter. net* or *www.macosxautomation.com*) and download any actions you'd like.

If the action's programmers did their jobs right, you can just download the action and run the installer (or double-click the action to install it automatically). The next time you open Automator, the new action will be listed in the correct category in the Library list.

Tip: Some programs, such as Microsoft Office, Fetch, OmniOutliner, Pixelmator, and Transmit, include built-in Automator actions. No additional installation is needed; Automator just sees them and they show up in its Library.

Once in Automator, you can use your new actions just as you'd use the ones that came bundled with your Mac: dragging and dropping them in whatever order you want, customizing their settings, and so on.

Before you run any new actions, though, look at the Description field to discover the actions' inputs and outputs. With that information in hand, you'll never accidentally connect, say, your new Sauté Vegetables action to an unrelated action like Burn a Disc.

And, finally, if you're interested in writing your own Automator actions (Warning: programming experience necessary), visit *http://developer.apple.com/documentation/ AppleApplications/Conceptual/AutomatorConcepts/Automator.html* for an introduction.

Watch Me Do Mode

Sometimes, you'll run into a task that Automator can't accomplish with *any* action, no matter how nicely you ask: opening multiple folders of bookmarks in several Safari windows, for example, or automating some no-name program that doesn't know anything about Automator and doesn't come with any actions.

Enter Watch Me Do. In this mode, you click a Record button. The Automator window disappears, and a black "Automator: Recording" window takes its place. From now until you hit the Stop button, every mouse click and keystroke is *recorded*, step by step, into Automator. Later, you can survey the list of steps you took and clean them up.

When you run the workflow, your mouse actually moves to reproduce your clicks, and the Mac actually types the same keystrokes you did. It's like watching a ghost control your computer, or maybe a really annoying little brother who won't stop mimicking you.

You can even manipulate the individual steps—delete one, for example, or edit the playback speed, or change how long it takes before the step "times out" (gives up).

It's far easier to create workflows using Watch Me Do than by having to drag the correct actions into the correct sequence; you're leaving even more of the programming to Automator.

Unfortunately, there are drawbacks to Watch Me Do, too:

- The conditions on the screen when you run the action must be *identical* to the way they were when you recorded. If some window isn't the same size, or in the same position, or if some button isn't where it used to be, the workflow derails.

- Watch Me Do relies on the Mac's accessibility features—the same ones that form the guts of VoiceOver and other tools for the disabled—and different programs have been "accessibilitized" to wildly varying degrees. You can record and play back steps that involve System Preferences with amazing success, for example. But operating other programs can be hopeless.

That's why Watch Me Do may seem incredibly flaky. For best results, use keystrokes and keyboard shortcuts as much as possible, and avoid the mouse.

Here's an example.

Change your startup disk

If you use Boot Camp to run Windows on your Mac (Chapter 8), you may find yourself having to open the Startup Disk pane of System Preferences with alarming frequency. And, unfortunately, there's no Change Startup Disk action in Automator to make that job less repetitive.

Fortunately, Watch Me Do *can* automate the process, so you can switch your startup disk with one click on an Automator-created application on your desktop or Dock. Creating the workflow is simple:

1. **Create a new workflow (⌘-N). Double-click Application in the template-selection panel.**

 Since you're just going to work with Watch Me Do, you won't be messing with any predefined actions this time.

2. **Click the Record button.**

 The Automator window disappears, and the black Recording window pops up. Everything you do is being recorded right into Automator.

3. **Click System Preferences in the Dock.**

 If System Preferences isn't in your Dock, put it there before beginning the recording. (It's in your Applications folder.) Choosing its name from the menu or from Launchpad generally doesn't work, thanks to some typical Watch Me Do flakiness.

4. **In System Preferences, click Startup Disk, and then click either your Windows partition or your Mac partition.**

 Later, you can create a second workflow to choose your other disk, if you want.

5. **Press ⌘-Q to quit System Preferences.**

 You've switched the disk and are ready to wrap up the workflow.

Tip: If you want the workflow to do the restarting, too, you can click the Restart button and follow the prompts. But you'll need to make sure another program is open with an unsaved document, so you'll have the chance to cancel the restart process. Otherwise, Automator will just quit and the computer will restart before you have a chance to stop recording and save the workflow.

6. **Click Stop in the Recording window.**

 The Automator window reopens with a new Watch Me Do action in your workflow (Figure 7-17). The Events list shows you everything you did, step by step—right down to pressing ⌘-Q to quit System Preferences in step 5.

When you run the workflow, you'll see your cursor magically move from one step to the next, all by itself (well, with a *little* help from Automator). It repeats every hesitation, misstep, and pause in your original mouse motion. Fortunately, you can speed up a particular step by up to 10 times using the Playback Speed slider (also shown in Figure 7-17).

Figure 7-17:
After you've recorded a Watch Me Do workflow, the steps you took appear here. You can drag to rearrange them; click one and press Delete to eliminate it; or adjust the speed.

All in all, the mantra to use when dealing with Automator and Watch Me Do is simple: If you can perform a task with a specific action, *use the action.* Use the Watch Me Do mode sparingly, and when you do, *take your time.* It doesn't behave well when you move too fast.

AppleScript

AppleScript is a powerful computer language that's been around since the days of Mac OS 7. Despite its maturity, however, AppleScript is often criticized by seasoned Mac programmers for being too simple, too easy to learn, and too much like English.

Of course, those are precisely the traits you *want* in a computer language—assuming, of course, that you want to use a computer language at all. If you're an everyday Mac fan—as opposed to some computer-science PhD—AppleScript is by far the easiest programming language to use for automating your Mac.

You can think of AppleScript programs (called *scripts*) as software robots. A simple AppleScript might perform some daily task, like backing up your Documents folder. A more complex script can be pages long. In professional printing and publishing, where AppleScript has hard-core fans, a script might connect to a photographer's hard drive elsewhere on the Internet, download a photo from a predetermined folder, color-correct it in Photoshop, import it into a specified page-layout document, print a proof copy, and send a notification email to the editor—automatically.

Even if you're not aware of it, you use the technology that underlies AppleScript all the time. Behind the scenes, numerous components of your Mac communicate by sending *Apple Events,* which are messages bearing instructions or data that your programs send to one another.

AppleScript has several important advantages over Automator—not the least of which is its even greater power. It comes with a dedicated program just for writing out these scripts. It's the AppleScript Editor program that's sitting in your Applications→Utilities folder. (It was called Script Editor before Snow Leopard.)

Still, AppleScript is a *very* deep subject—so deep, in fact, that you'd need an entire book to do it justice. This chapter is an appetizer; a book like *AppleScript: The Missing Manual* is the seven-course meal.

Tip: You can also download an entire chapter about AppleScript from this book's "Missing CD" page at *www.missingmanuals.com*.

Two Sample AppleScripts

Here are a couple of very simple AppleScripts, just to give you a taste:

Open a folder

The first one opens your Applications folder. Sure, you can do that in the Finder easily enough, but this one works no matter what program you're in.

FREQUENTLY ASKED QUESTION

The Scripts Menu

Hey, what happened to that handy Scripts menu? There were some pretty cool little tools in there!

Don't worry. It's still there; out of the box, it's just hidden. You can turn it back on with AppleScript Editor.

Open the program, go to AppleScript Editor→Preferences→General, and click "Show Script menu in the menu bar" (shown here). If you want to see some sample scripts that Apple has kindly provided for you, click "Show Computer scripts." Voila! The menu is back! Now you've got a nice little place to organize your scripts and workflows (you can add Automator workflows to the Scripts menu, too).

If you've used the Scripts menu in the past, you might remember there were around 100 sample scripts in there.

Some of those scripts have gone to the great hard drive in the sky, but there are still some gems, like Convert to PDF (under Printing Scripts), which you can use to change a selected JPEG on your Desktop to a PDF. Some of the missing ones you might remember have been reincarnated as Services. Or they're functions you can now do with Automator, like renaming or renumbering Finder files en masse (check out the Rename Finder Items action). Others are available as Services you can download from *www.macosxautomation.com*.

For an overview of some of the scripts listed in the Scripts menu, download the "What's in the Script Menu" appendix from this book's "Missing CD" page at *www.missingmanuals.com*.

Open up AppleScript Editor (which is in your Launchpad, under Utilities). Type this:

```
tell application "Finder"
activate
open folder "Applications" of the startup disk
end tell
```

The result looks like Figure 7-18.

Figure 7-18:
If you've never seen an AppleScript before, you may be surprised at how simple it looks. As you can probably guess from the commands in the window, this script simply opens the Applications folder in the Finder.

Now try it. Click the Run button. The first thing AppleScript Editor does is check your script for typos and syntax; if all is well, you'll see the script format itself, putting the verbs in bold, indenting pairs of matched commands, and so on. If that part went well, the script runs—and your Applications folder appears before you. Woo-hoo!

Now you can save your script (File→Save); choose Application as the file type. In the unlikely event that this was an actual *useful* script, instead of a lame sample, you could stash the new program on your Dock for anytime access.

So what do those commands mean? Here's the rundown:

- **tell application "Finder"** tells OS X which program is supposed to obey the following commands.

- **activate** brings the Finder to the foreground, much as you would by clicking its Dock icon.

- **open folder "Applications" of the startup disk** tells the Finder to open a new window, displaying the Applications folder on your main hard drive.

- **end tell** directs the Finder to go about its regular business, ignoring further Apple-Script commands.

Tip: You can also edit this script to suit your needs. Try replacing "Applications" with "Users," for example, to make the script open the Users folder instead.

The metronome script

OS X comes stocked with dozens of programs—everything but the kitchen sink. All right, everything but the kitchen sink and a *metronome*. How are you ever going to play the piano in even rhythm without a steady clicking sound provided by your Mac? Sure, sure, you can use GarageBand's metronome in a pinch, but that's like using an industrial pile driver to kill an ant.

Instead, you can use AppleScript to do the job for you. Open a new document in Script Editor (File→New, or ⌘-N), and type this:

```
display dialog "Welcome to the AppleScript Metronome"
set bpm to the text returned of (display dialog ¬
"How many beats per minute?" default answer 60)
set pauseBetweenBeeps to (60 / bpm)
repeat
beep
delay pauseBetweenBeeps
end repeat
```

Note: Don't actually type the ¬ character. That's programmerese for, "This is really all supposed to be on the same line, but I ran out of space on the page."

When you run this script, you see a dialog box that asks how many beats per minute you want the metronome to tick. Whatever number you type (for example, *120)* gets stored in a variable—a temporary holding tank within the script—that you've named *bpm*.

Next, the script calculates how long it must pause between beeps, and puts that fraction of a second into the "pauseBetweenBeeps." If you told the script to beep 120 times per minute, for example, "pauseBetweenBeeps" would be 0.5, since the script would have to pause half a second between beeps.

Finally, the script creates an endlessly repeating loop: beeping, pausing for the proper period, and then repeating.

Click Run to test out your script, and click Stop when you've had enough beeping.

Note: Believe it or not, even grandpappy AppleScript gets updates from time to time.

For example, AppleScript Editor now lets you to start writing a new script from a prebuilt template (choose File→New from Template). Templates are included for writing droplet scripts, file processing scripts, iChat scripts (which have been updated to work with , Mail rule action scripts, and some others. It's a great way to get started, but you still need to know enough to fill that template wrapper with the guts of your script.

Furthermore, for the geekiest of the geeky, it's now possible to write Cocoa-AppleScript programs right in AppleScript Editor. Before Lion, you needed Apple's developer tools to do this. Warning: This requires an understanding of AppleScript and Cocoa, the programming technology used to write serious Mac programs. (In fact, it's what Apple's own programs, such as Mail and iPhoto, are written in).

AppleScript vs. Automator

AppleScript has hundreds and hundreds of uses: automating layout workflows that are too complicated for Automator, controlling programs that Automator doesn't recognize, and programming things that Automator can't handle.

Yet if all you do is look at AppleScript as a second choice to Automator, you're missing out on a lot of power. Truth is, AppleScript lets you do more than Automator will probably let you do in the next 10 *years*; it's just a lot more powerful.

In the end, stick with Automator for simple things. If you need to use AppleScript to automate some aspect of your Mac, though, take pride; you're stepping up to a true power tool. (You can even combine the two, building AppleScripts right into your Automator workflows, thanks to the Run AppleScript action.)

Happy automating!

Windows on Macintosh

T he very moment Apple announced in 2006 that all new Mac models would come with Intel chips inside, the geeks and the bloggers started going nuts. "Let's see," they thought. "Macs and PCs now use exactly the same memory, hard drives, monitors, mice, keyboards, networking protocols, *and processors.* By our calculations, it ought to be possible make a Mac run Windows!"

Now, some in the Cult of Macintosh were baffled by the very idea. Who on earth, they asked, wants to pollute the magnificence of the Mac with a headache like Windows?

Lots of people, as it turns out. Think of all the potential switchers who are tempted by the Mac's sleek looks, yet worry about leaving Windows behind entirely. Or the people who love Apple's iLife programs, but have jobs that rely on Microsoft Access, Outlook, or some other piece of Windows corporateware. Even true-blue Mac fans occasionally look longingly at some of the Windows-only games, Web sites, or movie download services they thought they'd never be able to use.

So hackers set about trying to make Windows run on Intel Macs almost immediately. But they were wasting their time; within weeks, Apple did the job for them—by inventing Boot Camp.

Actually, today, there are two ways to run Windows 7 (or later) on a Mac:

- **Restart it in Boot Camp.** Boot Camp is a little Apple program that lets you *restart* your Mac into Windows.

 At that point, it's a full-blown Windows PC, with no trace of the Mac on the screen. It runs at 100 percent of the speed of a real PC, because it is one. Compatibility with

Windows software is excellent. The only downsides: Your laptop battery life isn't as good, and you have to restart the Mac *again* to return to the familiar world of OS X.

Tip: What's cool, though, is that even when you're running Windows, you can still access your Mac files and folders, as described below.

- **Run Windows in a window.** For $80 or so, you can eliminate the Boot Camp Bummer—the business of having to restart the Mac every time you want to switch its operating-system personality. You can buy a program like Parallels or VMware Fusion, which let you run Windows *in a window.*

 You're still running OS X, and all your Mac files and programs are still available. But you've got a parallel universe—Microsoft Windows—running in a window simultaneously.

 Compared with Boot Camp, this *virtualization software* offers only 90 percent of the speed and 90 percent of the software compatibility. But for thousands of people, the convenience of eliminating all those restarts—and gaining the freedom to copy and paste documents between OS X and Windows programs—makes the Windows-in-a-window solution nearly irresistible.

Tip: There's nothing wrong with using *both* on the same Mac, by the way. In fact, both Parallels and Fusion can use the *same copy of Windows* as Boot Camp, so you save disk space and don't have to manage two different Windows worlds.

Both techniques require you to provide your own copy of Windows. And both are described on the following pages.

FREQUENTLY ASKED QUESTION

The Virus Question

Doesn't running Windows on my Mac mean that I'll be exposed to the nightmare of viruses and spyware, just like the rest of the Windows world?

Yep!

If you install Windows on your Mac, you should also install Windows antivirus and antispyware software to protect that half of the computer. The world is crawling with commercial programs that do the job. There are also lots of free programs, like Microsoft Security Essentials, which protects you against both viruses and spyware.

The good news is that even if your Windows installation gets infected, the Mac side of your computer is unaffected. Just as OS X can't run Windows-only software like, say, Microsoft Access, it also can't run Windows virus software.

Some people, therefore, run Windows naked—without virus protection (especially when using Windows-in-a-window programs like Parallels and VMware Fusion). If a virus does strike, no big deal; they just drag the infected copy of Windows to the Trash and install a fresh one!

Boot Camp

To set up Boot Camp, you need the proper ingredients (plus an Intel-based Mac, which, since you have Mountain Lion, you obviously have):

- **A copy of Windows 7.** That's right: Mountain Lion requires the Home Premium, Business, or Ultimate editions of Windows 7.

- **At least 10 gigs of free hard drive space** on your built-in hard drive, or a second internal drive. (You can't install Windows on an external drive using Boot Camp.)

- **A wired keyboard and mouse**—or Apple Bluetooth wireless versions—is required for the installation process. You can use a Bluetooth keyboard and mouse once the installation is complete.

Then you're ready to proceed.

Installing Boot Camp

Open your Applications→Utilities folder. Inside, open the program called Boot Camp Assistant.

On the Introduction screen, you can print the instruction booklet, if you like (although the following pages contain the essential info). There's a lot of good, conservative legalese in that booklet: the importance of backing up your whole Mac before you begin, for example.

Click Continue. You arrive at the Select Tasks screen, where you have three options:

- **Create a Windows 7 install disk.** If you see this checkbox at all, it means that you have a recent MacBook Air or another Mac that has no DVD drive. And you're in luck: you can install a disk-image (downloadable) copy of Windows 7, which Microsoft sells. When you click Continue, Boot Camp Assistant will copy the Windows 7 disk image to a USB flash drive that you insert (you'll need one with 4 gigs of memory or more).

 From now on, you'll be able to install Windows *and* Boot Camp from that one flash drive.

- **Download the latest Windows support software from Apple.** One of Boot Camp's primary jobs is to teach Windows to recognize and operate all your Mac's hardware components: keyboard, trackpad, camera, WiFi, and so on. And as you may know, Windows does that by requiring an installed *driver* (software nugget) for each one of these components. Well, guess what? Out of the box, Windows does not know about any Apple hardware elements. Surprise, surprise.

 So your first job is to create an installation disk that contains these drivers. It can be a blank CD or DVD, or some kind of external disk (a flash drive or hard drive) that's been formatted in a way that Windows understands. (The USB flash drive option is especially handy if you have a laptop with no DVD drive, like a MacBook Air.)

Note: The required format for the external drive is, rather unappetizingly, called MS-DOS (FAT). If you decide to use a flash drive or a hard drive as your drivers-installation disk, first use Disk Utility to format it in MS-DOS (FAT) format. Otherwise, this driver-installation business won't work.

- **Install Windows 7.** This option will guide you through partitioning (subdividing) your hard drive, and installing Windows 7 onto one of the partitions.

Once those setup tasks are complete—you've prepared the flash drive and downloaded the drivers—you're asked to *partition*, or subdivide, your hard drive. You're setting aside a certain amount of space that will hold your copy of Windows and all the PC software you decide to install. This partitioning process doesn't involve erasing your whole hard drive; all your stuff is perfectly safe. (You can't install Boot Camp if your hard drive is already partitioned—except for Mountain Lion's own Recovery partition, of course.)

The dialog box offers a Divide Equally button, but it also lets you drag a space-divider handle to divide up your drive space between the Mac and Windows sides (Figure 8-1). Use your experience running Windows on a real PC, if you have one, to decide how big your Windows "hard drive" should be.

Most people choose to dedicate a swath of the main internal hard drive to the Windows partition. But if you have a second internal hard drive, you can also choose one of these options:

- **Create a Second Partition.** The Boot Camp Assistant carves out a Windows partition from *that* drive.

- **Erase Disk and Create a Single Partition for Windows.** Just what it says.

On the Start Windows Installation screen, you're supposed to—hey!—start the Windows installation. Grab your Windows 7 DVD and slip it into the Mac. Its installer goes to work immediately.

Following the "I agree to whatever Microsoft's lawyers say" screen, Microsoft's installer asks which partition you want to put Windows on. It's *really* important to pick the right one. Play your cards wrong, and you could erase your whole *Mac* partition.

Choose the one called "Disk 0 Partition 3 BOOTCAMP." (The number may be different, but it will say "BOOTCAMP.")

Then click "Drive options (advanced)," click Format, click OK, and finally click Next. Your Windows partition is now formatted (it uses the NTFS formatting scheme, if anybody asks).

Now your Mac looks just like a PC that's having Windows installed. Be patient; sit around for half an hour as the Windows installer flits about, restarts, does what it has to do.

Don't click any Cancel buttons. If you get a complaint that the software hasn't passed Windows Logo testing, click Continue Anyway. If things seem to stall, look for hidden windows that need your attention.

When it's all over, a crazy, disorienting sight presents itself: your Mac, running Windows. There's no trace of the familiar desktop, Dock, or menu; it's Windows now, baby.

Figure 8-1:
How much hard drive space do you want to dedicate to your "PC"? It's not an idle question; whatever you give Windows is no longer available for your Mac. Drag the vertical handle between the Mac and Windows sides of this diagram.

> Boot Camp Assistant
>
> **Create a Partition for Windows**
>
> Each operating system requires its own partition on the disk. Drag the divider to set the size of the partitions, or click one of the buttons.
>
> "Macintosh HD" will be partitioned as:
>
> Mac OS X
> 278 GB
> 218 GB free
>
> Windows
> 19 GB
>
> Divide Equally
>
> Go Back Partition

Walk through the Windows setup screens, creating an account, setting the time, and so on.

At this point, your Mac is actually a true Windows PC. You can install and run Windows programs, utilities, and even games; you'll discover that they run *really* fast and well.

But as Windows veterans know, every hardware feature of Windows requires a *driver*—a piece of software that tells the machine how to communicate with its own monitor, networking card, speakers, and so on. And it probably goes without saying that Windows doesn't include any drivers for *Apple's* hardware components.

That's why, at this point, you need the disc or flash drive you created earlier. It contains all the drivers for the Mac's graphics card, Ethernet and WiFi networking, audio input and output, built-in camera, brightness and volume keys, e key, multitouch trackpad gestures, and Bluetooth transmitter. (It also installs a new Control Panel icon and system-tray pop-up menu, as described later in this chapter.)

When you insert this disc or flash drive, the drivers installer opens and begins work automatically. (If it doesn't, double-click the *setup.exe* file in the WindowsSupport or Boot Camp folder.)

Click past the Welcome and License Agreement screens, and then click Install. You'll see a lot of dialog boxes come and go; just leave it alone (and don't click Cancel).

Tip: If the installation seems to stall, Windows may be waiting for you to click OK or Next in a window that's hidden behind other windows. Inspect the taskbar and look behind open windows.

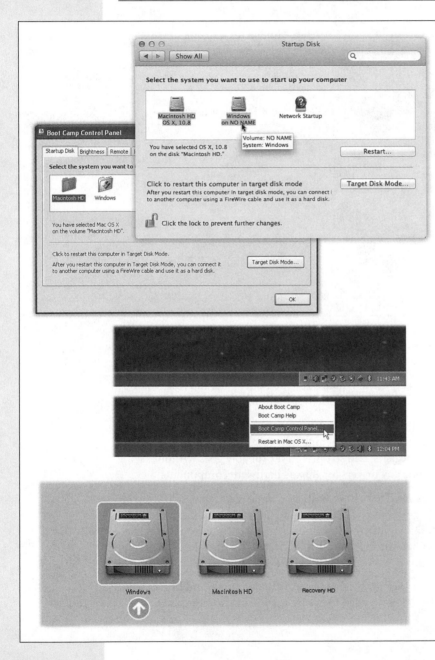

Figure 8-2:
Top: To choose your preferred operating system—the one that starts up automatically unless you intervene—choose ⌘→*System Preferences. Click Startup Disk, and then click the icon for either OS X or Windows. Next, either click Restart (if you want to switch right now) or close the panel. The identical controls are available when you're running Windows, thanks to the new Boot Camp Control Panel.*

Middle: To open the Boot Camp control panel, choose its name from its icon in the Windows system tray.

Bottom: This display, known as the Startup Manager, appears when you press Option during startup. It displays all the disk icons, or disk partitions, that contain bootable operating systems. Just click the name of the partition you want, and then click the Continue arrow.

When it's all over, a dialog box asks you to restart the computer; click Restart. When the machine comes to, it's a much more functional Windows Mac. (And it has an online Boot Camp Help window waiting for you on the screen.)

Note: Once you're running Windows, you might wonder: How am I supposed to right-click? I don't have a two-button mouse or two-button trackpad!

Yes, you do. See page 237 for a panoply of options.

Forth and Back, Windows/Mac

From now on, your main interaction with Boot Camp will be telling it what kind of computer you want your Mac to be today: a Windows machine or a Mac.

Presumably, though, you'll prefer one operating system *most* of the time. Figure 8-2 (top and middle) shows how you specify your favorite.

Tip: If you're running Windows and you just want to get back to OS X right now, you don't have to bother with all the steps shown in Figure 8-2. Instead, click the Boot Camp system-tray icon and, from the shortcut menu, choose Restart in OS X.

From now on, each time you turn on the Mac, it starts up in the operating system you've selected.

If you ever need to switch—when you need Windows just for one quick job, for example—press the Option key as the Mac is starting up. You'll see something like the icons shown in Figure 8-2 (bottom).

Keyboard Translation Guide

Now, if you really want to learn about Windows, you need *Windows 7: The Missing Manual* or *Windows 8: The Missing Manual.*

But suggesting that you go buy *another* book would be tacky. So here's just enough to get by.

First of all, a Mac keyboard and a Windows keyboard aren't the same. Each has keys that would strike the other as extremely goofy. Still, you can trigger almost any keystroke Windows is expecting by substituting special Apple-keystrokes, like this:

Windows keystroke	Apple keystroke
Ctrl-Alt-Delete	Control-Option-Delete
Alt	Option
⊞ key	⌘
Backspace	Delete
Delete (forward delete)	⌦ (on laptops, Fn-Delete)
Enter	Return or Enter
Num lock	Clear (laptops; Fn-F6)
Print Screen	F14 (laptops: Fn-F11)
Print active window	Option-F14 (laptops: Option-Fn-F11)

The keyboard shortcuts in your programs are *mostly* the same as on the Mac, but you have to substitute the Ctrl key for the ⌘ key. So in Windows programs, Copy, Save, and Print are Ctrl-C, Ctrl-S, and Ctrl-P.

Similarly, the Alt key is the Windows equivalent of the Option key.

Tip: You know that awesome two-finger scrolling trick on Mac laptops? It works when you're running Windows, too.

If you really want to understand how your Mac keyboard corresponds to your old PC keyboard, don't miss Apple's thrilling document on the subject at *http://support. apple.com/kb/HT1167.*

Accessing Mac Files from the Dark Side—and Vice Versa

When you've started up in one operating system, it's easy to access documents that "belong" to the other one. For example:

- When you're running OS X, you can get to the documents you created while you were running Windows, which is a huge convenience. Just double-click the Windows disk icon (called NO NAME or Untitled), and then navigate to the Documents and Settings→[your account name]→My Documents (or Desktop).

 You can only copy files *to* the Mac side, or open them without the ability to edit them.

Removing Windows

Maybe you're a switcher who held onto Windows because you were worried that you'd need it. Maybe you're finished with the project, the job, or the phase of life that required you to use Windows on your Mac. But one way or another, there may come a time when you want to get rid of your Windows installation and reclaim all the hard drive space it was using.

You can, and better yet, the process doesn't touch anything that's already on the Mac side. You don't have to erase your entire hard drive or anything—OS X simply erases what's on the Windows partition of your hard drive, and then adds that disk space back to your main, *Mac* partition.

To do this, start by making sure you've rescued anything worth saving from the Windows side of your computer—it's about to be erased.

Start up in OS X, quit all open programs, and make sure nobody's logged in but you. Now open up the Boot Camp Assistant program in your Applications→Utilities folder.

On the Select Tasks screen, click "Install or remove Windows 7 or a later version." On the next screen, you're warned: "The Windows volume and all of its contents will be permanently lost." But you knew that. Click Restore.

That's all there is to it.

Special notes for special setups: If you installed Windows on a separate hard drive, rather than a partition of your main hard drive, don't bother with all this. Just erase the Windows hard drive using Disk Utility, as described in Chapter 11, and format it as a Mac drive.

On the other hand, if your Mac has more than one internal hard drive and you created a Windows partition on one of them (rather than taking it over completely), then open Boot Camp Assistant as described above. Click the partition with Windows on it, and then click "Restore to a single Mac OS partition." Then click Continue.

Tip: You can rename the Windows disk, if you want, so it doesn't say NO NAME the rest of its life—as long as you do it while you're running Windows.

- When you're running Windows, you can get to your Mac documents, too. Click Start→Computer. In the resulting window, you'll see an icon representing your Mac's hard drive partition. Open it up.

 You can see and open these files. But if you want to edit them, you have to copy them to your Windows world first—onto the desktop, for example, or into a folder. (The Mac partition is "read-only" in this way, Apple says, to avoid the possibility that your Mac stuff could get contaminated by Windows viruses.)

Tip: If you did want to edit Mac files from within Windows, one solution is to buy a $50 program called MacDrive (*www.mediafour.com*). Another solution: Use a disk that both OS X and Windows "see," and keep your shared files on *that.* A flash drive works beautifully for this. So does a shared drive on the network.

Windows in a Window

The problem with Boot Camp is that every time you switch to or from Windows, you have to close down everything you were working on and restart the computer—and reverse the process when you're done. You lose 2 or 3 minutes each way. And you can't copy and paste between Mac and Windows programs.

There is another way: an $80 utility called Parallels Desktop for Mac (*www.parallels. com*), and its rival, VMware Fusion (*www.vmware.com*). These programs let you run Windows and OS X *simultaneously;* Windows hangs out in a window of its own,

Figure 8-3:
The strangest sight you ever did see: OS X and Windows. On the same screen. At the same time. Courtesy of VMware Fusion. Parallels is very similar.

while the Mac is running OS X (Figure 8-3). You're getting about 90 percent of Boot Camp's Windows speed—not fast enough for 3-D games, but plenty fast for just about everything else.

Once again, you have to supply your own copy of Windows for the installation process. This time, though, it can be any version of Windows, all the way back to Windows 3.1—or even Linux, FreeBSD, Solaris, OS/2, or MS-DOS.

Having virtualization software on your Mac is a beautiful thing. You can be working on a design in iWork, duck into a Microsoft Access database (Windows only), look up an address, copy it, and paste it back into the Mac program.

And what if you can't decide whether to use Boot Camp (fast and feature-complete, but requires restarting) or Parallels/Fusion (fast and no restarting, but no 3-D games)? No problem—install both. They coexist beautifully on a single Mac and can even use the same copy of Windows.

Together, they turn the Macintosh into the Uni-Computer: the single machine that can run nearly 100 percent of the world's software catalog.

Virtualization Tip-o-Rama

Mastering Parallels or Fusion means mastering Windows, of course, but it also means mastering these tips:

- You don't *have* to run Windows in a window. With one keystroke, you can make your Windows simulator cover the entire screen. You're still actually running two operating systems at once, but the whole Mac world is hidden for the moment so you can exploit your full screen. Just choose View→Full Screen.

POWER USERS' CLINIC

Beyond the Big Names

Parallels and VMware Fusion are bloodthirsty rivals. New versions tumble out with alarming frequency, each designed to one-up the competitor's.

Both also let you specify which program—Mac or Windows—opens when you double-click documents of specific types (like .jpeg or .doc). That's yet another way Windows becomes a full player on the Mac team.

Still, these aren't the only options. Several efforts are afoot to create software that lets you run Windows software without Windows. The most promising one is a $60 program called CrossOver Impersonator (*www.codeweavers.com*). It's a

commercialized version of Wine, a Unix-based Windows simulator.

Sure enough, CrossOver-compatible Windows programs open up and run in OS X just as though they were real Mac programs—without your having to own, install, or fire up a copy of Windows itself.

Unfortunately, the list of compatible programs is tiny. The CrossOver Web site lists 9,000 Windows apps that work, but only about 1,000 of them work perfectly. Still, you owe it to yourself to check the list to see if what you need is CrossOver-friendly.

Tip: Or use the keystroke Control-⌘-F (Parallels) or Control-⌘-Return (Fusion) to enter and exit Full Screen mode. (These keystrokes tend to change from version to version. You've been warned.)

- Conversely, both Parallels and Fusion offer something called *Coherence* or *Unity* mode, in which there's no trace of the Windows desktop. Instead, each Windows program floats in its own disembodied window, just like a Mac program; the OS X desktop lies reassuringly in the background.

Tip: In Fusion's Unity mode and Parallels' Coherence mode, you can access your Computer, Documents, Network, Control Panel, Search, and Run commands right from Fusion's or Parallels' Dock icon or launch palette, so you won't even care that there's no Start menu.

In Parallels, press Control-⌘-Enter to enter or exit Coherence mode. In Fusion, hit Control-⌘-U for Unity mode.

Tip: In Fusion, in Unity mode, you can use the usual Mac keystrokes for Cut, Copy, and Paste within Windows applications (⌘-X, ⌘-C, and ⌘-V). In Parallels, on the other hand, you can remap *all* Windows Ctrl-key shortcuts to the ⌘ key in Preferences.

- To send the "three-fingered salute" to shut down, restart, or lock Windows (usually Control-Alt-Delete), press Control-Option-Delete (Fusion) or Control-Fn-Alt-Delete (Parallels). Or use the Send Control-Alt-Delete command in the menus.

- You can drag files back and forth between the Mac and Windows universes. Just drag icons into, or out of, the Windows window.

- If you have a one-button mouse, you can "right-click" in Parallels by Control-Shift-clicking. In Fusion, Control-click instead. On Mac laptops, you can right-click by putting two fingers on the trackpad as you click.

- When you quit the virtualization program, you're not really shutting down the PC; you're just *suspending* it, or putting it to sleep. When you double-click the Parallels/VMware icon again, everything in your Windows world is exactly as you left it.

- Your entire Windows universe of files, folders, and programs is represented by a single file on your hard drive. In Parallels, it's in your Home→Documents→Parallels folder. In Fusion, it's in your Home→Documents→Virtual Machines folder.

That's super convenient, because it means you can back up your entire Windows "computer" by dragging a single icon to another drive. And if your Windows world ever gets a virus or spyware infestation, you can drag the entire thing to the Trash—and restore Windows from that clean backup.

Life with Microsoft Exchange

In the corporate world, Microsoft Exchange is the 800-pound gorilla. It's the networking software that runs the email, address book, and calendars for hundreds or

thousands of employees. All of this communicates with a central master database whose heart beats away in some closet or back room at your company's headquarters.

For years, Macs have been second-class citizens in Corporate America. As long as they couldn't talk to the Exchange brain, they weren't much use outside the graphic-design department. (You could buy add-on software or muck with workarounds, but you always felt like a weirdo.)

Now, however, Exchange compatibility is built in. In the Mac's Calendar, your company's Exchange calendar shows up. In Contacts, your company's names and addresses show up. In Mail, you can get all your corporate email. Best of all, this information shows up side-by-side with your own personal data, so you can have it all in one place. All the conveniences of OS X now apply to your corporate email: Spotlight, Quick Look, data detectors, and so on.

If you're lucky—that is, if your company is using Exchange 2007 or later (Service Pack 1, Update Rollup 4 and later)—setting this up could not be easier.

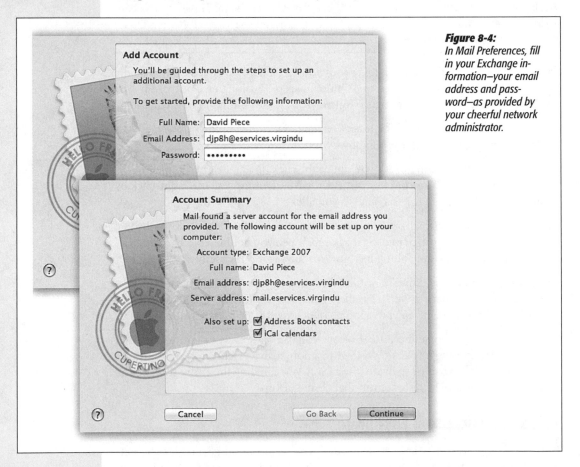

Figure 8-4:
In Mail Preferences, fill in your Exchange information—your email address and password—as provided by your cheerful network administrator.

Connecting to Exchange

To connect to your company's Exchange system, open Mail (Chapter 18). Choose Mail→Preferences. Click the **+** below the list of email accounts; proceed as shown in Figure 8-4. (You can also set up your Exchange information in the System Preferences→Mail, Contacts & Calendars pane. Just click the big Microsoft Exchange button to begin.)

When you click Continue, one of two things happens:

- A message says, "Mail found a server account for the email address you provided. The following account will be set up on your computer." You're all set.

 That box offers an "Also set up" item, featuring two delicious checkboxes: "Contacts contacts" and "Calendar calendars." Hard to think why you'd want to turn these off; they'll do all the work for you.

- Your Mac doesn't find the server. In that case, either (a) your company doesn't use Exchange 2007 or later, or (b) your network geek hasn't turned on Exchange Autodiscover. In that case, you have no choice but to call that person over to your desk and either (a) harangue him for not turning on Autodiscover, or (b) have him fill in the server address and other boxes by hand.

Exchange in Mail

Once everything is set up, open Mail. If you have a lot of mail, it may take time for Mail to synchronize with the Exchange server and display your messages. But it gets there eventually. Your Exchange account appears with its own heading, beneath your personal accounts (Figure 8-5).

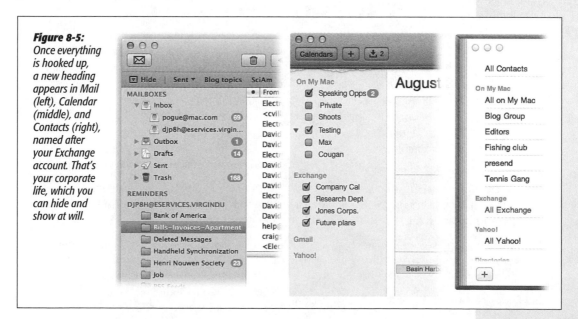

Figure 8-5:
Once everything is hooked up, a new heading appears in Mail (left), Calendar (middle), and Contacts (right), named after your Exchange account. That's your corporate life, which you can hide and show at will.

Now you can send and receive email, create notes and to-do items, respond to emailed invitations, and so on. All the Mail features described in Chapter 18 are ready to go: Spotlight can search all your accounts simultaneously, Smart Folders can round up messages from one account or all of them, Quick Look can show you attachments without your having to open them in a separate program, and so on.

Exchange in Calendar

Your corporate appointments now show up in the Mac's calendar (Chapter 11), neatly filed under their own heading in the Calendars list (Figure 8-5, middle). Each appointment category shows up with its own checkbox, as usual, so you can hide and show them as you see fit—even when they're mixed right in with your personal agenda.

The big payoff here is scheduling meetings; you get to use Calendar's invitations feature (page 399).

Exchange in Contacts

Your company's Global Address Lists show up in Contacts (Chapter 18) as a group on the Groups page (choose View→Groups, or press ⌘-3, or click the two-silhouette bookmark), as shown at right in Figure 8-5. You can work with your contacts on the server just as you would with your own addresses: Put them in groups, click an address to see where it is in Google Maps, and so on. When you're addressing an email message or a calendar invitation, the autocomplete feature now proposes names from both your personal and corporate address books.

GEM IN THE ROUGH

Delegating Your Calendars

Once you're all Exchanged up, you can even delegate your calendar—that is, permit someone else on your corporate network to see (and, if you wish, edit) your calendar from across the network. That's handy when you're a busy executive and you want your personal assistant to help you manage your busy life, or when you're going to be out of town and you've authorized a trusted minion to carry on with your calendar in your absence.

(This is not the same as publishing your calendar as described in Chapter 11. Your Exchange calendar isn't actually going to move. It'll sit right there on the server—you're just giving someone else access to it.)

To set this up, choose Calendar→Preferences→Accounts. (If you have more than one account, choose the one you want to share from the Accounts list.)

Click Delegation. Click Edit. On the Manage Account Access

screen, click +, and type the name of the person you want to share your calendar with. You can also specify how much access you want that person to have; Read Only means they can just see your life, and Read & Write means they can actually edit it. You can grant different levels of access to your calendar and your Tasks list.

Finally, click Done.

Now change hats. Suppose you're the trusted assistant.

On your Mac, choose Calendar→Preferences→Accounts. You'll find the account that's been shared with you on "Delegation – Accounts I can access."

Finally, turn on the Show checkbox. Close the Preferences dialog box to return to the main Calendar display. Here, your boss's calendars (appointment categories) show up in the left-side list; turn on the checkboxes of the ones you want to appear on the calendar grid.

Part Three:
The Components
of OS X

3

System Preferences

The hub of Mac customization is System Preferences, the modern-day successor to the Control Panel (Windows) or the ancient Control Panels (previous Mac systems). Some of its panels are extremely important, because their settings determine whether or not you can connect to a network or go online to exchange email. Others handle the more cosmetic aspects of customizing OS X.

This chapter guides you through the entire System Preferences program, panel by panel.

Tip: Only a system administrator (page 502) can change settings that affect everyone who shares a certain machine: most of its Network settings, Energy Saver settings, and so on. If you see a bunch of controls that are dimmed and unavailable, now you know why.

A tiny 🔒 in the lower-left corner of a panel is the other telltale sign. If you, a nonadministrator, would like to edit some settings, then call an administrator over to your Mac and ask him to click the 🔒, input his password, and supervise your tweaks.

The System Preferences Window

You can open System Preferences in dozens of ways:

- Choose its name from the menu.

- Jump directly to a System Preferences pane by pressing Option as you tap keys on the top row of your keyboard: Option-🔳 for Mission Control preferences, Option-volume key (◀, ◀), or ◀))) for Sound prefs, Option-brightness keys (☀ or

☀) or Option-keyboard-brightness key (☀ or ☀) for the Displays prefs. At that point, you can click Show All or press ⌘-L to see the full spread.

- If you know the name of the System Preferences panel you want, it's often quicker to use Spotlight. To open the iCloud panel, for example, hit ⌘-space, type *iclo*, and then press Return. See Chapter 3 for more on operating Spotlight from the keyboard.

- If you put the System Preferences icon in your *Dock* (Chapter 4), you can open it *and* jump to a particular panel in one smooth move: Click-and-hold the System Preferences icon. You get a pop-up menu of every System Preferences panel.

Suppose, then, that by hook or by crook, you've figured out how to open System Preferences. You'll notice that, at first, the rows of icons are grouped according to function: Personal, Hardware, and so on (Figure 9-1, bottom). But you can also view them in

Figure 9-1:
You can view System Preferences icons alphabetically (top), rather than in rows of categories (bottom); just choose View→Organize Alphabetically. Non-Apple preference panes appear in a category called Other.

Super-top-secret trick: If you choose Customize (from the View menu or, believe it or not, the Show All button, the icons here sprout checkboxes. You can turn off—and hide—the icons you never use. (You can still choose their names from the View menu.)

tidy alphabetical order, as shown at top in Figure 9-1. That can spare you the ritual of hunting through various rows just to find a certain panel icon whose name you already know. (Quick, without looking: Which row is Date & Time in?) This chapter describes the various panels following this alphabetical arrangement.

Either way, when you click one of the icons, the corresponding controls appear. To access a different preference pane, you have a number of options:

- **Fast:** When System Preferences first opens, the insertion point is blinking in the System Preferences search box. (If the insertion point is *not* blinking there, then press ⌘-F.) Type a few letters of *volume, resolution, wallpaper, wireless,* or whatever feature you want to adjust. In a literal illustration of Spotlight's name, the System Preferences window darkens *except* for the icons where you'll find relevant controls (Figure 9-2). Click the name or icon of the one that looks the most promising.

Figure 9-2:
Even if you don't know which System Preferences panel contains the settings you want to change, Spotlight can help. Type into the box at the top, and watch as the "spotlight" shines on the relevant icons.

- **Faster:** Click the Show All icon in the upper-left corner of the window (or press ⌘-L, a shortcut worth learning). Then click the icon of the new panel you want.

- **Fastest:** Choose any panel's name from the View menu—or from the System Preferences Dock icon pop-up menu described above.

Here, then, is your grand tour of all 29 of the built-in System Preferences panes. (You may have a couple more or fewer, depending on your Mac model and whether you've installed any non-Apple panes.)

Note: Don't freak out: A few panels have been renamed in the last couple of versions of OS X and therefore appear in new alphabetical positions. The panel formerly called Appearance is now called General. The one formerly known as Accounts has been renamed Users & Groups. Speech is now Dictation & Speech, and Universal Access is now Accessibility.

Accessibility

The Accessibility panel (formerly Universal Access) is designed for people who type with one hand, find it difficult to use a mouse, or have trouble seeing or hearing. (These features can also be handy when the mouse is broken or missing.)

Accessibility is a huge focus for Apple. In fact, there's a whole Apple Web site dedicated to explaining all these features: *www.apple.com/accessibility*. Here, though, is an overview of the noteworthiest features, broken down according to the tabs at the left side.

Figure 9-3:
You'll be amazed at just how much you can zoom into the Mac's screen using this Accessibility pane. In fact, there's nothing to stop you from zooming in so far that a single pixel nearly fills the entire monitor. (That may not be especially useful for people with limited vision, but it can be handy for graphic designers learning how to reproduce a certain icon, dot by dot.)

Display

If you have trouble seeing the screen, then, boy, does OS X have features for you.

"Invert colors" swaps the colors of the screen, so that text appears white on black—an effect that some people find easier to read. (This option also freaks out many Mac fans who turn it on by *mistake*. They think the Mac's expensive monitor has just gone loco. Now you know better.)

"Use grayscale" banishes all color from your screen. This is another feature designed to improve text clarity, but it's also a dandy way to see how a color document will look when printed on a monochrome laser printer.

The "Enhance contrast" slidermakes blacks blacker and whites whiter, further eliminating in-between shades and thereby making the screen easier to see.

At the bottom of this window, you'll find the Cursor Size slider. It's a godsend not only to people with failing vision, but also to anyone using one of Apple's large, super-

high-resolution screens; as the pixel density increases, the arrow cursor gets smaller and smaller. This slider lets you make the arrow cursor larger—much larger, if you like—making it much easier to see.

Zoom

This feature lets you enlarge the area surrounding your cursor in any increment. It's just incredibly useful, incredibly often, especially if you have over-40 eyes.

Tip: If you have a laptop or a Magic Mouse, just using the Control-key trick described in the box on page 372 is a far faster and easier way to magnify the screen. It works even when *this* one is turned off.

To make it work, press Option-⌘-8 as you're working. You can further adjust the magnification by pressing Option-⌘-plus (to zoom in) or Option-⌘-minus (to zoom out). With each press, the entire screen image gets larger or smaller, creating a virtual monitor that follows your cursor around the screen.

You're offered an array of customization options. For example, you can substitute the Option or ⌘ key, if Control isn't working out for you. And you can turn on a pixel-smoothing feature that adds a certain blurriness to the zoomed-in image. Finally, you can switch between Fullscreen (the whole monitor is your view) or Picture-in-Picture (the zoomed-in portion stays within a picture-in-picture rectangle on the screen, as shown in Figure 9-4).

Figure 9-4:
This inset window makes it easier for you to keep your bearings. It zooms into the screen only within this inset window.

If you click More Options, you can specify how you want to scroll around within your zoomed-in screen image. The factory setting, "Continuously with pointer," is actually pretty frustrating; the whole screen shifts around whenever you move the cursor. ("So the pointer is at or near the center of the image" is very similar.) "Only when

the pointer reaches an edge" is a lot less annoying and lets you *use* the cursor (to click buttons, for example) without sending the entire screen image darting away from you.

Tip: The sliders at the top of this dialog box limit the degree of zooming in and zooming out. However, even if you've adjusted them, you can always *override* your slider settings by pressing Option-⌘-plus or Option-⌘-minus.

When "Picture-in-picture" is turned on, the dialog box that appears when you click More Options is totally different. It offers these choices:

- **Stationary.** The inset remains parked on the screen. You can't move or resize it—at least not once you've left the Options dialog box.

Tip: You *can* change its size and position for good, though, by clicking the Adjust Size and Location button in the corner of the Options dialog box. You'll be offered the chance to drag the edges of the little inset window. When you like the result, click OK.

- **Follow mouse cursor.** The inset window follows your cursor around, as though you're moving a high-tech magnifying glass over a map.

UP TO SPEED

System Preferences: Under the Hood

The entire System Preferences program is nothing more than a series of graphical front ends for underlying Unix settings. (If you know Unix and feel so inclined, you can, in fact, bypass the System Preferences panel completely. Using the defaults command, you can use OS X's Terminal program to make any of the changes described in this chapter—and many others.)

The individual preferences panes are represented by package icons in your various Library folders. For example, icons that Apple supplies with Mountain Lion are in System→Library→PreferencePanes. OS X also looks for preferences modules in the Network→Library→PreferencePanes folder, if there is one.

Now suppose you've downloaded some new preferences module and you want to install it. Just double-clicking a downloaded System Preferences pane does the trick.

If you prefer manual control, you can put a downloaded module into your Home→Library→PreferencePanes folder. (To get to your Library folder, which is usually invisible, press the Option key; choose Go→Library in the Finder.)

The beauty of this arrangement, of course, is that everyone who shares the Mac now can see a different assortment of customized preference panes.

If you're an administrator, you can use the PreferencePanes folder in the Mac's main Library folder; it lets everyone with an account on the Mac (Chapter 13) access your newly added panes.

When you install some new System Preferences pane like Growl, Perian, or TiVo Desktop, it takes the form of a new icon in one of those four PreferencePanes folders. That's good to know when the day comes when you want to remove one of these add-on panes. Usually, you remove these non-Apple preference panes by Control-clicking (or right-clicking) them and choosing Remove Preference Pane from the shortcut menu; but in a pinch, you could also delete one by removing it from one of these special folders.

Within the System Preferences program, any new panes you add in this way appear in a new row of icons labeled Other (when you're viewing System Preferences in Category view).

- **Tiled along edge.** The magnified inset becomes much bigger—in fact, it becomes an enormous rectangular swath at the left side of your screen. The image scrolls as you move your cursor around.

Tip: One of the best options here is "Enable temporary zoom." What that means is that at any time, in any program, you can summon the magnified-inset window at your cursor location by holding down your Control and Option keys together. (It works only if Zoom is turned *on* in Accessibility.) It's a great way to dip into a magnified view of something on your screen, briefly.

VoiceOver

VoiceOver makes the Mac *read out loud* every bit of text that's on the screen. See page 634.

Audio

If you have trouble hearing the Mac's sounds, the obvious solution is to increase the volume, which is why this panel offers a link to the Sound preferences pane.

Audio is especially important when the Mac tries to get your attention by beeping. For those situations, turn on "Flash the screen when an alert occurs" (an effect you can try out by clicking the Test Flash Screen button). Now you'll see a white flash across the entire monitor whenever the Mac would otherwise beep—not a bad idea on laptops, actually, so that you don't miss beeps when you've got the speakers muted.

The "Play stereo audio as mono" option is intended for people with hearing loss in one ear. This way, you won't miss any of the musical mix just because you're listening through only one headphone.

Keyboard

This panel offers two clever features designed to help people who have trouble using the keyboard.

- **Sticky Keys** lets you press multiple-key shortcuts (involving keys like Shift, Option, Control, and ⌘) one at a time instead of all together.

 To make Sticky Keys work, first turn on Enable Sticky Keys. Then go to work on the Mac, triggering keyboard commands as shown in Figure 9-5.

 If you press a modifier key *twice,* meanwhile, you lock it down. (Its onscreen symbol gets brighter to let you know.) When a key is locked, you can use it for several commands in a row. For example, if a folder icon is highlighted, you could double-press ⌘ to lock it down—and then type O (to open the folder), look around, and then press W (to close the window). Press the ⌘ key a third time to "un-press" it.

Tip: The checkbox called "Press the Shift key five times to turn Sticky Keys on or off" (click Options to see it) gives you the flexibility of turning Sticky Keys on and off at will, without even taking a trip to System Preferences. Whenever you want to turn on Sticky Keys, press the Shift key five times in succession. You'll hear a special clacking sound effect alerting you that you just turned on Sticky Keys. (Repeat the five presses to turn Sticky Keys off again.)

- **Slow Keys,** on the other hand, doesn't register a key press at all until you've held down the key for more than a second or so—a feature designed to screen out accidental key presses.

If you click Options and then turn on "Use click key sounds," you'll hear a little typing sound each time you press a key—but none of these key presses registers unless you hold the key down for a moment. (Use the Acceptance Delay slider to govern this threshold.)

You hear a different sound when the Mac actually accepts the key press—and, of course, you see the letter you typed appear onscreen.

Figure 9-5:
Whenever you want to press a multiple-key keystroke like Shift-⌘-D, press them one at a time. You'll see ghost images of these keys superimposed on your screen, as though to show you which keystrokes you've added to your temporary collection. To "un-press" a key you've already pressed, press it again twice.

Mouse & Trackpad

Mouse Keys is designed to help people who can't use the mouse—or who want more precision when working in graphics programs. It lets you click, drag, and otherwise manipulate the cursor by pressing the keys on your numeric keypad. (It's not very useful on keyboards that don't *have* separate numeric keypads, like laptops.)

When Mouse Keys is turned on, the 5 key acts as the clicker—hold it down for a moment to "click the mouse," do that twice to double-click, and so on. Hold down the 0 key to lock down the mouse button, and the period key to unlock it. (The amount of time you have to hold them down depends on how you've set the Initial Delay slider.)

Move the cursor around the screen by pressing the eight keys that surround the 5 key. (For example, hold down the 9 key to move the cursor diagonally up and to the right.) If you hold one of these keys down continuously, the cursor, after a pause, begins to move smoothly in that direction—according to the way you've adjusted the sliders called Initial Delay and Maximum Speed.

Tip: The checkbox, in Options, called "Press the Option key five times to turn Mouse Keys on or off" saves you the trouble of opening System Preferences.

Speakable Items

Here's the final resting place for Speakable Items, formerly known as PlainTalk, commonly known as "the feature that lets you give your Mac spoken commands." Once you set things up properly, you can say things like "Open Safari," "Close window," or even trigger menu commands by voice.

Because it's a little clunky to set up—and not mind-blowingly accurate—PlainTalk never really caught on; not one person in a thousand uses it. Still, if you think it's worth a 15-minute test drive, you'll find full instructions in the free Appendix to this chapter, "PlainTalk spoken commands.pdf." It's on this book's "Missing CD" page at *www.missingmanuals.com*.

Bluetooth

Bluetooth is a short-range, low-power, wireless *cable-elimination* technology. It's designed to connect gadgets in pairings that make sense, like cellphone+earpiece, Mac+wireless keyboard, phone+portable speaker, or Mac+cellphone (for *tethering*, where you connect the Mac to the phone so the laptop can get online).

Now, you wouldn't want the guy in the next cubicle to be able to operate *your* Mac using *his* Bluetooth keyboard. So the first step in any Bluetooth relationship is *pairing*, or formally introducing the two gadgets that will be communicating. Here's how that goes:

1. **Open System Preferences→Bluetooth (Figure 9-6).**

 Make sure the On checkbox is turned on. (The only reason to turn it off is to save laptop battery power.) Also make sure Discoverable is turned on; that makes the Mac "visible" to other Bluetooth gadgets in range.

 If you intend to send a file to another Mac, set up that other machine by visiting System Preferences→Sharing; turn on the Bluetooth Sharing checkbox.

2. **Click the + button below the list at left (or Set Up New Device, if you've never done this before).**

 The Bluetooth Setup Assistant opens. After a moment, it displays the names of all Bluetooth gadgets it can sniff out: nearby headsets, laptops, cellphones, and so on. Usually, it finds the one you're trying to pair.

3. **Click the gadget you want to connect to, and then click Continue.**

If you're pairing a mobile phone or something else that has a keypad or keyboard, the Mac now displays a large, multiple-digit *passcode*. It's like a password, except you'll have to input it only this once, to confirm that *you* are the true owner of both the Mac and the gadget. (If it weren't for this passcode business, some guy next to you at the airport could enjoy free laptop Internet access through the cellphone in *your* pocket.)

Figure 9-6:
Top: This panel reveals a list of every Bluetooth gadget your Mac knows about. Click a Bluetooth device to see details.

Middle: The Bluetooth Setup Assistant scans the area for Bluetooth gadgets and, after a moment, lists them. Click one and hit Continue.

Bottom: Where security is an issue, you get the chance to pair your Bluetooth device with the Mac. To prove that you're really the owner of both, the Mac displays a one-time password, which you have 30 seconds to type into the phone. Once that's done, you're free to use the phone's Internet connection without any further muss, fuss, or passwords.

At this point, the phone, computer, or palmtop displays a message to the effect that you have 30 seconds to type that passcode. Do it. When the gadget asks if you want to pair with the Mac and connect to it, say yes. (If you're pairing one Mac

with another, just click Continue on both machines; you *see* the same passcode on both but don't have to type it.)

Tip: Some Bluetooth phones, including the iPhone, can even get your laptop onto the Internet via the cellular airwaves. No WiFi required—the phone never even leaves your pocket, and your laptop can get online wherever there's a cellphone signal. It's called *tethering.*

This is a special setup, however, involving signing up with your cell carrier (and paying an additional monthly fee). If you've signed up, then turn on the third option here (Access the Internet).

When it's all over, click Done on the Mac that will do the sending. The new gadget is listed in the left-side panel, in the list of Bluetooth cellphones, headsets, and other stuff that you've previously introduced to this Mac.

Advanced Options

If you click Advanced, you arrive at a pop-up panel with a few more tweaky Bluetoothisms:

- **Open Bluetooth Assistant at startup if no keyboard is detected.** Here's where you can tell the Bluetooth Setup Assistant to open up automatically when the Mac thinks no keyboard is attached (because it assumes that you have a wireless Bluetooth keyboard that has yet to be set up).

- **Open Bluetooth Assistant at startup if no mouse or trackpad is detected.** Same deal, this time suggesting that the Assistant will open if the Mac can't find a trackpad or mouse. Once again, the Mac is assuming that you'll be wanting to connect a *wireless* one.

- **Allow Bluetooth devices to wake this computer.** Turn this on if you want to be able to wake up a sleeping Mac when you press a key, just like a wired keyboard does.

- **Reject incoming audio requests.** Ordinarily, the Mac happily connects to sound sources like Bluetooth cellphones, music players, and so on. If you're concerned about some random person connecting to your Mac with an unauthorized music player, then turn this on; your Mac is now off limits to audio gadgets.

- **Serial ports.** This list identifies the simulated ports (such as Bluetooth-PDA-Sync) that some Bluetooth devices use to connect to your Mac.

Tip: If you Option-click the Bluetooth menulet (❋), you get a couple of lines of secret Bluetooth details. The menu reveals the name of your Mac, as it will appear to other Bluetooth wireless gadgets; and the version of Bluetooth you're running.

CDs & DVDs

This handy pane (Figure 9-7) lets you tell the Mac what it should do when it detects that you've inserted a CD or DVD. For example, when you insert a music CD, you probably want iTunes (Chapter 12) to open automatically so you can listen to the songs or convert them to MP3 or AAC files on your hard drive. Similarly, when you insert a picture CD (such as a Kodak Photo CD), you probably want iPhoto to open in readiness to import the pictures into your photo collection. And when you insert a DVD from Blockbuster, you probably want the Mac's DVD Player program to open.

Figure 9-7:
You can tell the Mac exactly which program to launch when you insert each kind of disc, or tell it to do nothing at all.

For each kind of disc (blank CD, blank DVD, music CD, picture CD, or video DVD), the pop-up menu lets you choose options like these:

- **Ask what to do.** A dialog box appears that asks what you want to do with a newly inserted blank disc.

- **Open (iDVD, iTunes, iPhoto, DVD Player…).** The Mac can open a certain program automatically when you insert the disc. When the day comes that somebody writes a better music player than iTunes, or a better digital shoebox than iPhoto, then you can use the "Open other application" option.

- **Run script.** If you've become handy writing or downloading AppleScript programs (Chapter 7), you can schedule one of your own scripts to take over from here. For example, you can set things up so that inserting a blank CD automatically copies your Home folder onto it for backup purposes.

- **Ignore.** The Mac won't do anything when you insert a disc except display its icon on the desktop. (If it's a blank disc, the Mac does nothing at all.)

Note: If your Mac doesn't have a DVD drive (if it's a MacBook Air, for example), you see only three pop-up menus here. They govern what happens when you insert a music CD, picture CD, or video DVD, and refer to situations when you've attached an external drive.

Date & Time

Your Mac's conception of what time it is can be very important. Every file you create, save, or even open is stamped with this time, and every email you send or receive is marked with it. As you might expect, setting your Mac's clock is what the Date & Time pane is all about.

Date & Time Tab

Click the Date & Time tab. If your Mac is online, turn on "Set date & time automatically" and be done with it. Your Mac sets its own clock by consulting a highly accurate scientific clock on the Internet. (No need to worry about daylight saving time, either; the time servers take that into account.)

If you're not online and have no prospect of getting there, you can also set the date and time manually. To change the month, day, or year, click the digit that needs changing and then either (a) type a new number, (b) press the ↑ or ↓ keys, or (c) click the little arrow buttons. Press the Tab key to highlight the next number. (You can also specify the day of the month by clicking a date on the minicalendar.)

To set the time of day, use the same technique—or, for more geeky fun, you can set the time by dragging the hour, minute, or second hands on the analog clock.

Finally, click Save. (If you get carried away with dragging the clock hands around and lose track of the *real* time, click the Revert button to restore the panel settings.)

Tip: If you prefer seeing 24-hour "military time" notation on your menu bar (that is, *17:30* instead of *5:30 p.m.*)—click the Clock tab and turn on "Use a 24-hour clock."

Note, however, that this affects only the menu bar clock. If you'd like to reformat the menu bar clock *and* all other dates (like the ones that show when your files were modified in list views), click the Open Language & Text button at the bottom of the Date & Time pane. Once there, click the Formats tab. There you'll see a Customize button for Times, which leads you to a whole new world of time-format customization. You can drag elements of the current time (Hour, Minute, Second, Millisecond, and so on) into any order you like, and separate them with any desired punctuation. This way, you can set up your date displays in (for example) the European format, expressing April 13 as 13/4 instead of 4/13).

Time Zone Tab

You'd be surprised how important it is to set the time zone for your Mac. If you don't do so, the email and documents you send out—and the Mac's conception of what documents are older and newer—could be hopelessly skewed.

OS X can set its own time zone *automatically.* That's an especially useful feature if you're a laptop warrior who travels a lot. (And how does it know where you are? See the box on page 346.)

If you turn on "Set time zone automatically using current location" (Figure 9-8), the Mac will think for a moment. Then, if the WiFi gods are smiling, it will, before your eyes, drop a pin onto the world map to represent your location—and set the time

zone automatically. (The world map dims to show that you can no longer set your location manually.)

Often, though, you'll be told that the Mac is "Unable to determine current location at this time." In that case, specify your location manually, as shown in Figure 9-8.

Figure 9-8:
To set your time zone the quick and dirty way, click a section of the map to indicate your general region of the world. To teach the Mac more precisely where you are in that time zone, use the Closest City pop-up menu. (Or, instead of using the pop-up menu with the mouse, you can also highlight the text in the Closest City box. Then start typing your city name until the Mac gets it.)

Clock Tab

In the Clock pane, you can turn the menu-bar clock on or off. You can choose between two different clock styles: digital (3:53 p.m.) or analog (a round clock face). You also get several other options for the digital clock display: whether to show seconds, designations for a.m. and p.m., the day of the week, a blinking colon, and a 24-hour clock.

Tip: At the bottom of the dialog box, you'll find a feature called "Announce the time." At the intervals you specify, the Mac can speak, out loud, the current time: "It's 10 o'clock." If you tend to get so immersed in "working" that you lose track of time, OS X just removed your last excuse. The menu-bar clock can show not just the time and day of the week, but also today's *date*. Turn on the "Show the day of the week" and "Show date" checkboxes if you want to see, for example, "Wed May 9 7:32 PM" on your menu bar.

If you decide you don't need all that information—if your menu bar is crowded enough as it is—you can always look up today's day and date just by *clicking* the time

on your menu bar. A menu drops down revealing the complete date. The menu also lets you switch between digital and analog clock types and provides a shortcut to the Date & Time Preferences pane.

Tip: This one's for Unix geeks only. Use *sudo*, type date *mmddhhmmyyyy.ss*, and press Return. (Of course, replace that code with the actual date and time you want, such as *040517552013*.00 for April 5, 2013, 5:55 p.m.) You might find this method faster than the System Preferences route.

Desktop & Screen Saver

This panel offers two ways to show off Mac OS X's glamorous graphics features: *desktop pictures* and *screen savers*.

Desktop Pictures

Mountain Lion comes with an expanded collection of desktop pictures, ranging from *National Geographic*–style nature photos to plain solid colors. To install a new background picture, first choose one of the image categories in the list at the left side of the window, as shown in Figure 9-9.

Your choices include Desktop Pictures (muted, soft-focus swishes and swirls and a few nature shots); Nature (bugs, water, outer space); Plants (flowers, soft-focus leaves); Art (a collection of famous paintings by Monet, Dégas, Seurat, and other canvas su-

FREQUENTLY ASKED QUESTION

How the Mac Knows Where You Are

OK, I'll bite. To set my time zone automatically, the Mac has to know where I am. It doesn't have GPS. So how does it do that?

Metropolitan areas today are blanketed by overlapping WiFi signals. At a typical Manhattan intersection, you might be in range of 20 base stations. Each one broadcasts its own name and unique network address (its MAC address—nothing to do with Mac computers) once every second. Although you'd need to be within 150 feet or so to *connect*, a laptop or phone can detect this beacon signal from up to 1,500 feet away.

So Apple had a huge idea: Suppose you could correlate all those beacon signals with their physical locations. Why, you'd be able to simulate GPS—without the GPS!

But to create that correlation, you'd have to send thousands of data recorders out into the world, combing every street, block, and neighborhood, constantly recording WiFi hot spot anmes and their coorinates.

Apple actually did that. In fact, it's constantly doing that. The data recorders are called iPhones.

That's right: All those tens of millions of iPhones are quietly recording the locations and names of WiFi hot spots all over the world, and transmitting them (anonymously, of course) back to Apple. (Neither these phones nor the Mac ever has to *connect* to these base stations. They're just reading the one-way beacon signals.)

To figure out where it is, the Mac sniffs around for WiFi base stations. If it finds any, it transmits their IDs back to Apple, which looks up those network addresses—and sends coordinates back to the Mac over the Internet.

That accuracy is good only to within 100 feet at best, and of course the system fails completely once you're out of populated areas—or whenever your Mac doesn't have WiFi or an Internet connection. On the other hand, it works fast, and it works indoors, which GPS definitely doesn't.

perheroes); Black & White (breathtaking monochrome shots); Abstract (swishes and swirls with wild colors); Patterns (a pair of fabric closeups); and Solid Colors (simple grays, blues, and greens). Some of them are new in Mountain Lion, and really nice.

Tip: You can choose *any* solid color—not just one of the preselected shades Apple gives you. Click Custom Color and go nuts.

Figure 9-9:
Using the list of picture sources at left, you can preview an entire folder of your own images before installing one as your new desktop picture. Use the + button to select a folder of assorted graphics—or, if you're an iPhoto veteran, click an iPhoto album name, as shown here. Clicking one of the thumbnails installs the corresponding picture on the desktop.

Using your own pictures

Of course, you may feel that decorating your Mac desktop is much more fun if you use one of your *own* pictures. You can use almost any graphics file: JPEG, GIF, TIFF, Photoshop, and even PDF. (Guess you could use the PDF option to help teach yourself your camera's user guide by staring at your desktop every morning.)

That's why icons for your own Pictures folder and iPhoto and Aperture albums also appear here, along with a + button that lets you choose *any* folder of pictures. When you click one of these icons, you see thumbnail versions of its contents in the main screen to its right. Just click the thumbnail of any picture to apply it immediately to the desktop. (There's no need to remove the previously installed picture first.)

Tip: If there's a certain picture you like, but it's not in any of the listed sources, you can drag its image file onto the *well* (the miniature desktop displayed in the Desktop panel). A thumbnail instantly appears in the well, and a moment later the picture is plastered across your monitor.

Making the picture fit

No matter which source you use to choose a photo of your own, you have one more issue to deal with. Unless you've gone to the trouble of editing your chosen photo so that it matches the precise dimensions of your screen (1920 × 1080 pixels, for example), it probably isn't exactly the right size.

Tip: The top 23 pixels of your graphic will be partly obscured by OS X's translucent menu bar. Then again, you can make the menu bar *stop* being translucent—by turning off the "Translucent menu bar" checkbox shown in Figure 9-9.

Fortunately, OS X offers a number of solutions to this problem. Using the pop-up menu just to the right of the desktop preview well, you can choose any of these options:

- **Fill Screen.** Enlarges or reduces the image so that it fills every inch of the desktop without distortion. Parts may get chopped off, but this option never distorts the picture.

- **Fit to Screen.** Your photo appears as large as possible without distortion *or* cropping. If the photo doesn't precisely match the proportions of your screen, then you get "letterbox bars" on the sides or at top and bottom. Apple provides a color-swatch button next to the pop-up menu shown in Figure 9-9. When you click it, the Color Picker appears so you can specify a color for those letterbox bars.

- **Stretch to Fill Screen.** Makes your picture fit the screen exactly, come hell or high water. Larger pictures may be squished vertically or horizontally as necessary, and small pictures are drastically blown up *and* squished, usually with grisly results.

- **Center.** Centers the photo neatly on the screen. The edges of the picture may be chopped off. If the picture is smaller than the screen, it sits smack in the center of the monitor at actual size, leaving a swath of empty border all the way around. (Use the swatch button just to the right of the pop-up menu to specify a color for that border.)

- **Tile.** This option makes your picture repeat over and over until the multiple images fill the entire monitor. (If your picture is larger than the screen, no such tiling takes place. You see only the top center chunk of the image.)

Auto picture changing

The novelty of any desktop picture, no matter how interesting, is likely to fade after several months of all-day viewing. That's why the randomizing function is so delightful.

Turn on "Change picture" at the bottom of the dialog box. From the pop-up menu, specify when you want your background picture to change: "every day," "every 15 minutes," or, if you're *really* having trouble staying awake at your Mac, "every 5 sec-

onds." (The option called "when waking from sleep" refers to the *Mac* waking from sleep, not you.)

Finally, turn on "Random order," if you like. If you leave it off, your desktop pictures change in alphabetical order by file name.

Now, at the interval you specified, your desktop picture changes automatically, smoothly cross-fading between the pictures like a slideshow. You may never want to open another window, because you'll hate to block your view of the show.

Screen Saver

On the Screen Saver panel, you can create your own screen-saver slideshows—an absolute must if you have an Apple Thunderbolt Display and a cool Manhattan loft apartment.

Tip: Of course, a screen saver doesn't really save your screen. Flat-panel screens, the only kind Apple sells, are incapable of "burning in" a stationary image of the sort that originally inspired the creation of screen savers years ago.

No, these screen savers serve two unrelated functions. First, they mask what's on your screen from passersby whenever you leave your desk. Second, they're kind of fun.

When you click a module's name in the Screen Saver list, you see a mini version of it playing back in the preview screen. Click the preview to give the module a dry run on your full screen. When you've had enough of the preview, just move the mouse or press any key. You return to the Screen Saver panel.

In Mountain Lion, the Screen Saver module has been given a deep cleaning and an architectural overhaul. It now offers two categories of screen savers.

Slideshows

At the top of the scrolling list of icons at left, Apple has installed 14 "slideshows"—attractive animations that gracefully fling photos around in different show-offy ways—that began life in programs like iPhoto.

At right, use the Source pop-up menu to specify which photos you want included in the slideshow. You can use any of the photo sets that Apple provides (National Geo-

GEM IN THE ROUGH

Secrets of the Screen Saver Modules

The canned screen saver modules are stored in your System→Library→Screen Savers folder. If you Control-click (right-click) one of the icons inside and choose Show Package Contents from the shortcut menu, you'll find a Contents→Resources folder that contains the individual image files for some of the slideshowish modules (the outer-space photos for the Forest screen saver, for example).

Why bother? Because some of these spectacular photos make really good desktop pictures. You're free to copy them out of the Resources folder for that purpose.

graphic, Aerial, Cosmos, Nature Patterns); you can choose Choose Folder to specify some photos of your own from a folder on your Mac; or you can choose Photo Library to see a list of your iPhoto or Aperture albums. Each creates an amazingly dramatic, almost cinematic experience, worthy of setting up to "play" during dinner parties like the lava lamps of the '70s.

"Shuffle slide order," of course, scrambles the photo sequence so that it's different every time. Wouldn't want you to get bored staring at your screen, now.

Tip: Once a slideshow screen saver kicks in, you can control it as you would a real slideshow. Press the ← and → keys to visit previous or subsequent photos. That's great for those times when someone passing your Mac says, "Hey, what was that?"

Screen savers

Beneath the list of slideshows, you'll find the icons for seven more traditional, non-photographic slideshow displays. Each has options worth exploring. For example:

- **Flurry.** Flaming, colorful, undulating arms of fire, which resemble a cross between an octopus and somebody arc welding in the dark. If you click Screen Saver Options, you can control how many streams of fire appear at once, the thickness of the arms, the speed of movement, and the colors.

- **Arabesque.** Patterns of small circles that come and go, shrink and grow; drugged-out randomness.

- **Shell.** Five swirling fireworksy spinners, centered around a bigger one.

- **Message.** The Apple logo and the computer's name, faintly displayed on the monitor. (These elements shift position every few minutes.) Lets corporate supervisors glance over at the screens of unattended Macs to find out which employees aren't at their desks.

Tip: If you click Options, you can type in replacement text. Instead of your Mac's name bouncing around, your supervisor can see, for example, "This Mac temporarily unassigned."

- **iTunes Artwork.** This module builds a gigantic mosaic of album art from your music collection. The tiles periodically flip around, just to keep the image changing. (The Options button lets you specify how many rows of album-art squares appear, and how often the tiles flip.)

Tip: If you point to an album cover while this screen saver is playing, a big ▶ button appears. If you click it, the Mac starts playing the corresponding album. (Of course, that means clicking no longer exits the screen saver. Press a key to wake up the Mac instead.)

- **Word of the Day.** A parade of interesting words drawn from the Dictionary program. You're invited to tap the D key to open the dictionary to that entry to read more. Build your word power!

Tip: Click Options to specify *which* dictionary you want: the standard New Oxford American or the Japanese one.

- **Random.** The Mac chooses a different screen saver each time. Surrender to the power of chance!

No matter which screen-saver mode you choose, you can also turn on "Show with clock." This option superimposes the current time on whatever screen saver you've selected. You'd be surprised at how handy it can be to use your Mac as a giant digital clock when you're getting coffee across the room.

Note: You can stop searching now: It's true. In Mountain Lion, you can no longer install different screen-saver styles. And you no longer have a choice of different presentations for your own folders, like the amazing Collage mosaic (which built up one giant photo by using hundreds of smaller photos as individual pixels).

Activating the screen saver

You can control when your screen saver takes over your monitor in a couple of ways:

- **After a period of inactivity.** Using the "Start after" pop-up menu, you can set the amount of time that has to pass without keyboard or mouse activity before the screen saver starts. The duration can be as short as 1 minute or as long as 1 hour, or you can choose Never to prevent the screen saver from ever turning on by itself.

- **When you park your cursor in the corner of the screen.** If you click the Hot Corners button, you can turn each corner of your monitor into a *hot corner* (Figure 9-10).

Figure 9-10:
Click the Hot Corners button to open this "sheet," which lets you designate certain corners of your screen as instant-activation spots, or never-come-on spots. Sliding the mouse to the Start Screen Saver corner, for example, turns on your screen saver right away.

If you work in a business, or in a nosy family, it might be worth noting here that you can set things up so that your password is required to exit the screen saver. Visit System Preferences→Security & Privacy, and turn on "Require password immediately after sleep or screen saver begins."

Dictation & Speech

Your Mac's ability to speak—and to be spoken to—is described in juicy detail within other chapters. To learn about Mountain Lion's new dictation feature, see page 245; for details on its ability to speak to you, see page 630.

Displays

This is the center of operations for all your monitor settings. Here you set your monitor's resolution, calibrate color balance and brightness, and turn AirPlay on and off—a cool new Mountain Lion feature that duplicates whatever's on your Mac screen on a TV set. Wirelessly.

Tip: You can open up this panel with a quick keystroke from any program on the Mac. Just press Option as you tap one of the screen-brightness keys on the top row of your keyboard.

The specific controls depend on the kind of monitor you're using, but here are the ones you'll most likely see.

Display Tab

This tab, newly redesigned in Mountain Lion, is the main headquarters for your screen controls. It governs these settings:

- **Resolution.** All Mac screens today can make the screen picture larger or smaller, thus accommodating different kinds of work. You perform this magnification or reduction by switching among different *resolutions* (measurements of the number of dots that compose the screen).

 When you use a low-resolution setting, such as 800 × 600, the dots of your screen image get larger, thus enlarging (zooming in on) the picture—but showing a smaller slice of the page. Use this setting when playing a small Web movie, for example, so that it fills more of the screen. (Lower resolutions usually look blurry on flat-panel screens, though; see the box below.) At higher resolutions, such as 1280 × 800, the screen dots get smaller, making your windows and icons smaller,

FREQUENTLY ASKED QUESTION

Blurry Flat-Panel Screens

Yucko! I tried the 800 × 600 setting on my laptop, and everything got all blurry and big! How do I fix it?

On any flat-panel screen—not just laptop screens—only one resolution setting looks really great: the maximum one. That's what geeks call the native resolution of that screen.

That's because on flat-panel screens, every pixel is a fixed size. At lower resolutions, the Mac does what it can to blur together adjacent pixels, but the effect is fuzzy and unsatisfying. (On a bulky CRT monitor, the electron gun can actually make the pixels larger or smaller, so you don't have this problem.)

but showing more overall area. You could use this kind of setting when working on two-page spreads in your page-layout program, for example.

If you select "Best for built-in display," the Mac uses the highest resolution possible for your Mac's screen—the one that makes it look sharpest. The list of other resolution settings your monitor can accommodate—800 × 600, 1024 × 768, and so on—doesn't appear unless you turn on Scaled.

Note: In previous OS X versions, you could adjust the resolution of your monitor without having to open System Preferences, by choosing from the Displays menulet on your menu bar. Unfortunately, it's no longer available in Mountain Lion.

- **Brightness.** This slider lets you make the screen look good in the prevailing lighting conditions. Of course, most Apple keyboards have brightness-adjustment *keys,* so this software control is included just for the sake of completeness.

- **Automatically adjust brightness.** Your laptop's light sensor dims the screen automatically in dark rooms—*if* this checkbox is turned on.

Note: If you have one of those increasingly rare CRT (that is, non-flat) screens, you get some additional controls. For example, a Geometry tab appears that lets you adjust the position, size, and angle of the screen image on the glass itself—controls that can be useful in counteracting distortion in aging monitors.

Arrangement Tab

From the dawn of the color-monitor era, Macs have had a terrific feature: the ability to exploit multiple monitors all plugged into the computer at the same time. Any Mac with a video-output jack (laptops, iMacs), or any Mac with a second or third video card (Mac Pros) can project the same thing on both screens (*mirror mode*); that's useful in a classroom when the "external monitor" is a projector.

Tip: The standard video card in a Mac Pro has jacks for one or two monitors. By installing more video cards, you can get up to *six* monitors going at once.

But it's equally useful to make one monitor act as an *extension* of the next. For example, you might have your Photoshop image window on your big monitor but keep all the Photoshop controls and tool palettes on a smaller screen. Your cursor passes from one screen to another as it crosses the boundary. To set this up, just hook up the monitor or projector and then choose Detect Displays from the Displays *menulet.*

When you open System Preferences, you see a different Displays window on each screen, so that you can change the color and resolution settings independently for each. Your Displays menulet shows two sets of resolutions, too—one for each screen.

If your Mac can show different images on each screen, then your Displays panel offers an Arrangement tab, showing a miniature version of each monitor. By dragging these icons around relative to each other, you can specify how you want the second monitor's image "attached" to the first. Most people position the second monitor's image to the right of the first, but you're also free to position it on the left, above, below, or even directly on top of the first monitor's icon (the last of which produces a video-mirroring setup). For the least likelihood of going insane, consider placing the real-world monitor in the same position.

Tip: There's good news about multiple monitors in Mountain Lion: You can now use full-screen mode on both monitors. (In Lion, the external monitor displayed nothing but wallpaper.)

For committed multiple-monitor fanatics, the fun doesn't stop there. See the microscopic menu bar on the first-monitor icon? You can drag that tiny strip onto a different monitor icon, if you like, to tell Displays where you'd like your menu bar to appear. (And check out how most screen savers correctly show different stuff on each monitor!)

Tip: If you close your laptop while it's connected to an external monitor, the machine doesn't go to sleep. Instead, it keeps the external monitor on. The laptop remains on, so you can keep right on working, as though the laptop were the brains for a big-screen Mac.

Color Tab

This pane offers a list of *color profiles* for your monitor (or, if you turn off "Show profiles for this display only," for *all* monitors). Each profile represents colors slightly differently—a big deal for designers and photo types.

When you click Calibrate, the Display Calibrator Assistant opens to walk you through a series of six screens, presenting various brightness and color-balance settings in each screen. You pick the settings that look best to you; at the end of the process, you save your monitor tweaks as a ColorSync profile, which your Mac uses to adjust the screen for improved color accuracy.

Dock

See Chapter 4 for details on the Dock and its System Preferences pane.

Energy Saver

The Energy Saver program helps you and your Mac in a number of ways. By blacking out the screen after a period of inactivity, it prolongs the life of your monitor. By putting the Mac to sleep after you've stopped using it, Energy Saver cuts down on electricity costs and pollution. On a laptop, Energy Saver extends the length of the battery charge by controlling the activity of the hard drive and screen.

Best of all, this pane offers the option to have your computer turn off each night automatically—and turn on again at a specified time in anticipation of your arrival at the desk.

Sleep Sliders

The Energy Saver controls are different on a laptop Mac and a desktop Mac, but both present a pair of sliders (Figure 9-11).

Figure 9-11:
Top: Here's what Energy Saver looks like on a laptop. In the "Display sleep" option, you can specify an independent sleep time for the screen.

Bottom: Here are the Schedule controls—the key to the Mac's self-scheduling abilities.

The top slider controls when the Mac will automatically go to sleep—anywhere from 1 minute after your last activity to Never. (Activity can be mouse movement, keyboard action, or Internet data transfer; Energy Saver won't put your Mac to sleep in the middle of a download.)

At that time, the screen goes dark, the hard drive stops spinning, and your processor chip slows to a crawl. Your Mac is now in *sleep* mode, using only a fraction of its usual

electricity consumption. To wake it up when you return to your desk, press any key. Everything you were working on, including open programs and documents, is still onscreen, exactly as it was. (To turn off this automatic sleep feature entirely, drag the slider to Never.)

The second slider controls when the *screen* goes black to save power. Yes, you can make the screen go to sleep independently of the Mac itself, although there's no screamingly obvious reason why you'd want to do that.

Checkbox Options

Below the sliders, you see a selection of additional power-related options. On a laptop, the two tabs at the top of the dialog box let you create different settings for the two states of life for a laptop: when it's plugged in (Power Adapter) and when it's running on battery power (Battery). That's important, because on a laptop, every drop of battery power counts. Here's what you may see:

- **Put the hard disks to sleep when possible.** This saves even more juice—and noise—by letting your drives stop spinning when not in use. This option appears

Mysteries of the Battery Menulet

If you've got a laptop, don't miss the checkbox in Energy Saver called "Show battery status in the menu bar." It puts a handy status indicator (⬭) in the menu bar that keeps you informed of your battery's life.

Without clicking the menulet, all you see is an icon that represents how full the battery charge is. If you turn on Show Percentage from the menulet's actual menu, then the menulet can also show how much charge remains, in percentage form.

If you click the menulet, however, you can see an estimate of actual time remaining on your battery charge, in hours:minutes form. (If the battery is charging, then you can click this menulet to see how much time until the battery is fully recharged, like this: "0:24 Until Full.") Either way, the readout is counting down (or up) to that joyous moment.

If you're seeing only the battery icon (no text) in the menu bar, here's what the readouts mean:

Power cord in the battery. The laptop is plugged in, and the battery is 100 percent charged. Ready to roll, Captain!

Lightning bolt in the battery. The laptop is plugged in, but the battery is still charging.

Superimposed X. The laptop is plugged in, but the battery isn't in right, is missing, or isn't getting a charge for some other reason.

Emptying black battery. The laptop is running off of battery power and has at least 25 percent power left. (The width of the bar reveals how much charge is left.)

Emptying red battery. The laptop is running off of battery power but has less than 25 percent charge remaining.

A nearly invisible red bar means you have less than 9 minutes left. Save those documents, buddy.

(Bonus tip: If you Option-click the menulet, you see a health report for your battery. It might say, for example, "Condition: Normal." When the condition needs your attention—when it says "Service Battery," "Replace Soon," "Replace Now," or "Check Battery," you don't have to press Option. You'll see that message every time you open the menulet.)

on both the Battery and Power Adapter tabs, so you can control it independently for each power source.

- **Slightly dim the display while on battery power.** You see this checkbox only on the Battery tab for a laptop. It means "Don't use full brightness, so I can save power."

Tip: And when your laptop is plugged in, the sudden dimming of the screen becomes a handy signal that you've lost power. Maybe your power cord needs replugging, the power strip went out, or there's a massive blackout in your half of the country.

- **Enable Power Nap.** For details on this new Mountain Lion feature, see the box below.
- **Wake for Wi-Fi network access.** This option (on the Power Adapter tab) lets you access a sleeping Mac from across the network. How is that possible? See the box on the facing page.

Note: The wording of this option reflects how your Mac can connect to a network. If it can connect either over an Ethernet cable or a wireless hot spot, it says, "Wake for network access." If it's not a wireless Mac, you'll see, "Wake for Ethernet network access." If it's a MacBook without an Ethernet adapter, it says, "Wake for Wi-Fi network access." On a laptop, the "wake" feature is available only when the machine's lid is left open and you're plugged into a power outlet.

Power Nap

Power Nap, new in Mountain Lion, is an ingenious and extremely useful feature for laptops. (Specifically, it's useful for owners of flash-storage laptop models that were introduced in 2012 or later, like the Retina Display laptops or the 2012 MacBook Airs. On older laptops, it doesn't appear at all.)

Anyway, when you turn on Enable Power Nap on the Energy pane of System Preferences, the Mac keeps updating Internet data even while it's closed and asleep. About once every hour, it wakes itself—without activating any fans or lights—long enough to check for mail, calendar updates, Photo Stream updates, software updates, and so on. When you wake up the laptop later, you'll be delighted to find that it's completely up to date, with new email waiting and all of your iCloud programs (Notes, Messages, Reminders, and so on) up to date. And the lid was closed the whole time!

Most of those network functions take place even when the laptop's on battery power. But when it's plugged in, Power Nap also performs two more time-consuming functions: Time Machine backups and App Store software updates.

Of course, Power Nap means that your laptop isn't quite as somnolent as it used to be while the lid was closed—it's using a little more battery power.

Power Nap comes set to work only when your laptop is plugged into a power outlet, but you can make it work on battery power, too (Apple says that the battery hit is very slight). You'll find separate on/off switches on each of the Energy Saver tabs. On the Battery tab, it says "Enable Power Nap while on battery power"; on the Power Adapter tab, it says "Enable Power Nap while plugged into a power adapter."

- **Restart automatically if the computer freezes.** This option is handy if you leave your Mac unattended and access it remotely, or if you use it as a network file server or Web server. It ensures that, if your lonely Mac seizes up or crashes, it will start itself right back up again. (This checkbox appears only on desktop Macs.)

Tip: If you've also turned off (or left off) "Ask to keep changes when closing documents" and "Close windows when quitting an application" in System Preferences→General, then your Mac will both restart *and* restore everything you were doing. You may, in fact, never even realize that a crash or freeze occurred while you were away! (The telltale sign: Any Web pages you had logged into, like a banking Web site, will have logged you out.)

- **Show battery status in the menu bar.** This on/off switch (laptops only) controls the battery menulet described in the box on page 357.

Scheduled Startup and Shutdown

By clicking the Schedule button, you can set up the Mac to shut itself down and turn itself back on automatically (Figure 9-11, bottom).

If you work from 9 to 5, for example, you can set the office Mac to turn itself on at 8:45 a.m. and shut itself down at 5:30 p.m.—an arrangement that conserves electricity, saves money, and reduces pollution, but doesn't inconvenience you in the least.

GEM IN THE ROUGH

Auto-Wake for Network Access

You should put your Mac to sleep as much as possible; you'll save power, money, and pollution. Unfortunately, a sleeping Mac is useless on your network. For example, you can't access files on it from another machine.

But Wake on Demand gives you the best of both worlds. It keeps a sleeping Mac available on the network, so you can wake it up remotely when you need it.

How can you do that? Is the Mac sleeping, or isn't it?

Yes, it's sleeping. But before it dozes off, it hands off its list of available network services—file sharing, screen sharing, iTunes , sharing, printer sharing, and so on—to your Apple wireless base station. The base station becomes your sleeping Mac's agent, continuing to broadcast the available features of the sleeping Mac (via Apple's Bonjour networking technology) to the rest of the network.

To make this work, you need an AirPort wireless base station or a Time Capsule, running the latest Apple firmware. If you're using a WPA or WPA2 password on your base station or Time Capsule, it can't be in "bridge mode" (you'd know if you'd turned that on). Only Macs made since late 2008 can be awakened over a wireless network (all Macs can be awakened over an Ethernet wired network). To find out if yours is eligible, open System Information (page 467); under the Network heading, click Wi-Fi and look to see if Wake on Wireless is listed as Supported.

(Longtime Mac nuts may observe that "Wake for network access" has been available in Energy Saver for years. That older method, however, worked only on wired networks, not wireless.)

Once you've turned on Wake on Demand, by the way, you might hear brief sounds from the DVD drive, hard drive, or fans, even when the Mac is asleep. That's normal; it means the Mac is checking in with the Bonjour sleep switchboard.

That's right: Even your Mac sometimes stirs in its sleep.

In fact, you may come to forget that you've set up the Mac this way, since you'll never actually see it turn itself off.

Note: The Mac doesn't shut down automatically if you've left unsaved documents open onscreen. It will go to sleep, though.

General

This panel is mostly about how things look on the screen: windows, menus, buttons, scroll bars, and fonts. (It used to be called Appearance, but "General" is more like—yes, you guessed it—the iPhone and the iPad.) Nothing you find here lets you perform any *radical* surgery on the overall OS X look—but you can tweak certain settings to match your personal style.

Changing Colors

Two pop-up menus let you crank up or tone down OS X's overall colorfulness:

- **Appearance.** Choose between Blue and Graphite. Blue refers to OS X's factory setting—bright, candy-colored progress bars, menu, and pulsing OK buttons—and those shiny red, yellow, and green buttons in the corner of every window. If you, like some graphics professionals, find all this circus-poster coloring a bit distracting, then choose Graphite, which renders all those interface elements in various shades of gray.

- **Highlight color.** When you drag your cursor across text, its background changes color to indicate that you've selected it. Exactly what color the background becomes is up to you—just choose the shade you want using the pop-up menu. The Highlight color also affects such subtleties as the lines on the inside of a window as you drag an icon into it.

If you choose Other, the Color Picker palette appears, from which you can choose any color your Mac is capable of displaying.

Sidebar Icon Size

This pop-up menu controls the size of the icons in the Sidebar (page 19), as you'd expect. But you might not guess that it also controls the *type size* of those icons. And you'd *definitely* not guess that it simultaneously adjusts the size and type of the mailbox icons in the Mail program.

Tweaking the Scroll Bars

These options control the scroll bars of all your windows—including the controversial *removal* of scroll bars in Lion/Mountain Lion.

- **Show scroll bars.** If you choose "Automatically based on mouse or trackpad," then OS X makes the scroll bars appear or not based on what you have plugged in.

If you have a trackpad or a Magic Mouse, for example, Apple assumes that you'll learn to scroll by dragging your fingers—so it figures you won't be needing the scroll bars at the edges of the windows. Therefore, the scroll bars appear only when you're actually scrolling (and then only to show you where you are in the window).

But if you have no way of using touch gestures—for example, if you have a regular mouse or Apple's own Mighty Mouse—then scroll bars are always visible, so you don't freak out.

"When scrolling" means that the scroll bars pop into view during the actual scroll, when your mouse or fingers-on-trackpad are actually in motion. And Always, of course, restores the pre-Lion scroll bar behavior; the scroll bars never disappear.

- **Click in the scroll bar to.** For details on "Jump to the next page" and "Jump to the spot that's clicked," see the box on page 34.

Ask to Keep Changes when Closing Documents

This option is for people who liked the old "Save changes before closing?" message that appears when you close a document—instead of the new AutoSave feature (page 220). If you turn this item on, AutoSave will still be there in case your program crashes, for example. But when you close that document or its program, you'll be *asked* whether or not you want to preserve the changes you've made since your last manual Save. AutoSave programs like Pages and TextEdit, in other words, will work just like they used to—and the way all other programs do.

Close Windows When Quitting an Application

Here it is: the master on/off switch for the Mountain Lion feature responsible for reopening your last-used documents and windows each time you open a window.

Usually, the auto-reopening feature saves you time and helps you resume your mental flow—but if you find it disturbing (or if you're worried about someone else discovering what you're up to), turn on this checkbox.

Number of Recent Items

Just how many of your recently opened documents and applications do you want the Mac to show using the Recent Items command in the menu? Pick a number from the pop-up menus. For example, you might choose 30 for documents, 20 for programs, and 5 for servers.

Use LCD Font Smoothing When Available

The Mac's built-in text-smoothing (*antialiasing*) feature is supposed to produce smoother, more commercial-looking text anywhere it appears on your Mac: in word processing documents, email messages, Web pages, and so on.

Experiment with the on/off checkbox to see how you like the effect. Either way, it's fairly subtle (see Figure 9-12). Furthermore, unlike most System Preferences, this one has no effect until the next time you open the program in question. In the Finder, for example, you won't notice the difference until you log out and log back in again.

Turning Off Text Smoothing for Font Sizes __ and Smaller

At smaller type sizes (10-point and smaller), you might find that text is actually *less* readable with font smoothing turned on. It all depends upon the font, the size, your monitor, and your taste. For that reason, this pop-up menu lets you choose a cutoff point. If you choose 12 here, for example, then 12-point (and smaller) type still appears crisp and sharp; only larger type, such as in headlines, displays the graceful edge smoothing. You can choose a size cutoff as low as 4-point.

(None of these settings affect your printouts, only the onscreen display.)

Smoothing is turned on.

Smoothing is turned off.

Figure 9-12:
The same 24-point type with text smoothing turned on (top) and off, shown magnified for your inspection pleasure. You don't get a choice of degrees of smoothing—it's just on or off.

iCloud

This pane is, of course, the master setup page for Apple's free iCloud synchronization service. For complete details on setting up iCloud and using it, see Chapter 17.

Keyboard

The changes you make on this panel are tiny but can have a cumulatively big impact on your daily typing routine. The options have been organized on two panes: Keyboard and Keyboard Shortcuts.

Keyboard

On this pane, you have these choices:

- **Key Repeat Rate, Delay Until Repeat.** In Mountain Lion, holding down letter and number keys no longer makes them repeat, much to the disappointment of people who like to type, for example, "AAAAAARRRRRRGGGGHHH!" Instead, holding down a key produces a palette of alternative accented versions of that letter, like é, è, ê, ë, and so on.

 Only the punctuation keys still repeat, so at least you can still type ****** or ????? or !!!!!!!.

 There are sneaky ways to make your regular keys repeat, as they did in days gone by; see page 240. In the meantime, these two sliders govern the repeating behavior of the punctuation keys. On the right: a slider that determines how long you must

hold down a key before it starts repeating (to prevent triggering repetitions accidentally). On the left: a slider that governs how fast each key spits out characters once the spitting has begun.

- **Use all F1, F2, etc. keys as standard function keys.** This option appears *only* on laptops and aluminum-keyboard Macs. It's complicated, so read page 197 slowly.

- **Adjust keyboard brightness in low light.** This setting appears only if your Mac's keyboard does, in fact, light up when you're working in the dark—a showy feature of many Mac laptops. You can specify that you want the internal lighting to shut off after a period of inactivity (to save power when you've wandered away, for example), or you can turn the lighting off altogether. (You can always adjust the keyboard brightness manually, of course, by tapping the ☼ and ☼ keys.)

- **Show Keyboard & Character Viewer in menu bar.** You can read all about these special symbol-generating windows on page 254. For years, the on/off switch for these handy tools has been buried in the International pane of System Preferences; now there's a duplicate on/off switch here, for your convenience. (An Input Sources button is here, too; it takes you directly to that same pane, so that you can specify which languages you plan to use.)

- **Modifier Keys.** This button lets you turn off, or remap, the functions of the Option, Caps Lock, Control, and ⌘ keys. It's for Unix programmers whose pinkies can't adjust to the Mac's modifier-key layout; for anyone using a PC keyboard on which the Option (Alt) and ⌘ (Windows) keys are in the "wrong" positions relative to each other; and for anyone who keeps hitting Caps Lock by accident during everyday typing.

Keyboard Shortcuts

This pane lets you make up new keystrokes for just about any function on the Mac, like capturing a screenshot, operating the Dock, triggering one of the Services, or operating a menu in *any program* from the keyboard. You can come up with keyboard combinations that, for example, are easier to remember, harder to trigger by accident, or easier to hit with one hand.

Step-by-step instructions for using this pane appear on page 213.

Language & Text

The primary job of this pane, once called International, is to set up your Mac to work in other languages. If you bought your Mac already set up in your own language—you're already using the only language, number format, and keyboard layout you'll ever need—then you can ignore most of this panel. But when it comes to showing off OS X to your friends and loved ones, the "wow" factor on the Mac's polyglot features is huge.

Details appear on page 251.

Mail, Contacts & Calendars

This System Preferences pane is identical to the one in the iPhone and iPad. It's a single, handy, central place to set up your email, calendar, and address-book accounts (Gmail, Yahoo, Exchange, Twitter, Vimeo, Flickr, and so on).

To get started entering your account names and passwords, click one of the big-name logos (Gmail, Yahoo, whatever)—or click the **+** button below the list. The Mac is smart enough to feed the account information here into the right programs (Mail, Calendar, Contacts, and the Share buttons described on page 268).

Mission Control

Mission Control, the joint venture of the Exposé, Spaces, and Dashboard window-management features, is described in detail in Chapter 5—and so is this joint-venture control panel.

Mouse

This pane looks different depending on what kind of mouse (if any) is attached to your Mac.

Tracking Speed, Double-Click Speed

It may surprise you that the cursor on the screen doesn't move five inches when you move the mouse five inches on the desk. Instead, the cursor moves farther when you move the mouse faster.

How *much* farther depends on how you set the first slider here. The Fast setting is nice if you have an enormous monitor, since you don't need an equally large mouse pad to get from one corner to another. The Slow setting, on the other hand, forces you to pick up and put down the mouse frequently as you scoot across the screen. It offers very little acceleration, but it can be great for highly detailed work like pixel-by-pixel editing in Photoshop.

The Double-Click Speed setting specifies how much time you have to complete a double-click. If you click too slowly—beyond the time you've allotted yourself with this slider—the Mac "hears" two *single* clicks instead.

Note: On a laptop without any mouse attached, the Mouse pane still appears in System Preferences—but its sole function is to help you "pair" your Mac with a wireless Bluetooth mouse. At that point, the Mouse pane looks just as it does on a desktop Mac.

The Mighty Mouse and Magic Mouse

Just by looking, you'd never know that these Apple mice have both a right button and a left button. Once you turn on the two-button feature in System Preferences (Figure 9-13), though, each side clicks independently.

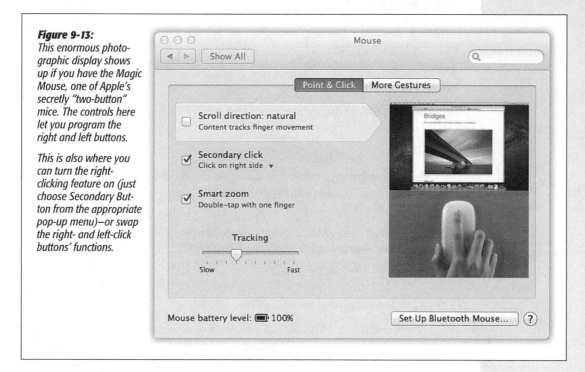

Figure 9-13:
This enormous photographic display shows up if you have the Magic Mouse, one of Apple's secretly "two-button" mice. The controls here let you program the right and left buttons.

This is also where you can turn the right-clicking feature on (just choose Secondary Button from the appropriate pop-up menu)—or swap the right- and left-click buttons' functions.

The Magic Mouse is especially useful in Mountain Lion. Its unusually flat, broad top surface is also a trackpad. You can drag your finger across its surface to trigger many of OS X's trackpad gestures.

The Mighty Mouse is the white mouse that has come with desktop Macs since 2005.

Network

See Chapters 14 and 21 for the settings you need to plug in for networking.

Notifications

Here's where you customize Mountain Lion's new Notification Center, which gets its own big writeup in Chapter 10.

Parental Controls

These controls are described at length in Chapter 13.

Print & Scan

Chapter 15 describes printing, scanning, and faxing. This panel offers a centralized list of the printers, scanners, and fax modems you've introduced to the Mac.

Security & Privacy

See Chapter 13 for details on locking up your Mac.

Sharing

OS X is an outstanding, upstanding network citizen, flexible enough to share its contents with other Macs, Windows PCs, people dialing in from the road, and so on. On this panel, you'll find on/off switches for each of these sharing channels.

In this book, many of these features are covered in other chapters. For example, **Screen Sharing** and **File Sharing** are in Chapter 14, **Printer Sharing** and **Scanner Sharing** are Chapter 15, **Internet Sharing** is in Chapter 17, and **Web Sharing** and **Remote Login** are in Chapter 21.

Here's a quick rundown on the other items:

- **DVD or CD Sharing.** This feature was added to accommodate Macs that don't have built-in CD/DVD drives, like MacBook Airs and some Mac Minis. When you turn on this option, such driveless computers on the network can "see," and borrow, your Mac's DVD drive for the purposes of installing new software or running Mac disk-repair software. (Your drive shows up under the Remote Disc heading in the driveless Mac's Finder Sidebar.)

- **Remote Management.** Lets someone else control your Mac using Apple Remote Desktop, a popular add-on program for teachers and system administrators.

- **Remote Apple Events.** Lets AppleScript gurus (Chapter 7) send commands to Macs across the network.

- **Bluetooth Sharing.** This pane lets you set up Bluetooth file sharing, a way for other people near you to shoot files over to (or receive files from) your laptop—without hassle, or passwords. Page 264 has the details.

Software Update

Whenever Apple improves or fixes some piece of OS X or some Apple-branded program, the Software Update program can notify you, download the update, and install it into your system automatically. These updates may include new versions of programs like iPhoto and iMovie; drivers for newly released printers, scanners, cameras, and such; bug fixes and security patches; and so on.

In Mountain Lion, most of the actual downloading duties have been handed off to the Mac App Store app. All that's left of this preference pane are four checkboxes that govern the process:

- **Automatically check for updates.** This is where you grant permission to your Mac to ping the mother ship periodically to see if there are updates available. Turn it off, and you're stuck with today's software versions forever.

- **Download newly available updates in the background.** If you leave this option turned on, you'll still be notified before anything gets installed, but you won't have to wait for the downloading—the deed will already be done.

- **Install system data files and security updates.** If you turn this off, you won't get OS X updates as they come along—only updates to your apps.

 It's hard to think of a reason why you wouldn't want the latest, most refined versions of OS X. But maybe you rely on some obscure piece of software that really, really likes your Mac the way you have it today. You don't want to risk "breaking" that app when some new system patch comes along.

 Or maybe you want to read about Apple's system updates online before installing them yourself.

- **Automatically download apps purchased on other Macs.** Fascinating, Captain. This checkbox ensures that if you buy an app from the App Store on one of your other Macs, this Mac will download it automatically, so that you have it everywhere (assuming that both Macs are signed in with the same Apple ID.)

At the bottom of this dialog box, a message lets you know whether or not new software updates are waiting to be installed. If so, a Show Updates button appears. Click it to open the App Store to its Updates page.

Sound

Using the panes of the Sound panel, you can configure the sound system of your Mac in any of several ways.

Tip: Here's a quick way to jump directly to the Sound panel of System Preferences–from the keyboard, without ever having to open System Preferences or click Sound. Just press Option as you tap the ◀, ◀), or ◀)) key on the top row of your Apple keyboard.

Sound Effects Tab

"Sound effects" means *error beeps*—the sound you hear when the Mac wants your attention, or when you click someplace you shouldn't.

Just click the sound of your choice to make it your default system beep. Most of the canned choices here are funny and clever, yet subdued enough to be of practical value as alert sounds (Figure 9-14).

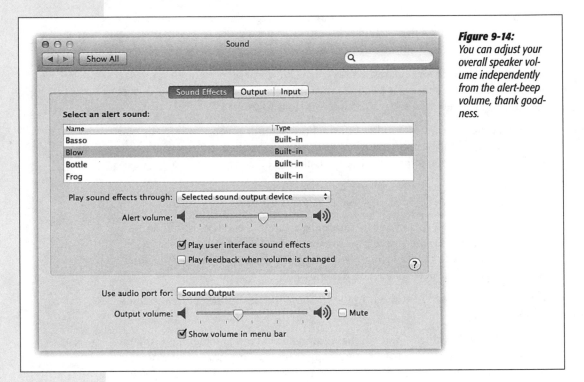

Figure 9-14:
You can adjust your overall speaker volume independently from the alert-beep volume, thank goodness.

As for the other controls on the Sound Effects panel, they include these:

- **Alert volume.** The *main* volume slider for your Mac is the "Output volume" slider at the bottom of the Sound pane. The "Alert volume" slider is *just* for error beeps; Apple was kind enough to let you adjust the volume of these error beeps independently.

- **Play user interface sound effects.** This option produces a few subtle sound effects during certain Finder operations: when you drag something off the Dock, into the Trash, or into a folder, or when the Finder finishes a file-copying job.

- **Play feedback when volume is changed.** Each time you press one of the volume keys (◂, ◂), ◂))), the Mac beeps (or, rather, pops) to help you gauge the current volume.

That's all fine when you're working at home. But more than one person has been humiliated in an important meeting when the Mac made a sudden, inappropriately loud sonic outburst—and then amplified that embarrassment by furiously and repeatedly pressing the volume-down key, beeping all the way.

If you turn off this checkbox, the Mac won't make any sound at all as you adjust its volume. Instead, you'll see only a visual representation of the steadily decreasing (or increasing) volume level.

Tip: The Shift key reverses the logic. So if you have "Play feedback" turned *on,* holding down Shift as you tap the volume keys makes them silent. If it's turned *off,* you can force the volume-gauging beeps to play by pressing Shift as you tap the volume keys.

- **Use audio port for: Sound Output/Sound Input.** Most Mac laptops have only a single audio jack on the side—a miniplug that can accommodate either an audio *output* device like headphones or speakers, or an *input* device (that is, a microphone). Here you tell your laptop which of these personalities you want that jack to have.

Output Tab

"Output" means speakers or headphones. For most people, this pane lists only Internal Speakers (and a Balance slider for left-to-right stereo balancing).

This panel is more useful when you've connected external speakers, a Bluetooth or USB phone headset, or an AirPlay receiver like an Apple TV—and then clicked its name. All Mac audio now flows to that device. OS X will even remember your volume setting for each gadget independently.

Tip: Here's a much quicker way to change your audio input or output: Press Option as you click the ◀⁍) menulet. You get a secret pop-up menu that lists your various microphones, speakers, and headphones, so you can switch things without a visit to System Preferences.

Input Tab

This panel lets you specify which sound source you want the Mac to "listen to," if you have more than one connected: external microphone, internal microphone, line input, USB headset, or whatever. It also lets you adjust the sensitivity of that microphone—its *input volume*—by dragging the slider and watching the real-time Input level meter above it change as you speak. Put another way, it's a quick way to see if your microphone is working.

The "Use ambient noise reduction" is great if you make podcasts or use dictation software. It turns any mike into what amounts to a noise-canceling microphone, deadening the background noise while you're recording.

If you'd prefer even more control over your Mac's sound inputs and outputs, don't miss the rewritten Audio MIDI Setup program in your Applications→Utilities folder.

Spotlight

Here's how you tell the Mac (a) which categories of files and information you want the Spotlight search feature to search, (b) which folders you *don't* want searched, for privacy reasons, and (c) which key combination you want to use for summoning the Spotlight menu or dialog box. Details are in Chapter 3.

Startup Disk

Use this panel to pick the System folder your Mac will use the next time it starts up—when you're swapping between OS X and Windows (running with Boot Camp), for example. Check out the details in Chapter 8.

Time Machine

Here's the master on/off switch and options panel for Time Machine, which is described in Chapter 6.

Trackpad

You may love your Mac laptop now, but wait until you find out about these special features. They make your laptop *crazy* better. It's one of Mountain Lion's most famous characteristics—that you can point, click, scroll, right-click, rotate things, enlarge things, hide windows, and switch programs, all on the trackpad itself, without a mouse and without ever having to lift your fingers. (You can do most of this on a desktop Mac, too, if it has an Apple Magic Mouse, or an external trackpad like Apple's Magic Trackpad.)

Apple keeps adding new "gestures" with each new laptop, so yours may not offer all these options. And even in Mountain Lion, you might see different options and layouts depending on what Mac you have.

On the latest Macs, you see something like Figure 6-3 on page 239: three tabs. Each offers on/off switches or pop-up menus that govern how you do pointing, clicking, scrolling, and other mouselike maneuvers. Each time you click one, the right half of the dialog box plays a tidy, looping movie that shows you that technique clearly and visibly.

Here's what's on the three main tabs.

Point & Click

- **Tap to Click.** Usually, you touch your laptop's trackpad only to move the cursor. For clicking and dragging, you're supposed to push down on the clicker (either the button *beneath* the trackpad or, on recent models, the lower half of the actual trackpad surface).

 Many people find, however, that it's more direct to tap and drag directly on the trackpad, using the same finger that's been moving the cursor. That's the purpose

of this checkbox. When it's on, you can tap the trackpad surface to register a mouse click at the location of the cursor. Double-tap to double-click.

- **Secondary click.** This means "right-click." As you know, right-clicking is a huge deal on the Mac; it unleashes useful features just about everywhere.

 On all Mac laptops, you can trigger a right-click by clicking with your thumb while resting your index and middle fingers on the trackpad.

 On the latest laptops—the ones without a separate clicker button—this pop-up menu offers you three other options. You can click with two fingers; click once in the lower-right corner of the trackpad; or click once in the lower-left corner. Weird, but wonderful.

- **Look up.** This gesture lets you tap the trackpad (*don't* click—just touch the surface without clicking) to bring up a handy dictionary definition for the word you're double-tapping. It doesn't work in all programs.

- **Three-finger drag.** This option lets you move a window around the screen, or change its size and shape, without actually clicking. Instead, you rest three fingers on the trackpad and drag. For example, move a window by pointing to the title bar and then dragging three fingers. Make it wider by pointing to its right or left edge and then dragging three fingers. Change its shape by pointing to the lower-right corner and then dragging three fingers.

- **Tracking speed.** This is a duplicate of the Tracking Speed slider described under "Mouse" earlier in this chapter—but it lets you establish an independent tracking speed for the *trackpad*.

Scroll & Zoom

- **Scroll direction: natural.** And here it is, the heart of Mountain Lion's most controversial feature: scrolling *up* when you drag your fingers (or the scroll wheel, or the scroll bar) *up*. That's exactly the opposite of what we've been doing for years.

 If you can't stand this new arrangement, turn it off here. But first read the discussion on page 12.

- **Zoom in or out.** If you've used an iPhone, this one will seem familiar. What it means is, "Put two fingers on the trackpad and spread them apart to *enlarge* what's on the screen. Slide two fingers *together* to shrink it down again." It doesn't work in every program—it affects pictures and PDFs in Preview, photos in iPhoto, text in Safari, text in a TextEdit window —but it's great when it does.

- **Smart zoom.** On the iPhone/iPad, you can double-tap a block of text or a graphic on a Web page to enlarge just that block to full-screen size. The "smart" element of this is the way the software senses that block's borders and zooms in exactly right.

 Now you can do that on your Mac, too. Double-tap your trackpad (touch, don't click) with *two* fingers to do it.

- **Rotate.** Place two fingers on the trackpad, and then twist them around an invisible center point, to rotate a photo or a PDF document. This doesn't work in all programs or in all circumstances, but it's great for turning images upright in Preview, iPhoto, Image Capture, and so on.

More Gestures

- **Swipe between pages.** Drag two fingers horizontally across the trackpad to skip to the next or previous page or image in a batch. Here again, this feature doesn't work in all programs, but it's great for flipping through images or PDF pages in Preview or iPhoto, or to go back or forward a page in Safari.

 The tiny pop-up menu here lets you *change* the swiping gesture. You can swipe with two fingers, three fingers, or—if you're a fan of variety—two *or* three fingers.

- **Swipe between full-screen apps.** If you've embraced Lion's new full-screen feature, or its Mission Control feature, you'll definitely want to learn this one. Here's the gesture that lets you flip between full-screen apps: either with four fingers on the trackpad or (if you change the setting using the pop-up menu) three.

- **Notification Center.** As noted on page 376, you can summon Mountain Lion's new Notification Center by swiping leftward with two fingers onto the trackpad from beyond its right edge.

- **Mission Control.** This gesture lets you enter and exit Mission Control (Chapter 5) by swiping up or down with three fingers. (You can change it to *four* fingers.)

- **App Exposé.** If this checkbox is on, you can trigger App Exposé (page 199) by swiping three fingers downward. (You can change the setting to *four* fingers.)

Note: If you study those last two paragraphs carefully, you'll realize that the four-finger swipe has different *levels.* Starting from whatever you're doing, a four-finger swipe *up* takes you into Mission Control. From there, *two* swipes down takes you into App Exposé.

Similarly, from within App Exposé, *two* swipes upward enters Mission Control.

Zooming In, the Shortcut Way

It's been one of the Mac's standout features forever: You can zoom into the screen image, magnifying the whole thing, just by dragging two fingers up or down the trackpad while you're pressing the Control key. You can zoom in so far that the word "zoom" in 12-point type fills the entire monitor. (If you have a mouse, turning the wheel or trackpea while pressing Control does the same thing.)

This feature comes in handy with amazing frequency. It's great for reading Web pages in tiny type, or enlarging Web movies, or studying the dot-by-dot construction of a button or icon that you admire. Just Control-drag upward to zoom in, and Control-drag downward to zoom out again.

The on/off switch for this feature is in System Preferences→Accessibility→Zoom. It's called "Use scroll gesture with modifier keys to zoom." As a bonus, you can change the Control key to one of the other modifier keys. And the Zoom Style pop-up menu lets you limit the magnification to a "picture-in-picture" inset window, rather than full screen.

- **Launchpad.** Launchpad (page 164) wouldn't be very useful if it took several steps to open. Fortunately, this option lets you fire up Launchpad by pinching on the trackpad with three fingers and your thumb. (You can also exit Launchpad by *spreading* those four fingers.)

- **Show Desktop.** You can spread three fingers and your thumb to trigger Desktop Exposé (page 200). Once there, *pinch* those fingers to return to what you were doing.

Note: Here again, Apple has created *levels* of four-finger pinching. Pinching once opens Launchpad; spread *twice* from there to show the desktop. Likewise, pinching *twice* from Show Desktop takes you straight into Launchpad.

At the bottom of the Trackpad pane, a Set Up Bluetooth Trackpad button appears. Use it to pair your Mac with a wireless external trackpad—like Apple's own Magic Trackpad.

Users & Groups

This is the master list of people who are allowed to log into your Mac. (In previous Mac OS X versions it was called Accounts.) It's where you can adjust their passwords, startup pictures, self-opening startup items, permissions to use various features of the Mac, and other security tools. All of this is described in Chapter 13.

OS X: THE MISSING MANUAL

Reminders, Notes & Notification Center

Y ou've come at last to the summit of the mountain, the heart of the matter, the core of the apple: the three new features that make Mountain Lion Mountain Lion. These three new apps have arrived, fully grown, on the Mac after a long and storied childhood on the iPhone and iPad. They are, of course, Reminders, Notes, and the Notification Center.

Their appearance in OS X makes perfect sense. First, of course, they're great day-to-day apps that can really, truly make you better organized. You'll feel less helpless in the modern maelstrom of obligations and to-do lists.

But more important, they make sense because of iCloud.

Reminders, Notes, and Notification Center like to be *synchronized* across all your Apple gadgets. Take some notes when you're at a meeting with your iPad, and presto—they magically appear on your Mac. Add a To Do item on your Mac when you're on a phone call, and shazam—you'll find it on your iPhone when you're out and about. Create an appointment on your desktop Mac's calendar, and kaboom—you'll be reminded of it when you're on the road using your laptop. We've waited a very long time for this.

If you've used one of these features on your iPhone, iPod Touch, or iPad, you'll feel right at home when you encounter them on the Mac. This, of course, is the beauty of submitting yourself to an all-powerful technological mother ship like Apple: Everything looks and works the same on different gadgets. But read along anyway; there are differences here and there.

Notification Center

A notification is an important status message. On the iPhone, you get one every time a text message comes in, an alarm goes off, a calendar appointment is imminent, or your battery is running low.

iPhone apps use this mechanism, too. Nowadays, you get a message when your friends post updates on Facebook or Twitter. When your flight is two hours from takeoff. When a new Groupon discount becomes available. When your online Scrabble or chess partner makes another move.

It's no different on your Mac. Mail and Messages might want to let you know that a new message has arrived. Game Center might want you to realize that it's your move. The Calendar app might want to flag you that an important meeting is about to start.

Figure 10-1:
Left: In Mountain Lion, all Mac features get your attention in the same quiet, uniform way: with a bubble like this one.

Right: Here's the Notification Center, where all those incoming messages pile up, for your inspection pleasure.

In Mountain Lion, you'll know when some app is trying to get your attention: A subtle message bubble slides into view at the top right of your screen (Figure 10-1, left). Some of these alerts slide away again after 5 seconds; others require you to click a button, like Close, Snooze, or Show (which opens the program that's waving its little hands in your face).

Note: Only apps you got from the Mac App Store can tap into the Notification Center. Other programs will still use whatever alert mechanisms they always have—pop-up dialog boxes, for example.

But what if you miss one? Or you decide to act on it later? Thought you'd never ask.

On the iPhone or iPad, all of those "Hey you!" messages collect on a single screen called the Notification Center. So it occurred to somebody at Apple: Why should that handiness be confined to the phone?

In Mountain Lion, the Notification Center looks exactly the same as it does on the mobile devices (Figure 10-1, right).

To make it appear on a laptop, swipe two fingers *onto* the trackpad from the right. (Start the swipe off to the right of the trackpad. It's the first time you've ever crossed the edge of the trackpad with a Mac gesture. Weird.)

You can also open the Notification Center by clicking the ☰ in the upper-right corner of your screen. That's a handy trick if your Mac doesn't have a trackpad—if it's an iMac, for example. (You can also set up a keystroke or a "hot corner" to open the Notification Center, if you like. See pages 213 and 176.)

Either way, the Notification Center slides onto the screen like a classy black window shade, printed in white with every recent item of interest; whatever *was* on your screen gets shoved temporarily off to the left side of your screen.

Tip: To close the Notification Center, swipe the opposite way (left to right) with two fingers. Or just click any other part of the screen. Or click the ☰ again. Or press the Esc key.

Here you'll find all your apps' notifications, as well as all of your Mac's messages, reminders, upcoming appointments, and so on.

Once the center is open, you can have three kinds of fun:

FREQUENTLY ASKED QUESTION

Shutting Up the Bubbles

I don't need the distraction of those message bubbles in the corner of my screen. Can't they be shut up?

If you're in a hurry, you can get rid of one with a right-swipe on it (two fingers on a trackpad, one on a Magic Mouse).

But to truly shut them up, just Option-click the ☰ button in your menu bar. That stifles all bubbles for the rest of the day (or until you Option-click it again).

There's also a longer method for slowpokes: open the Notification Center and scroll *up*. There, *above* the list of notifications, is a hidden on/off switch for those alerts and

> Fri Jul 20 12:08 AM 🔍 ☰
> Show Alerts and Banners ON ⬤
> 🐦 Click to Tweet 📘 Click to Post
> ⊕ App Store ✕

banners. You can always slide the switch back On when you're ready to be bombarded.

Either way, when you're hunkering down for a work session, feel free to shut alerts off. Your messages will quietly pile up in the Notification Center, but they won't pop up on your screen individually as they happen.

And by the way: Notification Center *automatically* shuts up its alert bubbles whenever you're giving a Keynote presentation from your Mac or connected to a projector. Nothing worse than an audience of 500 witnessing the embarrassing subject lines of your incoming email.

- Scroll the list to see more of it.

- Click an item in the Notification Center to open the relevant app for more details. For example, click an appointment listed there to open its information panel in Calendar. Click the name of a software update to open the Mac App Store program to read about it and download it. Click a message's name to open Mail, where you can read the entire message.

- Click the little ⊗ to dismiss one app's entire list of notifications once you've seen them. (The app is free to fill up your Notification Center again, once it has something to say.)

Tweeting or Facebooking

If you've told Mountain Lion the details of your Twitter or Facebook accounts, then a strange little surprise awaits you at the top of the Notification Center: "Click to Tweet" and "Click to Post" (to Facebook) buttons. As you'd guess, these buttons let you post something to Twitter or Facebook right from there, without having to open some special app or going to the corresponding Web page.

Note: You can hide these buttons, if you like. Open System Preferences→Notifications, and turn off "Show share button in Notification Center" for each service.

When you click one of these buttons, you get the little pop-up card illustrated in Figure 6-13 in Chapter 6.

And what do these buttons have to do with notifications? Absolutely nothing. They're here in the Notification Center because Apple wanted them to be available anytime, anywhere, no matter what program you're using—and the Notification Center is a perfect always-available dashboard.

Customizing the Notification Center

You can (and should) specify *which* apps are allowed to junk up your Notification Center. Open System Preferences→Notifications to see the list of apps that might want to get your attention in the master Notifications list (Figure 10-2).

Tip: A faster way to get to the proper System Preferences pane is built right into the Notification Center itself. Click the tiny ▦ icon at the very bottom of the panel.

This is also the place where you can specify the *order* of the various apps' notifications in the center. Use the Sort Notification Center pop-up menu at the bottom of the window. If you choose By Time, then the apps with the newest alerts appear at the top. But if you tap Manually, then you can simply drag the app names up or down in the list to specify their top-to-bottom order on the Notification Center list.

Out of the box, the following OS X programs are listed in the Notification Center:

- **Share Buttons** lets you hide the "Click to Tweet" and "Click to Post" (Facebook) buttons at the top of the Notification Center.

- **Calendar** lets you know about imminent appointments.

- **FaceTime** tells you when you've missed an incoming call.

- **Game Center** flags you when somebody has invited you to a game or wants to become your friend.

- **Mail** lets you know when you've received a new message. (Mercifully, Mail's Preferences→General tab lets you limit these alerts, so you won't be buried in a barrage of meaningless heads-up bubbles. You can tell Mail to alert you only when somebody in your Contacts list has written to you, only when a message lands in a smart mailbox folder, only when you get email from someone you've designated as a VIP—or whenever any message lands either in your Inbox or all mailboxes.

- **Messages** lets you know when somebody has sent you an instant message.

- **Reminders**—well, you can guess.

- **Safari.** Certain Web sites, if they're open in Safari, can send you notifications (known as HTML Web notifications).

- **Twitter** pops up whenever somebody has mentioned you on Twitter or tried to reach you with a direct message.

- **Facebook** governs the appearance of updates from your Facebook friends.

Of course, other companies' apps may appear in this list, too.

Figure 10-2:
Here, in System Preferences, you can specify which apps are permitted to intrude on the precious billboard that is your Notification Center—and how they're permitted to intrude.

Individual apps, including Mail and Calendar, may offer additional controls in their Preferences boxes. For example, in Calendar, you can turn off notifications from shared calendars and from meeting invitations.

Now it's time to change the settings for one app at a time. Click an app's name to see its individual Notifications settings (Figure 10-2—the Calendar app, in this example).

For example, as hinted above, different apps can get your attention in different ways:

- **None.** If certain apps seem to bug you with news you really don't care about, you can make them shut up forever. Tap None to squelch their notifications altogether. They won't bother you with pop-up messages, although they can still insert items into the Notification Center panel.

- **Banners.** This option is illustrated in Figure 10-1. It makes incoming notifications slide quietly and briefly onto the top right of your screen. Each message holds still long enough for you to read it, but it doesn't interrupt your work and goes away automatically after a few seconds. Banners are a good option for things like Facebook and Twitter updates, and incoming text and email messages.

- **Alerts.** A message slides into the upper-right corner of your screen and doesn't go away until you click a button to dismiss it. You might use this option for apps whose messages are too important to miss, like alarms and flight updates.

At the bottom of the Notifications window, you get three more settings for each app:

- **Show in Notification Center: __ Recent Items.** Use this pop-up menu to specify how *many* rows of information you want to reserve for this app in the Notification Center. You might care to see only the one most recent message from your Scrabble app, but all 20 of your recent Reminders.

Tip: If you turn off this checkbox, the app disappears from the Notification Center completely. You can still get its alert messages, but you just won't see them listed in the Notification Center panel.

Another way to achieve the same effect: Drag the app's name down to the bottom of the list, below the Not in Notification Center heading.

- **Badge app icon.** If you turn this option on, then each app's actual icon (in your Launchpad and on your Dock) sprouts a red circled number, exactly as on the iPhone and iPad. This number lets you know how many times it's tried to flag you about something. The number goes away once you've opened the app and dealt with whatever is bugging it.

- **Play sound when receiving notifications.** Some apps play a sound when a new notification arrives. For example, Calendar dings to remind you of an upcoming event, and Game Center plays a sound when you get a friend request or game invitation. It's a little extra insurance that you won't miss a nudge, but here's where you can turn these sounds off.

Tip: If this Notification Center thing gets you fired up, then you should probably know about Growl, too. It's a free program that creates an effect very similar to Notification Center—but with far more customization. You can make the alerts appear in a different corner of your screen, for example, or change how they look. Growl is available on this book's "Missing CD" page at *www.missingmanuals.com*.

Reminders

Here's another gift to you from the iPhone: Reminders. It's a program that not only records your life's little tasks, but also reminds you about them when the time comes. If you have a laptop, Reminders can even remind you about something based on *where you are,* just as it does on the iPhone and iPad. For example, it can remind you to feed your cats when you arrive home each day—or it can ask you if you've turned off the gas burners when you leave your vacation house.

Figure 10-3:
To open the Details panel, double-click the reminder item in the list, or click the ⓘ *button to its right.*

Here, you can make your reminder pop up at a certain time or place, create an auto-repeating schedule for it, assign a priority level to it, or just type in some notes about it.

To close the panel, click Done or click anywhere else in Reminders.

If you have an iCloud account, your reminders sync across all your gadgets. Create or check off a task on your iPhone, and you'll also find it created or checked off on your Mac, iPhone, iPad, iPod Touch, or PC. (Yes, you can get iCloud syncing on your PC. See *www.apple.com/icloud/setup/pc.html*).

The iCloud account also explains why the location feature is useful even if you have a desktop Mac that doesn't move around a lot. You can program a reminder on your Mac—and your *phone or tablet* will alert you when you move into or away from a specified place.

Tip: If you have an iPhone—oh, wow. Siri and Reminders are a match made in heaven. "Remind me to file the Jenkins report when I get to work." "Remind me to set the TiVo for tonight at 8." "Remind me about Timmy's soccer game a week from Saturday." "Add waffles to my Groceries list." Speech recognition rocks when it comes to leaving notes for yourself. And iCloud will take care of copying each reminder from one to the other.

Once you've opened Reminders (Figure 10-3), you record a new task by clicking the + button in the upper right, or choose File→New Reminder (⌘-N). A new blank line appears in your list. Type your reminder.

Later, as you go through life completing tasks, click the checkbox next to each one. Doing that makes the item seem to disappear—but in fact, it whips into a separate list called Completed (the top of the list, shown in Figure 10-3).

The Details Bubble

If you double-click an item's name (or click its ❶ button), you open the Details bubble. See Figure 10-3.

Here are the options you'll find:

- **On a Day.** Reminders can remind you at a certain time on a certain date. In the Details bubble, next to "remind me," turn on On a Day. The proposed time is the next "o'clock"—if it's 12:15 now, the app suggests 1:00. But you can tap the date to open a clickable mini-calendar (to change the date), or click the digits of the time to edit them.

- **At a location.** If you turn on this checkbox, your Mac or phone will use its location circuits to remind you of this item when you arrive at a certain place or leave a certain place. (Your laptop will remind you, if it's turned on and within a WiFi hot spot. But more often, this option will be useful if you have an iPhone or iPad that's on the same iCloud account. Record the reminder on your Mac—receive the reminder on your phone.)

 The little pop-up menu here proposes Current Location—wherever you are at the moment. That's handy if, for example, you're dropping off your dry cleaning and want to remember to pick it up the next time you're driving by.

 But you can tap that line to specify Home (your home address, as you've set it up in Contacts). You can also start typing any city name, or the name of any person in your Contacts whose address you've specified. You'll even see "Porky Pig Home" and "Porky Pig Work," if Porky has a couple of addresses on file.

 The final step here is to tap either Leaving or Arriving. Later, your gadgets will remind you at the appointed time, or as you approach (or leave) the appointed address. It's fairly mind-blowing the first few times it happens.

- **Repeat.** Reminders can remind you about things that recur in your life, like quarterly tax payments, haircuts, and anniversaries. Tap Repeat if you want this reminder to appear every day, week, two weeks, month, or year. (This option appears only if you've turned on the On a Day option.)

- **Priority.** Tap this pop-up menu to specify whether this item has High, Medium, or Low priority—or None. You'll see one, two, or three exclamation marks (!!!)

next to each item in your Reminders list, indicating its urgency. In some of the calendar programs that sync with Reminders, you can sort your task list by priority.

- **Notes.** Here's a handy place where you can record freehand notes about this item: an address, a phone number, details of any kind.

Click Done to close the Details bubble and record your changes.

Figure 10-4:
Click a date to see what to-do items are staring you down for that date. Click the ◀ and ▶ buttons to move to different months. Once you've clicked away from the current month, a • appears next to the month name; click it to jump back to this month.

The Calendar of Deadline Hell

As you now know, Reminders can give you warnings of upcoming deadlines and to-do items. You don't have to wait until it gives you a reminder, though.

Below the list of lists, you'll see a tiny ▦ icon. Click it to view the mini-calendar; see Figure 10-4.

Lists

Handily enough, you can create *more than one* to-do list, each with its own name: a Groceries list, Kids' Chores, a running tally of expenses, and so on. Here's a great way to log what you eat if you're on a diet, or to keep a list of movies people recommend.

If you share an iCloud account with another family member, you might create a different Reminder list for each person. (Of course, now you run the risk that your spouse might sneakily add items to *your* to-do list!)

If you have an Exchange account, one of your lists can be synced to your corporate Tasks list. It doesn't offer all the features of the other lists in Reminders, but at least it's kept tidy and separate. (Just set up your Exchange account in System Preferences→Mail, Contacts, Calendars.)

The list of lists is the dark-gray panel at the left side of Reminders; it's visible in Figure 10-3. If you don't see it—if you're feeling a little listless—click the ▣ button at the lower-left corner of the window.

At the outset, the list of lists lists only two lists: Completed and Reminders. But you can create others. Click the **+** button at the bottom-left corner, or choose File→New List. If you have any kind of online account set up, like an iCloud account, you'll then have to specify either On My Mac or "[the account's name]" from the submenu.

In any case, you've just made a new list called New List. Type to rename it to "Groceries list," "Movies list," whatever you like. (You can also get rid of a list by clicking it and then pressing the Delete key.)

Tip: You can view the contents of more than one list simultaneously. Just Shift-click the names of the lists you want in the left column; the right-side pane displays a unified, combined list of all their contents.

You can also open a list into a window of its own, just by double-clicking its name in the left column.

Once you've created some lists, you have two ways to switch among them:

- **Swipe two fingers across the trackpad.** The lists slide into view as though they're successive photos in a slideshow.

- **Click a different list in the list of lists.** Or press the ↑ and ↓ keys to "walk" through the list.

You can assign a task to a different list by dragging it. Click any blank part of its line (not the text itself), and drag carefully onto the name of a different list in the List list at left.

Syncing Reminders

Once you've set up a few reminders in Reminders, you'll marvel as it gracefully integrates with the Notification Center when it wants your attention.

But the real power of Reminders becomes apparent when you see it auto-synchronize your to-do lists across other gadgets, like iPhones, iPads, iPod Touches, other Mountain Lion Macs, and even Windows PCs.

To give it permission for that kind of sharing, open System Preferences→iCloud and turn on the Calendars & Reminders checkbox.

Note, however, that Reminders can also coordinate with the to-do list features of Exchange and so-called CalDAV services (Yahoo is one). To set them up, open System Preferences→Mail, Contacts, Calendars. Tap the account you want (like Exchange or Yahoo); finally, turn the Calendars & Reminders switch On.

That should do it. Now your to do lists are synced, both ways.

Tip: You can also export your lists as .ics files, which you can then import into Google Calendar or another program. Just click the list and then choose File→Export. You can also *import* an existing .ics file (from another computer, for example) into a Reminders list you've selected: it's File→Import, of course.

By the way, you can also create lists that live only on your Mac and don't get synced anywhere else. To create such a list, click the **+** button below the list of lists; from the pop-up menu, choose On My Mac. Type a name for your new list, content that anything you put there won't get synced anywhere else.

Notes

The Notes app is simple in the extreme; it's the digital version of a little lined 3 × 5 pad. Still, it's nice to be able to jot down lists, recipes, driving directions, and brainstorms—especially because they all sync effortlessly to your phone, tablet, and other computers.

The first time you open Notes, you see what looks like a yellow, lined legal pad—complete with the ragged remnants of previous pages that somebody has torn off. Real cute.

To create a new page of notes, choose File→New Note (⌘-N), or click the **+** button at lower left. Once the new lined page appears, type away (Figure 10-5).

Figure 10-5:
The first line of each page becomes the name of that note, as represented in the searchable list of notes (center column).

In this illustration, somebody has also opened up the Folders list, the skinny column at far left. Here, you can choose which account's notes you want to see: your iCloud notes, Gmail, Exchange, or what have you.

Interior Design

You can dress up your Mac's Notes pages far more elaborately than you can on the iPhone. For example:

- You have full control over fonts, type sizes, colors, paragraph alignment, and indentation, using the commands in the Format menu. Notes can even create automatic bulleted, dashed, or numbered lists; check out the Format→Lists submenus.

- You can paste or drag photos and other graphics into your notes, too—or even documents, like PDF files, Word documents, or Excel spreadsheets. Drag such a document into a note from the desktop; there it becomes an icon that you can double-click to open later.

- You can drag or paste a link into a note. Later, when you click it (or, on the phone or iPad, tap it), it opens into the corresponding Web site.

Note: Not all interior decoration gets synced to your phone or tablet. Pictures, for example, don't survive the transition, and not all of your Mac fonts are available on your phone. But for the first time, Notes' typographical skills extend beyond Marker Felt and Helvetica.

A couple of handy icons appear at the bottom of each Notes page. You can click 🗑 to delete the current note. Or you can click ↰ to send the note to someone, either by email or in Messages (Chapter 20).

Tip: You can also print a note; choose File→Print. Just pointing that out.

As you create more pages, the Notes list (the center column in Figure 10-5) becomes more useful. It's your table of contents for the Notes pad. It displays the first lines of your notes (most recent at the top), along with the time or date you last edited them. (The **+** button appears here, too.) To open a note, tap its name.

There's a search box here, too. You can search all your notes instantly—not just their titles, but also the text inside them.

Pinning Notes

Here's an undocumented special: If you double-click a note's name, it opens into a new window. Just the note, without the "table of contents" panel. This note stays open, floating on your screen! Figure 10-6 shows the idea. Just remember that this configuration remains in place only while Notes, the program, is open.

Tip: Notes is a card-carrying full-screen app, as described on page 12.

Notes Folders

Chances are fairly good that your Mac's screen is bigger than your phone's. So Apple gave the Mac version of Notes a few features that require some extra space—and one of them is the side panel of Notes folders. That is, you can organize your notes into various categories, for ease of wading through them. (Any folders you create on the Mac also show up on your iPhone/iPad.)

The key to understanding this feature is the slide-out Folders list, which you can see in Figure 10-5. You can make it appear either by clicking the little ▤ icon or by

choosing View→Show Folders List. You can hide it again by clicking the ▤ button next to it. Either way, you can adjust the Folder list's width by dragging the vertical line at its right edge.

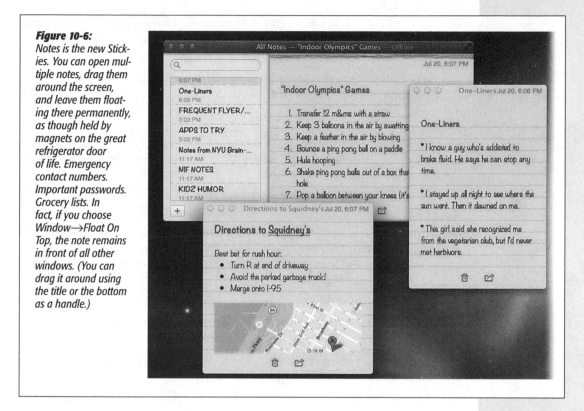

Figure 10-6:
Notes is the new Stickies. You can open multiple notes, drag them around the screen, and leave them floating there permanently, as though held by magnets on the great refrigerator door of life. Emergency contact numbers. Important passwords. Grocery lists. In fact, if you choose Window→Float On Top, the note remains in front of all other windows. (You can drag it around using the title or the bottom as a handle.)

To make a new folder, choose File→New Folder; name the folder and then press Enter. You can then drag existing notes into its name in the Folders list. (The usual rules apply: You can select a swath of notes in a list by clicking the first, then Shift-clicking the last. Or you can click individual, nonconsecutive notes by clicking with the ⌘ key pressed.)

Tip: If you press Option as you drag a note, you make a copy of it in the new folder instead of moving the original.

Click a folder's name to see the notes inside it. (Click "All [account name]" to see all the notes in that account.)

To create a new note within a folder, click the folder's name first. If you don't click any folder's name before you create the note, it goes into the general Notes category.

You can also rename a folder (Control-click its name; choose Rename Folder), delete one (Control-click its name; choose Delete Folder), put one inside another (drag its

name), and move a folder to a different account—for example, from your iCloud account to your Google one—by dragging it.

Syncing Notes

The real beauty of this app is that it can synchronize your collection of Notes with all kinds of other Apple gear—iPhones, iPads, and other Mountain Lion Macs—so the same notes are waiting for you everywhere you look.

Just make sure Notes is turned on in System Preferences→iCloud (on your Mac), and in Settings→Mail, Contacts, Calendars→iCloud (on your phone or tablet). The rest is automatic.

Tip: If you're using the Folders feature, here's how to see them on your phone or tablet: Tap the Accounts button in the upper-left corner of the Notes window. The list of accounts and folders appears, much as it does on your Mac.

Notes Accounts

Notes can also show you the contents of the Notes modules on Google, Yahoo, AOL, or another IMAP email account. You'll see each account's worth of notes in the Folder list, as you can see in Figure 10-5—and from there, you can drag notes hither and yon, among accounts, with abandon.

To set this up, open System Preferences→Mail, Contacts, Calendars. Tap the account you want (Exchange, Gmail, Yahoo, AOL, or whatever); finally, turn the Notes switch On.

That should do it. Now each account's notes appear under its own heading in the Folders list. And your notes are synced, both ways.

All of this makes life a little more complex, of course. For example, when you create a note, you have to worry about which account it's about to go into. To do that, be sure to specify an account name (and a folder within it, if necessary) *before* you create the new note.

Tip: If you look at the icon for the Notes program, you might describe it as "a lined, yellow pad with some illegible handwriting on it." Ah, but that's where you're wrong—it's not completely illegible.

If you open your Applications folder, switch to Icon view, and use the slider to make the icons as big as possible, you'll see that the scrawl is actually a bit of famous text. "Here's to the crazy ones. The misfits. The rebels. The troublemakers. The round pegs in the square holes. They're not fond of rules…"

The handwriting is pretty terrible. But it is, in fact, the text of the famous Apple "Think Different" TV ad that Steve Jobs had created when he returned to Apple in 1997.

The Other Free Programs

R ight out of the box, OS X comes with a healthy assortment of about 50 freebies: programs for sending email, writing documents, doing math, even playing games. Some have been around for years. Others, though, have been given extreme makeovers in Mountain Lion. They're designed not only to show off some of OS X's most dramatic technologies, but also to let you get real work done without having to invest in additional software.

Your Free OS X Programs

A broad assortment of programs sit in the Applications folder in the main hard drive window, and another couple dozen less frequently used apps await in the Applications→Utilities folder.

This chapter guides you through every item in your new software library, one program at a time. (Of course, your Applications list may vary. Apple might have blessed your particular Mac model with some bonus programs, or you may have downloaded or installed some on your own.)

Tip: A reminder: You can jump straight to the Applications folder in the Finder by pressing Shift-⌘-A (the shortcut for Go→Applications), or by clicking the Applications folder icon in the Sidebar. You might consider adding the Application folder's icon to the Dock, too, so you can access it no matter what program you're in. Shift-⌘-U (or Go→Utilities) takes you, of course, to the Utilities folder.

Address Book

The old Address Book program has been renamed Contacts, and it's described in Chapter 18.

App Store

See the beginning of Chapter 5 for full details on the Mac App Store.

Automator

This software-robot program is introduced in Chapter 7.

Calculator

The Calculator is much more than a simple four-function memory calculator. It can also act as a scientific calculator for students and scientists, a conversion calculator for metric and U.S. measures, and even a currency calculator for world travelers.

The little Calculator widget in the Dashboard is quicker to open, but the standalone Calculator program is far more powerful. For example:

- Calculator has three modes: Basic, Advanced, and Programmer (Figure 11-1). Switch among them by choosing from the View menu (or pressing ⌘-1 for Basic, ⌘-2 for Advanced, or ⌘-3 for Programmer).

Figure 11-1:
The Calculator program offers a four-function Basic mode, a full-blown scientific calculator mode, and a programmer's calculator (shown here, and capable of hex, octal, decimal, and binary notation). The first two modes offer a "paper tape" feature (Windows→Paper Tape) that lets you correct errors made way back in a calculation. To edit one of the numbers on the paper tape, drag through it, retype, and then click Recalculate Totals. You can also save the tape as a text file by choosing File→Save Tape As, or print it by selecting File→Print Tape.

- You can operate Calculator by clicking the onscreen buttons, but it's much easier to press the corresponding number and symbol keys on your keyboard.

- As you go, you can make Calculator speak each key you press. The Mac's voice ensures that you don't mistype as you keep your eyes on the receipts in front of you, typing by touch.

 Just choose Speech→Speak Button Pressed to turn this feature on or off. (You choose *which* voice does the talking in the Speech panel of System Preferences.)

- Press the C key to clear the calculator display.

- Once you've calculated a result, you can copy it (using Edit→Copy, or ⌘-C) and paste it directly into another program.

- Calculator even offers Reverse Polish Notation (RPN), a system of entering numbers that's popular with some mathematicians, programmers, and engineers, because it lets them omit parentheses. Choose View→RPN to turn it on and off.

Tip: How cool is this? In most programs, you don't need Calculator or even a Dashboard widget. Remember that the Spotlight menu is a calculator, too. Type or paste an equation into the Spotlight search box; instantly, the answer appears in the results menu.

Conversions

Calculator is more than a calculator; it's also a conversion program. No matter what units you're trying to convert—meters, grams, cubic inches, miles per hour, euros—Calculator is ready.

Now, the truth is, the Units Converter widget in Dashboard is simpler and better than this older Calculator feature. But if you've already got Calculator open, here's the drill:

1. **Clear the calculator (for example, type the letter C on your keyboard). Type in the starting measurement.**

 To convert 48 degrees Celsius to Fahrenheit, for example, type *48*.

2. **From the Convert menu, choose the kind of conversion you want.**

 In this case, choose Temperature. When you're done choosing, a dialog box appears.

3. **Use the pop-up menus to specify which units you want to convert to and from.**

 To convert Celsius to Fahrenheit, choose Celsius from the first pop-up menu, and Fahrenheit from the second.

4. **Click OK.**

 That's it. The Calculator displays the result—in degrees Fahrenheit, in this example.

The next time you want to make this kind of calculation, you can skip steps 2, 3, and 4. Instead, just choose your desired conversion from the Convert→Recent Conversions submenu.

Calculator is especially amazing when it comes to *currency* conversions—from pesos to American dollars, for example—because it actually does its homework. It goes online to download up-to-the-minute currency rates to ensure that the conversion is accurate. (Choose Convert→Update Currency Exchange Rates.)

Tip: If you're working with big numbers, don't forget to turn on View→Show Thousands Separators. Calculator will add commas (like 1,242,939) to help you read your big numbers more easily.

Calendar

In Mountain Lion, the calendar program that was called iCal for many years is now called Calendar, so that it matches up better with the iPhone and iPad.

Calendar is not so different from those "Hunks of the Midwest Police Stations" paper calendars that people leave hanging on the walls for months past their natural life span. In fact, in the extreme makeover of Calendar, it looks more than ever like a physical calendar.

Tip: Calendar's Dock icon displays today's date—even when Calendar isn't running.

But Calendar offers several advantages over paper calendars. For example:

- It can automate the process of entering repeating events, such as weekly staff meetings or gym workouts.

- Calendar can give you a gentle nudge (with a sound, a dialog box, or even an email) when an important appointment is approaching.

- Calendar can share information with Contacts, with Mail, with your iPod/iPad/iPhone, with other Macs, or with "published" calendars on the Internet. Some of these features require one of those iCloud accounts described in Chapter 17. But Calendar also works fine on a single Mac, even without an Internet connection.

- Calendar can subscribe to other people's calendars. For example, you can subscribe to your spouse's calendar, thereby finding out when you've been committed to after-dinner drinks on the night of the big game on TV. You can also tell Calendar to display your online calendars from Google and Yahoo, or even your company's Exchange calendar (Chapter 8).

Working with Views

When you open Calendar, you see something like Figure 11-2. By clicking one of the View buttons above the calendar, or by pressing ⌘-1, ⌘-2, ⌘-3, or ⌘-4, you can switch among these views:

- **Day** looks exactly like a day-at-a-time desk calendar. On the right-side "page," you see today's schedule on an hour-by-hour chart. On the left "page," you get a simple list of appointments for today and the next few days.

If you choose Calendar→Preferences, you can specify what hours constitute a workday. This is ideal both for those annoying power-life people who get up at 5 a.m. for two hours of calisthenics and for the more reasonable people who sleep until 11 a.m.

Tip: Calendar provides three quick ways to get to the current day's date. Click Today (upper-right corner, between the ◄ and ►), choose View→Go to Today, or press ⌘-T.

Figure 11-2:
In Calendar, the ◄ and ► buttons at top right take you to the previous or next day, week, month, or year (depending on your current view). In the new Day view, shown here, you can click the tiny numbers on the mini-calendar (top left of page) to change days. Double-click any appointment to open its Info balloon, shown in Figure 11-4.

• **Week** fills the main display area with seven columns, reflecting the current week. (You can establish a five-day workweek instead in Calendar→Preferences.)

Tip: If you double-click the date above the calendar, you open the Day view for that day.

• **Month** shows the entire month that contains today's date. Double-click a date number to open the Day view for that date.

Tip: If a Month-view square is too small to show everything you've got scheduled that day, you'll see a notation at the bottom of the square like, "3 more..." Sometimes, making the window bigger (or full screen) helps make more room, or you can just double-click the date's number to switch to Day view and see everything at once.

To save space, Calendar generally doesn't show you the *times* of your appointments in Month view. If you'd like to see them anyway, choose Calendar→Preferences, click General, and turn on "Show event times." Now each event's starting time appears in light gray, off to the right.

Tip: If your mouse has a scroll wheel, you can use it to great advantage in Calendar. For example, when entering a date, turning the wheel lets you jump forward or backward in time. It also lets you change the priority level of a To Do item you're entering, or even tweak the time zone as you're setting it.

• **Year** view displays a "heat map" of the entire year (Figure 11-3).

Figure 11-3:
Mountain Lion's Year view shows the entire year. The colors of the squares are a "heat map" that indicate how hectic your schedule is. If this book were in color, you'd see a range of shades from light yellow (not very busy) to deep red (you're in big trouble). Double-click a date to open the Day view for that date.

In any of the views, *double-click* an appointment to see more about it. The very first time you do that, you get the summary balloon shown at top right in Figure 11-4. If you want to make changes, you can then click the Edit button to open a more detailed view.

Tip: In Week or Day view, Calendar sprouts a handy horizontal line that shows where you are in time right now. (Look in the hours-of-the-day "ruler" down the left side of the window to see this line's little red bulb.) A nice touch, and a handy visual aid that can tell you at a glance when you're already late for something.

Also in any view, you can switch into full-screen view by clicking the ⬈ icon in the upper-right corner of the window. See page 12 for more on full-screen view.

Making an Appointment

The basic Calendar calendar is easy to figure out. After all, with the exception of one unfortunate Gregorian incident, we've been using calendars successfully for centuries.

Even so, there are two ways to record a new appointment: using the mouse, or using the new Quick Event box.

The mousy way

You can quickly record an appointment using any of several techniques, listed here in order of decreasing efficiency:

- In Month view, double-click a blank spot on the date you want. Type the name of the event and a time slot—for example, *Sales meeting 9am-4:30*. (See "The Quick Event way," below, for details on how Calendar interprets these time notations.)

- In Day or Week view, double-click the starting time to create a one-hour appointment. Or drag vertically through the time slots that represent the appointment's duration. Either way, type the event's name inside the newly created colored box.

- In any view, Control-click or right-click a date and choose New Event from the shortcut menu. Type the event's name.

 Unless you use the drag-over-hours method, a new event believes itself to be one hour long. But in Day or Week view, you can adjust its duration by dragging the bottom edge vertically. Drag the dark top bar up or down to adjust the start time.

In many cases, that's all there is to it. You've just specified the day, time, and title of the appointment. Now you can get on with your life.

Tip: If the Edit balloon is blocking a part of the calendar you need to see, no biggie: Just drag the balloon out of the way, using any blank spot as a handle.

The Quick Event way

In the *Quick Event* method, the program spares you the trouble of manually selecting dates, start times, and end times. Instead, the program understands notations like "7 pm Friday," and puts your new appointment into the right time slot automatically.

To use this feature, press ⌘-N. (Or click the **+** button—top left of the window—or choose File→New Event). The Quick Event box appears. Proceed as shown in Figure 11-4.

Note: Calendar proposes adding the new appointment to your *default calendar*—that is, the category you use most often (read on for details on these calendar categories). Supposedly, you've already told it which category is your preferred one by using the Calendar→Preferences→General→Default Calendar pop-up menu.

But as you add a new appointment this way, you can override that setting by *holding down* the **+** button. You get a pop-up menu of your calendar categories; only after you click the one you want do you see the Quick Event box shown in Figure 11-4.

Into the Quick Event box, you're supposed to type the name of your appointment and its date and time. For example, you could type *Report deadline Aug 12,* or *"Titanic 2: The Return" Sat 7 pm,* or *Cara date 11-11:15am.*

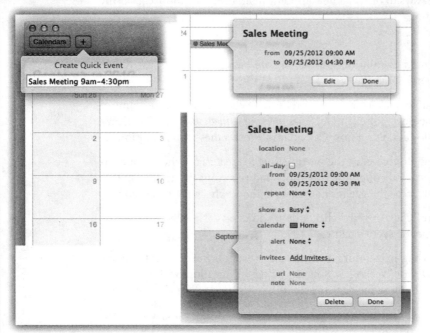

Figure 11-4:
Left: Type an event's name and time slot— for example, "Sales meeting 9am-4:30." Press Enter. Marvel as Calendar interprets the times you typed and inserts "Sales meeting" into the right time slot.

Right: All the details for an appointment appear right in this balloon/box, shown here in both its collapsed (top) and expanded views.

When you press Return, Calendar interprets what you typed, using these rules:

- If you didn't specify an ending time, Calendar sets the appointment to 1 hour long.

- If you didn't enter *any* time information, Calendar figures you meant an all-day event like a birthday, holiday, or deadline.

- If you typed *breakfast* or *morning,* Calendar sets the appointment to start at 9 a.m.; *lunch* or *noon,* it starts at 12 p.m.; *dinner* or *night,* it starts at 8 p.m.

- If you enter a weekday (for example, *Chicago Monday*), Calendar assumes you mean the very next occurrence of that day. (If that's not what you want, enter the date, like *Chicago Jul 3.)*

- If you enter a time but not a date or day (for example, *Fishing 3:30 pm*), Calendar assumes you mean today.

Alarms, repeats, and other details

No matter which method you use to create the basic event (the mouse way or the Quick Event way), you're now presented with the information balloon shown at lower right

in Figure 11-4. Here's where you go to town filling in the details. (This same balloon will appear when you double-click any existing appointment later.)

Tip: After you've already edited an appointment once, the full info balloon is a little more effort to open; double-clicking an event produces only the summary balloon shown in Figure 11-4 at top.

The short way to open the full balloon is to click the appointment and then press ⌘-E (which is short for Edit→Edit Event). The long way is to double-click the appointment to get the summary balloon and then click Edit inside it.

But the *best* solution to this problem is to avail yourself of an option in Calendar→Preferences→Advanced. It's the checkbox called "Open events in separate windows." Now when you double-click an appointment in Calendar, it opens immediately into a full-size Details window, saving you that intermediate step forever. (You can close the window with a quick ⌘-W.)

For each appointment, you can Tab your way to the following information areas:

- **subject.** That's the large, bold type at the top—the name of your appointment. For example, you might type *Fly to Phoenix.*

- **location.** This field makes a lot of sense; if you think about it, almost everyone needs to record *where* a meeting is to take place. You might type a reminder for yourself like *My place,* a specific address like *212 East 23,* or some other helpful information, like a contact phone number or flight number.

- **all-day.** An "all-day" event, of course, refers to something that has no specific time of day associated with it: a holiday, a birthday, a book deadline. When you turn on this box, you see the name of the appointment jump to the top of the Calendar screen, in the area reserved for this kind of thing.

- **from, to.** You can adjust the times shown here by typing, clicking buttons, or both. Press Tab to jump from one setting to another, and from there to the hours and minutes of the starting time.

Note: The little calendar that pops up when you click the date is new in Mountain Lion. It's handier than typing a date manually.

For example, start by clicking the hour, and then increase or decrease this number either by pressing ↑ and ↓ or by typing a number. Press Tab to highlight the minutes and repeat the arrow-buttons-or-keys business. Finally, press Tab to highlight the AM/PM indicator, and type either *A* or *P*—or press ↑ or ↓—to change it, if necessary.

Tip: If you specify a different ending date, a *banner* appears across the top of the calendar.

- **time zone.** This option appears only after you choose Calendar→Preferences→Advanced and then turn on "Turn on time zone support." And you would do *that* only if you plan to be traveling on the day this appointment comes to pass.

Once you've done that, a time zone pop-up menu appears. It starts out with "America/New York" (or whatever your Mac's usual time zone is); if you choose Other, a tiny world map appears. Click the time zone that represents where you'll be when this appointment comes due. From the shortcut menu, choose the major city that's in the same zone you'll be in.

Tip: The time zone pop-up menu remembers each new city you select. The next time you travel to a city you've visited before, you won't have to do that clicking-the-world-map business.

Now, when you arrive in the distant city, use the time zone pop-up menu at the top-right corner of the Calendar window to tell Calendar where you are. You'll see all of Calendar's appointments jump, like magic, to their correct new time slots.

- **repeat.** The pop-up menu here contains common options for recurring events: every day, every week, and so on. It starts out saying None.

Once you've made a selection, you get an *end* pop-up menu that lets you specify when this event should *stop* repeating. If you choose "Never," you're stuck seeing this event repeating on your calendar until the end of time (a good choice for recording, say, your anniversary, especially if your spouse might be consulting the same calendar). You can also turn on "After (a certain number of times)," which is a useful option for car and mortgage payments. And if you choose "On date," you can specify the date when the repetitions come to an end; use this option to indicate the last day of school, for example.

"Custom" lets you specify repeat schedules like "First Monday of the month" or "Every two weeks."

- **show as (busy/free/tentative/out of office).** This little item shows up only if you've subscribed to a calendar server, like an Internet-based calendar (in geek-speak, a CalDAV server) or your company's Exchange calendar (Chapter 8). It communicates to your colleagues when you might be available for meetings.

Note: If your calendar comes from a CalDAV server, then your only options are "busy" and "free." The factory setting for most appointments is "busy," but for all-day events it's "free." Which is logical; just because it's International Gecko Appreciation Day doesn't mean you're not available for meetings (rats!).

You might think: "Well, *duh*—if I've got something on the calendar, then I'm obviously busy!" But not necessarily. Some Calendar entries might just be placeholders, reminders to self, TV shows you wanted to watch, appointments you'd be willing to change—not things that would necessarily render you unavailable if a better invitation should come along.

- **calendar.** A *calendar,* in Calendar's terminology, is a subset—a category—into which you can place appointments. You can create one for you, one for family-only events, one for book-club appointments, and so on. You can hide and show these categories at will. Details begin on page 402.

Tip: Use this same pop-up menu to *change* an appointment's category. If you filed something in "Company Memos" that should have been in "Sweet Nothings for Honey-Poo," then open the event's information balloon and reassign it. Quick.

- **alert.** This pop-up menu tells Calendar how to notify you when a certain appointment is about to begin. Calendar can send four kinds of flags to get your attention. It can display a message (with a sound, if you like), send you an email, run a script of the sort described in Chapter 7, or open a file on your hard drive. (You could use this unusual option to ensure that you don't forget a work deadline by having Calendar fling the relevant document open in front of your face at the eleventh hour.)

 Once you've specified an alarm type, a new pop-up menu appears to let you specify how much advance notice you want for this particular appointment. If it's a TV show, a reminder 5 minutes before airtime is fine. If it's a birthday, you might set up a two-day warning, so there's time to buy a present. In fact, you can set up more than one alarm for the same appointment, each with its own advance-warning interval.

- **invitees.** If the appointment is a meeting or some other gathering, you can type the participants' names here. If a name is already in your Contacts program, Calendar proposes autocompleting the name for you.

 If you separate several names with commas, Calendar automatically turns each into a shaded oval button. You can click it for a pop-up menu of commands like Remove Attendee and Send Email. (That last option appears only if the person in Contacts has an email address, or if you typed a name *with* an email address in brackets, like this: *Chris Smith <chris@yahoo.com>.*)

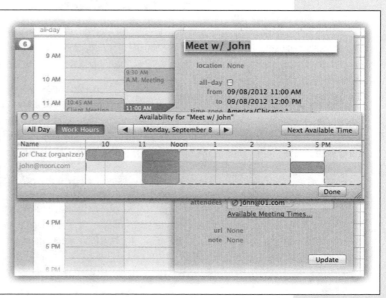

Figure 11-5:
If you and your invitees are on the same calendar server (a corporate Exchange server, for example), this handy scrolling display lets you spot times when your invitees are free for a meeting. You can either drag the vertical block (which represents your proposed meeting) to a different time slot, or click Next Available Time. That makes Calendar automatically seek a time slot where everybody's free. Good luck with that.

Tip: If you and your invitees are on the same CalDAV or Exchange calendar service—usually, this means coworkers at the same company—Calendar can show a "time map" of the invitees' days, all in a handy scrolling window, so you can find a time when everybody's free. To see this map, click the Available Meeting Times link beneath the addresses of the invitees you've specified, or choose Window→Availability Panel (see Figure 11-5).

Once you've specified some attendees, a Send button appears in the Info box. If you click it, Calendar fires up Mail and prepares ready-to-send messages, each with an *iCal.ics* attachment: a calendar-program invitation file. See the box below.

- **attachments.** This option lets you fasten a file to the appointment. It can be anything: a photo of the person you're meeting, a document to finish by that deadline, the song that was playing the first time you met this person—whatever.

- **url.** A *URL* is a Uniform Resource Locator, better known as a Web address, like *www.apple.com*. If there's a URL relevant to this appointment, by all means type it here. Type more than one, if it'll help you; just be sure to separate them all with commas.

- **note.** Here's your chance to customize your calendar event. You can type, paste, or drag any text you like in the note area—driving directions, contact phone numbers, a call history, or whatever.

Your newly scheduled event now shows up on the calendar, complete with the color coding that corresponds to the calendar category you've assigned.

UP TO SPEED

Inviting Guests

The truth is, this business of automatic invitations to Calendar events hasn't really caught on yet. Unless you've hooked up Calendar to your company's Exchange server (Chapter 8), the invitations system is still fairly complicated, and it requires compatible software on the receiving end.

When you click Send at the bottom of the info balloon, your guests receive your invitation. If they use Calendar, the invitation appears in their Notifications panels. (To open the Notifications panel, click the tiny envelope icon in the lower-left corner of the window.) They can click Accept, Decline, or Maybe.

In your Notifications window, you then see the status of each invitee's name: a checkmark for Accepted, an X for Declined, a ? for Maybe, and an arrow for Not Yet Responded.

(Your guests, meanwhile, will be delighted to find that the appointment automatically appears on their calendars once they commit.)

Now, suppose you send an invitation to your sister, who doesn't have a Mac. She just gets an email message that says, "Chris Smith has invited you to the event: Company Hoedown, scheduled for February 02, 2013 at 3:00 PM. To accept or decline this invitation, click the link below." Unfortunately, there generally *is* no link. She just has to know to open the .ics attachment.

If she uses a calendar program that understands this attachment, the appointment appears on her calendar, and her RSVP shows up in your Calendar Notification panel.

What to Do with an Appointment

Once you've entrusted your agenda to Calendar, you can start putting it to work. Calendar is only too pleased to remind you (via pop-up messages) of your events, reschedule them, print them out, and so on. Here are a few of the possibilities.

Editing events

To edit a calendar event's details, you have to open its Info balloon (Figure 11-4).

If you just want to change an event's name, Option-double-click it right in place. And if you want to change only an appointment's "calendar" category, Control-click (or right-click) anywhere on the appointment and, from the resulting shortcut menu, choose the category you want. In both cases, you bypass the need to open the Info balloon.

You don't have to bother with this if all you want to do is reschedule an event, however, as described next.

Rescheduling events

If an event in your life gets rescheduled, you can drag an appointment block vertically in a Day- or Week-view column to make it later or earlier the same day, or horizontally to another date in any view. (If you reschedule a recurring event, Calendar asks if you want to change only *this* occurrence, or this *and* all future ones.)

If something is postponed for, say, a month or two, you're in trouble, since you can't drag an appointment beyond its month window. You have no choice but to open the Info balloon and edit the starting and ending dates or times—or just cut and paste the event to a different date.

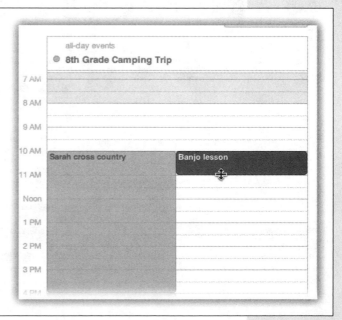

Figure 11-6:
You can resize any Calendar event just by dragging its bottom border. As your cursor touches the bottom edge of an event, it turns into a double-headed arrow. You can now drag the event's edge to make it take up more or less time on your calendar.

Lengthening or shortening events

If a scheduled meeting becomes shorter or your lunch hour becomes a lunch hour-and-a-half (in your dreams), changing the length of the representative calendar event is as easy as dragging the bottom border of its block in any column view (see Figure 11-6).

Tip: In Week view, if you've grabbed the *bottom* edge of an appointment's block so that the cursor changes, you can drag *horizontally* to make an appointment cross the midnight line and extend into a second day.

Printing events

To commit your calendar to paper, choose File→Print, or press ⌘-P. The resulting Print dialog box lets you include only a certain range of dates, only events on certain calendars, with or without To Do lists or mini-month calendars, and so on.

Deleting events

To delete an appointment, just select it and then press the Delete key. If you delete a recurring event (like a weekly meeting), Calendar asks whether you want to delete only that particular instance of the event, or the whole series from that point forward.

Searching for Events

You should recognize the oval text box at the top of the Calendar screen immediately: It's almost identical to the Spotlight box. This search box is designed to let you hide all appointments except those matching what you type into it. Figure 11-7 has the details.

Figure 11-7:
As you type into the search box (top right), Calendar sprouts a list of suggestions ("Location contains 'trip,'" "Notes contains 'trip,'" and so on). Click one to create a "search token" exactly like the ones that Spotlight and Mail use (page 116). Here again, they let you build up complex searches, bubble by bubble.

Double-click any row of the list to jump to and highlight the corresponding event on the calendar and open up its summary balloon.

The "Calendar" Category Concept

Just as iTunes has *playlists* that let you organize songs into subsets and iPhoto has *albums* that let you organize photos into subsets, Calendar has *calendars* that let you organize appointments into subsets. They can be anything you like. One person might have calendars called Home, Work, and TV Reminders. Another might have Me, Spouse 'n' Me, and Whole Family. A small business could have categories called Deductible Travel, R&D, and R&R.

To create a calendar, choose File→New Calendar. From the pop-up menu, specify *where* you want this category to live: either On My Mac (which means "on your Mac")—or, if you've subscribed to an online calendar or two, the name of the online account, like Google or Exchange. Type a name that defines the category in your mind.

Tip: Click a calendar name *before* you create an appointment. That way, the appointment will already belong to the correct calendar.

To see your list of categories, click the Calendars button (upper left of the window). A sidebar list appears (which is a huge relief to anyone who suffered through the self-collapsing bubble list in the Lion version of this program). To change the color-coding of your category, Control-click (right-click) its name in this pop-up list; from the shortcut menu, choose Get Info. The Calendar Info box appears. Here, you can change the name, color, or description of this category—or turn off its alarms.

You assign an appointment to one of these categories using the pop-up menu (on its Info balloon), or by Control-clicking (right-clicking) an event and choosing a calendar name from the shortcut menu. After that, you can hide or show an entire category of appointments at once just by turning on or off the appropriate checkbox in the Calendars pop-up list.

Tip: Calendar also has calendar *groups:* calendar containers that consolidate the appointments from several *other* calendars. (For example, you could have a calendar group called Kids, containing the individual calendars for each of your offspring. Super-calendars like this make it easier to manage, hide, show, print, and search subsets of your appointments.

To create a calendar group, choose File→New Calendar Group. Name the resulting item in the Calendar list; for the most part, it behaves like any other calendar. Drag other calendar names onto it to include them. Click the flippy triangle to hide or show the component calendars.

"Publishing" Calendars to the Web

One of Calendar's best features is its ability to post your calendar on the Web, so that other people (or you, on a different computer) can subscribe to it, which adds *your* appointments to *their* calendars. Anyone with a Web browser—or only people you designate—can also *view* your calendar, right online.

For example, you might use this feature to post the meeting schedule for a club that you manage, or to share the agenda for a series of upcoming financial meetings that all your coworkers will need to consult.

The steps for sharing a calendar depend on whether or not you have an iCloud account. Voilà.

Publishing

If you don't have iCloud: If you don't have an iCloud account, then you'll need a Web site of your own, where your online calendar can be hung. And it has to be a WebDAV-compatible server (ask your Web-hosting company). You know what? It might just be easier to sign up for a free iCloud account and do it that way.

In any case, begin by making sure that the Calendars list is open. Click the calendar you want to share. Choose Edit→Publish Calendar.

Tip: You have to perform this step individually for each calendar category. If you want to publish more than one calendar simultaneously, then create a calendar *group*, and publish *that*.

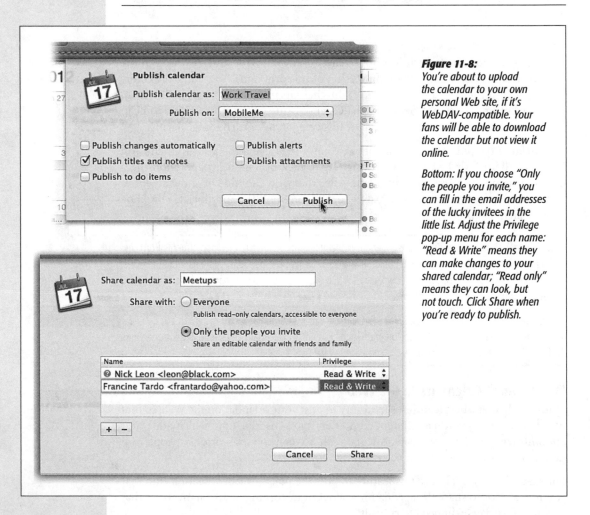

Figure 11-8:
You're about to upload the calendar to your own personal Web site, if it's WebDAV-compatible. Your fans will be able to download the calendar but not view it online.

Bottom: If you choose "Only the people you invite," you can fill in the email addresses of the lucky invitees in the little list. Adjust the Privilege pop-up menu for each name: "Read & Write" means they can make changes to your shared calendar; "Read only" means they can look, but not touch. Click Share when you're ready to publish.

The dialog box shown at top in Figure 11-8 appears. This is where you specify your Web address, its password (if necessary), and how your saved calendar is going to look and work. If you turn on "Publish changes automatically," then whenever you edit the calendar, Calendar connects to the Internet and updates the copy there. (Otherwise, you can right-click the calendar's name and choose Refresh whenever you want to update the Web copy.)

When you click Publish, your Mac connects to the Web and then shows you the Web address (the URL) of the finished page, complete with a Send Mail button that lets you fire the URL off to your colleagues.

Tip: Whenever you want to send someone the subscription information, click the calendar category you've published and choose Edit→Send Publication Email. Calendar will prepare an outgoing email message containing details on subscribing to your calendar.

To stop publishing that calendar, click its name in the Calendars pop-up list and then choose Edit→Stop Publishing.

If you have iCloud: In the list of categories, click the calendar you want to publish. It has to be one of the ones in the iCloud ("@me.com") group.

Choose Edit→Share Calendar. In the resulting dialog box (Figure 11-8, bottom), specify Everyone (anyone online can see, but not edit, the calendar) or "Only the people you invite." If you invite people, you can specify whether each person can just see the appointments, or be able to edit them, too. That's a delightful, two-way collaboration—a terrific way for a couple or a family to coordinate everyone's calendars, for example. See Figure 11-8 for details.

Later, you can modify the settings by clicking the little "shared" icon (.ꙮ) to open the Get Info box. Or you can stop sharing by clicking the calendar name and then choosing Edit→Stop Sharing or Edit→Stop Publishing.

Tip: You can also share an iCloud calendar at *icloud.com*. Just click the .ꙮ icon beside a calendar's name.

Subscribing

If somebody else has published a calendar, you can subscribe to it by choosing File→New Calendar Subscription. In the Subscribe to Calendar dialog box, type in the Internet address you received from the person who published the calendar.

You can also provide your own name for this category, specify how often you want your own copy to be updated (assuming you have a full-time Internet connection), and indicate whether or not you want to be bothered with the publisher's alarms and notes.

When it's all over, you see a new "calendar" category in your left-side list, representing the published appointments.

Tip: Want to try it out right now? Visit *www.icalshare.com*, a worldwide clearinghouse for sets of Calendar appointments. You can subscribe to calendars for shuttle launches, Mac trade shows, National Hockey League games, NASCAR races, soccer matches, the *Iron Chef* and *Survivor* TV shows, holidays, and much more. You'll never suffer from empty-calendar syndrome again.

Google and Yahoo Calendars

If you maintain a calendar online—at *www.google.com/calendar* or *http://calendar. yahoo.com*, for example, you may take particular pleasure in discovering how easy it is to bring those appointments into Calendar. It's one handy way to keep, for example, a husband's and wife's appointments visible on each other's calendars.

Setting this up is ridiculously easy (see Figure 11-9).

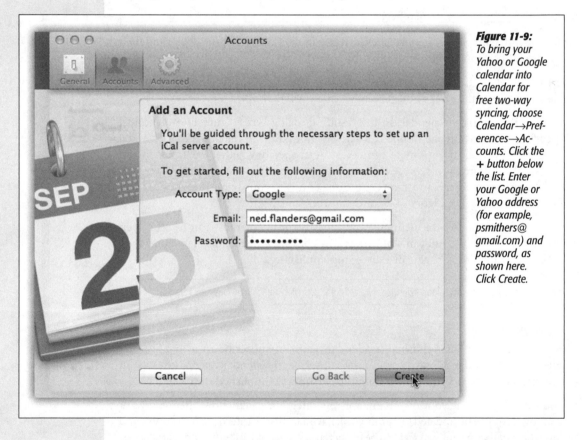

Figure 11-9:
To bring your Yahoo or Google calendar into Calendar for free two-way syncing, choose Calendar→Preferences→Accounts. Click the + button below the list. Enter your Google or Yahoo address (for example, psmithers@ gmail.com) and password, as shown here. Click Create.

In a minute or so, you'll see all your Google or Yahoo appointments show up in Calendar. (Each Web calendar has its own heading in the left-side list.) Better yet: It's a two-way sync; changes you make to these events in Calendar show up on the Web, too.

Syncing Calendar with Your iPhone, iPad, and Other Computers

Here's the real magic of Calendar, iCloud, and the rest of Apple's software archipelago: Your calendar can be auto-synced among all your machines, like your iPhone, iPad, and Macs. Add an appointment on your phone, change an appointment on your iPad, whatever—all your other gadgets are wirelessly and automatically synced to match. See Chapter 17 for details on this amazing setup.

Note: Wondering where the To Do list feature went? It was in iCal—it's gone in Calendar. Well, that's because Mountain Lion has its own full-blown Reminders app, described in Chapter 10.

Chess

Mountain Lion comes with only one game, but it's a beauty (Figure 11-10). It's a traditional chess game played on a gorgeously rendered board with a set of realistic 3-D pieces.

Note: The program is actually a sophisticated Unix-based chess program, Sjeng, that Apple packaged up in a new wrapper.

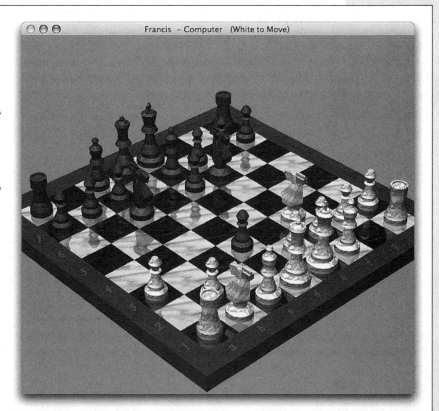

Figure 11-10:
You don't have to be terribly exact about grabbing the chess pieces when it's time to make your move. Just click anywhere within a piece's current square to drag it into a new position on the board (shown here in its Marble incarnation). And how did this chessboard get rotated like this? Because you can grab a corner of the board and rotate it in 3-D space. Cool!

Playing a Game of Chess

When you launch Chess, you're presented with a fresh, new game that's set up in Human vs. Computer mode—meaning that you, the Human (light-colored pieces) get to play against the Computer (your Mac, on the dark side). Drag the chess piece of your choice into position on the board, and the game is afoot.

If you choose Game→New Game, however, you're offered a pop-up menu with choices like Human vs. Computer, Human vs. Human, and so on. If you switch the pop-up menu to Computer vs. Human, then you and your Mac trade places; the Mac takes the white side of the board and opens the game with the first move, and you play the black side.

Tip: The same New Game dialog box also offers a pop-up menu called Variant, which offers three other chess-like games: Crazyhouse, Suicide, and Losers. The Chess help screens (choose Help→Chess Help, and then click "Starting a new chess game") explain these variations.

On some night when the video store is closed and you're desperate for entertainment, you might also want to try the Computer vs. Computer option, which pits your Mac against itself. Pour yourself a beer, open a bag of chips, and settle in to watch until someone—either the Mac or the Mac—gains victory.

Chess Prefs

Choose Chess→Preferences to find some useful controls like these:

- **Style.** Apple has gone nuts with the computer-generated materials options in this program. (Is it a coincidence that Steve Jobs was also the CEO of Pixar, the computer-animation company?)

 In any case, you can choose all kinds of wacky materials for the look of your game board (Wood, Metal, Marble, or *Grass*) and for your playing pieces (Wood, Metal, Marble, or *Fur*).

- **Computer Plays.** Use this slider to determine how frustrated you want to get when trying to win at Chess. The farther you drag the slider toward the Stronger side, the more calculations the computer runs before making its next move—and, thus, the harder it gets for you to outthink it. At the Faster setting, Chess won't spend more than 5 seconds ruminating over possible moves. Drag the slider all the way to the right, however, and the program may analyze *each move* for as long as 10 fun-filled hours. This hardest setting, of course, makes it all but impossible to win a game (which may stretch on for a week or more anyway).

 Choosing the Faster setting makes it only mildly impossible.

- **Speech.** The two checkboxes here let you play Chess using the Mac's built-in voice-recognition features, *telling* your chess pieces where to go instead of dragging them, and listening to the Mac tell you which moves it's making.

Studying Your Games

You can choose Game→Save to save any game in progress, so you can resume it later.

To analyze the moves making up a game, use the Window→Game Log command, which displays the history of your game, move by move. A typical move would be recorded as "Nb8 – c6," meaning the knight on the b8 square moved to the c6 square. Equipped with a Chess list document, you could recreate an entire game, move by move.

Contacts

Here's the old Address Book program, now renamed so that it matches the iPhone and iPad version. See the end of Chapter 18 for details.

Dashboard

Dashboard, described in Chapter 5, is a true-blue, double-clickable application. As a result, you can remove its icon from your Dock, if you like.

Dictionary

For word nerds everywhere, the Dictionary (and thesaurus) is a blessing—a handy way to look up word definitions, pronunciations, and synonyms (Figure 11-11). To be precise, OS X comes with electronic versions of multiple reference works in one:

- The entire New Oxford American Dictionary. The *third* edition, actually. You'll note that its entries give you more examples, background, and tables that help to differentiate fine shades of meaning (look up *weak* for an example).

- The complete Oxford American Writer's Thesaurus.

- Two venerable guides to British English: the Oxford Dictionary of English and Oxford Thesaurus of English.

- A dictionary of Apple terms, from "A/UX" to "Xsan." (Apparently there aren't any Apple terms that begin with Y or Z.)

- Wikipedia. This famous citizen-created encyclopedia isn't actually on your Mac. Dictionary just gives you an easy way to search the *online* version, and display the results right in the comfy Dictionary window.

• Dictionaries in Japanese, French, Spanish, German, and Chinese.

Tip: You don't ordinarily see these reference books. You have to turn them on in Dictionary→Preferences.

OS X also comes with about a million ways to look up a word:

- **If you have a trackpad, point to a word in a basic Mac program, and then double-touch the trackpad (don't actually click) with three fingers.** That's the gesture for the same dictionary panel described above. (It doesn't work unless you've turned it on in System Preferences→Trackpad.)

- **Double-click the Dictionary icon.** You get the window shown at top in Figure 11-11. As you type into the Spotlight-y search box, you home in on matching words; click a word, or highlight it and press Return, to view a full, typographically elegant definition, complete with sample sentence and pronunciation guide.

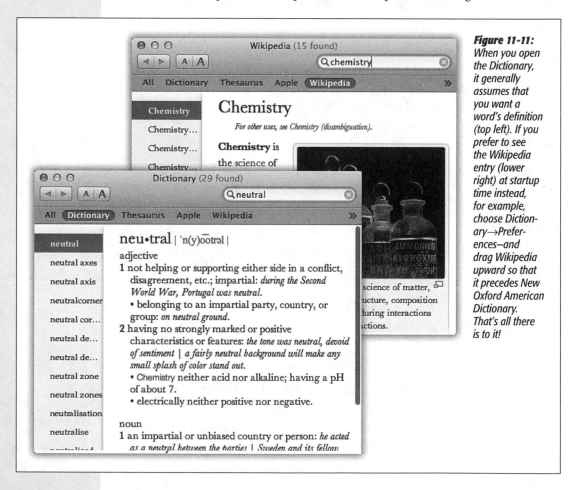

Figure 11-11:
When you open the Dictionary, it generally assumes that you want a word's definition (top left). If you prefer to see the Wikipedia entry (lower right) at startup time instead, for example, choose Dictionary→Preferences—and drag Wikipedia upward so that it precedes New Oxford American Dictionary. That's all there is to it!

Tip: And if you don't recognize a word in the definition, click *that word* to look up *its* definition. (Each word turns blue and underlined when you point to it, as a reminder.) You can then click again in *that* definition—and on, and on, and on.

(You can then use the ⊖ and ⊕ buttons on the toolbar, or the ⌘-[and ⌘-] keystrokes to go back and forward in your chain of lookups. Hold down the ⊖ for a pop-up menu of recent lookups.)

It's worth exploring the Dictionary→Preferences dialog box, by the way. There you can choose U.S. or British pronunciations and adjust the font size.

- **Press** ⊙. Yes, the Dictionary is one of the widgets in Dashboard (page 182).

- **Control-click (right-click) a highlighted word in a Cocoa program.** From the shortcut menu, choose Look Up [word]. You get a panel that pops out of the highlighted word or the Dictionary program opens to that word.

- **Use the *dict://* prefix in Safari.** This might sound a little odd, but it's actually ultra-convenient, because it puts the dictionary right where you're most likely to need it: on the Web.

 Turns out that you can look up a word (for example, *preposterous*) by typing *dict:// preposterous* into the address bar—the spot where you'd normally type *http://www. whatever.* When you hit Return, Dictionary opens automatically and presents the search results from all of its resources (dictionary, thesaurus, Apple terms, and Wikipedia).

- **Point to a word in a basic Mac program, and then press Control-⌘-D.** That keystroke makes the definition panel sprout right from the word you were pointing to. (The advantage here, of course, is that you don't have to highlight the word first.) "Basic Mac program," in this case, means one of the Apple standards: Mail, Stickies, Safari, TextEdit, Messages, and so on.

The *front matter* of the Oxford American Dictionary (the reference section at the beginning) is here, too. It includes some delicious writers' tools, including guides to spelling, grammar, capitalization, punctuation, chemical elements, and clichés, along with the full text of the Declaration of Independence and the U.S. Constitution. Just choose Go→Front/Back Matter—and marvel that your Mac comes with a built-in college English course.

Tip: Got a big screen or poor eyesight? Then bump up the type size. Dictionary's toolbar has bigger/smaller buttons, and there's a Font Size pop-up menu in the Preferences window.

DVD Player

DVD Player, your Mac's built-in movie projector, is described in Chapter 11.

FaceTime

FaceTime is Apple's video-chat program. It lets you make free video calls to other Macs, or to i-gadgets like iPhones, iPads, and iPod Touches. (This assumes of course, that you and your conversation partner both have high-speed Internet connections. You also both need Macs with Mac OS 10.6.6 or later, and cameras, either built-in or external. And you need an Apple ID; see the box below. If this is your first time enter your Apple ID and password on the right side of the window, and click Sign In.)

Tip: For the first time since FaceTime's debut in 2009, you can now make calls over the cellular network—not just WiFi. This is a news bulletin primarily for iPhone owners, of course, who used to be limited to making FaceTime calls when at home, at work, or in some other indoor WiFi location. Thank you, Mountain Lion!

To make a video call, open FaceTime. It starts out looking a little weird—the panel that displays the actual video (you, at first) is tall and skinny, as though you're us-ing—what else?—an iPhone.

Place a FaceTime Call

Now you have to choose someone to call. Ironically, this setup step usually begins with a more old-fashioned communication—a phone call or a text message, for example. ("Want to FaceTime now?")

The panel on the right side of the window offers three tab buttons (at the bottom). Click Contacts to see everyone in your OS X address book. If there *is* nobody in your address book, click the + button at upper right and enter the FaceTime contact information of your first calling buddy. If you're calling an iPhone, the contact info should be a phone number. For any other machine, it's an email address. Click Done when you've entered the information.

(As in the actual Contacts app, you can put people into groups, like "Work" or "Social Circle." If you plan to use this feature, be sure to click Groups and select the proper one *before* you click + to add a new person.)

UP TO SPEED

The Apple ID

Once you become a member of the Apple cult, the key that unlocks all Apple doors is your Apple ID. The same email address and password gets you into the iTunes Store, the Apple Store, the App Store, Messages, iCloud, FaceTime, and almost any other Apple service that requires you to log in. In the unlikely event that you don't yet have an Apple ID, you can get one by filling out the form at *https://appleid. apple.com*.

You can also create a new account right from within Face-Time. Choose FaceTime→Preferences, click Account, and then click Create New Account.

Tip: If you're smart, you'll pluck out the people you plan to FaceTime with most frequently and put them into your Favorites list (the first tab at the bottom). To do that, click the person's name on the Contacts tab and then click Add to Favorites. (If there's more than one email address or phone number, a subsequent screen lets you click the one you want to use.)

To remove someone from the Favorites list, click the Edit button (on the Favorites tab) and then click the ⊖ button next to the person's name.

Figure 11-12:
Yes, Messages also offers video calls—but FaceTime doesn't need as fast an Internet connection. You'll often be able to make FaceTime video calls in situations when Messages gives up.

All right then. To make the actual call, take one of these steps:

- **Click the person's** name in your Favorites list.

- **Click the Recents tab,** where you'll see a list of FaceTime calls you've recently made or received. Click the person's name.

Tip: If you right-click (or Control-click) FaceTime's Dock icon, you get a handy pop-up menu of Recent Calls. In other words, if you keep FaceTime in your Dock, you can place a new call to somebody on the spur of the moment, whatever you're doing, without having to open FaceTime first.

• **Click Contacts.** Click Groups, if you use the Groups feature, and click the group the person is in. Use the search box, or just scroll, to find the person you want to call. Click the name; if you have multiple email addresses or phone numbers for that person, click the one you want.

In any case, your Mac now attempts to connect to your FaceTime-equipped buddy. After a moment, the video image of *you* is replaced by the video image of your calling buddy (Figure 11-12). If you both have fast Internet connections, and if the other guy has a recent Mac (with a so-called FaceTime HD camera), the video should look pretty amazing—hi-def, actually.

Once You're Connected

Once the FaceTime session has begun, just talk normally. You're on camera!

Here's some of the fun you can have during your call:

• **Resize the window.** Drag any window edge, click the Zoom button (upper left), or choose Window→Zoom to make the window fill the screen.

• **Go full-screen.** Click the ⬈ button (upper right) to make the window fill your entire screen. (Click it again to restore the window.)

Tip: You can also enter or exit full-screen mode by spreading or pinching two fingers on your trackpad.

• **Move the inset.** The little picture-in-picture rectangle shows *you*. You can drag it to a different corner of the video window, if you like.

• **Rotate the screen.** If you're calling an iPad/iPhone/iPod Touch, the shape of the video-image rectangle changes automatically to match. But you can change the orientation of the window yourself, too. Either use the Video menu (choose Use Portrait or Use Landscape), or click the curved arrow in the inset that shows you, or use the Rotate gesture on your trackpad (two fingers, rotate).

• **Mute the mike.** Either choose Video→Mute, or click the ⬙ button at the bottom of the video window. The video continues. This is handy when you have to make ugly throat-clearing sounds or yell at your kid in the background.

• **Pause the call.** You can also pause the audio *and* video, for use when you have to perform small acts of personal grooming. To do that, choose FaceTime→Hide FaceTime, or Control-click the FaceTime icon in the Dock and choose Hide from the shortcut menu.

Tip: The call is also paused whenever you minimize FaceTime.

Receiving Calls

Life is even simpler when somebody calls *you*. You hear the little chirpy incoming-call sound, and a message appears on your screen. (If iTunes is playing music, it pauses automatically. Sweet.)

Click Accept to start the call, or Decline if now is not the time. (In that case, your caller will be told that you're not available.)

FaceTime doesn't have to be running for you to receive a call. That's generally a cool feature—but if you really don't want to be interrupted, you can hang up a digital "Do Not Disturb" sign in any of these ways:

• In FaceTime, choose FaceTime→Turn FaceTime Off.

• In FaceTime, choose FaceTime→Preferences; click the Off switch.

• Control-click (or right-click) the FaceTime icon in the Dock; from the shortcut menu, choose Turn FaceTime Off.

• Sign out of FaceTime. (Choose FaceTime→Preferences, click Account, and then click Sign Out.)

Font Book

For details on this font-management program, see Chapter 14.

Game Center

The Mac has had its share of games over the years, but it's never been much of a haven for gamers. That's not going to change dramatically with Mountain Lion, but the new Game Center app does make the Mac a little bit more of a hospitable place for the games people play.

Game Center began life on iPhones and iPads in 2010 as a way to compare scores with friends and challenge buddies to games. Several updates and 130 million people later, Game Center on iPhones/iPads is a certified hit.

Little wonder then, that Apple would want to create a Mac version of Game Center to promote gaming on the Mac. It performs the same functions as the iPhone version of Game Center—but opens up the possibility of playing games on your Mac against people with phones and tablets. (That miracle, of course, is possible only in cases when the same game is available on those different gadgets.) Someday soon, Apple hopes, there will be one glorious, universal game ecosystem of Apple machines.

Getting Started

When you open the Game Center app, start by signing in. If you've used Game Center on your phone or tablet, your Apple ID appears automatically; just type your password. From there, Game Center imports everything—your nickname, your list of existing Game Center friends, and even the photo you use to identify yourself.

If this is your first time with Game Center, fill in your Apple ID (page 412) and password. You're asked to create a nickname—"AngriestBird" or "BobSmith2000," for example. This nickname is public and can appear on the leaderboards for games (scoreboards that show the highest point winners); you can also use this nickname

when you play games against other people. Within your Game Center account, you can also turn two settings on and off: One lets friends invite you to play games; the other makes your public profile visible to other Game Center members.

That public profile includes space for a short description and photo of yourself. You can grab a picture from a list of recent photos (any images you've used as your Messages icon, for example), Apple's standard OS X icons, or a photo you take with your Mac's built-in camera. The Mac's Game Center gives you a few more photo editing options than you get in the iOS version: In addition to zooming and placing the image, you can also apply a filter, giving your photo a tinted, distorted, or pixelated look.

Tip: Any change you make to your Game Center profile on a Mac will also show up on Game Center on your iPhone or iPad—and vice versa.

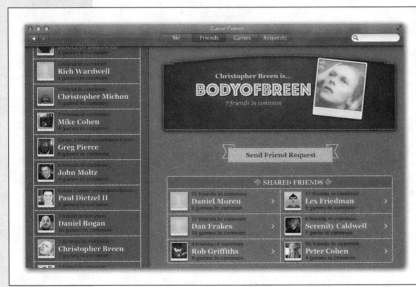

Figure 11-13:
You can sort the Friends list alphabetically, by how recently your friends have played a game, or by the total points they've accumulated in Game Center apps.

Once all that's in place, the Me tab in Game Center displays your nickname, that clever little phrase you wrote, and your picture. Beneath that, multicolored banners display the number of Game Center–compatible games you own (either iOS or Mac games), the number of Game Center friends you have, and—perhaps most significantly—the number of points you've accrued from your gaming activities.

Points and Achievements

Points play a leading role in Game Center. You earn them by racking up achievements in Game Center-compatible apps. Smash enough blocks in one of the many versions of Angry Birds, or expand your territory in Civilization, and you unlock achievements in those games; those achievements translate to points, which show up in your Game Center profile.

Those points also provide a way to measure your personal worth against your friends'. On Game Center's Friends tab, your friends appear in a pane on the left side of the Friends window (Figure 11-13).

If you click a friend's name in that left pane, you get a choice of three views: the games your friends play, the names of their friends, and the number of points they've tallied. The points view features a side-by-side comparison showing your respective accomplishments in commonly played games, so you can settle once and for all who's tops at Cubemen. (Game Center also shows the points your friends have racked up in games you don't own, which is Apple's way of suggesting that maybe you should download more games.)

Making Friends

Of course, before you can compare your scores with your friends', it helps to *have* some friends. (Insert your own joke about hardcore gamers here.)

You can invite your real-life pals to join you in Game Center by clicking the Add Friends banner near the top of the left-hand pane on the Friends window. You get a pop-up message window, where you can type in a person's Game Center nickname or email address to send a friend invitation. (Email is probably the better choice, as you may not know your friend's Game Center nickname; he might not even be signed up to the service.) You can also issue invitations from the Requests tab, which is where you typically accept invitations that come in from other Game Center users who want to befriend you.

But what if you don't have any existing friends, or at least none that you know are on Game Center? Above the Add Friends banner, a Friend Recommendations button brings up a list of potential buddies. These are strangers, of course, but they're based on friends and games you have in common. Clicking on one of those names takes you to a page that shows common friends, if any, and a Send Friend Request banner.

You can also find gaming companions through your other Game Center friends. Just click one of your friends' names, and then select the Friends view on her page to see who she hangs out with in Game Center (when she's not matching scores with you, of course). The list of her Game Center friends appears under a list of shared friends and notes how many games you have in common with this would-be buddy.

Finding Games

Game Center can also help you find games to play—well, at least games that are designed to tie in with Game Center. The top of the Games tab features a Recommendations section that takes you to a list of suggested games. Game Center bases these recommendations on what you already own, what your friends play, and popular App Store downloads.

At Mountain Lion's debut, there weren't many Game Center-compatible games; building up the catalog will take the world's game companies some time. While you wait, you can always fool around with the Chess game that comes with Mountain Lion; it's Game Center-ready.

Managing Game Center

You get to most of the Game Center management features from the Me tab. That's where you can change your photo and status message, manage your privacy settings, and even sign out of Game Center. But there's another aspect of Game Center that you manage in a completely different place.

Game Center notifies you whenever anyone asks to friend you or accepts your Game Center invitation. These notifications usually appear as banners, flashing in your upper-right corner briefly before they disappear. You can, of course, shut them up; open System Preferences→Notifications, click Game Center, and customize the settings as described on page 380.

GarageBand

GarageBand, Apple's do-it-yourself music construction kit, isn't actually part of OS X. If you have a copy, that's because it's part of the iLife suite that comes on every new Mac (along with iMovie and iPhoto).

iChat

Fooled you! There's no such thing as iChat anymore. It's now called Messages, and it's described in Chapter 20.

Image Capture

This unsung little program was originally designed to download pictures from a camera and then process them automatically (turning them into a Web page, scaling them to emailable size, and so on). Of course, after Image Capture's birth, iPhoto came along, generally blowing its predecessor out of the water.

Even so, Apple includes Image Capture with OS X for these reasons:

- Image Capture is a smaller, faster app for downloading all or only some pictures from your camera (Figure 11-14). iPhoto can do that nowadays, but sometimes that's like using a bulldozer to get out a splinter.

- Image Capture can grab images from scanners, too, not just cameras.

- Image Capture can download your *sounds* (like voice notes) from a digital still camera; iPhoto can't.

You can open Image Capture in either of two ways: You can simply double-click its icon in your Applications folder, or you can set it up to open automatically whenever you connect a digital camera and turn it on. To set up that arrangement, open Image Capture manually. Using the "Connecting this camera opens:" pop-up menu, choose Image Capture.

Tip: Image Capture remembers your setting here separately for each camera. For example, you can set it up so that when you connect your fancy SLR camera, Aperture opens; when you connect your spouse's pocket camera, iPhoto opens; and when you connect your iPhone, Image Capture opens, so you can quickly grab the best shots and email them directly.

Once Image Capture is open, it looks like Figure 11-14. When you connect your camera, cellphone, or scanner, its name appears in the left-side list. To begin, click it. After a moment, Image Capture displays all the photos on the camera's card, in either list view or icon view (your choice).

Figure 11-14:
In many ways, Image Capture is like a mini iPhoto; use the slider in the lower right to change the thumbnail sizes. Use the "Delete after import" checkbox (lower left) if you want your camera's card erased after you slurp in its photos. You can choose the individual pictures you want to download, rotate selected shots (using the buttons at the top), or delete shots from the camera.

Import To:

Use this pop-up menu to specify what happens to the imported pictures. Image Capture proposes putting photos, sounds, and movies from the camera into your Home folder's Pictures folder. But you can specify any folder (choose Other from the pop-up menu).

Furthermore, there are some other very cool options here:

- **iPhoto.** Neat that you can direct photos from your camera *to* iPhoto *via* Image Capture. Might come in handy when you didn't *expect* to want to load photos into your permanent collection, but you change your mind when you actually look them over in Image Capture.

- **Preview** opens the fresh pictures in Preview so you can get a better (and bigger) look at them.

- **Mail** sends the pix directly into the Mac's email program, which can be very handy when the whole point of getting the photos off the camera is to send them off to friends.

- **Build web page** creates an actual Web page of your downloaded shots. Against a dark-gray background, you get thumbnail images of the pictures in a Web page document called *index.html*. Just click one of the small images to view it at full size, exactly as your Web site visitors will be able to do once this page is actually on the Web. (Getting it online is up to you.)

Note: Image Capture puts the Web page files in a Home folder→Pictures→Webpage on [today's date and time] folder. It contains the graphics files incorporated into this HTML document; you can post the whole thing on your Web site, if you like.

Image Capture automatically opens up this page in your Web browser, proud of its work.

- **MakePDF.** What is MakePDF? It's a little app you didn't even know you had.

When you choose this option, you wind up with what looks like a Preview window, showing thumbnails of your photos. If you choose Save right now, you'll get a beautiful, full-color PDF of the selected photos, ready to print out and then, presumably, cut apart with scissors or a paper cutter. But if you use the Layout menu, you can choose different layouts for your photos: 3 × 5, 4 × 6, 8 × 10, and so on.

And what if a photo doesn't precisely fit the proportions you've selected? The Crop commands in the Layout menu (for example, "Crop to 4 × 6") center each photo within the specified shape and then trim the outer borders if necessary. The Fit commands, on the other hand, *shrink* the photo as necessary to fit into the specified dimensions, sometimes leaving blank white margins.

Note: The "crop" commands never touch the actual downloaded photos. The downloaded image files themselves retain their full sizes and resolutions.

- **Other.** The beauty of the Image Capture system is that people can, in theory, write additional processing scripts. Once you've written or downloaded them, drop them into your System→Library→Image Capture→Automatic Tasks folder. Then enjoy their presence in the newly enhanced Import To pop-up menu.

Tip: You can set up Image Capture to download everything on the camera *automatically* when you connect it. No muss, no options, no fuss.

To do that, connect the camera. Click its name in the Devices list. Then, from the "Connecting this camera opens" pop-up menu, choose AutoImporter. From now on, Image Capture downloads all pictures on the camera each time it's connected. When the downloading process is complete, a little green checkmark appears on the thumbnail of each imported photo.

Import Some, Import All

Clicking Import All, of course, begins the process of downloading the photos to the folder you've selected. A progress dialog box appears, showing you thumbnail images of each picture that flies down the wire.

If you prefer to import only *some* photos, select them first. (In list view, you click and Shift-click to select a bunch of *consecutive* photos, and ⌘-click to add *individual* photos to the selection. In icon view, you can both ⌘-click and *Shift*-click to select individual photos.) Then click Import.

Scanning

If you own a scanner, chances are good that you won't be needing whatever special scanning software came with it. Instead, OS X gives you two programs that can operate any standard scanner: Image Capture and Preview. In fact, the available controls are identical in both programs.

To scan in Image Capture, turn on your scanner and click its name in the left-side list. Put your photos or documents into the scanner.

Note: You can share a scanner on the network, if you like, by turning on Scanner Sharing in System Preferences→Sharing. That's sort of a weird option, though, for two reasons. First, what do you gain by sitting somewhere else in the building? Do you really want to yell or call up to whoever's sitting next to the scanner: "OK! Put in the next photo!"?

Second, don't forget that anyone else on the network will be able to see whatever you're scanning. Embarrassment may result. You've been warned.

Now you have a couple of decisions to make:

- **Separate and straighten?** If you turn on "Detect separate items" in the Scan Size menu, OS X will perform a nifty little stunt indeed: It will check to see if you've put *multiple* items onto the scanner glass, like several small photos. (It looks for rectangular images surrounded by empty white space, so if the photos are overlapping, this feature won't work.)

 If it finds multiple items, Image Capture automatically straightens them, compensating for haphazard placement on the glass, and then saves them as individual files.

- **Where to file.** Use the "Scan to" pop-up menu to specify where you want the newly scanned image files to land—in the Pictures folder, for example. You have some other cool options beyond sticking the scans in a folder; for example, you can send the resulting image to iPhoto, Preview, or Mail.

Once you've put a document onto it or into it, click Scan. The scanner heaves to life. After a moment, you see on the screen what's on the glass. It's simultaneously been sent to the folder (or post-processing task) you requested using the "Scan to" pop-up menu.

More power to you

As you can see, Apple has tried to make *basic* scanning as simple as possible: one click. That idiotproof method gives you very few options, however.

If you click Show Details before you scan, though, you get a special panel on the right side of the window that's filled with useful scanning controls (Figure 11-15).

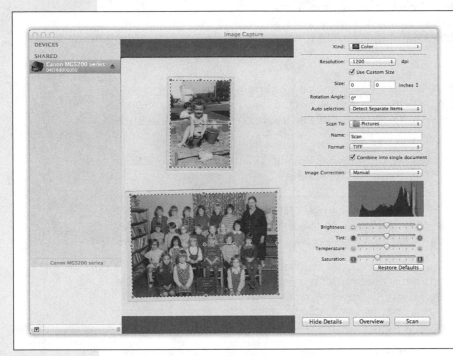

Figure 11-15:
When you use the Show Details button, you get a new panel on the right, where you can specify all the tweaky details for the scan you're about to make: resolution, size, and so on. See how the three photos have individual dotted lines around them? That's because Detect Separate Items is turned on. These will be scanned into three separate files.

Here are some of the most useful options:

- **Resolution.** This is the number of tiny scanned dots per inch. 300 is about right for something you plan to print out; 75 is standard for graphics that will be viewed on the screen, like images on a Web page.

- **Name.** Here, specify how you want each image file named when it lands on your hard drive. If it says *Scan,* then the files will be called *Scan 1, Scan 2,* and so on.

- **Format.** Usually, the file format for scanned graphics is TIFF. That's a very high-res format that's ideal if you're scanning precious photos for posterity. But if these images are bound for the Web, you might want to choose JPEG instead; that's the standard Web format.

- **Image Correction.** If you choose Manual from this pop-up menu, then, incredibly, you'll be treated to a whole expando-panel of color correction tools: brightness, tint, saturation, a histogram, and so on.

Opening the Details panel has another handy benefit, too: It lets you scan only a *portion* of what's on the scanner glass.

Once you've put the document or photo into the scanner, click Overview. Image Capture does a quick pass and displays on the screen whatever is on the glass. You'll see a dotted-line rectangle around the entire scanned image—unless you've turned on "Detect separate images," in which case you see a dotted-line rectangle around *each* item on the glass.

You can adjust these dotted-line rectangles around until you've enclosed precisely the portion of the image you want scanned. For example, drag the rectangles' corner handles to resize them; drag inside the rectangles to move them; drag the right end of the line inside the rectangle to rotate it; preview the rotation by pressing Control and Option.

Finally, when you think you've got the selection rectangle(s) correctly positioned, click Scan to trigger the actual scan.

Note: These instructions apply to the most common kind of scanner—the *flatbed* scanner. If you have a scanner with a document feeder—a tray or slot that sucks in one paper document after another from a stack—the instructions are only slightly different.

You may, for example, see a Mode or Scan Mode pop-up menu; if so, choose Document Feeder. You'll want to use the Show Details option described above. You may also be offered a Duplex command (meaning, "scan both sides of the paper"—not all scanners can do this).

iMovie, iPhoto

Here's another pair of iLife apps—not really part of OS X, but kicking around on your Mac because iLife comes with all new Macs.

Tip: Masterfully written, in-depth guides to these programs are available in the form of *iMovie '11 & iDVD: The Missing Manual* and *iPhoto '11: The Missing Manual*. (Corresponding Missing Manual titles are available for earlier versions of these programs, too.)

iTunes

iTunes is Apple's beloved digital music–library program. Chapter 12 tells all.

Launchpad

See Chapter 5 for the full story about the program-opening Home screen.

Mail

See Chapter 18 for the missing Mail manual.

Messages

See Chapter 20 for details on Messages, the Mac's instant-messaging/audiochat/videochat/text-messaging program.

Mission Control

Chapter 5 covers Mountain Lion's window-management tool.

Notes

This app, new in Mountain Lion, is meant to mimic (and sync with) the equivalent app on iPhones and iPads. Chapter 10 tells all.

Photo Booth

It may be goofy, it may be pointless, but the Photo Booth program is a bigger time drain than Solitaire, the Web, and *Dancing with the Stars* put together.

It's a match made in heaven for any Mac with a video camera above the screen, but you can also use it with a camcorder, iSight, or Webcam. (Photo Booth doesn't even open if your Mac doesn't have *some* kind of camera.)

Open this program and then peer into the camera. Photo Booth acts like a digital mirror, showing whatever the camera sees—that is, you.

But then click the Effects button. You enter a world of special visual effects—and we're talking *very* special. Some make you look like a pinhead, or bulbous, or like a Siamese twin; others simulate Andy Warhol paintings, fisheye lenses, and charcoal sketches (Figure 11-16). In fact, there are five whole pages of effects, nine previews on a page. (The last two pages hold *backdrop* effects, described below.)

To page through them, click the left or right arrow buttons, or press ← or →, or swipe with two fingers on your trackpad (one finger on the Magic Mouse).

GEM IN THE ROUGH

De-Mirrorizing Your Photos

Technically, Photo Booth acts like a mirror, not a camera. That is, every picture you take is actually flipped, left-to-right. If there's ever text in the picture—something written on your T-shirt, for example—or if you ever examine the way your hair is parted, you'll realize that every image is backwards.

That's why you can click a thumbnail at the bottom of the window and then choose Edit→Flip Photo (⌘-F). You've just made the photo match what a camera would have seen.

Or choose Edit→Auto Flip New Photos if you want Photo Booth to do the flipping *for* you from now on.

The first page contains eight effects that were new in Lion, some of which use sophisticated face-recognition smarts to track your face as it moves around the frame. That's how Dizzy and Lovestruck are able to keep the animated birds or hearts circling your head, and how Chipmunk, Nose Twirl, and Bug Out are able to distort your cheeks, nose, and eyeballs even as you move around.

Some of the effects have sliders that govern their intensity; you'll see them appear when you click the preview.

Still Photos

When you find an effect that looks appealing (or unappealing, depending on your goals here), click the camera button, or press ⌘-T. You see and hear a 3-second countdown, and then *snap!*—your screen flashes white to add illumination, and the resulting photo appears on your screen. Its thumbnail joins the collection at the bottom.

Tip: If that countdown is getting on your nerves, *Option*-click the camera button. You can get rid of the screen flash, too, by *Shift*-clicking. Needless to say, if you press Option *and* Shift, you get neither the countdown nor the flash.

Figure 11-16:
The Photo Booth effects must have been dreamed up one night in the midst of a serious beer party at Apple. They're disturbingly creative. If you decide that you really look best without any help from Apple's warped imagery, click the Normal icon in the center.

Click an effect

Space Alien / Nose Twirl / Chipmunk / Lovestruck / Normal / Dizzy / Blockhead / Bug Out / Frog

Still 4-Up Movie Effects pages Finished shots

4-Up Photos

If you click the 4-Up button identified in Figure 11-16, then when you click the Camera icon (or press ⌘-T), the 3-2-1 countdown begins, and then Photo Booth snaps *four* consecutive photos in 2 seconds. You can exploit the timing just the way you would in a real photo booth—make four different expressions, horse around, whatever.

The result is a single graphic with four panes, kind of like what you get at a shopping-mall photo booth. (In Photo Booth, they appear rakishly assembled at an angle; but when you export the image, they appear straight, like panes of a window.) Its icon plops into the row of thumbnails at the bottom of the window, just like the single still photos.

Movies

Photo Booth can also record *videos*, complete with those wacky distortion effects. Click the third icon below the screen, the Movie icon (Figure 11-16), and then click the camera button (or press ⌘-T). You get the 3-2-1 countdown—but this time, Photo Booth records a video, with sound, until you click the Stop button. (The little digital

GEM IN THE ROUGH

Still and Video Backdrops

Photo Booth and Messages are cousins, and they're closer than ever. One particular feature, in fact, is identical in each: custom backdrops. You can replace the actual, mundane background of your office or den with something far more exciting: a rushing waterfall, for example, or a rider's-eye view of a roller coaster. In fact, you can use any photo or video you want as the background.

It's just like the bluescreen or greenscreen technology that Hollywood uses to put actors someplace they're not—but without the bluescreen or greenscreen.

To replace your background in Photo Booth, click Effects. The fourth page of effects offers eight *canned* backgrounds, prepared by Apple for your enjoyment: various spectacular stills (cloudscape, color dots, the moon) and videos (Eiffel Tower plaza, aquarium, roller coaster, tropical beach, Yosemite waterfall).

The final page offers eight empty preview squares. You're supposed to drag a still or a video from your desktop (or iPhoto) into these empty squares, making them not so empty.

In any case, prepare the backdrop by clicking one of the preview squares. Photo Booth says, "Please step out of the frame." Do it. Photo Booth is going to memorize what its field of view looks like without you in it, so that when you reappear, it can tell *you* apart from your boring office background.

Now, when you record the movie or take the photo, you'll be amazed to discover that Photo Booth has just transplanted you to the far more exotic locale you selected. (Alas, blotches may result if the background includes movement or highly contrasting elements.)

counter at left reminds you that you're still filming.) When it's over, the movie's icon appears in the row of thumbnails, ready to play or export.

Tip: If you click a movie's thumbnail after recording it, a Trim button appears at the right end of the scroll bar. When you click it, yellow trim handles appear at both ends of the scroll bar (the same ones you'd see when trimming a video on the iPhone or iPad, or in iPhoto). Drag them inward to trim off any dead air at the beginning or end of your video clip. Hit the space bar to check your work. If the trim is OK, click the ● button to confirm the trim.

Exporting Shots and Movies

To look at a photo or movie you've captured, click its thumbnail in the scrolling row at the bottom of the screen. (To return to camera mode, click the ◉ button.)

Fortunately, these masterpieces of goofiness and distortion aren't locked in Photo Booth forever. You can share them with your adoring public in any of these ways:

- Click the photo or movie, and then choose File→Export. You're asked to name and save the exported image or video.

Tip: If you choose File→Export Original instead, the exported photo or video lacks any of the effects that you've applied. You get the original, undistorted, underlying photo—a useful new option in Mountain Lion.

- Drag a thumbnail out of the window to your desktop.

- Control-click (or right-click) a thumbnail. From the shortcut menu, choose Reveal in Finder. You're taken to the actual image or movie file on your hard drive, ready for copying, moving, deleting, renaming, or whatever.

Note: These files are stored in a single icon, a package file, that sits in your Home→Pictures folder. It's called Photo Booth Library. You'll find one JPEG apiece for single shots, four JPEG files for a 4-up, and a MOV file for videos.

- Click Email to send the photo or movie as an outgoing attachment in Mail.

- Click the Add to iPhoto button to import the shot or movie into iPhoto.

- Click User Picture to make this photo represent you on the Login screen.

- Click Buddy Picture to make this photo represent you in Messages (Chapter 20).

Tip: You can choose one frame of a Photo Booth movie to represent you. As the movie plays, click the Pause button, and then drag the scroll-bar handle to freeze the action on the frame you want. Then click User Picture or Buddy Picture.

Similarly, you can click your favorite *one pane* of a 4-up image to serve as your account photo—it expands to fill the Photo Booth screen—before clicking User Picture or Account Picture.

And speaking of interesting headshots: If you export a 4-up image and choose it as your Buddy Picture, you'll get an *animated* buddy icon. That is, your tiny icon cycles

among the four images, creating a crude sort of animation. It's sort of annoying, actually, but all the kids are doing it.

As you set off on your Photo Booth adventures, a note of caution: Keep it away from children. They won't move from Photo Booth for the next 12 years.

Tip: Photo Booth is one of the certified full-screen apps. Click the ⬚ icon in the upper right to make the app fill your screen, for added graphic juiciness.

Preview

Preview is OS X's scanning software, graphics viewer, fax viewer, and PDF reader. It's always been teeming with features that most Mac owners never even knew were there—but now it's a flagship OS X program, offering all of Apple's pet cutting-edge features like Autosave, Versions, and full-screen mode. In fact, in Mountain Lion, Preview also gains the ability to save files online, in your iCloud locker (page 255). And its Share icon (⤴) lets you send an document to somebody else by email, AirDrop, or Messages, or send an open graphic via Facebook, Twitter, or Flickr (page 268).

Tip: Preview can even open Microsoft Office documents (Word, PowerPoint, Excel) and iWork documents (Pages, Numbers, Keynote). You can't edit them in Preview, but you can read them, search them, and print them. No longer must you pay homage to Microsoft's bottom line just to have a look at the documents people send you.

Importing Camera Photos

Preview can import pictures directly from a digital camera (or iPhone), meaning that there are now *three* OS X apps that can perform that duty. (iPhoto and Image Capture are the other two.) It's sometimes handy to use Preview for this purpose, though, because it has some great tools for photos: color-correction controls, size/resolution options, format conversion, and so on.

The actual importing process, though, is *exactly* like using Image Capture. Connect your camera, choose File→Import from [your camera's name], and carry on as described on page 418.

Operating Your Scanner

Preview can also operate a scanner, auto-straighten the scanned images, and export them as PDF files, JPEG graphics, and so on.

This, too, is *exactly* like using Image Capture to operate your scanner. Only the first step is different. Open Preview, choose File→Import from Scanner→[your scanner's name], and proceed as described on page 421.

Clearly, Apple saved some time by reusing some code.

Multiple Pages, Multiple Views

One hallmark of Preview is its effortless handling of *multiples:* multiple fax pages, multiple PDF files, batches of photos, and so on. The key to understanding the possibilities is mastering the Sidebar, shown in Figure 11-17. The idea is that these thumbnails let you navigate pages or graphics without having to open a rat's nest of individual windows.

Tip: You can drag these thumbnails from one Preview window's Sidebar into another. That's a great way to mix and match pages from different PDF documents into a single new one, for example.

Figure 11-17:
The Sidebar can display thumbnails, a table of contents, or annotations, or it can appear as a full-screen array of thumbnail images. Drag the central scroll bar to make the Sidebar bigger; drag the lower-right corner of the Sidebar to make the whole Preview window bigger.

To hide or show the Sidebar, chose one of these three commands from the View menu:

- **Thumbnails.** This standard view (Figure 11-17, left) offers a scrolling vertical list of miniature pages or photos. Click one to see it at full size in the main window. Make the thumbnails larger or smaller by dragging the window/Sidebar dividing line.

- **Highlights & Notes.** Preview, in Mountain Lion, is a better PDF editor than ever. If you add comments and highlighting to a PDF document, as described later in this section, you can view all of them in this tidy list—and click one to jump to it .

- **Table of Contents.** If you're looking over photos, this option turns the Sidebar into a scrolling list of their names. If you've opened a group of PDFs all at once, you see a list of them. Or, if you have a PDF that contains chapter headings, you see them listed in the Sidebar as, yes, a table of contents.

- **Contact Sheet.** When you choose this view, the *main* window scrolls away, leaving you with a full screen of thumbnail miniatures. It's like a light table where you can look over all the photos or PDF pages at once. Make them bigger or smaller using the slider in the lower left.

Tip: You can also change among these views by pressing the keyboard shortcuts Option-⌘-1, -2, -3, and -4.

Preview as Graphics Viewer

Preview is surprisingly versatile. It can display and manipulate pictures saved in a wide variety of formats, including common graphics formats like JPEG, TIFF, PICT, and GIF; less commonly used formats like BMP, PNG, SGI, and TGA; and even Photoshop, EPS, and PDF graphics.

Tip: Don't miss the Tools→Show Magnifier command. It gives you a loupe: a magnifying circle (or, in a PDF document, a magnifying rectangle) that lets you inspect part of your graphic or PDF file more closely.

Bunches o' graphics

If you highlight a group of image files in the Finder and open them all at once (for example, by pressing ⌘-O), Preview opens the first one but lists the thumbnails of the whole group in the Sidebar. You can walk through them with the ↑ and ↓ keys, or you can choose View→Slideshow (Shift-⌘-F) to open a full-screen slideshow.

Scaling and Resampling

When you're fooling around with a picture's size and resolution in the Change Size dialog box, you might find that a couple of the options take a little explaining.

If "Scale proportionally" is turned on, Preview changes the Height number when you change the Width number, and vice versa. In other words, it won't let you change the *shape* of the photo; that's why a little padlock icon appears to bracket the Height and Width boxes.

If "Resample image" is turned off, then Preview adjusts the image's size by making the exist-

ing dots bigger or smaller—but never changes the *number* of dots. (That's why a padlock bracket links all three boxes together. For example, you can make the image larger—but you'll lower the number of dots per inch.)

If "Resample image" is turned *on,* then you're giving Preview permission to add or subtract pixels as necessary to scale the photo up or down. Of course, it can't create detail that wasn't there in the original, but if you're scaling the picture *up,* it does a decent job of generating new pixels by averaging the colors of the neighboring ones.

Tip: You can change the order of the photos just by dragging them around in the Sidebar, in any of its views.

Cropping graphics

To crop graphics in Preview, drag across the part of the graphic that you want to keep. To redraw, drag the round handles on the dotted rectangle; or, to proceed with the crop, choose Tools→Crop. (The keyboard shortcut is ⌘-K.)

Since Preview is an Autosave program, you can always return to the original if you change your mind someday.

Tip: You can also rotate an image—even a PDF document—in 90-degree increments and then flip it vertically or horizontally, using the commands in the Tools menu. In fact, if you select several thumbnails in the Sidebar first, you can rotate or flip them all simultaneously.

Fixing up photos

Preview is no Photoshop, but it's getting closer every year. Let us count the ways:

- **Choose Tools→Show Inspector.** A floating palette appears. Click the first tab to see the photo's name, when it was taken, its pixel dimensions, and so on. Click the second one for even more geeky photo details, including camera settings like the lens type, ISO setting, focus mode, whether the flash was on, and so on. The third tab lets you add keywords, so you'll be able to search for this image later us-

Figure 11-18:
Humble little Preview has grown up into a big, strong mini-Photoshop. You can really fix up a photo if you know what you're doing, using these sliders. Or you can just click the Auto Levels button. It sets all those sliders for you, which generally does an amazing job of making almost any photo look better.

ing Spotlight. (The fourth is for PDF documents only, not photos; it lets you add annotations. A fifth tab appears only in PDF documents—for rotating, cropping, and resizing the file.)

- **Choose Tools→Adjust Color.** A translucent, floating color-adjustment palette appears, teeming with sliders for brightness, contrast, exposure, saturation (color intensity), temperature and tint (color cast), sharpness, and more. See Figure 11-18.

- **Choose Tools→Adjust Size.** This command lets you adjust a photo's resolution, which comes in handy a lot. For example, you can scale an unwieldy 10-megapixel, gazillion-by-gazillion-pixel shot down to a nice 640 × 480 JPEG that's small enough to send by email. Or you can shrink a photo down so it fits within a desktop window, for use as a window background.

 There's not much to it. Type in the new print dimensions you want for the photo, in inches or whatever units you choose from the pop-up menu. If you like, you can also change the resolution (the number of pixels per inch) by editing the Resolution box.

Cutting people out of backgrounds

Here's a Photoshoppy feature you would never, ever expect to find in a simple viewer like Preview: You can extract a person (or anything, really) from its background. That's handy when you want to clip yourself out of a group shot to use as your Messages portrait, when you want to paste somebody into a new background, or when you break up with someone and want them out of your photos.

If the background is simple—mostly a solid color or two—you can do this job quickly. Start by making sure the toolbar is visible (⌘-B). From the Select pop-up menu, choose Instant Alpha.

This feature is extremely weird, but here goes: Click the first background color you want to eliminate. Preview automatically dims out *all* the pixels that match the

UP TO SPEED

Another Way to Cut People Out of Backgrounds

If the background of your graphic isn't primarily solid colors, the Instant Alpha feature won't help you much. Fortunately, you have another, cruder option: Manually drag around the person.

Again, start by making sure the toolbar is visible (⌘-B). From the Select pop-up menu, choose Smart Lasso.

Now carefully trace the person or thing that you'll want to extract. Preview marks your tracing with a fat red line. (Zoom in for tight corners by pressing ⌘-+.) Continue until you've

made a complete closed loop. Or just let go to say, "Connect where I am now with where I started."

(Hit Esc to erase the line and start over—or give up.)

Once you've isolated the person you want to keep, you can use Edit→Copy so that the person is ready to paste somewhere else. Or you can reverse the selection, so that the background is selected, so that you can get rid of it. Do that with a quick Edit→Invert Selection. Now you can hit the Delete key to lose the background.

color you clicked. Click again in another area to add more of the background to the dimmed patch.

Actually, if you click and *drag* a tiny distance, you'll see sensitivity-percentage numbers appear next to your cursor. They indicate that the more you drag, the more you're expanding the selection to colors *close* to the one you clicked. The proper technique, then, isn't click-click-click; it's drag-drag-drag.

When it looks like you've successfully isolated the subject from the background, press the Delete key. You've just chopped out the background.

You've just created a graphic with an *alpha channel*, which, in computer-graphics terms, is a special mask that can be used for transparency or blending. The background you deleted—the empty gray part—appears transparent when you export it (File→Export) and then import it into certain graphically sophisticated programs. For example:

- **iMovie.** You can drag your exported graphic directly onto a filmstrip in an iMovie project. The white areas of the exported Preview image become transparent, so whatever video is already in the filmstrip plays through it. Great for opening credits or special effects.

- **Preview.** Yes, Preview itself recognizes incoming alpha channels. So after you cut the background out of Photo A, you can select what's left (press ⌘-A), copy it to the Clipboard (⌘-C), open Photo B, and then paste (⌘-V). The visible part of Photo A gets pasted into the background of Photo B.

- **Photoshop, Photoshop Elements.** Of course, these advanced graphics programs recognize alpha channels, too. Paste in your Preview graphic; it appears as a layer, with the existing layers shining through the empty areas.

Tip: Here's a great way to create a banner or headline for your Web page: Create a big, bold-font text block in TextEdit. Choose File→Print; from the PDF pop-up button, choose Open PDF in Preview.

In Preview, crop the document down and save it as a PNG-format graphic (because PNG recognizes alpha channels). Then use the Instant Alpha feature to dab out the background and the gaps inside the letters. When you import this image to your Web page, you'll find a professional-looking text banner that lets your page's background shine through the empty areas of the lettering.

Converting file formats

Preview doesn't just open all these file formats—it can also convert among most of them. You can pop open some old Mac PICT files and turn them into BMP files for a Windows user, pry open a TIFF file from a scanner and turn it into a JPEG for use on your Web site, and so on.

Tip: What's even cooler is you can open raw PostScript files right into Preview, which converts them into PDF files on the spot. You no longer need a PostScript laser printer to print out high-end diagrams and page layouts that come to you as PostScript files. Thanks to Preview, even an inkjet printer can handle them.

All you have to do is open the file you want to convert and choose File→Export. In the dialog box that appears, choose the new format for the image using the Format pop-up menu (JPEG, TIFF, PNG, or Photoshop, for example); if you press the Option key, you're offered even more file types. Finally, click Save to export the file.

Preview as PDF Reader

Preview is a nearly full-blown equivalent of Adobe Reader, the free program used by millions to read PDF documents. It lets you search PDF documents, copy text out of them, add comments, fill in forms, click live hyperlinks, add highlighting, circle certain passages, type in notes—features that used to be available only in Adobe's Acrobat Reader. And now, in the Mountain Lion version, you can even fill out *PDF forms*, typing into imaginary boxes on the electronic document.

Tip: Don't forget that Preview is one of OS X's certified full-screen apps. That is, you can make it fill your screen, border to border, by clicking the ⬓ icon in the upper-right corner, as described on page 12. You can also flip through the pages of a PDF using the "next page" gesture: a two-finger swipe on the trackpad.

Here are the basics:

• Zoom in and out using ⌘-plus and ⌘-minus.

Tip: Another way to get a closer look: press the ` key (upper-left of your keyboard), or choose Tools→Show-Magnifier. Now a big magnifying glass follows your cursor; you can even press + or − to zoom in or out within it. Dismiss the magnifier by pressing ` again.

• Use the View menu commands to control how the PDF document appears: as two-page spreads; as single scrolling sheets of "paper towel"; with borders that indicate ends of pages; and so on.

• Press the space bar to page through a document (add Shift to page *upward*. The Page Up and Page Down keys do the same thing.)

Tip: Some PDF documents include a table of contents, which you'll see in Preview's Sidebar, complete with flippy triangles that denote chapter headings (Figure 11-17). Use the ↑ and ↓ keys to walk through these chapter headings, and then expand one that looks good by pressing the → key. Collapse it again with the ← key.

In other words, you expand and collapse flippy triangles in Preview just as you do in a Finder list view. (The View→Sidebar submenu also includes Expand All and Collapse All commands.)

• Bookmark your place by choosing Bookmarks→Add Bookmark (⌘-D); type a clever name. In future, you'll be able to return to that spot by choosing its name from the Bookmarks menu.

These remain living, editable entities even after the document is saved and re-opened. These are full-blown Acrobat annotations; they'll show up when your PDF document is opened by Acrobat Reader or even on Windows PCs.

- Turn smoothing on or off to improve readability. To find the on/off switch, choose Preview→Preferences, and click the PDF tab. Turn on "Smooth line art and text." (Though antialiased text generally looks great, it's sometimes easier to read very small type with antialiasing turned off. It's a little jagged, but clearer nonetheless.)

- To find a word or phrase somewhere in a PDF document, press ⌘-F (or choose Edit→Find→Find) to open the Find box—or just type into the ⚲ box at the top of the Sidebar, if it's open. Proceed as shown in Figure 11-19.

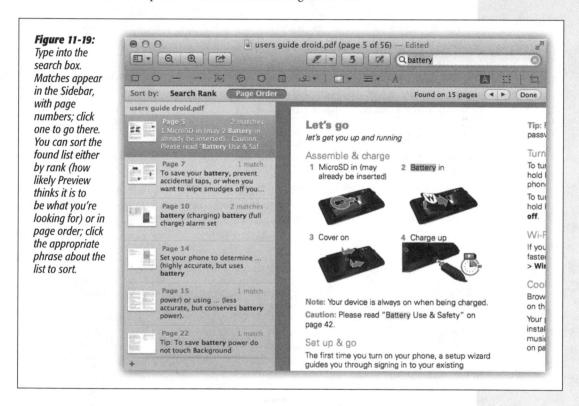

Figure 11-19:
Type into the search box. Matches appear in the Sidebar, with page numbers; click one to go there. You can sort the found list either by rank (how likely Preview thinks it is to be what you're looking for) or in page order; click the appropriate phrase about the list to sort.

The search results show a snippet of the actual text surrounding each "find," along with the number of matches per page, and even a thumbnail of the page itself. It's all about context, baby.

- If you want to copy material out of a PDF document—for pasting into a word processor, for example, where you can edit it—click the Text tool (the letter A on the toolbar) or choose Tools→Text Tool. Now you can drag through some text (and even graphics) and then choose Edit→Copy, just as though the PDF document were a Web page. You can even drag across page boundaries.

Tip: Ordinarily, dragging across text selects the text from one edge of the page to the other, even if the PDF document is laid out in columns. But Preview is a bit smarter. It can tell if you're trying to get the text in only one column and highlights just that part automatically.

- You can save a single page from a PDF as a TIFF file to use it in other graphics, word processing, or page layout programs that might not directly recognize PDF.

To extract a page, use the usual File→Export command, making sure to choose the new file format from the pop-up menu. (If you choose a format like Photoshop or JPEG, Preview converts only the currently selected page of your PDF document. That's because there's no such thing as a multipage Photoshop or JPEG graphic. But you already knew that.)

Tip: In Mountain Lion, you can also scan a new page directly into an open PDF document. Just choose File→Import from Scanner.

- Add keywords to a graphic or PDF (choose Tools→Show Inspector, click the ⌕ tab, click the **+** button). Later, you'll be able to call up these documents with a quick Spotlight search for those details.

Annotations

You can type notes (in a box or a bubble), add clickable links (to Web addresses or other spots in the document), or use circles, arrows, rectangles, strikethrough, underlining, or colored highlighting to draw your PDF eaders' attention to certain sections. (You can dress up photos this way, too.) The trick is to open the Edit toolbar, as shown in Figure 11-20.

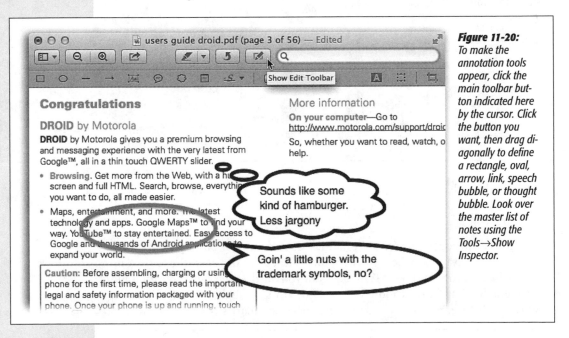

Figure 11-20:
To make the annotation tools appear, click the main toolbar button indicated here by the cursor. Click the button you want, then drag diagonally to define a rectangle, oval, arrow, link, speech bubble, or thought bubble. Look over the master list of notes using the Tools→Show Inspector.

Once you've made an annotation, you can drag it around, drag its control dots to change its shape, edit the text inside it, and so on.

Later, you can view a tidy list of all such annotations by choosing View→Highlighting and Notes.

Tip: On the Highlights and Notes panel, Preview ordinarily displays each text note with your name and the date. If you'd rather not have that info added, choose Preview→Preferences, click PDF, and then turn off "Add name to annotations.

Signing PDF Documents with Your Real Signature

Of OS X's 47,000 features, very few are quite as slick or useful as the PDF signature option. It lets your Mac *take a picture* of your actual written signature, which Preview then stores so that you can slap it into the PDF documents that will come through your life.

The first step is to teach Preview what your signature looks like. To do that, sign your name on a piece of plain white paper, using black ink. On the Edit toolbar, click the Signature pop-up menu, _S_, and choose Create Signature from Built-in Camera. (You'll see your actual camera name, like iSight Camera or FaceTime HD Camera. And if you don't see the Edit toolbar, which is shown in Figure 11-19, choose View→Show Edit Toolbar.) Now proceed as shown in Figure 11-21.

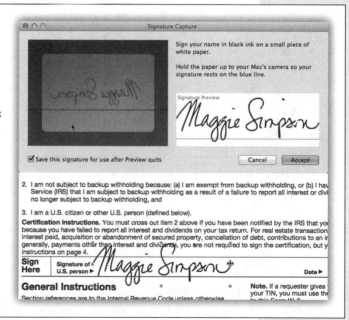

Figure 11-21:
Hold up your written signature page in front of your Mac's camera. Make sure it's big enough to fill the box on the left side—never mind that it appears backwards—and position it so that it sits on the blue line, as shown here. After a moment, your isolated, beautifully photographed signature appears in the Preview box.

When the positioning looks good, click Accept. You've just stored your signature. (You have to do this only once—per signature, anyway.)

When the time comes to sign a document, make the Edit toolbar visible. From the *S* pop-up menu, choose the signature's name. (Preview can store more than one signature; that's why this step is necessary.)

Now just click the document where you want the signature to appear. If there's a line you're supposed to sign on (such as a "Sign here" line), Preview is smart enough to shrink your scanned signature so that it fits on the line. Nice, huh?

You can delete signatures (and add new ones), if you like, using the Manage Signatures dialog box. Choose Manage Signatures from the *S* pop-up menu on the Edit toolbar.

Fill in PDF Forms

Here's a new Mountain Lion feature that could save a lot of trees: fill-innable PDF forms.

Lots and lots of PDF documents are forms that you're supposed to fill out—from the IRS tax forms to school permission slips. Preview is smart enough to recognize boxes to fill in, lines to type on, and checkboxes to click, meaning that you don't have to print, fill out, and then scan these things anymore. And it manages to find those lines, text boxes, and checkboxes on *any* PDF document, not just those that were originally designed to be filled in by PDF form-filling software. See Figure 11-22.

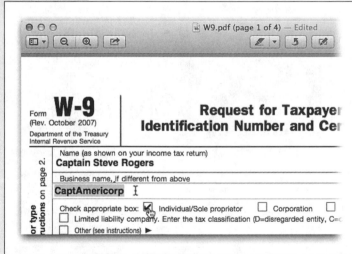

Figure 11-22:
When you fill in a form, the cursor changes automatically into an insertion point when it detects a box or a line that you can fill in. And it turns into a pointing-finger icon when it's over a checkbox, as shown here. Click to put an X in that box; click again to remove the X. It's hours of fun for the whole family!

When you're finished, save the document as you would any other. Amazingly, you'll be able to edit your responses when you open the PDF document again later.

The Toolbar

There's a lot you can do with Preview's toolbar. You can customize it (by choosing View→Customize Toolbar), rearrange its icons (by ⌘-dragging them sideways), and remove icons (by ⌘-dragging them downward).

Reminders

This Mountain Lion's marquee new program gets its own section in Chapter 10.

QuickTime Player

There's a lot to say about QuickTime player, but it's all in Chapter 16.

Safari

The secrets of Apple's Web browser are revealed in Chapter 19.

Stickies

Stickies creates virtual Post-it notes that you can stick anywhere on your screen—a triumphant software answer to the thousands of people who stick notes on the edges of their actual monitors. Like the Stickies widget in Dashboard, you can open this program with a keystroke (highlight some text, and then press Shift-⌘-Y)—but the program is a lot more powerful than the widget.

You can use Stickies to type quick notes and to-do items, paste in Web addresses or phone numbers you need to remember, or store any other little scraps and snippets of text you come across. Your electronic Post-it notes show up whenever the Stickies program is running (Figure 11-23).

Creating Sticky Notes

The first time you launch Stickies, a few sample notes appear automatically, describing some of the program's features. You can quickly dispose of each sample by clicking the

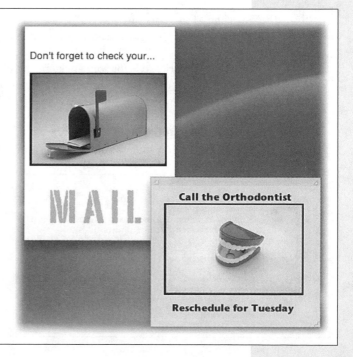

Figure 11-23:
In the old days of the Mac, the notes you created with Stickies were text-only, single-font deals. Today, however, you can use a mix of fonts, text colors, and styles within each note. You can even paste in graphics, sounds, and movies (like PICT, GIF, JPEG, QuickTime, AIFF, whole PDF files, and so on), creating the world's most elaborate reminders and to-do lists.

close button in the upper-left corner of each note or by choosing File→Close (⌘-W). Each time you close a note, a dialog box asks if you want to save it. If you click Don't Save (or press ⌘-D), the note disappears permanently.

To create a new note, choose File→New Note (⌘-N). Then start typing or:

- Drag text in from any other program. Or drag text clippings from the desktop directly into your note. You can also drag a graphics file into a note to add a picture. You can even drag a sound or movie in.

- Drag the icon of a PDF file into a note. (Stickies can even accommodate multipage PDF files. At first, you see only the first page, but the scroll bar reveals the rest.)

- Choose File→Import and select any plain text file or RTF (Rich Text Format) document to bring it into a note.

- Drag URLs into a note directly from a Web browser's address bar.

Tip: If one particular note contains your most important information—your to-do list, say—you can force it to remain in front of all other windows, even if Stickies itself gets shunted to the background. Just click the note, and then choose Note→Floating Window.

- In TextEdit, Mail, Pages, Safari, Messages, Stickies itself, and other standard Apple programs, you can select a chunk of text and then choose Make New Sticky Note from the program's Services menu, or press Shift-⌘-Y. This command launches Stickies, creates a new note, and fills it with your selected text—all in one step.

Note: All your notes are stored in a file called *StickiesDatabase*, located in your Home→Library folder. You're free to copy it, pass it along, and so on, just as you would any file.

Have a favorite style for your sticky notes? First create a new note, choosing the color and text style you like and setting it to the size you prefer. Then choose Note→Use as Default. All new notes you create now appear in the size, font, and color you've chosen.

Growing and Shrinking Notes

Stickies includes a few built-in tricks for managing a deskful of notes:

Figure 11-24:
If the first line of text gets truncated, as in the third note shown here, you can tug the right corner of the note and drag it wider without de-miniaturizing it.

Pick up theater tickets!

Compliment Brooks on his tie

Don't forget to check your...

Return "Sgt. Bilko" to Blockbuster

Ideas for next week's offsite

- There's a small resize handle on the lower-right corner of each note. Drag it to make notes larger or smaller onscreen.

- Use the small triangle in the upper-right corner of each note to zoom and shrink note windows with a single click. The first click expands a note nearly to full-screen size. Another click pops the note back down to normal size.

- The best option: Double-click anywhere along the dark strip at the top of each note to collapse it into a compact one-line mininote, as shown in Figure 11-24. You also can collapse a selected note by choosing Window→Collapse (⌘-M).

Tip: The most efficient way to use Stickies is to keep the notes in their collapsed state, as shown in Figure 10-24. When a note is collapsed, the first line of text shows up in tiny type in the collapsed title bar of the note, so you don't have to expand the note to remember what's in it. Plenty of notes can be summed up in a couple of words ("Pick up dry cleaning," "Call Mom"), so you may even be able to leave your notes this way.

Formatting Notes

Stickies has word processor-like commands for creating designer sticky notes, with any combination of fonts, colors, and styles (explore the Font menu). You can also choose from six background colors from the Color menu.

Saving Sticky Notes

The notes you create in Stickies last only as long as you keep them open. If you close a note to get it out of the way (and click Don't Save in the confirmation box), it vanishes permanently.

If you want to preserve the information you've stuffed into your notes in a more permanent form, use File→Export Text to save each note as a standalone TextEdit document. When you use the Export Text command, you have the following options:

- **Plain Text.** This option saves your note as a plain text file, with neither formatting nor pictures.

- **RTF.** RTF stands for Rich Text Format, a special exchange format that preserves most formatting, including font, style, and color choices. You can open the resulting RTF file in just about any word processor with all your formatting still intact.

- **RTFD.** RTFD, a strange and powerful variant of RTF, is a Rich Text Format document *with attachments*. How do you "attach" items to an RTFD file? Drag the icon of an actual application (Preview, Calculator, or whatever) or a multipage PDF file, into a sticky note. The icon for the program or document appears in the note, but double-clicking the icon doesn't do anything. When you export the note as an RTFD file, the result is a TextEdit document that has embedded within it the *entire* program or document you dragged in. The program icon appears just as it did in the sticky note, but if you double-click the icon, the program actually opens. (For more about RTFD files, see the box on page 447.)

You can also paste a graphic into your sticky note. When you export the note as an RTFD document, the resulting *package* file includes a graphics file of the format you pasted.

System Preferences

This program opens the door to the nerve center of OS X's various user preferences, settings, and options. Chapter 9 covers every option in detail.

TextEdit

TextEdit is a basic word processor—but it's not nearly as basic as people think it is. You can create real documents with real formatting, using style sheets, colors, automatic numbering and bullets, tables, and customized line spacing. You can even open, edit, and create Microsoft Word documents. If you had to, you could write a children's book in TextEdit, and it would look pretty decent.

Better yet, TextEdit (Figure 11-25) is now a showcase for Mountain Lion's iPaddish features, like full-screen mode, Autosave, and Versions (see Chapter 5). It can also save your files into your iCloud locker, as described on page 255.

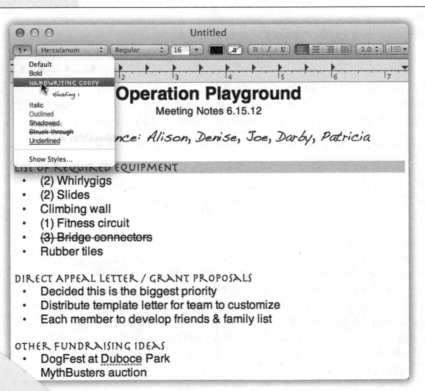

Figure 11-25:
The text ruler gives you control over tab stops, paragraph justification, and so on. Pressing ⌘-R makes it appear and disappear. On the toolbar, the Style pop-up menu lists canned sets of character and paragraph formatting, so you can apply them consistently through-out a document.

And TextEdit works with OS X's long list of built-in text-editing features: smart links, smart quotes, smart dashes, smart copy/paste, abbreviation expansion, auto–typo correction, data detectors, and so on. They're all described in Chapter 6.

Tip: In Mountain Lion, for the first time, you can magnify the type size of a TextEdit document just the way you do on an iPhone or an iPad: by pinching or spreading. That is, spread two fingers on your trackpad to enlarge the type, or pinch on the trackpad to shrink it. Best. Tip. Ever.

TextEdit's Two Personalities

The one confusing aspect of TextEdit is that it's both a *plain text editor* (no formatting; globally compatible) and a true *word processor* (fonts, sizes, styles; compatible with other word processors). Here's the scheme:

- You can change a plain text document to a formatted one by choosing Format→ Make Rich Text. The ruler appears automatically to remind you that a new world of formatting has just become available.

- Conversely, you can change a formatted document (a Word file you've opened, for example) to a plain text document by choosing Format→Make Plain Text. An alert message appears to point out that you're about to lose all formatting.

- If you know what kind of document you *always* want to open, go to the TextEdit→ Preferences dialog box; on the New Document tab, select Rich Text or Plain Text. That's what you'll get each time you choose File→New.

UP TO SPEED

The Deal with Microsoft Word

Yes, it's true: Humble TextEdit can open and create Microsoft Word documents! Your savings: the $400 price of Microsoft Office!

Well, sort of.

When you open a Microsoft Word document in TextEdit, most of the formatting comes through alive: bold, italic, font choices, colors, line spacing, alignment, and so on. Even very basic tables make it into TextEdit, although with different column widths.

A lot of Word-specific formatting does not survive crossing the chasm, however: borders, style sheets, footnotes, and the like. Bullets and numbered lists don't make it, either, even though TextEdit can create its own versions of these. And TextEdit doesn't recognize the comments and tracked changes your collaborators might use to mark up your manuscript.

Saving a new TextEdit document as a Word document is a better bet, because Word understands the many kinds of formatting that TextEdit can produce—including bullets, numbering, and tables. (You can create a Word file the first time you save it from TextEdit, or you can convert a document into Word format later by choosing File→Duplicate, then File→Save.)

The one disappointment is that Word doesn't recognize any style sheets you've set up in TextEdit. The formatting applied by those style names survives—just not the style names themselves.

Even so, a built-in Word-document editor is a huge, huge step for the Mac operating system. It means that in many cases, you can be a first-class citizen on the playing field of American business. Nobody ever needs to know that you're (a) using a Mac, and (b) not using the real Microsoft Word.

Tip: Here's also where you can turn on smart links, smart quotes, smart dashes, and the other smart text-processing features described in Chapter 6.

Working in TextEdit

As you begin typing, all the usual word processing rules apply, with a few twists:

- Choose bold, italic, and font sizes using the new formatting toolbar. (You can still use the commands in the Format menu.) You can even create subscripts or super-scripts, change the color of the text (Format→Font→Show Colors), and so on.

- Common paragraph-alignment options—Align Left, Align Right, Center, Justify— are all available as toolbar buttons and also reside in the Format→Text submenu. Adjust the line spacing (single, double, or any fraction or multiple) using the Spacing pop-up menu in the toolbar.

- The toolbar also offers automatic bulleting and numbering of paragraphs. Just choose the numbering style you prefer from the pop-up menu at the right end of the toolbar.

- You can select several nonadjacent bits of text *simultaneously.* To pull this off, highlight your first piece of text by dragging, and then press ⌘ as you use the mouse to select more text. Bingo: You've highlighted two separate chunks of text.

 When you're done selecting bits of text here and there, you can operate on them en masse. For example, you can make them all bold or italic in one fell swoop. You can even use the Cut, Copy, and Paste commands, as described in the next section. When you cut or copy, the command acts upon all your selections at once.

 You can also drag any *one* of the highlighted portions to a new area, confident that the other chunks will come along for the ride. All the selected areas wind up consolidated in their new location.

Tip: If you *Option*-drag one of the highlighted bits, you *copy* all selected chunks, leaving the originals in place.

- Similarly, you can use the Find command. To do that, choose Edit→Find→Find (or just press ⌘-F). Fill in the search box; the sought-for term appears highlighted everywhere in your document at once. (You can also search and *replace,* using the other commands in the Edit→Find submenu.)

- If you Option-drag vertically, you can freely select an arbitrary column of text (not necessarily the entire page width). This technique is very useful when you want to select only one column in a multicolumn layout, or when you want to select the numbers in a list and format them all at once.

Style Sheets

A *style* is a prepackaged collection of formatting attributes that you can apply and reapply with a click of the mouse (bold, 24-point Optima, double-spaced, centered, for instance). You can create as many styles as you need: chapter headings, sidebar

styles, and so on. You end up with a collection of custom-tailored styles for each of the repeating elements of your document.

Once you've created your styles, you can apply them as you need them, safe in the knowledge that they'll be consistent throughout the document. During the editing process, if you notice that you accidentally styled a *headline* using the *Subhead* style, you can fix the problem by simply reapplying the correct style.

Note: Unlike a real word processor, TextEdit doesn't let you *change* a style's formatting and thereby update every occurrence of it. Fortunately, you *can* search for all occurrences of a style and change them all simultaneously (see the next page).

- **Creating a named style.** To create a style, format some text so it looks the way you like it, complete with font, color, line spacing, tab settings, and so on.

 Then, from the ¶ pop-up menu at the left end of the toolbar, choose Show Styles (Figure 11-26, top). Click Add to Favorites, type a name for the style, turn on both checkboxes (Figure 11-26, bottom), and then click Add.

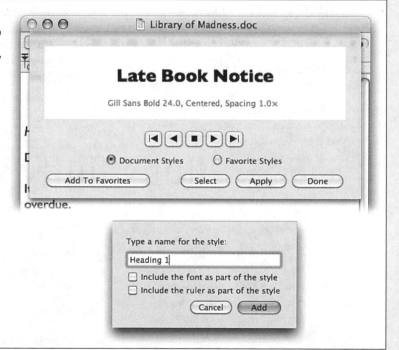

Figure 11-26:
Top: Highlight the text you want to format. Then, from the ¶ pop-up menu in the toolbar, choose Show Styles. With each click of the ▶ button, you summon a snippet of the next chunk of formatting. When you find one you like, you can either click Apply (to zap the highlighted text into submission) or Add To Favorites (to reuse this canned style later). In the latter case, you can give the new style a name (bottom).

- **Applying a style.** Later, when you want to reuse the formatting you set up, highlight some text and then choose the appropriate name from the ¶ pop-up menu. TextEdit applies the formatting immediately.

Tip: If you simply click inside a paragraph, applying a style affects only paragraph attributes, like line spacing, tab stops, and alignment. If you highlight a random chunk of text instead, applying a style affects only character attributes, like the font and type size. If you highlight an entire paragraph, however, both text and paragraph formatting appear.

- **Deleting a style.** To delete a superfluous style, choose Show Styles from the ¶ pop-up menu on the toolbar. Click the Favorite Styles button, choose the unwanted style's name from the pop-up menu, and then click Remove From Favorites. (Deleting a style doesn't affect any formatting that's already in your document; it just removes the name from the Styles menu.)

- **Replacing all occurrences.** You can highlight every occurrence of a certain style at once—and then change, copy, or delete them all at once.

Advanced Typography in TextEdit

If you just sprayed your coffee upon reading the heading of this sidebar, you're forgiven. Advanced typography in TextEdit? Isn't that a little bit like saying, "advanced page layout in Notepad"?

Not at all. TextEdit is a gleaming showcase for OS X's typographical smarts.

Most of the commands in the Format→Font submenu should be familiar to you: Bold, Italic, Underline, and so on. But a few were once found only in expensive page-layout programs like InDesign and QuarkXPress. For example:

Kern. Use these commands, such as Tighten and Loosen, to nudge the letters of the selected text closer together or farther apart–an especially useful feature when you're fiddling with headlines and headings.

There are no controls to set how much you want to kern the text, but you can apply these commands repeatedly to the same text selection to intensify them. If you want your text to be very tight, for example, just keep choosing the Tighten command. The characters creep closer and closer together until they crash into one another.

Ligature. Ligatures are letter pairs, such as fl and ff, that, in fancy typesetting, are often conjoined into special combi-

nation characters, as shown here. If you choose Format→ Font→Ligature→Use Default (or Use All), then TextEdit displays these letter pairs with the appropriate ligatures. (This works only if the font you're using has those ligatures built into it. New York, Charcoal, Apple Chancery, and all Adobe Expert fonts do, for example, but many other fonts don't.)

Baseline. The baseline is the imaginary "floor" for text characters in a line of type. You can push text above this line or sink it below the baseline using the Raise and Lower commands in the Baseline submenu. The Superscript and Subscript commands, meanwhile, shift characters far above or below the baseline, so you can write stuff like "H_2O."

Character Shape. In a few fonts, such as Adobe Expert fonts, this submenu offers a choice between Traditional Form and specialized type treatments like Small Caps.

Copy Style/Paste Style. If mastering the Styles pop-up menu (described on the next page) is too much effort, these commands offer another way to copy and paste just the font formatting to other text—the font, color, style, and size, but none of the actual text or paragraph attributes, such as alignment.

To make this work, choose Show Styles from the ¶ pop-up menu. Choose the style you want to work on. (If "Document styles" is selected, click the ▶ button to page through the styles; if "Favorite styles" is selected, choose from the pop-up menu.) Then click Select.

In the little details sheet that appears, click the options you want, and then click Select. TextEdit highlights every occurrence of that style in the entire document (or selection). At this point, you can use any of the usual text-formatting controls to modify them all simultaneously.

- **Formatting by example.** In TextEdit, you can also use Option-⌘-C and Option-⌘-V (Format→Font→Copy Style and Format→Font→Paste Style) to grab formatting from one place in your document and reuse it elsewhere. (Of course, you can't apply styles in text-only documents.)

Tables

Tables can make life a heck of a lot easier when you want to create a resumé, agenda, program booklet, list, multiple-choice test, Web page, or another document where numbers, words, and phrases must be aligned across the page. In the bad old days, people did it by pressing the Tab key to line up columns—a technique that turned into a nightmare as soon as you tried to add or delete text. But using a word processor's *table* feature is light-years easier and more flexible, because each row of a table expands to contain whatever you put into it. Everything else in its row remains aligned.

Tip: Tables are sometimes used for designing Web pages. Even though you can't see the table outlines, many a Web page is filled with columns of text that are aligned invisibly by tables. And now that TextEdit can save your work as an HTML document, it's suddenly a viable candidate for designing basic Web pages.

GEM IN THE ROUGH

Files Within Files Within Files

It's no surprise that you can include formatted text and pictures in a TextEdit document, but here's a shocker: You can also embed an entire program or document within a TextEdit file.

Try this experiment: Create a new TextEdit document in Rich Text mode. Drag a couple of program icons into the TextEdit document. Do the same with some documents that were created using native OS X programs (another TextEdit document, for example).

When you save the file, OS X saves embedded copies of the applications and documents you dragged into the TextEdit document itself. (The TextEdit file is saved in RTFD, a Rich Text Format document with attachments.)

Once you've saved the file, you can double-click any of the icons in it to launch the embedded items. In a single TextEdit document, you could launch the Chess, DVD Player, and Mail programs—all right from within the file.

To make things even wilder, it's possible to drag a TextEdit file containing embedded items into another TextEdit file, saving a file within a file within a file.

One important point: The double-clickable icons you create in TextEdit using this method are not aliases or links to your original documents and programs. They're actual, full copies. If you embed a 100 MB program into a TextEdit document, you'll end up with a 100 MB TextEdit file!

• **Create a table** by choosing Format→Table. The floating Table palette appears (Figure 11-27). Use it to specify how many rows and columns you want. The placeholder table in your document adjusts itself in real time.

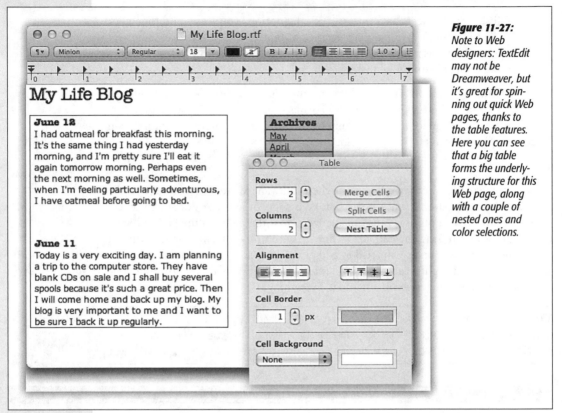

Figure 11-27:
Note to Web designers: TextEdit may not be Dreamweaver, but it's great for spinning out quick Web pages, thanks to the table features. Here you can see that a big table forms the underlying structure for this Web page, along with a couple of nested ones and color selections.

• **Format the table** using the other controls in the Table palette. The Alignment controls let you specify how the text in the table cells hugs its border. Cell Border controls the thickness of the line around the selected cells' borders (or, if you enter 0, makes the table walls invisible). The color swatch next to Cell Border specifies the color of the solid lines. The Cell Background controls let you color in the table cells with colors of your choice. (Choose Color Fill from the pop-up menu, and then click the color swatch.) This is an especially valuable option for Web designers.

• **Adjust the rows and columns** by dragging the cell borders.

• **Merge two selected cells** by clicking Merge Cells in the Table palette. Once you've done that, you can use the Split Cell button to split them apart again. (Split Cell doesn't work except in cells you've previously merged.)

- **Nest one table inside a cell of another** by clicking in the cell and then clicking Nest Table. Change the numbers in the Rows and Columns boxes to set up its dimensions (Figure 11-27).

TextEdit as Web Designer

The Table palette isn't the only clue that Apple intends TextEdit to be a quick-and-dirty Web page design program. Consider these other tools:

- You can easily add graphics to the page by dragging or pasting them into a document. The program understands TIFF, PICT, JPEG, and GIF formats.

- You can add Web-style hyperlinks by highlighting "Click here" (or whatever the link says), choosing Edit→Add Link, and then entering the Web address in the resulting dialog box. Or just drag a link in from Safari, Mail, or another program. (To edit the link later, Control-click it, and then choose Edit Link.)

Tip: Of course, you can also have TextEdit convert typed links into clickable ones *automatically* as you type them. That's the purpose of the Smart Links option in TextEdit→Preferences.

- To save a brand-new document as an HTML (Web page) file, choose File→Save; from the File Format pop-up menu, choose Web Page. (To save an existing TextEdit document as an HTML file, choose File→Duplicate, then File→Save; choose Web Page from the pop-up menu.)

- Don't miss the HTML options in TextEdit→Preferences. On the Open and Save tab, you can specify what kind of HTML document you want to produce, what cascading style sheets (CSS) setting you want, and whether or not you want TextEdit to include code to preserve blank areas (white space) in your layout.

Tip: When you open a Web page document—that is, an HTML document—TextEdit is faced with a quandary. Should it open up the page as though it's a Web page, interpreting the HTML code as though it's a browser? Or should it reveal the underlying HTML code itself?

Actually, that's up to you. When you choose File→Open, turn on "Ignore rich text commands" to make the document open up as HTML code. (To make this change permanent, turn on the same checkbox on the Open and Save pane of the TextEdit→Preferences dialog box.)

The TextEdit Preferences

Most of the settings in the TextEdit Preferences→New Document pane have no effect on documents that are *already* open—only on documents you open or create from now on. Most of the settings are self-explanatory; nonetheless, handy explanatory balloons appear if you point to an option without clicking. Here are a few settings that may not be immediately clear:

- **Font.** If Helvetica 12 doesn't float your boat, you can change TextEdit's starting font. In fact, you can set *two* default fonts—one for Rich Text documents and another one for Plain Text files.

Note: By definition, plain text files don't have any formatting. So whatever font you choose here for plain text files is for your viewing pleasure only. If you plan to send the file to anyone else, remember that the font choice won't be saved with the document.

- **Window Size.** These settings have no effect unless you're in Wrap to Window mode, in which the text rewraps to fit the window width, as opposed to Wrap to Page mode. (You choose these options from TextEdit's Format menu.)

 If you *are* in Wrap to Window mode, then these dimensions determine the size of the window that appears each time you create a new TextEdit document.

- **Properties.** These boxes—Author, Company, and Copyright—are some of the tags that Spotlight inspects when it searches your Mac. If you'd like to be able to round up your documents by these characteristics, fill them in here to specify the information you want to use for *most* documents. (To fill them in differently for individual documents, choose File→Show Properties instead.)

- **Options.** These are the on/off switches for the various typing aids described in Chapter 6: smart quotes, data detectors, text replacement, and so on.

TextEdit's Other Writing Tools

TextEdit includes a few other very useful document-editing tools:

- **Allow Hyphenation.** When you select this command from the Format menu, TextEdit breaks up words by syllable and inserts hyphens when necessary in order to create more visually pleasing line breaks.

Tip: It's especially important to turn this feature on if your paragraph alignment is set to Justify, or if you create narrow columns of text. If hyphenation is turned off, TextEdit won't break up long words at the end of a line—even if it leaves big, ugly gaps between words.

- **Prevent Editing.** When you turn this option on (again, in the Format menu), you're locked out. You can select and copy text to your heart's content, but you can't change anything. Prevent Editing mode can be useful if you want to prevent yourself from making accidental changes to a file, but it's not much of a security feature. (All anyone has to do is choose Format→Allow Editing to regain full editing privileges.)

- **Spelling and Grammar.** These aren't TextEdit features; they're system-wide OS X features, and they're described in Chapter 6.

Time Machine

This marquee feature of OS X is described in Chapter 6.

Utilities: Your OS X Toolbox

The Utilities folder (inside your Applications folder) is home to another batch of freebies: a couple of dozen tools for monitoring, tuning, tweaking, and troubleshooting your Mac.

The truth is, you're likely to use only about six of these utilities. The rest are very specialized gizmos primarily of interest to network administrators or Unix geeks who are obsessed with knowing what kind of computer-code gibberish is going on behind the scenes.

Tip: Even so, Apple obviously noticed that as the sophistication of OS X fans grows, more people open the Utilities folder more often. That's why there's a menu command and a keystroke that can take you there. In the Finder, choose Go→Utilities (Shift-⌘-U).

Activity Monitor

Activity Monitor is designed to let the technologically savvy Mac fan see how much of the Mac's available power is being tapped at any given moment.

The Processes table

Even when you're only running a program or two on your Mac, dozens of computational tasks (*processes*) are going on in the background. The top half of the dialog box, which looks like a table, shows you all the different processes—visible and invisible—that your Mac is handling at the moment.

Check out how many items appear in the Process list, even when you're just staring at the desktop. It's awesome to see just how busy your Mac is! Some are easily recognizable programs (such as Finder), while others are background system-level operations you don't normally see. For each item, you can see the percentage of the CPU being used, who's using it (either your account name, someone else's, or *root*, meaning the Mac itself), whether or not it's been written as a 64-bit app, and how much memory it's using.

Or use the pop-up menu above the list to see views like these:

- **All Processes.** This is the complete list of running processes; you'll notice that the vast majority are little Unix applications you never even knew you had.

- **All Processes, Hierarchically.** In Unix, one process launches another, creating a tree-like hierarchy. The big daddy of them all is the process called *launchd*. Here and there, you'll see some other interesting relationships: For example, the Dock launches DashboardClient.

- **My Processes.** This list shows only the programs that pertain to *your* world, your login. There are still plenty of unfamiliar items, but they're all running to serve *your* account.

- **System Processes.** These are the processes run by *root*—that is, opened by OS X itself.

- **Other User Processes.** Here's a list of all *other* processes—"owned" by neither root nor you. Here you might see the processes being run by another account holder, for example (using Fast User Switching), or people who have connected to this Mac from across a network or the Internet.

- **Active Processes, Inactive Processes.** Active processes are the ones that are actually doing something right now; inactive are the ones that are sitting there, waiting for a signal (like a keypress or a mouse click).

- **Windowed Processes.** Now *this* is probably what you were expecting: a list of actual programs with actual English names, like Activity Monitor, Finder, Safari, and Mail. These are the only ones running in actual windows, the only ones that are *visible*.

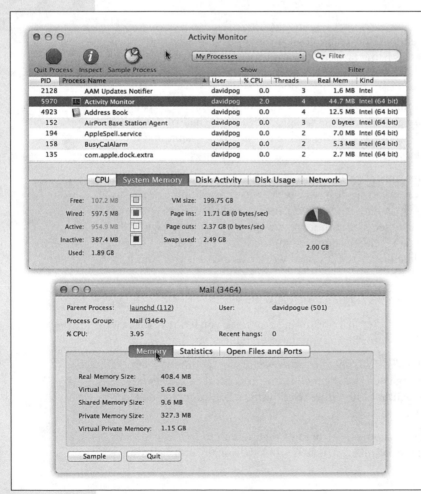

Figure 11-28:
The many faces of Activity Monitor.

Top: It can be a graph of your processor (CPU) activity, your RAM usage at the moment, your disk capacity, and so on. For most people, only the processes listed here with tiny icons beside their names are actual windowed programs—those with icons in the Finder, the ones you actually interact with.

Don't miss the top-left Quit Process button. It's a convenient way to jettison a locked-up program when all else fails.

Bottom: If you double-click a process's name, you get a two- or three-tab dialog box that offers stunningly complete reams of data (mostly of interest only to programmers) about what that program is up to. (The Open Files and Ports tab, for example, shows you how many files that program has opened, often invisibly.)

The System monitor tabs

At the bottom of Activity Monitor, you're offered five tabs that reveal intimate details about your Mac and its behind-the-scenes efforts (Figure 11-28):

- **CPU.** As you go about your usual Mac business, opening a few programs, playing QuickTime movies, playing a game, and so on, you can see the CPU graphs rise and fall, depending on how busy you're keeping the CPU. You see a different bar for each of your Mac's cores (independent sub-chips on your processor), so you can see how efficiently OS X is distributing the work among them.

Tip: You may also want to watch this graph right in your Dock (choose View→Dock Icon→Show CPU Usage) or in a bar at the edge of your screen (choose Window→Floating CPU Window→Horizontally).

Finally, there's the View→Show CPU History command. It makes a resizable, real-time monitor window float on top of all your other programs, so you can't miss it.

- **System Memory.** Here's a colorful graph that reveals the state of your Mac's RAM at the moment.

 The number below the graph shows how much memory is installed in your Mac. If, when your Mac is running a typical complement of programs, the Wired number plus the Active number nearly equals your total RAM amount, it's time to consider buying more memory. You're suffocating your Mac.

- **Disk Activity.** Even when you're not opening or saving a file, your Mac's hard drive is frequently hard at work, shuffling chunks of program code into and out of memory, for example. Here's where the savvy technician can see exactly how frantic the disk is at the moment.

- **Disk Usage.** This little graph offers one of the quickest ways to check out how full your hard drive is. (If you have more than one drive—say, a flash drive, tape-backup drive, or whatever—choose another drive's name from the pop-up menu.)

- **Network.** Keep an eye on how much data is shooting across your office network with this handy EKG-ish graph.

AirPort Utility

You use the AirPort Utility to set up and manage AirPort base stations (Apple's wireless WiFi networking routers).

If you click Continue, it presents a series of screens, posing one question at a time: what you want to name the network, what password you want for it, and so on. Once you've followed the steps and answered the questions, your AirPort hardware will be properly configured and ready to use.

AppleScript Editor

This little program, formerly called Script Editor, is where you can type up your own *AppleScripts,* as described at the end of Chapter 7.

Audio MIDI Setup

This program has a split personality; its name is a description of its two halves:

- **Audio.** When you first open Audio MIDI Setup, you see a complete summary of the audio inputs and outputs available on your Mac right now. It's a lot like the Sound pane of System Preferences, but with a lot more geeky detail. Here, for example, you can specify the recording level for your Mac's microphone, or even change the audio quality it records.

 For most people, this is all meaningless, because most Macs have only one input (the microphone) and one output (the speakers). But if you're sitting in your darkened music studio, which is humming with high-tech audio gear whose software has been designed to work with this little program, you'll smile when you see this tab.

 There's even a Configure Speakers button, for those audiophilic Mac fans who've attached stereo or even surround-sound speaker systems to their Macs.

Tip: Using the ✿ menu at the bottom of the window, you can turn your various audio inputs (that is, microphones, line inputs, and so on) on or off. You can even direct your Mac's system beeps to pour forth from one set of speakers (like the one built into your Mac), and all other sound, like music, through a different set.

- **MIDI.** MIDI stands for Musical Instrument Digital Interface, a standard "language" for inter-synthesizer communication. It's available to music software companies who have written their wares to capitalize on these tools.

 When you choose Window→Show MIDI Window, you get a window that represents your recording-studio configuration. By clicking Add Device, you create a new icon that represents one of your pieces of gear. Double-click the icon to specify its make and model. Finally, by dragging lines from the "in" and "out" arrows, you teach your Mac and its MIDI software how the various components are wired together.

Bluetooth File Exchange

One of the luxuries of using a Mac that has Bluetooth is the ability to shoot files (to colleagues who own similarly clever gadgets) through the air, up to 30 feet away. Bluetooth File Exchange makes it possible, as described on page 264.

Boot Camp Assistant

This program helps you create (or destroy) a partition of your hard drive to hold a copy of Microsoft Windows. Details in Chapter 8.

ColorSync Utility

If you use ColorSync, then you probably know already that this utility is for people in the high-end color printing business. Its tabs include these two:

- **Profile First Aid.** This tab performs a fairly esoteric task: repairing ColorSync profiles that may be "broken" because they don't strictly conform to the *ICC profile* specifications. (ICC [International Color Consortium] profiles are part of Apple's ColorSync color management system.) If a profile for your specific monitor or

printer doesn't appear in the Profiles tab of this program when it should, Profile First Aid is the tool you need to fix it.

- **Profiles.** This tab lets you review all the ColorSync profiles installed on your system. The area on the right side of the window displays information about each ColorSync profile you select from the list on the left.

The **other tabs** are described on page 607.

Console

Console is a viewer for all of OS X's logs—the behind-the-scenes, internal Unix record of your Mac's activities.

Opening the Console log is a bit like stepping into an operating room during a complex surgery: You're exposed to stuff the average person just isn't supposed to see. (Typical Console entries: "kCGErrorCannotComplete" or "doGetDisplayTransferBy-Table.") You can adjust the font and word wrapping using Console's Font menu, but the truth is that the phrase "CGXGetWindowType: Invalid window -1" looks ugly in just about *any* font!

Console isn't useless, however. These messages can be of significant value to programmers who are debugging software or troubleshooting a messy problem, or, occasionally, to someone you've called for tech support.

For example, your *crash logs* are detailed technical descriptions of what went wrong when various programs crashed, and what was stored in memory at the time.

Unfortunately, there's not much plain English here to help you understand the crash, or how to avoid it in the future. Most of it runs along the lines of "Exception: EXC_BAD_ACCESS (0x0001); Codes: KERN_INVALID_ADDRESS (0x0001) at 0x2f6b657d." In other words, it's primarily for the benefit of programmers. Still, tech-support staff may occasionally ask to see the information in one of these logs.

DigitalColor Meter

DigitalColor Meter can grab the exact color value of any pixel on your screen, which can be helpful when matching colors in Web page construction or other design work. After launching the DigitalColor Meter, just point anywhere on your screen. A magnified view appears in the meter window, and the RGB (red-green-blue) color value of the pixels appears in the meter window.

Here are some tips for using the DigitalColor Meter to capture color information from your screen:

- To home in on the exact pixel (and color) you want to measure, drag the Aperture Size slider to the smallest size—one pixel.

- Press ⌘-X (View→Lock X) to freeze your cursor at its current horizontal position; you can now move it only horizontally. Or press ⌘-Y (View→Lock Y) to freeze your cursor at its current vertical position. You can also lock the cursor in both

directions. (Press the keystroke again to unlock.) The idea is to make it easier for you to snap exactly the pixel you want.

- When the Aperture Size slider is set to view more than one pixel, DigitalColor Meter measures the *average* value of the pixels being examined.

Disk Utility

This important program serves two key functions:

- It serves as OS X's own little Norton Utilities: a powerful hard drive administration tool that lets you repair, erase, format, and partition disks. You'll probably use Disk Utility most often for its *Repair Permissions* feature, which solves an uncanny number of weird little Mac glitches. But it's also worth keeping in mind in case you ever find yourself facing a serious disk problem.

- Disk Utility also creates and manages *disk images,* electronic versions of disks or folders that you can exchange electronically with other people.

The following discussion tackles the program's two personalities one at a time.

Disk Utility, the hard drive repair program

Here are some of the tasks you can perform with this half of Disk Utility:

- Repair folders, files, and programs that don't work because you supposedly don't have sufficient "access privileges." This is by far the most common use of Disk Utility, not to mention the most reliable and satisfying. Using the Repair Disk Permissions button fixes an *astonishing* range of bizarre OS X problems, from programs that won't open to menulets that freeze up the works.

- Get size and type information about any disks attached to your Mac.

- Fix disks that won't appear on your desktop or behave properly.

- Completely erase disks—including rewritable CDs and DVDs (such as CD-RW and DVD-RW discs).

- Partition a disk into multiple *volumes* (that is, subdivide a drive so that its segments appear on the desktop with separate disk icons).

Tip: Disk Utility can even create or enlarge disk partitions without requiring you to erase the entire hard drive. Details below.

- Set up a *RAID array* (a cluster of separate disks that acts as a single volume).

Note: Disk Utility can perform *some* of its magic on the startup disk—the disk that's running OS X at the moment. For example, it can check the disk for damage, fix the permissions of the disk, or even adjust its partitions.

But any other operation, like reformatting, erasing, or actually repairing the disk, still requires the Mac to start up from a different disk (an external hard drive, for example, or Mountain Lion's secret recovery partition). Otherwise, it'd be like a surgeon performing an appendectomy on himself—not a great idea.

The left Disk Utility panel lists your hard drive and any other disks in or attached to your Mac at the moment. When you click the name of your hard drive's mechanism, like "500 GB Hitachi iC25N0…" (not the "Macintosh HD" volume label below it), you see a panel with five tabs, one for each of the main Disk Utility functions:

• **First Aid.** This is the disk-repair part of Disk Utility, and it does a terrific job at fixing many disk problems. When you're troubleshooting, Disk Utility should always be your first resort.

To use it, click the icon of a disk and then click either Verify Disk (to get a report on the disk's health) or Repair Disk (which fixes whatever problems the program finds). In other words, First Aid attempts to perform the same healing effects on a sick hard drive as, say, a program like Norton Utilities.

If Disk First Aid reports that it's unable to fix the problem, *then* it's time to invest in a program like DiskWarrior (*www.alsoft.com*).

You may wind up using the Verify and Repair Disk *Permissions* buttons even more often. Their function is to straighten out problems with the invisible Unix file permissions that keep you from moving, changing, or deleting files or folders. (The occasional software installer can create problems like this.) You'd be surprised how often running one of these permission checks solves little OS X glitches.

Chapter 13 has a much more detailed discussion of permissions.

POWER USERS' CLINIC

Partition Adjustments on the Fly

You can expand, shrink, or create partitions without having to erase the whole hard drive. If you're into partitioning at all, this is a *huge* convenience.

Expanding a partition. Suppose, for example, that your main hard drive has two partitions: a main one (200 gigs) and a secondary one (50 gigs) that used to hold all your photos and movies. But you've outgrown the second partition and have moved all those photos and movies to their own external hard drive. Wouldn't it be nice to add the newly unoccupied 50 gigs to your main partition?

You can do that without having to erase the whole hard drive. (This process, however, nukes everything on the *second* partition, so make sure you're prepared to lose it all.)

Open Disk Utility. Click the name of the hard drive (for example, "Hitachi HTS541616J9SA00"—*not* "Macintosh HD"). Click Partition. You see a display like the one in Figure 11-29.

Click the second partition (or third, or whatever partition is *just after* the one you want to expand) and then click the − button below the list. Poof! It's gone.

Now you can drag the main partition's bottom edge downward (or type a new size into the Size box), expanding it into the free area. Take a deep breath, and then click Apply.

Shrinking a partition. In Figure 11-29, you can see that a portion of the first partition is lightly shaded. (It's blue in real life.) The blue represents data; you can't shrink a partition so much that it crowds out your files. You can, however, shrink the partition to eliminate empty space. Just drag the lower edge of its map chunk upward.

Creating new partitions. Anytime there's leftover space on the drive, you can create *new* partitions from it. To do that, click the **+** button, and proceed as described in Figure 11-29.

- **Erase.** Select a disk, choose a format—*always* Mac OS Extended (Journaled), un-less you're formatting a disk for use on a Windows PC—give it a name, and then click Erase to wipe a disk clean.

Tip: The Erase tab is the key to using FileVault on flash drives and other external drives, as described in Chapter 13. In other words, you can encrypt external disks so that nobody can access them without a password. The trick is to erase the drive using "Mac OS Extended (Journaled, Encrypted)" format.

- **Partition.** With the Partition tools, you can erase a hard drive in such a way that you subdivide its surface. Each chunk is represented on your screen by another hard drive icon (Figure 11-29).

Figure 11-29:
Partitioning your drive with Disk Utility no longer involves erasing it completely. Select the drive you want to partition from the list on the left, and then click the Partition tab. Click the + button for each new partition you want.

Now drag the horizontal dividers in the Volumes map to specify the relative sizes of the partitions you want to create. Assign a name and a format for each partition in the Volume Information area, and then click Apply.

There are some very good reasons *not* to partition a drive these days: A partitioned hard drive is more difficult to resurrect after a serious crash, requires more naviga-tion when you want to open a particular file, and offers no speed or safety benefits.

On the other hand, there's one very good reason *to* do it: Partitioning is the only way to use Boot Camp, described in Chapter 8. When you're using Boot Camp, your Mac is a Mac when running off of one partition, and a Windows PC when starting up from another one. (But you don't use Disk Utility in that case; use Boot Camp Assistant.)

- **RAID.** RAID stands for Redundant Array of Independent Disks and refers to a special formatting scheme in which a group of separate disks are configured to work together as one very large, very fast drive. In a RAID array, multiple disks share the job of storing data—a setup that can improve speed and reliability.

 Most Mac owners don't use or set up RAID arrays, probably because most Mac owners have only one hard drive (and Disk Utility can't make your startup disk part of a RAID array).

 But if you're using multiple hard disks—in a Mac Pro, for example—you can use Apple RAID to merge them into one giant disk. Just drag the icons of the relevant disks (or disk partitions) from the left-side list of disks into the main list (where it says, "Drag disks or volumes here to add to set"). Use the RAID Type pop-up menu to specify the RAID format you want to use. (Stripe is a popular choice for maximizing disk speed; Mirror RAID is extra safe, because it creates a perfect backup clone of your main drive.) Name your new mega-disk, and then click Create. The result is a single "disk" icon on your desktop that actually represents the combined capacity of all the RAID disks.

- **Restore.** This tab lets you make a perfect copy of a disk or a disk image, much like the popular shareware programs Carbon Copy Cloner and SuperDuper. You might find this useful when, for example, you want to make an exact copy of your old Mac's drive on your new one. You can't do that just by copying your old files and folders manually. If you try, you won't get the thousands of *invisible* files that make up OS X. If you use the Restore function, though, they'll come along for the ride.

 Start by dragging the disk or disk image you want to copy *from* into the Source box. Then drag the icon of the disk you want to copy *to* into the Destination box.

Tip: If you want to copy an online disk image onto one of your disks, you don't have to download it first. Just type its Web address into the Source field.

If you turn on Erase Destination, then Disk Utility obliterates all the data on your target disk before copying the data. If you leave this checkbox off, however, Disk Utility simply copies everything onto your destination, preserving all your old data in the process (although it replaces files that have the same names and locations as the ones you're copying).

Finally, click the Restore button. (You might need to type in an administrator password.) Restoring can take a long time for big disks, so go ahead and make yourself a cup of coffee while you're waiting.

Disk Utility, the disk-image program

Disk images are very cool. Each one is a single icon that behaves precisely like an actual disk—a flash drive or hard drive, for example—but can be distributed electronically. For example, a lot of OS X apps arrive from your Web download in disk-image form, as shown below.

Disk images are popular for software distribution for a simple reason: Each image file precisely duplicates the original master disk, complete with all the necessary files in all the right places. When a software company sends you a disk image, it ensures that you'll install the software from a disk that *exactly* matches the master disk.

As a handy bonus, you can password-protect a disk image, which is the closest OS X comes to offering the ability to password-protect an individual folder.

It's important to understand the difference between a *disk-image file* and the *mounted disk* (the one that appears when you double-click the disk image). If you flip back to page 161 and consult Figure 5-2, this distinction should be clear.

Tip: After you double-click a disk image, click Skip in the verification box that appears. If something truly got scrambled during the download, you'll know about it right away—your file won't decompress correctly, or it'll display the wrong icon, for example.

In fact, you can make Disk Utility always skip that verification business, which is a relic from the days of floppy disks. To do so, choose Disk Utility→Preferences, and turn off "Check images on locked media."

GEM IN THE ROUGH

The Sparse Image

One of the coolest Disk Utility features is also one of the most buried.

Turns out you can make a nice, hermetically sealed, password-protected disk image that starts out small but magically increases as you stuff more files into it. If the usual disk image is like a steel bucket—a fixed size forever—a sparse image is like an accordion file folder.

Choose File→New→Blank Disk Image. In the resulting dialog box, name the file you're creating (which you'll double-click to make the virtual disk appear), as well as the virtual disk itself.

From the Encryption pop-up menu, choose one of the two scrambling methods that will password-protect your disk image. Finally, from the Image Format pop-up menu—this is the key step—choose "sparse bundle disk image."

Click Create. Make up a password (type it twice); store in your Keychain, if you like (meaning you won't need to enter the password whenever you are logged into your Mac). Then click Create.

Now, on your desktop, there's a disk image file with the suffix ".sparseimage." It occupies only 26 MB on your hard drive to start with.

From the Volume Size pop-up menu, choose the maximum size this disk image will ever be. The beautiful part is that it will probably never occupy that much disk space; it starts out small and slowly expands only as necessary. But you're setting the maximum here.

Double-click it and enter your password to bring the actual virtual disk icon to your desktop. You can now start filling the disk image up with private stuff. The .sparseimage file will grow automatically to accommodate it—but only as necessary.

You can create disk images, too. Doing so can be very handy in situations like these:

- You want to create a backup of an important CD. By turning it into a disk-image file on your hard drive, you'll always have a safety copy, ready to burn back onto a *new* CD. (This is an essential practice for educational CDs that kids will be handling soon after eating peanut butter and jelly.)

- You want to replicate your entire hard drive—complete with all its files, programs, folder setups, and so on—onto a new, bigger hard drive (or a new, better Mac), using the Restore feature described earlier.

- You want to back up your entire hard drive, or maybe just a certain chunk of it, onto an iPod or another disk. (Again, you can later use the Restore function.)

- You want to send somebody else a copy of a disk via the Internet. You simply create a disk image, and then send *that*—preferably in compressed form.

Here's how to make a disk image.

- **To image-ize a disk or partition.** Click the name of the disk in the list, where you see your currently available disks. (The topmost item is the name of your *drive*, like "484.0 MB MATSHITA DVD-R" for a DVD drive or "74.5 GB Hitachi" for a hard drive. Beneath that entry, you generally see the name of the actual partition, like "Macintosh HD," or the CD's name as it appears on the screen.)

 Then choose File→New→Disk Image from [the disk or partition's name].

- **To image-ize a folder.** Choose File→New→Disk Image from Folder. In the Open dialog box, click the folder you want, and then click Image. Either way, the next dialog box (Figure 11-30) offers some fascinating options.

Figure 11-30:
These two pop-up menus let you specify (a) what kind of disk image you want, and (b) whether or not you want it password-protected. The latter option is great when you want to password-protect one folder, without bothering with your entire Home folder.

- **Image Format.** If you choose "read/write," your disk image file, when double-clicked, turns into a superb imitation of a hard drive. You can drag files and folders onto it, drag them off of it, change icons' names on it, and so on.

If you choose "read-only," however, the result behaves more like a CD. You can copy things off of it but not make any changes to it.

The "compressed" option is best if you intend to send the resulting file by email, post it for Web download, or preserve the disk image on some backup disk for a rainy day. It takes a little longer to create a simulated disk when you double-click the disk image file, but it takes up a lot less disk space than an uncompressed version.

Finally, choose "DVD/CD master" if you're copying a CD or a DVD. The resulting file is a perfect mirror of the original disc, ready for copying onto a blank CD or DVD when the time comes.

- **Encryption.** Here's an easy way to lock private files away into a vault that nobody else can open. If you choose one of these two AES encryption options (choose AES-128, if you value your time), you'll be asked to assign a password to your new image file. Nobody can open it without the password—not even you. On the other hand, if you save it into your Keychain (page 542), it's not such a disaster if you forget the password.

- **Save As.** Choose a name and location for your new image file. The name you choose here doesn't need to match the original disk or folder name.

When you click Save (or press Return), if you opted to create an encrypted image, you're asked to make up a password at this point.

Otherwise, Disk Utility now creates the image and then *mounts* it—that is, turns the image file into a simulated, yet fully functional, disk icon on your desktop.

When you're finished working with the disk, eject it as you would any disk (Control-click it and choose Eject, for example). Hang onto the .dmg disk image file itself, however. This is the file you'll need to double-click if you ever want to recreate your "simulated disk."

Turning an image into a CD

One of the other most common disk-image tasks is turning a disk image *back* into a CD or DVD—provided that your Mac has a CD or DVD burner, of course.

All you have to do is drag the .dmg file into the Disk Utility window, select it, and click the Burn icon on the toolbar (or, alternatively, Control-click the .dmg icon and choose Burn from the shortcut menu). Insert a blank CD or DVD, and then click Burn.

Grab

Grab takes pictures of your Mac's screen, for use when you're writing up instructions, illustrating a computer book, or collecting proof of some secret screen you found buried in a game. You can take pictures of the entire screen (press ⌘-Z, which for once in its life does *not* mean Undo) or capture only the contents of a rectangular selection (press Shift-⌘-A). When you're finished, Grab displays your snapshot in a new window, which you can print, close without saving, or save as a TIFF file, ready for emailing or inserting into a manuscript.

Now, as experienced Mac enthusiasts already know, the Mac operating system has long had its *own* built-in shortcuts for capturing screenshots: Press Shift-⌘-3 to take a picture of the whole screen, and Shift-⌘-4 to capture a rectangular selection. (See page 611 for all the details.)

Tip: Don't forget that you can choose different, easier-to-remember keyboard shortcuts for these functions, if you like. Just open System Preferences→Keyboard→Keyboard Shortcuts, click Screen Shots, click where it now says Shift-⌘-3 (or whatever), and then press the new key combo.

So why use Grab instead? In many cases, you shouldn't. The Shift-⌘-3 and Shift-⌘-4 shortcuts work like a dream. But there are some cases when it might make more sense to opt for Grab. Here are three:

- Grab can make a *timed* screen capture (choose Capture→Timed Screen, or press Shift-⌘-Z), which lets you enjoy a 10-second delay before the screenshot is actually taken. After you click the Start Timer button, you have an opportunity to activate windows, pull down menus, drag items around, and otherwise set up the shot before Grab shoots the picture.

Figure 11-31:
Unlike the Shift-⌘-3 or Shift-⌘-4 keystrokes, Grab lets you include the pointer/cursor in the picture—or hide it. Choose Grab→Preferences and pick one of the eight pointer styles, or choose to keep the pointer hidden by activating the blank button in the upper-left corner.

- With Grab, you have the option of including the cursor in the picture, which is extremely useful when you're showing a menu being pulled down or a button being clicked. (OS X's screenshot keystrokes, by contrast, always eliminate the pointer.) Use the technique described in Figure 11-31 to add the pointer style of your choice to a Grab screenshot.

Tip: If you're really going to write a book or manual about OS X, the program you need is Snapz Pro X; a trial version is available from this book's "Missing CD" at *www.missingmanuals.com*. It offers far more flexibility.

Grapher

This little unsung app is an amazing piece of work. It lets you create 2-D or 3-D graphs of staggering beauty and complexity.

When you first open Grapher, you're asked to choose what kind of virtual "graph paper" you want: two-dimensional (standard, polar, logarithmic) or three-dimensional (cubic, spherical, cylindrical). Click a name to see a preview; when you're happy with the selection, click Open.

Figure 11-32:
In general, you type equations into Grapher just as you would on paper (like z=2xy). If in doubt, check the online help, which offers enough hints on functions, constants, differential equations, series, and periodic equations to keep the A Beautiful Mind guy busy for days.

Now the main Grapher window appears (Figure 11-32). Do yourself a favor. Spend a few wow-inducing minutes choosing canned equations from the Examples menu, and watching how Grapher whips up gorgeous, colorful, sometimes animated graphs on the fly.

POWER USERS' CLINIC

For Mathematicians (and Physicists, Scientists, and Students) Only

If you're into math, science, or studying math or science, Grapher is a tremendous addition to OS X. There's a whole lot to it—but if you're just getting started, here are a few features not to miss.

You can calculate values, intercepts, derivatives, and integrals (even indefinite integrals) by using the Equation→Evaluation and Equation→Integration commands.

Some useful ready-made equation components await in the pop-up button at the right side of the equation text box. Using the Sum and Product symbols, for example, you can quickly calculate summations and products.

That same pop-up menu can help you generate piecewise, parametric, and other specialized kinds of graphs (this means you, math students).

When you're ready to plug in an equation of your own, type it into the text box at the top of the window. If you're not such a math hotshot, or you're not sure of the equation format, work from the canned equations and mathematical building blocks that appear when you choose Equation→New Equation from Template or Window→Show Equation Palette (a floating window containing a huge selection of math symbols and constants).

Tip: If you don't know the keystroke that produces a mathematical symbol like π or θ, you can just type *pi* or *theta*. Grapher replaces it with the correct symbol automatically.

Once the graph is up on the screen, you can tailor it like this:

- **To move a 2-D graph** in the window, choose View→Move Tool and then drag; to move a 3-D graph, ⌘-drag it.

- **To rotate a 3-D graph,** drag in any direction. If you add the Option key, you flip the graph around on one axis.

- **To change the colors, line thicknesses, 3-D "walls," and other graphic elements,** click the ❶ button (or choose Window→Show Inspector) to open the formatting palette. The controls you find here vary by graph type, but rest assured that Grapher can accommodate your every visual whim.

- **To change the fonts and sizes,** choose Grapher→Preferences. On the Equations panel, the four sliders let you specify the relative sizes of the text elements. If you click the sample equation, the Font panel appears, so you can go to town fiddlingf with the type.

- Add your own captions, arrows, ovals, or rectangles using the Object menu.

When it's all over, you can preserve your masterpiece using any of these techniques:

- **Export a graphic** by choosing File→Export.

- **Copy an equation to the Clipboard** by Control-clicking it and choosing Copy As→TIFF (or EPS, or whatever) from the shortcut menu. Now you can paste it into another program.

- **Export an animated graph** by choosing Equation→Create Animation. The resulting dialog box lets you specify how long you want the movie to last (and a lot of other parameters).

Tip: If you Shift-drag the starting or ending images at the bottom, you can change their size.

Finally, click Create Animation. After a moment, the finished movie appears. If you like it, choose File→Save As to preserve it on your hard drive for future generations.

Java Preferences

Java is a programming language used by a lot of corporate programs. These apps can run on any kind of computer (Mac, Windows, Linux).

To run a Java program, you need a Java *runtime* (sort of a playback engine)—and Mountain Lion doesn't come with one. So the first time you open Java Preferences, or any Java program, the Mac offers to download and install one.

In any case, Java Preferences contains a bunch of advanced settings that geeks can use to modify how Java runs on their Macs.

Keychain Access

Keychain Access memorizes and stores all your secret information—passwords for network access, file servers, FTP sites, Web pages, and other secure items. For instructions on using Keychain Access, see Chapter 13.

Migration Assistant

This little cutie automates the transfer of all your stuff from another Mac, or, in Mountain Lion, even a Windows PC, to your current Mac: your Home folder, network settings, programs, and more. This comes in extremely handy when you buy a newer, better Mac—or when you need Time Machine to recover an entire dead Mac's worth of data. (It can also copy everything over from a secondary hard drive or partition.) The instructions on the screen guide you through the process (see Appendix A).

Network Utility

Network Utility gathers information about Web sites and network citizens. It offers a suite of standard Internet tools like netstat, ping, traceroute, DNS lookup, and whois—advanced tools, to be sure, but ones that even Mac novices may be asked to fire up when calling a technician for Internet help.

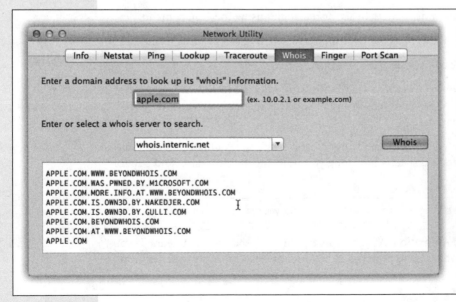

Figure 11-33:
The whois tool is a powerful part of Network Utility. First enter a domain that you want information about, and then choose a whois server (you might try whois. networksolutions. com). When you click the whois button, you get a surprisingly revealing report about the owner of the domain, including phone numbers and contact names.

Otherwise, you probably won't need to use Network Utility to get your work done. However, Network Utility can be useful when you're doing Internet detective work.

- **Whois** ("who is") can gather an amazing amount of information about the owners of any particular domain (such as apple.com)—including name and address info, telephone numbers, and administrative contacts. It uses the technique shown in Figure 11-33.

- Use **Ping** to enter an address (either a Web address like *www.google.com* or an IP address like 192.168.1.110), and then "ping" (send out a "sonar" signal to) the server to see how long it takes for it to respond to your request. Network Utility reports the response time in milliseconds—a useful test when you're trying to see if a remote server (a Web site, for example) is up and running. (The time it takes for the ping to report back to you also tells you how good your connection to it is.)

- **Traceroute** lets you track how many "hops" are required for your Mac to communicate with a certain server (an IP address or Web address). You'll see that your request actually jumps from one *trunk* of the Internet to another, from router to router, as it makes its way to its destination. You'll learn that a message sometimes crisscrosses the entire country before it arrives at its destination. You can also see how long each leg of the journey took, in milliseconds.

RAID Utility

This program is used with an Apple RAID (multiple-disk system) card.

System Information

System Information (formerly called System Profiler) is a great tool for learning exactly what's installed on your Mac and what's not—in terms of both hardware and software. The people who answer the phones on Apple's tech-support line are particularly fond of System Profiler, since the detailed information it reports can be very useful for troubleshooting nasty problems.

There are three ways to open System Information. Two of them involve a preliminary visit to the new dialog box shown in Figure 11-34, which is a faster, better-designed, more consolidated view of the system information you might care most about.

Anyway, here are the three ways:

- **Slow.** Choose →About This Mac. You get a bare-bones info screen that reveals your OS X version, your Mac's memory amount, and what processor it has inside.

Tip: If you click your OS X version number twice in the About box, you get to see your Mac's serial number!

If you then click More Info, you get the About This Mac details screen, shown in Figure 11-34. If that information isn't all you need, then click System Report to open the actual System Information program.

- **Medium.** Burrow into your Applications→Utilities folder; double-click System Information.

• **Fast.** Hold down the Option key, which makes the →About This Mac command *change* to say System Information. Choose it, then proceed as shown in Figure 11-34.

Figure 11-34:
This dialog box gives you a plain-English display of the Mac details you probably care the most about: memory, screen, storage, serial number, OS X version, and so on. (Click the tabs across the top for more details.) To proceed from here to the full System Information program, click System Report.

When System Information opens, it reports information about your Mac in a list down the left side (Figure 11-35).

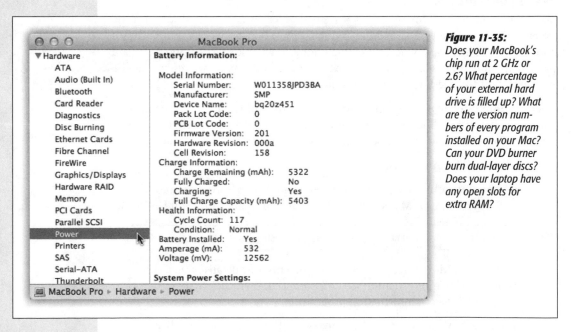

Figure 11-35:
Does your MacBook's chip run at 2 GHz or 2.6? What percentage of your external hard drive is filled up? What are the version numbers of every program installed on your Mac? Can your DVD burner burn dual-layer discs? Does your laptop have any open slots for extra RAM?

The details fall into these categories:

- **Hardware.** Click this word to see precisely which model Mac you have, what kind of chip is inside (and how many), how much memory it has, and its serial number.

 If you expand the flippy triangle, you get to see details about which **Memory** slots are filled and the size of the memory module in each slot; what kind of **Disc Burning** your Mac can do (DVD-R, DVD+R, and so on); what **PCI Cards** are installed in your expansion slots; what **Graphics/Displays** circuitry you have (graphics card and monitor); what's attached to your SATA bus (internal drives, like your hard drive); what's connected to your **Thunderbolt, USB,** and **FireWire** chains, if anything; and much more.

- **Network** reveals details what **WiFi** components you have, what Internet connection **Locations** you've established, and so on.

- **Software** shows which version of OS X you have and what your computer's name is, as far as the network is concerned ("Chris's Computer," for example).

 The **Applications** list documents every program on your system, with version information. It's useful for spotting duplicate copies of programs.

Tip: The right-hand column of the Applications list identifies each program as being PowerPC, Intel, or Universal. An Intel app runs only on Macs with Intel processors (that is, all of them since about 2006). A PowerPC program runs at full speed on pre-Intel Macs, but not at all in Mountain Lion. A Universal program can run natively—at full speed—on either Intel-based Macs or earlier models. This list is a handy summary of which programs have been updated for the Intel generation.

Similar information shows up in the **Extensions** panel. Extensions are the drivers for the Mac's various components, which sit in the System→Library→Extensions folder. Whatever is in that folder is what you see listed in this panel. Other categories include self-explanatory lists like **Fonts, Preference Panes,** and **Startup Items.**

Finally, the **Logs** panel reveals your Mac's secret diary: a record of the traumatic events that it experiences from day to day. (Many of these are the same as those revealed by the Console utility; see page 454.)

Tip: If any of these screens is showing you more technical information than you'd like, use the File→Show Less Information command to pare down the overload to just the human-recognizable items.

Saving a report

To create a handsomely formatted report that you can print or save, choose File→Export as Text, and then choose Rich Text Format from the File Format pop-up menu. Note, however, that the resulting report can be well over 500 pages long. In many cases, you're better off simply making a screenshot of the relevant Profiler screen, as described on page 611, or saving the thing as a PDF file.

Terminal

Underneath its shiny skin, OS X is actually Unix, one of the oldest and most respected operating systems in use today. But you'd never know it by looking; Unix is a world without icons, menus, or dialog boxes. You operate it by typing out memorized commands at a special prompt, called the command line. The mouse is almost useless here.

Wait a minute—Apple's ultramodern operating system, with a command line?! What's going on? Actually, the command line never went away. At universities and corporations worldwide, professional computer nerds still value the efficiency of pounding away at the little *C:* or *$* prompts.

You never *have* to use OS X's command line. In fact, Apple has swept it pretty far under the rug. There are, however, some tasks you can perform *only* at the command line.

Terminal is your keyhole into OS X's Unix innards. There's a whole chapter on it waiting for you on this book's "Missing CD" page at *www.missingmanuals.com*.

VoiceOver Utility

For details on this screen-reader software, see page 634.

The Developer Tools

The Mac App Store offers a free download for Mountain Lion: a batch of programs known as the Developer Tools or Xcode. They're for programmers who write OS X and iPhone software; you'll need some of these programs if you want to get into some of the more esoteric (or, as some would say, fun) OS X tricks and tips.

To install these tools, search the App Store for *Xcode*. You wind up with a new folder called Developer on your hard drive. Its Applications→ Utilities folder contains programs that are user-friendly enough even for nonprogrammers.

CrashReporterPrefs, for example, lets you tell OS X when to display the Application Unexpectedly Quit dialog box. If you choose Server, you'll never see one of those annoying dialog boxes again.

In Developer→Applications→Graphics Tools, you'll find Quartz Composer Visualizer. This program lets you build screen savers, animations, and other graphical goodies without writing a single line of code.

Finally, don't miss Core Image Fun House (also in Developer→Applications→Graphics Tools). It's intended to be a showcase for OS X's Core Image technologies, which constitute a ready-to-use photo-transformation toolkit that software companies can build into their programs. Fun House lets you apply dozens of mind-blowing visual effects to your images and movies with a few clicks. (You can even adjust filters in real time, so you can see the result of your modifications as you make them.) You can export the result.

CDs, DVDs, iTunes & AirPlay

D isks, it appears, just can't get a break. Show me a disk technology, and I'll
show you a spinning storage medium that the world eventually abandoned,
usually led by Apple. Think about it: The iMac was the first brand-name
computer to arrive without a floppy disk drive (1998). The MacBook Air and iPad
don't have CD/DVD drives. These days, even Windows PC manufacturers have left
the floppy drive for dead. Joining it in the great CompUSA in the sky: Zip disks, Jaz
disks, SyQuest disks, SuperDisks, Peerless disks…

Disks Today

So what's springing up to take their places? Let us count the disks.

Hard Drives

Thanks to the Mac's Thunderbolt, FireWire, or USB jacks, it's easier than ever to at-
tach an external hard drive for extra storage.

CDs, DVDs

CDs and DVDs may be fading from the scene, but they're not gone yet. These disc
drives are still built into every desktop Mac and many laptop models—and even if
you have a laptop without a drive built-in, you can buy an external one. Which is
handy if you have a many-hour flight ahead of you and want to watch some movies
you picked up at the library.

CD-ROM stands for "compact disc, read-only memory"—in other words, you can't
freely add and delete files from one, as you can from a hard drive. But most Macs can

also record onto blank CDs, of course, and blank DVDs, too, thanks to a built-in CD/DVD burner. A burner can record onto either of two kinds of blank discs:

- **CD-R.** You can fill this type of disc with your own files—once. (The R stands for *recordable.*) The disc can't be erased. Once you've grasped that much, you'll probably also understand the term DVD-R (and the nearly identical "plus" versions, CD+R and DVD+R).

Note: A Mac can accept either kind of blank disc: the -R type or the +R type. They're technically different, but since your Mac can handle either type, just buy whichever is on sale.

- **CD-RW.** The initials stand for *rewritable;* using Disk Utility, you can erase one of these discs and rerecord it, over and over again. Of course, CD-RW and DVD-RW blank discs are somewhat more expensive than the one-shot kind.

The standard Mac drive can also play DVD movies that you've rented or bought, but you may also occasionally use it for *data* DVDs—that is, DVDs that contain Mac files or software installers.

If your Mac has a drive, it's what Apple calls a t. This drive, actually made by a company like Pioneer or Panasonic, can play *and* record CDs *and* DVDs. You could, for example, use blank DVDs as backup disks that hold 4.7 GB or 8.5 GB each. (That's 4.7 gigs for regular blank DVDs and 8.5 gigs on the newer, more expensive dual-layer blanks.)

If you've used iMovie to edit your home camcorder footage, you can also save your masterpiece onto one of these DVDs for playback in standard home DVD players—the perfect way to distribute it to friends and family with spectacular quality.

Flash Drives

The most recent invention is among the most convenient: tiny, keychain-sized *flash drives* or *thumb drives*, which plug directly into your USB jack and serve as low-capacity hard drives with no moving parts. Inside, they contain nothing but RAM—pure memory.

Flash drives are fantastic, usually inexpensive gadgets that hold as much as 256 gigabytes. They work on any Mac or Windows PC and don't require any drivers or special software installation. Ask for one for your birthday.

Disks In, Disks Out

When you insert a disk, its icon may show up in any of three places (depending on your Finder preferences): on the right side of the desktop (Figure 12-1), in the Computer window, and in the Sidebar (page 19). To see what's on a disk you've inserted, double-click its icon.

Note: You can make the Mac work like Windows, if you choose. For example, to open a single window containing the icons of all currently inserted disks, choose Go→Computer (which produces the rough equivalent of the Computer window).

To complete the illusion that you're running Windows, you can even tell OS X not to put disk icons on the desktop at all. Just choose Finder→Preferences, click General, and turn off the four top checkboxes—"Hard disks," "External disks," "CDs, DVDs, and iPods," and "Connected servers." They'll no longer appear on the desktop—only in your Computer window. (You can stop them from appearing in the Sidebar, too, by clicking the Sidebar button in the Finder preferences and turning off the same checkboxes.)

Figure 12-1:
If you visit the Finder→Preferences command, you can turn on the checkboxes to make all kinds of disks appear on your desktop (shown here: hard drive, CD, iPod, memory card). But chances are pretty good you won't be seeing many floppy disk icons.

In Mountain Lion, if you right-click a disk icon, the shortcut menu contains a new Encrypt command. You're offered the chance to make up a password for that disk; the rest is automatic.

Oh yeah—don't forget the password. There's no back door.

To remove a disk from your Mac, use one of these methods:

- Hold down the ⏏ key on your keyboard. Mac keyboards, both on laptops and desktops, have a special Eject key (⏏), usually in the upper-right corner. Hold it down for a moment to make a CD or DVD pop out. (If you don't have an ⏏ key, hold down F12 instead.)

- Drag its icon onto the Trash icon. For years, this technique has confused and frightened first-time Mac users. Their typical reaction: Doesn't the Trash mean "delete"? Yes, but only when you drag *file or folder* icons there—not *disk* icons. Dragging a disk icon into the Trash (at the end of the Dock) makes the Mac spit the disk out. (If you drag a *disk image* icon or the icon of a networked disk, this maneuver *unmounts* them—that is, gets them off your screen.)

The instant you begin dragging a disk icon, the Trash icon on the Dock changes form, as though to reassure the novice that dragging a disk icon there will only eject the disk. As you drag, the wastebasket icon morphs into a giant-sized ⏏ logo.

- Highlight the disk icon, and then choose File→Eject (or press ⌘-E). The disk pops out.

- Control-click (or right-click) the disk icon. Choose Eject from the shortcut menu.

- Click the ⏏ button next to a disk's name in the Sidebar.

Any of these techniques also work to get network disks and disk images off your screen.

Note: If you try to eject a disc and the Mac tells you, "This disk is in use," the message tells you exactly which program is still holding onto the disk. Switch to that program, close whatever document is causing the problem, and then eject the disk.

Startup Disks

When you turn the Mac on, it hunts for a *startup disk*—that is, a disk containing a System folder. If you've ever seen the dispiriting blinking folder icon on a Mac's screen, you know what happens when the Mac *can't* find a startup disk. It blinks like that forever, or until you find and insert a disk with a viable System folder on it.

Usually, a startup disk is a DVD or a hard drive (internal or external—any properly formatted USB, FireWire or Thunderbolt drive). You can even put a stripped-down, emergency copy of Mountain Lion onto a flash drive and start up your Mac that way; see page 796.

UP TO SPEED

Mac OS Extended Formatting

Whether you use Disk Utility to erase a disk (or when you first install OS X and elect to erase the hard drive in the process), you'll be confronted with a choice between formatting options called Mac OS Extended and Unix File System (UFS). (Depending on the kind of disk, you may also see an option to create a DOS-formatted disk for use in Windows machines.)

Mac OS Extended or Mac OS Extended (Journaled) refers to the HFS Plus filing system, a disk format that has been proudly maximizing disk space for Mac fans since Mac OS 8.1. (For a definition of journaling, see page 792.)

OS X still accepts disks that were prepared using the older, Mac OS Standard formatting–the ancient HFS (hierarchical filing system) format–but you can't use one as your startup disk, and any file names longer than 31 characters will appear chopped off.

As for the Unix File System option, it's exclusively for use on computers that run Unix (the pure variety, not the dressed-up version that is OS X).

Selecting a Startup Disk

It's perfectly possible to have more than one startup disk simultaneously attached to your Mac. Some veteran Mac fans deliberately create other startup disks—using external hard drives, for example—so that they can easily start the Mac up from a backup disk, or from a different version of the OS.

Only one System folder can be operational at a time. So how does the Mac know which to use as its startup disk? You make your selection in the Startup Disk pane of System Preferences (Figure 12-2).

Tip: If you're in a hurry to start the machine up from a different disk, just click the disk icon and then click Restart in the System Preferences window. You don't have to close the System Preferences window first.

Figure 12-2:
In the Startup Disk pane of System Preferences, the currently selected disk—the one that will be "in force" the next time the machine starts up—is always highlighted. You also see the System folder's version, the name of the drive it's on, and its actual name.

Erasing a Disk

OS X doesn't have an Erase Disk command at the desktop. When you want to erase a disk (such as a DVD-RW disc), you're supposed to use Disk Utility, which sits in your Applications→Utilities folder. This is the same program you use to erase, repair, or subdivide *(partition)* a hard drive.

Once you've opened Disk Utility, click the name of the disk (in the left-side list), click the Erase tab, and then click the Erase button.

You won't be able to do so, though, if:

- The disk is a standard CD-ROM, DVD, a previously recorded CD-R disc, or a disk elsewhere on the network.

- You're trying to erase the startup disk. You can't wipe out the disk that contains the currently running System folder any more than you can paint the floor directly beneath your feet. (To erase your built-in hard drive, for example, you must start up from the OS X DVD.)

Burning CDs and DVDs

Burning a CD or DVD is great for backing up stuff, transferring stuff to another computer (even a Windows PC), mailing to somebody, or offloading (archiving) older files to free up hard drive space. You can buy blank CDs and DVDs incredibly cheaply in bulk—$20 for 100 CDs, for example—via the Web.

You can burn a disc in either of two ways: with the blank disc inserted or without.

Burn Folders: Without the Disc

The *burn folder* is a special folder that you fill up by dragging file and folder icons to it. Then, when you're ready to burn, you just insert the blank disc and go.

The burn-folder concept has a lot going for it:

- **No wasted hard drive space.** When you use a burn folder, you're not using up any additional disk space as you load up a disc with files and folders. Instead, the Mac just sets aside *aliases* of the files and folders you want to burn. Aliases take up negligible hard drive space. When you finally burn the disc, the designated material is copied directly onto the CD or DVD.

- **Easy reuse.** You can keep a burn folder on your desktop, prestocked with the folders you like to back up. Each time you burn a disc, you get the latest version of those folders' contents, and you're saved the effort of having to gather them each time.

- **Prepare ahead of time.** You can get a CD or DVD ready to burn without having a blank disc on hand.

Here's how you use burn folders:

1. **Create a burn folder.**

 To make a burn folder appear on your desktop, choose File→New Burn Folder. To create one in any other window, Control-click (or right-click) a blank spot inside that window and, from the shortcut menu, choose New Burn Folder.

 Either way, a new folder appears, bearing the universal Mac "burn" symbol (☢).

2. **Rename it.**

 Its name is highlighted, so you can just start typing to rename it. Press Return when you're finished.

3. **Load up the folder by dragging files and folders onto it.**

 If you double-click the burn folder to open its window (Figure 12-3), you'll notice that you're not actually copying huge files. You're simply making a list of aliases.

Tip: At the bottom of the burn folder's window, the "minimum disc size" display keeps track of how much stuff you've loaded up so far, so you can gauge if it will fit on one disc.

Figure 12-3:
Top: A burn folder looks like any ordinary folder–except that it has that radioactive logo on it. You can drag files and folders right into its window; OS X displays only aliases for now, but when you burn the disc, the actual files and folders will be there.

If you open the burn folder, you find an unusual strip across the top. Its most important feature is the Burn button at the right.

Bottom: Ready to proceed, Captain.

4. **Decorate the window, if you like.**

 You can choose list view or icon view; you can drag the icons into an arrangement you like; you can change the background color of the window; and so on. One nice feature of the Mac (which is not available on The Other OS) is that the look of a window is preserved when you burn it to CD.

5. **Click the Burn button in the upper-right corner of the window, or choose File→ Burn Disc.**

 The message shown at bottom in Figure 12-3 appears.

6. **Insert a blank disc.**

 If you have a slot-loading Mac, slip the disc into the slot. If your Mac has a sliding CD/DVD tray instead, open it first by pressing the button on the tray, or pressing your ⏏ key for about a second.

Tip: Once you've inserted a CD or DVD into your tray, you can close it either by pushing gently on the tray or by pressing the ⏏ key again.

One last confirmation box appears, where you can name the disc and choose a burning speed for it.

7. **Click Burn (or press Return).**

The Mac's laser proceeds to record the CD or DVD, which can take some time. Feel free to switch into another program and continue using your Mac. When it's all over, you have a freshly minted CD or DVD, whose files and folders you can open on any Mac or Windows PC.

When You Have a Blank Disc on Hand

If you have a blank disc ready to go, burning is even simpler.

Start by inserting the disc. After a moment, the Mac displays a dialog box asking, in effect, what you want to do with this blank disc (unless you've fiddled with your preference settings). See Figure 12-4 for instructions.

You inserted a blank DVD. Choose an action from the pop-up menu or click Ignore.

Action: Open Finder

☐ Make this action the default

(?) Eject Ignore OK

Figure 12-4:
Choose Open Finder if you plan to copy regular Mac files onto the CD or DVD, or Open iTunes if you plan to burn a music CD using iTunes. (Click "Make this action the default" if you figure you'll always answer this question the same way.) Click OK.

To burn the disk, drag its icon onto the Burn icon in the Dock, or choose File→Burn Disc.

If you choose Open Finder, the disc's icon appears on the desktop after a moment; its icon also appears in the Sidebar, complete with the Burn symbol (☢).

At this point, you can begin dragging files and folders onto the disc's icon, or (if you double-click the icon) into its window. You can add, remove, reorganize, and rename the files on it just as you would in any standard Finder window. All you're really doing is dragging aliases around; the real files are left untouched on your hard drive. You can also rename the CD or DVD itself just as you would a file or folder.

When the disc's icon contains the files and folders you want to immortalize, do one of these things:

- Choose File→Burn [the disc's name].

- Click the ☢ button next to the disc's name in the Sidebar.

- Click the Burn button in the upper-right corner of the disc's window.

- Drag the disc's icon toward the Trash icon in the Dock. As soon as you begin to drag, the Trash icon turns into the yellow ☢ logo. Drop the disc's icon onto it.

- Control-click (or right-click) the disc's icon; from the shortcut menu, choose Burn [the disc's name].

In any case, the dialog box shown at bottom in Figure 12-4 now appears. Click Burn. When the recording process is over, you'll have yourself a DVD or CD that works in any Mac or PC.

Here are a few final notes on burning CDs and DVDs at the desktop:

- Not sure what kinds of discs your Mac can burn? Choose ⌘→About This Mac, and click More Info. In the resulting dialog box, click the Storage tab. There it is, plain as day: a list of the formats your machine can read and write (that is, burn). For example, you might see: "CD-Write: -R, -RW. DVD-Write: -R, -RW, +R, +RW."

- If you do a lot of disc burning, a full-fledged CD-burning program like Toast (*www.roxio.com*) adds myriad additional formatting options that let you make startup CDs, video CDs, and so on.

- When you insert a CD-*RW* or DVD-*RW* disc that you've previously recorded, the box shown at the top in Figure 12-4 doesn't appear. Instead, the disc's icon simply appears on the desktop as though it's an ordinary CD. Before you can copy new files onto it, you must erase it using Disk Utility, as described in the previous section.

- The discs that your Mac burns work equally well on Macs and Windows (or Linux) PCs. If you plan to insert a CD or DVD into a PC, however, remember that Windows doesn't permit certain symbols in a Windows filename (\ / : * ? " < > |). You'll run into trouble if any of your file names contain these symbols. In fact, you won't be able to open any folders on your disc that contain illegally named files.

iTunes: The Digital Jukebox

iTunes, in your Applications folder, is the ultimate software jukebox (Figure 12-5). It can play music CDs, tune in to Internet radio stations, load up your iPod, iPhone, or iPad, and play back digital sound files (including the Internet's favorite format, MP3 files) and other popular audio formats. It can also turn selected tracks from your music CDs *into* MP3 files, so that you can store favorite songs on your hard drive to play back anytime—without having to dig up the original.

iTunes also lets you record your own custom audio CDs that contain only the good songs. Finally, of course, iTunes is the shop window for the online iTunes Store, which sells music, TV shows, movies, and iPhone/iPad apps.

iTunes can also burn *MP3 CDs,* music CDs that fit much more than the usual 74 or 80 minutes of music onto a disc (because they store songs in MP3 format instead of AIFF). Not all CD players can play MP3 discs, however, and the sound quality is slightly lower than standard CDs.

The first time you run iTunes, you're asked (a) whether you want iTunes to be the program your Mac uses for playing music files from the Internet, (b) whether you want it to ask your permission every time it connects to the Internet, and (c) whether you want the program to scan your Home folder for all music files already on it. (You can decline to have your hard drive scanned at this time. Later, you can always drag it, or any other folder, directly into the iTunes window for automatic scanning.)

Tip: The following pages present a mini-manual on iTunes. For the full scoop, plus coverage of the iPod and the iTunes Store, consult *iPod: The Missing Manual*.

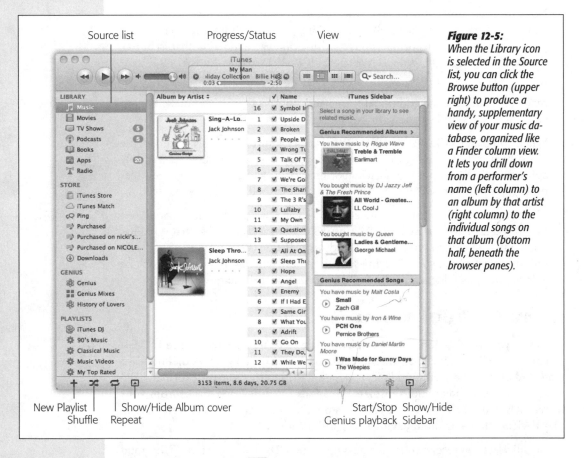

Figure 12-5:
When the Library icon is selected in the Source list, you can click the Browse button (upper right) to produce a handy, supplementary view of your music database, organized like a Finder column view. It lets you drill down from a performer's name (left column) to an album by that artist (right column) to the individual songs on that album (bottom half, beneath the browser panes).

By now, the layout of iTunes should look familiar: a Source list at the left side, acting as a table of contents for the larger window to the right. It's the same layout used in Finder windows (the Sidebar), iPhoto, Image Capture, and other Apple programs.

The major headings in iTunes's list are Library, Store, Devices, Shared, Genius, and Playlists. (You may not see all of them.) Here's what they do.

Library

The items in this list represent all your music and videos: Music, Movies, TV Shows, Podcasts, and so on. They include both your own stuff—songs you copied off of music CDs, for example—and material you bought from the iTunes Store online.

Note: When you first open iTunes, it offers to search your hard drive for the kinds of files it can play—every song in formats like MP3, AIFF, WAV, AAC, and Apple Lossless, for example. It then copies all such files into your Home→Music→iTunes→iTunes Music folder. But you don't ever need to muck around in there; use iTunes to manage your collection instead.

When you click Music, the main iTunes window is organized much like a Finder window, with columns indicating the song length, artist, album, and so on. As always, you can rearrange these columns by dragging their headings, sort your list by one of these criteria by clicking its heading, reverse the sorting order by clicking the heading a second time, and so on.

Or click one of the View buttons next to the search box to display your music as a list, a list with album covers, a grid of album covers—or as Cover Flow, which lets you flip through album covers as though they're sitting in a record-store bin.

To find a particular song or video, just type a few letters into the Spotlight-ish search box above the list. iTunes hides all but the ones that match.

Store

The iTunes Store is easy to figure out. By clicking the tabs across the top of the window, you can search or browse for music, movies, TV shows, iPhone and iPad apps, free podcasts, not-free audio books, and more. Sure, you may go broke, but at least you'll be entertained.

Use the Search Music Store box (top-right corner) to find the songs or performers you're interested in. Double-click a song or video to hear or view a 60-second excerpt.

If you decide to buy a song, sign in with your Apple account (page 142). When you click the Buy button next to a song's name, iTunes downloads it to your Mac. Behind the scenes, it goes into your Home→Music→iTunes Music folder. But for your purposes, it shows up in the Store→Purchased category in the Source list for convenient access.

Devices

These icons represent other gadgets that iTunes can talk to. If you insert a CD, it shows up here. If you attach an iPod, iPad, or iPhone, its icon appears here, too. Click any one of these icons to see what's on it. And if you don't have *any* of these things attached, the Devices category doesn't appear at all.

Shared

You can share songs and playlists with up to five networked computers in either of two ways:

- **Stream the music and videos.** In this setup, the music someone else chooses to share with you is played over the network from that Mac to your Mac. You could, for example, tap into your roommates' jazz collection without getting up from your desk, and they can sample the zydeco and Tejano tunes from your World Beat playlist.

To set this up, choose iTunes→Preferences→Sharing. Turn on "Share my library on my local network," and specify which playlists you want to share. You can require a password, if you like; set it up here. Then click OK.

Suddenly, your copy of iTunes shows up in the Shared lists of your network buddies. They can expand the flippy triangles to see and play your movies and music files (but not your audio books).

- **Copy the music and videos to your Mac from another one.** In this scenario, you can enjoy the music and movies even when the original computer is turned off. This feature, called Home Sharing, even works between Macs and PCs.

To get started, sit at Computer A. Choose Advanced→Turn On Home Sharing. You're asked for your Apple account information. Click Create Home Share and then Done.

Now, if you open iTunes on Computer B, you'll see Computer A listed in the Shared category at left. Click it to see what's in *its* copy of iTunes. You can play that stuff—even sitting at Computer B—and even copy it to Computer A. (Just drag the songs or videos you want into the appropriate category—Music, Movies, TV Shows, and so on—at the *top* of your Source list. Or, in the Show menu at the bottom of the iTunes window, choose "Items not in my library"; select the files you want to import, and then click Import.)

Note: There's some fine print. Up to five computers can do this Home Share business. They all have to sign in with the same Apple account, and they all have to be on the same network (meaning inside the same building).

Genius

Genius, according to Apple, assembles lists of "songs that sound great together," whatever that means. (It seems to mean "songs that have the same degree of rockiness.")

To get started, choose Store→Turn On Genius (unless it's already on); click Turn On Genius to dismiss the explanation screen; sign in with your Apple ID. Agree to the fine print.

Now click a song in your library that you want to serve as the anchor—the "seed" song—that you want to match. Then proceed in one of these three ways:

- **Create a Genius playlist.** Click the ❄ button at lower right. Presto: a new playlist, filed in your Source list under Genius. (Its name is Genius. Pure genius!) Play it to see how iTunes did at matching your original song's feel.

At the top of the window, you can use the Limit To pop-up menu to specify how many songs are in this playlist, the Refresh button to try again matching your "seed" song, or the Save Playlist button to turn this iTunes guess into a proper playlist.

- **Create a Genius mix.** There's also such a thing as a Genius *Mix,* which, unlike a playlist, never ends. It's more like a radio station, eternally plucking songs from your collection that all match one another (or, as Apple would say, "sound great together"). Just click Genius Mixes in the Source list; you'll see a couple of starter mixes to get you going. Click one to hear it.

- **Shop for Genius suggestions.** If you click a song name and then click the tiny, boxed ▶ button to the *right* of the �֍ button, you get a new Genius panel hugging the right side of the iTunes window. It shows other songs and albums from the iTunes store that Apple thinks you'd like, based on whatever song you clicked.

Playlists

Apple recognizes that you may not want to listen to *all* your songs every time you need some tunes. That's why iTunes lets you create *playlists*—folders in the Source list that contain, and play back, only certain songs (or videos). In effect, you can devise your own albums, like one called Party Tunes, another called Blind Date Music, and so on.

Creating playlists

To create a new playlist, click the **+** button in the lower-left corner of the window, or choose File→New Playlist (⌘-N). Alternatively, if you've already highlighted certain songs—by ⌘-clicking them or Shift-clicking them—you can choose File→New Playlist from Selection.

A new playlist appears as an icon in the Source list. You can rename this playlist by double-clicking it, and add songs to it by dragging them out of the main list into the icon.

Tip: Deleting a song from a playlist doesn't delete it from the Library (or your hard drive). Similarly, it's fine to add the same song to as many different playlists as you like, since you're not actually increasing the size of your Library. (You might be starting to pick up a running theme in Apple's software. Playlists work just like albums in iPhoto, or the Sidebar in the Finder.)

Smart playlists

Smart playlists constantly rebuild themselves according to criteria you specify. You might tell one smart playlist to assemble 45 minutes' worth of songs you've rated higher than four stars but rarely listen to, and another to list your most-often-played songs from the '80s.

Tip: To rate a song, make the window wide enough that you can see the Rating column. (If you don't see this column, Control-click any column heading and choose Rating from the list of options.) Then just click the Rating column for a selected song. The appropriate number of stars appears—one, two, three, four, or five—depending on the position of your click. You can change a song's rating as many times as you like—a good thing, considering the short shelf life of a pop hit these days.

To make a smart playlist, choose File→New Smart Playlist (Option-⌘-N)—or just Option-click the + button beneath the Source list. The dialog box shown in Figure 12-6 appears. The controls here are designed to set up a search of your music database. Figure 12-6, for example, illustrates how you'd find up to 74 minutes of Beatles tunes released between 1965 and 1968—that you've rated three stars or higher and that you've listened to no more than twice.

Figure 12-6:
A smart playlist is a powerful search command for your iTunes database. You can set up certain criteria, like the hunt for particular Beatles tunes illustrated here. The "Live updating" checkbox makes iTunes keep this playlist updated as your collection changes, as you change your ratings, as your play count changes, and so on.

When you click OK, your smart playlist is ready to show off. When you click its name in the Source list, the main song list updates itself according to your criteria and any changes in your music collection. (Smart playlists get transferred to your iPod or iPhone but don't continue to update themselves there.)

Audio CDs

If you insert a music CD while iTunes is open, the songs on it immediately show up in the list.

FREQUENTLY ASKED QUESTION

Autoplaying Music CDs

How do I make music CDs automatically play when they're inserted into the Mac?

First, make sure iTunes is slated to open automatically when you insert a music CD. You do that on the CDs & DVDs panel of System Preferences (use the "When you insert a music CD" pop-up menu).

Then all you have to do is make sure iTunes knows to begin playing automatically once it launches. Choose iTunes→Preferences, click the General icon if necessary; from the "When you insert a CD" pop-up menu, choose Begin Playing. Click OK.

From now on, whenever you insert a music CD, iTunes will open automatically and begin playing.

At first, they may appear with the exciting names "Track 01," "Track 02," and so on. But after a moment, iTunes connects to the Internet and compares your CD with the listings at *www.gracenote.com,* a global database of music CDs and their contents. If it finds a match among the thousands of CDs there, it copies the album and song names into iTunes, where they reappear every time you use this particular CD.

You can play the CD just as you would anything else in iTunes: by tapping the space bar, for example.

Tip: If you connect an iTunes-compatible portable MP3 player to your Mac (the iPod isn't the only one), its name, too, shows up in the left-side Source list. You can add songs to your player (by dragging them onto its icon), rename or reorder them, and so on.

Copying (ripping) CD songs to your hard drive

Once you copy your favorite audio CDs onto your hard drive, you can play them whenever you like, without the original CD.

To *rip* a CD (as aficionados would say) like this, make sure that only the songs you want to capture have checkmarks in the main list. Choose a format for the files you're about to create, if you like—MP3, for example, or AAC (better quality/size tradeoff, but less compatible with other gadgets)—by clicking the Import Settings button. Finally, click the Import CD button at the lower-right corner of the window.

Figure 12-7:
Watch the display at the top of the window to see how long the conversion is going to take, and which song iTunes is working on. As iTunes finishes processing each song, you see a small, circled checkmark next to its name in the main list to remind you that you've got it on board.

When it's all over (see Figure 12-7), you'll find the imported songs listed in your Library. (Click Music in the left-side Source list.) From there, you can drag them into any other "folder" (playlist), as described above.

The iPod, iPhone, and iPad

Unless you're just off the shuttle from Alpha Centauri, you probably already know that the iPod is Apple's tiny, elegant music player. It, and its pals the iPhone and iPad, are designed to integrate seamlessly with iTunes.

All you have to do is connect the i-gadget to the Mac via its white USB cable. The gizmo's icon shows up in the iTunes Source list. Click its icon to view its contents—and click the tabs (Music, TV Shows, Podcasts, and so on) to specify what Mac material you'd like copied over to it.

Playing with Playback

To play a song or video, double-click it. Or click iTunes's Play button (▶) or press the space bar. The Mac immediately begins to play the songs whose names have check-marks in the main list, or from the CD currently in your Mac.

Tip: The central display at the top of the window shows not only the name of the song and album, but also where you are in the song, as represented by the diamond in the horizontal strip. Drag this diamond, or click elsewhere in the strip, to jump around in the song.

To view the current music's sound levels, click the tiny triangle at the left side of this display to see a pulsing VU meter, indicating the various frequencies.

As music plays, you can control and manipulate the music and the visuals of your Mac in all kinds of interesting ways. Some people don't move from their Macs for months at a time.

Turning on visuals

Visuals are onscreen light shows that pulse, beat, and dance in sync to the music. (For real party fun, invite some people who grew up in the '60s to your house to watch.)

WORKAROUND WORKSHOP

iPod Independence

Out of the box, the iPod (or iPad, or iPhone) and iTunes come set for automatic synchronization. That is, as soon as you hook them together, iTunes sends your complete music library (the contents of your Library "folder" in iTunes) to the iPod. The iPod's songs and playlists always match the Mac's.

Apple's idea here was to ensure that you don't use the iPod as a convenient piracy machine. Your iPod gets its music from your Mac, it but can't put its songs onto a Mac.

At least that's the theory. But what if your hard drive self-destructs, vaporizing the 945 MP3 files that you've made from your paid-for CD collection? You legally own those

copies. Shouldn't you have the right to retrieve them from your own iPod?

If you believe the answer is yes, a quick search at *www.download.com* for the word "iPod" will bring up a list of programs like Senuti (iTunes spelled backward, get it?), which let you copy music from the iPod to the Mac.

These programs know that the name of the super-secret music folder on the iPod, called *iPod_Control*, is invisible, which is why you can't see it on your desktop without the help of these utilities.

To summon this psychedelic display, choose View→Show Visuals, or just press ⌘-T. The show begins immediately—although it's much more fun if you choose View→Enter Full Screen (Control-⌘-F) so the show takes over your whole monitor. True, you won't get a lot of work done, but when it comes to stress relief, visuals are a lot cheaper than a hot tub.

Keyboard control

You can control iTunes's music playback using its menus, of course, but the keyboard can be far more efficient. Here are a few of the control keystrokes worth noting:

Function	Keystroke
Play, Pause	space bar
Next song/previous song	↑, ↓ or ←, →

GEM IN THE ROUGH

Internet Radio and Podcasts

Audio CDs and MP3 files aren't the only sources of musical and spoken sound you can listen to as you work. iTunes also lets you tune in to hundreds of Internet-based radio stations, which may turn out to be the most convenient music source of all. They're free, they play 24 hours a day, and their music collections make yours look like a drop in the bucket. You can also download and listen to podcasts, which are like Web-distributed personal radio shows—some commercial (like NPR) and some homemade (sometimes *very* homemade).

For radio, click Radio in the left-side Source list. (If you don't see Radio there, choose iTunes→Preferences→General, and turn on Radio.)

In the main list, if you're connected to the Internet, you'll see categories like Blues, Classic Rock, Classical, and so on, as shown here. Click the flippy triangle to see a list of Internet radio stations in that category.

When you see one that looks interesting, double-click it. (The higher the number in the Bit Rate column, the better the sound quality.) Wait a moment for your Mac to connect

to the appropriate Internet site, and then let the music begin!

Without add-on shareware (like Audio Hijack Pro), there's no easy way to capture Internet broadcasts or save them onto your hard drive. You can, however, drag a radio station's name into the Music list (in the Source list), or even a playlist, to make it easier to access later on. If you discover other Internet radio stations that sound interesting, choose Advanced→Open Stream, type in the station's Web address (URL), and press Return.

To grab a podcast, click iTunes Store in the Source list. At the top of the screen, click Podcasts. Now iTunes lets you browse its vast list of available podcasts. When you click one that looks promising, you can either listen to it on the spot, or—and here's the real fun—click Subscribe.

Once you do that, a new icon called Podcasts appears in your Source list; click it to find the latest episodes of the podcasts you've subscribed to. Sync those babies to your iPod or iPhone, and you've got interesting material—or, at least fresh material—to listen to every day of the week.

Louder, quieter	⌘-↑, ⌘-↓
Rewind, fast-forward	Option-⌘-←, Option-⌘-→
Eject the CD	⌘-E
Turn Visuals on	⌘-T
Turn Visuals off	⌘-T or mouse click
Full-screen mode	Control-⌘-F
Exit full-screen visuals	⌘-T, ⌘-F, Esc, or mouse click

Tip: You can also control CD playback from the Dock. Control-click (or right-click) the iTunes icon to produce a pop-up menu offering playback commands like Pause, Next Song, and Previous Song, along with a display that identifies the song currently being played.

Playing with the graphic equalizer

If you choose Window→Equalizer, you get a handsome control console that lets you adjust the strength of each musical frequency independently (Figure 12-8).

Figure 12-8:
Drag the sliders (bass on the left, treble on the right) to accommodate the strengths and weaknesses of your speakers or headphones (and listening tastes). Or save yourself the trouble— use the pop-up menu above the sliders to choose a canned set of slider positions for Classical, Dance, Jazz, Latin, and so on. These settings even transfer to the iPod.

Sound Check: Preventing ear-blast syndrome

Here's a clever touch: In iTunes→Preferences→Playback, you see a checkbox called Sound Check. Its function is to keep the playback volume of all songs within the same basic level so you don't have to adjust the volume to compensate for different recorded levels. (This setting, too, gets transferred to your iPod, iPad, or iPhone.)

Come to think of it, you could while away quite a few happy afternoons just poking through the Preferences dialog box. It grows richer with every successive version of iTunes.

Burning Music CDs

iTunes can record selected sets of songs, no matter what the original sources, onto a blank CD. When it's all over, you can play the burned CD on a standard CD player, just as you would a CD from the record store—but this time, you hear only the songs you like, in the order you like, with all the annoying ones eliminated.

Start by creating a playlist for the CD you're about to make. Click its icon in the left-side Source list to see the list you've built. Drag songs up or down in the list to change their playback order. Keep these points in mind:

- The readout at the bottom of the list shows how much time the songs will take.

- About 74 or 80 minutes of regular audio files fit on one CD. But if you make an *MP3 CD*, you can fit at least 10 times as much—12 hours of music on a single disc!

The fine print: Not all CD players can play MP3 CDs (check the manual or the side of the CD player's box). Also note that your MP3 CD can't include songs you've bought in Apple's iTunes music store; iTunes won't convert them into the MP3 format.

To burn an MP3 CD, see Figure 12-9.

Figure 12-9:
To burn an MP3 CD, click the playlist, insert a blank CD, and then click Burn Disc (lower-right corner of the window). This box appears. Here you can select MP3 CD. If you're burning a regular audio CD instead, you can specify how much gap you want between the songs.

- You can control how many seconds of silence iTunes leaves between tracks on your custom CD, too. Use the Gap Between Songs pop-up menu shown in Figure 12-9.

When everything is set up, click the Burn Disc button in the playlist window. Specify your CD options (Figure 12-9), insert a blank CD into the Mac, and go read a book; the burning process takes some time. Feel free to work in other programs while iTunes chugs away.

DVD Movies

Watching movies on your Mac screen couldn't be simpler: Just insert a movie DVD. Unless you've fiddled with your preference settings, the DVD Player program opens and begins playing the movie in full-screen mode. (Even the menu bar disappears. To make it reappear, move your cursor to near the top of the screen.)

Note: If DVD Player *doesn't* open automatically when you insert a DVD movie, you can open it yourself. It's sitting there in your Applications folder. (Then fix the problem, using System Preferences CDs & DVDs.)

Playing a Movie

Once DVD Player starts playing your movie, you can move your mouse to the bottom of the screen, at any time, to bring up the control bar (Figure 12-10).

Figure 12-10:
Top: Even in full-screen mode, you can control the playback and navigate the disc using the new, translucent, pop-up control bar.

One especially cool feature is the new Player Settings button. It opens the Zoom controls window shown here, which gives you manual control over the width and height of the picture on your screen.

Don't miss the scrubber bar at the very bottom, either. It lets you scroll directly to any spot in the DVD.

Bottom: When you're not in full-screen mode, you get a separate, floating "remote control." It has most of the same controls, but they're arranged with a more 1999 sort of design aesthetic.

Scrubber bar

Languages, Subtitles

Eject DVD

Click to see elasped time/ time remaining

Picture controls

Exit full screen

Slo Mo
Frame Advance
Return to Movie

Subtitles
Language
Angle

Previous chapter/Next chapter
(Hold to scan backward/forward)

Or just use the keyboard controls, which appear here in this clip 'n' save cheat sheet:

Function	Keystroke
Play, Pause	space bar
Fast-forward, rewind	Shift-⌘-→, Shift-⌘-← (press repeatedly to cycle to 3, 8, 16, and 32 times normal speed)
Skip forward/back 5 seconds	Option-⌘-→, Option-⌘-←
Louder, quieter	⌘-↑, ⌘-↓
Mute/Unmute	Option-⌘-↓
Next/previous "chapter"	→, ←
Full-screen mode on/off	⌘-F
Half, normal, maximum size	⌘-1, ⌘-2, ⌘-3
Eject	⌘-E
Add a bookmark	⌘-= (equal sign)

Language Fun

Most Hollywood DVDs have been programmed with onscreen subtitles to help those with hearing impairments and people sitting in noisy bars. The Subtitle button offers a pop-up menu of alternative languages and subtitle options.

Tip: For real fun, turn on English subtitles but switch the soundtrack to a foreign language. No matter how trashy the movie you're watching, you'll gain much more respect from your friends and family when you tell them you're watching a foreign film.

Bookmarks and Video Clips

Two DVD Player features are designed to help you flag and return to favorite moments or scenes in a DVD movie.

FREQUENTLY ASKED QUESTION

Region Changing

The first time I tried to play a DVD, I got this weird message about initializing the region code. What's up with that?

Hollywood generally releases a movie in different parts of the world at different times. A movie may come out on video in the U.S. when it's just hitting screens in Europe. We certainly can't have people watching a DVD before the movie studio says it's OK! That's why many discs are region-locked, so that they play back only on players in certain geographic regions.

As a DVD player in disguise, your Mac is just doing its duty. You can change its region (you'll be offered the chance to do so when you insert a region-locked DVD from another region), but only five times—and then it's frozen forever in the fifth version.

The dialog box shows you which region your DVD is designed for: 1 for the U.S. and Canada; 2 for Japan, Europe, South Africa, and the Middle East; 3 for Southeast and East Asia; 4 for Australia, New Zealand, Pacific Islands, Central America, Mexico, South America, and the Caribbean; 5 for Eastern Europe, Africa, and North Korea; 6 for China; and 8 for airplanes, cruise ships, and so on. Any DVD that you burn yourself is assigned region 0, meaning that it will play anywhere.

(There's no region 7. Maybe it's reserved for the empty spot in movie executives' hearts.)

- **Bookmarks.** Each time you find a spot you'll want to find again later (during playback or when paused), hit ⌘-= (equal sign), or choose Controls→New Bookmark. DVD Player invites you to name the bookmark. You can also accept its proposal of 1:23:15 (or whatever the hours:minutes:seconds count happens to be).

Figure 12-11:
When you choose Controls→New Video Clip, this box appears. Find the starting point of the scene you want to capture and then click the upper Set button. Now play or navigate to the end of the scene, and click the lower Set button. When you click Save, you're invited to name the scene. From now on, you can play the scene by choosing from the Go→Video Clips submenu.

GEM IN THE ROUGH

Picture Controls

Every TV set has picture controls—settings that change the proportions and color of the picture; why not your Mac?

If you click the "Picture controls" button on the toolbar (identified in Figure 12-10), you get this little-known floating control. It's actually three dialog boxes in one; if you click the ▶ button in its title bar, you can choose the one you want.

Video Zoom controls the aspect ratio (proportions) of the picture. It's handy when the DVD you're playing doesn't quite match the size and shape of your screen. When you turn it On (upper left), you can choose Auto Zoom (the Mac's best fit), or you can adjust the horizontal and vertical sliders. (The Lock Aspect Ratio checkbox keeps them linked so you don't distort the image.) Or you can use the pop-up menu that starts out saying Manual, and choose a preset, like Widescreen. You can even save your tweakings under a new preset name, for use later on your oddball system.

Video Color adjusts the tint, brightness, contrast, and so on. And Audio Equalizer lets you adjust the sound characteristics to suit your particular speakers/headphones and your particular ears. It works just like the one described in Figure 12-8.

Once you click OK, you can use the Go→Bookmarks submenu to jump from one bookmark to another.

Tip: Ordinarily, DVD Player is smart enough to begin playing back a movie from the point where you stopped, even if you ejected the DVD in the meantime and three years have gone by.

But when you create a bookmark, the "Name your bookmark" dialog box offers you the chance to define a default bookmark. That means, "Next time you insert this disc, play back from here instead of where I stopped."

- **Video Clips.** A video clip is exactly the same as a bookmark, except that you're supposed to designate a starting point *and* an ending point. (Don't get excited; a video clip isn't a standalone file that's saved on your computer, and you can't send it or share it. It works only within DVD Player.)

 Figure 12-11 shows how you create and use a video clip.

Chapter Thumbnails

A standard Hollywood DVD comes programmed with chapters—invisible markers that let you jump from the beginning of one important scene to the next. To see them in DVD Player, just move your mouse to the top of the screen. A row of chapter thumbnail images appears, which you can click to jump around in.

You can create your own scene thumbnails, too. That might not be an especially tempting feature when you're playing Hollywood DVDs. But on homemade DVDs, made either by you or by somebody else, these custom scene markers can be handy signposts.

First choose Window→Chapters (⌘-B) to open the new chapter thumbnail palette. Here you'll find the existing scene breaks, which may or may not already have "poster frame" images.

GEM IN THE ROUGH

Parental Controls

The DVD parental controls in Mountain Lion aren't much. You can't say, for example, "Don't play anything rated PG-13 or above"; you have to rate each DVD yourself, one at a time.

But that's better than nothing.

Insert the DVD you're worried about. Choose File→Get Disk Info. Click the Parental Controls tab.

Click the 🔒 button and enter your administrator's password. (Unless, of course, your 8-year-old is the administrator of this Mac instead of you, in which case this DVD is the least of your problems.)

Now you can select either "Always ask for authorization" or "Always allow to be played," depending on your feelings about the movie. Click OK.

All you've done so far, however, is to specify what happens when you turn on parental controls—and you haven't done that yet. Choosing Features→Enable Parental Control does the trick.

When parental control is turned on, nobody can watch the "Always ask for authorization" DVDs without correctly inputting your administrator's password.

Which nobody knows except you. (Right?)

All the action takes place in the Action menu (✿) at the bottom of the panel. For example, it contains the Generate Missing Thumbnails command, for use on DVDs that have chapter breaks but no little poster frames to represent them.

Whether there's a poster frame for a particular chapter or not, you can substitute an image of your own. Find the exact frame of the movie that you think looks better than what's already in the Chapters palette; click the chapter in the palette, and, from the ✿ pop-up menu, choose Use Current Frame for Thumbnail. Presto: You've replaced the unhelpful (or nonexistent) chapter image with one that works better.

The Big Picture

Now, watching a movie while sitting in front of your Mac is not exactly the great American movie-watching dream. Fortunately, every recent Mac has a video-output jack; with the proper cables, you can connect the Mac to your TV for a much more comfortable movie-watching experience.

Of course, if you have an Apple TV, then you can pull off the same stunt without any wires at all, using AirPlay. Read on.

AirPlay

If you'd shown this new Mountain Lion feature to the masses in 2005 or so, they'd have fallen down and worshiped it as a god.

Today, we're used to wireless everything. But this is pretty cool: With one click, you can send whatever is on your Mac's screen to your TV's screen, in hi-def. No wires.

That stunt premiered on the iPad 2 and iPhone 4S. But on the Mac, AirPlay becomes far more useful. Now you can present photo slideshows on the TV from your laptop. Or play movies you've found online. Or give presentations from PowerPoint or Keynote. Or present software lessons to a class.

There is a catch, of course: This trick requires both a recent Mac model (mid-2011 or later) and an Apple TV. That's a tiny, $100 black box that connects to a hi-def TV and lets you watch videos from services like YouTube, Netflix, MLB.TV, NBA, NHL, and Vimeo. It can also play videos, music, and photos from Macs or PCs on the network.

But with AirPlay, the Apple TV (and therefore your TV) can now play anything you can see on your Mac, including services like Hulu that aren't available on the Apple TV alone. You can play your iTunes music while watching those cool screensavery visualizers on your HDTV. And you can carry your $100 Apple TV around with you to corporate boardrooms to project your pitches, rather than a $1,500 projector.

Tip: The Mac and the Apple TV have to be on the same wireless network—but that doesn't mean they need a WiFi *hotspot*. You may remember that your laptop can create its own WiFi network (see page 550). This *ad hoc* network isn't connected to the Internet, of course, but other *gadgets* can connect to it. So if you're someplace without a WiFi hotspot, you can still use AirPlay. Just create an ad hoc network on your laptop, and then choose that as your Apple TV's network!

Using AirPlay is so simple, it would confuse only an AirHead. See Figure 12-12 for instructions.

Figure 12-12:
Make sure the Apple TV is on the same WiFi network as your Mac. At that point, the AirPlay menulet appears automatically.

Top: From it, choose the name of your Apple TV, and presto: Whatever's playing on your Mac simultaneously plays on your big screen, both stereo audio and 720p hi-def video.

To stop sending your Mac's A/V to your TV, choose "Air-Play Mirroring: Off" from the same menulet.

Bottom: Specify which screen you want to impose its shape and resolution: the Mac or the TV.

"Match Desktop Size"

Once you turn on AirPlay, the AirPlay menulet lets you make an additional choice. A menu section called "Match Desktop Size To:" lets you choose either This Mac or Apple TV (or whatever you named your Apple TV).

Your Mac and your TV probably don't have the same proportions and resolution. So the menu is asking: Which screen "wins"?

The factory setting is "Apple TV." Your TV screen will be completely filled, although you might see black letterbox bars on your Mac's screen. But if you're watching TV shows or movies, for example, you won't care.

If you choose "This Mac" instead, the picture will look normal on your Mac, but you might see black letterbox bars on the TV. That might be better for a PowerPoint or Keynote presentation, for example, where you want the TV to show *exactly* what the Mac shows.

Your choice here may affect the magnification of the image on your TV, too, since its resolution and your Mac's probably don't match.

System Preferences

In System Preferences→Displays, you'll find an AirPlay Mirroring pop-up menu that duplicates the AirPlay menulet described above. You'll also find a checkbox called "Show mirroring options in the menu bar when available." That's the on/off switch for the AirPlay menulet. When this option is turned on, and the Mac uses The Force to detect the presence of a nearby Apple TV, the AirPlay menulet appears automatically.

AirPlay Sound

Not all Macs have the hardware horsepower to send video to an Apple TV; those made before mid-2011, for example, probably don't. But even those Macs can still send *audio* to your Apple TV (or your AirPort Express base station), and from there to what's presumably a better sound system than your Mac's puny built-in speakers.

The official way to do that: open System Preferences→Sound→Output. Click the name of the Apple TV or AirPort Express in the list of speakers.

But there are two faster ways:

• Press Option as you open the ß menulet. The items in this menu magically sprout previously invisible choices—like Apple TV and your other AirPlay gear.

• If you just want to play music that's in iTunes, you can choose your Apple TV's name (or AirPort Express's name) from the pop-up button in the lower right corner of the window.

Part Four:
The Technologies
of OS X

4

Accounts, Security & Gatekeeper

In an era when *security* is the hottest high-tech buzzword, Apple was smart to make security a focal point for OS X. It was already virus-free and better protected from Internet attacks than Windows. But OS X 10.8 is the most impenetrable Mac system yet, filled with new defenses against the dark arts. This chapter covers the whole range of them.

On the premise that the biggest security threat of all comes from other people in your home or office, though, the most important security feature in OS X is the *accounts* system.

Introducing Accounts

The concept of *user accounts* is central to OS X's security approach. Like the Unix under its skin (and also like recent versions of Windows), OS X is designed from the ground up to be a *multiple-user* operating system. That is, you can set up your OS X so that everyone must log in—click his name and type his password—when the computer turns on (Figure 13-1).

Upon doing so, you discover the Macintosh universe just as you left it, including these elements:

- Your documents, files, and folders.

- Your preference settings in every program you use: Web browser bookmarks and preferred home page; desktop picture, screen saver, and language; icons on the desktop and in the Dock—and the size and position of the Dock itself; and so on.

- Email account(s), including personal information and mailboxes.

• Your personally installed programs and fonts.

• Your choice of programs that launch automatically at startup.

This system lets different people use it throughout the day, without disrupting one another's files and settings. It also protects the Mac from getting fouled up by mischievous (or bumbling) students, employees, and hackers.

Figure 13-1:
When you set up several accounts, you don't turn on the Mac so much as sign into it. A command in the menu called Log Out summons this sign-in screen, as does the Accounts menu described later in this chapter. Click your own name, and type your password (if any), to get past this box and into your own stuff.

Casey McUser Dale McRobin Robin McCasey

If you're the only person who uses your Mac, you can safely skip most of this chapter. The Mac never pauses at startup time to demand the name and password you made up when you installed OS X, because Apple's installer automatically turns on something called *automatic login* (page 520). You *will* be using one of these accounts, though, whether you realize it or not.

Furthermore, when you're stuck in line at the Department of Motor Vehicles, you may find the concepts presented here worth skimming, as certain elements of this multiple-user system may intrude upon your solo activities—and figure in the discussions in this book—from time to time.

Tip: Even if you don't share your Mac with anyone and don't create any other accounts, you might still be tempted to learn about the accounts feature because of its ability to password-protect the entire computer. All you have to do is turn *off* the automatic login feature described on page 520. Thereafter, your Mac is protected from unauthorized fiddling when you're away from your desk or if your laptop is stolen.

The First Account

When you first installed OS X, whether it was 10.8 or an earlier version, you were asked for a name and a password. You were creating the first *user account* on your Macintosh. Since that fateful day, you may have made a number of changes to your desktop—adjusted the Dock settings, set up your folders and desktop the way you like them, added some bookmarks to your Web browser, and so on—without realizing that you were actually making those changes only to *your account.*

You've probably been saving your documents into your own Home folder, which is the cornerstone of your account. This folder, generally named after you and stashed in the Users folder on your hard drive, stores not only your own work, but also your preference settings for all the programs you use, special fonts you've installed, your own email collection, and so on.

Now then: Suppose you create an account for a second person. When she turns on the computer and signs in, she finds the desktop exactly the way it was factory-installed by Apple—stunning outer-space desktop picture, Dock along the bottom, and so on. She can make the same kinds of changes to the Mac that you've made, but nothing she does affects *your* environment the next time you log in.

In other words, the multiple-accounts feature has two components: first, a convenience element that hides everyone else's junk; and second, a security element that protects both the Mac's system software and everybody's work.

Creating an Account

Suppose somebody new joins your little Mac family—a new worker, student, or love interest, for example. And you want to make that person feel at home on your Mac.

Begin by opening System Preferences (Chapter 9). In the System Preferences window, click Users & Groups (which used to be called Accounts). You have just arrived at the master control center for account creation and management (Figure 13-2).

To create a new account, start by unlocking the Users & Groups panel. That is, click the 🔒 at lower left, and fill in your own account name and password.

Now you can click the **+** button beneath the list of accounts. The little panel shown at bottom in Figure 13-2 appears.

Phase 1: Choose an Account Type

As though this business of accounts and passwords wasn't complicated enough already, OS X offers several *types* of accounts. And you're expected to specify *which* type each person gets at the moment you create an account.

To do that, open the New Account pop-up menu (Figure 13-2, bottom). Its five account types are described on the following pages.

Administrator accounts

If this is your own personal Mac, then just beneath your name on the Users & Groups pane of System Preferences, it probably says *Admin*. This, as you could probably guess, stands for Administrator.

Because you're the person who originally installed OS X, the Mac assumes that you are its *administrator*—the technical wizard in charge of it. You're the teacher, the parent,

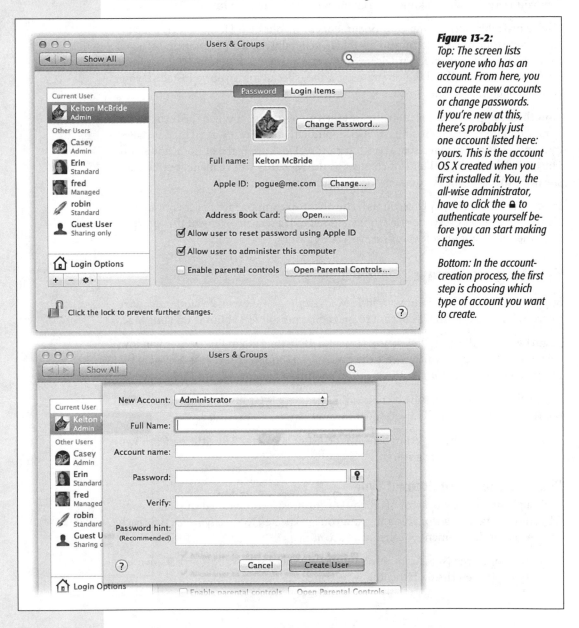

Figure 13-2:
Top: The screen lists everyone who has an account. From here, you can create new accounts or change passwords. If you're new at this, there's probably just one account listed here: yours. This is the account OS X created when you first installed it. You, the all-wise administrator, have to click the ⚿ to authenticate yourself before you can start making changes.

Bottom: In the account-creation process, the first step is choosing which type of account you want to create.

the resident guru. You're the one who will maintain this Mac. Only an administrator is allowed to do the following:

- Install new programs into the Applications folder.

- Add fonts that everybody can use.

- Make changes to certain System Preferences panes (including Network, Date & Time, Energy Saver, and Startup Disk).

- Use some features of the Disk Utility program.

- Create, move, or delete folders outside of your Home folder.

- Decide who gets to have accounts on the Mac.

- Open, change, or delete anyone else's files.

- Bypass FileVault using a recovery key (page 538).

The administrator concept may be new to you, but it's an important pill to swallow. For one thing, you'll find certain settings all over OS X that you can change *only* if you're an administrator—including many in the Users & Groups pane itself. For another thing, administrator status plays an enormous role when you want to network your Mac to other kinds of computers, as described in the next chapter. And, finally, in the bigger picture, the fact that the Mac has an industrial-strength accounts system, just like traditional Unix and recent Windows operating systems, gives it a fighting chance in the corporations of America.

As you create accounts for other people who'll use this Mac, you're offered the opportunity to make each one an administrator just like you. Needless to say, use discretion. Bestow these powers only upon people as responsible and technically masterful as yourself.

Standard accounts

Most people, on most Macs, are ordinary *Standard* account holders. These people have everyday access to their own Home folders and to the harmless panes of System Preferences, but most other areas of the Mac are off limits. OS X won't even let them create new folders on the main hard drive, except inside their own Home folders (or in the Shared folder described starting on page 526).

A few of the System Preferences panels display a padlock icon (🔒). If you're a Standard account holder, you can't make changes to these settings without the assistance of an administrator. Fortunately, you aren't required to log out so that an administrator can log in and make changes. You can just call the administrator over, click the padlock icon, and let him type in his name and password (if, indeed, he feels comfortable with you making the changes you're about to make).

Managed accounts with Parental Controls

A *Managed* account is the same thing as a Standard account—except that you've turned on Parental Controls. (These controls are described later in this chapter.) You can turn a Managed account into a Standard account just by turning off Parental Controls, and vice versa.

That is, this account usually has even fewer freedoms—because you've limited the programs this person is allowed to use, for example. Use a Managed account for children or anyone else who needs a Mac with rubber walls.

Sharing Only account

This kind of account is extremely useful—*if* your Mac is on a network (Chapter 14).

See, ordinarily, you can log in and access the files on your Mac in either of two ways:

• In person, seated in front of it.

• From across the network.

This arrangement was designed with families and schools in mind: lots of people sharing a *single* Mac.

This setup gets a little silly, though, when the people on a home or office network each have their *own* computers. If you wanted your spouse or your sales director to be able to grab some files from you, you'd have to create full-blown accounts for them on *your* Mac, complete with utterly unnecessary Home folders they'd never use.

That's why the *Sharing Only* account is such a great idea. It's available *only* from across the network. You can't get into it by sitting down at the Mac itself—it has no Home folder!

Finally, of course, a Sharing Only account holder can't make any changes to the Mac's settings or programs. (And since they don't have Home folders, you also can't turn on FileVault for these accounts.)

In other words, a Sharing Only account exists *solely* for the purpose of file sharing on the network, and people can enter their names and passwords *only* from other Macs.

Once you've set up this kind of account, all the file-sharing and screen-sharing goodies described in Chapter 14 become available.

Group

A *group* is just a virtual container that holds the names of other account holders. You might create one for your most trusted colleagues, another for those rambunctious kids, and so on—all in the name of streamlining the *file-sharing privileges* feature described on page 558. The box on the facing page covers groups in more detail.

The Guest account

For years, OS X offered a special account called the *Guest* account. It was great for accommodating visitors, buddies, or anyone else who was just passing through and

wanted to use your Mac for a while. If you let such people use the Guest account, your own account remained private and un-messed-with.

Note: The Guest account isn't listed among the account *types* in the New Account pop-up menu (Figure 13-2). That's because there's only *one* Guest account; you can't actually create additional ones.

But it's still an account type with specific characteristics. It's sitting right there in the list of accounts from Day One.

But in the early days of the Guest account, there was a problem: Any changes your friend made—downloading mail, making Web bookmarks, putting up a raunchy desktop picture—would still be there for the *next* guest to enjoy, unless you painstakingly restored everything back to neutral. The Guest account was like a hotel room shared by successive guests. And *you* were the maid.

Today, though, any changes your guest makes while using your Mac are automatically erased when she logs out. Files are deleted, email is nuked, setting changes are forgotten. It's like a hotel that gets demolished and rebuilt after each guest departs.

POWER USERS' CLINIC

Creating Groups

Changing permissions settings on a networked Mac, or one with a lot of account holders, is a lot easier if you sweep all your minions into subsets called groups.

This process used to require a complicated series of Unixy steps that, if not performed carefully, could seriously foul up your Mac.

But in OS X, you can create a group as easily as you'd create an account. And in the same place: the Users & Groups pane of System Preferences.

Click the tiny 🔒 in the lower-left corner. When prompted, type in your administrator's name and password, and then click OK. The Mac is just making sure that somebody with a clue is at the helm.

Now click the **+** button as though you were about to create a new account. But from the New Account pop-up menu (shown at bottom in Figure 13-2), choose Group. Type a name for the new group (Accounting, Kids, or whatever), and then click Create Group.

Now you see something like the list shown here: checkboxes for all this Mac's account holders. Turn on the checkboxes for the ones you consider worthy of being a part of this group.

You can create as many groups as you like. Later, when it comes time to share a folder or file, you'll save time by choosing a group name instead of setting these permissions one person at a time.

As noted above, the Guest account is permanently listed in the Users & Groups panel of System Preferences. Ordinarily, though, you don't see it in the login screen list; if you're normally the only person who uses this Mac, you don't need to have it staring you in the face every day.

So to use the Guest account, bring it to life by turning on "Allow guests to log into this computer." You can even turn on the parental controls described earlier in this chapter by clicking Open Parental Controls, or permit the guest to exchange files with your Mac from across the network (Chapter 13) by turning on "Allow guests to connect to shared folders."

Just remember to warn your vagabond friend that once he logs out (and acknowledges the warning), all traces of his visit are wiped out forever.

At least from your *Mac.*

Phase 2: Name, Password, and Status

All right. So you clicked the **+** button. And from the New Account pop-up menu, you chose the type of account you wanted to create.

Now, on the same starter sheet, it's time to fill in the most critical information about the new account holder:

- **Name.** If it's just the family, this could be "Chris" or "Robin." If it's a corporation or school, you probably want to use both first and last names.

- **Account Name.** You'll quickly discover the value of this Account Name, particularly if your name is, say, Alexandra Stephanopoulos. Before Lion, it was called the *short name*; it's meant to be an abbreviation of your actual name.

 When you sign into your Mac in person, you can use either your full name or account (short) name. But when you access this Mac by dialing into it or connecting from across the network (as described in the next chapter), the short version is more convenient.

 As soon as you tab into this field, the Mac proposes a short name for you. You can replace the suggestion with whatever you like. Technically, it doesn't even have to be shorter than the "long" name, but spaces and most punctuation marks are forbidden.

- **Password, Verify.** Here's where you type this new account holder's password (Figure 13-2). In fact, you're supposed to type it twice, to make sure you didn't introduce a typo the first time. (The Mac displays only dots as you type, to guard against the possibility that somebody is watching over your shoulder.)

 The usual computer book takes this opportunity to stress the importance of a long, complex password—a phrase that isn't in the dictionary, something that's made up of mixed letters and numbers. This is excellent advice if you create sensitive documents and work in a big corporation.

But if you share the Mac only with a spouse or a few trusted colleagues in a small office, you may have nothing to hide. You may see the multiple-users feature more as a convenience (keeping your settings and files separate) than a protector of secrecy and security. In these situations, there's no particular urgency to the mission of thwarting the world's hackers with a convoluted password.

In that case, you may want to consider setting up *no* password—leaving both password blanks empty. Later, whenever you're asked for your password, just leave the Password box blank. You'll be able to log in that much faster each day.

Tip: Actually, having *some* password comes in handy if you share files on the network, because Mac A can *store* your name and password from Mac B—and therefore you can access Mac B without entering your name and password *at all.* So consider making your password something very short and easy, like the apostrophe/quote mark—the ' key. It's a real password, so it's enough for Mac A to memorize. Yet when you *are* asked to enter your password—for example, when you're installing a new program—it's incredibly fast and easy to enter, because it's right next to the Return key.

- **Password Hint.** If your password is the middle name of the first person who ever kissed you, for example, your hint might be "middle name of the first person who ever kissed me."

 Later, if you forget your password, the Mac will show you this cue to jog your memory.

When you finish setting up these essential items, click Create User. If you left the password boxes empty, the Mac asks for reassurance that you know what you're doing; click OK.

You then return to the Users & Groups pane, where you see the new account name in the list at the left side.

Here, three final decisions await your wisdom:

- **Apple ID.** Since the Apple ID (page 412) is growing in importance and features—App Store, iTunes Store, email address, Web site, iCloud, syncing, Back to My Mac, and so on—it's convenient to associate each account with its own Apple ID.

Tip: "Allow user to reset password using Apple ID" is a handy feature. It means that if this person ever forgets his password, he'll be offered, on the login screen, a chance to recover it by entering his Apple ID.

- **Allow user to administer this computer.** This checkbox lets you turn ordinary, unsuspecting Standard or Managed accounts into Administrator accounts, as described above. You know—when your kid turns 18.

- **Enable Parental Controls.** "Parental Controls" refers to the feature that limits what your offspring are allowed to do on this computer—and how much time a day they're allowed to spend glued to the mouse. Details are on page 510.

Phase 3: Choose a Picture

The usual sign-in screen (Figure 13-1) displays each account holder's name, accompanied by a little picture.

When you click the sample photo, you get a pop-up menu of Apple-supplied graphics; you can choose one to represent you. It becomes not only your icon on the sign-in screen, but also your "card" photo in the Contacts program and your icon in Messages.

If you'd rather supply your *own* graphics file—a digital photo of your own head, for example—then choose Edit Picture from the pop-up menu. As shown in Figure 13-3, you have several options:

- **Drag a graphics file directly into the "picture well" (Figure 13-3).** Use the cropping slider below the picture to frame it properly.

Figure 13-3:
Once you've selected a photo to represent yourself (left), you can adjust its position relative to the square "frame" (right), or adjust its size by dragging the slider. Finally, when the picture looks correctly framed, click Set. (The next time you return to the Images dialog box, you can recall the new image using the Recent Pictures pop-up menu.)

- **Click Choose.** You're shown a list of what's on your hard drive. Find and double-click the image you want.

- **Take a new picture.** If your Mac has a built-in camera above the screen, or if you have an external Webcam or a camcorder hooked up, then click the little camera button. The Mac counts down from 3 with loud beeps to help you get ready, and then takes the picture.

In each case, click Set to enshrine your icon forever (or until you feel like picking a different one).

Phase 4: Login Items (Startup Items)

There's one additional setting that your account holders can set up for themselves: which programs or documents open automatically upon login. (This is one decision an administrator *can't* make for other people. It's available only to whoever is logged in at the moment.)

To choose your own crew of self-starters, open System Preferences and click Users & Groups. Click your account. Click the Login Items tab. As shown in Figure 13-4, you can now build a list of programs, documents, disks, and other goodies that automatically launch each time you log in. You can even turn on the Hide checkbox for each one so that the program is running in the background at login time, waiting to be called into service with a quick click.

Figure 13-4:
You can add any icon to the list of things you want to start up automatically. Click the + button to summon the Open dialog box, where you can find the icon, select it, and then click Choose. Better yet, if you can see the icon in a folder or disk window (or on the desktop), just drag it into this list. To remove an item, click it in the list and then click the − button.

Don't feel obligated to limit this list to programs and documents, by the way. Disks, folders, servers on the network, and other fun icons can also be startup items, so that their windows are open and waiting when you arrive at the Mac each morning.

Tip: Here's a much quicker way to add something to the Login Items list: Control-click (or right-click) its Dock icon and choose "Open at Login" from the shortcut menu.

Parental Controls

If you're setting up a Standard/Managed account, the Parental Controls checkbox affords you the opportunity to shield your Mac—or its very young, very fearful, or very mischievous operator—from confusion and harm. This is a helpful feature to remember when you're setting up accounts for students, young children, or easily intimidated adults. (This checkbox is available for Admin accounts, too, but turning it on produces a "Silly rabbit—this is for kids!" sort of message.)

You can specify how many hours a day each person is allowed to use the Mac, and declare certain hours (like sleeping hours) off-limits. You can specify exactly who your kids are allowed to communicate with via email (if they use Mail) and instant messaging (if they use Messages), what Web sites they can visit (if they use Safari), what programs they're allowed to use, and even what words they can look up in the OS X Dictionary.

Here are all the ways you can keep your little Managed account holders shielded from the Internet—and themselves. For sanity's sake, the following discussion refers to the Managed account holder as "your child." But some of these controls—notably those in the System category—are equally useful for people of *any* age who feel overwhelmed by the Mac, are inclined to mess it up by not knowing what they're doing, or are tempted to mess it up deliberately.

GEM IN THE ROUGH

Logs

On the Web tab of the Parental Controls panel, you'll find a button called Logs. That, my friends, is Big Brother Central.

It gives you a complete rundown of what your kids have been up to. Its four categories—Websites Visited, Websites Blocked, Applications, and Messages—are extremely detailed. For example, in Applications, you can see exactly which programs your kids tried to use when, and how much time they spent in each one.

It's spying, sure, but it's for the good of the child. (Right?) Use the pop-up menus at the top to change the time period being reported (Today, This Week, or whatever)

and how they're grouped in the list—by date or by application/Web site.

If you see something that you really think should be off limits—a site in the Websites Visited list, an application, a Messages session with someone—click its name and then click Restrict. You've just nipped that one in the bud.

Conversely, if the Mac blocked a Web site that you think is really OK, click its name in the list, and then click Allow. (And if you're wondering what a certain Web page *is,* click it and then click Open.)

Note: If you apply any of these options to a Standard account, then the account type listed on the Users & Groups panel changes from "Standard" to "Managed."

To begin, click Open Parental Controls at the bottom of the Users & Groups pane. Click Enable Parental Controls, if necessary. Now you should see the screen shown in Figure 13-5.

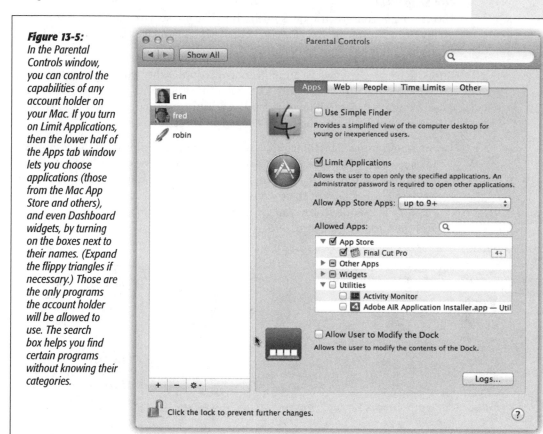

Figure 13-5:
In the Parental Controls window, you can control the capabilities of any account holder on your Mac. If you turn on Limit Applications, then the lower half of the Apps tab window lets you choose applications (those from the Mac App Store and others), and even Dashboard widgets, by turning on the boxes next to their names. (Expand the flippy triangles if necessary.) Those are the only programs the account holder will be allowed to use. The search box helps you find certain programs without knowing their categories.

Apps Tab

On this tab (Figure 13-5), you can limit which programs your Managed-account flock is allowed to use. (Limiting what people can do to your Mac when you're not looking is a handy feature under any shared-computer circumstance. But if there's one word tattooed on its forehead, it would be "Classrooms!")

At the bottom of the dialog box shown in Figure 13-5, you see a list of all the programs you've bought from the Mac App Store, all other programs, all Dashboard widgets, and all the apps in your Utilities folder. Only checked items will show up in the account holder's Applications folder. (If you don't see a program listed, then use the search box, or drag its icon from the Finder into the window.)

Note: This panel gives special attention to programs you've bought from the App Store (see Chapter 5). The Allow App Store Apps pop-up menu even lets you specify an appropriate age group for the permitted apps. If you choose "up to 9+," for example, your well-parented offspring will be allowed to use all App Store programs that have been rated for use by anyone who's 9 or older.

Use Simple Finder

If you're *really* concerned about somebody's ability to survive the Mac—or the Mac's ability to survive somebody—turn on Use Simple Finder. Then turn on the checkboxes of the programs that person is allowed to use.

Suppose you've been given a Simple Finder account. When you log in, you discover the barren world shown in Figure 13-6. There are only three menus (, Finder, and File), a single onscreen window, no hard drive icon, and a bare-bones Dock. The only folders you can see are in the Dock. They include these:

- **My Applications.** This folder holds aliases of the applications that the administrator approved. They appear on a strange, fixed icon view called "pages." List and column views don't exist. As a Simple person, you can't move, rename, delete, sort, or change the display of these icons—you can merely click them. If you have too many to fit on one screen, you get numbered page buttons beneath them, which you can click to move from one set to another.

Figure 13-6:
The Simple Finder doesn't feel like home— unless you've got one of those Spartan, space-age, Dr. Evil– style pads. But it can be just the ticket for less-skilled Mac users, with few options and a basic one-click interface. Every program in the My Applications folder is actually an alias to the real program, which is safely ensconced in the off-limits Applications folder.

- **Documents.** Behind the scenes, this is your Home→Documents folder. Of course, as a Simple Finder kind of soul, you don't *have* a visible Home folder. All your stuff goes in here.

- **Shared.** This is the same Shared folder described on page 526. It's provided so that you and other account holders can exchange material. However, you can't open any of the folders here, only the documents.

- **Trash.** The Trash is here, but you won't use it much. Selecting or dragging any icon is against the rules, so you're left with no obvious means of putting anything into your Trash.

The only program with its own icon on the Dock is the Finder.

To keep things extra-simple, OS X permits only one window at a time to be open. It's easy to open icons, too, because *one* click opens them, not two.

The File menu is stunted, offering only a Close Window command. The Finder menu gives you only two options: About Finder and Run Full Finder. (The latter command prompts you for an administrator's user name and password, and then turns back into the regular Finder—a handy escape hatch. To return to Simple Finder, just choose Finder→Return to Simple Finder.)

The menu is *really* bare-bones: You can Log Out, Force Quit, or go to Sleep. That's it. And there's no trace of Spotlight.

Otherwise, you can essentially forget everything else you've read in this book. You can't create folders, move icons, or do much of anything beyond clicking the icons that your benevolent administrator has provided. It's as though OS X moved away and left you the empty house.

Although the Simple Finder is simple, any program (at least, any that the administrator has permitted) can run from Simple Finder. A program running inside the Simple Finder still has all its features and complexities—only the Finder has been whittled down to its essence.

In other words, Simple Finder is great for streamlining the Finder, but novices won't get far combating their techno-fear until the world presents us with Simple iMovie, Simple Mail, and Simple Microsoft Word. Still, it's better than nothing.

Web Tab

This feature is designed to limit which Web sites your kid is allowed to visit.

Frankly, trying to block the racy stuff from the Web is something of a hopeless task; if your kid doesn't manage to get around this blockade by simply using a different browser, then he'll just see the dirty pictures at another kid's house. But at least you can enjoy the illusion of taking a stand, using approaches with three degrees of severity:

- **Allow unrestricted access to Web sites.** No filtering. Anything goes.

- **Try to limit access to adult Web sites automatically.** Those words—"try to"—are Apple's way of admitting that no filter is foolproof.

 In any case, OS X analyzes what's on a Web page that you try to call up and filters out Web sites with naughty material. These sites won't appear in Safari while this account holder is logged in. By clicking Customize and then editing the "Always allow" and "Never allow" lists, you can override its decisions on a site-at-a-time basis.

- **Allow access to only these Web sites.** This is the most restrictive approach of all: It's a *whitelist,* a list of the *only* Web sites your youngster is allowed to visit. It's filled with kid-friendly sites like Disney and Discovery Kids, but of course you can edit the list by clicking the **+** and **−** buttons below the list.

People Tab

Here you can control your kid's access to three realms of people: those on email, on Messages, and on Game Center. Turn on the checkboxes as you feel it's necessary.

Then build a list of email and chat addresses, corresponding to the people you feel comfortable letting your kid exchange emails and chats with. Click the **+** button below the list, type the address, and then press Return. Lather, rinse, repeat.

Tip: No, you can't drag cards in from Contacts; that would be much too simple. But after clicking the **+** button to create a new row in the list (in Edit mode), you can drag *just the email address* out of a Contacts card you've opened up. Or expand the resulting dialog box (click the ▾ button) and double-click someone in your address book.

Parental Remote Controls

It occurred to somebody at Apple that the Parental Controls feature might be especially useful in a classroom. That person further realized that it'd be very cool if you could adjust the settings for Macs A, B, C, and D while *seated* at Mac E. That is, the teacher might prefer not to have to scurry from kid's desk to kid's desk to make changes.

And that's why you can operate Parental Controls from another Mac on the same network.

Phase 1: While seated at the first kid's Mac, open System Preferences, open Parental Controls, click the 🔒, and then enter your password.

Now click the name of the account you want to manage remotely. Then, from the ✿ menu below the list of accounts, choose Allow Remote Setup. Close System Preferences.

Repeat for each account on each Mac that you'll want to manage from afar.

Phase 2: Go back to your teacher's desk. On your own Mac, choose Go→Connect to Server. In the resulting dialog box, click Browse.

Now you get a list of the other Macs on the network. Click one and enter an administrator's name and password for that Mac.

Now open System Preferences, click Parental Controls, click the 🔒, and then enter your password again. This time, you'll see a section in the Users & Groups list called Other Computers. Click the account name (on the kid's Mac) whose settings you want to change. Enter the administrator name and password of the remote computer one more time, and off you go!

For reasons explained in a moment, turn on "Send permission requests to" and plug in your own email address.

Now then: When your youngster uses Apple's Mail program to send a message to someone who's *not* on the approved list, or tries to chat with someone not on the list, she gets the message shown at top in Figure 13-7. If she clicks Ask Permission, then *your* copy of Mail shortly receives a permission-request message; meanwhile, the outgoing message gets placed in limbo in her Drafts folder.

If you add that person's address to the list of approved correspondents (Figure 13-7, bottom), then the next time your young apprentice clicks the quarantined outgoing message in her Drafts folder, the banner across the top lets her know that all is well—and the message is OK to go out.

Note: This feature doesn't attempt to stop email or chat using *other* programs, like Microsoft Outlook or Skype. If you're worried about your efforts being bypassed, block access to those programs using the Permitted Applications list described above.

Figure 13-7:
Top: If your kid tries to contact someone who's not on the Approved list, she can either give up or click Ask Permission.

Bottom: In the latter case, if you use Mail as your email program, you'll know about your kid's attempt. If you're convinced that the would-be correspondent is not, in fact, a stalker, you can grant permission by clicking Always Allow. Your young ward gets the good news the next time she visits her Drafts folder, where the message has been awaiting word from you, the Good Parent.

When your underling fires up Messages or Mail, she'll discover that her Buddy List is empty except for the people you've identified.

Handling the teenage hissy fit is your problem.

Time Limits

Clever folks, those Apple programmers. They must have kids of their own.

They realize that some parents care about *how many* hours their kids spend in front of the Mac, and that some also care about *which* hours (Figure 13-8):

Figure 13-8:
Top: If this account holder tries to log in outside the time limits you specify here, she'll encounter only a box that says, "Computer time limits expired." She'll be offered a pop-up menu that grants her additional time, from 15 minutes to "Rest of the day"—but it requires your parental consent (actually, your parental password) to activate.

Bottom: Similarly, as her time on the Mac winds down, she'll get this message. Once again, you, the all-knowing administrator, can grant her more time using this dialog box.

- **How much time.** In the "Weekday time limits" and "Weekend time limits" sections, turn on "Limit computer use to," and then adjust the slider.

- **Which hours.** In the "Bedtime" section, turn on the checkbox for either "School nights" or "Weekend," and then set the hours of the day (or, rather, night) when the Mac is unavailable to your young account holder.

In other words, this feature may have the smallest pages-to-significance ratio in this entire book. Doesn't take long to explain it, but it could bring the parents of Mac addicts a lot of peace.

Tip: When Time Limits have been applied, your little rug rats can now check to see how much time they have left to goof off on the Mac before your digital iron fist slams down. When they click the menu-bar clock (where it now says the current time), a menu appears, complete with a readout that says, for example, "Parental Controls: Time Remaining 1:29." Good parenting comes in many forms.

Other Tab

This tab offers a few miscellaneous options, including the following:

- **Hide profanity in Dictionary.** OS X comes with a complete electronic copy of the *New Oxford American Dictionary.* And "complete," in this case, means "it even has swear words."

Turning on "Hide profanity in Dictionary" is like having an Insta-Censor™. It hides most of the naughty words from the dictionary whenever your young account holder is logged in (Figure 13-9).

Figure 13-9:
Something's missing from the Dictionary when the Parental Control tool is turned on: dirty words.

Parental Controls

- **Limit printer administration.** When this checkbox is on, your underlings aren't allowed to change your Mac's printer settings. You wouldn't want them deleting or installing any printers, would you?

- **Limit CD and DVD burning.** When you first create Standard accounts, their holders are free to burn CDs or DVDs. But in a school lab, for example, you might want to turn off the ability to burn discs (to block software piracy). That's why this box is here.

- **Disable changing the password.** Pretty self-explanatory. This option prevents your unruly minions from changing their passwords. That's your job, after all.

Editing Accounts

If you're an administrator, you can change your own account in any way you like.

If you have any other kind of account, though, you can't change anything but your picture, password, Apple ID, and login items. If you want to make any other changes, you have to ask an admin to log in, make the changes you want made to your account, and then turn the computer back over to you.

Deleting Accounts

Hey, it happens: Somebody graduates, somebody gets fired, somebody dumps you. Sooner or later, you may need to delete an account from your Mac.

When that time comes, click the account name in the Users & Groups list and then click the minus-sign button beneath the list. OS X asks what to do with all the dearly departed's files and settings (Figure 13-10):

- **Save the home folder in a disk image.** This option represents the "I'll be back" approach. OS X preserves the deleted account holder's folders on the Mac, in a tidy digital envelope that won't clutter your hard drive and can be reopened in case of emergency.

 In the Users→Deleted Users folder, you find a disk image file (.dmg). If you double-click it, a new, virtual disk icon named for the deleted account appears on your desktop. You can open folders and root through the stuff in this "disk," just as if it were a living, working Home folder.

 If fate ever brings that person back into your life, you can use this disk image to reinstate the deleted person's account. Start by creating a brand-new account. Then copy the contents of the folders in the mounted disk image (Documents, Pictures, Desktop, and so on) into the corresponding folders of the new Home folder.

- **Do not change the home folder.** This time, OS X removes the *account*, in that it no longer appears in the Login list or in the Users & Groups panel of System Preferences—but it leaves the *Home folder* right where it is. Use this option if you don't intend to dispose of the dearly departed's belongings right here and now.

- **Delete the home folder.** This button offers the "Hasta la vista, baby" approach. The account and all its files and settings are vaporized forever, on the spot.

Note: If you delete a Shared Only account, you're not offered the chance to preserve the Home folder contents—because a Shared Only account doesn't *have* a Home folder.

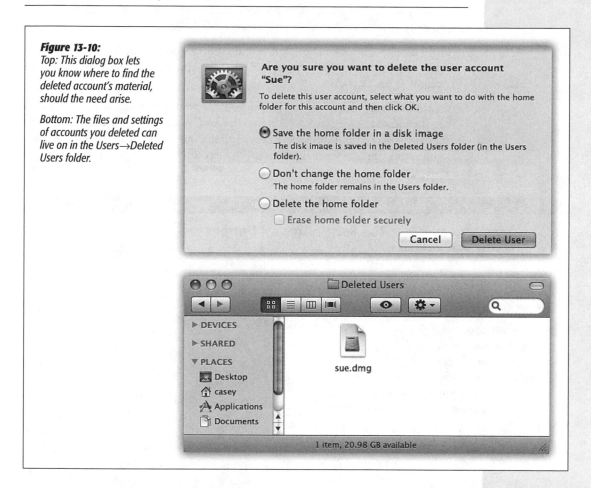

Figure 13-10:
Top: This dialog box lets you know where to find the deleted account's material, should the need arise.

Bottom: The files and settings of accounts you deleted can live on in the Users→Deleted Users folder.

Setting Up the Login Process

Once you've set up more than one account, the dialog box shown in Figure 13-1 appears whenever you turn on the Mac, whenever you choose →Log Out, or whenever the Mac logs you out automatically. But a few extra controls let you, an administrator, set up either more or less security at the login screen—or, put another way, build in less or more convenience.

Open System Preferences, click Users & Groups, click the and enter an admin password to prove your worthiness, and then click the Login Options button (Figure

13-11). Here are some of the ways you can shape the login experience for greater security (or greater convenience):

• **Automatic login.** This option eliminates the need to sign in at all. It's a timesaving, hassle-free arrangement if only one person uses the Mac, or uses it most of the time.

When you choose an account holder's name from this pop-up menu, you're prompted for his password. Type it and click OK.

From now on, the dialog box shown in Figure 13-1 won't appear *at all* at startup time. After turning on the machine, you, the specified account holder, zoom straight to your desktop.

Of course, everybody else must still enter their names and passwords. (And how can they, since the Mac rushes right into the Automatic person's account at startup time? Answer: The Automatic thing happens only at startup time. The usual login screen appears whenever the current account holder logs out—by choosing →Log Out, for example.)

POWER USERS' CLINIC

The Secret Account Options

Anyone who knows OS X very well might object to one sentence in this section: "If you're an administrator, you can change your own account in any way you like."

Because everybody knows that there's one aspect of an account that even an admin can't change: the account's *short name* (the account name, as opposed to the Full Name). Once that's created, it's yours forever, or at least until you delete the account.

Or at least that's what Apple wants you to think. There is, however, a secret way to pick a different short name. You can't easily *change* the one you created originally, but you can create *another* one—shorter, more memorable—that *also* works when you're logging in or authenticating yourself.

To find it, Control-click (or right-click) the account's name in

the list at the left side of the Users & Groups panel in System Preferences. From the shortcut menu, choose Advanced Options.

The strange and wonderful Advanced Options panel appears. Right there in the middle is an "Account name" box, but don't edit that; it won't work.

Instead, click the **+** button below the Aliases list. You're offered the chance to type in an *alternative* account name. Do it and then click OK. You can create as many of these aliases as you like.

When it's all over, click OK. The next time you log into your Mac, you can use your new, improved short name instead of the old one.

Rejoice that you lived to see the day.

- **Display login window as.** Under normal circumstances, the login screen presents a list of account holders when you power up the Mac, as shown in Figure 13-1. That's the "List of users" option in action.

 If you're especially worried about security, however, you might not even want that list to appear. If you turn on "Name and password" (Figure 13-11), then each person who signs in must type both his name (into a blank that appears) *and* his password—a very inconvenient, but more secure, arrangement.

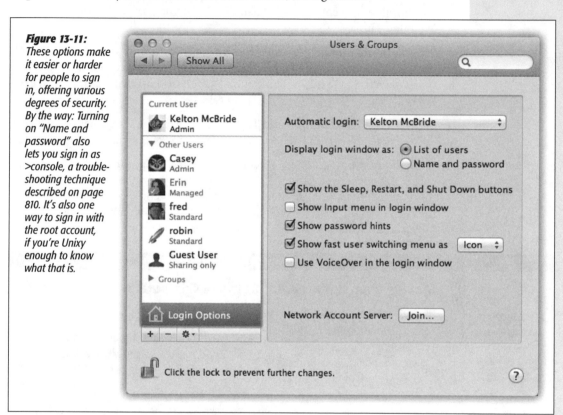

Figure 13-11:
These options make it easier or harder for people to sign in, offering various degrees of security. By the way: Turning on "Name and password" also lets you sign in as >console, a trouble-shooting technique described on page 810. It's also one way to sign in with the root account, if you're Unixy enough to know what that is.

- **Show the Sleep, Restart, and Shut Down buttons.** Truth is, the OS X security system is easy to circumvent. Truly devoted evildoers can bypass the standard login screen in a number of different ways: restart in FireWire disk mode, restart at the Unix Terminal, and so on. Suddenly, these no-goodniks have full access to every document on the machine, blowing right past all the safeguards you've so carefully established.

 One way to thwart them is to use FileVault (page 535). Another is to turn off this checkbox. Now there's no Restart or Shut Down button to tempt mischief-makers. That's plenty of protection in most homes, schools, and workplaces; after all, Mac people tend to be *nice* people.

But if you worry that somebody with a pronounced mean streak might restart simply by pulling the plug, then either use FileVault or set the *Firmware password*, as described in the box on the facing page.

• **Show Input menu in login window.** If the Input menu is available at login time, it means that people who use non-U.S. keyboard layouts and alphabets can use the login features without having to pretend to be American. (You can't use fancy non-Roman alphabets like Japanese or Russian for your password. But at least this option will let you enter your full name in the language of your choice. Greetings, Mr. Bond-san.)

• **Show password hints.** OS X is kind enough to display your password hint ("middle name of the first person who ever kissed me") after you've typed it wrong three times when trying to log in. This option lets you turn off that feature for an extra layer of security. The hint will never appear.

• **Show fast user switching menu as:** The Fast User Switching feature lets you switch to another account without having to log out of the first one, as described on page 527.

If you do turn on Fast User Switching, a new menu appears at the upper-right corner of your screen, listing all the account holders on the machine. Thanks to this pop-up menu, you can now specify what that menu looks like. It can display the current account holder's full name (Name), the short name (Short Name), or only a generic torso-silhouette icon (Icon) to save space on the menu bar.

POWER USERS' CLINIC

Moving Your Home Folder Between Computers

OS X proposes putting all the account holders' Home folders in one special folder (Users) on the main hard drive. But being able to put your Home folder on a different disk can have its advantages, too. If you bring your files back and forth between home and work, for example, you might find it convenient to keep your entire life on an iPod or some other portable disk. In corporate environments, a network administrator may want you to keep your Home folder elsewhere on the Windows network. (Yes, OS X is that compatible.)

You can do it, but it takes a few steps.

Begin by copying your Home folder to the iPod (or wherever). You can do it in the Finder, just by dragging the folder's icon as usual.

Now open the Users & Groups pane of System Preferences. Control-click (or right-click) your account's name; from the

shortcut menu, choose Advanced Options.

In the Advanced Options dialog box, in the Home Directory box, type the folder path to your new Home folder—or just click Choose and show OS X where it is.

Now restart the Mac. Log back in, and test the new Home-folder arrangement. If everything is working perfectly, you can delete the original from the internal hard drive.

If your intention is to take the external hard drive back and forth to work, repeat the procedure on the Mac at work.

Just make sure the external drive is plugged in, powered up, and running before you try to log in; otherwise, the Mac won't be able to find the Home folder at all and will give you an error message.

- **Use VoiceOver in the login window.** The VoiceOver feature (page 634) is all well and good if you're blind. But how are you supposed to log in? Turn on this checkbox, and VoiceOver speaks the features on the Login panel, too.

Tip: Actually, there's one more, rather secret login option—and if you're a laptop lugger, you might really like it. You can create a message that appears on the login screen whenever you—or, rather, *not* you—turns on the computer. For example, it could be an "If found, contact…" message. Or a "$500 reward" message.

To set it up, open System Preferences→Security & Privacy→General. Click the 🔒, authenticate yourself, and then turn on "Show a message when the screen is locked." Click Set Lock Message, and then type your message. (Press Option-Return to create a new paragraph.) And hope whoever finds your laptop has a conscience.

Signing In, Logging Out

Once somebody has set up your account, here's what it's like getting into, and out of, an OS X machine. (For the purposes of this discussion, "you" are no longer the

The Firmware Password Utility

After all this discussion of security and passwords, it may come as a bit of a shock to learn that enterprising villains can bypass all of OS X's security features in 10 seconds. If you haven't turned on FileVault, their nefarious options include using the Unix console described in Appendix B, single-user mode, FireWire disk mode, and so on.

But there is one way to secure your Mac completely: by turning on the very secret, little-known firmware password.

To find it, restart your Mac while pressing ⌘-R. That starts up Mountain Lion's Recovery console (page 803).

Once you've chosen your language, choose Utilities→Firmware Password Utility.

When you run this utility, enter an administrator's password. Now turn on "Require password to change firmware settings," as shown here. Then make up a password—your

firmware password—that will be required to start up from anything but the internal drive.

Next, you're asked for an administrator's password. Finally, a message tells you, "The settings were successfully saved." Restart the Mac.

From now on, whenever you attempt to start up in anything but the usual way, you're asked to type the firmware password. Holding down the C key to start up from a CD, holding down N to start up from a NetBoot server, pressing T to start up in Target Disk Mode, pressing D to start up from the installation DVD in diagnostic mode, pressing ⌘-V to start up in Verbose mode, ⌘-S to start up in Single-user mode, ⌘-Option-P-R to reset the parameter RAM, pressing Option to start up from a different system disk, pressing Shift to enter Safe Boot mode—none of it works without the master firmware password.

administrator—you're one of the students, employees, or family members for whom an account has been set up.)

Identifying Yourself

When you first turn on the Mac—or when the person who last used this computer chooses →Log Out—the login screen shown in Figure 13-1 appears. At this point, you can proceed in any of several ways:

- **Restart.** Click if you need to restart the Mac for some reason. (The Restart and Shut Down buttons don't appear here if the administrator has chosen to hide them as a security precaution.)

- **Shut Down.** Click if you're done for the day, or if sudden panic about the complexity of user accounts makes you want to run away. The computer turns off.

FREQUENTLY ASKED QUESTION

The Forgotten-Password Survival Guide

Help—I forgot my password! And I never told it to anybody, so even the administrator can't help me!

No problem. Your administrator can simply open up System Preferences, click Users & Groups, click your account name, and then click Reset Password to re-establish the password.

But you don't understand. I am the administrator! And I'm the only account!

Lucky for you, Apple has provided you with not one, not two, but three safety nets. None of them work, however, unless your friendly neighborhood administrator turned them on in advance.

First: On your third attempt to type your password correctly, the Mac shows you your password hint (if you have one, and if the administrator left the Hint option turned on).

Second: If the administrator has turned on the "Allow user to reset password using Apple ID" in System Preferences→Users & Groups, then you can click the ? button right there in the Password box when you're logging in. A tiny message appears, letting you know that, "If you forgot your password, you can reset it using your Apple ID."

To proceed, click the ⊕ button to bring up the Reset Password dialog box. Enter your Apple ID and password, and then click Reset Password. A message appears to let you

know that changing your account password will also create a new Keychain (page 542). (The old one is still around, ready to be unlocked if you remember the old password at some point.) Click OK. Now enter a new password (twice) and password hint, and then click Reset Password.

You've just reset your account password. Click Continue Log In to finish logging in with your new, improved, not-forgotten password.

Third: If the administrator has turned on FileVault, described later in this chapter, then you can use its recovery key to log in, in a pinch. Before Lion, it was called the master password, but the point is the same: It's a last-ditch, emergency, backup password.

If you have your recovery key, read on. (If not, and you opted to store it with Apple, call Apple tech support; they'll give it to you. If not, and you didn't store it with Apple, you're completely out of luck. Your hard drive is encrypted, and you can't do anything but erase it and kiss your files goodbye.)

Anyway, restart the Mac. On the login screen, click your name; then click the ? button. If the hint appears and it helps you out, great. If not, click "Reset it using your Recovery Key," type in your recovery key, and then praise the Apple gods that this final safety net actually worked.

- **Log In.** To sign in, click your account name in the list. If you're a keyboard speed freak, you can also type the first letter or two—or press the up or down arrow keys—until your name is highlighted. Then press Return.

Either way, the password box appears now (if a password is required). If you accidentally click the wrong person's name on the first screen, you can click Back. Otherwise, type your password, and then press Return (or click Log In).

You can try as many times as you want to type the password. With each incorrect guess, the entire password box shudders violently from side to side, as though shaking its head no. (If you see a strange ⇧ icon in the password box, guess what? You've got your Caps Lock key on, and the Mac thinks you're typing an all-capitals password.)

If you try unsuccessfully three times, your hint appears—if you've set one up. And if even that safety net fails, you can use your Apple ID as the key to resetting your password. See the box on the facing page.

Once you're in, the world of the Mac looks just the way you left it (or the way an administrator set it up for you). Everything in your Home folder, all your email and bookmarks, your desktop picture and Dock settings—all of it unique to you.

Unless you're an administrator, you're not allowed to install any new programs (or, indeed, to put anything at all) into the Applications folder. That folder, after all, is a central software repository for *everybody* who uses the Mac, and the Mac forbids everyday account holders from moving or changing all such universally shared folders.

Logging Out

When you're finished using the Mac, choose →Log Out (or press Shift-⌘-Q). A confirmation message appears; if you click Cancel or press Esc, you return to whatever you were doing. If you click Log Out or press Return, you return to the screen shown in Figure 13-1, and the entire sign-in cycle begins again.

Tip: If you press Option as you choose →Log Out (or as you press Shift-⌘-Q), the confirmation box doesn't appear.

Sharing Across Accounts

It's all fine to say that every account is segregated from all *other* accounts. It's nice to know your stuff is safe from the prying eyes of your coworkers or family.

But what about collaboration? What if you *want* to give some files or folders to another account holder?

You can't just open up someone else's Home folder and drop it in there. Yes, every account holder has a Home folder (all in the Users folder on your hard drive). But if you try to open anybody else's Home folder, you'll see a tiny red ⊖ icon superimposed on almost every folder inside, telling you, "Look, but don't touch."

Fortunately, there are a couple of wormholes between accounts (Figure 13-12):

- **The Shared folder.** Sitting in the Users folder is one folder that doesn't correspond to any particular person: Shared. Everybody can freely access this folder, inserting and extracting files without restriction. It's the common ground among all the account holders on a single Mac. It's Central Park, the farmers' market, and the grocery-store bulletin board.

Figure 13-12:
Top: In other people's Home folders, the Public folder is available for your inspection. It contains stuff that other people have "published" for the benefit of their coworkers.

Middle: In the Public folder is the Drop Box, which serves the opposite purpose. It lets anyone else who uses this Mac hand in files to you; they, however, can't see what's in it.

Bottom: Inside the Users folder (to get there from a Home folder, press ⌘-↑) is the Shared folder, a wormhole connecting all accounts. Everybody has full access to everything inside.

- **The Public folder.** In your Home folder, there's a folder called Public. Anything you copy into it becomes available for inspection or copying (but not changing or deleting) by any other account holder, whether they log into your Mac or sign in from across the network.

- **The Drop Box.** And *inside* your Public folder is another cool little folder: the Drop Box (not to be confused with the free online Dropbox service). It exists to let *other* people give files to *you,* discreetly and invisibly to anyone else. That is, people can drop files and folders into your Drop Box, but they can't actually *open* it. This folder, too, is available both locally (in person) and from across the network.

Fast User Switching

The account system described so far in this chapter has its charms. It keeps everyone's stuff separate, it keeps your files safe, and it lets you have the desktop picture of your choice.

Unfortunately, it can go from handy to hassle in one split second. That's when you're logged in, and somebody else wants to duck in just for a second—to check email or a calendar, for example. What are you supposed to do—log out completely, closing all your documents and quitting all your programs, just so the interloper can look something up? Then afterward, you'd have to log back in and fire up all your stuff again, praying that your inspirational muse hasn't fled in the meantime.

Fortunately, that's all over now. Fast User Switching lets Person B log in and use the Mac for a little while. All *your* stuff, Person A, simply slides into the background, still open the way you had it; see Figure 13-13.

FREQUENTLY ASKED QUESTION

Shared Data Files

My wife and my 8-year-old kid share my Mac. Over the years, we've amassed a fabulous collection of MP3 files, but at the moment, I'm the only one who sees them in iTunes. This business of separate environments for every account holder is all well and good, but what about when we want to access the same files—like our iTunes Library?

The problem is that the iTunes Library is stored in the Music folder of just one person. Fortunately, the solution is easy enough.

Whoever is the administrator—probably your 8-year-old—should move the iTunes Music folder (currently inside somebody's Music→iTunes folder) to the Users→Shared folder. Now it's available to everybody.

At this point, each account holder can log in, fire up iTunes, choose iTunes→Preferences→Advanced, and click the Change button to choose the relocated iTunes Music folder in the Shared folder. To update the list of songs, you should also drag the folder into each account holder's iTunes window.

From now on, each person will be able to see and access the entire library of iTunes tunes. Your underlings won't be able to rename songs, convert them to other formats, and so on, but they'll still enjoy the flexibility to build individual playlists.

When Person B is finished working, you can bring your whole work environment back to the screen without having to reopen anything. All your windows and programs are still open, just as you left them.

Figure 13-13:

Top: The appearance of the Accounts menu lets you know that Fast User Switching is turned on. The circled checkmark indicates people who are already logged in, including those who have been "fast user switched" into the background. The dimmed name shows who's logged in right now.

Bottom: When the screen changes from your account to somebody else's, your entire world slides visibly offscreen as though it's mounted on the side of a rotating cube—a spectacular animation made possible by OS X's Quartz Extreme graphics software.

To turn on this feature, open the Users & Groups panel of System Preferences (and click the 🔒, if necessary, to unlock the panel). Click Login Options, and turn on the "Show fast user switching menu as" checkbox. (You can see this option in Figure 13-11.)

The only change you notice immediately is the appearance of your own account name in the upper-right corner of the screen (Figure 13-13, top). You can change what this menu looks like by using the "Show fast user switching menu as" pop-up menu, also shown in Figure 13-11.

That's all there is to it. Next time you need a fellow account holder to relinquish control so you can duck in to do a little work, just choose your name from the Accounts menu. Type your password, if one is required, and feel guiltless about the interruption.

And now, the finer points of Fast User Switching:

- Depending on how many programs are open and how much memory the Mac has, switching accounts may entail a delay and some hard drive activity. That's OS X's virtual memory scheme "setting down" what was in memory in *your* account to make room for the incoming account's stuff.

- To exit an open account, choose →Log Out as usual. Or just choose Login Window from the Accounts menu. It ensures that you can get to your own account no matter whose is running at the moment.

- Weirdly enough, a bunch of account holders can be using the same program simultaneously in their own parallel universes. Even if Microsoft Word was open in your account, Chris, Casey, and Robin can each open the same copy of the same program simultaneously when they fast-switch into their own accounts.

- You can't make changes to accounts (in System Preferences) that are still logged in. Nor, as you'd expect, can you turn off Fast User Switching while other people are logged in. Can't turn on FileVault, either.

- If you try to shut the Mac down or restart it while other people are logged in, a dialog box tells you, "There are currently logged in users who may lose unsaved changes if you shut down this computer." And you're asked to type in an administrator's name and password to establish that you know what the heck you're doing.

 Here's a moral dilemma for the modern age: If you proceed by typing the password and clicking Shut Down, you shut down all accounts that were open in the background *and* any open documents. If you click Cancel, you can't shut down the Mac until you hunt down the account holders whose stuff is still open in the background so they can log out.

Tip: You can avoid this awkward situation in either of two ways: (1) Trust one another completely, or (2) Save all your documents before you let anyone else cut in and send your account to the background.

- Remember the Shared folder (in the Users folder on the hard drive)? It's still the wormhole connecting all accounts. If you want to share a file with another account holder, put it there.

- Your account isn't anesthetized completely when it's switched into the background. In fact, it keeps on doing whatever you set it to doing. If you were downloading some big file, for example, it keeps right on downloading when the next guy logs in.

Six OS X Security Shields

OS X has a spectacular reputation for stability and security. At this writing, there still hasn't been a single widespread OS X virus—a spectacular feature that makes Windows look like a waste of time. There's also no Windows-esque plague of spyware (downloaded programs that do something sneaky behind your back).

The usual rap is, "Well, that's because Windows is a much bigger target. What virus writer is going to waste his time on a computer with 8 percent market share?"

That may be part of the reason OS X is virus-free. But OS X was also built more intelligently from the ground up. Listed below are a few of the many drafty corners of a typical operating system that Apple has solidly plugged:

- The original Windows XP came with five of its *ports* open. OS X has always come from the factory with all of them shut and locked.

 Ports are channels that remote computers use to connect to services on your computer: one for instant messaging, one for Windows' remote-control feature, and so on. It's fine to have them open if you're expecting visitors. But if you've got an open port that exposes the soft underbelly of your computer without your knowledge, you're in for a world of hurt. Open ports are precisely what permitted viruses like Blaster to infiltrate millions of PCs. (Microsoft finally closed those ports in Windows XP Service Pack 2.)

- In OS X, no program (like a virus) can install itself without your awareness. You're notified at every juncture when anything is trying to install itself on your Mac. In fact, every time you try to download something, either in Safari or Mail, that contains *executable code* (a program, in other words), a dialog box warns you that it could conceivably harbor a virus—even if your download is compressed as a .zip file (Figure 13-14).

Figure 13-14:
The Mac makes darned sure that no program ever runs without your knowledge (which is how Windows PCs get viruses and spyware). It tries to protect you, for example, when you open a new program or when you first double-click a program that came from the Internet.

- Unlike certain other operating systems, OS X doesn't even let an administrator touch the files that drive the operating system itself without pestering you to provide your password and grant it permission to do so. An OS X virus could theoretically wipe out all your files, but it wouldn't be able to access anyone else's stuff—and it couldn't touch the operating system itself.

- You probably already know about the Finder's Secure Empty Trash option (page 94). But an option on the Erase tab of the Disk Utility program can do the same super-erasing of *all free space* on your hard drive. We're talking not just erasing, but recording gibberish over the spots where your files once were—once, seven

times, or *35* times—utterly shattering any hope a hard-disk recovery firm (or spy) might have had of recovering passwords or files from your hard drive.

- Safari's Private Browsing mode means you can freely visit Web sites without leaving any digital tracks—no history, no nothing.

Those are only a few tiny examples. Here are a few of OS X's big-ticket defenses.

Gatekeeper

This security feature is new in Mountain Lion, and it's going to send every Eastern European teenage hacker into therapy.

Nasty programs aren't very common on the Mac to begin with. But now, unless you turn Gatekeeper off, downloading a program that's secretly designed to damage your Mac is virtually impossible.

Gatekeeper won't even let you install programs that haven't been proven to be safe (Figure 13-15).

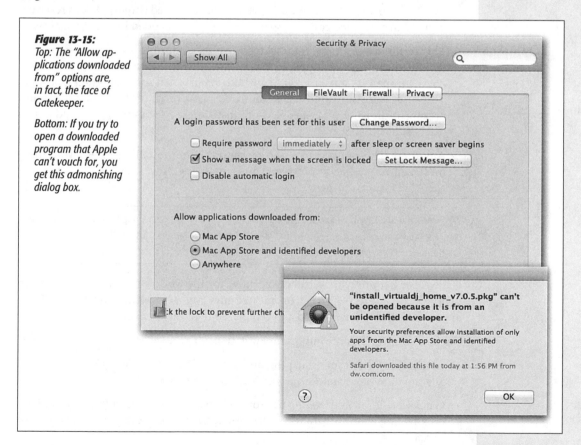

Figure 13-15:
Top: The "Allow applications downloaded from" options are, in fact, the face of Gatekeeper.

Bottom: If you try to open a downloaded program that Apple can't vouch for, you get this admonishing dialog box.

There's no Gatekeeper app or even a Gatekeeper System Preferences icon. Instead, to find Gatekeeper, you open System Preferences→Security & Privacy→General. At the bottom of this screen (Figure 13-15, top), you see three options. These three humble buttons are Gatekeeper.

Your choices, under "Allow applications downloaded from," are:

- **Mac App Store.** This is the safest option. Every program that Apple allows into its Mac App store is safe. Each has been tested by Apple to make sure that, among other things, it's both *sandboxed* (blocked from accessing parts of the Mac that it doesn't need) and *digitally signed* (set up to notify that Mac if it's been altered in any way since it left the software company).

 So what happens if you try to download a program that didn't come from the App Store? The Mac won't let you install it, period.

- **Mac App Store and identified developers.** This option, the factory setting, lets you download and install both App Store programs and those from "identified developers." That means software companies that have registered with Apple and received, in turn, an encrypted code (a "certificate") that's embedded in their programs.

 This certificate lets Apple track who created the app, and also digitally signs it, as described above. Now, Apple may not know this software company, and Apple doesn't inspect its software. But if anybody reports that some program is actually a virus in disguise, Apple can instantly add that program to its blacklist—and prevent millions of other people from installing it. (Mountain Lion updates its blacklist once a day.)

- **Anywhere.** This button turns Gatekeeper off (after presenting an "Are you sure?" message). You're free to download and install any programs you want, with no checking for their hygiene.

Tip: Don't turn on Anywhere just because there's one particular non-kosher app you want to run. In that case, it's smarter to leave Gatekeeper turned on—and override Gatekeeper just for that one app. To do so, Control-click (or right-click) the program's icon; from the shortcut menu, choose Open.

Gatekeeper is a pretty powerful disincentive for the world's bad eggs; if millions of people leave Gatekeeper turned on, the bad guys might as well not even bother. Their apps will never be downloaded and can therefore never spread.

There are, however, some important limitations to note:

- Gatekeeper doesn't uninstall programs you've already installed. (Once you've run any program once, Gatekeeper never checks it again.)

- Gatekeeper is intended to stop bad software that you get by *downloading*. It doesn't do anything about programs you've installed from, for example, a DVD or USB drive.

- It doesn't stop Flash and Java programs.

Overall, Gatekeeper is a pretty convincing barrier to a Windows-like nightmare scenario, where some virus breaks out into the wild and takes down hundreds of thousands of computers. If most people leave the factory setting selected—and they will—that outcome is virtually impossible.

The Firewall

If you have a broadband, always-on connection, you're open to the Internet 24 hours a day. It's theoretically possible for some cretin to use automated hacking software to flood you with data packets or take control of your machine. OS X's *firewall* feature puts up a barrier to such mischief. To turn it on, click the 🔒 on the Firewall pane, authenticate yourself, and then click Start.

Note: You don't need to turn on this firewall if your Mac connects to the Internet through a wired or wireless router (including the AirPort base station). Virtually every router already has a built-in firewall that protects your entire network. (Similarly, if you're using the Internet Sharing feature described on page 650, turn on the firewall only for the *first* Mac, the one connected right to the Internet.)

In short: Use the firewall only if your Mac is connected *directly* to a cable modem, DSL box, or dial-up modem.

Fortunately, it's not a *complete* barrier. One of the great joys of having a computer is the ability to connect to other computers. Living in a cement crypt is one way to avoid getting infected, but it's not much fun.

Therefore, you can turn the firewall on by opening System Preferences→Security→Firewall tab, authenticating, and clicking Turn On Firewall. But you can also fine-tune the blockade.

To do that, click Firewall Options; you see something like Figure 13-16 at top. As you can sort of tell, OS X lets you allow or block Internet connections individually for *each program* on your Mac. Here's what you'll find there:

- **Block all incoming connections.** This option might be better known as Paranoid Mode. You're allowed to do email and basic Web surfing and a few other deep-seated services that OS X needs to get by. But all other kinds of network connections are blocked, including screen sharing, iTunes music sharing, and so on. This is a hard-core, meat-fisted firewall that, for most people, is more trouble than it's worth.

Tip: As you can tell from the wording of this item, OS X's firewall blocks only *incoming* connections, which covers most of the dangerous stuff. But if you'd also like your Mac to block *outgoing* Internet connections, you can install a shareware firewall program like LittleSnitch. It's available on this book's "Missing CD" page at *www.missingmanuals.com*.

- **[List of individual programs].** If the firewall is on but you haven't turned on "Block all," then the Mac uses this list of individual programs and features to determine what's allowed to accept network connections.

Above the horizontal line (Figure 13-16, bottom), features of OS X itself are listed. They get added to this list automatically when you turn them on in System Preferences: File Sharing, Printer Sharing, and so on.

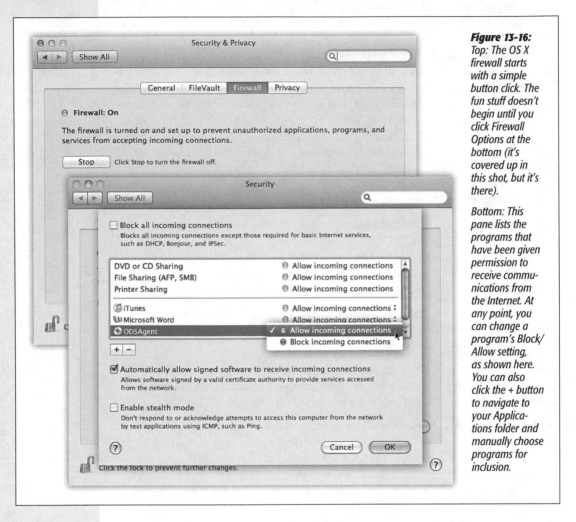

Figure 13-16:
Top: The OS X firewall starts with a simple button click. The fun stuff doesn't begin until you click Firewall Options at the bottom (it's covered up in this shot, but it's there).

Bottom: This pane lists the programs that have been given permission to receive communications from the Internet. At any point, you can change a program's Block/ Allow setting, as shown here. You can also click the + button to navigate to your Applications folder and manually choose programs for inclusion.

Non-Apple programs can gain passage through your firewall, too. You can add one to the list manually by clicking the **+** button below the list and choosing it by hand; or you can simply respond to the request box that pops up whenever a new program wants to accept incoming Internet connections.

Click Allow for each such request (unless, of course, you see a request for an app called SneakyPoisonVirus or something). As you do so, their names get added to the list of programs in this dialog box.

For each program, you can use the pop-up menu beside its name to specify either "Allow incoming connections" or "Block incoming connections," depending on your level of paranoia.

Note: From time to time, some program will ask for permission to accept incoming messages from its mother ship online. If it's a program you trust, click Allow.

- **Automatically allow signed software to receive incoming connections.** *Signed* software means programs that Apple recognizes as coming from legitimate companies. Anything from Adobe or Microsoft, for example, has got to be OK, right? (Insert your own wisecrack here.)

Note: OK, technically, a signed program is one whose authenticity is confirmed by a third party—a "certificate authority" company like VeriSign or GoDaddy. A system of invisible *keys* (security numbers) confirms that the software did indeed come from the creators it claims it came from, no matter how many detours it took to reach you.

One more point: When you explicitly grant permission to a program, as described below, *you're* signing that program.

If this checkbox is *not* turned on, then each time you run a new program for the first time, you'll be interrupted so that the Mac can ask if it's OK to permit Internet connections. The "signed software" box cuts down on the interruptions, since well-known apps are assumed not to be viruses or spyware.

- **Enable stealth mode.** This is designed to slam shut the Mac's back door to the Internet. See, hackers often use automated hacker tools that send out "Are you there?" messages. They're hoping to find computers that are turned on and connected full time to the Internet. If your machine responds, and they can figure out how to get into it, they'll use it, without your knowledge, as a relay station for pumping out spam or masking their hacking footsteps.

"Enable stealth mode," then, makes your Mac even more invisible on the network; it means your Mac won't respond to the electronic signal called a *ping*. (On the other hand, *you* won't be able to ping your machine, either, when you're on the road and want to know if it's turned on and online.)

Note: You might have noticed that there doesn't seem to be any option to turn on *firewall logging,* which creates a little text file where OS X records every attempt that anyone from the outside makes to infiltrate your Mac. Logging is available, though—in fact, it's turned on all the time. To view the log, open the Applications→Utilities→Console program. In the left-side list, expand the */private/var/log* heading, and click *appfirewall.log.*

FileVault

FileVault is one of OS X's most powerful security features. Understanding what it does, however, may take a little slogging.

As you know, the accounts system is designed to keep people out of one another's stuff. Ordinarily, for example, Chris isn't allowed to go rooting through Robin's email and files.

Until FileVault came along, though, there were all kinds of ways to circumvent this protection system. A sneak or a show-off could start up the Mac in FireWire disk mode, for example, or even remove the hard drive and hook it up to a Linux machine or another Mac.

In each case, they'd then be able to run rampant through everybody's files, changing or trashing them with abandon. For people with sensitive or private files, the result was a security hole bigger than Oprah's bank account.

FileVault is an extra line of defense. When you turn on this feature, your Mac automatically *encrypts* (scrambles) *everything* on your startup hard drive—not just what's in your Home folder. Every time you create or save a new file, it, too, is insta-encrypted.

Note: FileVault uses something called XTS-AES 128 encryption. How secure is that? It would take a password-guessing computer *149 trillion years* before hitting pay dirt. Or, in more human terms, slightly longer than two back-to-back Kevin Costner movies.

This means that unless someone knows (or can figure out) your password, FileVault renders your files unreadable for anyone but you and your computer's administrator—no matter what sneaky tricks they try to pull. (You can, if you like, authorize other account holders to get in, too.)

You won't notice much difference when FileVault is turned on. You log in as usual, clicking your name and typing your password. Only a slight pause as you log out indicates that OS X is doing some housekeeping on the encrypted files: freeing up some space and/or backing up your home directory with Time Machine.

Tip: This feature is especially useful for laptop owners. If someone swipes or "borrows" your laptop, they can't get into your stuff without the password.

Here are some things you should know about FileVault's protection:

- **It's useful only if you've logged out.** Once you're logged in, the entire drive is unlocked and accessible. If you want the protection, log out before you wander away from the Mac.

- **An administrator can access your files, too.** According to OS X's caste system, anyone with an Administrator account can theoretically have unhindered access to his peasants' files—even with FileVault on—if that administrator has the master password (the recovery key) described below.

- **FileVault 2 relies on the Recovery HD partition.** You can read about this secret chunk of your hard drive on page 802. For now, the point is that if you've deliberately reformatted your hard drive in some nonstandard way, you may not be able to use FileVault 2.

- **FileVault can encrypt external drives, too—even flash drives.** The controls to do this, though, are in a totally different place—not in System Preferences at all. Instead, open Disk Utility (in your Utilities folder). Erase the external drive using Mac OS Extended (Journaled, Encrypted) format. (And, yes, you have to *erase* the drive before you can encrypt it.)

Note: Pre-Lion machines won't be able to access a drive you've encrypted in this way.

- **Old FileVault still works.** If you upgraded your Mac from Snow Leopard, and you were using FileVault before, the protected accounts still work as they always have. But you won't be able to use FileVault 2 unless you first turn the old FileVault *off* for those old accounts. That's a good idea anyway, since FileVault 2 is so much better.

- **You can turn FileVault off at any time.** Just revisit the FileVault pane in System Preferences. (It takes time to decrypt your drive, but you can keep right on working.)

- **If you forget your password** *and* **your administrator forgets the recovery key, you're toast.** If this happens, your data is *permanently lost*. You have no choice but to erase your hard drive and start from scratch.

To turn FileVault on, proceed like this:

1. **In System Preferences, click Security & Privacy, and then click FileVault. Click the 🔒, authenticate yourself, and then click Turn On FileVault.**

 A list of account holders appears (Figure 13-17, top). The button next to each one, Enable User, might sound like you're about to lead someone into drug addiction, but it's actually your chance to specify who else can unlock the disk by logging in.

Note: If an account has *no* password, you have to add one first. Click the Set Password button that appears.

Virtual Memory, Security, and You

Virtual memory is a trick that computers use to keep a lot of programs open at once—more, in fact, than they technically have enough memory (RAM) for. How do they manage to keep so many software balls in the air? Easy: They set some of them down on the hard drive.

When you bring Photoshop to the front, OS X frees up the necessary memory for it by storing some of the *background* programs' code on the hard drive. When you switch back to, say, Safari, OS X swaps Photoshop for the Safari code it needs from the hard drive, so that the frontmost program always has full command of your actual memory.

Sophisticated software snoopers could, in theory, sneak up to the Mac while you're logged in but away from your desk. Using a built-in Unix command called *strings,* the no-goodniks could actually *read* what's stored on the hard drive in that virtual-memory swap file—in particular, your passwords.

When you turned on the old FileVault, your *virtual memory swap files* were also encrypted.

But in Mountain Lion, your virtual memory swap files are encrypted *all the time,* automatically and invisibly, so nobody can read them.

2. **For each person you want to be able to log into this Mac with her own password, click Enable User. Type in that person's password and click OK. When you're finished, click Continue.**

(Anyone in this list to whom you *don't* give access can still use the Mac—but only after persuading an administrator to come over and type in his name and password.)

Now, in huge type, the Mac displays your *recovery key*.

The recovery key is an override password that gives an administrator full power to access any account, even without knowing the account holder's password, or to turn off FileVault for any account.

The thinking goes like this: Yeah, yeah, the peons with Standard accounts forget their *account* passwords all the time. But with FileVault, a forgotten password would mean *the entire hard drive is locked forever*—so Apple gave you, the technically

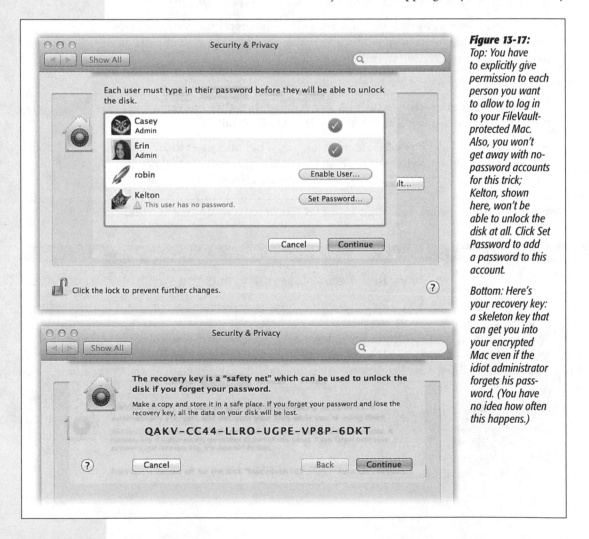

Figure 13-17:
Top: You have to explicitly give permission to each person you want to allow to log in to your FileVault-protected Mac. Also, you won't get away with no-password accounts for this trick; Kelton, shown here, won't be able to unlock the disk at all. Click Set Password to add a password to this account.

Bottom: Here's your recovery key: a skeleton key that can get you into your encrypted Mac even if the idiot administrator forgets his password. (You have no idea how often this happens.)

savvy administrator, a back door. (And you, the omniscient administrator, would *never* forget the recovery key—right?)

3. **Print or copy down the recovery key. Click Continue.**

 Because a forgotten password and recovery key could be absolutely devastating to your life, Apple handles this whole business like nuclear secrets (and so should you). Now, for example, a message appears that says, "Apple can store the recovery key for you." It's a really great idea to take advantage of this option.

 If you click "Store the recovery key with Apple," then the box expands and you're asked to type in the answers to three security questions (you can choose the questions from the pop-up menus): "What's your maternal grandmother's middle name?" for example. Don't mess this up; if you can't remember the answers, you won't get your recovery key from Apple.

4. **After answering the "Store the recovery key" screen, click Continue. On the following screen, click Restart.**

 When you log in again, the Mac begins the process of encrypting your entire hard drive. This process takes a long time (the FileVault pane in System Preferences shows you the estimated remaining time), but you can keep using your Mac in the meantime; in theory, you won't feel much of a slowdown at all while the encrypting is going on. You can even restart or shut down the computer.

 You shouldn't notice any speed hit as you work with an encrypted disk, either. You'll notice only a few small security-related changes. For example, you'll be asked for your password every time you wake the computer or exit the screen saver.

UP TO SPEED

Password Hell

In OS X, you have quite a few different passwords to keep straight. Each one, however, has a specific purpose:

Account password. You type this password in at the normal login screen. You can't get into anyone else's account with it—only yours. Entering this password unlocks FileVault, too.

Administrator password. You're asked to enter this password whenever you try to install new software or modify certain system settings. If you're the only one who uses your computer (or you're the one who controls it), your administrator password *is* your account password. Otherwise, you're supposed to go find an administrator (the parent, teacher,

or guru who set up your account to begin with) and ask that person to type in his name and password once he's assessed what you're trying to do.

Recovery key. Think of this password as a master key. If anyone with FileVault forgets her account password, the administrator who knows the master password can unlock the account. This master password also lets an administrator change an account's password right at the login screen, whether FileVault is turned on or not.

Root password. This password is rarely useful for anything other than Unix hackery; you know who you are.

Note: Actually, there's one more change. When FileVault is turned on, you won't see the icon for the Recovery HD appear when you hold down the Option key at startup. It's still there, though, and you can still start up with the Recovery HD by pressing ⌘-R as your Mac starts up.

Logout Options

As you read earlier in this chapter, the usual procedure for finishing up a work session is for each person to choose →Log Out. After you confirm your intention to log out, the login screen appears, ready for the next victim.

But sometimes people forget. You might wander off to the bathroom for a minute, but run into a colleague there who breathlessly begins describing last night's date and proposes finishing the conversation over pizza. The next thing you know, you've left your Mac unattended but logged in, with all your life's secrets accessible to anyone who walks by your desk.

You can tighten up that security hole, and many others, using the options in the Security & Privacy→General panel of System Preferences:

- **Require password [immediately] after sleep or screen saver begins.** This option gives you a password-protected screen saver that locks your Mac when you wander away. Now, whenever somebody tries to wake up your Mac after the screen saver has appeared (or when the Mac has simply gone to sleep according to your settings in the Energy Saver panel of System Preferences), the "Enter your password" dialog box appears. No password? No access.

 The pop-up menu here (which starts out saying "immediately") is a handy feature. Without it, the person most inconvenienced by the password requirement would be *you*, not the evil snitch from Accounting; even if you just stepped away to the bathroom or the coffee machine, you'd have to unlock the screen saver with your password. It would get old fast.

 Instead, the password requirement can kick in only after you've been away for a more serious amount of time—5 minutes, 15 minutes, an hour, whatever. You can still put the Mac to sleep, or you can still set up your screen saver to kick in sooner than that. But until that time period has passed, you'll be able to wake the machine without having to log in.

 (Super-geeky bonus fact: You can use a Unix command in Terminal, described on page 469, to specify *any* time interval—not just the canned choices in the pop-up menu. The magic command is *defaults -currentHost write com.apple.screensaver askForPasswordDelay -int 1800,* where the final number specifies how many seconds should elapse before a password is required.)

- **Disable automatic login.** This is just a duplicate of the Automatic Login on/off switch described on page 520. Apple figured that this feature really deserved *some* presence on a control panel called Security & Privacy.

- **Show a message when the screen is locked.** Whatever you type into this box will appear on the login screen (where you click your name in the list) or the screen saver..

If you click the Advanced button (it's at the bottom of the Security & Privacy pane of System Preferences), you get these three bonus tweaks:

- **Require an administrator password to access system preferences with lock icons.** Ordinarily, certain System Preferences changes require an administrator's approval—namely, the ones that affect the entire computer and everyone who uses it, like Date & Time, Users & Groups, Network, Time Machine, and Security & Privacy. If you're *not* an administrator, you can't make changes to these panels until an administrator has typed in her name and password to approve your change.

 However, once Mr. Teacher or Ms. Parent has unlocked *one* of those secure preference settings, they're *all* unlocked. Once the administrator leaves your desk, you can go right on making changes to the *other* important panels (Network *and* Time Machine *and* Security & Privacy) without the administrator's knowledge.

 Unless this "Require an administrator password" box is turned on, that is. In that case, an Administrative account holder has to enter her name and password to approve *each* of those System Preferences panes individually.

- **Log out after [60] minutes of inactivity.** You can make the Mac sign out of your account completely if it figures out that you've wandered off (and it's been, say, 15 minutes since the last time you touched the mouse or keyboard). Anyone who shows up at your Mac will find only the standard login screen.

- **Automatically update safe downloads list.** This option refers to Apple's master list of viruses and spyware, which Mail and Safari block automatically. That list, of course, is changing all the time as Apple discovers new nasties; this option tells your Mac to update itself with Apple's master list automatically.

The Password Assistant

Plenty of software features require you to make up a password: Web sites, accounts, networked disks, and so on. No wonder most people wind up trying to use the same password in as many situations as possible. Worse, they use something easily guessable

Figure 13-18:
Anyplace you're supposed to make up a password, including in the Users & Groups pane of System Preferences, a key icon appears. When you click it, the Password Assistant opens. Use the pop-up menu and the Length slider to specify how long and unguessable the password should be. The Quality graph shows you just how tough it is to crack this password.

(In the Type pop-up menu, you might wonder about FIPS-181. It stands for the Federal Information Processing Standards Publication 181, which sets forth the U.S. government's standard for password-generating algorithms.)

like their names, kids' names, spouse's names, and so on. Even regular English words aren't very secure, because hackers routinely use *dictionary attacks*—software that tries to guess your password by running through every word in the dictionary—to break in.

To prevent evildoers from guessing your passwords, OS X comes with a good-password suggestion feature called the Password Assistant (Figure 13-18). It cheerfully generates one suggestion after another for impossible-to-guess passwords (*recharges8@ exchangeability,* anyone?).

Fortunately, *you* won't have to remember most of them, thanks to the Keychain password-memorizing feature described at the end of this chapter. (The only password you have to memorize is your account password.)

The Keychain

The information explosion of the computer age may translate into bargains, power, and efficiency, but as noted above, it carries with it a colossal annoyance: the proliferation of *passwords* we have to memorize. Shared folders on the network, Web sites, FTP sites—each requires another password.

Apple has done the world a mighty favor with its *Keychain* feature. Whenever you log into OS X and type in your password, you've typed the master code that tells the computer, "It's really me. I'm at my computer now." From that moment on, the Mac *automatically* fills in every password blank you encounter, whether it's a Web site in Safari, a shared disk on your network, a wireless network, an encrypted disk image, or an FTP (File Transfer Protocol) program like Transmit or Cyberduck. With only a few exceptions, you can safely forget *all* your passwords except your login password.

These days, all kinds of programs and services know about the Keychain and offer to store your passwords there. For example:

- In Safari, whenever you type your name and password for a certain Web page and then click OK, a dialog box asks: "Would you like to save this password?" (See Figure 13-19, top.)

Note: This offer is valid only if, in Safari→Preferences→AutoFill tab, "User names and passwords" is turned on. If not, the "Would you like to save this password?" message never appears.

Note, too, that some Web sites use a nonstandard login system that also doesn't produce the "Would you?" message. Unless the Web site provides its own "Remember me" or "Store my password" option, you're out of luck; you'll have to type in this information with every visit.

- When you connect to a shared folder or disk on the network, the opportunity to save the password in your Keychain is equally obvious (Figure 13-19, bottom).

- You also see a "Remember password (add to Keychain)" option when you create an encrypted disk image using Disk Utility.

- Mac email programs, like Mail and Entourage/Outlook, store your email account passwords in your Keychain. So do FTP programs; check their Preferences dialog boxes.

- Your iCloud account information is stored in the Keychain, too (as you entered it on the iCloud pane of System Preferences).

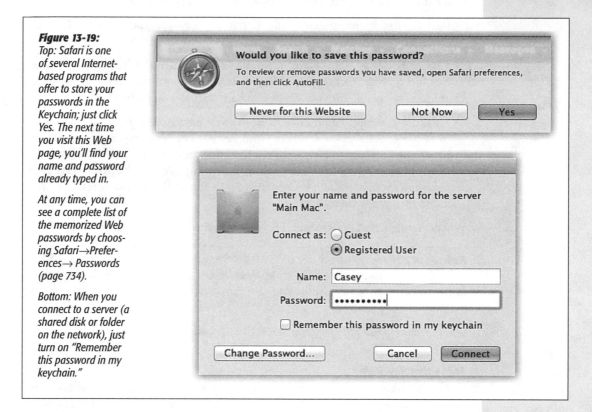

Figure 13-19:
Top: Safari is one of several Internet-based programs that offer to store your passwords in the Keychain; just click Yes. The next time you visit this Web page, you'll find your name and password already typed in.

At any time, you can see a complete list of the memorized Web passwords by choosing Safari→Preferences→ Passwords (page 734).

Bottom: When you connect to a server (a shared disk or folder on the network), just turn on "Remember this password in my keychain."

- A "Remember password" option appears when you type in the password for a wireless network or an AirPort base station.

- The iTunes program memorizes your iTunes Store password, too.

Locking and unlocking the Keychain

If you work alone, the Keychain is automatic, invisible, and generally wonderful. Login is the only time you have to type a password. After that, the Mac figures, "Hey, I know it's you; you proved it by entering your account password. That ID is good enough for me. I'll fill in all your other passwords automatically." In Apple parlance, you've *unlocked* your Keychain just by logging in.

But there may be times when you want the Keychain to *stop* filling in all your passwords, perhaps only temporarily. Maybe you work in an office where someone else might sit down at your Mac while you're getting a candy bar.

Of course, you can have OS X lock your Mac—Keychain and all—after a specified period of inactivity (page 541).

But if you want to lock the Keychain *manually,* so that no passwords are autofilled in until you unlock it again, you can use any of these methods. Each requires the Keychain Access program (in your Applications→Utilities folder):

- **Lock the Keychain manually.** In the Keychain Access program, choose File→Lock Keychain "login" (⌘-L), or just click the big 🔒 button in the toolbar (Figure 13-20).

- **Choose Lock Keychain "login" from the Keychain menulet.** To put the Keychain menulet on your menu bar, open Keychain Access, choose Keychain Access→Preferences→General. Turn on "Show keychain status in menu bar."

- **Lock the Keychain automatically.** In the Keychain Access program, choose Edit→Change Settings for Keychain [your name]. The resulting dialog box lets you set up the Keychain to lock itself, say, 5 minutes after the last time you used your Mac, or whenever the Mac goes to sleep. When you return to the Mac, you're asked to re-enter your account password in order to unlock the Keychain, restoring your automatic-password feature.

Whenever the Keychain is locked, OS X no longer fills in your passwords.

Note: As noted above, you unlock your Keychain using the same password you use to log into OS X, but that's just a convenience. If you're really worried about security, you can choose Edit→Change Password for Keychain [your name], thereby establishing a *different* password for your Keychain, so that it no longer matches your login password.

Of course, doing so also turns off the automatic-Keychain-unlocking-when-you-log-in feature.

Managing Keychain

To take a look at your Keychain, open the Keychain Access program. By clicking one of the password rows, you get to see its attributes—name, kind, account, and so on (Figure 13-20).

Tip: The primary purpose of the Keychain is, of course, to type in passwords for you automatically. However, it's also an excellent place to record all kinds of private information just for your own reference: credit card numbers, ATM numbers, and so on. Simply choose File→New Password Item (if it's a name and password) or File→New Secure Note Item (if you just want to type a blob of very, very private text).

No, the Mac won't type them in for you automatically anywhere, but it will maintain them in one central location that is, itself, password-protected.

Multiple Keychains

By choosing File→New Keychain, you can create more than one Keychain, each with its own master password. On one hand, this might defeat the simplicity goal of the Keychain. On the other hand, it's conceivable that you might want to encrypt all your business documents with one master password and all your personal stuff with another, for example.

If you do have more than one Keychain, you can view all of them by clicking the little Show Keychains button at the lower-left corner of the Keychain Access window; now you see a list of all your Keychains (including some maintained by OS X itself). Click their names to switch among them.

Figure 13-20:
In the main Keychain list, you can double-click a listing for more details about a certain password–including the actual password it's storing. To see the password, turn on "Show password." The first time you try this, you're asked to prove your worthiness by entering your Keychain password (usually your account password). If you then click Always Allow, you won't be bothered for a password-to-see-this-password again.

Keychain files

Keychains are represented by separate files in your Home→Library→Keychains folder. Knowing that can be handy when you want to delete a Keychain or copy it to another Mac—your laptop, for example. (Then again, the File→Export command may be even more convenient.)

And Four Privacy Shields

In Apple's mind, there's a difference between security (protecting your Mac) and privacy (protecting your information from distribution).

The Privacy tab in the Security & Privacy pane of System Preferences harbors four fairly random privacy-related options:

Location Services

Location Services means "knowing where I am." It's the feature that lets your laptop figure out its own time zone automatically, for example, or that lets a weather Web site show your *local* weather the first time you visit.

Every time a program wants to use your current location for its own features, you'll be asked about it. (The Mac figures out your location based on its proximity to known WiFi networks.) Each time you say OK, the program that did the asking installs its own name into the list here.

You can turn off the checkboxes of the programs you'd rather didn't know where you are, or you can turn off location tracking altogether by turning off the "Enable location services" box.

Contacts

Some programs work better if you allow them to access your database of names and addresses. For example, Skype wants access so that it can incorporate *your* address book into *its* address book. This list shows all of the programs that access your Contacts—and offers checkboxes to turn off that access.

Twitter, Facebook

Here, you'll see programs that want to access your Twitter and Facebook accounts. Once again, you can turn off their access, if you like.

Diagnostic and Usage Data

If you turn on this box, your Mac will automatically and quietly send data to Apple about what's going on with your Mac (anonymously, of course—Apple won't know it's you). The transmissions include details about crashes and freezes, what programs and hardware you use, what software versions and peripherals you have, and so on.

None of this is transmitted unless you turn this box on.

Incidentally, you have another chance to turn on automatic reporting: when a program, or your Mac, crashes. At that time, a message invites you to send a crash report to Apple; you can click either OK or No Thanks. You can also turn on "Don't ask me again," which makes your OK or No Thanks decision permanent. (What you're actually doing with that "Don't ask me again" option, of course, is changing the status of this checkbox here in the Security & Privacy pane of System Preferences. That's how you can change your mind later.

Tip: Want to *see* the sort of information being sent? Open the Console app in Applications→Utilities. In the toolbar, click Show Log List, if necessary. Next to Diagnostic and Usage Information, click Show, if necessary. Under the subheadings here, you can read the sort of reports that Apple gets if you permit automatic sending. (*Understanding* the gobbledygook is another story.)

Networking, File Sharing & AirDrop

Networks are awesome. Once you've got a home or office network, you can copy files from one machine to another—even between Windows PCs and Macs—just as you'd drag files between folders on your own Mac. You can send little messages to other people's screens. Everyone on the network can consult the same database or calendar, or listen to the same iTunes music collection. You can play games over the network. You can share a single printer or cable modem among all the Macs in the office. You can connect to the network from wherever you are in the world, using the Internet as the world's longest extension cord back to your office.

In OS X, you can even do *screen sharing*, which means that you, the wise computer whiz, can see what's on the screen of your pathetic, floundering relative or buddy elsewhere on the network. You can seize control of the other Mac's mouse and keyboard. You can troubleshoot, fiddle with settings, and so on. It's the next best thing to being there—often, a lot *better* than being there.

Note: This chapter concerns itself with *local* networking—setting up a network in your home or small office. But don't miss its sibling, Chapter 17, which is about hooking up to the somewhat larger network called the Internet.

Wiring the Network

Most people connect their computers using one of two connection systems: Ethernet or WiFi.

Note: Until OS X Lion came along, Apple had its own name for WiFi: AirPort. That's what it said in System Preferences→Network, for example, and that's what the 🛜 menulet was called.

AirPort was a lot cleverer, wordplay-wise, than the meaningless "WiFi." Unfortunately, not many people realized that AirPort was the same thing as what the rest of the world called WiFi. So at least in the onscreen references, these days, Apple gives AirPort a new name: WiFi.

Ethernet Networks

Every Mac (except the MacBook Air) and every network-ready laser printer has an Ethernet jack (Figure 14-1). If you connect all the Macs and Ethernet printers in your small office to a central Ethernet hub, switch, or *router*—a compact, inexpensive box with jacks for five, 10, or even more computers and printers—you've got yourself a very fast, very reliable network. (Most people wind up hiding the hub in a closet and running the wiring either along the edges of the room or inside the walls.) You can buy Ethernet cables, plus the hub, at any computer store or, less expensively, from an Internet-based mail-order house; none of this stuff is Mac-specific.

Tip: If you want to connect only two Macs—say, your laptop and your desktop machine—you don't need an Ethernet hub. Instead, you just need a standard Ethernet cable. Run it directly between the Ethernet jacks of the two computers. (You don't need a special *crossover* Ethernet cable, as you did with Macs of old.) Then connect the Macs as described in the box on page 550.

Or don't use Ethernet at all; just use a FireWire cable or a person-to-person WiFi network.

Ethernet jack Ethernet hub

Figure 14-1:
Every Mac except the Air has a built-in Ethernet jack (left). It looks like an overweight telephone jack. It connects to an Ethernet router or hub (right) via an Ethernet cable (also known as Cat 5 or Cat 6), which ends in what looks like an overweight telephone-wire plug (also known as an RJ-45 connector).

Ethernet is the best networking system for many offices. It's fast, easy, and cheap.

WiFi Networks

WiFi, known to the geeks as 802.11 and to Apple fans as AirPort, means wireless networking. It's the technology that lets laptops get online at high speed in any WiFi "hotspot." Hotspots are everywhere these days: in homes, offices, coffee shops, hotels, airports, and thousands of other places.

Tip: At *www.jiwire.com,* you can type in an address or a city and learn exactly where to find the closest WiFi hotspots.

When you're in a WiFi hotspot, your Mac has a very fast connection to the Internet, as though it's connected to a cable modem or DSL.

WiFi circuitry comes preinstalled in every new Mac. This circuitry lets your machine connect to your network and the Internet without any wires at all. You just have to be within about 150 feet of a *base station* or (as Windows people call it) *access point,* which must in turn be physically connected to a network and Internet connection.

If you think about it, WiFi is a lot like a cordless phone, where the base station is, well, the base station, and the Mac is the handset.

The base station can take any of these forms:

- **AirPort base station.** Apple's sleek, white, squarish base stations ($100 to $180) permit as many as 50 computers to connect simultaneously.

UP TO SPEED

AirPort a, b, g, and n: Regular or Supersized?

In the short history of wireless networking, WiFi gear has come in several variants, bearing the absurdly user-hostile names 802.11b, 802.11g, 802.11a, 802.11n, and so on.

The difference involves the technical specs of the wireless signal. Original AirPort uses the 802.11b standard; AirPort Extreme uses 802.11g; the current AirPort cards and base stations use 802.11n.

So what's the difference? Equipment bearing the "b" label transfers data through the air at up to 11 megabits per second; the "g" system is almost five times as fast (54 megabits a second); and "n" is supposed to be four times as fast as that.

(Traditionally, geeks measure network speeds in megabits, not megabytes. If you're more familiar with megabytes, though, here's a translation: The older AirPort gear has a top speed of 1.4 megabytes per second, versus more than 6 megabytes per second for the AirPort Extreme stuff.)

(Oh, and while we're using parentheses here: The only place you'll get the quoted speeds out of this gear is on the moon. Here on earth, signal strength is affected by pesky things like air, furniture, walls, floors, wiring, phone interference, and antenna angles. Speed and signal strength diminish proportionally as you move away from the base station.)

Now, each successive version of the WiFi base station/laptop circuitry standard is backward-compatible. For example, you can buy a new, 802.11n base station, and still connect to it from your ancient 802.11g PowerBook. You won't get any greater speed, of course—that would require a laptop with an 802.11n transmitter—but you'll enjoy the greater range in your house.

It's important to understand, though, that even the most expensive, top-tier cable modem or DSL service delivers Internet information at only about half a megabyte per second. The bottleneck is the Internet connection, not your network. Don't buy newer AirPort gear thinking that you're going to speed up your email and Web activity.

Instead, the speed boost you get with AirPort Extreme is useful only for transferring files between computers and gadgets on your own network (like the bandwidth-hungry Apple TV)—and playing networkable games.

And one more note: All WiFi gear works together, no matter what kind of computer you have. There's no such thing as a "Windows" wireless network or a "Macintosh" wireless network. Macs can use non-Apple base stations, Windows PCs can use AirPort base stations, and so on.

The less expensive one, the AirPort Express, is so small it looks like a small white power adapter. It also has a USB jack so you can share a USB printer on the network. It can serve up to 10 computers at once.

- **A Time Capsule.** This Apple gizmo is exactly the same as the AirPort base station, except that it also contains a huge hard drive so that it can back up your Macs automatically over the wired or wireless network.

- **A wireless broadband router.** Linksys, Belkin, and lots of other companies make less expensive WiFi base stations. You can plug the base station into an Ethernet router or hub, thus permitting 10 or 20 wireless-equipped computers, including Macs, to join an existing Ethernet network without wiring. (With all due non-fanboyism, however, Apple's base stations and software are more polished and satisfying to use.)

Tip: It's perfectly possible to plug a WiFi base station into a regular router, too, to accommodate both wired and wireless computers.

- **Another Mac.** Your Mac can also *impersonate* an AirPort base station. In effect, the Mac becomes a software-based base station, and you save yourself the cost of a separate physical base station.

- **A modem.** A few, proud people still get online by dialing via modem, which is built into some old AirPort base station models. The base station is plugged into a phone jack. Wireless Macs in the house can get online by triggering the base station to dial by remote control.

Tip: If you connect through a modern router or AirPort base station, you already have a great firewall protecting you. You don't have to turn on OS X's firewall.

GEM IN THE ROUGH

Networking Without the Network

In a pinch, you can connect two Macs without any real network at all. You can create an Ethernet connection without a hub or a router—or an AirPort connection without a WiFi base station.

To set up the wired connection, just run a standard Ethernet cable between the Ethernet jacks of the two Macs. (You don't need to use an Ethernet crossover cable, as you did in days of old.)

To set up a wireless connection, from your 🛜 menulet,

choose Create Network. Make up a name and password for your little private network, and then click OK. On the second Mac, choose 🛜→Join Network, enter the same private network name, and then click Join.

At this point, your two Macs belong to the same ad hoc micro-network. If you've shared some folders on the first Mac, its name (like "Casey's iMac") now appears in the Sidebar of the second Mac. Click it to see what's on it. From here, proceed exactly as described on page 561.

You use the AirPort Utility (in your Applications→Utilities folder) to set up your base station; if you have a typical cable modem or DSL, the setup practically takes care of itself.

Whether you've set up your own wireless network or want to hop onto somebody else's, Chapter 17 has the full scoop on *joining* WiFi networks.

Cell Networks

If you have an iPhone or a similar cellphone, you may be able to get your Mac online even when you're hundreds of miles from the nearest Ethernet jack or WiFi hotspot. Thanks to *tethering,* your phone can act as an Internet antenna for your laptop, relying on the slow, expensive, but almost ubiquitous *cellular* network for its connection. Details are on page 647.

FireWire Networks

Apple is busily phasing out the convenient, fast *FireWire* jacks on its Macs. But if you have two FireWire-equipped Macs, you can create a blazing-fast connection between them with nothing more than a FireWire cable. Details are in the free downloadable appendix to this chapter called "FireWire Networking." It's available on this book's "Missing CD" page at *www.missingmanuals.com.*

File Sharing: Three Ways

When you're done wiring (or not wiring, as the case may be), your network is ready. Your Mac should "see" any Ethernet or shared USB printers, in readiness to print (Chapter 15). You can now play network games or use a network calendar. And you can now turn on *File Sharing,* one of the most useful features of all.

In File Sharing, you can drag files back and forth between different Macs (or even Windows PCs) on the network, exactly as though the other computer's folder or disk is a hard drive connected to your own machine. You can see the idea in Figure 14-2.

The thing is, it's not easy being Apple. You have to write *one* operating system that's supposed to please *everyone,* from the self-employed first-time newbie to the network administrator for NASA. You have to design a networking system simple enough for the laptop owner who just wants to copy things to a desktop Mac when returning from a trip, yet secure and flexible enough for the network designer at a large corporation.

Clearly, different people have different attitudes toward the need for security and flexibility.

That's why OS X offers *three ways* to share files, striking three different positions along the Simplicity-to-Flexibility Spectrum:

- **The easiest way: AirDrop.** This feature is dreamy—if there are other people in your house or office who have wireless Macs running Lion or Mountain Lion. Imagine this: You open the AirDrop folder, where you see everybody else's icons. To give someone a file, you drop its icon on that person's face. Done.

• **What used to be the easiest way: the Public folder.** Every account holder has a Public folder. It's free for anyone else on the network to access. Like a grocery store bulletin board, there's no password required. Super-convenient, super-easy.

There's only one downside, and you may not care about it: You have to move or copy files *into* the Public folder before anyone else can see them. Depending on how many files you want to share, this can get tedious, disrupt your standard organizational structure, and eat up disk space.

• **The flexible way: any folder.** You can also make *any* file, folder, or disk available for inspection by other people on the network. This method means that you don't have to move files into the Public folder, for starters. It also gives you elaborate control over who is allowed to do what to your files. You might want to permit your company's executives to see *and* edit your documents, but allow the peons in Accounting just to see them. And Andy, that unreliable goofball in Sales? You don't want him even *seeing* what's in your shared folder.

Of course, setting up all those levels of control means more work and more complexity.

The following pages tackle these three methods one at a time.

Figure 14-2:
Here's the master switch that makes your Public folder (and any other folders you designate) available to other people on the network. You can edit the Computer Name, if you like. Your Mac will appear on the network with this name. Make it nice and descriptive, such as Front Desk iMac.

AirDrop

AirDrop is one of Mountain Lion's star attractions. It's a breakthrough in speed, simplicity, and efficiency. There's no setup, no passwords involved. It lets you copy files to someone else's Mac up to 30 feet away, instantly and wirelessly; you don't need an Internet connection or even a WiFi network. It works on a flight, a beach, or a sailboat in the middle of the Atlantic. It also works if you are on a WiFi network, doing other things online.

Figure 14-3:
Top: If there are other Lion or Mountain Lion Macs within about 30 feet, you see their logged-in users' icons here. Usually, the icons display the Mac owners' account pictures; but if they have facial photos in your Contacts, then you see those instead.

Bottom: Here's what you see if you're the recipient (and have clicked Save in the confirmation box). To find your newly arrived goodies, open your Downloads folder.

To give someone a file, you and your lucky recipient must each open your respective AirDrop window. Then you have a choice:

Drag into the AirDrop window

Open the AirDrop window. To do that, click the AirDrop icon (at the top of the Sidebar in any Finder window), choose Go→AirDrop, or press Shift-⌘-R.

Note: If you don't see AirDrop in the Sidebar, and you're sure you're using Lion or Mountain Lion, it's because somebody turned off its checkbox in Finder→Preferences→Sidebar. Hiding the AirDrop icon in this way means you can't use the feature at all, at least not by dragging an icon into a window. You can still use the Share button as described below.

The window shown in Figure 14-3 appears. After a moment, it fills up with icons for everyone nearby who's running a wireless Lion or Mountain Lion Mac—and has opened their AirDrop windows. They don't have to do anything else; their icons show up automatically in *your* AirDrop window.

Now drag a file or folder icon, or several, onto the icon of the intended recipient. When the Mac asks if you're sure, click Send or press Return.

The recipient now sees a message that says, "[Other guy's Mac] wants to send you [the file's name]." And there are three options: Save and Open, Decline, and Save.

If the lucky winner clicks one of the Save buttons, then the file transfer proceeds automatically. A progress bar wraps *around* the other person's icon in the AirDrop window—cute. The transfer is encrypted, so evildoers nearby have no clue what you're transferring (or even *that* you're transferring).

The file winds up in the other guy's Downloads folder.

Tip: The Downloads folder generally sits on the Dock, so it's easy to find. But your recipient can also choose Go→Downloads, or press Option-⌘-L, to jump there.

Use the Share Sheet

In Mountain Lion, there's another, more direct way to send a file by AirDrop. Click the icon of the file you want to send (or select several). Now choose the Share→Air-Drop command.

And where is that command? Everywhere. It's in the shortcut menu that appears when you Control-click (right-click) an icon. It's in the ➦ icon at the top of every Finder window, and at the top of every Quick Look window. (See page 268 for more on the Share button.)

Now a miniature version of the AirDrop window appears; see Figure 14-4.

Once you've clicked the recipient's icon, and the recipient agrees to receive (by clicking Save and Open, or Save), the transfer begins, just as described above.

Figure 14-4:
The icons of nearby AirDrop-happy Macs show up in this fun-sized version of the regular AirDrop window. You've already said which files you want to send; now you just have to specify who gets them. Click the Mac's icon and then click Send.

All right. So if AirDrop is so great, why doesn't it wipe out all other forms of file transfer and save this book a bunch of pages? Because (a) it works only on *Macs running Lion or Mountain Lion,* (b) it works only *wirelessly,* and (c) it's a one-way street. Other people can't *take* files from your Mac—you have to shove the files to them.

Note: Actually, there's another limitation: AirDrop doesn't work on some older Macs. It works on the MacBook Pro (made since late 2008), MacBook Air (late 2010), MacBook (late 2008), iMac (early 2009), Mac mini (mid-2010), and Mac Pro (mid-2010).

If you can get past those limitations, though, there's a lot of great stuff in AirDrop:

- If you see someone's name beneath her icon in the AirDrop window, that means that she's in your Contacts *and* has signed in with her Apple ID. That's an extra bit of confidence that she is who her icon says she is.

- AirDrop works by creating a temporary two-computer wireless network. That's why it works even if you're not in a WiFi hotspot. It does, however, require both computers to have WiFi turned *on,* which you can check by opening the 🛜 menu.

- If *you're* the one receiving a file, you can cancel a half-finished transfer by clicking the ⊗ button on the progress bar that wraps around the sender's icon in the AirDrop window. (Another way: If your Downloads folder is set to Stack view, you can click the ⊗ button in the corner of the file's icon.)

- AirDrop doesn't work unless both of you have opened your AirDrop windows in the Finder. If you close your AirDrop window, or even click outside that window, your Mac disappears from everyone else's AirDrop screens.

Sharing Your Public Folder

AirDrop is the simplest and happiest way to share files, no doubt about it. But it requires Lion/ Mountain Lion on both Macs, it works only wirelessly, and it's a one-way street (you have to initiate the file handoff).

The next simplest file-sharing method eliminates all those limitations. It's the Public-folder method.

Inside your Home folder, there's a folder called Public. (Inside *everybody's* Home folder is a folder called Public.)

Anything you put into this folder is automatically available to everyone else on the network. They don't need a password, they don't need an account on your Mac—they just have to be on the same network, wireless or wired. They can put files here *or* copy things out.

To make your Public folder available to your networkmates, you have to turn on the File Sharing master switch. Choose →System Preferences, click Sharing, and then turn on File Sharing (as shown back in Figure 14-2).

Now round up the files and folders you want to share with all comers on the network and drag them into your Home→Public folder. That's all there is to it.

Note: You may notice that there's already something in your Public folder: a folder called Drop Box. It's there so that other people can give *you* files from across the network, as described later in this chapter.

So now that you've set up Public folder sharing, how are other people supposed to access your Public folder? See page 561.

Sharing Any Folder

If the Public-folder method seems too simple and restrictive, then you can graduate to the "share any folder" method. In this scheme, you can make *any* file, folder, or disk available to other people on the network.

The advantage here is that you don't have to move your files into the Public folder; they can sit right where you have them. And this time, you can set up elaborate *sharing privileges* (also known as *permissions*) that grant individuals different amounts of access to your files.

This method is more complicated to set up than that Public-folder business. In fact, just to underline its complexity, Apple has created two different setup procedures. You can share one icon at a time by opening its Get Info window; or you can work in a master list of shared items in System Preferences.

The following pages cover both methods.

The Get Info method

Here's how to share a Mac file, disk, or folder disk using its Get Info window.

The following steps assume that you've turned on →System Preferences→Sharing→File Sharing, as shown in Figure 14-2.

1. Highlight the folder or disk you want to share. Choose File→Get Info.

The Get Info dialog box appears (Figure 14-5). Expand the General panel, if it's not already visible.

Note: Sharing an entire disk means that every folder and file on it is available to anyone you give access to. On the other hand, by sharing only a folder or two, you can keep *most* of the stuff on your hard drive private, out of view of curious network comrades. Sharing only a folder or two does *them* a favor, too, by making it easier for them to find the files they're supposed to have. This way, they don't have to root through your entire drive looking for the folder they actually need.

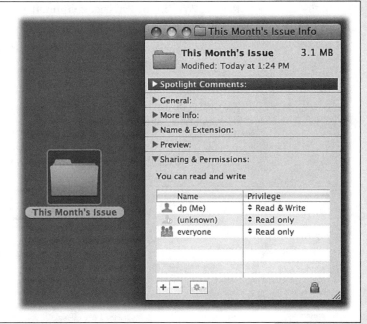

Figure 14-5:
The file-sharing permissions controls are here, in the Get Info box for any file, folder, or disk.

2. Turn on "Shared folder."

Enter your administrative password, if necessary.

Tip: To help you remember what you've made available to other people on the network, a gray banner labeled "Shared Folder" appears across the top of any Finder window you've shared. It even appears at the top of the Open and Save dialog boxes.

OK, this disk or folder is now shared. But with whom?

3. **Expand the Sharing & Permissions panel, if it's not already visible. Click the 🔒 icon and enter your administrator's password.**

The controls in the Sharing & Permissions area spring to life and become editable. At the bottom of the Info panel is a little table. The first column can display the names of individual account holders, like Casey or Chris, or *groups* of account holders, like Everyone or Accounting Dept.

The second column lists the *privileges* each person or group has for this folder.

Now, the average person has no clue what "privileges" means, and this is why things get a little hairy when you're setting up folder-by-folder permissions. But read on; it's not as bad as it seems.

4. **Edit the table by adding people's names. Then set their access permissions.**

At the moment, your name appears in the Name column, and it probably says Read & Write in the Privilege column. In other words, you're currently the master of this folder. You can put things in, and you can take things out.

If you just want to share files with *yourself*, so you can transfer them from one computer to another, you can stop here.

If you want to share files with *other* people—well, at the moment, the privileges for Everyone are probably set to "Read only." Other people can see this folder, but they can't do anything with it.

Your job is to work through this list of people, specifying *how much* control each person has over the file or folder you're sharing.

Figure 14-6:
This list includes every ac-count holder on your Mac, plus groups you've set up, plus the contents of your ad-dress book. One by one, you can add them to the list of lucky sharers of your files or folders—and then change the degree of access they have to the stuff you're sharing.

To add the name of a person or group, click the **+** button below the list. The list shown in Figure 14-6 appears.

Now click a name in the list. Then, from the Privilege pop-up menu, choose a permissions setting.

- **Read & Write** has the most access of all. This person, like you, can add, change, or delete any file in the shared folder, or make any changes she likes to a document. Give Read & Write permission to people you trust not to mess things up.

- **Read only** means "Look, but don't touch." This person can see what's in the folder (or file) and can copy it, but he can't delete or change the original. It's a good setting for distributing company documents or making source files available to your minions.

- **Write only (Drop Box)** means that other people can't even open the folder. They can drop things *into* it, but it's like a mail slot: The letter disappears into the slot, and then it's too late for them to change their minds. As the folder's owner, you can do what you like with the deposited goodies. This drop-box effect is great when you want students, coworkers, or family members to be able to *turn things in* to you—homework, reports, scandalous diaries—without running the risk that someone else might see those documents. (This option doesn't appear for documents—only disks and folders.)

- **No access** is an option only for Everyone. It means that other people can see this file or folder's icon but can't do a thing with it.

Tip: Usually, you'll want the privileges for the folder to also apply to everything *inside* it; it would be a real drag to have to change the sharing privileges of the contents one icon at a time. That's why the ✿ menu at the bottom of the Get Info box has a command called "Apply to enclosed items."

5. **Close the Get Info window.**

 Now the folder is ready for invasion from across the network.

The System Preferences method

It's very convenient to turn on sharing one folder at a time, using the Get Info window. But there's another way in, too, one that displays *all* your shared stuff in one handy master list.

To see it, choose →System Preferences. Click Sharing. Click File Sharing (and make sure it's turned on).

Now you're looking at a slightly different kind of permissions table, shown in Figure 14-7. It has *three* columns:

- **Shared folders.** The first column lists the files, folders, and disks you've shared. You'll probably see that every account's *Public* folder is already listed here, since they're all shared automatically. (You can turn *off* sharing for a Public folder, too, just by clicking it and then clicking the **–** button.)

But you can add more icons to this list. Either drag them into the list directly from the desktop or a Finder window, or click the **+** sign, navigate to the item you want to share, select it, and then click Add. Either way, that item now appears in the Shared Folders list.

Figure 14-7:
Hiding in System Preferences is a list of every disk and folder you've shared. To stop sharing something, click it and click the — button. To share a new disk or folder, drag its icon off the desktop, or out of its window, directly into the Shared Folders list.

- **Users.** When you click a shared item, the second column sprouts a list of *who* gets to work with it from across the network. You're listed here, of course, since it's your stuff. There's also a listing here for Everyone, which really means, "everyone *else*"—that is, everyone who's not specifically listed here.

You can add to this list, too. Click **+** to open the person-selection box shown in Figure 14-6. It lists the other account holders on your Mac, and some predefined groups, as well as the contents of your Contacts.

Note: *Most of the Contacts people don't actually have accounts on this Mac, of course. If you choose some-body from this list, you're asked to make up an account password. When you click Create Account, you've actually created a* Sharing Only *account on your Mac for that person, as described on page 504. When you return to the Accounts pane of System Preferences, you'll see that new person listed.*

Double-click a person's name to add her to the list of people who can access this item from over the network, and then set up the appropriate privileges (described next).

To *remove* someone from this list, just click the name and then click the **–** button.

- **Users.** This *third* column lets you specify how much access each person in the *second* column has to this folder. Your choices, once again, are **Read & Write** (full access to change or delete this item's contents); **Read Only** (open or copy, but can't edit or delete); and **Write Only** (**Drop Box**), which lets the person put things *into* this disk or folder, but not open it or see what else is in it.

 For the Everyone group, you also get an option called **No Access,** which means that this item is completely off limits to everyone else on the network.

And now, having slogged through all these options and permutations, your Mac is ready for invasion from across the network.

Accessing Shared Files

The previous pages have described *setting up* a Mac so people at other computers can access its files. There's an easy, limited way (use the Public folder) and a more elaborate way (turn on sharing settings for each folder individually).

Now comes the payoff to both methods: sitting at another computer and *connecting* to the one you set up. There are two ways to go about it: You can use the Sidebar, or you can use the older, more flexible Connect to Server command. The following pages cover both methods.

Connection Method A: Use the Sidebar

Suppose, then, that you're seated in front of your Mac, and you want to see the files on another Mac on the network. Proceed like this:

1. **Open any Finder window.**

 In the Shared category of the Sidebar at the left side of the window, icons for all the computers on the network appear. See Figure 14-8.

Tip: The same Sidebar items show up in the Save and Open dialog boxes of your programs, too, making the entire network available to you for opening and saving files.

If you don't see a certain Mac's icon here, it might be turned off, it might not be on the network, or it might have File Sharing turned off.

Note: Or it might not have the right file-sharing *type* turned on. To check, open System Preferences→Sharing; click Sharing, and then Options. You'll see checkboxes for AFP and SMB; your computers can't see each other if they don't have one of these options in common.

If you don't see any computers at all in the Sidebar, then *your* computer might not be on the network. Or maybe you've turned off the checkboxes for Connected Servers and Bonjour Computers in Finder→Preferences→Sidebar.

Tip: If the other Mac is just asleep, it still shows up in the Sidebar, and you can wake it up to get at it. How is that possible? Through the miracle of the Wake for Network Access feature described on page 359.

Figure 14-8:
Macs appear in the Sidebar with whatever names they've been given in System Preferences→Sharing. Their tiny icons usually resemble the computers themselves. Other computers (like Windows PCs) look like generic PCs.

If there are a lot of computer icons in the Sidebar, or if you're on a corporate-style network that has the sub-chunks known as *workgroups*, you may also see an icon

What You Can See

Precisely which other folders you can see on the remote Mac depend on what kind of account you have there: Guest, Standard, or Administrator. (See the previous chapter.)

If you're using the Guest account, you can see only the Public folders. The rest of the Mac is invisible and off limits to you. (You may see additional folders if somebody turned on sharing for them.)

If you have a Standard account, you can see other people's Public and Drop Box folders, plus your own Home folder. (Again, somebody may have made other folders available.)

If you're an administrator, you get to see icons for the account holders' Public folders and the hard drive itself to

which you're connecting. In fact, you even get to see the names of any other disks connected to that Mac.

If you, O lucky administrator, open the hard drive, you'll discover that you also have the freedom to see and manipulate the contents of the Applications, Desktop, Library, and Users→Shared folders.

You can even see what folders are in other users' Home folders, although you can't open them or put anything into them.

Finally, there's something called the root user. This account has complete freedom to move or delete any file or folder anywhere, including critical system files that could disable your Mac. It also requires a degree in Unix.

called All. Click it to see the full list of network entities that your Mac can see: not just individual Mac, Windows, and Unix machines, but also any "network neighborhoods" (limbs of your network tree). For example, you may see the names of network zones (clusters of machines, as found in big companies and universities).

Or, if you're trying to tap into a Windows machine, open the icon representing the *workgroup* (computer cluster) that contains the machine you want. In small office networks, it's usually called MSHOME or WORKGROUP. In big corporations, these workgroups can be called almost anything—as long as it's no more than 15 letters long with no punctuation. (Thanks, Microsoft.)

If you *do* see icons for workgroups or other network "zones," double-click until you're seeing the icons for individual computers.

Note: If you're a network nerd, you may be interested to note that OS X can "see" servers that use the SMB/CIFS, NFS, FTP, and WebDAV protocols running on OS X Server, Unix, Linux, Novell NetWare, and Windows servers (NT, 2000, XP, Vista, and Windows 7). But the Sidebar reveals *only* the shared computers on your *subnet* (your local, internal office network). (It also shows Back to My Mac if it's set up; see page 584.)

2. **Click the computer whose files you want to open.**

 In the main window, you now see the Public Folder icons for each account holder on that computer: Mom, Dad, Sissy, whatever, as shown in Figure 14-8. (They *may* have shared other folders with you, too.) If you have an account on the other computer, you'll see a folder representing *your* stuff, too. At this point, you're considered a guest.

Note: This amount of access depends on a setting in System Preferences→Users & Groups. Click the Guest account to see it: "Allow guests to connect to shared folders." That checkbox is usually turned on—but it's something to check if you can't seem to connect.

 From here, the remaining instructions diverge, depending on whether you want to access *other* people's stuff or *your* stuff. That's why there are two alternative versions of step 3 here:

3a. **If you want to access the stuff that somebody else has left for you, double-click that person's Public folder.**

 Instantly, that folder's contents appear in the Finder window.

 In this situation, you're only a guest. You don't have to bother with a password. On the other hand, the only thing you can generally see inside the other person's account folder is his Public folder.

Tip: Actually, you *might* see other folders here—if the account holder has specifically shared them *and* decided that you're important enough to have access to them.

One thing you'll find inside the Public folder is the Drop Box folder. This folder exists so that you can *give* files and folders to the other person. You can drop any of your own icons onto the Drop Box folder—but you can't open the Drop Box folder to see what *other* people have put there. It's one-way, like a mail slot in somebody's front door.

If you see anything else at all in the Public folder you've opened, then it's stuff the account holder has copied there for the enjoyment of you and your networkmates. You're not allowed to delete anything from the other person's Public folder or make changes to anything in it.

You can, however, open those icons, read them, or even copy them to *your* Mac— and then edit *your* copies.

3b. **To access your own Home folder on the other Mac, click the Connect As button (Figure 14-9). Sign in as usual.**

When the "Connect to the file server" box appears, you're supposed to specify your account name and password (from the Mac you're tapping into). This is the same name and password you'd use to log in if you were actually sitting at that machine.

Type your account name (long or short version) and password. And if you didn't set up a password for your account, leave the password box empty.

Tip: The dialog box shown in Figure 14-9 includes the delightful and timesaving "Remember this password in my keychain" option, which makes the Mac memorize your password for a certain disk so you don't have to type it—or even see this dialog box—every darned time you connect. (If you have no password, though, the "Remember password" doesn't work. You'll have to confront—and press Return to dismiss—the "Connect to the file server" box every time.)

When you click Connect (or press Return or Enter), the other Mac's icon shows up in your Sidebar, and its contents appear in the main window. (The other Mac's icon may also show up on the desktop, if you've turned on the "Connected Servers" option in Finder→Preferences→Sidebar.)

GEM IN THE ROUGH

Faster Ways to Connect Next Time

If you expect that you might want to access a shared disk or folder again later, take a moment to make an alias of it. The easiest way is to press Option-⌘ as you drag it out of the window where it first appears.

Next time, you can bring it back to your screen just by double-clicking the alias. And if you turned on "Remember this password in my keychain," you won't even be asked for your name and password again.

Similarly, if you put an alias like this onto the Dock, you can bring it back to your screen later just by clicking its icon.

You can even drag the alias into the Login Items window described on page 509. Now the disk appears on your desktop automatically each time you log in—the most effortless arrangement of all.

Tip: Once you've connected to a Mac using your account, the other Mac has a lock on your identity. You'll be able to connect to the other Mac over and over again during this same computing session, without ever having to retype your password.

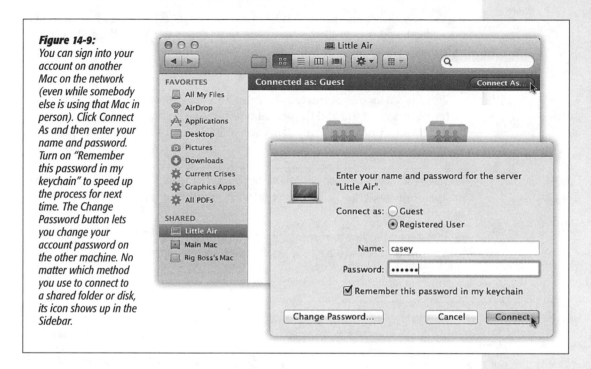

Figure 14-9:
You can sign into your account on another Mac on the network (even while somebody else is using that Mac in person). Click Connect As and then enter your name and password. Turn on "Remember this password in my keychain" to speed up the process for next time. The Change Password button lets you change your account password on the other machine. No matter which method you use to connect to a shared folder or disk, its icon shows up in the Sidebar.

In the meantime, you can double-click icons to open them, make copies of them, and otherwise manipulate them exactly as though they were icons on your own hard drive. Depending on what permissions you've been given, you can even edit or trash those files.

Tip: There's one significant difference between working with "local" icons and working with those that sit elsewhere on the network. When you delete a file from another Mac on the network, either by pressing the Delete key or by dragging it to the Trash, a message appears to let you know that you're about to delete that item instantly and permanently. It won't simply land in the Trash "folder," awaiting the Empty Trash command.

You can even use Spotlight to find files on that networked disk. If the Mac across the network is running Leopard or a later OS X version, in fact, you can search for words *inside* its files, just as though you were sitting in front of it. If not, you can still search for text in files' names.

Connection Method B: Connect to Server

The Sidebar method of connecting to networked folders and disks is practically effortless. It involves nothing more than clicking your way through folders—a skill that, in theory, you already know.

But the Sidebar method has its drawbacks. For example, the Sidebar doesn't let you type in a disk's network address. As a result, you can't access any shared disk *on the Internet* (an FTP site, for example), or indeed anywhere beyond your local subnet (your own small network).

Fortunately, there's another way. When you choose Go→Connect to Server, you get the dialog box shown in Figure 14-10. You're supposed to type in the address of the shared disk you want.

For example, from here you can connect to:

- **Everyday Macs on your network.** If you know the IP address of the Mac you're trying to access (you geek!), you can type nothing but its IP address into the box and then hit Connect. Or you can just type its Bonjour name, something like this: *afp://upstairs-PowerMac.local/.*

Tip: To find out your Mac's IP address, open the Network pane of System Preferences. There, near the top, you'll see a message like this: "AirPort is connected to Tim's Hotspot and has the IP address 192.168.1.113." That's your IP address.

To see your Bonjour address, open the Sharing pane of System Preferences. Click File Sharing. Near the top, you'll see the computer name with ".local" tacked onto its name—and hyphens instead of spaces—like this: Little-MacBook.local.

Figure 14-10:
The Sidebar method of connecting to shared disks and folders is quick and easy, but it doesn't let you connect to certain kinds of disks. The Connect to Server method entails plodding through several dialog boxes, but it can find just about every kind of networked disk.

After you enter your account password and choose the shared disk or folder you want, you're connected exactly as though you had clicked Connect As (Figure 14-9).

The next time you open the Connect to Server dialog box, OS X remembers that address, as a courtesy to you, and shows it pre-entered in the Address field.

- **Macs across the Internet.** If your Mac has a permanent (static) IP address, the computer itself can be a server, to which you can connect from anywhere in the world via the Internet. Details on this procedure are in Chapter 21.

- **Windows machines.** Find out the PC's IP address or computer name, and then use this format for the address: *smb://192.168.1.34* or *smb://Cheapo-Dell*.

 After a moment, you're asked to enter your Windows account name and password, and then to choose the name of the shared folder you want. When you click OK, the shared folder's contents appear in the window, ready to use, and the computer's icon appears in your Sidebar. (More on sharing with Windows PCs later in this chapter.)

Tip: If you know the name of the shared folder, you can add that after a slash, like this: *smb://192.168.4.23/ sharedstuff.* You save yourself one dialog box.

- **NFS servers.** If you're on a network with Unix machines, you can tap into one of their shared directories using this address format: *nfs://Machine-Name/pathname*, where *Machine-Name* is the computer's name or IP address, and *pathname* is the folder path to the shared item you want.

- **FTP servers.** OS X makes it simple to bring *FTP servers* onto your screen, too. (These are the drives, out there on the Internet, that store the files used by Web sites.)

 In the Connect to Server dialog box, type the FTP address of the server you want, like this: *ftp://www.apple.com*. If the site's administrators have permitted *anonymous* access—the equivalent of a Guest account—that's all there is to it. A Finder window pops open, revealing the FTP site's contents.

 If you need a password for the FTP site, however, you're now asked for your name and password.

GEM IN THE ROUGH

Hello, Bonjour

Throughout this chapter, and throughout this book, you'll encounter rituals in which you're supposed to connect to another Mac, server, or printer by typing in its IP address (its unique network address).

But first of all, IP addresses are insanely difficult to memorize (192.179.248.3, anyone?). Second, networks shouldn't require you to deal with them anyway. If a piece of equipment is on the network, it should announce its presence, rather than making you specifically call for it by name.

Now you can appreciate the beauty of Bonjour (once known as Rendezvous), an underlying OS X networking technology that lets networked gadgets detect one another on the network automatically and recognize one another's capabilities.

It's Bonjour at work, for example, that makes other Macs' names show up in your iTunes program so you can listen

to their music from across the network. Bonjour is also responsible for filling up your Bonjour buddy list in Messages automatically, listing everyone who's on the same office network; for making shared Macs' names show up in the Sidebar's Shared list; and for making the names of modern laser printers from HP, Epson, or Lexmark appear like magic in the list of printers in the Print dialog box.

It's even more tantalizing to contemplate the future of Bonjour. If electronics companies show interest (and some have already), you may someday be able to connect the TV, stereo, and DVD player with just a couple of Ethernet cables, or even wirelessly, instead of a rat's nest of audio and video cables.

For most of us, that day can't come soon enough.

Tip: You can eliminate that password-dialog-box step by using this address format: *ftp://
yourname:yourpassword@www.apple.com.*

Once you type it and press Return, the FTP server's icon appears in the Sidebar.
Its contents appear, too, ready to open or copy.

- **WebDAV server.** This special Web-based shared disk requires a special address
format, something like this: *http://Computer-Name/pathname.*

In each case, once you click OK, you may be asked for your name and password.

And now, some timesaving features in the Connect to Server box:

- Once you've typed a disk's address, you can click **+** to add it to the list of server
favorites. The next time you want to connect, you can just double-click its name.

- The clock-icon pop-up menu lists Recent Servers—computers you've accessed
recently over the network. If you choose one of them from this pop-up menu, you
can skip having to type in an address.

Tip: Like the Sidebar network-browsing method, the Connect to Server command displays each connected
computer as an icon in your Sidebar, even within the Open or Save dialog boxes of your programs. You
don't have to burrow through the Sidebar's Network icon to open files from them, or save files onto them.

Figure 14-11:
*To disconnect
from a shared
network disk or
folder, click the
other comput-
er's icon in the
Sidebar. Then
click Disconnect
at the top right
corner of the
window.*

Disconnecting Yourself

When you're finished using a shared disk or folder, you can disconnect from it as shown in Figure 14-11.

Disconnecting Others

In OS X, you really have to work if you want to know whether other people on the network are accessing *your* Mac. You have to choose System Preferences→Sharing→File Sharing→Options. There you'll see something like, "Number of users connected: 1."

Maybe that's because there's nothing to worry about. You certainly have nothing to fear from a security standpoint, since you control what they can see on your Mac. Nor will you experience much computer slowdown as you work, thanks to OS X's prodigious multitasking features.

Still, if you're feeling particularly antisocial, you can slam shut the door to your Mac. Just open System Preferences→Sharing and turn off File Sharing.

If anybody is, in fact, connected to your Mac at the time (*from* a Mac), you, the door-slammer, get to see the dialog box in Figure 14-12, which lets you send a little warning or farewell message to whomever's connected to your Mac.

Figure 14-12:
This dialog box asks you how much notice you want to give your coworkers that they're about to be disconnected, and what message to send them before the ax falls.

There may be users connected to this computer.
Enter the number of minutes before file sharing is turned off.

5

Message to connected users:

Yo, minions! Wrap it up. I'm headin' home for the night!

(optional)

Cancel OK

If nobody is connected right now, your Mac instantly becomes an island once again.

Networking with Windows

Microsoft Windows may dominate the corporate market, but there *are* Macs in the offices of America—and there *are* PCs in homes. Fortunately, Macs and Windows PCs can see each other on the network, with no special software (or talent) required.

In fact, you can go in either direction. Your Mac can see shared folders on a Windows PC, and a Windows PC can see shared folders on your Mac.

It goes like this.

Seated at the Mac, Seeing the PC

Suppose you have a Windows PC and a Mac on the same wired or wireless network. Here's how you get the Mac and PC chatting:

1. **On your Windows PC, share some files.**

 This isn't really a book about Windows networking (thank heaven), but here are the basics.

 Just as on the Mac, there are two ways to share files in Windows. One of them is super-simple: You just copy the files you want to share into a central, fully accessible

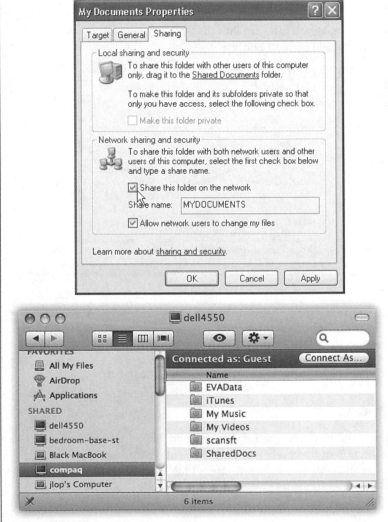

Figure 14-13:
Top: To share a folder in Windows, right-click it, choose Properties, and then turn on "Share this folder on the network." In the "Share name" box, type a name for the folder as it will appear on the network. (No spaces are allowed).

Bottom: Back in the safety of OS X, click the PC's name in the Sidebar. (If it's part of a workgroup, click All, and then your workgroup name first.)

Next, click the name of the shared computer. If the files you need are in a Shared Documents or Public folder, no password is required. You see the contents of the PC's Shared Documents folder or Public folder, as shown here. Now it's just like file sharing with another Mac.

If you want access to any other shared folder, click Connect As, and see Figure 14-14.

folder. As long as nobody has turned off the Guest-access feature, no passwords, accounts, or other steps are required.

In **Windows XP,** that special folder is the Shared Documents folder, which you can find by choosing Start→My Computer. Share it on the network as shown in Figure 14-13, top.

In **Windows Vista,** it's the Public folder, which appears in the Navigation pane of every Explorer window. (In Vista, there's one Public folder for the whole *computer,* not one per account holder.)

In **Windows 7,** there's a Public folder in each library. That is, there's a Public Documents, Public Pictures, Public Music, and so on.

TROUBLESHOOTING MOMENT

Windows 7 Tips

Windows 7 is a very Mac-like version of Windows, but making it share nicely with the Mac still requires a few setup steps.

First, make sure you've shared everything you want to share on the Windows 7 machine. For example, suppose you want to share your entire personal folder (the equivalent of the Mac's Home folder).

To do that, choose Start→ [your name]. In the window that opens, choose "Share with"→"Specific people." In the resulting dialog box, you'll see that you are already permitted to access this folder, as shown here; unless you want to add someone else, just click Share and then Done.

Now, on the Mac, in the Finder, choose Go→Connect to Server. Type smb:// SuperDell, or whatever your PC's name is. (And how do you find that out? Open the Start menu; right-click Computer; from the shortcut menu, choose Properties. You'll see the computer name in the middle of the resulting info screen.)

On the Mac, after typing the PC's name into the Connect to Server box, click Connect. After a moment, you're asked for your account name and password, as it appears on the *PC.*

Enter these credentials—turn on "Remember my password" if you want to be spared this rigmarole the next time—and then click Connect.

Now you're shown a list of disks and folders you shared on the Windows PC. Double-click the one you want. Presto: It appears in a Finder window, ready to access!

(If you discover you can copy stuff out of these folders but can't put stuff into them, check the sharing permissions on the Windows side.)

Finally, for heaven's sake, make an alias of the Windows folder or disk on the Mac so you can just double-click to open it the next time!

The second, more complicated method is the "share any folder" method, just as in OS X. In XP or Vista, you right-click the folder you want to share, choose Properties from the shortcut menu, click the Sharing tab, and turn on "Share this folder on the network" (Figure 14-13, top). In Windows 7, use the Share With menu at the top of any folder's window. See the box below for more details.

Repeat for any other folders you want to make available to your Mac.

2. On the Mac, open any Finder window.

The shared PCs may appear as individual computer names in the Sidebar, or you may have to click the All icon to see the icons of their *workgroups* (network clusters). Unless you or a network administrator changed it, the workgroup name is probably MSHOME or WORKGROUP. Double-click the workgroup name you want.

Tip: You can also access the shared PC via the Connect to Server command, as described on page 565. You could type into it *smb://192.168.1.103* (or whatever the PC's IP address is) or *smb://SuperDell* (or whatever its name is) and hit Return—and then skip to step 5. In fact, using the Connect to Server method often works when the Sidebar method doesn't.

TROUBLESHOOTING MOMENT

When the Mac Doesn't See the PC

Are you having trouble getting your PC's icon to show up in your Finder's Sidebar?

Now, you can probably connect to the PC using the Mac's Go→Connect to Server command, but the Sidebar would be a lot more convenient.

And the problem is probably that the Mac doesn't know anything about Windows workgroups.

Even a lowly home PC is part of a workgroup (a corporate cluster), whether it knows it or not. And until your Mac is part of that very tiny club, it won't be able to see your PCs, and they won't be able to see it.

So if you're having no luck with this whole Mac-PC thing, try this. First, find out what your PC thinks its workgroup is. (It's usually either WORKGROUP or MSHOME.) Click Start, and then right-click Computer. From the shortcut menu,

choose Properties. In the resulting info screen, you'll see the workgroup's name.

Now, on the Mac, open System Preferences. Click Network. Click the connection you're using (like WiFi or Ethernet). Click Advanced. Click WINS.

Now you see the peculiar controls shown here. Type the workgroup name into the box (if indeed it's not already a choice in the Workgroup pop-up menu). Click OK, and then click Apply.

Now your Windows PCs show up in the Sidebar, like magic.

Still having trouble? Open System Preferences→Security→Firewall. Make sure your Mac's firewall is either turned off or at least not set to "Block all incoming connections."

Now the names of the individual PCs on the network appear in your Finder window. (If you're running Windows 7, see the box on page 571.)

3. **Double-click the name of the computer you want.**

If you're using one of the simple file-sharing methods on the PC, as described above, that's all there is to it. The contents of the Shared Documents or Public folder now appear on your Mac screen. You can work with them just as you would your own files.

If you're not using one of those simple methods, and you want access to individual shared folders, read on.

Note: In Windows XP Pro, the next step won't work unless you turn *off* Simple File Sharing. To do that, choose Tools→Folder Options in any Explorer window. Click the View tab and turn off "Use simple file sharing."

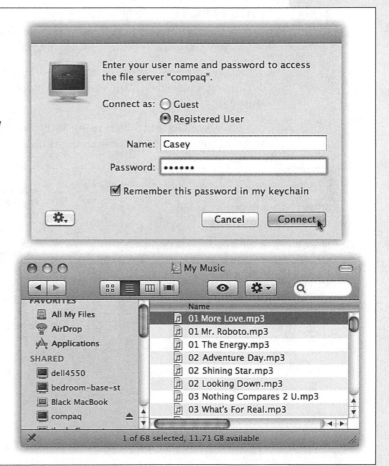

Figure 14-14:
Top: The PC wants to make sure you're authorized to visit it. Fortunately, you see this box only the very first time you access a certain Windows folder or disk; after that, you see only the box shown below.

Bottom: Here you see a list of shared folders on the PC. Choose the one you want to connect to, and then click OK. Like magic, the Windows folder shows up on your Mac screen, ready to use!

4. **Click Connect As.**

This button appears in the top-right corner of the Finder window; you can see it at bottom in Figure 14-13. Now you're asked for your name and password (Figure 14-14, top).

5. **Enter the name and password for your account on the PC, and then click OK.**

At long last, the contents of the shared folder on the Windows machine appear in your Finder window, just as though you'd tapped into another Mac (Figure 14-14, bottom). The icon of the shared folder appears on your desktop, too, and an Eject button (⏏) appears next to the PC's name in your Sidebar.

From here, it's a simple matter to drag files between the machines, open Word documents on the PC using Word for the Mac, and so on—exactly like you're hooked into another Mac.

Seated at the PC, Seeing the Mac

Cross-platformers, rejoice: OS X lets you share files in *both directions*. Not only can your Mac see other PCs on the network, but they can see the Mac, too.

On the Mac, open →System Preferences→Sharing. Click File Sharing (make sure File Sharing is turned on), and then click Options to open the dialog box shown in Figure 14-14.

Turn on "Share files and folders using SMB (Windows)" (Figure 14-15). Below that checkbox, you see a list of all the accounts on your Mac. Turn on the checkboxes to

☑ Share files and folders using AFP

 Number of users connected: 0

☑ Share files and folders using SMB (Windows)

 When you enable SMB sharing for a user account, you must enter the password for that account. Sharing files with some Windows computers requires storing the Windows user's account password on this computer in a less secure manner.

On	Account
☑	Casey
☑	Chris
☑	david
☐	Robin

(?) [Done]

Figure 14-15:
Prepare your Mac for visitation by the Windows PC. It won't hurt a bit. The system-wide On switch for invasion from Windows is the second checkbox shown here, in the System Preferences→Sharing→File Sharing→Options box.

Next, turn on the individual accounts of people you want to allow to connect from the PC. You'll be asked to enter their account passwords, too. Click Done when you're done.

specify *which* Mac user accounts you want to be able to access. You must type in each person's password, too. Click Done.

Before you close System Preferences, study the line near the middle of the window, where it says something like: "Other users can access your computer at afp://192.168.1.108 or MacBook-Pro." You'll need one of these addresses shortly.

Now, on **Windows XP,** open My Network Places; in **Windows Vista,** choose Start→Network; in **Windows 7,** expand the Network heading in the sidebar of any desktop window. If you've sacrificed the proper animals to the networking gods, your Mac's icon should appear in the network window, as shown in Figure 14-16, top.

Figure 14-16:
Top: Double-click the icon of the Mac you want to visit from your Windows machine (Vista is shown here).

Middle: Type your Mac's NetBIOS name in all capitals (or its IP address), then a backslash, and then your Mac account short name. (You can find out your Mac's NetBIOS name—that is, what Windows calls it—on the Network pane of System Preferences. Click Advanced, then WINS.)

Enter your Mac account's password, too. Turn on "Remember my password" if you plan to do this again someday. Click OK.

Bottom: Here's your Mac Home folder—in Windows! Open it up to find all your stuff.

Double-click the Mac's icon. Public-folder stuff is available immediately. Otherwise, you have to sign in with your Mac account name and password; Figure 14-16, middle, has the details.

In the final window, you see your actual Home folder—on a Windows PC! You're ready to open its files, copy them back and forth, or whatever (Figure 14-16, bottom).

If your Mac's icon *doesn't* appear, and you've read the troubleshooting boxes in this chapter, wait a minute or two. Try restarting the PC. In Windows XP, try clicking "Microsoft Windows Network" or "View workgroup computers" in the task pane.

If your Mac still doesn't show up, you'll have to add it the hard way. In the address bar of any Windows window, type *macbook-pro\chris* (but substitute your Mac's actual computer name and your short account name), taking care to use backslashes (\), not normal slashes (/). You can also type your Mac's IP address in place of its computer name.

In the future, you won't have to do so much burrowing; your Mac's icon should appear automatically in the My Network Places or Network window.

More Mac-Windows Connections

The direct Mac-to-Windows file-sharing feature of OS X is by far the easiest way to access each other's files. But it's not the only way. Chapter 6 offers a long list of other options, from flash drives to the third-party service Dropbox.

Screen Sharing

OS X has answered the prayers of baffled beginners and exasperated experts everywhere. Now, when a novice needs help from a guru, the guru doesn't have to run all the way downstairs or down the hall to assist. Thanks to OS X's screen-sharing feature, you can see exactly what's on the screen of another Mac, from across the network—and even seize control of the other Mac's mouse and keyboard (with the newbie's permission, of course).

(Anyone who's ever tried to help someone troubleshoot over the phone knows *exactly* how helpful this is. If you haven't, this small example may suffice: "OK, open the Apple menu and choose 'About This Mac.'" Pause. "What's the Apple menu?")

Nor is playing Bail-Out-the-Newbie the only situation when screen sharing is useful. It's also great for collaborating on a document, showing something to someone for approval, or just freaking each other out. It can also be handy when *you* are the owner of both Macs (a laptop and a desktop, for example), and you want to run a program that you don't have on the Mac that's in front of you. For example, you might want to adjust the playlist selection on the upstairs Mac that's connected to your sound system.

Or maybe you just want to keep an eye on what your kids are doing on the Macs upstairs in their rooms.

The controlling person can do *everything* on the controlled Mac, including running programs, messing around with the folders and files, and even shutting it down. You

can even press keystrokes on *your* Mac—⌘-Tab, ⌘-space, ⌘-Option-Escape, and so on—to trigger the corresponding functions on the *other* Mac.

OS X is crawling with ways to use screen sharing. You can do it over a network, over the Internet, and even during a Messages chat.

Truth is, the Messages method, described in Chapter 20, is much simpler and better than the small-network method described here. It doesn't require names or passwords, it doesn't require the same OS X version on both Macs, it's easy to flip back between seeing the other guy's screen and your own, and you can transfer files by dragging them from your screen to the other guy's (or vice versa).

Then again, the small-network method described here is built right into the Finder and doesn't require logging into Messages.

In the modern Mountain Lion screen sharing, you can log into a distant Mac and control it as though you were logged into your own account—*while somebody else is using it* and seeing a totally different screen! Read on.

Other Mac: Give Permission in Advance

As always, trying to understand meta concepts like seeing one Mac's screen on the monitor of another can get confusing fast. So in this example, suppose that you're seated at Your Mac, and you want to control Other Mac.

GEM IN THE ROUGH

Logging In with an Apple ID

In the bad old days, you couldn't share your screen or your files with other people unless you first created full-blown accounts for them on your Mac. You know: a Home folder, Music and Movies folders, and so on. That was an awful lot of disk space sacrificed, just so other people could visit your Mac over the network.

Nowadays, you can create a Sharing Only account for them. They can now share your screen or your files without actually having a presence on your hard drive.

In Mountain Lion, there's even a third option: They can exploit your shared screen or shared folders just by logging in with their Apple IDs. This way, you don't even have to set up a name and password for them on your Mac, and they don't have to learn another name and password. They don't have an account on your Mac at all—just a Contacts card.

To set this up, open Contacts. Make sure there's a card in

there for the person who will be visiting your Mac over the network. Make sure, furthermore, that the card includes the email address that person uses as an Apple ID.

Now visit System Preferences→Sharing. Click Screen Sharing. As shown in Figure 14-17, click the **+** sign. In the panel that appears, click Contacts, and double-click the name of the prospective visitor. You're asked to enter a screen-sharing password for this person (twice) and then click Create Account.

The visitor should make sure he's registered his Apple ID in his own account details for System Preferences→Users & Groups.

If so, then the setup is ready. When he attempts to connect to your Mac, he'll be able to use the "Using an Apple ID" option as his credentials. No account on your Mac is necessary!

Now, it would be a chaotic world if any Mac could randomly take control of any other Mac (although it sure would be fun). Fortunately, though, nobody can share your screen or take control of your Mac without your explicit permission.

To give such permission, sit down at Other Mac. Choose →System Preferences→Sharing, and then turn on Screen Sharing.

At this point, there are three levels of security to protect your Mac against unauthorized remote-control mischief:

- **Secure.** If you select All Users, then *anyone with an account on your Mac* will be able to tap in and take control anytime they like, even when you're not around. They'll just have to enter the same name and password they'd use if they were sitting in front of your machine.

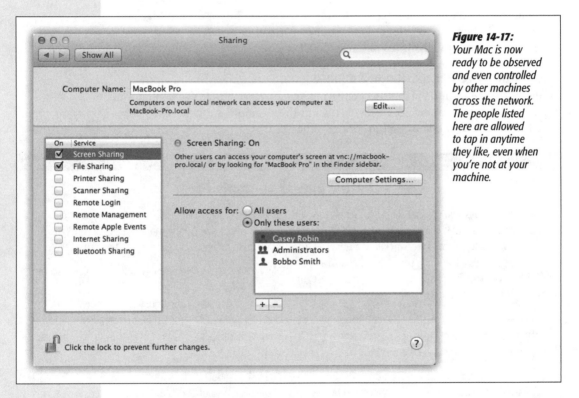

Figure 14-17:
Your Mac is now ready to be observed and even controlled by other machines across the network. The people listed here are allowed to tap in anytime they like, even when you're not at your machine.

If "anyone" means "you and your spouse" or "you and the other two fourth-grade teachers," then that's probably perfectly fine.

- **Securer.** For greater security, though, you can limit who's allowed to stop in. Click "Only these users" and then click the **+** sign. A small panel appears, listing everyone with an account on your Mac. Choose the ones you trust not to mess things up while you're away from your Mac (Figure 14-17).

Tip: You can permit people to see your Mac's screen remotely by entering their Apple ID and passwords. That's a lot simpler and less disk space than before, when each person had to have a full-blown *account* on your Mac, complete with Pictures folder, Movies folder, and so on. To set this up, see the box on page 577.

- **Securest.** If you click "Only these users" and then don't add *anyone* to the list, then only people who have Administrator accounts on your Mac (page 502) can tap into your screen.

Alternatively, if you're only a *little* bit of a Scrooge, you can set things up so that they can request permission to share your screen—as long as you're sitting in front of your Mac at the time and feeling generous.

Figure 14-18:
Top: Start by clicking Share Screen in the strip at the top of your Mac's window.

Middle: If you've been pre-added to the VIP list of authorized screen sharers, as already described, you can sign in with either your account name and password or your Apple ID. If not, you can request permission to share Other Mac's screen (provided the Mac owner has turned on that option in System Preferences→Sharing→Screen Sharing→Computer Settings). You'll be granted permission only if Other Mac's owner happens to be sitting in front of it at the moment and has opted to accept such requests.

Bottom: If you request permission, the other person (sitting at Other Mac) sees your request like this.

To set this up, click Computer Settings and then turn on "Anyone may request permission to share screen." Now your fans will have to request permission to enter, and you'll have to grant it (by clicking OK on the screen), in real time, while you're there to watch what they're doing.

Your Mac: Take Control

All right, Other Mac has been prepared for invasion. Now suppose you're the person on the other end. You're the guru, or the parent, or whoever wants to take control.

Sit at Your Mac elsewhere on your home or office network, and proceed like this:

1. **Open a Finder window. Expand the Shared list in the Sidebar, if necessary, so that you see the icon of Other Mac. Click it.**

 The dark strip at the top of the main window displays a button that wasn't there before: Share Screen (Figure 14-18, top).

2. **Click Share Screen.**

 Now you see the box shown at middle in Figure 14-18. It offers as many as three different ways for you to prove that you're not some East German teenage hacker. "By asking for permission" sends the other Mac's current operator a message asking if it's OK for you to take over.

 Most of the time, people choose "As a registered user," meaning, "I have a regular account on the Other Mac."

 But the "Using an Apple ID" option lets you enter an Apple ID and password instead, so the Other Mac's owner doesn't have to set up an account for you just so you can use screen sharing or file sharing. See the box on page 577.

Tip: In theory, you can also connect from across the Internet, assuming you left your Mac at home turned on and connected to a broadband modem, and assuming you've worked through the port-forwarding issue described on page 774.

In this case, though, you'd begin by choosing Go→Connect to Server in the Finder; in the Connect to Server box, type in *vnc://123.456.78.90* (or whatever your home Mac's public IP address is). The rest of the steps are the same.

3. **If you have a user account on Other Mac, click "As a registered user" and log in. If your Apple ID will suffice, click "Using an Apple ID" and supply your sharing password.**

 Your Mac, of course, *knows* your Apple ID already (because you've entered it in your account screen in System Preferences→User Accounts). It shows up here in the dialog box; all you have to do is enter your password.

4. **Click Connect.**

If you've signed in successfully, or if permission is granted, then you see the dialog box shown in Figure 14-19. If you choose "Connect to a virtual display," then you can use your account on the Other Mac even while somebody else is using her account. Simultaneously. Crazy stuff.

(The only evidence she'll have that you're rooting around behind the scenes is a tiny menu-bar icon that looks like this: ⊞.)

Note: If *nobody* is using Other Mac at the moment, then it doesn't matter which option you click. And if you enter the name and password of the person who's already logged in at the Other Mac, then you don't see the dialog box in Figure 14-19. You just jump right into screen sharing, as shown in Figure 14-20.

Figure 14-19:
The Mac wants to know if you want to view or control the screen that's in use right now by whoever's using Other Mac—or if you want to use the new "virtual display" option, where you take control of your account on the other Mac without disturbing the totally different activity of whomever is seated there.

5. **Click either "Ask to share the display" (to see the same thing as the Other Mac person) or "Connect to a virtual display" (to log into a different account and work independently).**

And now a weird and wonderful sight appears. As shown in Figure 14-20, your screen now fills with a *second* screen—from the other Mac. You have full keyboard and mouse control to work with that other machine exactly as though you were sitting in front of it.

Well, maybe not *exactly.* There are a few caveats and options.

- **Full-screen mode.** There it is, in the upper-right corner: the ⊡ button. If you click it, then your view of Other Mac expands to fill your screen, edge to edge; now there's *no sign at all* that you're actually using a different computer.

- **The speed-vs.-blurriness issue.** Remember, you're asking the other Mac to pump its video display across the network—and that takes time. Entire milliseconds, in fact.

So ordinarily, the Mac uses something called *adaptive quality,* which just means that the screen gets blurry when you scroll, quit a program, or do anything else that creates a sudden change in the picture. You can turn off this feature by choosing View→Full Quality. Now you get full sharpness all the time—but things take longer to scroll, appear, and disappear.

- **Mismatched screen sizes.** If the other screen is *smaller* than yours, no big deal. It floats at actual size on your monitor, with room to spare. But if it's the same size as yours or larger, then the other Mac's screen gets shrunk down to fit in a window.

 If you'd prefer to see it at actual size, choose View→Turn Scaling Off. Of course, now you have to *scroll* in the Screen Sharing window to see the whole image.

Tip: Another way to turn scaling on and off is to click the "Fit screen in window" button on the Screen Sharing *toolbar* (identified in Figure 14-20).

Figure 14-20:
Don't be alarmed. You're looking at the Other Mac's desktop in a window on your Mac desktop. You have keyboard and mouse control, and so does the other guy (if he's there); when you're really bored, you can play King of the Cursor. (Note the Screen Sharing toolbar, which has been made visible by choosing View→Show Toolbar.)

- **Observe Only.** In Observe Only mode, your cursor turns white, and you give up all your typing and clicking powers. In other words, you're playing "look, but don't touch." (To enter this mode, choose View→Switch to Observe Mode, or click the corresponding toolbar icon.)

 This is a handy option when the person at Other Mac just wants to give you a slideshow or a presentation, or when you just want to watch what he's doing when

you're on a troubleshooting hunt, or when he's freaked out by having you move the mouse or type stuff by remote control.

- **Manage the Clipboard.** You can actually *copy and paste* material from the remote-controlled Mac to your own—or the other way—thanks to a freaky little wormhole in the time-space continuum. In the Edit menu, choose Send Clipboard to put what's on *your* Clipboard onto *Other* Mac's Clipboard, or Get Clipboard to copy Other Mac's Clipboard contents onto *your* Clipboard. Breathe slowly and drink plenty of fluids, and your brain won't explode. (There are toolbar-button equivalents, too.)

- **Dragging files between computers.** Here's a crazy new one in Mountain Lion: You can now transfer files from one Mac to the other, just by dragging their icons. Drag the icon from the distant Mac clear out of its window, and pause over your own desktop until your cursor sprouts a green ✚ icon. When you let go, the files get copied to your own Mac.

- **Quitting.** When you hit the ⌘-Q keystroke, you *don't* quit Screen Sharing; you quit whatever program is running on the other Mac! So when you're finished having your way with the other computer, choose Screen Sharing→Quit Screen Sharing to return to your own desktop (and your own sanity).

The Toolbar

If you don't see the screen-sharing toolbar, you can summon it by choosing View→Show Toolbar. It starts out with buttons for Control (click to enter Observe Only mode), Fit to Window, Screen Capture (takes a picture of the screen), Get Clipboard, and Send Clipboard.

But if you Control-click (or right-click) the toolbar, you're offered a shortcut menu containing the usual controls over how the toolbar buttons appear (Icon and Text, Icon

GEM IN THE ROUGH

Screen Sharing with Windows and Other Oddball Machines

The beauty of Apple's screen-sharing technology is that it isn't Apple's screen-sharing technology. It's a popular open standard called VNC (Virtual Network Computing).

Once you've turned on Screen Sharing on your Mac, any computer on earth with a free VNC client program—sort of a viewer program—can pop onto your machine for a screen share. VNC clients are available for Windows, Linux, pre-Leopard Macs, and even some cellphones. (Not all VNC programs work with the Mountain Lion version of screen sharing, alas; some require updates.)

To prepare your Mac for invasion, open the Sharing pane

of System Preferences. Click Screen Sharing, and then click Computer Settings. Turn on "VNC viewers may control screen with password," and make up a password. (VNC doesn't know anything about OS X account passwords, so you're making up one password for sharing your whole Mac.)

Give that password to the lucky few who have your trust. Let them plug your Mac's public IP address into their VNC clients—or let them connect over your office network, using the address displayed on the Screen Sharing pane (*vnc:// MacBook-Pro,* for example)—and let the sharing begin.

Only, Use Small Size, and so on), plus a Customize Toolbar command that produces the box shown in Figure 14-21.

Figure 14-21:
In here, you can move the toolbar buttons around by dragging, change the assortment of available buttons, add gaps between the buttons (drag a Space or Flexible Space into position), and modify how the buttons appear.

Variations on Screen Sharing

The steps above guide you through screen sharing between two Macs running Mac OS 10.5 or later. But screen sharing is based on a standard technology called VNC, and OS X is bristling with different permutations.

Screen sharing through Messages

Two people who both have Mac OS 10.5 or later can perform exactly the same screen-sharing stunt *over the Internet.* No accounts, passwords, or setup are required—only the granting of permission by the other guy. Just initiate a Messages chat, and then proceed as described on page 767. It's really awesome.

Screen sharing the manual way

Screen Sharing is an actual, double-clickable program, with its own icon on your Mac. (It's in the System→Library→CoreServices folder.) When you double-click it, you can type in the public IP address or domain name of the computer you want to connect to, and presto: You're connected!

Screen sharing with Back to My Mac

Back to My Mac is intended to simplify the nightmare of remote networking. It works only if:

- You use iCloud.

- You have at least two Macs, both running Mac OS 10.7.2 or later.

- On each one, you've entered your Apple ID into the Users & Groups pane of System Preferences, and logged in.

Once that's all in place, your Macs behave exactly as though they're on the same home network, even though they can be thousands of miles apart across the network.

To set it up, proceed as shown in Figure 14-22.

From now on, on your laptop in New Zealand, you see an entry for Back to My Mac in the Sharing section of your Sidebar. Click to see the icon of your Mac back at home. At this point, you can connect to it for file sharing by clicking Connect As or take control of it by clicking Share Screen.

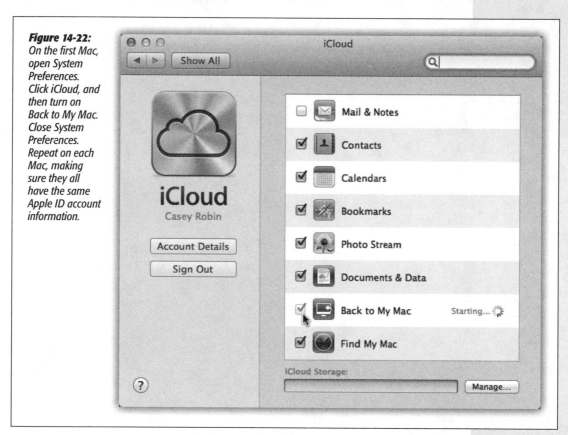

Figure 14-22:
On the first Mac, open System Preferences. Click iCloud, and then turn on Back to My Mac. Close System Preferences. Repeat on each Mac, making sure they all have the same Apple ID account information.

In theory, Back to My Mac spares you an awfully long visit to networking hell (including the port-forwarding headache described on page 774), because Apple has done all the configuration work for you.

In practice, not everyone can get Back to My Mac to work. Apple says the problems are related to firewalls, port-forwarding issues, and router incompatibilities. Apple also says you'll have the best luck on networks that involve only an AirPort base station—and not a hardware router.

All the technical details are available online. Visit *http://support.apple.com/kb/HT1109* to read more about the Back to My Mac issues.

More Dialing In from the Road

If you have a full-time Internet connection, a special thrill awaits. You can connect to your Mac from anywhere in the world via the Internet. If you have a laptop, you don't need to worry when you discover you've left a critical file on your desktop Mac at home.

OS X offers several ways to connect to your Mac from a distant location, including file sharing over the Internet, Back to My Mac, virtual private networking (VPN), FTP, and SSH (secure shell). Chapter 21 has the details.

Graphics, Fonts & Printing

The Macintosh may be only the 10 percent solution in the mainstream business world, but in the graphics and printing industries, it's the 800-pound gorilla. You'd better believe that when Apple designed OS X, it worked very hard to keep its graphics and printing fans happy.

This chapter tackles printing, faxing, fonts, graphics, ColorSync, and PDF, which OS X uses as an everyday exchange format—one of the biggest perks of using a Mac.

Mac Meets Printer

OS X used to come pre-loaded with the printing software for every conceivable printer model from every conceivable printer company—Epson, HP, Lexmark, Canon, and others, several gigabytes' worth. Clearly, most people wound up with about 900 wads of printing software they'd never use.

When you install Mountain Lion, though, you get *only* the printer drivers for the printers you actually have, or are nearby on the network. If you ever encounter a different printer model later, OS X offers to download it for you on the spot.

Setting Up a Printer

Setting up a printer is incredibly easy. The first time you want to print something, follow this guide:

1. **Connect the printer to the Mac, and then turn the printer on.**

 Inkjet printers connect to your USB jack. Laser printers hook up either to your USB jack or to your network (Ethernet or wireless).

2. **Open the document you want to print. Choose File→Print. In the Print dialog box, choose your printer's name from the Printer pop-up menu (or one of its submenus, if any, like Nearby Printers). See Figure 14-1.**

Cool! Wasn't that easy? Very nice how the Mac autodiscovers, autoconfigures, and autolists almost any USB, FireWire, Bluetooth, or Bonjour printer.

Have a nice afternoon. The End.

Figure 14-1:
Top: To introduce your Mac to a new printer, try to print something. If you have a USB printer or a "nearby" one, it's probably listed here already. Off you go.

If your printer isn't listed, choose Add Printer from this pop-up menu.

Bottom: Your Mac should automatically "see" any printers that are hooked up and turned on. Click the one you want, and then click Add.

Oh—unless your printer *isn't* listed in the Printer pop-up menu. In that case, read on.

Note: "Nearby Printers" refers to printers that aren't connected directly to your Mac but are accessible anyway: a printer connected to an Apple Time Capsule or an AirPort base station, certain network printers that speak Bonjour, or printers connected to other Macs that you've shared, as described later in this chapter.

3. From the Printer pop-up menu (Figure 14-1, top), choose Add Printer.

A special setup window opens (Figure 14-1, bottom), which is even better at auto-detecting printers available to your Mac. If you see the printer's name here, click it and then click Add.

You're all set. Have a good time.

Unless, of course, your printer *still* isn't showing up. Proceed to step 4.

4. Click the icon for the *kind* of printer you have: Default, IP, or Windows.

Default usually does the trick, especially if you have an inkjet printer. Choose IP if you have a network printer that's not showing up in Default—especially if you

TROUBLESHOOTING MOMENT

The Death of AppleTalk

Like most 800-pound-gorilla computer companies, Apple can be a frustrating partner. It throws its hairy weight behind some technology, gets all the other companies to adopt it—and then moves on to something else.

That's why AppleTalk is no longer with us, much to the dismay of thousands of Mac fans who own AppleTalk printers.

AppleTalk was a networking system that was part of the Mac since 1984. Hundreds of networkable printer models, especially laser printers, used this scheme to talk to Macs.

If yours is among them, you can still make your printer work. Follow steps 1 through 4 of "Setting Up a Printer" on these pages; in step 4, choose IP.

From the Protocol pop-up menu, choose "HP Jetdirect – Socket" (if you have an HP laser printer), or "Internet Printing Protocol – IPP" (for most other laser printers). If you and your company's network expert determine that the printer you want to use is, in fact, an LPD printer, then choose Line

Printer Daemon instead.

In any of these cases, you now have to fill in the IP address (network address) of the printer. On some printers, you can call up this information on the screen. On others, you have to print out that printer's configuration or test page. (On many HP laser printers, you do that by holding down a button while the printer turns on.) There's no solution to this except to cuddle up with the manual—or, faster yet, Google it ("HP LaserJet 1300 configuration page").

Once you've filled in the IP address, you can make up a name for this printer ("HP Hulk") and a location ("Next to the water cooler"), if you like. The Print Using pop-up menu is supposed to fill itself in with the correct printer-driver information; if it doesn't, you can choose the printer model (or, in a pinch, a very similar one) manually.

Click Add. You're off and printing!

have an old AppleTalk printer (see the box on page 589). And choose Windows if there's a Windows-only printer out there on your office network.

After a moment, the names of any printers that are turned on and connected appear in the printer list. For most people, that means only one printer—but one is enough.

5. **Click the name of the printer you want to use.**

As an optional step, you can open the Print Using pop-up menu at the bottom of the dialog box. Choose "Select a driver to use," and then, in the list that appears, choose your particular printer's model name, if you can find it. That's how your Mac knows what printing features to offer you when the time comes: double-sided, legal size, second paper tray, and so on.

6. **Click Add.**

After a moment, you return to the main Printer Browser window (Figure 14-1, top), where your printer now appears. You're ready to print.

Note: If you still don't see your printer's name show up, ask yourself: Is my Mac on a corporate network? Does the network have an LPR (Line Printer Remote) printer? If you and your company's network nerd determine that the printer you want to use is, in fact, an LPR printer, then click IP Printing at the top of the Printer Browser dialog box. Fill in the appropriate IP address and other settings, as directed by your cheerful network administrator.

Printer Preferences

If you're lucky enough to own several printers, repeat the steps above for each one. Eventually, you'll have introduced the Mac to all the printers available to it, so all their names show up in the printer list.

To see the printer list so far, open System Preferences→Print & Scan. You can have all kinds of fun here (Figure 14-2):

• **Choose a default printer.** As indicated by the Default Printer pop-up menu, OS X intends, conveniently enough, to use whichever printer you used for the last printout for the next one. Most people, after all, don't switch printers much.

Still, you can choose one particular printer from this pop-up menu to set it as the default printer—the one the Mac uses unless you intervene by choosing from the Printer pop-up menu in the Print dialog box (Figure 14-1).

• **Create desktop printer icons.** *This* handy, little-known feature gives you drag-and-drop access to your printers.

From the Print & Scan pane of System Preferences, just drag a printer's icon out of the window and onto the desktop (or wherever you like). Repeat for your other printers. From now on, you can print a document on a certain printer just by dragging the document's icon onto the appropriate printer icon.

- **Check the ink level.** Click a printer, and then click Options & Supplies, to see how your inkjet ink or laser-printer toner level is. That way, you won't be caught short when you're on a deadline and your printer is out of ink. You now get a bright yellow "low ink" warning in the dialog box that actually appears when you print.

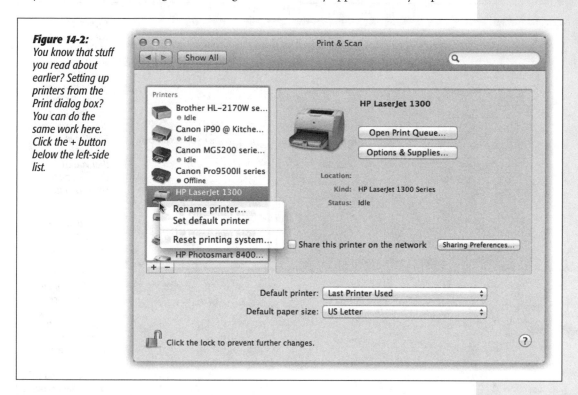

Figure 14-2:
You know that stuff you read about earlier? Setting up printers from the Print dialog box? You can do the same work here. Click the + button below the left-side list.

Making the Printout

You can't miss the Print dialog box. It appears, like it or not, whenever you choose File→Print in one of your programs.

The options you encounter depend on the printer you're using. They also depend on whether or not you *expand* the dialog box by clicking the Show Details button. That reveals a *lot* of useful options, including a handy preview; see Figure 14-3.

If you expand the box, the options you find vary by printer. But here are the common options:

- **Printer.** If you have more than one printer connected to your Mac, you can indicate which you want to use for a particular printout by choosing its name from this pop-up menu.

- **Presets.** Here's a way to preserve your favorite print settings: Once you've proceeded through this dialog box, specifying the number of copies, which printer trays you want the paper taken from, and so on, you can choose Save As from the

pop-up menu, and then assign your settings set a name (like "Borderless, 2 copies"). Thereafter, you'll be able to recreate that elaborate suite of settings simply by choosing its name from this pop-up menu.

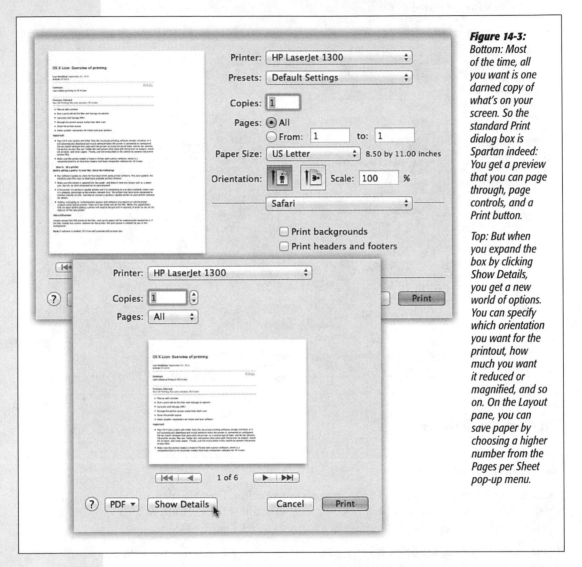

Figure 14-3:
Bottom: Most of the time, all you want is one darned copy of what's on your screen. So the standard Print dialog box is Spartan indeed: You get a preview that you can page through, page controls, and a Print button.

Top: But when you expand the box by clicking Show Details, you get a new world of options. You can specify which orientation you want for the printout, how much you want it reduced or magnified, and so on. On the Layout pane, you can save paper by choosing a higher number from the Pages per Sheet pop-up menu.

- **Copies.** Type the number of copies you want printed. The Collated checkbox controls the printing order for the various pages. For example, if you print two copies of a three-page document, the Mac generally prints the pages in this order: 1, 2, 3, 1, 2, 3. If you turn off Collated, on the other hand, it prints in this order: 1, 1, 2, 2, 3, 3.

- **Pages.** You don't have to print an entire document—you can print, say, only pages 2 through 15.

Tip: You don't have to type numbers into both the From and To boxes. If you leave the first box blank, the Mac assumes you mean "from page 1." If you leave the second box blank, the Mac understands that you mean "to the end." To print only the first three pages, in other words, leave the first box blank and type 3 into the second box. (These page numbers refer to the physical pages you're printing, not to any fancy numbering you've set up in your word processor. As far as the Print dialog box is concerned, the first printed page is page 1, even if you've told your word processor to label it page 455.)

- **Paper Size, Orientation.** Somebody at Apple finally realized how frustrating it was to have to open the Page Setup dialog box to change the paper-size and orientation settings, and then open the Print dialog box for other settings. Now, in most programs, these controls are duplicated right in the Print dialog box for your convenience.

- **PDF.** A *PDF* file, of course, is an Adobe Reader (Acrobat) document—a file that any Mac, Windows, Linux, or Unix user can view, read, and print using either Preview or the free Adobe Reader (included with every PC and Mac operating system).

 You can easily save any document as a PDF file instead of printing it—a truly beautiful feature that saves paper, ink, and time. The document remains on your hard drive, and the text inside is even searchable using Spotlight.

 And that's just the beginning. Apple has added a long list of additional PDF options (like password-protected PDFs, emailed ones, and so on). But Apple faced a design quandary: How could it offer a new list of PDF-related options without junking up the Print dialog box?

 Its solution was a strange little item called a pop-up *button,* shown in Figure 14-3, bottom. Use it like a pop-up menu. The command you'll use most often is probably Save as PDF, which turns the printout into a PDF file instead of sending it to the printer. For details on the other PDF-related options here, see page 598.

If you examine the unnamed pop-up menu just below the Presets pop-up menu, you'll find dozens of additional options. They depend on your printer model and the program you're using at the moment, but here are some typical choices:

- **Layout.** As described in Figure 14-3, you can save paper and ink or toner cartridges by printing several miniature "pages" on a single sheet of paper.

- **Paper Handling.** You can opt to print your pages in reverse order so they stack correctly, or you can print just odd or even pages so you can run them through again for double-sided printing.

- **Paper Feed.** If you chose the correct printer model when setting up your printer, then this screen "knows about" your printer's various paper trays. Here's where you specify which pages you want to come from which paper tray. (By far the most popular use for this feature is printing the first page of a letter on company letterhead, and the following pages on blank paper from a second tray.)

- **Cover Page.** Yes, that throwaway info page has made its way from the fax world into the hard-copy world.

- **Scheduler.** This option lets you specify *when* you want your document to print. If you're a freelancer, sitting at home with an inkjet on your desk, you might not immediately grasp why anyone wouldn't want the printouts *right now*. But try printing a 400-page catalog in a big office where other people on the network might conceivably resent you for tying up the laser printer all afternoon, and you'll get the idea.

- **ColorSync.** Most color printers offer this panel, where you can adjust the color settings—to add a little more red, perhaps. This is also where you indicate whose *color-matching system* you want to use: Apple's ColorSync, your printer manufacturer's, or none at all.

Then, below the light-gray line in this pop-up menu, you'll find a few options that are unique to the chosen printer or program. Some HP printers, for example, offer Cover Page, Finishing, and other choices. Other likely guest commands:

- **Quality & Media** (inkjet printers only). Here's where you specify the print quality you want, the kind of paper you're printing on, and so on. (The name of this panel varies by manufacturer.)

- **[Program Name].** Whichever program you're using—Mail, Word, Pages, or anything else—may offer its own special printing options on this screen.

- **Summary.** This command summons a text summary of all your settings so far.

Tip: Here's one for the technically inclined. Open your Web browser and enter this address: *http://127.0.0.1:631*. You find yourself at a secret "front end" for CUPS (Common Unix Printing System), the underlying printing technology for OS X. This trick lets your Mac communicate with a huge array of older printers that don't yet have OS X drivers. Using this administration screen, you can print a test page, stop your printer in its tracks, manage your networked printers and print jobs, and more—a very slick trick.

Printing

When all your settings look good, click Print (or press Return) to send your document to the printer.

Managing Printouts

After you've used the Print command, you can either sit there until the paper emerges from the printer, or you can *manage* the printouts-in-waiting. That option is attractive primarily to people who do a lot of printing, have connections to a lot of printers, or share printers with many other people.

Start by opening the printer's window. If you're already in the process of printing, just click the printer's Dock icon. If not, open →System Preferences→Print & Scan, click the printer's name, and then click Open Print Queue.

At this point, you see something like Figure 14-4: The printouts that will soon be sliding out of your printer appear in a tidy list.

Figure 14-4:
Waiting printouts appear in this window. You can sort the list by clicking the column headings (Name or Status), make the columns wider or narrower by dragging the column-heading dividers horizontally, or reverse the sorting order by clicking the column name a second time. The Supply Levels button opens a graph that shows how much ink each cartridge has remaining (certain printer models only).

Here are some of the ways in which you can control these waiting printouts, which Apple collectively calls the *print queue*:

- **Delete them.** By clicking an icon, or ⌘-clicking several, and then clicking the Delete toolbar button, you remove items from the list of waiting printouts. Now they won't print.

- **Pause them.** By highlighting a printout and then clicking the Hold button, you pause that printout. It doesn't print out until you highlight it again and then click the Resume button. (Other documents continue to print.) This pausing business could be useful when, for example, you need time to check or refill the printer, or when you're just about to print your letter of resignation as your boss drops by. (Maybe to offer you a promotion.)

- **Halt them all.** You can stop all printouts from a printer by clicking Pause Printer. (They resume when you click the button again, which now says Resume Printer.)

You can't rearrange printouts by dragging them in the queue list. But remember that you can resequence the printing order by choosing the Scheduler option; you can also drag waiting printouts *between* these lists, shifting them from one printer to another.

Tip: As you now know, the icon for a printer's queue window appears automatically in the Dock when you print. But it also *stays* in the Dock for the rest of the day; it doesn't disappear when the printing is complete.

If you wish it would, Control-click (or right-click) the printer's Dock icon; from the shortcut menu, choose Auto Quit.

Printer Sharing

Printer sharing is for people (or offices) with more than one Mac, connected to a network, who'd rather not buy a separate printer for each machine. Instead, you connect the printer to one Mac, flip a couple of software switches, and then boom: The other Macs on the network can send their printouts to the printer without actually being attached to it—even wirelessly, if they're on an AirPort network.

Note: Of course, this feature is most useful when you're sharing printers that can hook up to only one Mac at a time, like USB inkjet photo printers. Office laser printers are often designed to be networked from Day One.

Figure 14-5:
Top: On the Mac with the printer, open the Sharing panel of System Preferences. Turn on Printer Sharing, and then turn on the checkboxes for the printers you want to share. Switch to the Print & Scan pane, and turn on "Share this printer on the network" for the printer(s) you want to share.

Bottom: To use a shared printer elsewhere on the network, open the document you want to print, and then choose File→Print. In the Print dialog box, the shared printer is clearly identified under the Nearby Printers heading.

Setting up printer sharing is easy; see Figure 14-5, top. Then, to make a printout from across the network, see the instructions in Figure 14-5, bottom.

Tip: You can control *which* account holders on your network are allowed to use the printer you've shared. You know that idiot in Accounting who's always using up your cartridges by printing 200-page documents? Cut that sucker off! Just add the lucky guests' names to the Users column in System Preferences→Sharing→Printer Sharing, as shown in Figure 14-5.

If your PC-wielding friends install Bonjour for Windows (a free download from this book's "Missing CD" page at *www.missingmanuals.com*), they can even print to your Mac's shared printer, too.

Tip: Of course, your Mac (the one attached to the printer) must be turned on in order for the other computers to print. In part, that's because the documents-in-waiting from other people pile up on *your* hard drive.

Faxing

Apple giveth, and Apple taketh away. And Apple hath taken away faxing.

Apple has never been afraid to abandon technologies that strike it as obsolete, and faxing is one of them. Heck, Mountain Lion can't even fax if you have one of Apple's own USB fax modems.

If you still need to fax, you have a couple of options. First, you can sign up for a service like eFax or Faxaway, which let you send and receive faxes online. Second, you're welcome to buy a non-Apple fax modem, some of which work fine. Whatever you buy comes with its own software and instructions.

PDF Files

Sooner or later, almost everyone with a personal computer encounters PDF (portable document format) files. Many a software manual, Read Me file, and downloadable "white paper" comes in this format. Until recently, you needed the free program called Adobe Reader if you hoped to open or print these files. Windows devotees still do.

PDF files, however, are one of OS X's common forms of currency. In fact, you can turn *any document* (in any program with a Print command) into a PDF file—a trick that once required the $250 program called Adobe Acrobat Distiller. (Maybe Apple should advertise: "Buy Acrobat for $250, get OS X free—and $120 cash back!")

Note: All right, that joke about Acrobat is an exaggeration. OS X alone creates *screen-optimized* PDF files: compact, easy-to-email files that look good onscreen but don't have high enough resolution for professional printing. For high-end purposes and more optimization for specific uses (Web, fancy press machines, and so on), you still need a program like Adobe Acrobat, Illustrator, or InDesign.

But why would you want to create PDFs? What's the big deal about them? Consider these advantages:

- **Other people see your layout.** When you distribute PDF files to other people, they see precisely the same fonts, colors, page design, and other elements you put in your original document. And here's the kicker: They get to see all of this even if they don't *have* the fonts or the software you used to create the document. (Contrast with the alternative: Say you're sending somebody a Microsoft Word document. If your correspondent doesn't have precisely the same fonts you have, then he'll see a screwy layout. And if he doesn't have Word or a program that can open Word files, he'll see nothing at all.)

- **It's universal.** PDF files are very common in the Macintosh, Windows, Unix/Linux, and even smartphone worlds. When you create a PDF file, you can distribute it (by email, for example) without worrying about what kinds of computers your correspondents are using.

- **It has very high resolution.** PDF files print at the maximum quality of any printer. A PDF file prints great both on cheapo inkjets and on high-quality image-setting gear at professional print shops. (Right now you're looking at a PDF file that was printed at a publishing plant.)

- **You can search it.** A PDF file may look like a captured graphic, but behind the scenes, its text is still text; Spotlight can find a word in a PDF haystack in a matter of seconds. That's an especially handy feature when you work with electronic software manuals in PDF format.

Opening PDF Files

There's nothing to opening up a PDF file: Just double-click it. Preview takes over from there and opens the PDF file on your screen. (Or highlight its icon in the Finder and tap the space bar for a Quick Look at it.)

Creating PDF Files

Opening, schmopening—what's really exciting in OS X is the ability to create your *own* PDF files. The easiest way is to click the PDF pop-up button in the standard Print dialog box (Figure 14-6). When you click it, you're offered a world of interesting PDF-creation possibilities:

- **Open PDF in Preview** lets you convert whatever document you're on the verge of printing into a frozen PDF file that opens into Preview for your inspection. The point here is that you can have a look at it *before* you print it.

- **Save as PDF** saves your document to the disk as a PDF document instead of printing it.

- **Save as PostScript** gives you a PostScript file instead of a PDF. (PostScript is a format preferred by some designers and print shops. It consists of highly precise "what to draw" instructions for PostScript laser printers.)

- **Fax PDF** *faxes* a document instead of printing it, in the unlikely event that you have a Mountain Lion–compatible fax modem.

- **Add PDF to iTunes** converts the document into a PDF file and stores it in, of all places, iTunes. (Yes, iTunes can manage PDF documents.)

- **Mail PDF** generates a PDF file and then attaches it to an outgoing message in Mail. Great for exchanging layout-intensive documents with collaborators who don't have the same fonts, layout software, or taste as you.

- **Save PDF to Web Receipts Folder** is one of the simplest and sweetest features in all of OS X.

 You use it when you've just ordered something on a Web site, and the "Print this receipt" screen is staring you in the face. Don't waste paper and ink (and, later, time trying to find it!). Instead, use this command. You get a perfectly usable PDF version, stored in your Home→Documents→Web Receipts folder, where you can use Spotlight to find it later, when you need to consult or print it because your gray-market goods never arrived.

Note: You may see other commands here, too, as you install other companies' software programs.

Figure 14-6:
The PDF button is crawling with neat ways to process a document while it's still open—and you can add to this pop-up button's list, too. For example, you can create even more elaborate pathways for documents you want to print or convert to PDF using an Automator workflow (Chapter 7).

Fonts—and Font Book

OS X type is all smooth, all the time. Fonts in OS X's formats—called TrueType, PostScript Type 1, and OpenType—always look smooth onscreen and in printouts, no matter what the point size.

OS X also comes with a program that's *just* for installing, removing, inspecting, and organizing fonts. It's called Font Book (Figure 14-7), and it's in your Applications folder.

Where Fonts Live

Brace yourself. In OS X, there are *three* Fonts folders. The fonts you actually see listed in the Font menus and Font panels of your programs are combinations of these Fonts folders' contents.

Figure 14-7:
Each account holder can have a separate set of fonts; your set is represented by the User icon. You can drag fonts and font families among the various Fonts folders represented here—from your User account folder to the Computer icon, for example, making them available to all account holders.

Here's a rundown:

- **Your private fonts (your Home folder→Library→Fonts).** This Fonts folder sits right inside your own Home folder. You're free to add your own custom fonts to this folder. Go wild—it's your font collection and yours alone. Nobody else who uses the Mac can use these fonts; they'll never even know you have them.

Note: Your Home→Library folder is ordinarily hidden. The quickest way to see it is to press Option as you choose Go→Library in the Finder.

- **Main font collection (Library→Fonts).** Any fonts in this folder are available to everyone to use in every program. (As with most features that affect everybody who shares your Mac, however, only people with Administrator accounts can change the contents of this folder.)

- **Essential system fonts (System→Library→Fonts).** This folder contains the 35 fonts that the Mac itself needs: the typefaces you see in your menus, dialog boxes, icons, and so on. You can open this folder to *see* these font suitcases, but you can't do anything with them, such as opening, moving, or adding to them. Remember that, for stability reasons, the System folder is sealed under glass forever. Only the

Unix entity known as the *superuser* can touch these files—and even that person would be foolish to do so.

With the exception of the essential system fonts, you'll find an icon representing each of these locations in your Font Book program, described next.

Note: And just to make life even more exciting, Adobe's software installers may donate even *more* fonts to your cause, in yet *another* folder: your Home→Application Support folder.

Font Book: Installing and Managing Fonts

One of the biggest perks of OS X is its preinstalled collection of over 50 great-looking fonts—"over $1,000 worth," according to Apple, which licensed many of them from type companies. In short, fewer Mac users than ever will wind up buying and installing new fonts.

But when you do buy or download new fonts, you're in luck. There's no limit to the number of fonts you can install.

Looking over your fonts

Right off the bat, Font Book is great for looking at samples of each typeface. For example, click Computer, click the first font name, and then press the ↓ key. As you walk down the list, the rightmost panel shows you a sample of each font (Figure 14-7).

You can also click any font family's flippy triangle (or highlight its name and then press →) to see the font *variations* it includes: Italic, Bold, and so on.

Tip: When you first open Font Book, the actual text of the typeface preview (in the right panel) is pretty generic. Don't miss the Preview menu, though. It lets you substitute a full display of every character (choose Repertoire)—or, if you choose Custom, it lets you type your *own* text.

Printing a reference sheet

You can print a handy, whole-font sampler of any font. Click its name and then choose File→Print. In the Print dialog box, click the Show Details button to expand the dialog box, if necessary.

As shown in Figure 14-8, you can use the Report Type pop-up menu to choose from three reference-sheet styles:

- **Catalog** prints the alphabet twice (uppercase and lowercase) and the numbers in each selected font; use the Sample Size slider to control the size. This style is the most compact, because more than one print sample fits on each sheet of paper.

- **Repertoire** prints a grid that contains every single character in the font. This report may take more than one page per font.

- **Waterfall** prints the alphabet over and over again, with increasing type sizes, until the page is full. You can control which sizes appear using the Sample Sizes list.

When everything looks good, click Print.

Figure 14-8:
From the Report Type pop-up menu, choose the style you want. The preview screen shows you each one before you commit it to paper. Type-size controls always appear in the lower right.

Eliminating duplicates

Since your Mac accesses up to three folders containing fonts, you might wonder what happens in the case of *conflicts*. For example, suppose you have two slightly different fonts, both called Optima, which came from different type companies and are housed in different Fonts folders on your system. Which font do you actually get when you use it in your documents?

The scheme is actually fairly simple: OS X proceeds down the list of Fonts folders in the order shown on page 600, beginning with your own home Fonts folder. It acknowledges the existence of only the *first* duplicated font it finds.

If you'd rather have more control, open Font Book. A bullet (•) next to a font's name is Font Book's charming way of trying to tell you that you've got copies of the same font in more than one of your Fonts folders. You might have one version of Comic Sans in your own Home→Library→Fonts folder, for example, and another in your Mac's main Fonts folder.

Click the one you want to keep, and then choose Edit→Resolve Duplicates. Font Book turns off all *other* copies, and the bullet disappears.

Adding, removing, and hiding fonts

Here's what you can do with Font Book:

- **Install a font.** When you double-click a font file's icon in the Finder, Font Book opens and presents the typeface for your inspection pleasure. If you like it, click Install Font. You've just installed it into *your account's* Fonts folder so that it appears in the Font menus of all your programs. (If you'd rather install it so that it appears in *all* account holders' Font menus, see Figure 14-7.)

- **Remove a font.** Removing a font from your machine is easy: Highlight it in the Font Book list, and then press the Delete key. (You're asked to confirm the decision.) Before taking such a drastic and permanent step, however, keep in mind that you can simply *disable* (hide) the font instead. Read on.

- **Disable a font.** When you disable a font, you're simply hiding it from your programs. You might want to turn off a font so that you can use a different version of it (bearing the same name but from a different type company, for example), or to make your Font menus shorter, or to make programs like Microsoft Word start up faster. You can always turn a disabled font back on if you ever need it again.

Tip: How's this for a sweet feature? OS X can activate fonts *automatically* as you need them. When you open a document that relies on a font it doesn't have, OS X activates that font and keeps it available until that particular program quits.

Actually, it does better than that. If it doesn't see that font installed, it *searches your hard drive* on a quest to find the font—and then it asks you if you want it installed, so the document will look right.

To disable a font, just click it or its family name, and then click the checkbox button beneath the list (or press Shift-⌘-D). Confirm your decision by clicking Disable in the confirmation box. (Turn on "Do not ask me again" if you're the confident sort.)

The font's name now appears gray, and the word "Off" appears next to it, making it absolutely clear what you've just done. (To turn the font on again, highlight its name, and then click the now-empty checkbox button, or press Shift-⌘-D again.)

Note: When you install, remove, disable, or enable a font using Font Book, you see the changes in the Font menus and panels of your *Cocoa* programs immediately. You won't see the changes in open Carbon programs, however, until you quit and reopen them.

Font collections

A *collection*, like any of the ones listed in the first Font Book column, is a subset of your installed fonts. Apple starts you off with collections called things like PDF (a set of standard fonts used in PDF files) and Web (fonts you're safe using on Web pages—that is, fonts that are very likely to be installed on the Macs or Windows PCs of your Web visitors).

But you can create collections called, for example, Headline or Sans Serif, organized by font type. Or you can create collections like Brochure or Movie Poster, organized

by project. Later, you can switch these groups of fonts on or off at will, or jump right to them in programs that use the standard Fonts panel, which saves you time wading through hundreds of fonts.

To create a new collection, click the leftmost **+** button to create a new entry in the Collection column, whose name you can edit. Then click one of the font storage locations—User or Computer—and drag fonts or font families onto your newly created collection icon. (Recognize this process from playlists in iTunes, or albums in iPhoto?) Each font can be in as many different collections as you want.

To remove a font from the collection, click its name, and then press Delete. You're not actually removing the font from your Mac, of course—only from the collection.

Tip: Each time you create a new font collection, OS X records its name and contents in a little file in your Home folder→Library→FontCollections folder.

By copying these files into the Users→Shared folder on your hard drive, you can make them available to anyone who uses the Mac. If your sister, for example, copies a file from the Shared folder into her own Home folder→Library→FontCollections folder, she'll see the name of your collection in her own Fonts panel. This way, she can reap the benefits of the effort and care you put into its creation.

Smart Collections

New in Mountain Lion: Font Book can create a collection *for* you, too. If you choose File→New Smart Collection, a new dialog box lets you specify criteria for this always-updated collection. For example, you might use the + buttons to specify "Kind name is TrueType" and "Design style is Sans-serif." The effect is exactly like smart folders in the Finder (page 128) or smart playlists in iTunes (page 483): Once you set up the smartness, the set stays up to date as your font collection changes.

Font libraries

Don't get confused; a font *library* is not the same as a font *collection*.

A font library is a set of fonts *outside* Font Book that you can install or uninstall on the fly. They don't have to be in any of your Fonts folders; Font Book can install them from wherever they happen to be sitting on your hard drive (or even on the network). Font Book never copies or moves these font files as you install or remove them from libraries; it simply adds them to your Font menus by referencing them right where they sit.

Tip: That can be a handy arrangement if you periodically work on different projects for different clients. Why burden your day-to-day Font menu with the 37 fonts used by *Beekeeper Quarterly* magazine, when you need to work with those fonts only four times a year?

Once you've added some fonts to a library, you can even set up collections *within* that library.

To create a library, choose File→New Library; the library appears in the Collection list at the left side of Font Book. Now you can drag fonts into it right from the Finder, or set up collections inside it by highlighting the library's icon and choosing File→New Collection.

Exporting fonts

Next time you submit a design project to a print shop or a graphics bureau, you won't have to worry that they won't have the right fonts. It's easy to collect all the fonts you used in a document and export them to a folder, ready to submit along with your file.

Use the Services→Font Book→Create Collection From Text command. Font Book opens and shows you the new collection it's created, containing all the fonts used in your document. Click the collection, and then choose File→Export Collection. The software prompts you to name and choose a location for the exported fonts folder.

Note: The Create Collection From Text command doesn't work in all programs, but you can always build and export a collection manually.

Figure 14-9:
The Fonts panel, generally available only in Cocoa programs, offers elaborate controls over text color, shadow, and underline styles.

See the handy font sample shown here above the font lists? To get it, choose Show Preview from the ✿ pop-up menu. Or use the mousy way: Place your cursor just below the title bar (where it says Fonts) and drag downward.

The Fonts Panel

As noted in Chapter 5, some existing Mac programs have simply been touched up—
Carbonized, in the lingo—to be OS X–compatible. Choosing fonts in these programs
works exactly as it always has on the Mac: You choose a typeface name from the Font
menu or from a formatting palette.

Things get much more interesting when you use the more modern *Cocoa* programs,
like TextEdit, iMovie, Pages, Keynote, Numbers, iPhoto, and Mail. They offer a standard
OS X feature called the Fonts panel. If you're seated in front of your OS X machine
now, fire up TextEdit or Pages and follow along.

Choosing fonts from the Fonts panel

Suppose you've just highlighted a headline in TextEdit, and now you want to choose
an appropriate typeface for it.

In TextEdit, you open the Fonts panel (Figure 14-9) by choosing Format→Font→Show
Fonts (⌘-T). Just as in Font Book, the first column lists your Collections. The second
column, Family, shows the names of the actual fonts in your system. The third, Type-
face, shows the various style variations—Bold, Italic, Condensed, and so on—available
in that type family. (Oblique and Italic are roughly the same thing; Bold, Black, and
Ultra are varying degrees of boldface.)

The last column lists a sampling of point sizes. You can use the Size slider, choose from
the point-size pop-up menu, or type any number into the box at the top of the Size list.

Designing collections and favorites

At the bottom of the Fonts panel, the ✿ menu offers a few useful customization tools:

- **Add to Favorites.** To designate a font as one of your favorites, specify a font, style,
 and size by clicking in the appropriate columns of the Fonts panel. Then use this
 command.

 From now on, whenever you click Favorites in the Collections column, you'll see
 a list of the typefaces you've specified.

- **Show Preview.** The Fonts panel is great and all that, but you may have noticed
 that, until you choose this option, it doesn't actually *show* you the fonts you're
 working with—something of an oversight in a window designed to help you find
 your fonts. See Figure 14-9 for details. (Choose this command again—now called
 Hide Preview—to get rid of the preview.)

Tip: Once you've opened the Preview pane, feel free to click the different sizes, typeface names, and family
names to see the various effects.

- **Hide Effects.** The "toolbar" of the Fonts panel lets you create special text effects—
 colors, shadows, and so on—as shown in Figure 14-9. This command hides that
 row of pop-up buttons.

- **Color.** Opens the Color Picker, so you can specify a color for the highlighted text in your document.

- **Characters.** Opens the Character Viewer, so you can choose a symbol without having to remember the crazy keyboard combo that types it.

- **Typography.** Opens the Typography palette (see Figure 14-10).

Figure 14-10:
The Typography palette is a collapsible menagerie of fancy type effects, which vary by font. In this example, turning on Common Ligatures creates fused letter pairs like fl and fi; the Small Capitals option created the "Do Not Drink" style; and so on.

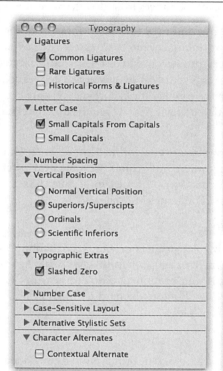

- **Edit Sizes.** The point sizes listed in the Fonts panel are just suggestions. You can actually type in any point size you want. By choosing this command, in fact, you can edit this list so that the sizes you use most often are only a click away.

- **Manage Fonts.** Opens Font Book, described earlier in this chapter.

ColorSync

As you may have discovered through painful experience, computers aren't great with color. Each device you use to create and print digital images "sees" color a little bit differently, which explains why the deep amber captured by your scanner may be rendered as chalky brown on your monitor, yet come out as a fiery orange on your Epson inkjet printer. Since every gadget defines and renders color in its own way, colors are often inconsistent as a print job moves from design to proof to press.

ColorSync attempts to sort out this mess, serving as a translator for all the different pieces of hardware in your workflow. For this to work, each device (scanner, monitor, printer, digital camera, copier, proofer, and so on) has to be calibrated with a unique *ColorSync profile*—a file that tells your Mac exactly how it defines colors. Armed with the knowledge contained in the profiles, the ColorSync software can compensate for the various quirks of the different devices, and even the different kinds of paper they print on.

Most of the people who lose sleep over color fidelity are those who do commercial color scanning and printing, where "off" colors are a big deal. After all, a customer might return a product after discovering, for example, that the actual product color doesn't match the photo on a company's Web site.

Getting ColorSync Profiles

ColorSync profiles for many color printers, scanners, and monitors come built into OS X. When you buy equipment or software from, say, Kodak, Agfa, or Pantone, you may get additional profiles. If your equipment didn't come with a ColorSync profile, let Google be your friend; they shouldn't be hard to find. Put new profiles into the Library→ColorSync→Profiles folder.

Default Profiles

In professional graphics work, a ColorSync profile is often embedded right in a photo, making all this color management automatic. Using the ColorSync Utility program (in Applications→Utilities), you can specify which ColorSync profile each of your gadgets should use. Click the Devices button, open the category for your device (scan-

POWER USERS' CLINIC

AppleScript and ColorSync

Using AppleScript, described in Chapter 7, you can harness ColorSync in elaborate ways. Just by dragging document icons onto AppleScript icons, for example, you can embed ColorSync profiles, modify the profiles already incorporated, remove profiles, review the profile information embedded in a graphic, and much more. Better yet, you don't even have to know AppleScript to perform these functions—just use the built-in AppleScripts that come with OS X.

To find them, open the Library→ColorSync→Scripts folder. Unfortunately, there aren't any instructions for using these eight ready-made AppleScripts. Nonetheless, Apple's real hope is that these example scripts give you a leg up on creating your own AppleScripts—that someday you, the print shop operator, will be able to automate your entire color processing routine using AppleScript and ColorSync.

ner, camera, display, printer, or proofer), click the model you have, and then use the Current Profile pop-up menu to assign a profile to it.

Tip: In the Displays pane of System Preferences, you'll find a Color tab. Its Calibrate button is designed to create a profile for your particular monitor in your particular office lighting—all you have to do is answer a few fun questions onscreen and drag a few sliders.

More on ColorSync

If you ache to learn more about ColorSync, you won't find much in OS X's Help system. Instead, search the Web. You'll find Googling *ColorSync* to be a fruitful exercise.

Graphics in OS X

Everywhere you look in OS X, you'll find visual effects that would make any other operating system think about early retirement.

For example: Menus are transparent, and when you release them, they fade away instead of snapping off. You can set Excel 3-D graphs to be slightly transparent so that they don't block other bars in a 3-D graph. When you paste files into windows in icon view, their icons fade into view. When you open an especially long message in Mail, its text fades in from white. When you use Launchpad, it fades in and out. And when you switch accounts using Fast User Switching, your work environment slides off the screen as though it's pasted on the side of an animated cube.

All these visual goodies owe their existence to Quartz (or its enhanced successor, Quartz Extreme, which is not available on older Macs).

Graphics Formats on the Mac

OS X understands dozens of Mac and Windows graphics file formats. Better yet, its Preview program can open such graphics and then export them in a different format, making it an excellent file-conversion program.

You can confidently double-click graphics files—from a digital camera, scanner, or Web download, for example—in any of these formats:

- **PICT files.** For almost 20 years, the PICT file was the graphics format Mac fans were most familiar with. It was the graphics format used by the Mac Clipboard, and it was the format created by the Shift-⌘-3 keystroke (see the end of this chapter).

 Unfortunately, no other kinds of computers could open these files, so PICT files gave conniptions to the equipment at printing shops. Now, after all these years, Apple is finally letting PICT slip away. The Preview program can no longer save graphics in the PICT format. It *can* open them, but only when it's running in 32-bit mode.

- **TIFF files.** The TIFF file format is a high-density, high-quality, uncompressed *bitmap*—that is, the Mac has memorized the color of each tiny dot in the file. Trying to enlarge one is like enlarging a fax: Make it too big, and the image breaks down into visible dots.

Nonetheless, TIFF files are very popular in the printing industry—most of the graphics in this book, for example, were stored as TIFF files. They print beautifully, work nicely in page-layout programs, and are understood by both Macs and Windows PCs. (They're also pretty big files.)

- **JPEG files.** This format is one of the most popular on the Web, particularly for photos or other high-quality, full-color artwork.

 What makes JPEG files ideal for online use is that they've been compressed (using a program like Photoshop). Just enough of the color data has been thrown out from the original file to make the image a quick download without noticeably affecting its quality.

- **GIF files.** GIF stands for *graphics interchange format.* Today, GIF files are used almost exclusively on the Web, usually for solid-colored graphics like cartoons, headlines, and logos. (A GIF file can have a maximum of 256 colors, which is not even close to the photorealism of, say, JPEG. That's what makes the GIF format inappropriate for photographs.)

- **PNG files.** As it turns out, one of the algorithms used by GIF files is, technically speaking, the property of a company called Unisys, which threatened to sue everybody who was creating GIF files. "No problem," said the World Wide Web Consortium. "We'll just come up with our own replacement—a file format that has no legal strings attached." What they created was PNG (for Portable Network Graphics). You can save Photoshop and Preview documents in PNG format, and every modern Web browser understands it. Screenshots you take in OS X (that is, captured images of the screen, as described in the following pages) are in the PNG format, too.

 PNG files don't lose quality when compressed, as JPEG files do. On the other hand, PNG files don't accommodate animation, as GIF files do. And when it comes to photos, they don't offer as impressive a size/quality balance as JPEG.

- **PDF (Adobe Reader) files.** As noted earlier in this chapter, the Mac traffics effortlessly in PDF files, meaning that you can distribute documents you create to almost anyone, confident that they'll be able to open and print your stuff regardless of what kind of computer, fonts, and programs they have.

- **Photoshop files.** If you're a graphic designer or Webmeister, this one is kind of neat: OS X can open (and Preview can even export) actual Photoshop files (except for so-called *16-bit RGB* files). In practical terms, the fact that OS X can open and display these files means that you could use a Photoshop masterpiece, complete with layers and transparency, as, for example, an OS X desktop background.

- **BMP files.** You can think of this graphics format as the PICT of the Windows world. It's nice that OS X can open (and Preview can export) them, especially because you may occasionally find .bmp files on the Web or attached to email messages.

- **Silicon Graphics, MacPaint, Targ.** Talk about obscure—you could go through your whole life without ever seeing a graphic in one of these formats. Silicon Graphics

is, unsurprisingly, the format created by Silicon Graphics computers. MacPaint is a black-and-white-only, 8 × 10–inch maximum, ancient Macintosh graphics format that disappeared from the scene in about 1988. And Targ (Targa) is the file format once used by products from Truevision.

Screen-Capture Keystrokes

If you're reading a chapter about printing and graphics, you may someday be interested in creating *screenshots*—printable illustrations of the Mac screen.

Screenshots are a staple of articles, tutorials, and books about the Mac (including this one). The Mac has a secret built-in feature that lets you make them—and includes some very cool conveniences.

Here's how to capture various regions of the screen.

The Whole Screen

Press Shift-⌘-3 to create a picture file on your desktop, in PNG format, that depicts the entire screen image. A satisfying camera-shutter sound tells you that you were successful. Each time you press Shift-⌘-3, you get another file on your desktop.

These files are named after the current time and date. They're called "Screen shot 2013-01-18 at 5.18.13 PM," "Screen shot 2013-01-18 at 5.18.32 PM," and so on.

You can open these files into Preview or any other graphics program, in readiness for editing, printing, or exporting in a different format.

Tip: It doesn't have to be Shift-⌘-3. You can change this keystroke, or any of these screenshot keystrokes, to anything you like. Open System Preferences→Keyboard→Keyboard Shortcuts→Screen Shots. Click the keystroke you want to change, press Return to highlight the current keyboard combo, and then press the new keystroke you prefer.

One Section of the Screen

You can capture just a rectangular *region* of the screen by pressing Shift-⌘-4. Your cursor turns into a crosshairs with two tiny digital readouts—the horizontal and vertical coordinates of your cursor on the screen at this moment. (The numbers are pixels, as measured from the upper-left corner of the screen, which has coordinates 0, 0.)

Now drag diagonally across the screen to capture only a rectangular chunk of it. When you drag and release the mouse, you hear the camera-click sound, and the screenshot file appears on your desktop as usual—containing only the rectangle you enclosed.

But that's just the beginning. Once you've begun dragging diagonally, while the mouse is still down, you can press any of these keys for special manipulation effects:

- **Space bar.** While you hold down the space bar with one hand, your selection rectangle is frozen in size and shape. With your mouse hand, you can move the cursor with the entire selection rectangle attached, the better to fine-tune your positioning relative to your target.

- **Shift key.** When you hit Shift, you confine the dragging action of your mouse to a single dimension: horizontal or vertical. Which dimension depends on how you move your mouse after you hit Shift.

 For example, suppose you drag out a two-inch square, and then you pause. With the mouse button still down, you press Shift. If you now continue to drag downward, the selected area maintains a fixed width; you're increasing only the rectangle's height.

- **Option key.** If you hold down Option after beginning to drag, you create a rectangular selection that grows from the center point outward. That is, it treats your initial click as the rectangle's center point, rather than as a diagonal corner.

- **Esc.** If you change your mind about taking a screenshot, tap Esc. The darkened selection area disappears, and you've exited screenshot mode.

A Dialog Box, Menu, Window, or Icon

Why fuss with cleaning up a screenshot after you've taken it? Using this trick, you can neatly snip *one screen element* out from its background.

Make sure the dialog box, menu, window, or icon is visible. Then press Shift-⌘-4. But *instead of* dragging diagonally, tap the space bar.

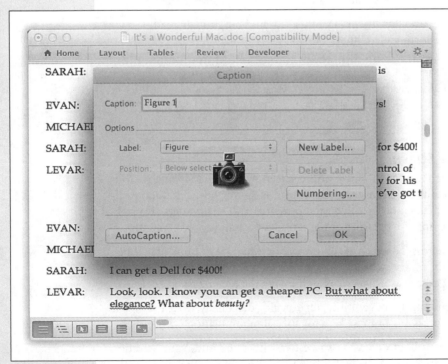

Figure 14-11:
To capture just one dialog box, use the old camera-cursor trick. That is, invoke Shift-⌘-4 and then tap the space bar to produce the cursor shown here. Click the element you want to snip from its background. (Press the space bar a second time to exit "snip one screen element" mode and return to "drag across an area" mode.) If you ever change your mind about taking any kind of screenshot, press ⌘-period or the Esc key.

Your cursor turns into a tiny camera (Figure 14-11). Move it so the misty-blue high-lighting fills the window or menu you want to capture—and then click. The resulting picture file snips the window or menu neatly from its background.

Pressing Shift-⌘-4 and then the space bar also captures the Dock in one quick snip. Once you've got the camera cursor, just click any *blank* spot in the Dock (between icons).

Tip: If you hold down the Control key as you click or drag (using any of the techniques described above), you copy the screenshot to your *Clipboard,* ready for pasting, rather than saving it as a new graphics file on your desktop.

OS X comes with other ways to create screenshots:

- **Grab.** Grab is a program in your Applications→Utilities folder. Grab's chief selling point is its *timer* option, which lets you set up the screen before it takes the shot.

- **Preview.** You can use the File→Take Screen Shot submenu commands to take screenshots (whole screen, selection, just one window) and open the result directly into Preview, rather than dumping the result onto your hard drive. The advantage here is that you can use all of Preview's image-manipulation skills—changing resolution, cropping, annotating, color-adjusting, exporting in various graphics formats—before committing the thing to your hard drive.

- **Services.** The Capture commands in the Services menu trigger the same screen-capturing function. They work, however, only when your cursor is in a Cocoa program that accepts pasted graphics (TextEdit, Stickies, and Pages, for example).

That's a lot of flexibility. But if you're really serious about capturing screenshots, you should opt instead for a program like Snapz Pro X (*www.ambrosiasw.com*), which can capture virtually anything on the screen—even movies of onscreen procedures, along with your narration—and save it in your choice of graphics format.

OS X: THE MISSING MANUAL

Sound, Movies & Speech

M acs have been capable of handing sound and graphics from Day One, years before the word *multimedia* was even coined. OS X's QuickTime technology plays digital movies and live "streaming" broadcasts from the Internet; its speech features let you command your Mac by voice or make your Mac talk back; and VoiceOver is a beefed-up talking-Mac feature for blind people.

This chapter covers it all: how to record sound and video, edit it, play it back—and how to make your Mac talkative.

Playing Sounds

You can have a lot of fun with digital sounds—if you know where to find them, where to put them, and how to edit them. You can play almost any kind of digitized sound files, even MP3 files, right in the Finder—if you put their windows into column view or Cover Flow view (or use Quick Look). But that's just the beginning.

Controlling the Volume

Adjusting the volume of your Mac's speakers couldn't be easier: Tap the ◀) and ◀)) keys on your keyboard. (The ◀ key next to them is the Mute button, which instantaneously cuts off all the Mac's sound—a wonderful feature when you find yourself trying to use the Mac surreptitiously in a library or a church.)

Alternatively, you can add the ◀)) menulet to your menu bar (Figure 15-1).

The Output tab of the System Preferences→Sound pane, by the way, is designed to let you adjust the left-to-right balance of your stereo speakers, if you have them. The stereo speakers on most Macs that have them (iMacs, laptops) are already perfectly

centered, so there's little need to adjust this slider unless you generally list to one side in your chair. (You might find additional controls here if you have extra audio gear—an old iSub subwoofer system, for example.)

Tip: In the Audio MIDI Setup program (in Applications→Utilities), you can set up and configure much fancier speaker setups, including 5.1 and 6.1 surround-sound systems.

Figure 15-1:
The tiny speaker silhouette in the upper-right corner of your screen turns into a volume slider when you click it. To make this sound menulet appear, open the Sound pane of System Preferences and turn on "Show volume in menu bar."

Alert Beeps and You

Alert beeps are the quacks, beeps, or trumpet blasts that say, "You can't click here." (Try typing letters into a dialog box where a program expects numbers, for example.)

Choosing an alert beep

To choose one that suits your personal taste, open System Preferences→Sound→Sound Effects. Press the ↑ and ↓ keys to walk through the 14 witty and interesting sound snippets you can use as error beeps. You can also drag the "Alert volume" slider to adjust the error beep volume relative to your Mac's overall speaker setting.

Adding new alert beeps

OS X's error beeps are AIFF sound files, a standard Mac/Windows/Internet sound format—which, as a testimony to its potential for high quality, is also the standard sound-file format for music CDs. (The abbreviation stands for *audio interchange file format,* if you're scoring at home.)

As with fonts, OS X builds the list of error beeps you see in the Sound pane of System Preferences from several folder sources:

- **System→Library→Sounds folder.** This folder contains the basic OS X set. Because it's in the System folder, it's off limits to manipulation by us meddlesome human beings. You can't easily delete one of the original OS X error beeps or add to this collection.

- **Home→Library→Sounds folder.** It's easy enough to add sounds for your own use—just put them in this folder. (Your Home→Library folder is usually invisible; to open it, press Option as you choose Go→Library in the Finder.)

- **Library→Sounds folder.** If you, an administrator, want to make a sound file available to all account holders on your Mac (if there are more than one), create a new Sounds folder in the main hard drive window's Library folder. Any sound files you put there now appear in every account holder's list of alert sounds.

The sound files you put into these folders must be in AIFF format, and their names must end with the extension *.aiff* or *.aif.*

Note: Any changes you make to these Sounds folders don't show up in the Sound pane until the next time you open it.

Recording Sounds

If you hope to record new sounds, you need a microphone. Your microphone situation depends on the kind of Mac you have:

- **Laptop, iMac.** You have a built-in microphone, usually a tiny hole near the screen.

- **Mac Pro, Mac mini.** You can plug in an external USB microphone or use an adapter (such as the iMic, *www.griffintechnology.com*) that accommodates a standard microphone.

The System Preferences→Sound→Input pane lets you choose which sound source you want the Mac to listen to: external USB microphone, built-in microphone, or whatever.

Tip: Actually, there's a quicker way to change audio inputs—if you know the secret. Option-click the ◀)) menulet, if you've installed it. The resulting menu lists all your audio inputs and outputs, making it simple to switch.

Making the Recording

Once you've got your microphone situation taken care of, you need to get your hands on some sound-recording software—like QuickTime Player, which is in your Applications folder. (You can use GarageBand to record sound, too, but that's often like using a pneumatic drill to get out a splinter.)

Choose File→New Audio Recording. Use the pop-up menu to specify the audio quality and sound source (Figure 15-2). Click the round, red Record button and begin to speak; click the square Stop button to finish up. Now you can use the volume slider and the ▶ button to listen to your masterpiece.

Tip: Don't adjust the tiny volume slider in the Audio Recording window unless you're wearing headphones. This slider lets you monitor the sound—and turning it up while the Mac's speakers are live risks producing the hideous shriek known as feedback.

Behind the scenes, the Mac has created a new AAC audio file called *Audio Recording. mov* in your Home→Movies folder. (Additional recordings are called Audio Recording 2, 3, 4, and so on.) You can double-click it to open it right back up into QuickTime

Player for trimming (read on). Or, if you think it needs more in-depth editing, you can open it with GarageBand and really go to town.

Note: You can record *video* in QuickTime Player just as easily. See page 624.

Figure 15-2:
There's a lot going on in this tiny window. The pop-up menu lets you choose audio quality and audio input. At bottom, as you record, you see a VU meter (audio level) and an indication of the recording's length and file size.

QuickTime Player

A QuickTime movie is a video file you can play from your hard drive, a CD or DVD, or the Internet. Like any movie, it creates the illusion of motion by flashing many individual frames (photos) per second before your eyes, while also playing a synchronized soundtrack.

The cornerstone of OS X's built-in movie-playback software is QuickTime Player, which sits in your Applications folder. Despite its name, QuickTime Player also lets you edit movies and even record new ones, either using your Mac's built-in camera or by recording screen activity. Finally, when everything looks good, you can post your masterpiece to YouTube, Facebook, Vimeo, or another online site.

You can open a movie file by double-clicking it. When QuickTime Player first opens, you get a very cool, borderless playback window. Just hit the space bar to play the movie.

There's a control toolbar at the bottom of the window (Figure 15-3), but it fades away after a few seconds—or immediately, if you move the cursor out of the frame. The toolbar reappears anytime your mouse moves back into the movie frame. These are the controls:

- **Rotate or flip.** The Edit menu contains commands for Rotate Right, Rotate Left, Flip Horizontal, and Flip Vertical. Those commands can be handy when a movie turns out to be flipped or rotated—or when you *want* to flip or rotate it for creative purposes.

- **Volume slider** (� ... ◄)). Click in the slider, or drag the dot, to adjust the volume—although it's actually easier to just tap the ↑ or ↓ keys.

Tip: To mute the sound, click the ◀ icon or press Option-↓. Press Option-↑ to make the volume slider jump to full-blast position.

- **Rewind, Fast-forward (◀◀, ▶▶).** By clicking one of these buttons, you get to speed through your movie at double speed, backward or forward, complete with sound. Click again for 4X speed, again for 8X.

Tip: You don't have to keep your mouse button pressed on these. Just click once and let QuickTime Player do the work. Click ▶ or tap the space bar to stop scanning.

Figure 15-3:
QuickTime Player displays this control bar only when you move your mouse into its window, or whenever playback is stopped.

- **Play/Pause (▶/❚❚).** Click ▶ to start playback, ❚❚ to pause/stop. Or just tap the space bar for both functions.

- **Scroll bar.** Drag the little diamond, or just click inside its track, to jump to a different spot in the movie. The counters at the beginning and end of the scroll bar tell you, in "hours:minutes:seconds" format, how far your playhead cursor has moved into the movie, and how far you are from the end. (Click the right-hand readout to see the total movie duration.)

Tip: You can also press the ← and → keys to step through the movie one frame at a time. If you press Option-← or Option-→, you jump to the beginning or the end of the movie. That's important to know, since there are no longer dedicated Jump to Start/Jump to End buttons on the control bar.

- **Window edges.** Drag any edge, or the lower-right corner, to make the window bigger or smaller. QuickTime Player always maintains the same *aspect ratio* (relative dimensions) of the original movie, so you won't accidentally squish it.

- **Share button ().** Click for a pop-up menu of choices for passing on this video to your adoring fans: via Email, Message, AirDrop, Facebook, YouTube, Vimeo, or Flickr. All of these options are described below.

- **Full Screen ().** Click to make the video fill your entire monitor, just as though you'd chosen View→Enter Full Screen. And what if the proportions of the movie don't quite match your screen? If you make the menu bar return by pointing to the top of your screen, then you can handle this problem using one of the choices in the View menu, described next.

Note: When you enter Full Screen mode, the movie doesn't begin playing automatically (unless it was already playing, of course). You have to tap the space bar to get the show under way.

Fancy Playback Tricks

Playing one movie, start to finish, is kid stuff. Here's what else QuickTime Player can do:

- **Change the screen size.** As noted above, you can drag the window to any size using the edges as handles. But the View menu commands are handy, too.

QuickTime Player vs. QuickTime Player 7 vs. QuickTime Player Pro

Hey! I paid $30 to upgrade the old QuickTime Player to the Pro version, so I could edit videos, copy/paste, combine tracks, export in different formats, stuff like that. I upgraded to Mountain Lion, and now Pro is gone! What's the deal!? Apple just trashed my $30 software?

Chillax, bro. It's all good.

True enough, the new QuickTime Player is intended to replace the old, free, pre–Snow Leopard program QuickTime Player (now called QuickTime Player 7). Apple figures: Look, the new app looks better, plays better, uploads movies to YouTube, and does basic editing really well. If you need fancier editing or exporting, well, your Mac came with iMovie, didn't it? You can always use that.

But not everybody wants to heave open the lumbering iMovie just for quick, simple editing jobs. And the old QuickTime Player had some nice features that the new

version lacks. For example, it could play back QuickTime VR (virtual-reality) movies, interactive QuickTime movies, and MIDI music files. And if you paid $30, you could turn it into QuickTime 7 Pro, which offered lots more editing features than even the Mountain Lion version of QuickTime Player does.

Fortunately, the old QuickTime Player is still around. If you had it already when you installed Mountain Lion, it got moved into the Applications→Utilities folder, bearing the name QuickTime Player 7. (If you had upgraded it to Pro, it still has the Pro features.) And if you don't have it, you can download it from *http://support.apple.com/kb/dl923*.

If you use the old app more often than you use the new Lion QuickTime Player, then you can reassign movies so that they open up in QuickTime Player 7 when double-clicked.

Happy QuickTiming!

Actual size represents the movie on your screen at its real size—no larger. (If it's truly huge, larger than your screen, it may be scaled *smaller* to fit. But that's a rarity.)

Fit to Screen fills your screen without cropping or distorting; the menu bar and other windows remain visible.

Fill Screen is especially satisfying, because it turns your entire monitor into a movie playback area.

Panoramic squishes the outer edges of the video, distorting them slightly, so that nothing gets chopped off *and* the movie fills the screen. (These two options are available only in Full Screen mode.)

Tip: These same options are available via keyboard shortcuts—⌘-1, ⌘-3, ⌘-4, and ⌘-5. There's even a little button on the control bar, second from right, that switches back and forth between Fit to Screen and Fill Screen. (This button appears only when you're already in Full Screen mode.)

Making the window larger may also make the movie coarser, because QuickTime Player simply enlarges every dot that was present in the original. Still, when you want to show a movie to a group of people more than a few feet back from the screen, these larger sizes are perfectly effective.

Tip: You can make the movie window bigger or smaller by pressing ⌘-plus (+) or ⌘-minus (-).

- **Play more than one movie.** You can open several movies at once and run them simultaneously. (Of course, the more movies you try to play at once, the jerkier the playback gets.)

- **Loop the movie.** When you choose View→Loop and then click Play, the movie repeats endlessly until you make it stop.

- **Navigate chapters.** A few movies, like the ones you buy or rent from Apple, come with built-in chapter markers, just like a DVD. They let you jump around in the film at your whim.

Editing movies

QuickTime Player is now QuickTime Editor. The program still doesn't offer selection handles, so you might think there's no way to select a portion of the middle of a movie (to chop it out, for example). But in fact, the new commands for trimming, splitting, and merging video clips let you perform just about any editing trick you can imagine. Read on.

- **Trimming video from the ends.** You can very easily trim dead space off the ends of a video. Figure 15-4 shows how.

You don't have to worry about damaging the original video when trimming—you couldn't modify the original if you tried. The instant you use the Trim command, QuickTime Player peels off the shortened version as a new, untitled movie, which you'll have to name and save separately (choose File→Export).

Figure 15-4:
Top: To trim a video, choose Edit→Trim or press ⌘-T. Drag the yellow handles inward to isolate the chunk you want to preserve. (You can click ▶ or tap the space bar to check your work.) When everything looks good, click Trim or press Return.

Bottom: If you choose View→Show Audio Track, then you can use the soundwaves as a guide to your precision editing.

- **Splitting a clip.** *Clips* are subsections of a movie. To chop a movie in two, move the playhead to the spot where you want the movie to split, and then choose Edit→Split Clip. As shown in Figure 15-5, a clips map appears at the bottom of the window, showing the two resulting clips.

- **Chopping video out of the middle.** If you want to trim some video from the *middle* of a movie, first open up the clips map. Then split the movie as described above. Once you've split a movie into a couple of clips, you can double-click *one* of the clips to produce trim handles *just for it.* In this way, you can cut unwanted sections from the *middle* of a video.

 Or just split the clip into three chunks—and delete the middle one.

- **Rearranging clips.** Once you've chopped up a video into subclips using the Split Clip command, you can drag them around within the map. (If you don't see the map, shown in Figure 15-5, then choose View→Show Clips.)

You can use the Cut, Copy, and Paste commands in the Edit menu, too, to move chunks around—even among different movies. (Just remember to first split the target movie at the spot where you want to paste the new clip. The pasted material appears just *after* whatever clip is currently highlighted.)

• **Combining movies.** Combining clips, as described above, is one way to merge videos together. But you can also merge entire movie files that are sitting in the Finder.

Start by opening the first movie. If you want the second movie to appear at the *end* of it, just choose Edit→Add Clip to End.

Tip: If you press Option, the command says Add Clip to Beginning. Sneaky!

Figure 15-5:
The Split Clip command chops the video into two clips—and produces the map shown at bottom. If you click a clip and then press the space bar to play the video, you'll see the red vertical line that represents the playhead. To chop one of your clips up into further subclips, move that red line into position and then use the Split Clip command again.

The Open dialog box now appears. Find and double-click the clip you want to tack on. Repeat as necessary.

You can also drag movie clips' icons from the desktop right into a movie window. QuickTime Player adds them to the end of the existing movie.

If you want the second movie to appear somewhere in the middle of the first movie, open up the clip map (View→Show Clips). Click the clip that appears right *before* the spot where the new movie will go. Choose Edit→Insert Clip After Selection; in the resulting dialog box, find and double-click the movie file you want to bring in.

Or drag a movie file from the Finder directly into the gap between two subclips.

Tip: QuickTime Player automatically shrinks or crops the incoming movies so that they fit the same "screen size" as the original. If they're *not* exactly the same size or proportions, you can then use the Edit→Clip Alignment submenu (Top, Left, Center, and so on) to specify which edge of the movie frame the imported video should hug.

Recording movies with QuickTime Player

QuickTime Player does more than *play* movies; it can also *record* them. Yes, your Mac is now a camcorder, and a darned handy one; you can pop out quick video greetings, gross out your former roommates, impress your coworkers with a dress rehearsal of your pitch, and so on.

Laptops and iMacs, of course, have a video camera built right in, above the screen. If you have another model, you can attach a Webcam, an old iSight camera, or even a FireWire camcorder.

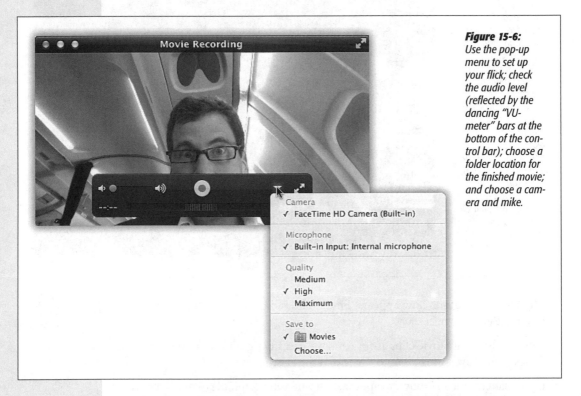

Figure 15-6:
Use the pop-up menu to set up your flick; check the audio level (reflected by the dancing "VU-meter" bars at the bottom of the control bar); choose a folder location for the finished movie; and choose a camera and mike.

Then open QuickTime Player and choose File→New Movie Recording. The preview window appears. Use the pop-up menu shown in Figure 15-6 to specify what mike and camera you want to use (in the unlikely event that you have more than one), what video quality you want, and where you want to store the result.

Then, to record, click the red Record button (or press the space bar). Do your schtick. Press the space bar again to stop recording.

Your new video appears in its own playback window. Check it out, trim it if necessary, and then shoot it off to iTunes, Vimeo, YouTube, or whatever.

Recording screen movies

You can also record movies *of the screen.*

Why is it useful to capture screen activity as a video? Because you can make mini-tutorials to give little lessons to techno-clueless relatives. You can make video podcasts that show how to do things in your software programs. You can preserve Web animations that you used to think you had no way to capture.

There are limitations. Your movies don't include the Mac's own sounds (game soundtracks and so on), so forget about capturing videos playing on YouTube. (It can record from the *mike*, though, so you can narrate what you're doing.)

But who cares? It's fantastically handy. And in Mountain Lion, you can capture only a *portion* of the screen—one particular window, for example—instead of being stuck with the entire monitor's worth.

To make a screen recording, choose File→New Screen Recording. Use the pop-up menu on the resulting Screen Recording panel to turn the microphone on or off, to choose a quality setting, and to indicate where you want the finished movie stored.

Tip: This pop-up menu also contains an option called Show Mouse Clicks in Recording. It helps your viewers understand when and where you actually clicked the mouse during the tutorial—by briefly displaying a little circle around the cursor each time you click. (It appears only in playback—not while you're recording.)

Finally, click the red Record button (or press Return), and then proceed as shown in Figure 15-7.

Figure 15-7:
This message appears when you tap the Record button. If you just click to start recording, you'll capture the entire monitor. But if you drag first, defining a rectangle, you'll capture only that area.

Press Return, or click Start Recording, to begin the capture. When you finally click the ■ button in the floating Screen Recording window, your finished movie appears in a regular playback window, ready to trim or to send away to your fans.

Internet Streaming QuickTime

QuickTime Player also lets you view "Internet slideshows," watch a couple of live TV stations, or listen to the radio—all as you work on your Mac, and all at no charge.

Streaming video from your browser

With ever-increasing frequency, Web sites advertise *streaming video* events, such as Apple keynote speeches and the occasional live rock concert. You'll find a note on a Web page, for example, that says, "Watch the live debate by clicking here on October 15 at 9:00 p.m. EST."

If you do so, you'll sometimes be able to watch it in your browser, and sometimes you'll be transported once again into QuickTime Player, which connects to the appropriate Internet "station" and plays the video in its window. (You can also choose File→Open Location from within QuickTime Player to type in the Web address.)

You don't have much control when watching a live broadcast. You generally can't rewind, and you certainly can't fast-forward. You may be able to pause the broadcast, but when you un-pause, you wind up at the current broadcast moment—not where you stopped.

Note: QuickTime Player can also play HTTP Live Streaming video, which is catching on for live broadcasts. One advantage: Because it uses the same "language" as ordinary Web pages, corporate firewalls and grouchy routers are less likely to block this kind of video.

Eleven Ways to Export Your Video

One of QuickTime Player's most important talents is *sharing* a video: posting it directly to Facebook, YouTube, Vimeo, Flickr, or your own Web site; converting it to the right format for an iPod, iPhone, or cellphone; stashing it in iTunes for easy transfer to your iPod/iPhone; handing it off to iMovie for further editing; saving it to the hard drive as a double-clickable movie; and so on.

Let us count the ways.

Post to YouTube, Vimeo, Flickr, Facebook

Apple makes much of the new ↱ button in Mountain Lion. But the truth is, that Share button has been around for a while—right here in QuickTime Player. As before, it offers one-click commands for posting to YouTube (the world's most popular and famous Web site for short videos), Vimeo (a less well-known, but classier, more high-def video-sharing site), Flickr (mainly a photo-sharing site, but it handles videos, too), or Facebook (the most visited Web site on earth).

All of these services require that you first sign up for a free account. (You do that online, not in QuickTime Player.)

have file-size limits, and movies are big. You'll be allowed to send the movie just fine, but the recipient's email system may reject it as being too big. You'll get a "bounce back" message, in that case.

The ↪ menu also offers commands like Message (sends the movie to someone's Mac, phone, or tablet via Messages, described in Chapter 20) and AirDrop (sends the movie to someone's Mac wirelessly, provided it's within 30 feet of you; see page 553).

Send to iTunes

The main reason you'd want to send your video to iTunes is because you have an iPod, iPhone, iPad, or Apple TV. Once it's in iTunes, you can sync your video easily to that other Apple gadget and have it ready to view at all times.

To make this transfer happen, choose File→Export To→iTunes. You see the dialog box in Figure 15-9. Click the appropriate gadget/screen size, and then click Share. When it's all over, your video will appear safely nestled in iTunes, in the Videos category, ready to watch or sync.

Figure 15-9:
This dialog box gives you three size choices for the movie you're exporting, which correspond to the screen sizes of the three Apple gadgets available. (The Computer option is just there in case you like to play videos right in iTunes, right on the screen. It's dimmed if the original movie isn't big enough to fill the screen.)

Post to a Web page

The File→Export To→Web command produces a dialog box with three options: WiFi, Cellular, and Broadband. Turn on as many of them as you like.

An Export Progress dialog box appears, and the Mac chews away at the job of creating differently sized versions of the movie, at different frame and data rates, for the different kinds of visitors your Web site might encounter.

When it's over, the dialog box displays a link to a Web page (an HTML document) that's been saved to your hard drive. Click the link to view the remarkable sight shown

in Figure 15-10. This Web page contains user-friendly instructions for embedding this movie on your own Web site (well, as user-friendly as HTML code fragments get). There's even a playable preview, so you can try the finished product before you post it online.

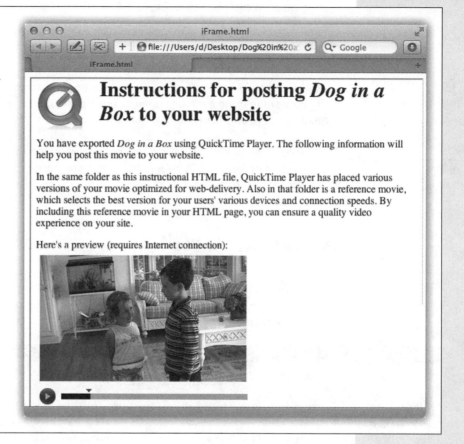

Figure 15-10:
This Web page explains that you've actually created as many as three different versions of your movie for the Web—plus a reference movie *that's smart enough to detect which Web visitor is using which kind of Internet connection, and to play the correctly sized version accordingly.*

Saving the finished movie

After you've edited a movie (or not), you can use the Export command to specify a new name for your masterpiece—and, if you wish, to convert it to a different format, depending on what kind of machine will be playing it.

When you choose File→Export, the Format pop-up menu offers these choices:

- **480p.** You're creating a video in H.264 format, with a resolution of 640 × 480 pixels (standard-definition TV size). It requires 3 megabits per second of Internet speed, which means that almost anyone can watch it online.

- **720p.** You're saving a high-definition H.264 video (1280 × 720 pixels). Requires more bandwidth to watch online: 7.5 Mbits per second.

- **1080p.** An even higher-def high-def movie (1920 × 1080). Requires 10 Mbits per second.

- **iPod Touch & iPhone 3GS.** This option makes a 480p copy of the movie, in MPEG format. Perfect size for the iPhone 3GS and iPod Touch (third generation or later). Also plays on computers and Apple TV.

- **iPad, iPhone 4 & Apple TV.** Creates a 720p (high-def) copy of the movie. Sized for the higher-resolution screens of the iPod touch (fourth generation), iPhone 4 or 4S, iPad, and Apple TV (second generation).

- **Audio Only.** This option lets you export just the *audio* from a movie. That's handy if you want to listen on your phone or iPod, post an interview online, or use the audio track in another movie.

Tip: Most people think that those are the only options—but there are a few more choices that can handle earlier gadgets. To see them, press Option as you open the Format pop-up menu. Now you also get choices for older iPods and iPhones (and for slower Internet connections—1.5 megabits a second), and first-generation Apple TVs.

The Mac Reads to You

As you may have noticed, Mountain Lion is quite talented when it comes to speech. Its abilities fall into three categories: typing out what you say, reading text aloud using a synthesized voice, and obeying spoken *commands*. For details on Mountain Lion's new dictation feature, see page 245. For more on the spoken commands thing, see page 341.

GEM IN THE ROUGH

Talking to Chess

If your friends and coworkers are, for some reason, still unimpressed by OS X and your mastery of it, invite them over to watch you play a game of chess with your Mac—by talking to it.

(Actually, this feature isn't purely for entertainment: Some chess players prefer to move without looking at the board. By speaking their moves to the computer—and having the computer respond by speaking its own moves—these people can play "blindfolded.")

Open the Chess program. Unless you've turned it off (in Chess→Preferences), the game's speech-recognition feature is already turned on. When it's on, the round Feedback window should be visible onscreen.

To learn how to speak commands in a way that Chess understands, click the small gray triangle at the bottom of the Speech Feedback window to open the Speech Commands window. As usual, it lists all the commands Chess can comprehend.

You specify the location of pieces using the grid of numbers and letters along the edges of the chessboard. The white king, for example, starts on square e1 because he's in the first row (1) and the fifth column (e). To move the king forward by one square, you'd say, "King e1 to e2."

As the Speech Commands window should make clear, a few other commands are at your disposal. "Take back move" is one of the most useful. When you're ready to close in for the kill, the syntax is: "Pawn e5 takes f6."

And smile when you say that.

But to make the Mac *talk*, read on.

Most Apple programs have a Start Speaking command built right in: Safari, Mail, TextEdit, Messages, Stickies, Pages, and so on. Just Control-click (or right-click) inside a window full of text and, from the pop-up menu, choose Speech→Start Speaking. How cool is that? Your Mac can read your email or a Web article to you while you're getting dressed.

You can add a Speak command in FileMaker Pro scripts. OS X's Chess and Calculator programs can talk back, too.

But that's kid stuff. Truth is, the Mac can read almost anything you like: text you pass your cursor over, alert messages, menus, and *any text document in any program.* It can speak in your choice of dozens of synthesizer voices, ages 8 to 50. Most read with a twangy, charmingly Norwegian accent—but some of the newest voices (like Alex, Jill, Samantha, and Tom) sound scarily like a professional human voice-over artist.

Note: This text-reading business is not the same thing as the Mac's VoiceOver feature. VoiceOver is designed to read everything on the screen, including pop-up menus, buttons, and other controls, to visually impaired Mac fans (and to permit complete control, mouse-free, of everything). Details are on page 634.

Setting Up the Mac's Voice

To configure the way the Mac talks, revisit the Dictation & Speech pane of System Preferences. Click the Text to Speech tab at the top of the window. As you can see in Figure 15-11, you can control which of the Mac's voices you want your computer to use, as well as how fast it should speak.

As shown in Figure 15-11, though, the Mac comes with a huge range of additional voices that you can add to the pop-up menu here.

Tip: Three of the American voices were new for Lion—Jill, Samantha, and Tom—and they sound great. But don't ignore the "international" voices just because you're an American English speaker. There are also new voices that speak English with British, South African, and Australian accents—always fun.

All of those new-in-Lion voices have to be downloaded, so you can't grab them without an Internet connection. They're huge files, too, so don't be impatient. (They're stored in your System→Library→Speech→Voices folder.)

Here are all the different occasions when the Mac can talk to you.

Announce when alerts are displayed

If you turn on this checkbox, you can make the Mac read aloud error messages and alert messages that may appear on your screen. If you click the Set Alert Options button, you'll find these useful controls:

- **Voice.** Use this pop-up menu to specify the voice you want reading your error messages. (It doesn't have to be the same as the standard Mac voice that's used for other purposes.)

- **Phrase.** Use this pop-up menu to specify which utterance the Mac speaks before the actual error message—for example, "*Excuse me!* The Trash could not be emptied," or "*Attention!* The document could not be printed."

Figure 15-11:
Top: At the outset, you see only six voices.

Bottom: Choose Customize to see the complete list of 27 American English voices (plus 51 international voices); turn on the checkboxes of the ones you want to have available. The Mac automatically downloads any international voices you select. Then, for 15 minutes of hilarity, try clicking the voices in turn to hear sample sentences. Drag the slider to affect how fast each one speaks. (Clearly, Apple's programmers had some fun with this assignment.)

If you choose "Next in the phrase list" or "Random from the phrase list" from this pop-up menu, you'll never hear the same expletive twice. Better yet, choose Edit Phrase List to open a dialog box where you can specify your own words of frustration. (Apple Inc. is not liable for any trouble you may get into with people in neighboring cubicles.)

- **Delay.** The ostensible purpose of the Talking Alerts feature is to get your attention if you've wandered away from your Mac—mentally or physically. The chances are slim, but an urgent problem might occur that, if left undetected, could land you in trouble. (A 500-page printout brought to its knees by a paper jam comes to mind.)

In other words, if you're still sitting in front of your Mac, you may not need the Mac to speak to get your attention; you could simply read the onscreen message. That's why you can set this slider to make the Mac wait, after the error message appears, for up to a minute before trying to flag you with its voice. That way it won't harangue you unnecessarily. (Click Play for a sense of how long the Mac will delay before speaking.)

Announce when an application requires your attention

A jumping Dock icon means that the program is trying to get your attention. It might be because your printer is out of paper, or it might be because you've tried to shut down but one program still has open, unsaved documents. In any case, now the Mac can tell you, in so many words, which program needs some loving care.

Speak selected text when the key is pressed

As promised, this is the feature that makes the Mac read you any Web page, any email message, any sticky note—a welcome break for sore eyes. Furthermore, if you do any kind of writing at all, you'll discover the value of having your material read back to you out loud; it's a proofreading technique that reveals all kinds of typos and wordos that you wouldn't catch just by reading, even if you read it 50 times.

The very first time you turn on this checkbox, the Mac prompts you to specify a keystroke. (Later, you can always change the keystroke by clicking Set Key.) Choose a keystroke that doesn't conflict with the program you're using, like Control-T.

Now go to the program where you'd like the reading to happen. Highlight some text (or press ⌘-A to select all of it). Then press the keystroke you specified. The Mac begins reading it aloud immediately. To interrupt the playback, press the same keystroke again.

And be glad you were alive to see the day.

Tip: If you have an iPod or iPhone, your Mac can convert any text or word-processing document into a spoken recording so you can listen to it when you're on the go. To pull this off, see page 288.

GEM IN THE ROUGH

Voices to Sing About

The Mac's built-in speaking voices are no end of fun, as noted in Figure 15-11.

Five of the voices, in fact, *sing* rather than speak. Good News sings to the tune of "Pomp and Circumstance," otherwise known as the Graduation March. Bad News sings to the tune of Chopin's *Prelude in C minor*, better known as the Funeral March. Cellos sings to the tune of Grieg's *Peer Gynt* suite. Pipe Organ sings to the tune of the Alfred Hitchcock TV theme. Bells sings the typical church-bell carillon melody.

In other words, these voices sing whatever words you type to those melodies. (To hear the melody in its entirety, don't use any punctuation.)

VoiceOver

The Mac has always been able to read stuff on the screen out loud. But Apple has taken this feature light-years further, turning it into a full-blown *screen reader* for the benefit of people who can't see. VoiceOver doesn't just read every scrap of text it finds on the screen—it also lets you control everything on the screen (menus, buttons, and so on) without ever needing the mouse.

On a Mac with a multitouch trackpad, you can interact with what's visible on the screen by using the trackpad itself as a map of the current window or screen area; VoiceOver speaks whatever's under your finger. You can flick in any direction to move to the next thing on the screen. You hear a sound whenever VoiceOver finds blank spaces on the screen, all in the name of helping you "feel" where everything is.

OS X can also read entire Web pages, navigate Web tables, hop from link to link, and so on. You can navigate by pressing arrow keys, using the mouse, or using the trackpad.

Obviously, learning VoiceOver is a *huge* task that can take days or weeks—but if it's your ticket to being able to use a computer at all, you'll probably be happy to have such a full-fledged monster of a program.

Ink: Handwriting Recognition

In the same way that your grandmother turned yesterday's dinner into today's sandwich (and tomorrow's soup), Apple recycled the handwriting technology of its failed Newton handheld and added it to OS X. It's now called Ink, and it does exactly what it used to: turn your handwriting into "typed" text in any program.

You can't very well write directly on your Apple Cinema Display (although that would be cool). So Ink appears in OS X only if you have a graphics tablet, one of those stylus-and-pad devices found generally only on the desks of graphic artists. (Wacom is the best-known tablet company, but there are a couple of others.)

Can Ink really replace the keyboard? Not for anything more than quick notes, that's for sure. But it can be handy when you're Web surfing, sketching, filling in database forms, and so on.

Still, let's face it: You could count on one hand the number of people with Wacom digitizing tablets who use them for handwriting input. And so, to avoid sacrificing any more old-growth trees to this book than absolutely necessary, the how-to for Ink is available as a free downloadable PDF appendix to this chapter. You'll find it on this book's "Missing CD" page at *www.missingmanuals.com*.

Part Five: OS X Online

5

Internet Setup & iCloud

A s Apple's programmers slogged away for months on the massive OS X project, there were areas where they must have felt like they were happily gliding on ice: networking and the Internet. For the most part, the Internet already runs on Unix, and hundreds of extremely polished tools and software chunks were already available.

There are all kinds of ways to get your Mac onto the Internet these days:

- **WiFi.** Wireless hotspots, known as WiFi (or, as Apple used to call it, AirPort), are glorious conveniences, especially if you have a laptop. Without stirring from your hotel bed, you're online at high speed. Sometimes for free.

- **Cable modems, DSL.** Over half of the U.S. Internet population connects over higher-speed wires, using *broadband* connections that are always on: cable modems, DSL, or corporate networks. (These, of course, are often what's at the other end of an Internet hotspot.)

- **Cellular modems.** A few well-heeled individuals enjoy the go-anywhere bliss of *USB cellular modems,* which get them online just about anywhere they can make a phone call. These modems are offered by Verizon, Sprint, AT&T, and so on, and usually cost $60 a month.

Note: A MiFi is sort of a cellular modem, too. It's a pocketable, battery-operated, portable hotspot. It converts the cellular signal into a WiFi signal, so up to five people can be online at once, while the MiFi itself sits happily in your pocket or laptop bag.

- **Tethering.** *Tethering* is letting your cellphone act as a glorified Internet antenna for your Mac, whether connected by a cable or a Bluetooth wireless link. You pay your phone company extra for this convenience.

- **Dial-up modems.** Their numbers are shrinking, but plenty of people still connect to the Internet using a modem that dials out over ordinary phone lines. The service is cheap, but the connection is slow.

This chapter explains how to set up each one of these. It also describes some of OS X's offbeat Internet featurettes. It tackles Internet Sharing, which lets several computers in the same household share a single broadband connection; the system-wide Internet bookmarks known as *Internet location files*; and iCloud, Apple's suite of free online syncing tools.

The Best News You've Heard All Day

If you upgraded to Mountain Lion from an earlier version of the Mac OS, breathe easy: You're already online, since the installer picked up your networking and Internet settings from that earlier installation. The moment you see the OS X desktop, you're ready to use the Internet (and skip the next 10 pages).

Read on, however, if you need to plug in the Internet settings manually. If you're setting up a new Mac, or if you simply want to create a new Internet account, you definitely have some typing to look forward to.

Tip: If you haven't yet set up an Internet connection, reading the next few pages will guide you through plugging the proper settings into System Preferences.

If you're more of a doer than a reader, however, you may prefer the "Assist me" button at the bottom of the Network pane of System Preferences. It asks how you want to connect to the Internet (by dial-up modem, DSL, cable modem, and so on) and then walks you through the process of typing in the settings, if necessary.

Network Central and Multihoming

In this chapter, you'll be spending a lot of time in the Network pane of System Preferences (Figure 17-1). (Choose →System Preferences; click Network.) This list summarizes the ways your Mac can connect to the Internet or an office network—Ethernet, WiFi, Bluetooth, cellular modem card, VPN (Chapter 21), and so on.

Multihoming

The *order* of the network connections listed in the Network pane is important. That's the sequence the Mac uses as it tries to get online. If one of your programs needs Internet access and the first method isn't hooked up, then the Mac switches to the next available connection automatically.

In fact, OS X can maintain multiple simultaneous network connections—Ethernet, WiFi, dial-up, even FireWire—with a feature known as *multihoming*.

This feature is especially relevant for laptops. When you open your Web browser, your laptop might first check to see if it's plugged into an Ethernet cable, which is the fastest, most secure type of connection. If there's no Ethernet, then it looks for a WiFi network.

Figure 17-1:
You set up all your network connections here, and you can connect to and disconnect from all your networks here. The listed network connections are tagged with color-coded dots. A green dot means turned on and connected to a network; yellow means the connection is working but some other setting is wrong (for example, your Mac can't get an IP address); red means there's no connection, or you haven't yet set up a connection.

Here's how to go about setting up the connection-attempt sequence you want:

1. **Open System Preferences. Click the Network icon.**

 The Network Status screen (Figure 17-1) brings home the point of multihoming: You can have more than one network connection operating at once.

2. **From the ✿ pop-up menu, choose Set Service Order.**

POWER USERS' CLINIC

PPPoE and DSL

If you have DSL service, you may be directed to create a *PPPoE service.* (You do that on the Network pane of System Preferences; click the **+** button, choose PPPoE, select the connection you're using to PPPoE, and then click Create.)

It stands for PPP over Ethernet, meaning that although your DSL "modem" is connected to your Ethernet port, you still have to make and break your Internet connections manually, as though you had a dial-up modem.

Fill in the PPPoE dialog box as directed by your ISP (usually just your account name and password). From here on in, you start and end your Internet connections exactly as though you had a dial-up modem.

Now you see the display shown in Figure 17-2. It lists all the ways your Mac knows how to get online, or onto an office network.

3. **Drag the items up and down the list into priority order.**

 If you have a wired broadband connection, for example, you might want to drag Built-in Ethernet to the top of the list, since that's almost always the fastest way to get online.

Figure 17-2:
The key to multihoming is sliding the network connection methods' names up or down. Note that you can choose a different connection sequence for each location. (Locations are described later in this chapter.)

4. **Click OK.**

 You return to the Network pane of System Preferences, where the master list of connections magically re-sorts itself to match your efforts.

Your Mac will now be able to switch connections even in real time, during a single Internet session. If lightning takes out your Ethernet hub in the middle of your Web surfing, your Mac will seamlessly switch to your WiFi network, for example, to keep your session alive.

All right, then: Your paperwork is complete. The following pages guide you through the process of setting up these various connections.

Broadband Connections

If your Mac is connected wirelessly or, um, *wirefully* to a cable modem, DSL, or office network, you're one of the lucky ones. You have a high-speed broadband connection to the Internet that's always available, always on. You never have to wait to dial.

Automatic Configuration

Most broadband connections require *no setup whatsoever.* Take a new Mac out of the box, plug in the Ethernet cable to your cable modem—or choose a wireless network from the menulet—and you can begin surfing the Web instantly.

That's because most cable modems, DSL boxes, and wireless base stations use *DHCP.* It stands for *dynamic host configuration protocol,* but what it means is: "We'll fill in your Network pane of System Preferences automatically." (Including techie specs like IP address and DNS Server addresses.)

Manual Configuration

If, for some reason, you're not able to surf the Web or check email the first time you try, it's remotely possible that your broadband modem or your office network *doesn't* offer DHCP. In that case, you may have to fiddle with the Network pane of System Preferences, preferably with a customer-support rep from your broadband company on the phone.

On the Network pane, click your Internet connection (Wi-Fi, Built-in Ethernet, cellular modem, whatever). Click Advanced; click TCP/IP. Now you see something like Figure 17-3. Don't be alarmed by the morass of numbers and periods—it's all in good fun. (If you find TCP/IP fun, that is.)

Note: There's a bright side to having a *static IP address,* an Internet address that's all your own and won't change: Because your Mac has this one reliable address, several cool OS X features are available to you. For example, it's easier to access your files from anywhere in the world, as described in Chapter 21.

Figure 17-3:
Here's the setup for a cable-modem account with a static IP address, which means you have to type in all these numbers yourself.

Ethernet Connections

The beauty of Ethernet connections is that they're super-fast and super-secure. No bad guys sitting across the coffee shop, armed with shareware "sniffing" software, can intercept your email and chat messages, as they theoretically can when you're on wireless.

And 99 percent of the time, connecting to an Ethernet network is as simple as connecting the cable to the Mac. That's it. You're online, quickly and securely, and you never have to worry about connecting or disconnecting.

WiFi Connections

Your Mac can communicate with a wireless base station up to 300 feet away, much like a cordless phone. Doing so lets you surf the Web from your laptop in a hotel room, for example, or share files with someone across the building from you.

Chapter 14 has much more information about *setting up* a WiFi network. The real fun begins, however, when it comes time to *join* one.

Sometimes you just want to join a friend's WiFi network. Sometimes you've got time to kill in an airport, and it's worth a $7 splurge for half an hour. And sometimes, at some street corners in big cities, WiFi signals bleeding out of apartment buildings might give you a choice of several free hotspots to join.

POWER USERS' CLINIC

The Super-Secret Hotspot Management Box

If you open System Preferences→Network, click Wi-Fi in the left-side list, and then click Advanced, you see the dialog box shown here. It lets you manage the list of WiFi hotspots that OS X has memorized on your travels.

For example, you can delete the old ones. Or you can drag the hotspots' names up and down the list to establish a priority for making connections when more than one is available.

Ordinarily, OS X memorizes the names of the various hotspots you join on your travels. It's kind of nice, actually, because

it means you're interrupted less often by the "Do you want to join?" box.

But if you're alarmed at the massive list of hotspots OS X has memorized—for privacy reasons, say—here's where you turn off "Remember networks this computer has joined."

Finally, for added security on your Mac, you can turn on checkboxes that prevent the unauthorized from making changes (creating computer-to-computer networks, changing networks, turning WiFi on or off) without an administrator's password.

Your Mac joins WiFi hotspots like this:

- First, it sniffs around for a WiFi network you've used before. If it finds one, it connects quietly and automatically. You're not asked for permission, a password, or anything else; you're just online. (It's that way, for example, when you come home with your laptop every day.) For details on this memorization feature, see the box on the facing page.

- If the Mac can't find a known hotspot, but it detects a new hotspot or two, a message appears on the screen, displaying their names. Double-click one to connect.

Tip: If you don't *want* your Mac to keep interrupting you with its discoveries of new hotspots—it can get pretty annoying when you're in a taxi driving through a city—you can shut them off. In System Preferences, click Network, click Wi-Fi, and then turn off "Ask to join new networks."

- If you're in the presence of a commercial hotspot—one that requires payment or reading some kind of insipid legal agreement—OS X opens a miniature Web page, shoving it right into your face, even if your Web browser isn't open; see Figure 17-4.

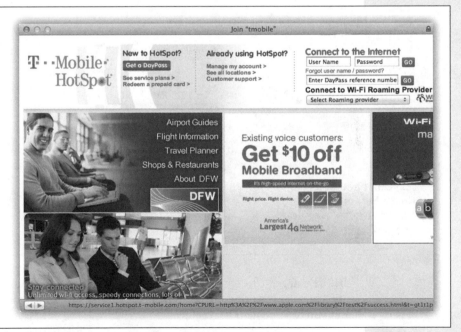

Figure 17-4:
OS X auto-opens a page like this whenever it senses that you're in a commercial WiFi network, one that requires you to sign in. (That's a big improvement from the old way, where you'd join a network and then have no clue that you wouldn't be able to get any further until you opened up your Web browser to find that login screen.)

- If you missed the opportunity to join a hotspot when the message appeared, or if you joined the wrong one or a non-working one, then you have another chance. You can always choose a hotspot's name from the 🛜 menulet, as shown in Figure 17-5. A 🔒 icon indicates a hotspot that requires a password, so you don't waste your time trying to join it (unless, of course, you *have* the password).

Tip: It always takes a computer a few seconds—maybe 5 or 10—to connect to the Internet over WiFi. In OS X, the 📶 menulet itself *pulses,* or rather ripples, with a black-and-gray animation to let you know you're still in the connection process. It's an anti-frustration aid. (Oh, and also, each hotspot's signal strength appears right in the menulet.)

Figure 17-5:
Top: Congratulations—your Mac has discovered new WiFi hotspots all around you! You even get to see the signal strength right in the menu. Double-click one to join it. But if you see a 🔒 icon next to the hotspot's name, beware: It's been protected by a password. If you don't know it, then you won't be able to connect.

Bottom: Later, you can always switch networks using the WiFi menulet.

Before you get too excited, though, some lowering of expectations is in order. There are a bunch of reasons why your 📶 menulet might indicate that you're in a hotspot, but you can't actually get online:

- **It's locked.** If there's a 🔒 next to the hotspot's name in your 📶 menulet, then the hotspot has been password protected. That's partly to prevent hackers from "sniffing" the transmissions and intercepting messages, and partly to keep random passersby like you off the network.

- **The signal isn't strong enough.** Sometimes the WiFi signal is strong enough to make the hotspot's name show up in your 📶 menu but not strong enough for an actual connection.

- **You're not on the list.** Sometimes, for security, hotspots are rigged to permit only *specific* computers to join (see the box below), and yours isn't one of them.

- **You haven't logged in yet.** Commercial hotspots (the ones you have to pay for) don't connect you to the Internet until you've supplied your payment details on a special Web page that appears automatically when you open your browser, as described below.

- **The router's on, but the Internet's not connected.** Sometimes wireless routers are broadcasting, but their Internet connection is down. It'd be like a cordless phone that has a good connection back to the base station in the kitchen—but the phone cord isn't plugged into the base station.

Commercial Hotspots

Choosing the name of the hotspot you want to join is generally all you have to do—if it's a *home* WiFi network.

Unfortunately, joining a *commercial* WiFi hotspot—one that requires a credit card number (in a hotel room or an airport, for example)—requires more than just connecting to it. You also have to *sign into* it before you can send so much as a single email message.

POWER USERS' CLINIC

The Secret WiFi Menulet—and a Word About MAC Addresses

Here's something not one Mac fan in a thousand knows about: a secret diagnostic mode in the 📶 menulet.

Turns out that if you press the Option key as you open the 📶 menulet, you get a special treat: a faint gray *interior* menu that identifies some diagnostic details of your current wireless network. You get to see the hotspot's channel, your current data rate, and the BSSID (address of the base station you're using).

In Mountain Lion, this secret menu also offers direct access to a hidden app called WiFi Diagnostics. It's for troubleshooting; it can capture network traffic, create a diagnostic report, or log all events for debugging purposes.

```
📶 ◀) 🔋 (2:30)  Fri Sep 25  3:32 PM
Wi-Fi: On
Turn Wi-Fi Off

✓PNet                              📶
   PHY Mode: 802.11g
   BSSID: 0:3:93:ea:d2:25
   Channel: 10 (2.4 GHz)
   Security: None
   RSSI: –56
   Transmit Rate: 54

Join Other Network...
Create Network...
Open Network Preferences...
```

By the way: This WiFi network isn't password-protected (there's no 🔒 next to its name), and yet it won't get you online. Why not? Because some hotspots are so restrictive that the network administrator has to register *each MAC address* that's allowed to use it.

A MAC address has nothing to do with Macintosh computers. It stands for Media Access Control, although the equivalent term, Ethernet Hardware Address, is much more descriptive. It's a unique identifier for your networking card, whether it's your Ethernet card or your WiFi circuitry.

MAC-address filtering is another, even more exclusive, way to keep the unwashed masses from using a hotspot.

To do that, open your Web browser—if, in fact, OS X doesn't auto-open the sign-up screen (page 643). You'll see the "Enter your payment information" screen either immediately or as soon as you try to open a Web page of your choice. (Even at free hotspots, you might have to click OK on a welcome page to initiate the connection.)

Supply your credit card information or (if you have a membership to this WiFi chain, like Boingo or T-Mobile) your name and password. Click Submit or Proceed, try *not* to contemplate how this $8 per hour is pure profit for somebody, and enjoy your surfing.

Cellular Modems

WiFi hotspots are fast and usually cheap—but they're *spots.* Beyond 150 feet away, you're offline.

No wonder laptop luggers across America are getting into *cellular* Internet services. All the big cellphone companies offer USB sticks that let your laptop get online at high speed *anywhere* in major cities. No hunting for a coffee shop; with a cellular Internet

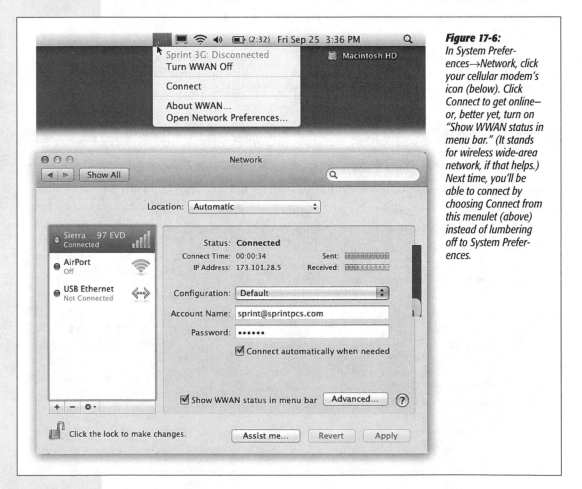

Figure 17-6:
In System Prefer-ences→Network, click your cellular modem's icon (below). Click Connect to get online–or, better yet, turn on "Show WWAN status in menu bar." (It stands for wireless wide-area network, if that helps.) Next time, you'll be able to connect by choosing Connect from this menulet (above) instead of lumbering off to System Prefer-ences.

service, you can check your email while zooming down the road in a taxi. (Outside the metropolitan areas, you can still get online wirelessly, though much more slowly.)

Verizon, Sprint, and AT&T all offer cellular Internet networks with speeds approaching a cable modem's. So why isn't the world beating a path to this delicious technology's door? Because it's expensive—$60 a month on top of your phone bill.

To get online, insert the USB stick; it may take about 15 seconds for the thing to latch onto the cellular signal.

Now you're supposed to make the Internet connection using the special "dialing" software provided by the cellphone company. Technically, though, you may not need it. You can start and stop the Internet connection using the menulet—no phone-company software required (see Figure 17-6).

Tethering

If you have an iPhone, Android phone, or another app phone, you don't even need a cellular modem; you've already got one. Most app phones nowadays offer *tethering*, where the cellphone tunes into the Internet for the benefit of your laptop (or even your desktop computer). The phone connects to your laptop either with a USB cable or wirelessly (Bluetooth or WiFi).

The nice part is that you can get online almost anywhere there's cellphone coverage. The less-nice part is that the connection isn't always blazing fast, and you have to pay your cellphone company for the privilege. (It's usually $20 or $30 on top of your regular monthly phone plan; for that, you're allowed to send and receive 2 gigabytes of data each month. If you go over the limit, you pay overage fees. Good luck figuring that out.)

Here's a typical example: Suppose you have an iPhone. You open Settings→General→Network→Personal Hotspot. You turn it on. You assign a password to your private little hotspot. The iPhone asks how you'll be connecting to the phone; let's say you tap Wi-Fi.

Now, on your laptop, you choose your iPhone's name from the 🛜 menulet. You enter your hotspot password (just this time—later, your laptop will remember), and presto: Your laptop is online. A bright blue "Personal Hotspot: 1 Connection" banner appears on your iPhone to remind you, and your 🛜 menulet changes to become the International Symbol for Apple Tethering: ➰.

Now, tethering eats up your phone's battery like crazy; you'll be lucky to get 3 hours out of it. So you probably shouldn't count on watching Netflix on your laptop via your phone.

But for email, emergency Web checks, and other mobile crises, tethering is a convenient, useful feature. And when you're on the road for a couple of weeks, it's a heck of a lot cheaper than paying your hotel $13 a night for WiFi.

Dial-Up Modem Connections

If you ask Apple, dial-up modems are dead. Macs don't even come with built-in modems anymore. You can get a non-Apple USB modem for $50, but clearly, Apple is trying to shove the trusty dial-up technology into the recycling bin.

Still, millions of people never got the memo. If you're among them, then you need to sign up for Internet service. Once you've selected a service provider, you plug its settings into the Network pane of System Preferences. You get the necessary information directly from your ISP by consulting either its Web page, the instruction sheets that came with your account, or a help-desk agent on the phone.

Further details on OS X's dial-up modem setup are in the free appendix to this chapter, "Setting Up a Dial-Up Connection." It's available on this book's "Missing CD" page at *www.missingmanuals.com*.

Switching Locations

If you travel with a laptop, you know the drill. You're constantly opening up System Preferences→Network so you can switch between Internet settings: Ethernet at the office, WiFi at home. Or maybe you simply visit the branch office from time to time,

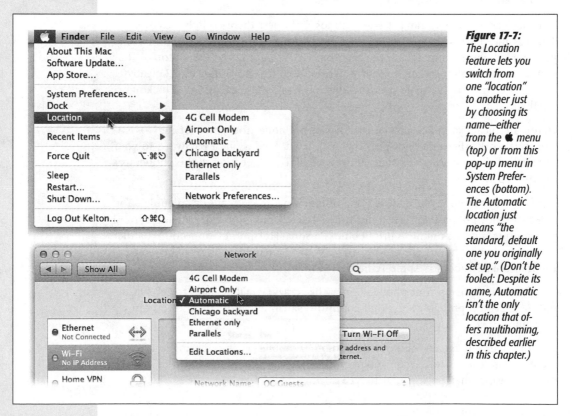

Figure 17-7:
The Location feature lets you switch from one "location" to another just by choosing its name—either from the menu (top) or from this pop-up menu in System Preferences (bottom). The Automatic location just means "the standard, default one you originally set up." (Don't be fooled: Despite its name, Automatic isn't the only location that offers multihoming, described earlier in this chapter.)

and you're getting tired of having to change the local access number for your ISP each time you leave home (and return home again).

The simple solution is the →Location submenu, which appears once you've set up more than one Location. As Figure 17-7 illustrates, all you have to do is tell it where you are. OS X handles the details of switching Internet connections.

Creating a New Location

To create a *Location,* which is nothing more than a set of memorized settings, open System Preferences, click Network, and then choose Edit Locations from the Location pop-up menu. Continue as shown in Figure 17-8.

Tip: You can use the commands in the ⚙ menu to rename or duplicate a Location.

Figure 17-8:
When you choose Edit Locations, this list of existing Locations appears; click the + button. A new entry appears at the bottom of the list. Type a name for your new location, such as Chicago Office or Dining Room Floor.

When you click Done, you return to the Network panel. Take this opportunity to set up the kind of Internet connection you use at the corresponding location, just as described on the first pages of this chapter.

If you travel regularly, you can build a *list* of Locations, each of which "knows" the way you like to get online in each city you visit.

A key part of making a new Location is putting the various Internet connection types (Ethernet, Wi-Fi, Modem, Bluetooth) into the correct order. Your connections will be slightly quicker if you give the modem connection priority in your Hotel setup, the WiFi connection priority in your Starbucks setup, and so on.

You can even turn off some connections entirely. For example, if you use nothing but a cable modem when you're at home, you might want to create a location in which *only* the Ethernet connection is active. Use the Make Service Inactive command in the ⚙ menu.

Conversely, if your laptop uses nothing but WiFi when you're on the road, your Location could include *nothing* but the Wi-Fi connection. You'll save a few seconds each

time you try to go online, because your Mac won't bother hunting for an Internet connection that doesn't exist.

Making the Switch

Once you've set up your various Locations, you can switch among them using the ⌘→Location submenu, as shown in Figure 17-7. As soon as you do so, your Mac is automatically set to get online the way you like.

Tip: If you have a laptop, create a connection called Offline. From the Show pop-up menu, choose Network Port Configurations; make *all* the connection methods in the list inactive. When you're finished, you've got yourself a laptop that will *never* attempt to go online. It's the laptop equivalent of Airplane Mode on a cellphone.

Internet Sharing

If you have cable modem or DSL service, you're a very lucky individual. You get terrific Internet speed and an always-on connection. Too bad only one computer in your household or office can enjoy these luxuries.

It doesn't have to be that way. You can spread the joy of high-speed Internet to every Mac (and PC) on your network in either of two ways:

- **Buy a router.** A *router* is a little box, costing about $50, that connects directly to the cable modem or DSL box. In most cases, it has multiple Internet jacks so you can plug in several Macs, PCs, and/or wireless base stations. As a bonus, a router provides excellent security, serving as a firewall to keep out unsolicited visits from hackers on the Internet.

- **Use Internet Sharing.** OS X's Internet Sharing feature is the software version of a router: It distributes a single Internet signal to every computer on the network. But unlike a router, it's free. You just fire it up on the one Mac that's connected directly to the Internet—the *gateway* computer.

 But there's a downside: If the gateway Mac is turned off or asleep, then the other machines can't get online.

Most people use Internet Sharing to share a broadband connection like a cable modem or DSL. But there are other times when it comes in handy. If you have a cellular modem, for example, you might want to share its signal via WiFi so the kids in the backseat can get online with their iPod Touches. You could even share a tethered Bluetooth cellphone's Internet connection with a traveling companion who needs a quick email check.

The only requirement: The Internet-connected Mac must have some *other* kind of connection (Ethernet, WiFi, Bluetooth, FireWire) to the Macs that will share the connection.

Turning On Internet Sharing

To turn on Internet Sharing on the gateway Mac, open the Sharing panel of System Preferences. Click Internet Sharing, as shown in Figure 17-9, but don't turn on the checkbox yet.

Figure 17-9:
Ka-ching! You and your buddy just saved money. In this example, an iPhone is getting this Mac online. But it's sharing that Internet connection with other Macs via WiFi. They can get online, too, even though they're not directly connected to the iPhone.

Before you do that, you have to specify (a) how the gateway Mac is connected to the Internet, and (b) how it's connected to the other Macs on your network:

- **Share your connection from.** Using this pop-up menu, identify how *this Mac* (the gateway machine) connects to the Internet—via Built-in Ethernet, Wi-Fi, cellular modem, or Bluetooth DUN (dial-up networking—that is, tethering to your cellphone).

- **To computers using.** Using these checkboxes, specify how you want your Mac to rebroadcast the Internet signal to the others. (It has to be a *different* network channel. You can't get your signal via WiFi and then pass it on via WiFi.)

Note: Which checkboxes appear here depends on which kinds of Internet connections are turned on in the Network pane of System Preferences. If the gateway Mac doesn't have WiFi circuitry, for example, or if WiFi is turned off in the current configuration, then the Wi-Fi option doesn't appear.

Now visit each of the other Macs on the same network. Open the Network pane of System Preferences. Select the network method you chose in the second step above: Wi-Fi, Built-in Ethernet, or FireWire. Click Apply.

If the gateway Mac is rebroadcasting using WiFi—by far the most common use of this feature—you have one more step. In your 📶 menulet, you'll see a strange new "hotspot" that wasn't there before, bearing the name of the gateway Mac. (It might say, for example, "Casey's MacBook Air.") Choose its name to begin your borrowed Internet connection.

As long as the gateway Mac remains on and online, both it and your other computers can get onto the Internet simultaneously, all at high speed, even Windows PCs. You've created a *software* base station. The Mac itself is now the transmitter for Internet signals to and from any other WiFi computers within range.

Tip: Now that you know how to let a wireless Mac piggyback on a wired Mac's connection, you can let a wired Mac share a *wireless* connection, too. Suppose, for example, that you and a buddy both have laptops in a hotel lobby. You're online, having paid $13 to use the hotel's WiFi network. If you set up Internet Sharing appropriately, your buddy can connect to your Mac via an Ethernet cable or even a FireWire cable and surf along with you—no extra charge.

Internet Sharing as a Bridge

Ordinarily, only one Mac has Internet Sharing turned on: the one that's connected directly to the Internet.

But sometimes, you might want another Mac "downstream" to have it on, too. That's when you want to *bridge* two networks.

Consider the setup shown here. There are really two networks: one that uses WiFi, and another connected to an Ethernet hub.

If you play your cards right, all these Macs can get online simultaneously, using a single Internet connection.

Set up the gateway Mac so that it's a WiFi base station, exactly

Gateway Mac:
Internet Sharing ON

To cable modem, DSL, or Bluetooth phone

Hub

Bridge Mac (with AirPort):
Internet Sharing ON

AirPort Macs

as described on these pages.

Start setting up the *bridge* Mac the way you'd set up the other WiFi Macs—with Wi-Fi selected as the primary connection method, and Using DHCP turned on in the Network panel.

Then visit the bridge Mac's Sharing panel. Turn on Internet Sharing here, too, but this time select "To computers using: Built-in Ethernet."

The bridge Mac is now on both networks. It uses the WiFi connection as a bridge to the gateway Mac and the Internet—and its Ethernet connection to share that happiness with the wired Macs in its own neighborhood.

iCloud

Apple's iCloud service may have opened for business in October 2011, but it's had a long and eventful history.

It began life in January 2000, when Apple CEO Steve Jobs explained to the Macworld Expo crowds that he and his team had had a mighty brainstorm: Apple controls *both ends* of the connection between a Mac and the Apple Web site. As a result, Apple should be able to create some pretty clever Internet-based features as a reward to loyal Mac fans. Later that same day, the Apple Web site offered a suite of *free* services called iTools.

Then the American technology bubble burst.

In 2002, those Internet services were reborn as something called .Mac, and you had to pay for them. In 2008, they were rebranded again as MobileMe, and you still had to pay for them ($100 a year).

But Apple was still clearly itchy on this subject, still not quite satisfied with its "we control both ends" product. So in the fall of 2011, the old suite of online services became free once again—and it was reborn as iCloud.

What iCloud Giveth

So what is iCloud? Mainly, it's these things:

- **A synchronizing service.** It keeps your calendar, address book, documents, reminders, notes, and photos updated and identical on all your gadgets: Mac, PC, iPhone, iPad, iPod Touch.

- **An online locker.** Anything you buy from Apple—music, TV shows, ebooks, and apps—is stored online, for easy access at any time. For example, whenever you buy a song or a TV show from the online iTunes store, it appears automatically on all your i-gadgets and computers. Your photos are stored online, too.

- **Back to My Mac.** This option to grab files from one of your other Macs across the Internet isn't new, but it survives in iCloud. See page 584.

- **Find My iPhone—and Mac.** Find My iPhone is one of iCloud's greatest features. It pinpoints the current location of your iPhone or iPad on a map. In other words, it's great for helping you find your i-gadget if it's been stolen or lost.

 You can also make your lost gadget start making a loud pinging sound for a couple of minutes by remote control—even if it was set to Vibrate mode. That's brilliantly effective when your phone has slipped under the couch cushions. In dire situations, you can even erase the phone by remote control, preventing sensitive information from falling into the wrong hands.

 This feature can find your *Mac,* too. That might seem like a silly idea; how often do you misplace your iMac? But remember that 75 percent of all computers Apple sells are laptops.

- **Automatic Backup.** iCloud can back up your iPhone, iPad, or iPod Touch—completely, automatically, and wirelessly (over WiFi, not over cellular connections). It's a quick backup, since iCloud backs up only the changed data.

If you ever want to set up a new i-gadget, or if you want to restore everything to an existing one, life is sweet. Once you're in a WiFi hotspot, all you have to do is re-enter your Apple ID and password in the setup assistant that appears when you turn the thing on. Magically, your gadget is refilled with everything that used to be on it.

Note: Well, *almost* everything. You get back everything you've bought from Apple (music, apps, books); photos and videos in your Camera Roll; settings, including the layout of your Home screen; text messages; and ringtones. Your mail and anything that came to the gadget from your computer (like music from iTunes and photos from iPhoto) have to be reloaded.

Much of this is based on the central Web site *www.icloud.com* (Figure 17-10).

Tip: You can get iCloud on your Windows PC, too, and enjoy all of its features there—including syncing to Microsoft Outlook. Just install the free iCloud control panel for Windows, which is available at *www.apple. com/icloud/setup/pc.html*.

Figure 17-10:
To switch among iCloud features, click the ☁ button that always appears in the upper-left corner of each feature's screen (like the calendar, shown at top). That summons the icons for the major iCloud Web-based features: email, address book, calendar, Find My iPhone (or Mac or iPad or iPod Touch), and iWork.

Starting Up iCloud

Whether you've upgraded from MobileMe or started fresh, your iCloud adventure begins in System Preferences; click the iCloud icon. Enter your Apple ID and password (page 412). Click Sign In.

Now the preference pane invites you to turn on two of the biggest iCloud features:

- **Use iCloud for contacts, calendars, and bookmarks.** It's hard to imagine that you'd turn off this option—it's the single most important iCloud feature—but this is the on/off switch if you're some kind of heretic.

- **Use Find My Mac.** This is the "find my lost laptop on a map" feature described on page 659. Click Next, and then confirm that you *really* want to use Find My Mac.

At last you arrive at the screen you'll see when you open the iCloud pane on System Preferences from now on (Figure 17-11).

Figure 17-11:
The headquarters of iCloud's features. You'll find a nearly identical panel on your iPhone, iPad, or iPod Touch (in Settings→iCloud).

Let your grand tour of iCloud's motley features begin.

iCloud Sync

For many people, this may be the killer app for iCloud right here: The icloud.com Web site, acting as the master control center, can keep multiple Macs, Windows PCs, and iPhones/iPads/iPod Touches synchronized. There's both a huge convenience fac-

tor—all your stuff is always on all your gadgets—and a safety/backup factor, since you have duplicates everywhere.

It works by storing the master copies of your stuff—email, notes, contacts, calendars, Web bookmarks, and documents—on the Web. (Or "in the cloud," as the product managers would say.)

Whenever your computers, or i-gadgets are online, they connect to the mother ship and update themselves. Edit an address on your iPhone, and you'll find the same change in Contacts (on your Mac) and Outlook (on your PC). Send an email reply from your PC at the office, and you'll find it in your Sent Mail folder on the Mac at home. Add a Web bookmark anywhere and find it everywhere else. Edit a spreadsheet in Numbers on your iPad, and find the same numbers updated on your Mac.

Actually, there's another place where you can work with your data: on the Web. At *www.icloud.com,* you can log in to find Web-based clones of Calendar, Contacts, Mail, and iWork.

To set up syncing, open System Preferences→iCloud. Turn on the checkboxes of the stuff you want to be synchronized all the way around:

- **Mail.** "Mail" refers to your actual email messages, plus your account settings and preferences from OS X's Mail program.

R.I.P. MobileMe

In many ways, iCloud is like MobileMe Plus. But in some ways, it's MobileMe Minus; some MobileMe features didn't survive the cut—and Apple shut MobileMe down for good on June 30, 2012. Here's what went away, along with some ideas for replacements:

iWeb. The beauty of this easy-to-use Web-site design program was that, with one click, you could publish your work on the actual Web—the MobileMe site "hosted" your pages.

The iWeb app still works, but you'll need a replacement hosting service. Or consider the free *weebly.com* service, which makes it super-simple to design and host a Web site.

The iDisk. This handy "virtual hard drive in the sky" was a great way to transfer big files between computers.

There are lots of things like the iDisk that are still around, even if they're not as well integrated into OS X. Dropbox and SugarSync, for example, let you create Finder folders that behave exactly like the iDisk. You can make them ap-

pear—and synchronize them—on any computer, or on the iPhone or iPad.

Photo Gallery. Apple's online galleries were a beautiful, uncluttered, and ad-free way to present your digital slide-shows to your adoring fans. And now they're gone (the galleries, not the fans).

There are lots of things like Photo Gallery, too, including SmugMug.com and Flickr.com. Some of them offer direct album publishing from iPhoto, just as the Photo Gallery used to. And, of course, there's Facebook.

Documents and data sync. iCloud still keeps the important stuff synchronized among your various gadgets—calendar, address book, email, and bookmarks, for example. But some of the things MobileMe could also sync no longer sync in iCloud: Dashboard widgets, Dock items, Keychains, and all the trappings of your email accounts, like settings, signatures, rules, and preferences.

- **Contacts.** This is a big one. There's nothing as exasperating as realizing that the address book you're consulting on your home Mac is missing somebody you're *sure* you entered—on your computer at work. This option keeps all your Macs' contacts synchronized. Delete a phone number at work, and you'll find it deleted on your Mac at home, too.

- **Calendars & Reminders.** Enter an appointment on your iPhone, and you'll find the calendar updated everywhere else, like in the Mac's Calendar program. Or make a reminder for yourself on the Mac—using Mountain Lion's new Reminders app—and have it remind you later on your phone. (No word from Apple on why these two different programs share a single on/off switch.)

- **Notes.** These are the notes you enter in the new Notes program (Chapter 10).

- **Safari.** If a Web site is important enough to merit bookmarking while you're using your laptop, why shouldn't it also show up in the Bookmarks menu on your desktop Mac at home, in your iPhone, or on your PC at work? This option syncs your Safari Reading List, too, and also iCloud Tabs (whatever tabs and windows were most recently open on your other Apple gadgets and Macs).

- **Photo Stream.** See the next page.

- **Documents and Data.** Numbers, Pages, and Keynote are available for Mac, iPhone/iPod Touch, and iPad. Therefore, you can store their documents online, where they're accessible from any of your Apple machines. Details are on page 225.

- **Back to My Mac.** See page 584 for details.

- **Find My Mac.** Read on.

To set up syncing, turn on the checkboxes for the items you want synced.

Note: *You may notice that there are no checkboxes here for syncing stuff you buy from Apple, like books, movies, apps, and music. They're not so much* synced *as they are* stored *for you online. You can download them at any time to any of your machines.*

The Price of Free

A free iCloud account gives you 5 gigabytes of online storage. That may not sound like much, especially when you consider how big some music files, photo files, and video files are.

Fortunately, nothing you buy from Apple—including music, apps, books, and TV shows—counts against that 5-gigabyte amount. Neither do the photos in your Photo Stream.

So what's left? Just email, settings, documents, and pictures you take with your iPhone, iPad, or iPod Touch—all stuff that doesn't take up much space.

You can, of course, expand your storage if you find 5 gigs constricting—for $2 a gigabyte a year. So you'll pay $20, $40, or $100 a year for an extra 10, 20, or 50 gigs. You can upgrade your storage right from your i-gadget or computer.

After the first sync with the first machine, you can turn on the checkboxes on the other computers and gadgets, too, in effect telling them to participate in the great data-sharing experiment.

Photo Stream

Every time a new photo enters your life—when you take a picture with an i-gadget, for example, or import one onto your computer—it gets added to your Photo Stream. In other words, it appears automatically on all your *other* iCloud machines. Here's where to find them:

- **iPhone, iPad, iPod Touch.** Open your Photos app. There it is: a new listing called Photo Stream. It shows the most recent 1,000 photos you've taken with any of your *other* i-gadgets, or that you've imported to your computer from a scanner or digital camera.

 Now, Apple realizes that your i-gadget doesn't have nearly as much storage available as your Mac or PC; you can't yet buy an iPad with 750 gigabytes of storage. That's why, on your iPhone/iPad/iPod, your Photo Stream consists of just the last 1,000 photos. (There's another limitation, too: The iCloud servers store your photos for

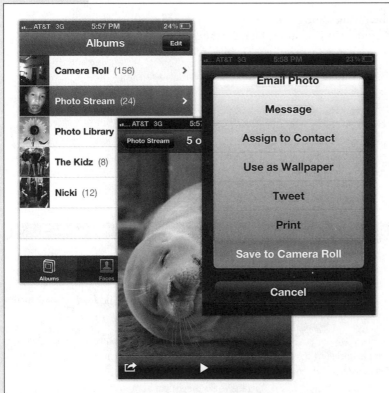

Figure 17-12:
Left: Why, look! It's photos you imported onto your Mac at home. How'd they get here on the iPhone? iCloud!

Middle: To rescue one of these photos from the 1,000-photo rule, open it. Then tap the ⤴ *button.*

Right: Finally, tap Save to Camera Roll. Now, even after that photo disappears from the Photo Stream, having been displaced by the 1,001st incoming photo, you'll still have your permanent copy.

30 days. As long as your gadgets go online at least once a month, they'll remain current with the photo stream.)

Once a photo arrives, you can save it to your Camera Roll, where it's permanently saved. See Figure 17-12.

Note: Photo Stream is the one iCloud feature that doesn't sync over the cellular airwaves. It sends photos around only when you're in a WiFi hotspot or connected to a wired network.

- **On the Mac or PC.** In iPhoto (Mac), your Photo Stream photos appear in a new album called, of course, Photo Stream. On a Windows PC, you get a Photo Stream folder in your Pictures folder.

 You don't have to worry about that 30-day, 1,000-photo business. Once pictures appear here, they're here until you delete them.

 This, in its way, is one of the best features in all of iCloudland, because it means you don't have to sync your iPhone over a USB cable to get your photos onto your computer. It all happens automatically, wirelessly over WiFi.

- **Apple TV.** When you're viewing your photos on an Apple TV, a new album appears there called Photo Stream. There they are, ready for showing on the big plasma.

If you bought your gadget/photo software/Apple TV before iCloud's debut, of course, you'll need a software update to add the Photo Stream feature.

Find My Mac, Find My iPhone

Did you leave your iPhone somewhere? Did your laptop get stolen? Has that mischievous 5-year-old hidden your iPad again?

Now you can check into iCloud.com to see exactly where your Mac, iPhone, or iPad is. You can even make it beep loudly for 2 minutes, so you can figure out which couch cushion it's under, or which jacket pocket you left it in. If the missing item is an iPad or an iPhone, you can make it beep even if the ringer switch is off, and even if the phone is asleep. You can also make a message pop up on the screen; if you actually left the thing in a taxi or on some restaurant table, you can use this feature to plead for its return. The bottom line: If you ever lose your Apple gear, you have a fighting chance at getting it back.

(That's *if* it's online, and *if* you turned on Find My Mac in the iCloud panel of System Preferences.)

If an ethical person finds your phone, you might get it back. If it's a greedy person who says, "Hey, cool! A free iPhone!" then maybe you can bombard him with so many of these messages that he gives it back in exasperation.

If not, you can either lock the gadget with a password (yes, by remote control) or even avail yourself of one more amazing last-ditch feature: Remote Wipe.

That means *erasing your data by remote control,* from wherever you happen to be. The evil thief can do nothing but stare in amazement as the phone, tablet, or Mac suddenly erases itself, winding up completely empty.

(If you ever get the phone back, you can just sync with iTunes, and presto! Your stuff is back on the phone—at least everything from your last sync.)

To set up your Mac so you can find it remotely, open System Preferences→iCloud. Make sure Find My Mac is turned on. That's all there is to it.

Later, if the worst should come to pass and you can't find your Mac, go to any computer and call up *www.icloud.com.* Log in with your Apple name and password.

Click the ☁ icon at upper left; in the list of iCloud features, click Find My iPhone. If you're asked for your password again, type it; Apple wants to make sure it's really, *really* you who's messing around with your account settings.

Finally, in the panel on the left side, click the name of your Mac.

Immediately, the Web site updates to show you, on a map, the current location of your Macs (and iPhones, iPod Touches, and iPads); see Figure 17-13.

Figure 17-13.
The location process can take a couple of minutes. You can zoom into or out of the map, click Satellite to see an overhead photo of the area, or click Hybrid to see the photo with street names superimposed.

Note: If they're not online, or if they're turned all the way off, you won't see their current locations. If your Mac is asleep, you won't find it, although if your i-gadget is asleep, you will.

If just knowing where the thing *is* isn't enough to satisfy you, click the little pushpin that represents your phone, and try one of these three buttons:

- **Display Message or Play Sound.** Click this button, type a message, and then click Send. Instantly, that message appears on the Mac's screen, wherever it is, no matter what app was running. Whoever's using it can't miss it, can't even do anything without dismissing the message.

 When it's all over, Apple sends an email confirmation to your @me.com address.

- **Lock.** What if you worry about the security of your Mac's info, but you don't want to erase it completely and just want to throw a low-level veil of casual protection over the thing? Easy: Lock it by remote control. The Lock button lets you make up a four-digit passcode (which overrides the one you already had on the phone, if any). Without it, the sleazy crook can't get into your phone without erasing it.

- **Remote Wipe.** This is the last-ditch security option, for when your immediate concern isn't so much the phone as all the private stuff that's on it. Click this button, confirm the dire warning box, and click Erase All Data. By remote control, you've just erased everything from your Mac, wherever it may be. (If it's ever returned, you can restore it from your Time Machine backup.)

 Once you've wiped the Mac, you can no longer find it or send messages to it using Find My Mac.

Email

Apple offers an email address as part of each iCloud account. Of course, you already *have* an email account. So why bother? The first advantage is the simple address: *YourName@me.com.*

Second, me.com addresses are integrated into OS X's Mail program, as you'll see in the next chapter. And, finally, you can read your me.com email from any computer anywhere in the world, via the iCloud.com Web site, or on your iPhone/iPod Touch/iPad.

To make things even sweeter, your me.com mail is completely synced. Delete a message on one gadget, and you'll find it in the Deleted Mail folder on another. Send a message from your iPad, and you'll find it in the Sent Mail folder on your Mac. And so on.

Books, Music, Apps, Movies: the Locker in the Sky

Apple, as if you hadn't noticed, has become a big seller of multimedia files. It has the biggest music store in the world. It has the biggest app store, for both i-gadgets and Macs. It sells an awful lot of TV shows and movies. Its ebook store, iBooks, is no Amazon.com, but it's chugging along.

When you buy a song, movie, app, or book, you've always been allowed to copy it to all your other Apple equipment—no extra charge. But iCloud automates, or at least formalizes, that process. Once you buy something, it's added to a tidy list of items that you can download to all your *other* machines.

Here's how to grab them:

- **iPhone, iPad, iPod Touch.** Open the App Store icon (for apps), the iBooks program (for books), or the iTunes app (for songs or TV shows; tap the category you want). Tap Updates. Tap Purchased. Tap Not on This iPhone (see Figure 17-14).

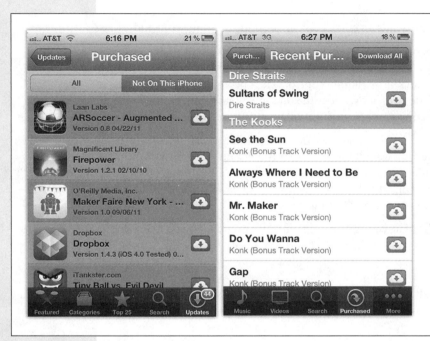

Figure 17-14:
Anything you've bought from Apple, like apps (left), music (right), TV shows, and ebooks, is always available to you, from any Mac or i-gadget, for re-downloading from the great Apple locker in the sky. Tap the cloud-with-arrow button to download something to the machine you're using now.

There they are: all the items you've bought on your *other* machines using the same Apple ID. To download anything listed here onto *this* machine, tap the cloud-with-arrow button. Or tap an album name to see the list of songs on it so you can download just *some* of those songs.

You can save yourself all that tapping by opening Settings→Store and turning the Automatic Downloads switches to On (for Music, Apps, and Books). From now on, whenever you're in WiFi, stuff you've bought on other Apple machines gets downloaded to this one *automatically*, in the background.

> **Note:** Any bookmark you set in an iBook book is synced to your other gadgets, too. The idea, of course, is that you can read a few pages on your phone in the doctor's waiting room, and then continue on your iPad from the same page on the train ride home.

- **Mac or PC.** Open the App Store program (for apps) or the iTunes app (for songs, TV shows, books, and movies). Under the Store heading, there they are: individual subheadings for each gadget you've used to buy stuff: "Purchased on iPhone," "Purchased on Mom's iPad," and so on. Or just click Purchased to view the entire list. There are all your purchases, ready to open or re-download if necessary.

Tip: To make this automatic, open iTunes. Choose iTunes→Preferences→Store. Under Automatic Downloads, turn on Music, Apps, and Books, as you see fit. Click OK.

Internet Location Files

An Internet location file is like a system-wide bookmark: When you double-click one, your Web browser opens to that page, or your email program generates an outgoing message to a predetermined addressee. You could put a folder full of location files for favorite Web sites into the Dock. Do the same with addresses to which you frequently send email. Thereafter, you save a step every time you want to jump to a particular Web page or to send email to a particular person—just choose the appropriate name from the Dock folder's Stack. (It's fine to rename them, by the way.)

UP TO SPEED

iTunes in the Cloud

Anything you've ever bought from the iTunes music store is now available for playing on any Apple gadget you own. We get it.

A lot of people, however, have music in their collections that *didn't* come from the iTunes store. Maybe they ripped some audio CDs into their computers. Maybe they acquired some music from, ahem, a friend.

What a sad situation! You've got some of your music available with you on any computer or mobile gadget, and some that's stranded at home on your computer.

Enter iTunes Match. It's an Apple service that lets you store your *entire* collection, including songs that didn't come from Apple, online, for $25 a year.

The iTunes software analyzes the songs in your collection. If it finds a song that's also available in iTunes, then—*bing!*—that song becomes available for your playback pleasure, without your actually having to transfer your copy to Apple. Apple says, in effect: "Well, our copy of the song is just as good as yours, so you're welcome to listen to our copy on any of your machines."

Truth is, in fact, Apple's copy is probably *better* than your copy. You get to play back the song at iTunes' 256-Kbps quality, no matter how grungy your own copy was.

If there's a song or two in your collection that are *not* among Apple's 20 million tracks, you can upload them to Apple.

The advantages of forking over the $25 a year are (a) you can listen to *all* your music from any computer/phone/tablet, (b) using the song-matching system saves you hours or days of uploading time, and (c) that audio-quality upgrade.

The disadvantage: You're paying $25 a year.

OS X: THE MISSING MANUAL

Mail & Contacts

E mail is a fast, cheap, convenient communication medium. In fact, these days, anyone who *doesn't* have an email address is considered some kind of freak.

If you do have an email address or two, you'll be happy to discover that OS X includes Mail, a program that lets you get and send email messages without having to wade through a lot of spam (junk mail). Mail is a surprisingly complete program, filled with shortcuts and surprises around every turn, and its Mountain Lion overhaul introduces a couple of clever and useful new features.

Setting Up Mail

Mail can't get your mail unless it knows the details of your email account. The first time you open Mail, then, it asks you for your name, email address, and email account password. If you use a common email service like Gmail, Yahoo, AOL, or Microsoft Exchange, or a common Internet provider like Verizon or Comcast, then you're in luck; Apple has rounded up the acronym-laden server settings for 30 popular mail services and taught Mail to fill them in for you.

All you have to do is type your email name and password into the box (Figure 18-1). If Mail recognizes the suffix (for example, *@gmail.com*), and if "Automatically set up account" is turned on, then Mail does the heavy lifting for you. Mail is ready to go online.

> **Note:** You can perform exactly the same account setup in the Mail, Contacts & Calendars pane in System Preferences. There's no advantage of one method or the other, except that the System Preferences pane lets you enter your account information for online calendars and address books, too.

Now, if you use a service provider that Mail doesn't recognize when you type in your email name and password—you weirdo—then you have to set up your mail account the long way. Mail prompts you along, and you confront the dialog boxes shown in Figure 18-2, where you're supposed to type in various settings to specify your email account. Some of this information may require a call to your Internet service provider (ISP).

Figure 18-1:
Mail takes the pain, agony, and acronyms out of setting up an email account on your Mac. Forget about remembering your SMTP server address (or even what SMTP stands for), and just type your email address and password into the box. If you use a mainstream mail service like Gmail, Hotmail, Yahoo, Comcast, or Verizon, then Mail configures your account settings automatically after you click the Create button.

Here's the rundown:

- **Add Account screen.** Here Mail wants to know your Full Name (it will appear in the From field of any email you send, so type it just the way you'd like it to appear); Email Address (the address you got when you signed up for Internet services, such as *billg@microsoft.com*); and Password (the name and password provided by your ISP).

- **Incoming Mail Server. This** is where you enter the information your ISP gave you about its mail servers. You specify your **Account Type** (what flavor of email account you have; check with your ISP if you're not sure which type you have); a **Description** (an affectionate nickname for your email account; for your reference only); the actual **Incoming Mail Server address** (which is usually related to the name of your ISP, such as *popmail.mindspring.com);* and the **User Name and password** provided by your ISP.

- **Incoming Mail Security.** Secure Sockets Layer? Kerberos Version 5? MD5 Challenge-Response? Only your Internet provider can tell you what to do on this screen.

- **Outgoing Mail Server.** The outgoing mail server (also called the *SMTP server*) usually looks something like *mail.mindspring.com.* Here again, the **Description** is optional, the **Outgoing Mail Server address** comes from your ISP, and the **User**

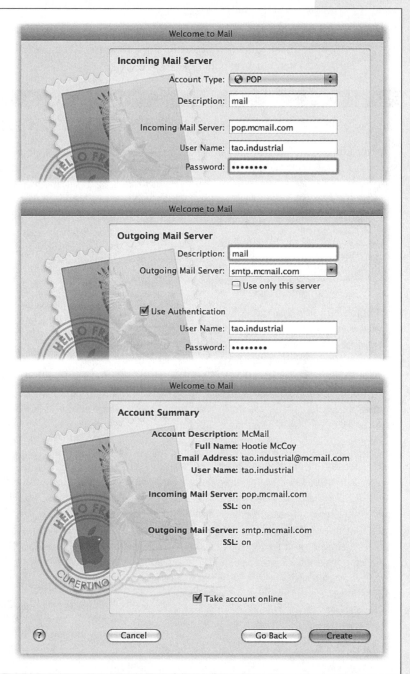

Figure 18-2:
These dialog boxes let you plug in the email settings provided by your Internet service. If you want to add another email account later, choose File→Add Account, and then enter your information in the resulting dialog box. (Or, if you like doing things the hard way, choose Mail→Preferences→Accounts tab, click the + in the lower-left corner of the window, and then enter your account information in the fields on the right.)

Authentication setting depends on your particular email provider. Your **User Name and password** are often the same for both incoming and outgoing servers.

- **Outgoing Mail Security.** Same thing here. Your ISP will have to tell you what settings to use.

When you've made it through the setup screens, turn on Take Account Online to make your new account "live." If you entered everything correctly, Mail checks for new mail right away.

POP, IMAP, Exchange, and Web-based Mail

When it comes to email, there are four primary flavors of *servers* (Internet computers that process email): *POP* (also known as POP3), *IMAP* (also known as IMAP4), *Exchange*, and *Web-based*. Each has its own distinct taste, with different strengths and weaknesses.

POP accounts (Post Office Protocol) are very common. Your Mac downloads your incoming mail from a POP server to your hard drive before you read it, which works fine as long as you're using only one computer for email.

The problem with POP, of course, is that things get complicated when you have more than one machine—a phone and a Mac, for example, or a laptop and a desktop. For example, if you usually use a desktop Mac, but you want to take your email along on the road on your laptop, you have to copy the Mail folder from your Home→Library folder into the corresponding location on your laptop's hard drive. That's the only way you'll see your messages and attachments in place when you open Mail on the laptop.

IMAP servers (Internet Message Access Protocol), a newer type, solve that problem. IMAP servers keep all your mail online, rather than making you store it on your hard drive; as a result, you can access the same mail regardless of the computer or phone you use. IMAP servers remember which messages you've read and sent, to boot. (With these accounts, you're not so much *downloading* mail as *synchronizing* your computer with what's online.) It's a great setup if, for example, you check your email on an iPhone, because the deletions and replies you process on the phone will be there on your Mac when you get home.

(You can opt for a Gmail or AOL account to be an IMAP account, too.)

Exchange servers are popular in corporations and some schools. Most of the time, employees tap into these servers using a Windows program like Outlook. Corporate geeks like Exchange servers because they're easy to set up and maintain, and because they offer many of the same features as IMAP servers. Luckily, Mail can read and send email through Exchange servers as though your Mac were just another beige PC.

Free, Web-based services like Hotmail, Yahoo, and Gmail also store your mail on the Internet, but you can use a Web browser on any computer to read and send messages. They're slower and more cumbersome to use than "regular" email accounts, but they're usually free.

Unfortunately, Mail can't check accounts that are entirely Web-based. Fortunately, the big-name Web-based email services also offer POP or IMAP servers. If you have a Gmail account, for example, you'll find that you can read your email using either a Web browser or Mail (see Gmail's help pages for details on making that work).

Conversely, more and more POP and IMAP accounts are also offering a *Web-based* component. For example, whoever provides your Internet service—EarthLink, Verizon, or Speakeasy, for instance—probably provides both POP service and a Web-based way of accessing your email, so you can access your mail either from home or from an Internet café in Bangladesh.

All Mail cares about, though, is whether your email account allows POP, IMAP, or Exchange access; what you do on the Web is, as far as Mail is concerned, your own business.

Importing Old Mail

Mail can also import your email collection from an email program you've used before—Thunderbird, Netscape/Mozilla, Eudora, or even a version of OS X Mail that's stored somewhere else (say, on an old Mac's hard drive). Importing is a big help in making a smooth transition between your old email world and your new one.

To bring over your old mail and mailboxes, choose File→Import Mailboxes. Figure 18-3 has the details.

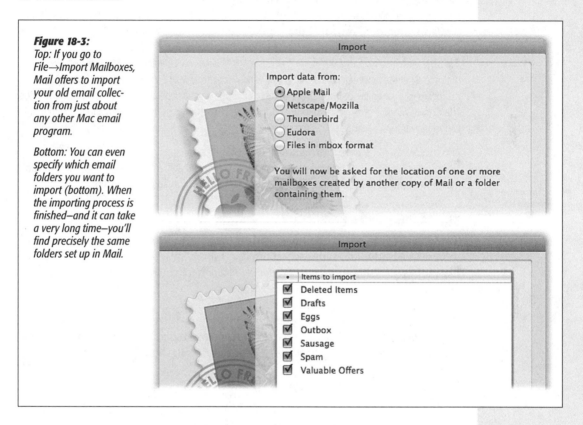

Figure 18-3:
Top: If you go to File→Import Mailboxes, Mail offers to import your old email collection from just about any other Mac email program.

Bottom: You can even specify which email folders you want to import (bottom). When the importing process is finished—and it can take a very long time—you'll find precisely the same folders set up in Mail.

Checking Your Mail

You get new mail and send mail you've already written using the Get Mail command. You can trigger it in any of several ways:

- Click the ✉ button on the toolbar.

- Choose Mailbox→Get All New Mail (or press Shift-⌘-N).

Note: If you have multiple email accounts, you can also use the Mailbox→Get New Mail submenu to pick just *one* account to check for new mail.

- **Control-click (or right-click) Mail's Dock icon, and choose Get New Mail from the shortcut menu.** (You can use this method from within any program, as long as Mail is already open.)

- **Wait.** Mail comes set to check your email automatically every few minutes. To adjust its timing or to turn this feature off, choose Mail→Preferences, click General, and then choose a time interval from the "Check for new messages" pop-up menu.

Now Mail contacts the mail servers listed in the Accounts pane of Mail's preferences, retrieving new messages and downloading any files attached to those messages. It also *sends* any outgoing messages that couldn't be sent when you wrote them.

Tip: The far-left column of the Mail window has a tiny Mail Activity monitor tucked away; click the second button (▣) at the lower-left corner of the Mail window to reveal Mail Activity. If you don't want to give up mailboxes-list real estate, or if you prefer to monitor your mail in a separate window, you can do that, too. The Activity window gives you a Stop button, progress bars, and other useful information. Summon it by choosing Window→Activity, or by pressing ⌘-0.

Also, if you're having trouble connecting to some (or all) of your email accounts, choose Window→Connection Doctor. There, you can see detailed information about accounts that aren't responding. If your computer's Internet connection is at fault, you can click Network Diagnostics to try to get back online.

The Mailboxes List

The mailboxes panel, the leftmost list on the screen, lists all your email accounts' folders (and subfolders, and sub-subfolders) for easy access. Mail looks quite a bit like iTunes (and iPhoto, and the Finder)—except here you have mailboxes where your iTunes Library and connected iPods would be.

Tip: You can also collapse or expand the various sections of the mailboxes list (On My Mac and Reminders, for example) by clicking the Hide or Show button next to each one. That button doesn't appear, however, until you *point* to the capitalized section title (like MAILBOXES or ON MY MAC).

Under the Mailboxes heading, you may find these folders:

- **Inbox** holds mail you've received. If you have more than one email account, you can expand the triangles to see separate folders for each of your accounts. You'll see this pattern repeated with the Sent, Junk, and other mailboxes, too—separate accounts have separate subheadings.

Tip: If Mail has something to tell you about your Inbox (like, for instance, that Mail can't connect to it), a tiny warning triangle (⚠) appears on the right side of the Mailboxes heading. Click it to see what Mail is griping about.

If you see a wavy ⬤ icon, that's Mail's way of announcing that you're offline. Click the icon to try to connect to the Internet.

- **VIPs** displays messages from the most important people in your life—those you've designated as VIPs (page 702). This folder doesn't appear if you haven't identified any VIPs.

Figure 18-4:
Mail can have several different layouts. In the standard three-column view (top), all your mailboxes are grouped tidily in the far-left column. You can hide that column, though, so that you have more space for reading (middle). You can also return to the pre-Lion layout (bottom), in which the messages list is above the message body.

Standard view (three columns) Standard view (folder column hidden)

Classic view

- **Flagged.** If you've flagged any messages, the flag headings appear here, too. (Flags are described later in this chapter.)

- **Outbox** holds mail you've written but haven't yet sent (because you were on an airplane when you wrote it, for example). If you have no mail waiting to be sent, then the Outbox disappears.

- **Drafts** holds messages you've started but don't want to send just yet.

- **Sent,** unsurprisingly, holds copies of messages you've sent.

- **Trash** works a lot like the Trash on your desktop, in that messages you put there don't actually disappear. They remain in the Trash folder until you permanently delete them—or until Mail's automatic trash-cleaning service deletes them for you.

- **Junk** appears when you use Mail's spam filter, as described later in this chapter.

- **Mail Activity.** You don't need to summon a separate window to see how much more of that message with the giant attachment the program still has to send. To reveal the Mail activity panel, click the tiny ◪ icon below the Mailboxes list.

Note: Some of the icons that traditionally occupied this list are no longer in Mountain Lion. Reminders and Notes aren't here, because they have their own apps now. RSS Feeds aren't here, either, because Mail no longer handles these Internet "news feeds."

Tailoring the Look of Mail

Apple put a lot of energy into exploiting the size and shape of your screen. In a program made for managing lists and reading messages, you need all the room you can get.

You've always been able to tweak Mail's look, layout, and proportions—but now you have both the Lion/Mountain Lion layout (three columns) and the Classic layout (list above, message below), which is still around for people who don't care for the new look. The following pages offer advice in modifying the design of *both* layouts.

Tweaking the three-column layout

The three-column view is shown in Figure 18-5. Here's some of the plastic surgery you can perform:

- **Try full-screen mode.** Click the ⬈ in the upper-right corner to make the Mail window expand to fill your monitor. (See page 12 for details on full-screen mode.) Full-screen mode is a natural for space-hungry email, especially on a small laptop screen.

GEM IN THE ROUGH

Favorites Bar Keyboard Shortcuts

One of the best parts of the new Favorites bar is that you have complete keyboard control over the buttons there.

The keystrokes ⌘-1 through ⌘-9 "click" the first nine buttons on the Favorites bar. Press ⌘-1, for example, to see what's in the first mailbox you've installed on the Favorites bar.

Even cooler yet, if you add the Control key, you now know the keyboard shortcuts for moving selected messages to those corresponding folders. For example, you can highlight a message and then press ⌘-Control-3, confident that you've just filed that message away in the third Favorites-bar folder.

That is, you can now file messages using only the keyboard—and when you're in the thick of things, the less time you spend using the mouse, the better.

Note: In full-screen mode, any *individual* message or note that you double-click pops front and center; the rest of the screen, including all your lists and panes and other messages, fades and becomes inactive. While that special effect certainly draws your attention to the *one* open message, it also means that you can't copy and paste from another message, refer to another message, or drag to or from another message.

If you want to do something like that, you have to exit full-screen mode first.

Figure 18-5:
Click an icon in the Mailboxes column to see its contents in the messages list. The messages list now shows you the first couple of lines of each message, along with photos of the senders, if available in your Contacts. Click one of the column headings (From, Subject, and so on) to sort your mail collection by that criterion.

- **Install folders onto the Favorites bar.** You can drag any icon in the mailboxes list onto the Favorites toolbar, where it becomes a button or a pop-up menu. The button works exactly like a folder: For example, you can drag a message onto one to file it there, or you can click one of these folder buttons (or use its pop-up menu) to see what's inside.

 The Favorites bar comes with starter buttons already installed, like Inbox, Sent, Notes, and so on. But you can, and should, install your *own* favorites there, and remove the ones you don't want. (To move a button around, ⌘-drag it. To get rid of it, just drag it away from the toolbar.)

Tip: You can also hide this new Favorites bar whenever you feel the urge. Choose View→Hide Favorites Bar, of course.

- **Hide the mailboxes panel completely.** To do that, click the ▼ button above it. Now you have much more screen space to work with.

Tip: Hey, here's a thought! *Combine* the previous two ideas. Install the most important folders onto the Favorites bar, so you can get at them, and *then* hide the mailboxes list. Now you have easy access to the most important folders, but your mailboxes list isn't eating up a lot of screen space. This glorious, space-efficient result is shown back in Figure 18-4, center.

- **Label the toolbar buttons.** Out of the box, the buttons on the toolbar (✉, 🗑, and so on) have no labels. But if you Control-click (or right-click) the toolbar, you get a pop-up menu that offers you other styles for those buttons: Icon & Text, Icon Only, Text Only (which is *very* space-efficient), and None (which is even more space-efficient—provided you know the keyboard shortcuts for all the buttons you've just hidden away).

- **Change the type size/icon size for the folders in the mailboxes panel.** To do that, open System Preferences→General. Use the "Sidebar icon size" pop-up menu to choose Small, Medium, or Large.

Note: Whatever size you choose here also affects the font and icon sizes in the *Finder window Sidebar*. Apple figures that if you're that eagle-eyed (or that vision-impaired), you'll want the same size adjustment in both apps.

- **Redesign the New Message window.** What signature do you want stamped on every outgoing message? Do you want the Cc and Bcc lines to show up? How about the Priority pop-up menu?

 You can make all these settings using the little ⬛▾ menu in the New Message window; see Figure 18-6.

- **Adjust the message window width.** Drag the very right edge of the window inward or outward to adjust the width of the message itself. Double-click the edge of the messages list to hide the *message* completely. Now you have only the mailboxes list and the very wide messages list; to read a message, you have to double-click it to open it into a new window. (Double-click the right edge of the window to restore the message-reading pane.)

- **Adjust the width of the mailboxes or messages list.** Similarly, you can drag the right edges of the first two columns to adjust their width. Or double-click the right edge to make the column exactly as wide as Mail thinks it should be.

- **Change what morsels show up in the messages list.** The messages list (center column) usually shows the sender's name, subject line, and the first few lines of the message itself (an iPhone/iPad feature brought to the Mac). But you can add additional info displays to the list—message size, mailbox, date sent, and so on—by choosing from the View→Message Attributes submenu.

- **Change what details show up in the header.** The *header* is the top part of a message, where you see the details of how the message reached you. Ordinarily, Mail shields you from the geekiest details of the header; if you really want to see it all, choose View→Message→All Headers.

But if you'd rather, you can tailor the standard header so that Mail always shows you exactly the information you want. In Mail→Preferences→Viewing, use the "Show header detail" pop-up menu to choose Custom. Now you can add just the details you always want to see: Attachments, Bcc, Cc, Flag, From, Reply-To, Resent-Cc, and so on.

Figure 18-6:
To redesign the New Message window, choose Customize from the little pop-up menu shown here (top). Now you get a full-scale model of the New Message window with all the available parts visible. Turn on the checkboxes of the pieces you want in your everyday email composing (bottom).

- **Control how many lines of preview text appear.** In Mail→Preferences→Viewing, you can use the List Preview pop-up menu to control how many lines of each message you want to appear, in light gray, as a preview of what's in the message itself. You can choose up to five lines, or choose None to hide the preview completely.

- **Sort the messages.** Use the "Sort by" pop-up menu above the messages list ("by Date," "by Attachment," "by Unread," and so on). Use the bottom two commands—Ascending or Descending—to control *which way* the sorting goes (A to Z, Z to A, or whatever).

Tip: If you click the "Sort by" bar above the message list, you jump directly to the top—just like you do on the iPhone or iPad. Some ideas, you just can't keep down.

Tweaking the Classic layout

Out of the box, Mail assumes a new three-column layout (Figure 18-4, top): mailboxes list at left, messages list in the middle, and the message itself at right.

There are two advantages to this layout. First, your Mac's screen is wider than it is tall, so *columns* of information make more sense than *horizontal* strips. Second, by devoting only about half of the screen to the message itself, the column of text is kept to a comfortable reading width; too wide, and your eyeballs have to scan across the whole screen, which is supposedly tiring.

But if you hate that layout, you can always go back to the older layout, shown in Figure 18-7, by choosing Mail→Preferences→Viewing and turning on "Show Classic layout."

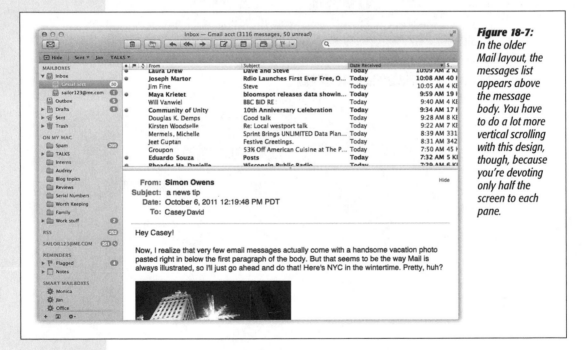

Figure 18-7:
In the older Mail layout, the messages list appears above the message body. You have to do a lot more vertical scrolling with this design, though, because you're devoting only half the screen to each pane.

You have a bunch of customization options here, too:

- **Adjust the columns.** You can make a column narrower or wider by dragging the right edge of its column *heading*, or rearrange columns by dragging their titles. Similarly, you can *sort* your email by clicking these column headings, exactly as in the Finder. Click a second time to reverse the sorting order. You can also control *which* columns appear using the commands in the View→Columns menu.

- **Hide the message body.** You can get rid of the message-reading pane altogether by double-clicking the divider line, double-clicking just above the vertical scroll bar, or dragging the divider line's handle all the way to the bottom of the screen. Bring it back by dragging the divider line up from the bottom.

- **Control the mailboxes pane.** Drag the thin vertical line that separates this tinted column from the white messages area to make the column wider or narrower. You can make the column disappear or reappear by choosing View→Hide Mailbox List (or View→Show Mailbox List), or by pressing Shift-⌘-M.

The toolbar

In either layout—Classic or Lion—you have full control over the toolbar, which works much like the Finder toolbar.

You can rearrange or remove icon buttons (by ⌘-dragging them); add interesting new buttons to the toolbar (View→Customize Toolbar); change its display to show just text labels or just icons (choose View→Customize Toolbar, and then use the Show pop-up menu); or hide the toolbar entirely (using the View→Hide Toolbar command).

Tip: Even when the toolbar is hidden, you can still hit Option-⌘-F to use the search box. (Press ⌘-F by itself to search the *current message.)*

Writing Messages

To send an email, click ⌨ in the toolbar or press ⌘-N. The New Message form, shown in Figure 18-8, opens. Here's how you go about writing a message:

1. **In the To field, type the recipient's email address.**

 If somebody is in your Contacts, type the first couple of letters of the name or email address; Mail automatically completes the address. (If the first guess is wrong, then type another letter or two until Mail revises its guess.)

Tip: If Mail constantly tries to autofill in the address of someone you don't really communicate with, you can zap that address from its memory by choosing Window→Previous Recipients. Click the undesired address, and then click Remove From List.

 As in most dialog boxes, you can jump from blank to blank (from To to Cc, for example) by pressing Tab. To send this message to more than one person, separate the addresses with commas: *bob@earthlink.net, billg@microsoft.com,* and so on.

Tip: If you send most of your email to addresses within the same organization (like *reddelicious@apple.com, grannysmith@apple.com,* and *winesap@apple.com*), Mail can automatically turn all *other* email addresses red. It's a feature designed to avoid sending confidential messages to outside addresses.

To turn this feature on, choose Mail→Preferences, click Composing, turn on "Mark addresses not ending with," and then type the "safe" domain (like *apple.com*) into the blank.

2. To send a copy to other recipients, enter their addresses in the Cc field.

Cc stands for *carbon copy.* Getting an email message where your name is in the Cc line implies: "I sent you a copy because I thought you'd want to know about this correspondence, but I'm not expecting you to reply."

Tip: If Mail recognizes the address you type into the To or Cc box (because it's someone in your Contacts, for instance), then the name turns into a shaded, round-ended box button. In addition to looking cool, these buttons sprout a ▾ when you point to them; when you click there, you get a list of useful commands (including Show Contact Card).

These buttons are also drag-and-droppable. For example, you can drag one from the To field to the Cc field, or from Contacts to Mail.

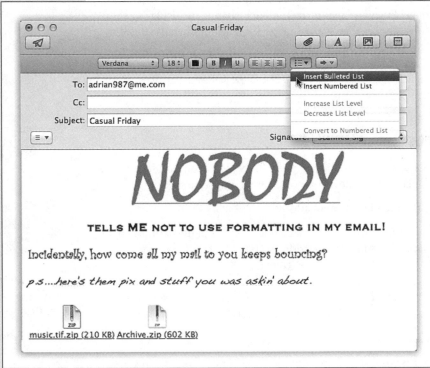

Figure 18-8:
If you want to use formatting, click the Show Format Bar icon (A) on the toolbar to open the Format bar—a strip of buttons for font, style, color, justification, bulleted lists, indentation, and so on. (The Format menu contains menu versions of the same stuff.)

3. Type the topic of the message in the Subject field.

It's courteous to put some thought into the subject line. (Use "Change in plans for next week," for instance, instead of "Yo.") On the other hand, don't put the *entire* message into the subject line, either.

4. Specify an email format.

There are two kinds of email: *plain text* and *formatted* (which Apple calls Rich Text). Plain text messages are faster to send and open, are universally compatible with the world's email programs, and are greatly preferred by many veteran computer fans. And even though the message itself is plain, you can still attach pictures and other files. (If you want to get really graphic with your mail, you can also use the *Stationery* option, which gives you preformatted message templates to drop in pictures, graphics, and text. Flip to page 683 for more on using stationery.)

Resourceful geeks have even learned how to fake some formatting in plain messages: They use capitals or asterisks instead of bold formatting *(*man* is he a GEEK!)*, and pseudo-underlines for emphasis *(I _love_ Swiss cheese!).*

By contrast, formatted messages sometimes appear without any formatting at all in some email programs.

UP TO SPEED

Bcc, Reply-To, and Priority

A blind carbon copy is a secret copy. This feature lets you send a copy of a message to somebody secretly, without any of the other recipients knowing that you did so. To view this field when composing a message (if it's not already visible), choose View→Bcc Address Field.

You can use the Bcc field to quietly signal a third party that a message has been sent. For example, if you send your co-worker a message that says, "Chris, it bothers me that you've been cheating the customers," you could Bcc your supervisor to clue her in without getting into trouble with Chris.

The Bcc box is useful in other ways, too. Many people send email messages (corny jokes, for example) to a long list of recipients. You, the recipient, have to scroll through the long list of names the sender placed in the To or Cc field.

But if the sender used the Bcc field to hold all the recipients' email addresses, you won't see anybody else's names at the top of the email. In the To box, you might see the sender's name, or "undisclosed recipients," or nothing at all. (Spammers have also learned this trick, which is why it usually looks like you're the only recipient of a junk message when there are actually millions of other people who received the same message.)

Another hidden field you can add to your messages is *Reply-To*. (Choose View→Reply-To Address Field.) That field has one simple purpose: to make the recipient's email program reply to a different email address than the one you sent the message from.

For example, if your business email address isn't working but you absolutely *have* to send a field report to your boss, you can send the message from your personal email account but put your business address in the Reply-To field. That way, when your boss emails you back to congratulate you, the email goes to your business account.

Finally, if you click the (≡ ▾) on the left side of an email message and choose Customize, you can enable one more hidden header option: Priority. (It's the pop-up menu with an exclamation mark in it.) If you turn on the checkbox next to that pop-up menu and click OK, all your email messages let you set how important they are on a three-tiered scale.

The good part about this system is that it lets your recipient see that an email you've sent is, for example, urgent. The bad part is that not every email program displays the priority of email—and even if your recipient's email program *does* display your message's priority, there's no guarantee that it'll make him respond any faster.

To control which kind of mail you send on a message-by-message basis, choose from the Format menu either Make Plain Text or Make Rich Text. To change the factory setting for new outgoing messages, choose Mail→Preferences; click the Composing icon; and choose from the Message Format pop-up menu.

(But note: Even if you choose Rich Text, Mail sends a plain text message if you don't actually *use* a formatting command—choose a new font, size, or whatever.)

Tip: If you plan to send formatted mail, remember that your recipients won't see the fonts you use unless their machines have the same ones installed. Bottom line: For email to Mac and Windows owners alike, stick to universal choices like Arial, Times, and Courier.

5. **Type your message in the message box.**

You can use all standard editing techniques, including dictation, copy and paste, drag and drop, and so on. If you selected the Rich Text style of email, you can use word processor–like formatting (Figure 18-8).

As you type, Mail checks your spelling, using a dotted underline to mark questionable words. You can read much more about OS X's built-in spelling/grammar checker (and typing expander) in Chapter 6.

If you're composing a long email message, or if it's one you don't want to send until later, press ⌘-S or choose File→Save. You've just saved the message in your Drafts folder. It'll still be there the next time you open Mail. To reopen a saved draft later, click the Drafts icon in the mailboxes column and then double-click the message you want to work on.

6. **Click Send ⊿ (or press Shift-⌘-D).**

Mail sends the message.

Tip: To resend a message you've already sent, click it and then choose Message→Send Again, or press Shift-⌘-D.

If you'd rather have Mail place each message you write in the Outbox folder instead of connecting to the Net when you click Send, choose Mailbox→Take All Accounts Offline. While you're offline, Mail refrains from trying to connect, which is a great feature when you're working on a laptop at 39,000 feet and didn't feel like paying for WiFi. (Choose Mailbox→Take All Accounts Online to reverse the procedure.)

Attaching Files to Messages

Sending little text messages is fine, but it's not much help when you want to send somebody a photograph, a sound, or a Word document. To attach a file to a message you've written, use one of these methods:

- Drag the icons you want to attach directly off the desktop (or out of a folder) into the New Message window. There your attachments appear with their own

hyperlinked icons (visible in Figure 18-8), meaning that your recipient can simply click to open them.

Tip: Exposé was *born* for this moment. Hit ⌘-F3 to make all open windows flee to the edges of the screen, revealing the desktop. Root around until you find the file you want to send. Begin dragging it; without releasing the mouse, press ⌘-F3 again to bring your message window back into view. Complete your drag into the message window.

Mail makes it look as though you can park the attached file's icon (or the full image of a graphics file) *inside* the text of the message, mingled with your typing. Don't be fooled, however; on the receiving end, all the attachments will be clumped together at the end of the message (unless your recipient also uses Mail or you've sent pictures with Stationery).

- Drag the icons you want to attach from the desktop onto Mail's *Dock icon*. Mail dutifully creates a new outgoing message, with the files already attached.

POWER USERS' CLINIC

Attachment Tricks

Nowadays, what's attached to an email message is often more important than the message itself. You might send a PowerPoint file to a coworker or send your aunt a picture of your new dog, for example, without bothering to write anything more than "See attached" in the body of the message.

That's why it's such a pain when email attachments don't go through properly—or when they're too big to send at all. Luckily, OS X provides three tools for making attachments smaller and more compatible with Windows, so you'll never get another frustrated "I *can't* see attached!" reply again.

If you're sending images along with your message, you can shrink them down right in Mail. Use the Image Size pop-up menu in the lower-right corner of the window to pick a smaller size for the images (like Medium or Small).

You can keep tabs on the total size of your attachments in the lower-left corner of the window, too. Ideally, you should keep the total under 2 MB, so dial-up sufferers don't get annoyed—and so your message doesn't get rejected by your recipient's ISP for being too big.

Use the Finder to compress big files before you send them. It makes the Finder create zip-compressed files, which gener-

ally take up much less space than the originals.

You can pick from two different formats for your attachments: normal or Windows-friendly. Normal attachments open correctly on both Macs and PCs. Trouble is, a normal attachment may show up on a PC accompanied by a useless second attachment whose name starts with "._" (which often frustrates your recipients).

Windows-friendly attachments, on the other hand, always work correctly on PCs—but when sent to Macs, they lose minor details like color labels and originating Web site information.

Bottom line: Unless you work in an all-Mac company, stick with the Windows-friendly setting.

To use the Windows-friendly setting for an open message, choose Edit→Attachments→Send Windows-Friendly Attachments. (If no message is open, the command says *Always Send Windows-Friendly Attachments* instead). You can also adjust the setting on a per-email basis using the Send Windows-Friendly Attachments checkbox at the bottom of the attachment dialog box.

- Click the () on the New Message toolbar, choose File→Attach Files, or press Shift-⌘-A. The Open File sheet appears so you can find the files you want to include. (You can choose multiple files simultaneously in this dialog box. Just ⌘-click or Shift-click them as though you were selecting them in a Finder window.)

Once you've selected them, click Choose File (or press Return). You return to the New Message window, where the attachments' icons appear, ready to ride along when you send the message.

To remove an attachment, drag across its icon to highlight it, and then press the Delete key. (You can also choose Message→Remove Attachments.)

Signatures

Signatures are bits of text that get stamped at the bottom of your outgoing email messages. A signature might contain a name, a postal address, a pithy quote, or even a scan of your *real* signature, as shown in Figure 18-9.

Figure 18-9:
After naming your signature in the middle pane and typing the text on the right, don't miss the Format menu, which you can use to dress up your signature with colors and formatting. You can even paste a picture into the signature box. Click OK when you're finished. (You can use formatted signatures only when sending Rich Text messages.)

You can customize your signatures by choosing Mail→Preferences→Signatures. Here's what you should know:

- **To build up a library of signatures that you can use in any of your accounts:** Select All Signatures in the leftmost pane, and then click the **+** button to add each new signature (Figure 18-9). Give each new signature a name in the middle pane, and then customize the signatures' text in the rightmost pane.

Tip: If you ever get tired of a signature, you can delete it forever by selecting All Signatures→[your signature's name], clicking the **−** button, and then clicking OK.

- **To make a signature available in one of your email accounts:** Drag the signature's name from the middle pane onto the name of the account in the leftmost pane. In other words, you can make certain signatures available to only your work (or personal) account, so you never accidentally end up appending your secret FBI contact signature to the bottom of a birthday invitation you send out.

- **To assign a particular signature to one account:** In the left pane, click an account; pick from the Choose Signature pop-up menu. Each time you compose a message from that account, Mail inserts the signature you selected.

Tip: To make things more interesting for your recipients, pick At Random; Mail selects a different signature each time you send a message. Or, if you're not that much of a risk-taker, choose In Sequential Order; Mail picks the next signature in order for each new message you write.

Remember that you can always change your signature on a message-by-message basis, using the Signature pop-up menu in any new email message.

- **To use the signature feature as a prefix in replies:** Turn on "Place signature above quoted text." If you turn on this setting, your signature gets inserted *above* any text that you're replying to, rather than below. You'd use this setting if your "signature" said something like, "Hi there! You wrote this to me!"

Tip: If you're into consistent typographical styling, also turn on "Always match my default font." That setting makes sure that any messages you send contain the signature in the same font as the rest of the message, lending it an air of professionalism.

Stationery

Rich Text—and even plain text—messages are fine for your everyday personal and business correspondence. After all, you really won't help messages like, "Let's have a meeting on those third-quarter earnings results" much by adding visual bells and whistles.

But suppose you have an occasion where you *want* to jazz up your mail, like an electronic invitation to a bridal shower or a mass-mail update as you get your kicks down Route 66.

These messages just cry out for Mail's *Stationery* feature. Stationery means colorful, predesigned mail templates that you make your own by dragging in photos from your own collection. Those fancy fonts and graphics will certainly get people's attention when they open the message.

Note: They will, that is, *if* their email programs understand HTML formatting. That's the formatting Mail uses for its stationery. (If *HTML* rings a bell, it's because this HyperText Markup Language is the same language used to make Web pages so lively and colorful.)

It might be a good idea to make sure everyone on your recipient list has a mail program that can handle HTML; otherwise, your message may look like a jumble of code and letters in the middle of the screen.

Here's how to make a stylized message with Mail Stationery:

1. **Create a new message.**

 Click File→New Message, press ⌘-N, or click the 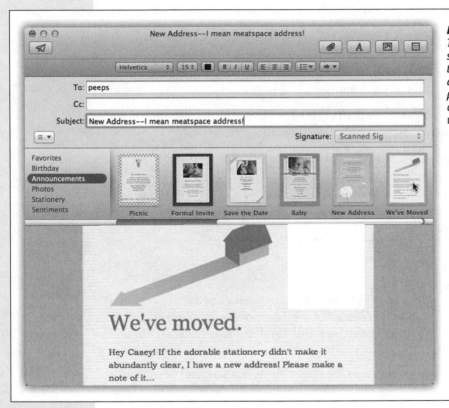 button on the Mail window toolbar.

2. **On the right side of the toolbar in the New Message window, click the 🔲 button.**

 A panel opens up, showing you all the available templates, in categories like Birthday and Announcements (Figure 18-10).

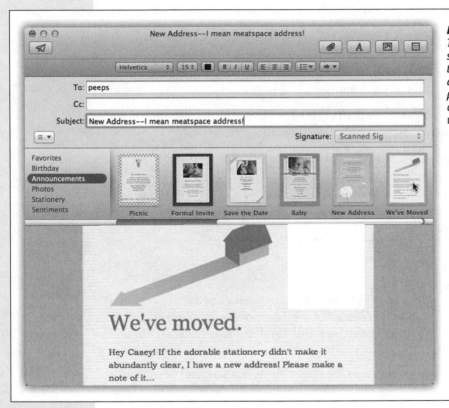

Figure 18-10:
To use Stationery, start by clicking a template, and then add your own text in place of the generic copy that comes with the template.

3. **Click a category, and then click a stationery thumbnail image to apply it to your message.**

 The body of your message changes to take on the look of the template.

4. **If you like what you see, click the 🔲 button on the toolbar again to fold up the stationery-picker panel.**

 Now, Apple's canned stationery looks fantastic. The only problem is, the photos on most of the templates are pictures of *somebody else's* family and friends. Unless you work for Apple's modeling agency, you probably have no clue who they are.

Fortunately, it's easy enough to replace those placeholder photos with your *own* snaps.

5. **Add and adjust pictures.**

Click the Photo Browser icon (▣) on the toolbar to open up a palette that lists all the photos you've stored in iPhoto, Aperture, and Photo Booth.

Tip: If you don't keep your pictures in any of those programs, you can drag any folder of pictures onto the Photo Browser window to add them.

Now you can drag your own pictures directly onto Apple's dummy photos on the stationery template. They replace the sunny models. You don't have to know a lick of HTML to use the templates—it's all drag, drop, and type, baby.

To resize a photo in the template, double-click it. A size slider appears. Drag the mouse around the photo window to reposition the picture relative to its frame.

6. **Select the fake text and type over it with what you really want to say.**

As you type, your words are autoformatted to match the template design.

Once you've got your message looking the way you want it, address it just as you would any other piece of mail, and then click the Send ✍ button to get it on its way.

Tip: You're not stuck with Apple's designs for your stationery templates; you can make your own. Just make a new message, style the fonts and photos the way you want them, and then choose File→Save as Stationery. You can now select your masterwork in the Custom category, which appears down at the end of the list in the stationery-picker panel.

If you decide that the message would be better off as plain old text, click Show Stationery on the message window. In the list of template categories, click Stationery and then Original to strip the color and formats out of the message.

Tip: If you find you're using one or two templates a lot (if, for example, all your friends are having babies these days), drag your frequently used templates into the Favorites category so you don't have to go wading around for them.

To remove one from Favorites, click it, and then click the ⊗ in the top-left corner of the thumbnail.

Reading Email

Mail puts all incoming email into your Inbox; the statistic after the word *Inbox* lets you know how many messages you haven't yet read. New messages are also marked with light-blue dots in the main list.

Tip: The Mail icon in the Dock also shows you how many new messages you have waiting; it's the number in the red circle. In Mail→Preferences→General, you can specify *which* mailbox it's tallying up—or have it tally up all of them.

Click the Inbox folder to see a list of received messages. If it's a long list, press Control-Page Up and Control-Page Down to scroll. (Page Up and Page Down without the Control key scroll the message pane instead.

Tip: If you ⌘-click more than one mailbox folder, you can combine them (and their total-message counts) into one unified messages list.

Click the name of a message once to read it in the message window, or double-click a message to open it into a separate window. (If a message is already selected, pressing Return also opens its separate window.)

When you click the name of a message in the messages list (or press the ↑ and ↓ keys to highlight successive messages in that list), you see the message itself, along with any attachments, in the message pane.

Tip: Instead of reading your mail, you might prefer to have OS X read it *to* you, as you sit back in your chair and sip a strawberry daiquiri. Highlight the text you want to hear (or choose Edit→Select All), and then choose Edit→Speech→Start Speaking. You'll hear the message read aloud, in the voice you've selected on the Speech pane of System Preferences (Chapter 9).

To stop the insanity, choose Edit→Speech→Stop Speaking.

At the top of each message, you see the *header*—a bunch of details like date, subject, to/from addresses, and so on. Figure 18-11 has more on headers.

Figure 18-11:
Top: The little blue Hide button pares down all this gunk to a simpler look—sender, subject, date. (Click Details to expand the header again.)

Bottom: If you point to the header without clicking, you get to see the ghosts of four useful buttons: Trash, Reply, Reply All, and Forward.

Once you've viewed a message, you can respond to it, delete it, print it, file it, and so on. The following pages should get you started.

Conversation View

Threading is one of the most useful mail-sorting methods to come along in a long time. It groups all messages that are part of the same back-and-forth conversation as a *single item* in the main messages list. (In this discussion, let's call that one item the *main message.* In Mail, it's always the most recent message in the conversation.)

Less sophisticated email programs figure out which messages go together by matching only their subject lines. But Mail is much smarter; it also studies the message headers, senders, recipients, and dates. Even if someone changes the subject line along the way, Mail still knows that a conversation is a conversation.

As shown in Figure 18-12, Conversation view, as Apple calls it, hides all the usual awful indents, repetitions, forwards of forwards, and so on. You see only neatly numbered scrolling blocks, each representing the *newly added* text in each back-and-forth.

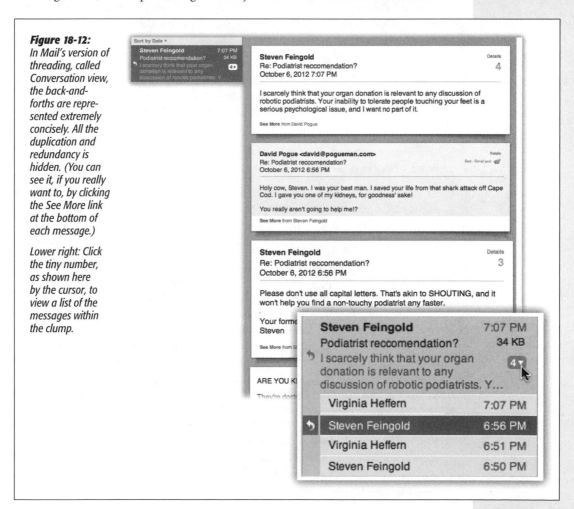

Figure 18-12:
In Mail's version of threading, called Conversation view, the back-and-forths are represented extremely concisely. All the duplication and redundancy is hidden. (You can see it, if you really want to, by clicking the See More link at the bottom of each message.)

Lower right: Click the tiny number, as shown here by the cursor, to view a list of the messages within the clump.

To turn on threading, choose View→Organize by Conversation. Each main message in the messages list sprouts a little numbered badge, like "3 ▸," to indicate messages that have been clustered together (Figure 18-12).

Note: When Organize by Conversation is turned on, you might be wondering: What happens to chronological order? In other words, if the messages in a certain thread took place over several days or weeks, where does Mail wind up listing them when it sorts your messages list by date?

Answer: They're all clumped together in the main message—the *most recent* message. That is, if the messages on a certain topic arrived July 1, 4, 7, and 11, you'll find all four grouped with the July 11 message. They're essentially pulled *out* of the chronological list to join the latest one, for your reviewing pleasure.

Here are some powerful ways to use threading:

- **View all the messages in a conversation** by clicking the main message in the messages list. In the message pane, you see all the back-and-forths, minus all the duplication and the replies to replies.

- **Expand a list of the messages in a conversation** by clicking the small gray number-of-messages badge—or by clicking the main message and then pressing the → key. A tiny message-conversation list sprouts out of the one listed message, as shown in the inset in Figure 18-12. (Or you can make *all* conversations display their submessages like this; to do that, choose View→Expand All Conversations.)

 Once you've expanded the mini-list, you can walk through it by pressing the up/down arrow keys.

 The messages from the current mailbox are numbered—those are the big gray digits in the upper-right corner. Those numbers help you figure out where you are in all the back-and-forths.

- **Examine messages from multiple mailboxes.** Normally, conversations display only messages held in the *same* mailbox, but that's not especially convenient when you want to see, for example, both messages you've received (from your Inbox) and your replies (from your Sent box). To work around that problem, click the Show Related Messages (⬛) button in the toolbar (or turn on "Include related messages" in Mail→Preferences→Viewing). These options mean, "Include messages in *other* mailboxes, too, like Sent messages—not just this one mailbox." Now your conversations seamlessly combine related messages from all mailboxes.

Note: When "Include related messages" is turned on, the related messages do *not* display the big gray numbers in the corner; only the ones in the current mailbox sprout numbers.

- **Move all the messages in a conversation to a new mailbox** by dragging the main message. You might find this useful, for example, when you've just finished a project and want to file away all the email related to it quickly. You can even delete all the messages in a thread at once by deleting its main entry.

Note: If you just drag *one* message of a conversation to a different folder, though, it becomes a "related" message, no longer numbered, as described in the previous Note.

- **Send someone all the messages in a thread** by selecting the main message and then clicking Forward as usual. Mail automatically copies all the messages of the thread into a new message, putting the oldest at the top. You might find this useful, for instance, when you want to send your boss all the correspondence you've had with someone about a certain project.

- **Manipulate an individual message in a conversation** by first clicking it in the message-reading pane. For example, if you have five messages in a conversation, and you want to forward only the juicy one, which happens to be message #2, click #2 and then use the Forward command—or Reply, Delete, or whatever. (You can also click one of the four light-gray buttons that appear when you point to the message header—Delete, Reply, Reply All, Forward.)

Tip: In Mail→Preferences→Viewing, you'll find a bunch of fine-tuning tweaks that apply to conversations. For example, you can ask that messages that are part of the same conversation show up highlighted in a color you choose—even when conversation grouping is turned *off.* And you can request that, when a conversation message is clicked in the messages list, the resulting messages are shown in reverse chronological order—oldest at the top.

Adding the Sender to Contacts

When you choose the Message→Add Sender to Contacts command, Mail memorizes the email address of the person whose message is on the screen. In fact, you can highlight a huge number of messages and add *all* the senders simultaneously using this technique.

Thereafter, you'll be able to address a new message to somebody just by typing the first few letters of her name or email address.

Data Detectors

Data detectors are described on page 256. They're what you see when OS X recognizes commonly used bits of written information: a physical address, a phone number, a date and time, a flight number, and so on. With one quick click, you can send that information into the appropriate OS X program, like Calendar, Contacts, the Flight Tracker widget in Dashboard, or your Web browser (for looking an address up on a map).

This is just a public-service reminder that data detectors are especially useful—*primarily* useful, in fact—in Mail. Watch for the dotted rectangle that appears when you point to a name, address, date, time, or flight number.

Opening File Attachments

Just as you can attach files to a message, so can people send files to you. Sometimes they don't even bother to type a note; you wind up receiving an empty email message with a file or two attached. Only the presence of the file's icon in the message body tells you there's something attached.

Tip: In Classic view, Mail doesn't ordinarily indicate the presence of attachments in the messages list. It can do so, however. Just choose View→Columns→Attachments. A new column appears in the messages list—at the far right—where you see a paper-clip icon and the number of file attachments listed for each message.

Mail stores downloaded files in a hidden folder on your hard drive. To bring them out into the open, you must proceed in one of these ways:

• Click the Quick Look button in the message header. Instantly, you're treated to a nearly full-size preview of the file's contents. Yes, Quick Look has come to email. It works exactly as described in Chapter 1.

Tip: If the attachments are pictures, then clicking Quick Look gives you a full-screen slideshow of every attached image. If you jiggle the mouse a little during the slideshow, you get a useful row of slideshow-control buttons along the bottom of the screen, too.

• Click the Save button in the message header to save it to your Downloads folder, nestled within easy reach in the Dock. (It's a pop-up menu, which is handy if there's more than one attachment. You can either save *all* attachments at once, or choose from the pop-up menu to save them individually.)

Tip: If you don't want to use the Downloads folder, you can choose a new autosave location for attachments by choosing Mail→Preferences→General→Downloads folder.

All the Little Symbols

The left edge of the messages list shows little symbols that let you know at a glance how you've processed certain messages. The most common one is, of course, the light-blue dot (⬤), which means "new message." (After reading a message, you can mark it once again as an *unread* message by choosing Message→Mark→As Unread [Shift-⌘-U]—or by Control-clicking the message's name and then choosing Mark→As Unread from the shortcut menu.)

You might also see these symbols, which represent messages you've replied to (↩), forwarded (➡), redirected (↪), or flagged (🚩).

A well-guarded secret, however, is that the "replied to" and "forwarded" symbols aren't just indicators—they're also *buttons.*

When you see one of these symbols next to your original message, click it to jump straight to your reply (or forwarded message). You're spared the trouble of having to search through all your mailboxes.

Incidentally, you may have noticed that Mail marks a message as having been read the moment you click it. You can change it back to unread by using its shortcut menu—but there's also a more permanent workaround.

If you hide the message pane by double-clicking the divider bar to its right (or, in Classic view, above it), Mail no longer marks messages "read" just because you clicked them in the list.

• Drag the attachment icon (it appears at the bottom of the message) out of the message window and onto any visible portion of your desktop or any visible folder window.

• Double-click the attachment's icon, or single-click the blue link underneath the icon. If you were sent a document (a photo, Word file, or Excel file, for example), it now opens in the corresponding program.

Note: After the attachment is open, use the File→Save As command to save the file into a folder of your choice. Otherwise, any changes you make to the document will be lost.

• Control-click (or right-click) the attachment's icon at the bottom of the message. From the shortcut menu, you can open it, save it, Quick Look it, and so on.

Replying to a Message

To answer a message, click the Reply ◄ button on the message toolbar (or choose Message→Reply, or press ⌘-R). If the message was originally addressed to multiple recipients, you can send your reply to everyone simultaneously by clicking Reply All ◄◄ instead (Shift-⌘-R).

A new message window opens, already addressed. As a courtesy to your correspondent, Mail places the original message at the bottom of the window, set off by a vertical bar, as shown in Figure 18-13.

In Mail messages formatted with Rich Text (not to be confused with Rich Text Format word processing format, which is very different), a reply includes the original message, marked in a special color (which you can change in Mail→Preferences) and with a vertical bar to differentiate it from the text of your reply. (In plain-text messages, each line of the reply is >denoted >with >brackets, although only your recipient will see them.)

The original sender's name is automatically placed in the To field. The subject is the same as the original subject with the addition of "Re:" (shorthand for Regarding). You're now ready to type your response.

At this point, you can add or delete recipients, edit the subject line or the original message, attach a file, and so on.

Tip: Use the Return key to create blank lines in the original message. Using this method, you can splice your own comments into the paragraphs of the original message, replying point by point. The brackets preceding each line of the original message help your correspondent keep straight what's yours and what's hers.

When you're finished, click Send (🖅).

Forwarding Messages

Instead of replying to the person who sent you a message, you may sometimes want to pass the note on to a third person.

To do so, click the Forward ➔ toolbar button (or choose Message→Forward, or press Shift-⌘-F). A new message opens, looking a lot like the one that appears when you reply. You may wish to precede the original message with a comment of your own, along the lines of: "Frank: I thought you'd be interested in this joke about your mom."

Finally, address it as you would any outgoing piece of mail.

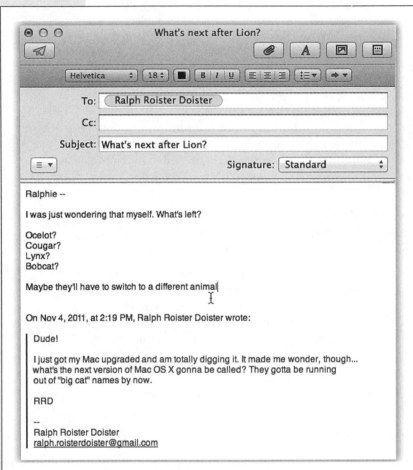

Figure 18-13:
If you highlight some text before clicking Reply, Mail pastes only that portion of the original message into your reply. That's a great convenience to your correspondent, who now knows exactly which part of the message you're responding to.

Redirecting Messages

A *redirected* message is similar to a forwarded message, with one useful difference: When you forward a message, your recipient sees that it came from you. When you redirect it, your recipient sees the *original* writer's name as the sender. In other words, a redirected message uses you as a low-profile relay station between two other people.

Treasure this feature. Plenty of email programs don't offer a Redirect command at all. You can use it to transfer messages from one of your own accounts to another, or to pass along a message that came to you by mistake.

To redirect a message, choose Message→Redirect, or press Shift-⌘-E. You get an outgoing copy of the message—this time without any quoting marks. (You can edit redirected messages before you send them, too, which is perfect for April Fools' Day pranks.

Printing Messages

Sometimes there's no substitute for a printout. Choose File→Print, or press ⌘-P to summon the Print dialog box.

Filing Messages

Mail lets you create new mailboxes (mail folders) in the mailboxes list. You might create one for important messages, another for order confirmations from Web shopping, still another for friends and family, and so on. You can even create mailboxes *inside* these mailboxes, a feature beloved by the hopelessly organized.

Tip: You can drag mailbox folders up and down in the list to rearrange them. Sweet.

Mail even offers *smart mailboxes*—self-updating folders that show you all your mail from your boss, for example, or every message with "mortgage" in its subject. It's the same idea as smart folders in the Finder or smart playlists in iTunes: folders whose contents are based around criteria you specify (Figure 18-14).

Figure 18-14:
Mail lets you create self-populating folders. In this example, the "New Mail from Mom" smart mailbox will automatically display all messages from her that you've received in the past week.

The commands you need are all in the Mailbox menu. For example, to create a new mailbox folder, choose Mailbox→New Mailbox, or click the **+** button at the bottom of the column. To create a smart mailbox, choose Mailbox→New Smart Mailbox.

Mail asks you to name the new mailbox. If you have more than one email account, you can specify which one will contain the new folder. (Smart mailboxes, however, always sit outside your other mailboxes.)

Tip: If you want to create a folder inside a folder, use slashes in the name of your new mailbox. (If you use the name *Cephalopods/Squid,* for example, then Mail creates a folder called Cephalopods, with a subfolder called Squid.) You can also drag the mailbox icons up and down in the drawer to place one inside another.

None of those tricks work for smart mailboxes, however. The only way to organize smart mailboxes is to put them inside a smart mailbox *folder,* which you create using Mailbox→New Smart Mailbox Folder. You might do that if you have several smart mailboxes for mail from your coworkers ("From Jim," "From Anne," and so on) and want to put them together in one collapsible group to save screen space.

When you click OK, a new icon appears in the mailboxes column, ready for use.

You can move a message (or group of messages) into a mailbox folder in any of three ways:

- Drag it out of the messages list onto a mailbox icon.

- Highlight one or more messages, and then choose from the Message→Move To submenu, which lists all your mailboxes.

- Control-click (or right-click) a message, or one of several that you've highlighted. From the resulting shortcut menu, choose Move To, and then, from the submenu, choose the mailbox you want.

Of course, the only way to change the contents of a *smart* mailbox is to change the criteria it uses to populate itself. To do so, double-click the smart mailbox icon and use the dialog box that appears.

Flagging Messages

Sometimes you'll receive email that prompts you to some sort of action, but you may not have the time (or the fortitude) to face the task at the moment. ("Hi there… it's

TROUBLESHOOTING MOMENT

Rebuilding Your Mail Databases

Mail keeps your messages in your Home→Library→Mail folder. (Your Library folder is usually invisible, but you can jump to it by pressing Option as you choose Go→Library in the Finder.)

Over time, as you add and delete hundreds of messages from these database files, some digital sawdust gets left behind, resulting in general Mail sluggishness. You also wind up with *massive* message files hidden on your hard drive, which can consume hundreds of megabytes of disk space. That's a particular bummer if you like to copy your message databases to your laptop when you go on a trip.

Fortunately, it's easy enough to *rebuild the message databases.* Doing so cleanses, repairs, and purges your message files. As a result, you wind up with a much more compact and healthy database.

To rebuild a mailbox, highlight it in the mailboxes column in Mail. (Highlight several by ⌘-clicking, if you like.) Then choose Mailbox→Rebuild. OS X takes several minutes (or hours, depending on the size of your mailboxes) to repair and compact your database—but if you're experiencing Mail weirdness or slowness, it's well worth the sacrifice.

me, your accountant. Would you mind rounding up your expenses for 1999 through 2011 and sending me a list by email?")

That's why Mail lets you *flag* a message, summoning a little flag icon in a new column next to the message's name. In fact, you can use seven differently *colored* flags.

These indicators can mean anything you like—they simply call attention to certain messages.

Once you've applied some flags, you can use their power in all kinds of ways. For example, you can view all of them in one place—in the Flagged folder that appears near the top of the mailboxes list.

You can also sort your mail list by flag color (choose Sort by→Flags at the top of the messages list). You can search for flagged messages using the search box. Better yet, you can view all messages with a certain flag color—magically rounded up from all your different accounts and mailboxes—by clicking the corresponding icon in the Flagged folder of the mailboxes list.

Tip: Just in case you don't find "Red," "Orange," "Yellow," and so on to be the most descriptive possible flag names, you can change them.

First, though, make sure you've applied a couple of flags to different messages already. That's necessary to make the Flagged mailbox appear in the mailboxes list. If you open the flippy triangle, you'll see the names of the flags you've applied so far. You can change a flag's name just the way you'd name a file—start by double-clicking it.

To flag a message in this way, select the message (or several messages) and then choose one of the colored flags in the Message→Flag submenu. Or Control-click (right-click) the message's name in the list and, from the shortcut menu, choose one of the seven flag colors. (To clear the flags, repeat the procedure, but use the Message→Flag→Clear Flag command instead.)

If you're using only one flag to simply mean "flag this," and you don't need all the colors, you can also press Shift-⌘-L.

Finding Messages

The box in the upper-right corner of the main mail window is Mail's own private Spotlight—a fast, powerful search command. That's essential when you have to deal with masses of email (see Figure 18-15).

This search box incorporates the same pop-up suggestions lists and "search tokens" as regular file searching in the Finder. Here's how it works:

1. **Press Option-⌘-F (or click in the search box).**

 The cursor jumps up there.

2. **Start typing what you're looking for.**

As you type, the messages list changes to show only the matching messages from all your mail folders.

If you see the message you're looking for, great. Click it, and off you go.

But this initial search is a pretty broad one. Mail is rounding up messages that match your search term *in any way.* If you type *veg,* you see messages from Murray Vegelstein, messages from vegan@militanteaters.org, and messages with the subject line "HOT DEALS IN VEGAS." All of them in one big stew.

To help you sort through it, Mail produces a Suggestions list, which sprouts from the search box. As in the Finder, it's Mail's way of asking what sort of *thing* your search term is. Is it a person? A subject? The status of a message? A date? Figure 18-15 shows the idea.

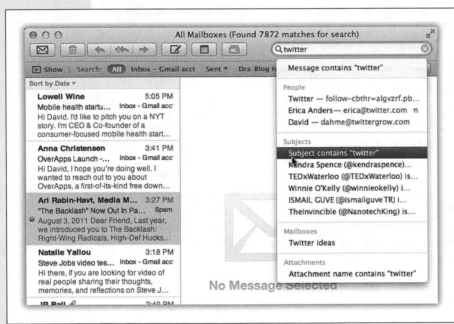

Figure 18-15:
You can jump to the search box by clicking or by pressing Option-⌘-F. As you type, Mail shrinks the list of messages— and simultaneously displays a list of suggestions. You can fine-tune your results using the mailbox buttons you've installed on the Favorites bar. To return to the full messages list, click the tiny ⊗ at the right side of the search box.

3. **Click the suggestion you want.**

 Mail filters the list. For example, if you click Murray Vegelstein, you'll see *only* the messages to or from Murray.

4. **Edit the search token.**

 The *search token* is the little bubble that appears in the search box after you've clicked one of the suggestions. You can click the little ▾ in the search token to change it. For example, if you've clicked somebody's name, that pop-up menu says To, From, or Entire Message (including the header and the body).

You can also type more into the search box to add *another* search token. For example, the first token might limit the search to messages from one person; you could then create another one that limits the search to a certain date.

Tip: Once you've built up a complicated search like this, save yourself the effort next time by *saving* that search. Click the Save button just below the search box. You get the Smart Mailbox dialog box, shown in Figure 18-15, already filled out with the search setup you've specified. All you have to do is give it a name and click OK to transform your search into a smart mailbox that you can open anytime.

You've done a lot of refining of this search. But you still haven't limited your results by *account or folder*. Mail is showing you results from either *all* mailboxes, or from only the most recent mailbox you've searched. Fortunately, your Favorites bar has now sprouted two new buttons: one called All, and one that names the folder you most recently clicked.

5. **Click a button on the Favorites bar to change which mailbox is being searched.**

 The results list updates itself.

Tip: If you ⌘-click *several* mail folders before you search, you can limit the search to that particular *set of* mailboxes. (In that case, you see a button on the Favorites bar called Selected Mailboxes.)

When you're finished hunting around, you can empty out the search box, and get back to your regularly scheduled lists of email, by clicking any other mailbox, or by clicking the ⊗ button at the right end of the search box.

A few last notes on searching:

- The Mail search is almost exactly like Finder searching, right down to the saved-search mechanism. See Chapter 3 for details.

- You can also search for certain text *within* an open message. Choose Edit→Find→ Find (or press ⌘-F) to bring up the Find dialog box (Figure 18-16).

Figure 18-16:
The Find box works just as it does in a word processor, except that the Replace function works only on messages you've written your-self—Mail doesn't let you change the words of mail you've received. (Lawyers would have a field day with that one.)

- As with regular Spotlight, Mail matches your search term by looking only at the *beginnings* of words. Searching for *flag* will find messages that contain the words *flagstone* and *flagellum,* but not *Redflag Incorporated.*

• In Mail→Preferences→General, you can specify whether or not you want Mail to include the Trash folder, Junk folder, and encrypted messages when you search all mailboxes.

Deleting Messages

Sometimes it's junk mail. Sometimes you're just done with it. Either way, it's a snap to delete a selected message, several selected messages, or a message that's currently before you on the screen. You can press the Delete key, click the Delete 🗑 button on the toolbar, choose Edit→Delete, or drag messages out of the list window and into your Trash mailbox—or even onto the Dock's Trash icon.

Tip: If you delete a message by accident, the Undo command (Edit→Undo or ⌘-Z) restores it.

All these commands move the messages to the Trash folder. If you like, you can then click its icon to view a list of the messages you've deleted. You can even rescue messages by dragging them back into a mailbox (back to the Inbox, for example).

Emptying the Trash folder

Mail doesn't vaporize messages in the Trash folder until you "empty the trash," just like in the Finder. You can empty the Trash folder in any of several ways:

• Click a message (or several) within the Trash folder list, and then click the Delete 🗑 icon on the toolbar (or press the Delete key). Now those messages are *really* gone.

• Choose Mailbox→Erase Deleted Items (Shift-⌘-Delete). (If you have multiple accounts, choose Erase Deleted Items→In All Accounts.)

• Control-click (or right-click) the Trash mailbox icon, and then choose Erase Deleted Items from the shortcut menu. Or choose the same command from the ✿ pop-up menu at the bottom of the window.

• Wait. Mail will permanently delete these messages automatically after a week.

 If a week is too long (or not long enough), you can change this interval. Choose Mail→Preferences, click Accounts, and select the account name from the list at left. Then click Mailbox Behaviors, and change the "Permanently erase deleted messages when" pop-up menu. If you choose Quitting Mail from the pop-up menu, Mail will take out the trash every time you quit the program.

Turning deleted mail invisible

Mail offers another—and very unusual—method of deleting messages that doesn't involve the Trash folder at all. Using this method, pressing the Delete key (or clicking the Delete 🗑 toolbar button) simply hides the selected message in the list. Hidden messages remain hidden, but they don't go away for good until you use the Rebuild Mailbox command described in the box on page 594.

If this arrangement sounds useful, choose Mail→Preferences; click Accounts and select the account from the list on the left; click Mailbox Behaviors; and then turn off the checkbox called "Move deleted messages to a separate folder" or "Move deleted

messages to the Trash mailbox." (The checkbox's wording depends on what kind of account you have.) From now on, messages you delete vanish from the list.

They're not really gone, however. You can bring them back, at least in ghostly form, by choosing View→Show Deleted Messages (or pressing ⌘-L). Using this system, in other words, you never truly delete messages; you just hide them.

At first, you might be concerned about the disk space and database size involved in keeping your old messages around forever like this. Truth is, OS X is perfectly capable of maintaining many thousands of messages in its mailbox databases—and with the sizes of hard drives nowadays, a few thousand messages aren't likely to make much of a dent.

Meanwhile, there's a huge benefit to this arrangement. At some point, almost everyone wishes he could resurrect a deleted message—maybe months later, maybe years later. Using the hidden-deleted-message system, your old messages are always around for reference. (The downside to this system, of course, is that SEC investigators can use it to find incriminating mail that you thought you'd deleted.)

When you do want to purge these messages for good, you can always return to the Mailbox Behaviors dialog box and turn the "Move deleted mail to a separate folder" checkbox back on.

Archiving messages

There's one final option for getting unwanted messages out of your hair: *archiving*. It just means, "Get it out of my sight for now." Archiving sweeps the selected message into a folder called Archived, where it will stay until you deal with it further (by moving or deleting it). There's one of these folders per account.

To archive a selected message, a group of selected messages, or a conversation, choose Message→Archive, or click the Archive icon on the toolbar.

Exporting Mailboxes

Time Machine (Chapter 6) keeps a watchful eye on your Mac and backs up its data regularly—including your email. If you ever delete a message by accident or otherwise make a mess of your email stash, you can duck into Time Machine right from within Mail.

But not everybody wants to use Time Machine, for personal reasons—lack of a second hard drive, aversion to software named after H.G. Wells novels, whatever.

Yet having a backup of your email is critically important. Fortunately, there's a second good way to back up your email—*export it*, like this:

1. **In the mailboxes column, choose which mailbox or mailboxes you want to archive.**

 If you have multiple mailboxes in mind, ⌘-click each one until you've selected all the ones you want.

2. At the bottom of the Mail window, open the ✿ pop-up menu and choose Export Mailbox(es).

You can also get to this command by choosing Mailbox→Export Mailbox.

3. **In the box that appears, navigate to the place you want to stash this cache of valuable mail, like a server, a flash drive, or a folder. Click Choose.**

Your exported mailboxes are saved to the location you've chosen. You can now go back to work writing new messages.

Later, if you need to pull one of those stashes back into duty, choose File→Import Mailboxes. Choose the Apple Mail option and then navigate back to the place where you stored your mailboxes.

Message Rules

Once you know how to create folders, the next step in managing your email is to set up a series of *message rules* (filters) that file, answer, or delete incoming messages automatically based on their contents (such as their subject, address, and/or size). Message rules require you to think like the distant relative of a programmer, but the mental effort can reward you many times over. Message rules turn Mail into a surprisingly smart and efficient secretary.

Setting up message rules

Here's how to set up a message rule:

1. **Choose Mail→Preferences. Click the Rules icon.**

The Rules pane appears, as shown at top in Figure 18-17.

2. **Click Add Rule.**

Now the dialog box shown at bottom in Figure 18-17 appears.

3. **Use the criteria options (at the top) to specify how Mail should select messages to process.**

For example, if you'd like the program to watch out for messages from a particular person, you would set up the first two pop-up menus to say "From" and "Contains," respectively.

POWER USERS' CLINIC

Secrets of the Mailbox Files

Mail keeps your messages in a series of mailbox folders in your Home→Library→Mail folder, inside folders (Outbox, Deleted Messages, and so on) named for each account.

Knowing this permits you to perform a number of interesting tricks. First of all, now you know what files to back up for safekeeping. (To see the invisible Library folder, press Option as you choose Go→Library in the Finder.)

Second, if you have messages on an old Mac that you'd like to copy to your new one, now you know where they're stored.

To flag messages containing *loan, $$$$, XXXX, !!!!,* and so on, set the pop-up menus to say "Subject" and "Contains."

Figure 18-17:
Top: Mail rules can screen out junk mail, serve as an email answering machine, or call important messages to your attention. All mail message rules you've created appear in this list. (The color shading for each rule is a reflection of the colorizing options you've set up, if any.)

Bottom: Double-click a rule to open the Edit Rule dialog box, where you can specify what should set off the rule and what it should do in response.

GEM IN THE ROUGH

The Email Answering Machine

If you're going on vacation, you can turn Mail into an email answering machine that sends a canned "I'm away until the 15th" message to everyone who writes you.

To do so, set the first set of pop-up menus in the Rules dialog box so that they say Account and the name of your account. In the bottom half of the dialog box, select Reply to Message from the pop-up menu. Click "Reply message text," and then type your outgoing message in the resulting box.

Keep in mind, though, that mail rules work only when Mail is open and connected to the Internet. If your computer is set to turn off after a certain period of time, therefore, make sure to disable that feature before you go on vacation.

Also: If you subscribe to mailing lists, set up another mail rule that intercepts and files them *before* your answering-machine rule kicks in. Otherwise, you'll incur the wrath of other Internet citizens by littering their email discussion groups with copies of your auto-reply message.

You can set up *multiple* criteria here to flag messages whose subjects contain any one of those common spam triggers. (If you change the "any" pop-up menu to say "all," then *all* the criteria must be true for the rule to kick in.)

4. **Specify which words or people you want the message rule to watch for.**

 In the text box to the right of the two pop-up menus, type the word, address, name, or phrase you want Mail to watch for—a person's name, or *$$$$*, in the previous examples.

5. **In the lower half of the box, specify what you want to happen to messages that match the criteria.**

 If, in steps 1 through 4, you've told your rule to watch for junk mail containing *$$$$* in the subject line, here's where you can tell Mail to delete it or move it into, say, a Junk folder.

 With a little imagination, you'll see how the options in this pop-up menu can do absolutely amazing things with your incoming email. Mail can colorize, delete, move, redirect, or forward messages—or even play a sound when you get a certain message.

 By setting up the controls as shown in Figure 18-17, for example, you'll have specified that whenever your mother sends something to you that mentions a visit, you'll hear a specific alert noise as the email is highlighted in a bright red, so it will jump out at you in the Inbox.

6. **In the very top box, name your mail rule. Click OK.**

 At this point, Mail offers to apply your freshly minted rule to all the messages that are in the mailboxes that are currently selected. It's your one chance to go back in time—because from now on, the rule will apply only to *new* messages. Click either Apply or Don't Apply.

 Now you're back to the Rules pane (Figure 18-17, top). Here you can choose a sequence for the rules you've created by dragging them up and down. Here, too, you can turn off the ones you won't be needing at the moment, but may use again one day.

Tip: Mail applies rules as they appear, from top to bottom, in the list. If a rule doesn't seem to be working properly, it may be that an earlier rule is intercepting and processing some messages before the "broken" rule even sees them. To fix this, try dragging the rule (or the interfering rule) up or down in the list.

VIPs

In the real world, VIPs are people who get backstage passes to concerts, or special treatment at business functions (it stands for "very important person"). In Mountain Lion, it means "somebody whose mail is important enough that I want it brought to my attention immediately when it arrives."

So who should your VIPs be? That's up to you. Your spouse, your boss, and your doctor come to mind.

To designate someone as a VIP, follow the steps shown in Figure 18-18. From now on, lots of interesting things happen:

- A new mailbox, called VIPs, appears in your mailboxes list. Click it to see all the mail from all your VIPs (even messages you've deleted). Or click the flippy triangle to see your VIPs' names, each representing messages from that person.

- A new menu button appears on your Favorites toolbar called VIPs. Click to see all VIP messages, or click the ▾ to see a pop-up menu of all the VIPs' names. Here again, the point is that you can jump to the messages from just that person.

- If you use iCloud, the same person is now a VIP on all your other Mountain Lion Macs, plus iPhones and iPads (running iOS 6 or later).

- Best of all, you can set up your Mac so that when a new message from a VIP comes in, an alert bubble appears in the top-right corner of your screen (Figure 18-18, bottom). That feature, of course, is part of Mountain Lion's new Notification Center feature, and it's described in Chapter 10. See the box on the next page for instructions on setting this up.

Figure 18-18:
Top: To designate a VIP, open a message she's sent you. Point to her name. A hollow star appears; click there. The star darkens. (Or choose Add to VIPs from the pop-up menu that appears when you point to her name.) Note: If that person one day insults you, fires you, or dumps you, you can remove her VIP status by clicking that same star again.

Bottom: OS X can alert you when VIP messages arrive.

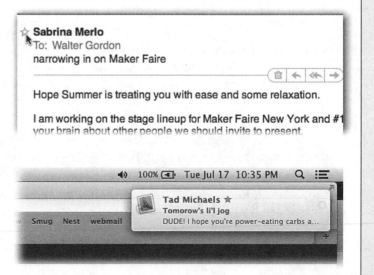

The Anti-Spam Toolkit

Spam, the junk that now makes up more than 80 percent of email, is a problem that's only getting worse. Luckily, you, along with Mail's advanced spam filters, can make it better—at least for *your* email accounts.

Using the Junk Mail Filter

You'll see the effects of Mail's spam filter the first time you check your mail: A certain swath of message titles appears in brown. These are the messages that Mail considers junk.

Note: Out of the box, Mail doesn't apply its spam-targeting features to people whose addresses are in your Contacts, to people you've emailed recently, or to messages sent to you *by name* rather than just by email address. You can adjust these settings in the Mail→Preferences→Junk Mail tab.

During your first couple of weeks with Mail, your job is to supervise Mail's work. That is, if you get spam that Mail misses, click the message, and then click the Junk button on the toolbar. On the other hand, if Mail flags legitimate mail as spam, slap it gently on the wrist by clicking the Not Junk button. Over time, Mail gets better and better at filtering your mail.

GEM IN THE ROUGH

When You Want to be Nudged About Incoming Mail

Mountain Lion's new Notification Center consolidates all the different programs and features that might want your attention—Mail, Reminders, Twitter, Facebook, software updates, and so on—into a single tidy list. See Chapter 10 for the full details.

But if a little Notification Center alert bubble appeared on your screen every time *any* new Mail message came in, you'd go quietly mad. Fortunately, a new Mail setting lets you tell Mail, "Don't disturb me unless it's really important. Like if it's from my accountant."

Here's how to set up this useful filter. Choose Mail→Preferences→General. See the "New message notifications" pop-up menu?

Here, you can choose **Inbox only** (all incoming messages trigger alert bubbles); **VIPs** (perhaps the most useful option—only messages from these essential people produce alerts); **Contacts** (messages from anyone in your address book trigger alerts—just not messages from strangers); or **All Mailboxes** (every single incoming message flags you).

You can also choose the name of a smart mailbox, if you've created one. That's a pretty potent feature. It means that you can set up incoming messages to alert you only if they match whatever criteria your smart mailbox uses. For example, you might not want to be disturbed except when a message comes from one of your best friends *and* it has an attachment *and* it mentions "money I owe you."

You may have noticed, by the way, that there's no option here for "Don't show me Mail message bubbles at all." That's because you do that in System Preferences.

Open System Preferences→Notifications, click Mail, and turn off Show in Notification Center. Now you'll be left in peace when new mail arrives, no matter who it's from.

The trouble with this so-called Training mode is that you're still left with the task of trashing the spam yourself, saving you no time whatsoever.

Once Mail has perfected its filtering skills to your satisfaction, though, open Mail's preferences, click Junk Mail, and then click "Move it to the Junk mailbox." From now on, Mail automatically files what it deems junk into a Junk mailbox, where it's much easier to scan and delete the messages en masse.

Tip: Don't miss the "Trust Junk Mail headers" option in the Junk Mail pane of the Preferences window. If you turn on that checkbox, then Mail takes your Internet provider's word that certain messages are spam, giving you a *double* layer of spam protection.

More Anti-Spam Tips

The Junk filter goes a long way toward cleaning out the spam from your mail collection—but it doesn't catch everything. If you're overrun by spam, here are some other steps you can take:

- **Rules.** Set up some message rules, as described on the preceding pages, that autoflag as spam messages that have subject lines containing trigger words like "Viagra," "Herbal," "Mortgage," "Refinance," "Enlarge," "Your"—you get the idea.

- **Create a private account.** If you're overrun by spam, consider sacrificing your current address, using it for the public areas of the Internet, like chat rooms, online shopping, Web site and software registration, and newsgroup posting. Reserve a separate email account for person-to-person email.

 Spammers use automated software robots that scour every public Internet message and Web page, recording email addresses they find. (In fact, that's probably how they got your address in the first place.)

 Using this technique, at least you're now restricting the junk mail to a secondary mail account.

- **For goodness' sake, don't *order* anything sold by the spammers.** If only one person in 500,000 does so, the spammer makes money.

Contacts (Address Book)

Contacts is OS X's little-black-book program—an electronic Rolodex where you can stash the names, job titles, addresses, phone numbers, email addresses, and Internet chat screen names of all the people in your life. It can also hold related information, like birthdays, anniversaries, and any other tidbits of personal data you'd like to keep at your fingertips (Figure 18-19).

The best part: It's *centralized.* This one address list appears everywhere: in Mail, Messages, and so on. And it synchronizes with your iPhone, iPad, and (via iCloud) your other computers.

Tip: In Mountain Lion, Apple changed the name of this program from "Address Book" to "Contacts." Why? To make it match the program's name as it appears on the iPhone and the iPad, of course.

By the way: If you find yourself accidentally typing "address book" into the Spotlight search feature from force of habit, you'll be pleased to discover that "Contacts" is the first search result. Apple's got your back.

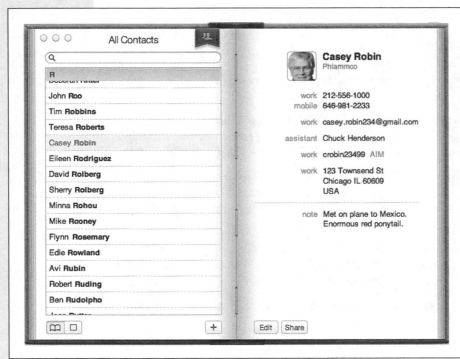

Figure 18-19:
Contacts is meant to look like a physical address book. On the left, the full list of names; on the right, the card for the one person whose name you've clicked. (You can hide the names list by choosing View→Card Only, or bring it back with View→List and Card.)

Once you make Contacts the central repository of all your personal contact information, you can call up this information in a number of convenient ways:

- **You can open Contacts and then search for a contact** by typing just a few letters in the search box.

- **Regardless of what program you're in,** you can use a single keystroke (the ⊙ key on aluminum keyboards) to summon the Contacts Dashboard widget. There you can search for any contact you want. When you're done, hide the widget with the same quick keystroke.

- **When you're composing messages in Mail,** Contacts automatically fills in email addresses for you when you type the first few letters.

Tip: If you choose Window→Address Panel (Option-⌘-A) from within Mail, you can browse all your addresses without even launching the Contacts program. Once you've selected the people you want to contact, just click the To button to address an email to them—or, if you already have a new email message open, to add them to the recipients.

- **When you use Messages to chat** with people in Contacts, the pictures you've stored of them automatically appear in chat windows.

- **The free iCloud service can synchronize your contacts** to the Web so you can see them while you're away from your Mac.

- **Contacts can sync with an iPod, iPhone, or iPad,** giving you a "little black book" that fits in your shirt pocket, can be operated one-handed, and comes with built-in musical accompaniment. You can have that happen wirelessly, using iCloud, or wirefully, when you connect your iPod/iPhone/iPad to your Mac. (To set this up, open iTunes while your i-gadget is connected. Click the i-gadget's icon; on the Contacts or Info tab, turn on Synchronize Contacts.)

You can find Contacts in your Applications folder or in the Dock.

Importing Addresses

The easiest way to add people to Contacts is to import them from another service, like Yahoo or Exchange, or another program, like Microsoft Outlook (for Mac) or Entourage.

Importing from Yahoo, Google, Exchange, or another Internet service

Contacts can synchronize its contacts with online Rolodexes that may be very important to you: your Gmail (Google) contacts, Yahoo contacts, iCloud address book, or your company's Microsoft Exchange master address book (Figure 18-20).

In Contacts, choose Contacts→Preferences→Accounts. There, staring you in the face, are checkboxes that let you sync your contacts with iCloud, Yahoo, Google. Turn on the checkbox you want, click Configure, agree to the legalese, enter your account information, and boom—you're done. Contacts is now synced with your online accounts. Change information in one place, and it's also changed in the other. Even your contacts' photos, if your online address book has them, show up in Contacts!

Tip: You can also enter this information in the Mail, Contacts & Calendars pane of System Preferences.

If some other online service maintains your address book, Contacts can sync with it, too, as long as it uses one of the standard sharing formats (Exchange, CardDAV, or Lightweight Directory Access Protocol, known by the pros as LDAP). To teach Contacts about those, choose Contacts→Preferences→Accounts. Click the **+** button in the lower left, enter your account information on the resulting screen, click Create, and away you go.

Note: Contacts may display an advanced Account Settings screen, where you have to enter more detailed information. If you're a hands-on sort of nerd, you can also force this screen to open on your command. To do that, press Option and point to the Create button, which now says Continue. Click it.

Figure 18-20:
Contacts can sync your digital Rolodex with online contact managers like Yahoo and Google. Turn on the appropriate checkbox to enter your account name and password. For other account types, like Exchange, click the + button below the list to begin.

Once you've set up a Contacts account, you can also change its settings, right there in the same Preferences dialog box. Specify how often you want your Mac to sync changes with the online account, for example.

Importing from another address-book program

Contacts can also slurp in contact info from other address-book or list programs, like Microsoft Outlook (Entourage), Palm Desktop, Excel, and others. Not directly, of course; that would be too easy. But most of those programs can *export* their information as an intermediary file in one of four popular formats: vCard, LDAP Interchange Format (LDIF), tab-delimited, or comma-separated value (CSV).

For example, Microsoft's programs can export addresses as vCards; Thunderbird can export in LDIF format; Excel can export tab-delimited or CSV files.

It's a fine art, this importing business; all kinds of things can go wrong. The fields (like Name, Street, Phone) may not be in the right order. Tab-separated export files may not have the right number of empty fields. And so on.

For best results, choose Contacts→Help, and search for "Importing contacts from other applications." The resulting page gives special tips for each kind of export/import file format. (Fortunately, if the fields are out of order, Contacts will offer you the chance to straighten them out.)

About vCards

Contacts exchanges contact information with other programs primarily through *vCards.* vCard is short for *virtual business card.* More and more email programs send and receive these electronic business cards, which you can identify by their .vcf file name extensions (if, that is, you've set your Mac to display these extensions).

If you ever receive an email with a vCard file attached, drag the .vcf file into your Contacts window to create an instant entry with a complete set of information. You can create vCards of your own, too. Just drag a name out of your Contacts and onto the desktop (or into a piece of outgoing mail).

Tip: In addition to letting you create vCards of individual entries, Contacts makes it easy to create vCards that contain several entries. To do so, ⌘-click the entries in the Name column that you want included, and drag them to the desktop. There they'll appear all together as a single vCard. You can even drag an item from the Group page to the desktop to make a vCard that contains all the group's entries.

Keep this trick in mind if you ever want to copy all your contacts from an old PC to a new Mac. By creating a single vCard containing all your contacts, you've made it trivial to import them into the copy of Contacts running on your new Mac.

Creating Address Cards

Each entry in Contacts is called a *card*—like a paper Rolodex card, with predefined spaces to hold all the standard contact information.

To add a new person, choose File→New Card, press ⌘-N, or click the **+** button beneath the Name column. Then type in the contact information, pressing the Tab key to move from field to field, as shown in Figure 18-21.

Tip: If you find yourself constantly adding the same fields to new cards, check out the Template pane of Contacts's Preferences (Contacts→Preferences). There you can customize exactly which fields appear for new cards.

Figure 18-21 shows some unusual fields that you can plug into your address cards. The phonetic first/last name fields (shown at top) let you store phonetic spellings of hard-to-pronounce names. There's a Birthday field and a place to store the Twitter name, too. To add fields like these, choose from the Card→Add Field menu.

Each card also contains a free-form Note field at the bottom, where you can type any other random crumbs of information you'd like to store about the person (pet's name, embarrassing nicknames, favorite Chinese restaurant, and so on).

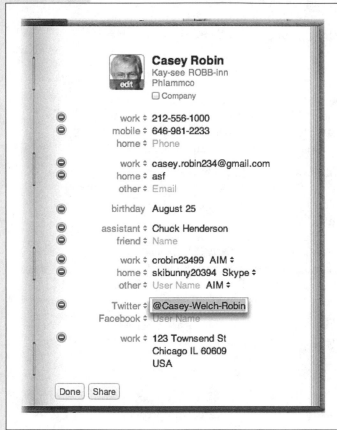

Figure 18-21:
If one of your contacts happens to have three office phone extensions, a pager number, two home phone lines, a cellphone, and a couple of fax machines, no problem—you can add as many fields as you need. Each time you fill up a phone, email, chat name, or address box, a new, empty one magically sprouts up to accommodate another one. Click a field's name to change its label; you can select one of the standard labels from the pop-up menu (Home, Work, and so on) or make up your own labels by choosing Custom.

Editing an address

When you create a new address card, you're automatically in Edit mode, which means you can add and remove fields and change the information on the card. To switch into Browse mode (where you can view and copy contact information but not change it), click the Edit button or choose Edit→Edit Card (⌘-L). You can also switch *out* of Browse Mode in the same ways.

Adding addresses from Mail

You can also make new contacts right in Mail, saving you the trouble of having to type names and email addresses manually. Select a message in Mail, and then choose Message→Add Sender to Contacts (Shift-⌘-Y). Presto: OS X adds a new card to the Contacts, with the name and email address fields already filled in. Later, you can edit the card in Contacts to add phone numbers, street addresses, and so on.

Tip: If you enter some people's birthdays in Contacts, they can show up automatically in Calendar. To make that happen, open Calendar, and then choose Calendar→Preferences→General. Turn on "Show Birthdays calendar."

Groups

A *group* is a collection of related address cards, saved under a single descriptive name (see Figure 18-22).

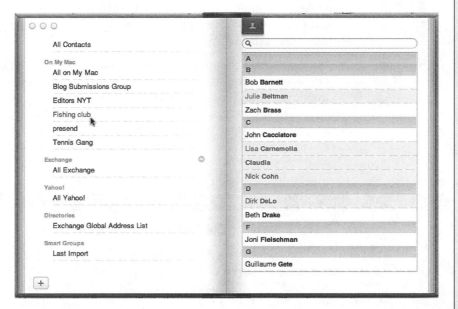

Figure 18-22:
If you regularly send out a family newsletter to 35 relatives, you might gather the address cards of all your assorted siblings, cousins, nieces, nephews, uncles, and aunts into a single group called Family. When addressing an outgoing message using Mail, you can type this group name to reach all your kin at once.

Organizing your contacts into groups can make them much easier to find and use—especially when your database of addresses climbs into the hundreds.

Tip: When you send an email message to a group en masse, how does Mail know *which* email address to use for each person?

Because you've *told* it. In Contacts, choose Edit→Edit Distribution List. A special dialog box appears, listing everyone in each group, along with each person's complete list of email addresses. (Use the tiny pop-up menu above the list to choose Phone or Address; that way, you can also indicate the preferred phone number and mailing address.) Just click the preferred email address to make it bold.

To see your groups, choose View→Groups, press ⌘-3, or click the red bookmark at the top of the page that shows individuals' names.

To create a group, click the **+** button at the bottom of the Group column in the Contacts window, or choose File→New Group (Shift-⌘-N.) Type a name for the newly spawned group icon in the Group column.

Now you have to fill up the group with the appropriate subset of names. There are three ways to do that:

- To turn a set of address cards into a group very quickly when you're in regular address-book mode (not Groups), select multiple entries from the Names column. You can do that either by Shift-clicking the names (to make contiguous selections) or by ⌘-clicking (for noncontiguous selections)—and then choose File→New Group From Selection. You end up with a new group containing all the selected names.

- While you're on the Groups page, click All Contacts at the top of the screen. Now your full names list appears on the right page; drag them directly onto the group names to put them there.

- If you're not on the Groups page, drag contacts up onto the Groups bookmark at the top of the page—leave the mouse button down as Contacts shows you the Groups page—and continue dragging onto the group's name.

Note: You're not *moving* those names; in essence, you're just creating *aliases* of them, just as you might put songs in different playlists in iTunes. The only exception is Exchange accounts; those names can exist in only one group or folder at a time.

TROUBLESHOOTING MOMENT

Resolving Conflicts and Duplicates

Suppose you tell Contacts to sync its information with one of your online accounts. And suppose that someone is listed in both places—with a different phone number in each place. Which address-book information "wins"? What's the Mac supposed to do?

Ask you, of course.

And that's exactly what it does.

The first warning you may see lets you know that the other address book is very different from the one on your Mac—more than, say, 25 percent different. If you know what you're doing, go ahead and click Sync Contacts. If you'd like to inspect the differences name by name, click Show Details instead. You'll see a summary box that indicates how many people need to be added to one list or the other, and how many people's information is different.

That "these two address books are radically different" warning isn't quite the same thing as the warning you may get about sync conflicts. That's when you've entered the same person into each address book source, but with different information. Maybe one has a different phone number, for example. If you click Review Now, you're shown one conflict after another—the complete address cards—so that you can make a ruling on which version "wins."

One other problem may crop up when you're combining accounts: You may wind up with duplicates.

Fortunately, Contacts is ready for you here. On the Groups page (press ⌘-3), click the account with the problem (or All Contacts). Choose Card→Look for Duplicates.

The program lets you know about any duplicates it finds, even if only the name is the same and everything else is different. It even flags cards that have duplicate bits of information, like the same phone number twice. All you have to do is click Merge; Contacts merges the multiple cards into a single one, preserving all the details that are unique to each. (If there were duplicate photos, whichever one was on the first card becomes the new photo.)

Once you've created some groups, you can even add groups to *other* groups, as though you were nesting folders. You might find it useful to keep a Nieces group and a Nephews group, for example, but to keep both groups inside a master Family group. To do this, create the two groups. Then drag each onto the Family group. Now, whenever you select Family, you'll see both Nieces and Nephews listed among the rest of the cards; double-click either group to see its members.

Tip: If, while viewing the list of groups, you Option-click someone's name in the main list, Contacts shows you all the groups and folders that person belongs to.

Smart groups

The Finder has smart folders, Mail has smart mailboxes, and iTunes has smart playlists; inevitably, Contacts has smart *groups.*

Smart address groups, like smart folders in the Finder, automatically populate themselves with items that match criteria you specify. For example, you might create a smart group called "Apple Employees" that lists all your contacts with "apple.com" in their email addresses. Or when you visit Detroit, you could whip up a group that lists everyone you know who lives there.

To create a smart group, choose File→New Smart Group (Option-⌘-N). Then use the resulting dialog box (which looks a lot like Mail's smart mailbox dialog box) to specify how you'd like the smart group to fill itself.

Once you're done, you can use your new smart group much like you'd use a regular group. You can't add contacts to a smart group yourself, but you can still send an email to all the members of a smart group, for example, or drag one to the Finder to create a composite vCard.

Removing someone from a group

To take someone out of a group, first click the group name, and then click the person's name in the Name column and press the Delete key. If you want to remove the person from Contacts *itself,* click Delete in the resulting dialog box. Otherwise, just click Remove from Group or press Return. Contacts keeps the card but removes it from the currently selected group.

Note: If you selected All Contacts in the Group column, rather than a specific group, you don't get a Remove from Group option. Instead, the Mac just asks you to confirm that you do, in fact, want to permanently remove the card.

Adding Pictures

You can dress up each Contacts entry with a photo. Whenever you're editing somebody's address book card, drag a digital photo—preferably 64 pixels square, or a multiple of that—onto the empty headshot square; the image shows up. Or double-click the picture well. Now you can choose from categories like Defaults (canned symbolic photos like animals and bugs); Recents (photos you've used recently); Camera (handy

if this person is *with* you—take a new photo); and Linked (photos from online services like Facebook). Don't miss the swirly button next to it, which lets you apply nutty Photo Boothish effects. At that point, you can enlarge, reposition, and crop the new photo. Click Done when you're done.

You don't necessarily have to use a photo, of course. You could add any graphic that you want to represent someone, even if it's a Bart Simpson face or a skull and crossbones. You can use any standard image file format in an address card—JPEG, GIF, PNG, TIFF, or even PDF. You can drag any of these directly into one of the squares here.

From now on, if you receive an email from that person, the photo shows up right in the email message—even on your phone or iPad.

Tip: If you've got snapshots in iPhoto, it's particularly easy to add a picture to any address card. Just drag a picture directly from the main iPhoto window to the picture frame on the address card to insert it.

Replacing and removing a picture

To replace a photo on an address card, just drag a new image on top of the old one. If you want to get rid of an existing picture without replacing it, select the card, and then choose Card→Clear Custom Image (or, in Edit mode, select the picture and then press Delete).

Free Headshots from Facebook

Yes, there's a little photo well on each card of your Contacts app. But here's a wild guess: Most of yours are empty. After all: Who's going to go to the trouble of hunting down headshots of 500 acquaintances, just so they fully illustrate their Contacts?

Fortunately, Mountain Lion stands ready to help. With one click, it can harvest headshots from the world's largest database of names and faces: Facebook. (This assumes you've installed the fall 2012 software update that brings Facebook to Mountain Lion.)

Visit System Preferences→Mail, Contacts, Calendars (or MCC, as they call it at Apple). Click your Facebook account to see the magical button: Get Profile Photos. When you click it, Mountain Lion goes online for a massive research mission. Using your contacts' names and phone numbers as matching criteria, it ventures off to Facebook, finds the profile photos of every one on your Contacts, and installs them into Contacts automatically.

Crazier still, it even grabs the headshots of people in your Contacts who *aren't your Facebook friends!*

If you have already a photo for somebody, don't worry; it doesn't get replaced. Of course, you can switch to the new Facebook profile picture if you prefer. Use the Linked heading in the photo picker as described above.

Tip: You can use the Get Profile Photos button even if you don't want your Facebook friends loaded into your copy of Contacts (by turning off Contacts in System Preferences→Mail, Contacts, Calendars→Facebook).

Finding an Address

You can search for a Contacts entry inside the currently selected group by typing a few letters of a name (or address, or any other snippet of contact information) in the search box. To search *all* your contacts instead of just the current group, click All Contacts in the Group list.

Tip: You can press ⌘-F to jump directly to the search field and start typing. Your savings: one mouse click.

With each letter you type, Contacts filters your social circle and displays the number of matches at the bottom. The matching records themselves appear in the Name column, the first of the matching card entries appears in the far-right pane, and the matching text itself appears highlighted in the matching card.

If Contacts finds more than one matching card, use the ↓ and ↑ keys, or Return and Shift-Return, to navigate through them.

Once you've found the card you're looking for, you can perform some interesting stunts. If you click the label of a phone number ("home" or "office," for example), you see the Show in Large Type option: Contacts displays the number in an absurdly gigantic font that fills the entire width of your screen, making it possible to read the

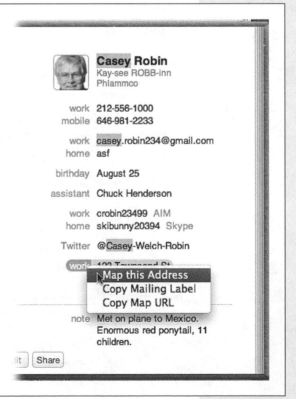

Figure 18-23:
The options that become available when you click the field labels on an address card vary according to field type. Pop-up menus let you send email, open a Web page, or view a map, depending on the type of field you've clicked.

New in Mountain Lion: The Send Message command. It sends an iMessage to the phone number or email address whose label you've clicked—if, in fact, it's an iMessages-registered number or address.

number as you dial from across the room. You can also click the label of an email address to create a preaddressed email message, or click a home page to launch your Web browser and go to somebody's site.

Tip: That same pop-up menu lists FaceTime. That is, you can begin a FaceTime video call right from the Contacts.

You can also copy and paste (or drag) address card info into another program or convert it into a Sticky Note.

Tip: Once you find a street address in your Contacts, you can find those coordinates on a map by Control-clicking (or right-clicking) the address's *label* and choosing Map This Address from the shortcut menu, as shown in Figure 18-23. Your Web browser obediently leaps up to display the address on a Google map.

Changing the Contacts Display

You can't do much to customize Contacts's appearance, but the Preferences pane (Contacts→Preferences) gives you at least a couple of options in the General pane that are worth checking out:

- **Show first name.** Choose to have names displayed with the first name followed by the last name, or vice versa.

- **Sort By.** Sort the entries in Contacts by either first or last name.

Printing Options

When you choose File→Print and click Show Details, the Style pop-up menu offers four ways to print whatever addresses are selected at the moment:

- **Mailing Labels.** This option prints addresses on standard sheets of sticky mailing labels—Avery, for example—that you buy at office-supply stores.

Tip: As you manipulate settings, you can see your changes in the preview pane on the left. If the preview is too small for you to see, use the Zoom slider. (It doesn't affect your printout.)

- **Envelopes.** This feature is great if you have bad handwriting; rather than hand addressing your envelopes, you can have Contacts print them out for you. Use the Layout pop-up menu to pick the size of your envelopes—it's usually listed on the outside of the envelope box.

Note: Both the Mailing Labels and Envelopes options print *only* the contacts for which you have, in fact, entered physical mailing addresses.

- **Lists.** If all you want is a paper backup of your Contacts entries, then use this setting. In the Attributes list, turn on the checkboxes of the fields you want printed—just name and phone number, for example.

- **Pocket Contacts.** This feature prints out a convenient *paper* address book from your virtual one. If you pick Indexed from the Flip Style pop-up menu, then each page's edge will even list the first letters of the last names listed on the page, making it a cinch to find the page with the address you want. (Here again, you can pick which fields you'd like to include—phone numbers, addresses, and so on.)

As you fiddle with the options presented here, you get to see a miniature preview, right in the dialog box, that shows what you're going to get.

No matter which mode you choose, the only cards that print are the ones that were selected when you chose File→Print. If you want to print *all* your cards, therefore, click All in the Group column before you print.

Figure 18-24:
To see which accounts Contacts is combining for you for this person, scroll to the bottom of the card. There, the Linked Cards section shows you which cards have been unified. It might list, for example, On My Mac, Yahoo, and Facebook. In other words, this card's underlying information comes from three different places: your Mac's own Contacts list, your Yahoo address book, and this person's Facebook page.

You can click one of these gray links to open the corresponding, underlying card from just that service, as shown below.

Facebook data
("f" logo)

Tip: You can combine the smart-groups feature with the printing features in one clever way: to print yourself a portable phone book when you're heading off for a visit to a different city. That is, set up a smart group that rounds up everyone you know who lives in Chicago, and then print that as a pocket address book.

Linked Cards

Contacts can sync up with different accounts. Yours might wind up containing three or four sets of names and numbers: one stored on your phone, one from an iCloud account, and a third from Facebook. In the old days, therefore, certain names might have shown up in the All Contacts list multiple times—not an optimal situation.

Now, as a favor to you, Contacts can display each person's name only once in the master All Contacts list. If you click that name, you open up a unified card for that person. It includes all the details from all the underlying cards from that person, cleanly merged into a virtual combined card. See Figure 18-24 for details.

You can also unlink one of the cards: tap the ⊖ button next to its account's name (you're just unlinking, not deleting any card). For that matter, you can manually link cards together, too. Select both (or several) by ⌘-clicking them. Then choose Card→Merge and Link Selected Cards.

Tip: It's OK to manually link Joe Carnelia's card with Joseph Carnelia's card this way–they're probably the same person. But don't link up *different* people's cards. Remember, the whole point is to make Contacts combine all the phone numbers, email addresses, and so on onto a single card–which, for two different people, could get confusing fast.

Clearly, this stuff gets complex. But in general, Contacts tries to do the right thing. For example, if you edit the information on the unified card, you're actually changing that information only on the card in the corresponding account. (Unless you add information to the *unified* card. In that case, the new data tidbit is added to *all* the underlying source-account cards.)

Tip: If you need to see two people's cards simultaneously, double-click each one in the list. That makes them open into individual windows.

Contacts Backups

Your Contacts may represent *years* of typing and compiling effort. Losing all that information to a corrupted database or a hard drive crash could be devastating. Here are three ways to protect your Contacts data:

- **Back up your entire Contacts database.** Choose File→Export→Contacts Archive. Store the resulting backup file on another drive, if you like. Later, you can use the File→Import command to find that data and slurp it back in.

- **Turn on iCloud syncing.** An iCloud account has its privileges—and one of them is automatic synchronizing with the iCloud mother ship online.

- **Back up your whole Mac with Time Machine.** Chapter 6 tells you how.

Safari

The Internet has come a long way since its early days in the 1960s, when it was a communications network for universities and the military. Today, that little network has morphed into an international information hub, an entertainment provider, and the world's biggest mall. For that, we can thank the development of the World Wide Web—the visual, point-and-click face of the Internet.

Apple is obviously intrigued by the possibilities of the Internet. With each new release of OS X, more clever tendrils reach out from the Mac to the world's biggest network: the Share button, integrated Facebook and Twitter, Dashboard, the Wikipedia link in the Dictionary program, Web clippings, Back to My Mac, and so on.

But Apple's most obvious Internet-friendly creation is Safari, a smartly designed window to the Web (available for OS X and, believe it or not, Windows). Most people go on safari to see mountain lions—but now there's a great Safari in Mountain Lion.

Herewith is what may be the world's best and most complete coverage of Safari, all in one place, so you can get right to work killing time online.

Browsing Basics

You probably know the drill when it comes to Web browsers. When you click an underlined *link* (*hyperlink*) or a picture button, you're transported from one Web page to another. One page might be the home page of General Motors; another might contain critical information about a bill in Congress; another might have baby pictures posted by a parent in Omaha.

Tip: Text links aren't always blue and underlined. In fact, trendy Web designers sometimes make it very difficult to tell which text is clickable and which is just text. When in doubt, move your cursor over something; if the arrow changes to a pointing-finger cursor, you've found yourself a link.

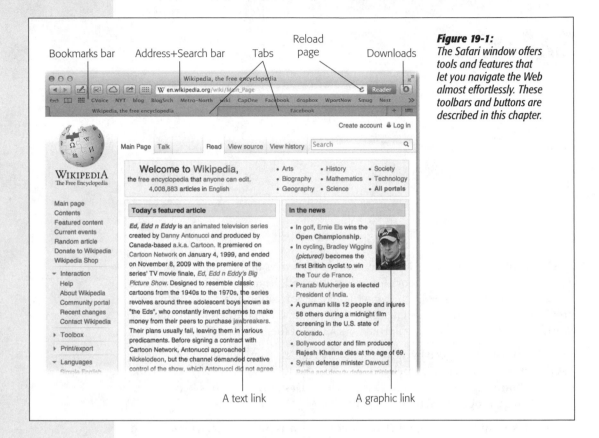

Figure 19-1:
The Safari window offers tools and features that let you navigate the Web almost effortlessly. These toolbars and buttons are described in this chapter.

The New, Unified Address/Search Bar

Often, of course, you'll want to type in a Web address; that's the purpose of the Address/Search bar identified in Figure 19-1. In Mountain Lion, a single, unified box serves as both the address bar and the search bar (Apple just calls it "the toolbar"). If you type a Web address there, like *amazon.com,* pressing Enter takes you to that Web site; if you type anything else, like *cashmere sweaters* or just *amazon,* pressing Enter gives you the Google search results for that phrase, as described next.

In general, it's handy to have a combined address bar/search bar (many other browsers work this way, too). Unfortunately, it means that you can no longer leave off the .com when you're typing an address—a longtime advantage of Safari's smart address bar.

Searching the Web

Press ⌘-L to deposit your insertion point inside the new unified toolbar, type something you're looking for—*phony baloney,* say—and then press Return. Safari takes you directly to the Google results page. As Figure 19-2 makes clear, Safari offers plenty of assistance as you type, in the form of Google suggestions and matching listings from your Bookmarks and History list.

Tip: You can turn off the Google suggestions in Safari→Preferences→Privacy. Turn on "Prevent search engine from providing suggestions."

Figure 19-2:
As you type, Safari offers autocomplete suggestions from Google's own Suggest feature; below that, it shows the matching pages that you've either book-marked or visited recently.

To spare yourself the tedium of typing, click the correct complete address with your mouse, or use the ↓ key to reach the desired listing and then press Return. The complete address you select pops into the toolbar.

If you prefer to use Bing or Yahoo for searching the Web instead of Google, open Safari→Preferences→General, and use the "Default search engine" pop-up menu.

Bonus Tip: If you Control-click (or right-click) a highlighted word or phrase on a Web page, you can choose Search with Google from the shortcut menu to search for that text. And, even cooler, this trick works in *all* Cocoa programs—not just Safari.

POWER USERS' CLINIC

The Ever-Shrinking SnapBack Feature

With every version of OS X, Apple seems to lose more enthusiasm for SnapBack. In Mountain Lion, even its little orange icon on the address bar (◄) has disappeared.

Still, SnapBack is hanging around in a bare-bones form, and it still does what it was designed to do: jump you back to the originating Google page of search results after you've burrowed from one link to another on a wild-link chase.

Try it. Do a search for something—"electric backscratcher," for example. Click one of the search results. Click a link on that page. Click another link on *that* page. No matter how far you get from your starting point, you can choose History→Search Results SnapBack (or press Option-⌘-S) to leap all the way back to the search-results page. From there, you can start barking up a different tree.

Address + Search Bar Tips

Because typing Internet addresses and searching for things are so central to the Internet experience and such a typo-prone hassle, the Address + Search bar is rich with features that minimize keystrokes. For example:

- **You don't have to click there before typing;** just press ⌘-L.

- **You can highlight the entire address** (so it's ready to be typed over with a new one) by clicking anywhere inside the bar. Or press ⌘-L.

- **You don't have to type out the whole Internet address.** You can omit the *http://* and *.www* portions; Safari fills in those standard address bits for you. To visit *http://www.nytimes.com,* for example, a speed freak might press ⌘-L to highlight the address bar, type *nytimes.com,* and then press Return.

- You're Web surfing, and you suddenly need to look up an appointment in Calendar. What do you do?

 The power user opens other programs right from within Safari by typing *ical://* in the address bar—or *ichat://, messages://,* or *addressbook://*—and then pressing Return. (Unfortunately, these Apple programs are generally the only ones that work with this URL-launching trick—and you have to use these apps' old names.)

 You can also type *mailto:* to open a new outgoing email message in your default email program, or *mailto:barney@dinosaur.com* to pre-address that outgoing message to Barney the Dinosaur. (Of course, remember to replace that email address with that of someone you'd actually like to contact.)

Tip: You might wonder why the View menu even offers you the chance to hide the address/search bar. If it were hidden, how could you use the Web?

Simple: Even with this bar hidden, you can briefly summon it by pressing ⌘-L. Type the address you want and then press Return to make the bar disappear again. That's good news for people with small screens—and for Mac trivia collectors.

Scrolling

You'll rarely do more page scrolling than you do in a Web browser. Scrolling is a *constant* activity.

Fortunately, Apple gives you about 11,339 different ways to do it.

You can use the regular scroll gesture (two fingers on the trackpad). You can also press your ↑ and ↓ keys to scroll one line at a time. Page Up and Page Down scroll in full-screen increments, while Home and End whisk you to the top or bottom of the current Web page. And if your mouse has a scroll wheel, it works, too. (Hold Shift while you're rolling the wheel to scroll *horizontally.*)

But maybe the best way of all is to *tap the space bar* each time you want to see more. Press Shift-space to scroll *up.* (The space bar serves its traditional, space-making function only when the insertion point is blinking in a text box or the address bar.)

Note: Let's raise our eyes to the heavens to give Apple a silent thanks. Scrolling happens to be one of the Safari features that Apple worked on in Mountain Lion. You should notice that scrolling is smooth and fluid, even when a page hasn't yet fully loaded.

Full Screen and Gestures

If any app is going to remind you of an iPhone/iPad, it's Safari. Once you enter full-screen mode by clicking the ⬈ button at upper right (see page 12), it's almost exactly like surfing the Web on the iPad. For example:

- **Zoom in and out with pinch and spread.** That is, put two fingers on your trackpad and spread them to magnify the Web page, or pinch to zoom out. Great when the type is a little too small.

- **Magnify just a block with a two-finger double-tap.** Most Web pages are subdivided into various rectangles of text or graphics. Just as on the iPhone/iPad, you can double-tap (with *two* fingers on your trackpad) to magnify only one single block of text or graphics. Repeat the process to zoom back out to regular size. (Note that this is *tapping,* not *clicking.)*

- **Use a two-finger swipe for Back and Next.** This one's really juicy. With two fingers on your trackpad, swipe left or right instead of clicking the ◀ or ▶ buttons. The great part is that if you do this *slowly,* you pull the previous or next page onto the screen *gradually,* giving you a chance to peek at it without actually moving to it.

Tip: Each time you open Safari, it brings up whatever pages you had open last. It's part of OS X's auto-resume feature.

Five Ways to Magnify a Page

If it seems as though a lot of Web sites are designed with type that's too small to read, it's not just you and your aging eyes. Often, it has to do with the high resolution of today's screens, which work by packing their pixels together more tightly—and making everything look smaller.

Fortunately, Safari is extremely well equipped to help you with this problem. In fact, it offers many solutions:

- **Enlarge the screen.** Press ⌘-plus or ⌘-minus to enlarge or reduce the entire Web page. Or use the two-finger "spread" gesture on your laptop trackpad. Or use the Zoom button, if you've added it to your toolbar. The advantage of this method is that the whole Web page's layout remains proportional.

- **Magnify a block.** Lightly double-tap (don't fully click) with *two fingers* on your trackpad to zoom into one block of text or graphics on a page, as described above.

- **Blow up just the text.** If you turn on View→Zoom Text Only, then all those short-cuts serve to magnify or shrink *only the text* on your page. Graphics remain at their original size. You're now distorting the original layout, but you're maximizing the amount of reading you can do before you have to scroll.

- **Zoom in the usual way.** Remember the Control-key zooming technique described on page 372? It's not the same thing as the ⌘-plus or ⌘-minus tricks, which keep the window frame and menu at normal size. The Control-key zooming technique magnifies *everything*—the entire screen, menus and all. It also doesn't keep text as sharp as the ⌘-plus/⌘-minus trick.

- **Specify a minimum type size.** This may be the best option of all, because it saves you all that zooming. Open Safari→Preferences→Advanced, and set the "Never use font sizes smaller than" option to, for example, 14 points. Now *every* Web page shows up with legible text. (Except a few oddballs that use weird coding to prevent text-size changing.)

Customizing the Toolbar

You can summon or dismiss a number of individual buttons on the toolbar, in effect customizing it (Figure 19-3). It's worth putting some thought into this tailoring, because some of these buttons' functions are really handy. So here's a catalog of your options:

- **Back/Forward.** Click the Back button (◄) to revisit the page you were just on. *Keyboard shortcut:* Delete, or ⌘-←, or ⌘-[, or a two-finger swipe left on the trackpad. (On a Mighty Mouse, that's a *one*-finger swipe.)

 Once you've clicked ◄, you can then click the ► button (or press ⌘-→, or ⌘-], or a two-finger swipe to the *right*) to return to the page you were on before you

Figure 19-3:
To summon this toolbar-tailoring screen, choose View→ Customize Toolbar. Then drag the buttons you want directly onto the address bar. In Mountain Lion, there are no longer text labels available for these icons. But all offer tooltip labels that you can read by pointing to the button without clicking.

clicked the Back button. Click and hold the ◄ or ► button for a drop-down list of *all* the Web pages you've visited during this online session.

That pop-up menu lists the sites by name, as in "The New York Times—Breaking News, World News & Multimedia." To view the actual *addresses* instead, Option-click (and hold the mouse down on) the ◄ or ► button.

- **Reading List.** This button hides or shows the Reading List, described at the beginning of this chapter.

- **iCloud Tabs.** New in Mountain Lion: A way to open whatever browser windows and tabs you had open on your other Apple gadget, like an iPhone or iPad or another Mountain Lion Mac. Thanks to the miracle of iCloud syncing, the last windows and tabs you had open on that other gadget (even if the gadget is turned off) show up here. See Figure 19-4.

Figure 19-4:
The iCloud Tabs concept is to unify your Macs and i-gadgets into one glorious, seamless Web-browsing experience. You're reading three browser windows and tabs of weight-lifting news on your phone—why not resume on the big screen when you get home and sit down in front of your Mac?

(You won't see these tabs unless the other gadget has iOS 6 or later and the other Macs have Mountain Lion or later. And, of course, the Safari checkbox has to be turned on in System Preferences→iCloud on the Macs, or Settings→iCloud on the phone or tablet.)

- **Share.** Yes, the new Mountain Lion Share button (📤) is also in Safari. Some of the features in this pop-up menu aren't new features: Add to Reading List, Add Bookmark, and Email Page, for example. But Message, Twitter, and Facebook are new. They let you send the current Web page as a text message, a tweet, or a Facebook update with a single click. See page 268 for details.

- **Top Sites.** This feature opens up the highly visual dashboard shown in Figure 19-5. These thumbnails represent what Safari has determined are your favorite Web sites, as calculated by how often and how recently you've visited them.

• **Home.** Click to bring up the Web page you've designated as your home page (in the Safari→Preferences→General tab).

Figure 19-5:
You can open the Top Sites display either by clicking the Top Sites button on the toolbar or by choosing History→Top Sites. Click a page to revisit it; a star in the corner means, "This page has changed since your last visit."

• **New Tab.** Creates a new tab (embedded window), described later in this chapter.

• **History.** Click to open the list of Web sites you've visited recently in a window—a much easier-to-navigate display than the History *menu*.

• **Bookmarks, Add Bookmark.** See page 728 for more on bookmarks.

• **Bookmarks Bar.** Hides or shows the horizontal toolbar that lists your favorite bookmarks. (The equivalent of choosing View→Bookmarks Bar.)

Tip: In Mountain Lion, you can rename a bookmark on the Boomarks bar just by click-and-holding on its name. You'll see it highlighted; you can just retype. No more right-clicking necessary!

• **AutoFill.** Click this button to make Safari fill in Web order forms with your name, address, and other information. See page 734.

• **Zoom.** You can adjust the size of a Web page's text using these buttons. When you visit a Web site designed for Windows computers—whose text often looks too small on Mac screens—you can use these buttons to bump up the size. The keyboard shortcuts are ⌘-plus or ⌘-minus.

- **Open in Dashboard.** This icon is the key to creating Dashboard *Web clips*, as described on page 194. Click this button, and then select the part of the page you want to widgetize. It's the equivalent of the File→Open in Dashboard command.

- **Mail.** Opens a new, outgoing email message in your email program. The subject line contains the *name* of the site you were visiting; the body contains the actual Web page—not just a link, as in the days before Mountain Lion. You can address the message, add a comment ("Re: your comment that 'no expert' recommends trampolines for children"), and send it.

- **Print.** You can add a printer icon to Safari for point-and-click paper action if you don't want to bother with ⌘-P.

Tip: Safari automatically shrinks your printouts, if necessary, by up to 10 percent, if doing so will avoid printing a second page with just one or two lines of text on it. Nice.

- **Downloads.** Here's that awesome Downloads button described at the beginning of this chapter. (It's available only as part of the standard toolbar; you can't install it independently.)

- **Web Inspector.** This button is intended for Web designers and programmers (it appears only if you've visited Safari→Preferences and turned on "Show Develop menu in menu bar"). Clicking it opens a technical-looking window that lists everything on the current Web page: documents, style sheets, and scripts. Using the

POWER USERS' CLINIC

Customizing Top Sites

Ordinarily, the Top Sites display changes over time, as your tastes and your activity change. But you can override Safari's attempt to curate this page in various ways. For example, you can pin a certain site so that it never leaves the Top Sites screen, or you can manually add a page.

It all happens when you click the Edit button in the lower left. Each thumbnail sprouts two buttons in the corner: the **×** button (this page will never again appear on Top Sites) and the thumbtack button (this page will always appear in Top Sites, even if you don't visit it much).

To add a new page to the Top Sites display, first open that page in another Safari window. Then highlight its address in the address bar and drag it right onto the Top Sites page. You can also drag a Web link from an email message, text document, Web page, or any other source to the Top Sites page.

You can reorder the thumbnails, too, just by dragging them around on this screen.

Finally, you can change the thumbnail size on this Edit screen, too. Use the Small/Medium/Large control in the lower right; the smaller the thumbnails, the more of them fit (24, 12, or six, respectively).

buttons across the top, you can also view statistics like how long each resource takes to load, and how much bandwidth (Internet data) this page requires.

- **Report Bug.** Ladies and gentlemen, this is Apple at its most humble. This insect-shaped button opens a tiny "Dear Apple" box, where you can tell Apple about a Safari feature or a Web page that doesn't work. If you click Options, you can even send Apple a screen illustration of, for example, a screwy Web page layout that Safari delivered.

- **Address/Search bar.** Yep, it's the toolbar, where you type in the Web address you want to call up.

The Stop/Reload button is built into the address bar, at the right end. Click the Stop button (or Esc, or ⌘-period) to interrupt the downloading of a Web page you've just requested—if you've made a mistake, for instance.

Once a page has finished loading, the Stop button turns into a Refresh button. Click this circular arrow (or press ⌘-R) if a page doesn't look or work quite right, or if you want to see the updated version of it (like for a breaking-news site that changes constantly). Safari redownloads the Web page and reinterprets its text and graphics.

Bookmarks

When you find a Web page you might like to visit again, bookmark it. Press ⌘-D, or choose Bookmarks→Add Bookmark, or drag the tiny Web-page icon from the address bar directly onto your Bookmarks bar.

As shown in Figure 19-6, Safari offers to add this Web page's name (or a shorter name that you specify for it) either to the Bookmarks menu or to the Bookmarks bar (described below). The next time you want to visit that page, just select its name in whichever location you chose.

Tip: Press Shift-⌘-D to add the bookmark to the menu instantly—no questions asked, no dialog box presented.

The ⌘ (Bookmarks) button on the toolbar opens the Bookmarks editing window (Figure 19-6). Here you can rearrange the names in your Bookmarks menu easily, or peruse them by scrolling through their giant Cover Flow thumbnails—a great feature in a Web browser, because a visual representation of a page is a lot more helpful than some Web address.

(Even without the ⌘ button, you can get there by choosing Bookmarks→Show All Bookmarks or by pressing Option-⌘-B.)

In the resulting organization window, drag the bookmarks up and down. Figure 19-6 also shows you how to perform more dramatic management tasks, like editing, renaming, or deleting bookmarks.

The Bookmarks menu is one way to maintain a list of Web sites you visit frequently. But opening a Web page from that menu requires *two mouse clicks*—an exorbitant expenditure of energy. The Bookmarks bar (View→Bookmarks Bar), on the other hand, lets you summon a few *very* favorite Web pages with only one click.

Tip: If you have a bunch of bookmarks stored in another Web browser, use that browser's export feature to save them to a file, and then use Safari's File→Import Bookmarks command to save you the time of re-entering the bookmarks by hand.

Figure 19-6 illustrates how to add buttons to, and remove them from, this toolbar.

Figure 19-6:
Top: Once you've got a juicy Web page on the screen, you can drag its page-logo icon (left end of the address bar) from the toolbar directly onto the Bookmarks bar or menu.

Second from top: Safari realizes that you may prefer a shorter name to appear on the space-limited bar, so it offers you the chance to type in a new label.

Third from top: When you click OK, the button appears on the bar. (You can also drag any link to the bar, such as a blue underlined phrase from a Web page, or even an icon from your desktop!) To remove a button, drag it off the bar.

Bottom: Click the ⌘ icon (left end of toolbar) to open the Organize Bookmarks window. Here you can drag names up or down to rearrange the list, or drag them into a submenu in the Bookmarks menu. (Create a submenu by clicking the + button below the list.) You can edit a bookmark by clicking once on its name or URL, or delete one by pressing Delete.

Tip: As shown in Figure 19-6, you can drag a link from a Web page onto your Bookmarks bar. But you can also drag a link directly to the desktop, where it turns into an *Internet location file.* Thereafter, to launch your browser and visit the associated Web page whenever you like, just double-click this icon.

Better yet, stash a few of these icons in your Dock or Sidebar for even easier access.

Status Bar

The status bar at the bottom of the window tells you what Safari is doing (such as "Opening page…" or "Done"). When you point to a link without clicking, the status bar also tells you which URL will open if you click it. For those two reasons, it's a very useful strip, but it doesn't appear when you first run Safari. You have to summon it by choosing View→Show Status Bar.

15 Tips for Better Surfing

Safari is filled with shortcuts and tricks for better speed and more pleasant surfing. For example:

The Reading List

The Reading List is a hide-able panel at the left side of the screen that lists Web pages you want to read later (Figure 19-7).

Until Mountain Lion, the Reading List didn't actually store the pages on the Mac; it basically stored a link to the bookmarked page, just like a bookmark. You couldn't read it later unless you were actually online.

In Mountain Lion, though, the Reading List actually stores each page you've requested. Better than that, actually: It store that page *and* any other pages necessary to continue reading an article that you've flagged.

Meanwhile, the Reading List still has some advantages over bookmarks. For example, it's faster to flag a Web page you like—you don't have to make up a name or a location for it, as with a bookmark. Also, the Reading List keeps track of what you've read; you can use the All/Unread buttons at the top of the list to view everything, or just what you haven't yet read. You might treat the Reading List as a list of pages you'll want to read *once* later, and use bookmarks for pages you like to revisit *frequently.*

To make matters even sweeter, iCloud synchronizes your Reading List among your Mac, iPhone, iPad, and so on—as long as you've turned on bookmark syncing. It's as though the Web always keeps your place.

To add a page to the Reading List, use one of these techniques:

- **Shift-click a link.** That simple trick adds the linked page to the Reading List. You don't have to *visit* the page itself (only the link to it), or even open the Reading List itself.

- **Use the menu.** If you're already *on* the page you might want to read later, choose Bookmarks→Add to Reading List, or press Shift-⌘-D.

- **Use the Share button.** You can also click the ⬆ button on the toolbar and choose Add to Reading List.

- **Use the Reading List.** If the Reading List is already open, just click Add Page to add the current page to the list.

You can view your saved pages by clicking the ⊶ button on the toolbar, or by choosing View→Show Reading List (Shift-⌘-L).

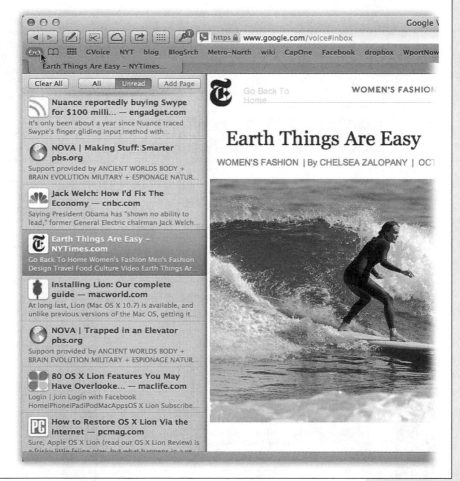

Figure 19-7:
To revisit a page you've set aside in the Reading List, just click it. Screen out the pages you've already read by clicking the Unread tab at the top. Delete an entry by clicking the ⊗ button that appears at the right side when you point there.

To read the pages in the Reading List, you can press Option-⌘-↓ or Option-⌘-↑ to move up and down your list.

Tip: If you're reading one article in your Reading List using the Reader feature described on the next page, and then select another article, it, too, will appear in Reader.

Reader

How can people read Web articles when there's Times-Square blinking going on all around them? Fortunately, you'll never have to put up with that again.

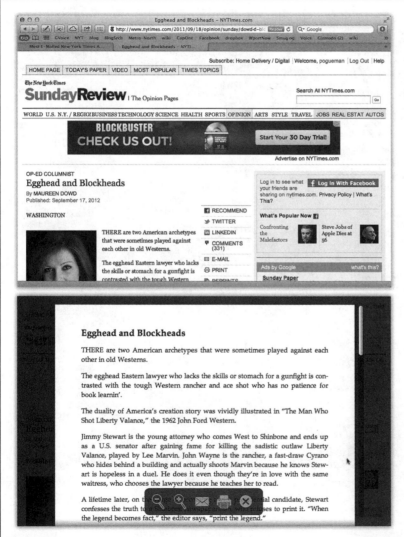

Figure 19-8:
Seriously, which way would you rather read an article? Like this (top)? Or in the calm peace of this (bottom)? Not only does Reader get rid of all the ads and clutter and blinking, it even knits together multipage articles into one seamless scrolling page. Use the space bar or two fingers to scroll, as usual. Point near the bottom of the page to produce a palette of useful buttons: "Zoom out," "Zoom in," "Mail this page," "Print this page," and "Hide Reader."

The Reader button in the address bar is amazing. With one click (or press Shift-⌘-R), it eliminates *everything* from the Web page you're reading except the text and photos. No ads, blinking, links, banners, promos, or anything else.

The text is also changed to a clean, clear font and size, and the background is made plain white. Basically, it makes any Web page look like a printed book page or a Kindle page, and it's glorious (Figure 19-8).

Figure 19-9:
Click the Downloads (⊙) button to view this list of recent downloads. Double-click an icon to open the download. Drag it out of the list onto your Desktop, or even onto a folder on the Desktop. You can even drag it onto a Dock icon to open that file with a particular program.

Click the ⊙ button to jump to the file wherever it's sitting in the Finder. To remove an item from the list, click it and then press Delete. (The Clear button erases the whole list.)

To exit Reader, press the same keyboard shortcut, or click the Reader button again.

Best. Feature. Ever.

The Download Manager

No browser has ever made tracking downloads simpler.

When you click a link to download something from a Web page, it *visibly* flies to the upper-right corner of the Safari window, where the Downloads button ⊙ appears. You can then monitor the progress of the download at a glance—because the Downloads button *fills up* with blue as the download completes.

15 Tips for Better Surfing

As Figure 19-9 shows, you can also view and manipulate a list of everything you've downloaded recently, all without leaving the comfort of whatever page you're on.

To pause downloading, click the ⊗ button next to the download's name. Later, you can generally pick up from where you left off by clicking the Resume (⏻) button.

Tip: In Safari→Preferences→General, you can opt to have your download listings removed from the Downloads window as soon as they've been successfully downloaded. You might want to do that for privacy reasons, or just because there's no reason to keep looking at them in the list once they're done.

Let AutoFill Do the Typing

Safari can remember user names, passwords, and other information you type into the text boxes you encounter in your Web travels.

To turn on this great feature, visit the Safari→Preferences→AutoFill tab. If you turn on "Using info from my Contacts card," then whenever you're supposed to fill in your shipping address on a Web form, you can click the AutoFill button in the address bar to have Safari fill in the blanks for you automatically. (If you don't see the AutoFill button, then choose Edit→AutoFill Form to do the deed instead.)

Alternatively, just click a text box—Name, for example—and start typing. As soon as Safari recognizes a familiar scrap of your contact information, it displays a pop-up suggestion below the text box. To accept the suggestion, click it (or press the ↓ arrow key and then press Return). To decline it, press Return, or just keep typing.

Figure 19-10:
Choose Safari→Preferences→Passwords to see this master list of all the Web-site user names and passwords Safari has memorized for you. It's easy enough to delete one. But maybe the more useful option is the "Show passwords" checkbox. After you authenticate with your account password, it shows you the actual passwords instead of dots—a great feature if, by some chance, you weren't born with a memory like an elephant's.

734 OS X: THE MISSING MANUAL

Tip: There's one more bit of memorizing that Mountain Lion can do for you. The first time you log into your Gmail, Yahoo, or AOL email account, Safari pops up a message that invites you to use that account as the source of your mail, calendar, and chat information for Mail, Calendar, and Messages. If you click Add Account, then OS X opens the corresponding app and fills in the account information automatically, based on what you just typed while logging in.

Memorized Passwords

If, in Preferences, you turn on "User names and passwords," then each time you type a password into a Web page, Safari offers to memorize it for you. It's a great time- and brain-saver, even though it doesn't work on all Web sites. (Of course, use it with caution if you share an account on your Mac with other people.)

Turn on Other Forms if you'd like Safari to remember the terms you've typed into search engines, shopping sites, online gaming sites, and so on.

[Thanks to Mountain Lion's new Passwords dialog box, it's now easy to see all the passwords Safari has saved for you—and to delete the ones you want Safari to "forget" —for security reasons, for example. See Figure 19-10.]

Where Am I?

Occasionally, you may wish you could view a little map that marks the path of the current Web page within its site. Ah, but Safari has already thought of that. See Figure 19-11.

Figure 19-11:
If you ⌘-click the title bar (centered just above the address bar), then Safari displays the "ladder" that shows the Web site's internal folder structure. That can be handy when you want to jump to this page's "parent" page.

Keyboard Control

Efficiency freaks generally prefer keyboard shortcuts to using the mouse, so Safari is filled with them.

Press Tab to jump from one text box or pop-up menu to the next on your Web page. Add the Option key to jump from one *link* to another (and when you highlight a link, press Return to "click" it).

Tip: For a shockingly complete list of Safari's keyboard shortcuts, open the Help menu. In the search box at the top of the menu, type *Safari shortcuts.* Wait a moment. Click "Safari shortcuts" in the list of Help topics.

Graphics Worth Saving

When you see a picture you'd like to keep, Control-click (or right-click) it and choose Save Image to Downloads (or Add Image to iPhoto Library, or just Save Image As) from the shortcut menu. Safari stores it as a new graphics file, freed from its birth-place on the Web. (You can specify where Safari saves downloaded pictures on the Safari→Preferences→General tab. In that case, the shortcut menu's wording changes to say, for example, "Save Image to 'Pictures.'")

Tip: You can also save a graphic to the desktop just by dragging it there, right out of the Safari window.

Saving Web Pages to Disk

You don't have to be connected to the Net to read a favorite Web page; you can tuck it away for later, thanks to the newly improved Reading List feature described earlier in this chapter.

The old way of saving a page, though, is still around. You can save it to your hard drive—to archive it for good, or to send it to somebody, for example—by choosing File→Save As.

At that point, to save the *entire* page, along with all its images, movies, and so on, choose Web Archive from the Format pop-up menu. (Choose Page Source only if you intend to *edit* the raw HTML Web documents and then repost them, or if you just want to study the underlying code.)

Tip: When you buy something online, don't waste paper by printing out the "This is your receipt" page. Instead, choose File→Print and, from the PDF pop-up button, choose Save PDF to Web Receipts Folder. Safari saves the page as a PDF file into a tidy folder (in your Home→Documents folder) called Web Receipts. Nice touch!

Sending a Page to a Friend

Safari provides two ways of telling a friend about the page you're looking at. You might find that useful when you come across a particularly interesting news story, op-ed piece, or burrito recipe.

- **The send-the-whole-page method.** While looking at a page, click the ⬆ button and choose Email This Page. You open a new Mail message with a copy of the *actual* Web page in the body. Address the message and click Send.

- **The send-a-link method.** To send just a *link* to the page you're looking at, install the Mail button (✉) onto the toolbar, as described earlier in this chapter. When you click it, Safari prepares an outgoing mail message containing only the *link* to the page you're on. Then proceed as usual, addressing the message and clicking Send.

Links take only a split second for your recipient to download, and they're guaranteed to display properly in all email programs. All your recipients have to do is click the link to open it in their Web browsers.

Tip: Or just press Shift-⌘-I. That keystroke sends a link to an outgoing mail message.

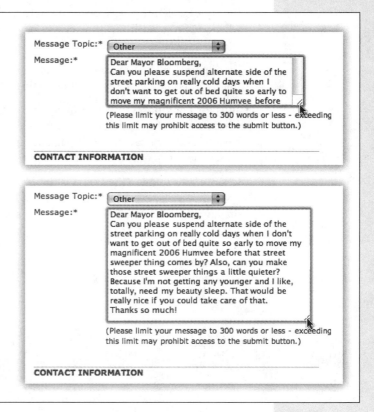

Figure 19-12:
This trick works on a Web page's text fields—comment boxes, forms to send a letter to the mayor, and so on. You can resize such boxes by dragging the three diagonal ribbed lines in the lower-right corner of the text field. The rest of the page adjusts itself to the new text-box size, and you have room to say what you need to say.

Expanding Web Forms

If the customer-service comment form on that corporate Web site doesn't give you enough room to rant properly, you can resize the text box right on the page—a *very* welcome feature. Figure 19-12 tells all.

Designate Your Start Page

What's the first thing you see when you open Safari? Is it the Apple news Web site? Is it the Top Sites display (Figure 19-5)?

Actually, that's up to you.

Choose Safari→Preferences→General tab. Here, the "New windows open with" pop-up menu offers choices like these:

• **Top Sites.** The thumbnail view of your favorites sites makes a great starting point.

- **Home Page.** If you choose this option, then Safari will open up with whatever page you've specified in the "Home page" box. Google—or its news page, *http://news. google.com*—is a good starting place. So is your favorite newspaper home page, or maybe *www.dilbert.com* for today's Dilbert cartoon.

 If you're already *on* the page you like, just click Set to Current Page.

- **Empty Page.** Some people prefer this setup, which makes Safari load very quickly when you first open it. Once this empty window opens, *then* you can tell the browser where you want to go today.

- **Bookmarks.** Whenever you open a new window or launch Safari, you see your full list of bookmarks. You can then choose exactly which page you want to open.

- **Tabs for Bookmarks Bar.** This intriguing option creates a row of tabs in a single window—one for *every* icon on your Bookmarks bar. The idea, of course, is to have not just one favorite Web page waiting for you in the morning, but *all* the ones you visit frequently, preloaded and ready to go.

- **Choose Tabs folder.** This option is similar to Tabs for Bookmarks Bar, except that it starts you off with tabs for *any* random bunch of Web sites—not just the ones on your Bookmarks bar. The trick is to build a *folder* full of bookmarks (Figure 19-6), and choose *that* as the basis for your auto-opening tabs.

Note: *An identical pop-up menu is available for "New tabs open with." That is, you can specify one starter-page preference for new* tabs, *and another for new* windows.

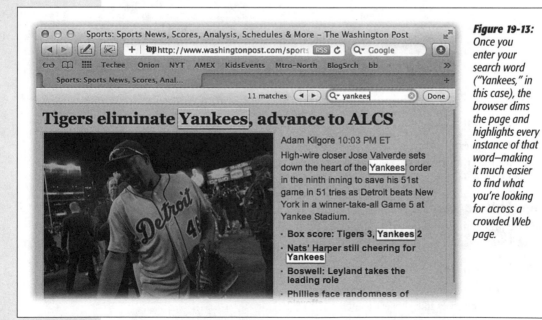

Figure 19-13:
Once you enter your search word ("Yankees," in this case), the browser dims the page and highlights every instance of that word—making it much easier to find what you're looking for across a crowded Web page.

Finding Text on Web Pages

The address/search bar can help you find Web sites that match your keywords. But some pages are so long, dense, or poorly designed that finding the words *on* the page needs a whole 'nother search engine. Fortunately, Safari's search-within-the-page function shines a light on the words or phrase you're seeking.

To use it, press ⌘-F and then type your search word into the Find box (Figure 19-13). As Safari locates the word or words, it displays them within a bright yellow box and dims the background of the rest of the page. The Find bar also tells you how many times the word or phrase occurs on the page; you can jump to each instance. Click the ❽ to start over with new search terms, or click Done to close the Find box and return to your normal browsing activity.

Tip: When you use the Find command, are you looking for words on the page that *begin* with your search term, or that contain them *anywhere?* You can now specify. Click the 🔍 in the search box and choose either Contains or Starts With from the pop-up menu.

Figure 19-14:
If you're having trouble reading the tiny type in a PDF, point your mouse to the bottom of it to invoke Safari's PDF toolbar. You can zoom out, zoom in, open the file in the Mac's Preview program, or even download it from the Web site with a well-placed click.

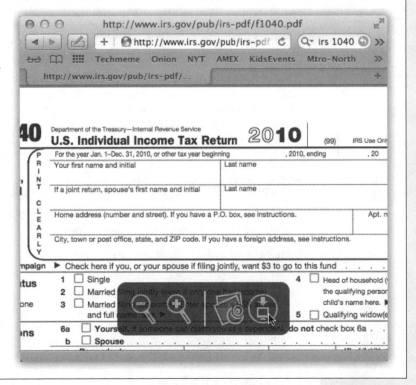

PDF Pages Online

PDF files are all over the Web as, among other things, forms to download, online brochures, and scanned book pages. But they aren't always especially readable in a browser window.

Unless, that is, you're using Safari. The next time you're squinting at a PDF in the window, point to the bottom edge of the document; you'll see a toolbar like the one in Figure 19-14 appear. With these four icons, you can zoom out, zoom in, open the file in Preview, or save the PDF file to your Downloads folder.

The History Menu

The History menu lists the Web sites you've visited in the past week or so, neatly organized into subfolders like Earlier Today and Yesterday. (A similar menu appears when you click *and hold* the ◀ or ▶ button.) These are great features if you can't recall the URL for a Web site you remember having visited recently.

Tip: See Safari's Help menu? It features a search box that lets you search all the *menu commands* in Safari—including Safari's History menu. That's just a *crazy* powerful feature. It means you can re-find a site without having to hunt through all the History submenus manually; just search for a word you remember in the title.

You can also view your History in a more expansive view—in Cover Flow view, in fact—by clicking the ▥ at the left end of your toolbar. You enter the Bookmarks-management view, described in Figure 19-6.

Tip: Having History available in the Bookmarks window is very handy, because you can drag a Web page from your History into your Bookmarks menu, folder, or bar. That is, you can bookmark a Web site long after your initial visit.

Tabbed Browsing

Beloved by hardcore surfers the world over, *tabbed browsing* is a way to keep a bunch of Web pages open simultaneously—in a single, neat window. Figure 19-15 illustrates.

Turning on tabbed browsing unlocks a whole raft of Safari shortcuts and tricks, which are just the sort of thing power surfers gulp down like Gatorade:

- If there's a certain set of Web sites you like to visit daily, put the bookmarks into one folder, using Bookmarks→Add Bookmark Folder and the Bookmarks organizer window (Figure 19-15). You can then load all of them into a single tabbed window, simply by selecting the resulting "folder" in the Bookmarks menu—or the Bookmarks bar—and choosing Open in Tabs from the submenu.

 The beauty of this arrangement is that you can start reading the first Web page while all the others load into their own tabs in the background.

Tip: Click the 🔖 icon at the left end of the Bookmarks bar. In the Bookmarks organizer, click the Bookmarks Bar item in the left-side list. Now you can see an Auto-Click checkbox for each listed folder.

If you turn on this checkbox, you'll be able to open all the bookmarks in that folder into tabs, all at once, merely by clicking the folder's name in the Bookmarks bar. (If you want to summon the *normal* menu from the folder, just hold the mouse button down.)

Figure 19-15:
Top: Set up tabbed browsing in Safari's Preferences→Tabs window. (For best results, turn on "When a new tab or window opens, make it active.")

Bottom: Now, when you ⌘-click a link, or type an address and press ⌘-Return or ⌘-Enter, you open a new tab, not a new window as you ordinarily would. You can now pop from one open page to another by clicking the tabs just under your Bookmarks bar, or close one by clicking its ⊗ button (or pressing ⌘-W).

- A variation on a theme: When you have a bunch of pages open in tabs, you can drag the tabs across the window to rearrange the order. When you have them the way you want them, Control-click (or right-click) a tab, and then choose Add Bookmark for These [*number*] Tabs from the shortcut menu. You can save your tabs to the Bookmarks bar and load all those pages with one click.

- If you Option-click a tab's ⊗ button, you close all the tabs *except* the one you clicked. The same thing happens if you hold down Option and choose File→Close Other Tabs, or if you press Option-⌘-W.

- If you Option-⌘-click a link, it opens in a separate window, rather than in a new tab. (When tabbed browsing is turned *off,* just ⌘-click a link to open a new window.)

- If you find yourself with a bunch of separate browser windows all over your screen, you can neatly consolidate them all into one nicely tabbed Safari window by choosing Window→Merge All Windows.

- If you Shift-⌘-click a link, Safari opens that page in a tab *behind* the one you're reading. That's a fantastic trick when you're reading a Web page and see a reference you want to set aside for reading next, but you don't want to interrupt whatever you're reading.

Tab View

In the olden days, the only indication you had of your open tab collection was pieces of their names, as revealed in the tab titles across the top of your Safari window. In Mountain Lion, however, there's a much more visual way to survey your tab domain: Tab View. Figure 19-16 explains all.

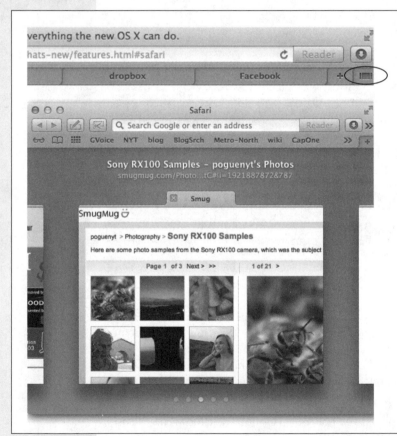

Figure 19-16:
Tab View gives you a horizontally scrolling parade of miniatures, so that you can easily spot what's in your open tabs.

To get here, pinch with two fingers on your trackpad, or click the new Tab View button at the right end of the tabs themselves (circled).

In Tab view, you can scroll among the tabs in the usual way (drag two fingers on your trackpad, for example). When you find the tab you want, press Enter or click.

You can also back out of Tab View without switching tabs at all, just by spreading two fingers on the trackpad.

Privacy and Security Features

Every year, there's another headline about some break-in where millions of credit card numbers are stolen by a hacker, sending panic into the hearts of the world's innocent

Web audiences. In Mountain Lion, Apple strikes back with some of its cleverest privacy and security features yet.

Erasing Your History

Some people find it creepy that Safari maintains a complete list of every Web site they've seen recently, right there in plain view of any family member or coworker who wanders by.

To delete just one particularly incriminating History listing, click the ⊞ icon at the left end of the Bookmarks bar; in the resulting Bookmarks organizer window, click History. Expand the relevant date triangle, highlight the offending address, and then press your Delete key. Click ⊞ again to return to normal browsing. You've just rewritten History!

Or, to erase the entire History menu, choose History→Clear History.

Of course, the History menu isn't the only place where you've left footprints. If you choose Safari→Reset Safari instead, you also erase all other shreds of your activities: any cookies (Web-page preference files) you've accumulated, your list of past downloads, the cache files (bits of the Web pages that a browser stores on your hard drive to save time when you return to the page they came from), and so on. This is good information to know; after all, you might be nominated to the Supreme Court someday.

Private Browsing

Of course, that's a lot of work just to cover your tracks; it also erases a lot of valuable cookies, passwords, and History entries you'd probably like to keep. Is all that really necessary just so you can duck in for an occasional look at the Hot Bods of the Midwestern Tax Preparers' Association Web site?

No, it's not. A feature called *private browsing* lets you surf without adding any pages to your History list, searches to your Google search suggestions, passwords to Safari's saved password list, or autofill entries to Safari's memory. (Apple says this feature is intended for use at public Macs, where you don't want to reveal anything personal to subsequent visitors. Ha!)

The trick is to choose Safari→Private Browsing *before* you start browsing. Once you OK the explanation box, Safari records nothing while you surf. As you'd hope, OS X won't use auto-resume the next time you open Safari, either—that is, the last page you'd opened won't reopen automatically

When you're ready to browse "publicly" again, choose Safari→Private Browsing once more so the checkmark goes away. Safari again begins taking note of the pages you visit—but it never remembers the earlier ones.

In other words, what happens in Private Browsing stays in Private Browsing.

Cookie Control—and Privacy Control

Cookies are something like Web page preference files. Certain Web sites—particularly commercial ones like Amazon.com—deposit them on your hard drive like little bookmarks so that they'll remember you the next time you visit.

Most cookies are perfectly innocuous—and, in fact, are extremely helpful, because they help Web sites remember your tastes. Cookies also spare you the effort of having to type in your name, address, credit card number, and so on every time you visit these Web sites.

But fear is widespread, and the media fans the flames with tales of sinister cookies that track your movements on the Web. If you're worried about invasions of privacy, Safari is ready to protect you.

Figure 19-17:
This dialog box is Privacy Central for the Safari browser. Here you can control which cookies you want to accept, you can remove any detritus commercial Web sites have bequeathed you, and you can get a handle on Web sites that try to track you.

POWER USERS' CLINIC

Who's My Real Host?

In Mountain Lion's Safari, you might notice something weird going on in the Address/Search bar. The first part of the Web site's address appears in black type, and the rest is in gray.

The idea is to help you identify the Web company that's hosting this page.

See, the bad guys these days use "phishing" scams. They send you a bogus email that looks like it's from your bank, or eBay, or PayPal. It warns you of "a problem with your account." Concerned, you click the ink to log into what looks exactly like your bank's site—but it's a fake, and you've just supplied your name and password to the bad guys.

By setting the mail host address (for example, *www.ebay.com*) apart from the rest of the gobbledygook, Safari makes it eaiser to distinguish the real sites from the phishing ones (for example, *www.interhost.com/ebay/accountservices.html*).

Once the browser is open, choose Safari→Preferences→Privacy tab (Figure 19-17). The "Block cookies" buttons in this dialog box are like a paranoia gauge. If you click Always, you create an acrylic shield around your Mac. No cookies can come in, and no cookie information can go out. You'll probably find the Web a very inconvenient place; you'll have to re-enter your information upon every visit, and some Web sites may not work properly at all.

A less-drastic choice is "From third parties and advertisers," which accepts cookies from sites you want to visit but blocks cookies deposited on your hard drive by sites you're not actually visiting—cookies an especially evil banner ad gives you, for example.

Note, too, the Details button. It reveals the shockingly complete list of every cookie you've accumulated so far—and offers you the chance to delete the ones that don't look so savory.

While you're in there, horrified at the number of cookies, notice that there's other stuff Web sites have dumped onto your Mac. There are things like cache files and local storage files (data that Web applications leave behind on your hard drive—something like cookies, except that Web sites can't retrieve this information later). All of it is available for your removal with one click on the Remove All Website Data button.

While you're in this box, you might discover two new checkboxes. "Ask websites not to track me" signs you up for a new online "Do not track" program. The problem is, of course, that this program is voluntary—and the sleazy operators just ignore it.

Finally, "Prevent search engine from providing suggestions" turns off the little pop-up lists of Google suggestions illustrated in Figure 19-2. If it creeps you out that Google is "monitoring" your search queries in order to provide suggestions, turn this checkbox on.

Then again, search suggestions are hardly your biggest worry about privacy these days.

GEM IN THE ROUGH

Safari Extensions

Safari extensions are little add-on, plug-in features, written by other people, that can make the Web a much better place.

Consider, for starters, the terrific ClickToFlash. Basically, it blocks all the Flash animations that turn Web pages into a blinking, flashing, animated mess. Anytime you'd normally see a Flash animation, you just get an empty gray box. And if you want to see that Flash? If it is, for example, a video you were hoping to watch? Well, as the name suggests, you just click inside the empty box to make the Flash load.

(You can also tell ClickToFlash not to block Flash on certain favorite Web sites.)

Another great one is A Cleaner YouTube, which presents each YouTube video on a simple, pure, plain white page, without the 50,000 elements of clutter and chaos. Facebook Cleaner is similar, but for Facebook.

You can find these and many other great Safari extensions at Apple's extensions gallery, *https://extensions.apple.com*.

Stifle Pop-Ups and Pop-Unders

The world's smarmiest advertisers inundate us with *pop-up* and *pop-under* ads—nasty little windows that appear in front of the browser window or, worse, behind it, waiting to jump out the moment you close your current window. They're often deceptive, masquerading as error messages or dialog boxes, and they'll do absolutely anything to get you to click inside them.

If this kind of thing is driving you crazy, choose Safari→Preferences→Security→Block Pop-Up Windows. It's a war out there—but at least you now have some ammunition.

Note: This feature doesn't squelch small windows that pop up when you click a link—only windows that appear unbidden.

Even unbidden windows, however, are sometimes legitimate (and not ads)—notices of new banking features, warnings that the instructions to use a site have changed, and so on. Safari can't tell these from ads and stifles them, too. So if a site you trust says, "Please turn off pop-up blockers and reload this page," then you know you're probably missing out on a *useful* pop-up message.

And one more thing: These days, the evildoers of the Internet have begun to attract your attention using other programming tricks that don't work by creating new windows (instead, they create new layers in your browser window). There's not much you can do about those nuisances.

Messages

Somewhere between email and the telephone lies the joyous communication tool called instant messaging. Plenty of instant messenger programs run on the Mac, but Mountain Lion comes with its very own instant messenger program called Messages. (It used to be called iChat.) It's built right into the system and ready to connect to your friends on the Yahoo, AIM, Jabber, Facebook, or Google Talk networks.

This chapter covers how to use Messages to communicate by video, audio, and text with your online pals.

Welcome to Messages

Messages does seven things very well:

- **Instant messaging.** If you don't know what instant messaging is, there's a teenager near you who does.

 Instant messaging combines the privacy of email and the immediacy of the phone. You type messages in a chat window, and your friends type replies back to you in real time.

 In this regard, Messages is a lot like the popular standalone messenger apps from AOL and Yahoo. But Messages lets you type back and forth with anyone from the AOL, Yahoo, Google Talk, and Facebook chat networks, all in a single program, which is a huge advantage. And Messages's visual design is pure Apple.

- **Unified chat/text messages with phones (iMessages).** This is huge. If you and your conversation partner both have iCloud accounts, then you can move freely from phone to tablet to Mac. Your conversation is auto-synced between gadgets. If you

started texting someone on the train home, you can sit down at your Mac and open Messages—and pick up right from where you left off.

You can also fire off a text message to somebody's *phone* while seated at your Mac—a mind-bending violation of the usual rules that limit text messages to the cellular network only.

The messages, which Apple calls iMessages, are a lot more flexible than regular text messages. They can be much longer than 160 characters. They can include photos, movies, or other kinds of files. They give you feedback that lets you know when a message has arrived on the recipient's gadget.

And above all, they don't count as text messages. They're routed through the Internet rather than the cellphone voice network. As far as your cellphone company is concerned, you're not texting at all, and therefore you don't have to pay for a texting plan.

- **Free long distance.** If your Mac has a microphone, and your buddy's does, too, the two of you can also chat *out loud,* by talking, using the Internet as a free long-distance phone. Wait, not just the two of you—the *10* of you, thanks to Messages's party-line feature.

- **Free videoconferencing.** If you and your buddies all have fast Internet connections and cameras like the ones built into most Mac models, then up to four participants can join in *video* chats, all onscreen at once, no matter where they happen to be in the world. This jaw-dropping visual stunt can bring distant collaborators face to face without plane tickets—and it costs about $99,900 less than professional videoconferencing gear.

- **File transfers.** Got an album of high-quality photos or a giant presentation file that's too big to send by email? Forget about using some online file-transfer service or networked server; you can drag that monster file directly to your buddy's Mac, through Messages, for a direct machine-to-machine transfer. (It lands in the other Mac's Downloads folder.)

- **Presentations.** You can open up most kinds of documents, at nearly full size, to show your video buddy, right there in the Messages window, without actually having to transfer them. That's Messages Theater.

- **Screen sharing.** Next time some parents or neighbors are throwing themselves upon your mercy for tech support, remember this: Messages lets you see their screen, and even control it, from across the Internet. Or you can volunteer your own screen for sharing, so you can demonstrate things to them.

iMessages

As you're about to discover, Messages is like an MP3 toothbrush or a carboat. It's a hybrid app—two very different functions mashed into a single body.

First, Messages is your Mac's gateway to *iMessages*. They're a lot like text messages on cell phones, except for the following:

- They're unlimited and free.

- There's almost no length limit.

- They can include photos, videos, and other huge files.

- They can go to Macs, iPhones, *and* tablets—and, in fact, they appear simultaneously on all of yours.

- Unlike traditional chat, your pal doesn't have to be online to get your message. An iMessage will be there when he turns his gadget on again.

The only requirement is that both of you, sender and receiver, have to have iCloud accounts (Chapter 17).

But Messages also does what its predecessor, iChat, did: It's a traditional chat program, capable of exchanging audio, video, and typed messages with people on other chat networks (AIM, Yahoo, and so on).

This chapter covers both of these major functions in turn. First up: iMessages.

Getting Started with iMessages

All right. You have an iCloud account, and you have at least one Apple machine. The first time you opened Messages, you were asked for your iCloud address (and offered the chance to get one). If you bowed out, you can still fill in that info in Mes-

Figure 20-1:
You have to specify an email address to anchor your iMessages life. You can specify more than one, actually (click the + button under "You can be reached for messages at"). If you do that, you should also choose one that Messages will use as your return address (the "Caller ID" address).

Turn on "Enable this account" to make it work. Turn on "Send read receipts" if you want your correspondents to know when you've read each of their messages.

sages→Preferences→Accounts. Basically, Messages keeps demanding your iCloud or Apple ID until you submit. See Figure 20-1.

Begin the iMessage Conversation

To begin a conversation with somebody who's on iCloud, start typing her name into the To box at the top of the Messages list. (If you don't see the To box, click the Compose button [☑]next to the search box.) As you type, Messages sprouts a list of matching names from your Contacts. Look for the blue speech bubble (💬) next to somebody's name, email address, or phone number. That's your cue that you've found someone on iCloud, someone with whom you can exchange iMessages.

Note: Until the fall of 2012, the only way to send a true iMessage (one that appears on all of your recipient's Apple gadgets) is to send it to an *email address* that he's registered with iCloud. If you address a message to a phone number, it goes only to that phone. With the fall update, however, it will be possible to register a phone number with iCloud, too, so that any message you send to an email address or a phone number arrives on all of your correspondent's Apple gadgets at once.

You can also click the ⊕ button to get a pop-up version of your Contacts, complete with a search bar at the top.

Once you've selected your lucky conversation partner(s), just type what you want to say into the iMessage box at the bottom of the window. Remember, this isn't a text message. You can type outrageously long messages; you can use fonts and colors; you can use the smiley-face pop-up menu (at the right end of the typing box) to insert emoticons and smileys.

You can even drag photos, movies, or other files (up to 100 megabytes!) into the typing box. They'll show up on the other guy's Mac, phone, or tablet just fine; he can double-click to open them up.

Now, if you have multiple Apple gadgets, and you've set up your iMessages email address or phone number in the Settings or System Preferences of each one, some mind-boggling stuff might start to happen. Your conversation appears simultaneously on all the gadgets.

That's extremely useful, because it means that you can (for example) start texting on your phone when you're out and about, and pick up seamlessly on your Mac when you get home, enjoying the real keyboard and big screen.

It's also sometimes weird, because the messages don't always arrive in order. Still, you usually get the gist.

Tip: If you're iMessaging on your Mac with your iPhone nearby, you might go crazy with all the phone's pinging and vibrating as it celebrates every incoming message. And turning it off, or putting it into Airplane mode, isn't the solution—once you turn it on again, it'll spend 20 minutes in paroxysms of dinging and vibrating as it downloads all the iMessages it missed.

No, the better solution is to open Settings→Sounds and turn Vibrate to Off. That takes care of the buzzing; now just turn your ringer switch off to silence the noise. Don't forget to undo all that when the chat concludes.

If you find that typing is losing too much emotional nuance, you can jump into a video call at any point—just click the FaceTime button (■◀) in the upper right of the Messages window and choose your long-suffering friend's name. The FaceTime app opens, and you can proceed as described on page 411.

As you get used to iMessages, you'll discover that they have many advantages over regular text messages. For example, the tiny word "received" appears beneath any message you send to let you know that your recipient's gadget has received it. If the recipient has turned on "Show read receipts" (Figure 20-1), you'll even see the word "read" to let you know that the person has actually *read* the message.

If you're in a back-and-forth conversation, the text messages show up on a single screen, scrolling up in conversation balloons like a chat session. While the other guy is typing, you see "…" in his balloon, so you know he's working on a response and not just ignoring you.

Finally, Messages means that you can *keep* your text messages. They're not locked onto your phone, like regular text messages, and they don't scroll away forever, like regular text messages. You can archive them, search them, copy and paste them, print them, forward them, and so on.

Messages blurs the line between text messages, chats, and email. And it gives birth to this frequently asked question: "Are you on the phone or the Mac?" For the first time, there's no way to know.

The Traditional Chat Networks

What's new in Messages, the big deal, is that iMessages thing. But under its skin, Messages is still iChat—an instant-messaging program that connects you to chat partners on several different networks: AOL Instant Messenger (AIM) , Yahoo, Jabber, or Google Talk.

Note: Jabber is a chat network whose key virtue is its *open-source* origins. In other words, it wasn't masterminded by some corporate media behemoth; it's an all-volunteer effort, joined by thousands of programmers all over the world. There's no one Jabber chat program (like AOL Instant Messenger). There are dozens, available for OS X, Windows, Linux, Unix, iPhone, and so on. They can all chat with one another across the Internet in one glorious frenzy of typing.

Behind the scenes, Google Talk uses the Jabber network, so Google Talk doesn't really count as a different network. But it does mean you can use Messages to converse with all those Google Talkers, too.

Finally, thanks to the Bonjour network-recognition technology, you can communicate with other Macs on your own office network without signing up for anything at all—and without being online. This is a terrific feature when you're sitting around a conference table, idly chatting with colleagues using your wireless laptop (and the boss thinks you're taking notes). It's also handy when you want to type little messages throughout the day to a family member downstairs, or a roommate 15 feet away.

Your contacts from all of these services are consolidated into a single buddy list.

You log into each network separately using the Messages→Accounts submenu, but you can also be logged into all of them at once. This is a great option if your friends are spread out among different chat networks.

Note: If you're on AOL's AIM service or Yahoo's Messenger service, why would you want to use Messages instead of those companies' dedicated chat programs? Easy: Because Messages is a nice, cleanly designed program that's free of advertisements, chatbots, and clunky interface elements.

On the other hand, there are some great chat apps that Messages can't touch. One is the popular Adium, a single program that works with Messages's chat services and many others, including MSN and ICQ. And then, of course, there's Skype, the granddaddy of all chat programs, which offers audio and video chats like Messages, but happily connects to Skype running on Windows, iPhones, Android phones, and so on.

Chatting and videoconferencing work identically on all of these networks. Keep that in mind as you read the following pages.

Setting Up Your Chat Accounts

When you open Messages for the first time, you're invited to enter (or sign up for) your iCloud or Apple account. Or, to use Messages with a different chat service, click Not Now; you're now offered a more generic Account Setup window; see Figure 20-2.

If you already have an AIM, Yahoo, Google Talk, or Jabber account, enter your name and password and click Continue. (If you're an America Online member, your existing screen name and password work for AIM purposes.)

If you don't have one, it's easy enough to get one. Sign up for a free account at the relevant company's Web site (at *gmail.com* or *yahoo.com*, for example).

You can also input account information later—the setup assistant isn't your only opportunity. You can do it in either of two places:

- In System Preferences, click Mail, Contacts & Calendars, described in Chapter 9.

- In Messages, choose Messages→Preferences, click the Accounts button, click the **+** button, and proceed as shown in Figure 20-2, bottom.

Once you've set up your accounts, you can activate or deactivate them either in Messages→Preferences→Accounts or by using the Messages→Accounts submenu. You might want to deactivate an account when, for example, you don't want to be bugged by the rabble on that particular service.

Note: Incidentally, it's possible to get good mileage out of Messages even if you don't have a chat account. Messages comes ready to connect you with other people in your building, over the office network, thanks to a technology called Bonjour. You can't add names to your Bonjour list; anyone who's on the network and running Messages appears there automatically.

The Buddy List

Once you've entered your account information, you're technically ready to start chatting. All you need now is a chatting companion, or, as he's called in instant-messaging

circles, a buddy. Messages comes with a unified Messages Buddies window where you can house the chat "addresses" for all your chat partners from all the different chat services, in a single list.

Tip: If you like, you can restore Messages to the old way of doing things, where each service (AIM, Yahoo, and so on) had its own separate buddy list window. To do that, choose Messages→Preferences→ General; turn off "Show all my accounts in one list." Now you can use the Window menu to reveal each service's buddy list separately.

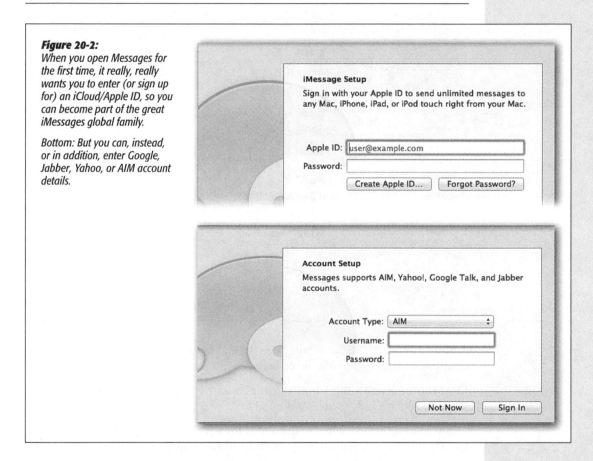

Figure 20-2:
When you open Messages for the first time, it really, really wants you to enter (or sign up for) an iCloud/Apple ID, so you can become part of the great iMessages global family.

Bottom: But you can, instead, or in addition, enter Google, Jabber, Yahoo, or AIM account details.

A tiny icon appears next to each name in your list, indicating that person's availability to chat—and what kinds of multimedia chats are available. A phone icon means "equipped for an audio chat"; a camcorder means "equipped for a video chat." The little colored dots mean "available" (green), "away" (red), "idle" (orange), and "undetermined—probably on a cellphone" (gray). A little .ɴ icon means you're chatting with someone on a cellphone.

Making a List

When you start Messages, your buddy list automatically appears (Figure 20-3). If you don't see it, choose Buddies from the Window menu.

Announce that you're available to chat, or display your current iTunes track

Choose your own buddy icon

Status indicators

Control-click for common commands (like "Invite to Audio Chat")

Capable of video chat

Invite for text, audio, or video chats (or screen sharing)

Add buddy

Figure 20-3:
Left: The Mountain Lion buddy list combines all your contacts from all chat services. Each chat account has its own status menu at the top.

Right: You can also choose Edit Status Menu to set up more creative alternatives to "Available" and "Away."

Adding a buddy to this list entails knowing that person's account name/address (for example, *bunnyface23@aim.com* or *harold1968@yahoo.com*).

Once you have it, click the **+** button in the bottom-left corner of the Buddies window; in the resulting window, click Add Buddy.

Down slides a sheet attached to the buddy list window, offering a window into your Contacts program (Chapter 18). Using the "Add to" pop-up menu, choose the service you want to use for chatting with this person (Yahoo, Google, AIM, whatever).

If your companion's chat address is already in Contacts, then double-click the person's name, or click it and then click Add.

If not, enter your pal's chat address in "Account name." Enter this person's real first and last names in the appropriate boxes, if you like.

Tip: Just to make things more complicated—er, flexible—Messages lets you organize buddies into groups, like Work, Family, and Fantasy Badminton League. Use the "Add to group" pop-up menu here to specify which group you want—or just choose Buddies to leave the new person in the general sloshing bucket of humanity.

When everything looks good, click Add.

Broadcasting Your Status

Using the pop-up menu just below your name (Figure 20-3, right), you can display your current mental status to *other* people's chat programs. You can announce that you're Available, Away, On the Phone, Drunk, and so on. (You have to choose Edit Status Menu for that last one; see Figure 20-3, right.)

Better yet, if you have music playing in iTunes, you can tell the world what you're listening to by choosing Current iTunes Song. (Your buddy can even click that song's name to open its screen on the iTunes Store, all for instant purchase gratification.)

For some people, by far the juiciest status option is Invisible (available for me.com and AIM accounts only). It's like a *Star Trek* cloaking device for your onscreen presence. Great for stalkers!

You can display the same status to your friends on all the different chat networks—Available, say, or Out to Lunch. Or you can set the status for each account separately, so that the lowlifes on Yahoo believe you to be "In a meeting" but the sophisticates on AIM realize that you're "Available."

To control whether your status message appears identically to all services, choose Use Same Status for All Accounts from the Status pop-up menu (Figure 20-3, right).

Tip: You can also add a Messages menulet to the top of your screen. Choose Messages→Preferences→General, and turn on "Show status in menu bar." From now on, you can change your status even when Messages isn't running. If other people see you as anything besides Offline or Invisible, they can send you a message—and Messages will open automatically.

GEM IN THE ROUGH

The Messages Chat Room

If everyone you want to include is a member of the same service, like Jabber, Yahoo, or me.com/AIM, there's another way to go about starting a group chat: Create a chat room. The advantage here is that you don't have to invite each member manually; you can just publicize the name of the room, and people can drop in at the appropriate time.

To create such a room, choose File→Go to Chat Room. Use the Account pop-up menu to specify which service you want, and then type a name for your room. Click Add.

Turn on Autojoin, if you like (it means, "Enter this room automatically whenever I'm online with that chat service"). Click Go. You're in!

Other people can enter your secret room by choosing File→Go to Chat Room, choosing the appropriate chat service, typing the room name, and then clicking Go.

If they don't know about the room, you can invite them yourself. Choose View→Show Chat Participants, click the + button, and then choose a buddy.

If you become a hard-core chataholic, don't miss the options in Messages→Preferences→General. Here you can set up automatic status changes.

For example, "Set my status to Away after the computer is inactive" changes your status to Away when you haven't touched your Mac in 15 minutes, or when the Mac goes to sleep or the screen saver kicks in. That way, people seeking your witty repartee won't think you're just ignoring them.

You can also select what happens when you return to your computer after your status has been set to Away.

Sorting and Sizing Your Friends

In View→Sort Buddies, you can rearrange your buddies as they're listed in the buddy list (by availability, name, or manually—drag the names up and down).

Once you get a lot of people piled on your list, all with their buddy pictures and audio/video chat icons, you may feel like Messages is taking up way too much screen real estate. If you want a more space-efficient view of your buddy list, go to the View menu and turn off Show Buddy Pictures, Show Audio Status, or Show Video Status. You can turn off Buddy Groups here as well, if you'd prefer to see your buddies in one undivided list.

Let the Chat Begin

As with any conversation, somebody has to talk first. In chat circles, that's called *inviting* someone to a chat.

POWER USERS' CLINIC

iTunes by Remote Control

Thanks to some sneaky AppleScripting (Chapter 7), you can use Messages as a glorified music-system remote control for another Mac. Specifically, you can sit at Mac #1, controlling the iTunes playback of Mac #2 elsewhere in the house. That's handy when Mac #2 is connected to your sound system and you really don't feel like getting up off the couch.

To set it all up, start on Mac #1, the one you'll be using in person. In Messages, choose Messages→Preferences→Accounts. Click Bonjour, and make sure Enable Bonjour Instant Messaging is turned on. Close the window.

On Mac #2, the one with iTunes, open Messages. Choose Messages→Preferences→Alerts. From the Event pop-up menu, choose Message Received. Turn on Run an

AppleScript Script, and then select iTunes Remote Control. applescript from the pop-up menu.

Now, while seated at Mac #1, you can control Mac #2's music playback by typing one-word commands into Messages. You can type any of these commands: play, pause, status, next, previous, mute, unmute, or help. After you type your command (like "mute" when the phone rings and you're blasting Lady Gaga), hit the Return key to make iTunes on the other Mac obey your orders.

You'll get responses in the Messages window, too. For example, if you enter "next," Messages types back, "Playing next track. Now playing 'In This Diary' by The Ataris.")

They Invite You

If someone invites you to chat, Messages opens automatically and displays an invitation message like the one in Figure 20-4. If the person initiating a chat isn't already in your buddy list, the note says, "[service] Message from [name of the person]."

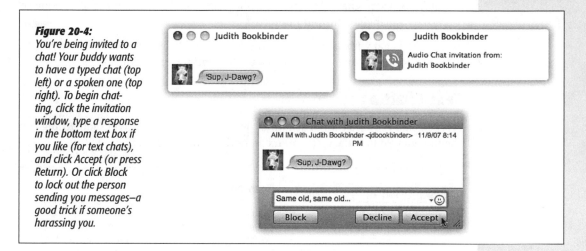

Figure 20-4:
You're being invited to a chat! Your buddy wants to have a typed chat (top left) or a spoken one (top right). To begin chatting, click the invitation window, type a response in the bottom text box if you like (for text chats), and click Accept (or press Return). Or click Block to lock out the person sending you messages—a good trick if someone's harassing you.

(If you've set your status to Offline, on the other hand, you won't see those invitation messages. You'll see me.com and AIM invitations once you're online again, but if the invites come from the other services, you've missed out.)

Tip: If you're getting hassled by someone on AIM or me.com, click his name in the buddy list, or in the window containing the invitation, and choose Buddies→Block Person. If the person isn't online at the time, go to Messages→Preferences→Accounts→Security and then click the button for "Block specific people." Click the Edit List button, and then type in the screen name of the person you want out of your IM life. (The other chat network types don't offer security options like this.)

You Invite Them

To begin a chat:

- **One-to-one typed conversations (instant messaging).** To message someone, double-click the person's name, type a quick invite ("You there?"), and press Return. You've just triggered what Apple calls an instant messaging session, which is a one-to-one affair.

Tip: If this person is on more than one chat network, then open the flippy triangle and choose the account you want to use. The flippy triangle is in the little strip called the Recipient bar; if you don't see it, choose View→Show Recipient Bar.

- **Multiperson typed conversations (chat).** To start a chat instead, click someone's name in the buddy list and then choose Buddies→Invite to Chat. Now, each time

you click the **+** button at the bottom of the Participants list, you choose another person to invite. (Or ⌘-click each name in the buddy list to select several people at once and then click the ⒜ button below the list to start the text chat.) Everyone sees all the messages anyone sends, and anyone can add new participants.

- **Audio or video chats.** To start an audio or video chat, click the microphone or movie-camera icon in your buddy list.

To initiate a chat with someone who isn't in the buddy list, choose File→New Chat. Type the account name, and then click OK to send the invitation.

Text Chatting

A typed chat works like this: Each time you or your chat partner types something and then presses Return, the text appears on both of your screens (Figure 20-5).

Figure 20-5:
As you chat, your comments always appear on the right. If you haven't yet created a custom icon, you'll look like a blue globe or an AOL running man. You can choose a picture for yourself either in your own Contacts card or right in Messages. And Web links your pals paste into messages are perfectly clickable—your Web browser leaps right up to take you to the site your friend has shared.

Messages displays each typed comment next to an icon, which can be any of these three things:

- **A picture the other person added.** If the buddy added her own picture—to her own copy of Messages, a Jabber program, AOL Instant Messenger, or Yahoo Messenger—it will be transmitted to you, appearing automatically in the chat window. Cool!

- **A picture you added.** If you've added a picture of that person to the buddy list or Contacts, you see it here instead. (After all, your vision of what somebody looks like may not match his own self-image.)

- **Generic.** If nobody's done icon-dragging of any sort, you get a generic silhouette icon.

To choose a graphic to use as your own icon, click the square picture to the right of your own name at the top of the buddy list. From the pop-up palette of recently selected pictures, choose Edit Picture to open a pop-up image-selection palette, where you can take a snapshot with your Mac's camera or choose a photo file from your hard drive. Feel free to build an array of graphics to represent yourself—and to change them in midchat, using this pop-up palette, to the delight or confusion of your conversation partner.

Tip: When you minimize the Messages message window, its Dock icon displays the icon of the person you're chatting with—a handy reminder that she's still there.

In-Chat Fun

Typing isn't the only thing you can do during a chat. You can also perform any of these stunts:

- **Format your text.** You can press ⌘-B or ⌘-I to make your next typed utterance bold or italic. Or change your color or font by choosing Format→Show Colors or Format→Show Fonts, which summons the standard OS X color or font palettes. (If you use some weird font that your chat partners don't have installed, they won't see the same typeface.)

- **Insert a smiley.** When you choose a face (like Undecided, Angry, or Frown) from this quick-access menu of smiley options (at the right end of the text-reply box), Messages inserts it as a graphic into your response.

 On the other hand, if you know the correct symbols to produce smileys—that :) means a smiling face, for example—you can save time by typing them instead of using the pop-up menu. Messages converts them into smiley icons on the fly, as soon as you send your reply.

- **Send a file.** Choosing Buddies→Send File lets you send a file to *all* the participants in your chat.

The Chat Transcript

When you close a chat by clicking the ⊗ in its left-side tab, Messages asks if you're sure you know what you're doing. If you proceed, you lose the transcript of that chat forever. That prose is hosed.

On the Messages→Preferences→Messages panel, you can turn on "Save history when chats are closed." From now on, the text of your conversations is automatically saved. You can retrieve them using the File→Recent Items command; by

starting another chat with the same person (the history reappears); or by opening your Library→Messages→Archives folder. (To get to your Library folder, press Option as you choose Go→Library in the Finder.)

If you do have "Save history" turned on, and you wind up having a particularly incriminating chat, you can tell Messages *not* to save its transcript by pressing ⌘-Delete.

Better yet, just drag the file's icon from the Finder into the box where you normally type. (This trick works well with pictures, because your conversation partner sees the graphic right in his Messages window. And it can handle files as big as 100 megabytes.)

This is a fantastic way to transfer a file that would be too big to send by email. A chat window never gets "full," and no attachment is too large to send.

This method halves the time of transfer, too, since your recipients get the file as you upload it. They don't have to wait 20 minutes for you to send the file and then another 20 minutes to download it, as they would with email or FTP.

If you have multiple conversations taking place—and are flinging files around to a bunch of people—you can keep an eye on each file's progress with the File Transfer Manager. Choose Window→File Transfers (or press Option-⌘-L) to pop open an all-in-one document delivery monitor.

- **Get Info on someone.** If you click a name in your buddy list and then choose Buddies→Show Info (or Control-click someone's name and choose Show Info from the shortcut menu), you get a little Info window about your buddy where you can edit her name, email address, and picture. (If you change the picture here, you'll see it instead of the graphic your buddy chose for herself.)

 If you click the Alerts tab at this point, you can make Messages react when this particular buddy logs in, logs out, or changes status—for example, by playing a sound or saying, "She's here! She's here!"

- **Send an Instant Message.** Not everything in a chat session has to be "heard" by all participants. If you choose Buddies→Send Instant Message, you get a private chat window, where you can "whisper" something directly to a special someone behind the other chatters' backs.

Figure 20-6:
Messages can look like almost anything. Here, for example, is what a chat looks like with the balloon effect turned off (giving you colored rectangles instead). You can even turn off pictures if they bother you. You can also hide the names. You can also change the color and typeface settings in the Messages→Preferences→Messages panel.

- **Send Email.** If someone messages you, "Hey, will you email me directions?" you can do so on the spot by choosing Buddies→Send Email. Your email program opens up automatically so you can send the note along; if your buddy's email address is part of his Contacts info, the message is even preaddressed.

Popping the Balloons

The words you might have for Messages's word-balloon design might be "cute" and "distinctive." But it's equally likely that your choice of adjectives includes "juvenile" and "annoying."

Fortunately, behind Messages's candy coating are enough options tucked away in the View→Messages menu that you'll certainly find one that works for you (see Figure 20-6).

Audio Chats

Messages becomes much more exciting when you exploit its AV Club capabilities. Even over slow Internet connections, you can conduct audio chats, speaking into your microphone and listening to the responses from your speaker.

If you have a broadband connection, though, you get a much more satisfying experience: Up to 10 of you can join in one massive, free conference call from across the Internet.

A telephone icon next to a name in your buddy list tells you that the buddy has a microphone and is ready for a free Internet "phone call." If you see what appear to be stacked phone icons, then your pal's Mac has enough horsepower to handle a multiple-person conference call.

To begin an audio chat, you have three choices:

- Click the telephone icon next to the buddy's name.

- Highlight someone in the buddy list, and then click the telephone icon at the bottom of the list.

- If you're already in a text chat, choose Buddies→Invite to Audio Chat.

Once your invitation is accepted, you can begin speaking to each other. The bars of the sound-level meter let you know that the microphone—which you've specified in the Messages→Preferences→Audio/Video tab—is working.

Tip: Although the audio is full duplex (you can hear and speak simultaneously, like a phone but unlike a walkie-talkie), there may be a delay, like you're calling overseas on a bad connection. If you can't hear anything at all, check out Messages's Help system, which contains some suggestions.

Video Chats

If you and your partner both have broadband Internet connections, even more impressive feats await. You can conduct a free video chat with up to four people, who show up on three vertical panels, gorgeously reflected on a shiny black table surface. This isn't the jerky, out-of-audio-sync, Triscuit-sized video of days gone by. If you've got the Mac muscle and bandwidth, your partners are as crisp, clear, bright, and smooth as television—and as big as your screen, if you like.

People can come and go; as they enter and leave the "videosphere," Messages slides their glistening screens aside, enlarging or shrinking them as necessary to fit on your screen.

Equipment Requirements

Everyone in a video chat has to be on the same service (me.com/AIM, Yahoo, or Jabber), and everyone needs pretty high-horsepower computers and Internet connections.

Tip: For better audio quality during your video calls—both hearing and broadcasting—wear a headset. For example, you can pair a wireless Bluetooth headset with your Mac in Messages→Preferences→Audio/Video→Set Up Bluetooth Headset. This fires up the Mac's Bluetooth Setup Assistant program to guide you through the process.

After you get your Bluetooth headset married to your Mac, go to →System Preferences→Output and select your headset in the list.

For example, your Mac needs a video camera (like the one that came built in), a camcorder, or a FireWire version of one of those golf-ball Webcams.

Tip: You and your buddy don't both need the gear. If only you have a camera, for example, you can choose Buddies→Invite to One-Way Video Chat (or Audio Chat). Your less-equipped buddy can see you, but has to speak (audio only) or type in response.

You need pretty decent Internet speeds, too.

Starting the Video Call

If you see a ◼◀ icon next to a buddy's name, you can have a full-screen, high-quality video chat with that person, because they, like you, have a suitable camera and a high-speed Internet connection. If you see a stacked camcorder icon, then that person has a Mac that's capable of joining a four-way video chat.

To begin a video chat, click the ◼◀ icon next to a buddy's name, or highlight someone in the buddy list and then click the camcorder icon at the bottom of the list. Or, if you're already in a text chat, choose Buddies→Invite to Video Chat.

A window opens, showing you. This Preview mode is intended to show what your buddy will see. (You'll probably discover that you need some kind of light in front of you to avoid being too shadowy.) As your buddies join you, they appear in their own windows (Figure 20-7).

And now, some video-chat notes:

- If your conversation partners seem unwilling to make eye contact, it's not because they're shifty. They're just looking at *you,* on the screen, rather than at the camera—and chances are you aren't looking into your camera, either.

Figure 20-7:
That's you in the smaller window. To move your own miniwindow, click a different corner, or drag yourself to a different corner. If you need to blow your nose or do something else unseemly, Option-click the microphone button to freeze the video and mute the audio. Click again to resume.

- Don't miss the ⬈ button in the upper-right corner of the window. It takes your video into full screen. Wild.

- If you're the one who started the call, then you can add more people by clicking the + button in the chat window, or dragging a buddy's name into the window. (If that person doesn't have a camera, she can still enjoy audio or typing privileges.)

- You can have video chats with Windows computers, too. Be prepared for disappointment, though; the video is generally jerky, small, and slightly out of sync. That's partly due to the cheap USB Webcams most PCs have, and partly due to the poor video codec (compression scheme) built into many Windows chat programs.

- You can capture a still "photo" of a video chat by ⌘-dragging the image to your desktop, or by choosing Video→Take Snapshot (Option-⌘-S). Or just use the Copy command (⌘-C) to copy an image of the chat to the Clipboard, ready for pasting in another program.

- Don't want to see yourself in the picture-in-picture window during your video chat? Choose Video→Hide Local Video.

- This cutting-edge technology can occasionally present cutting-edge glitches. The video quality deteriorates, the transmission aborts suddenly, the audio has an an-

noying echo, and so on. When problems strike, Messages Help offers a number of tips; the Video→Connection Doctor can identify your network speed. (Messages video likes lots of network speed.)

Tip: If the Messages video seems to be struggling too much to be worthwhile, consider using FaceTime instead. It's designed to deliver good video quality over less-beefy Internet connections.

- Just as you can save your typed transcripts of instant message conversations, you can record your audio and video chats. Once you start a chat, choose Video→Record Chat. Your buddy is asked if it's OK for you to proceed with the recording (to ward off any question of those pesky wiretapping laws); if permission is granted, then Messages begins recording the call.

 When you've got what you want, click Stop. Your recordings are automatically saved into Home→Documents→Messages (AAC files for audio conversations, MPEG-4 files for video chats). From there, you can drag them into iTunes to play or sync them up with an iPod or iPhone. Yes, you can now relive those glorious Messages moments when you're standing in line at the grocery store.

Bluescreen Backdrops and Video FX

If your video chats look like a bunch of cubicle-dwellers sitting around chatting at their desks, you can liven things up with one of Messages's most glamorous and jaw-dropping features: photo or video *backgrounds* for your talking head. Yes, now you can make your video chat partners think you're in Paris, on the moon, or even impersonating a four-panel Andy Warhol silkscreen.

Note: The Messages and Photo Booth backdrop effects require bandwidth, man, serious bandwidth—at least 128 Kbps for both upload and download speeds.

Here's how to prepare your backdrop for a video chat that's under way:

1. **Choose Video→Show Video Effects.**

 The Effects box appears, looking a lot like the one in Photo Booth (Chapter 11); visual backdrops are the same. Click the various squares to see how each effect will transform you in real time.

 The first three pages of effects all do video magic on you and everything else in the picture. The second two pages of effects, however, don't do anything to your image. Instead, they replace the background.

 This is the really amazing part. In TV and movies, replacing the background is an extremely common special effect. All you have to do is set up a perfectly smooth, evenly lit, shadowless blue or bright green backdrop behind the subject. Later, the computer replaces that solid color with a new picture or video of the director's choice.

 Messages, however, creates exactly the same special effect (Figure 20-8) without requiring the bluescreen or the greenscreen. Read on.

2. Click the background effect you want.

Suppose, for example, that you've clicked the video loop showing the Eiffel Tower with people walking around. At this point, a message appears on the screen that says, "Please step out of the frame."

Figure 20-8:
Top left: You have plenty of backgrounds to choose from for your next video chat. Click an effect to add it to your chat window. Click the small arrows at the bottom of the window to advance or retreat through the various effects styles. Click the Original square in the middle of the window to erase the effect and start again from scratch.

Lower right: Let the live bluescreen action begin!

3. Duck out of camera range (or move off to one side).

See, Messages intends to memorize a picture of the *real* background—without you in it. When you return to the scene, your high-horsepower Mac then compares each pixel of its memorized image with what it's seeing now. Any differences, it concludes, must be *you*. And *that* is how it can create a bluescreen effect without a bluescreen.

Note: To make this work, both the camera and the background must be perfectly still. If the lighting or the visuals shift or change in any way, you may get some weird, glitchy effects where your real background bleeds through.

4. When the screen says, "Background detected," step back into the frame.

Sacré bleu! You're now in virtual Paris. Go ahead and start the video chat with your friends, and don't forget your beret.

If you want to clear out the background, or change it, click the Original square in the middle of the Effects palette and then choose a different backdrop. (You can also change backdrops in midchat by clicking Effects again.)

If things get too weird and choppy onscreen, you can restore the normal background by choosing Video→Reset Background. (That's also handy if you suddenly have to have a video talk with your boss about your excessive use of Messages while he's away on his business trip.)

Tip: You can use one of your own photos or video clips as a Messages backdrop, too. In the Video Effects box, click the arrows on the bottom until you get to the screen with several blank User Backdrop screens. Next, drag a photo or video from the desktop directly onto one of the blank screens. Click it just like you would any of Apple's stock shots.

Juggling Chats and Windows

Once you become a Messages addict, you often wind up with multiple chats in progress. These days, Messages contains all your conversations in a single window, as shown in Figure 20-9.

Tip: You can press Control-Tab to switch from chat to chat in a multi-chat window. Add the Shift key to move the other way.

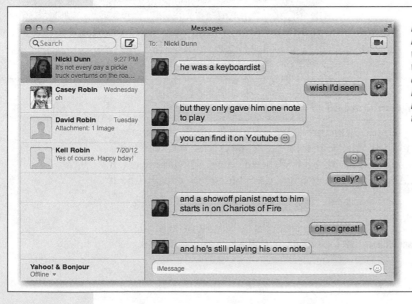

Figure 20-9:
Messages keeps tabs on your various simultaneous conversations—literally. Click the different tabs to switch chats. Double-click one to open it into its own window, without the tabs taking up space.

Sharing Your Screen

As you've seen already in this chapter, Messages lets you share your thoughts, your voice, and your image with the people on your buddy list. And now, for its next trick, it lets you share…your computer.

Messages's screen-sharing feature is a close relative of the *network* screen-sharing feature described in Chapter 14. It lets you not only *see* what's on a faraway buddy's screen, but also control it, taking command of the distant mouse and keyboard. (You can share your screen with the other guy, too.)

You can open folders, create and edit documents, and copy files on the shared Mac screen. Sharing a screen makes collaborating as easy as working side by side around the same Mac, except now you can be sitting in San Francisco while your buddy is banging it out in Boston.

And if you're the family tech-support specialist—but the family lives all over the country—screen sharing makes troubleshooting a heckuva lot easier. You can now jump on your Mom's shared Mac and figure out why the formatting went wacky in her Word document, without her having to attempt to *explain* it to you over the phone. ("And then the little thingy disappeared and the doohickey got scrambled…")

Tip: Once you're controlling someone else's screen remotely, your keyboard shortcuts operate their Mac instead of yours. Press ⌘-Tab to bring up the application switcher, hit ⌘-Q to quit a program, use all the Mission Control and Spotlight shortcuts, and so on.

To make Messages screen sharing work, you and your buddy must both be running Macs with OS X 10.5 (Leopard) or later. On the other hand, you can share over any account type: AIM, iCloud, Google Talk, Yahoo, Jabber, or Bonjour.

To begin, click the sharee's name in your buddy list.

POWER USERS' CLINIC

Messages Tweaks

If you've done nothing but chat in Messages, you haven't even scratched the surface. The Messages→Preferences dialog box gives you plenty of additional control. A few examples:

The Messages preference panel lets you design your chat windows–the background color, word balloon color, and typeface and size of text you type.

Here's a little tweak, right on the Messages pane, that nobody ever mentions: the preference setting called "Watch for my name in incoming messages." It alerts you anytime anyone, in any of the open chats, types your name, even if you're doing something else on the Mac. (As in, "Casey, are you there? Casey!? CASEY!!")

Finally, on the Alerts pane, you can choose how Messages responds to various events. For example, it can play a sound, bounce its Dock icon, or say something out loud whenever you log in, log out, receive new messages, or run an Apple-Script, as described earlier in this chapter.

- To share your screen, choose Buddies→Share My Screen with [person's name].

- To see his screen, choose Buddies→Ask to Share [person's name]'s Screen.

Note: Similar commands are available in the Screen Sharing pop-up button—the two overlapping squares at the bottom of the Buddies window.

Once the invitation is accepted, the sharing begins, as shown in Figure 20-10. To help you communicate further, Messages politely opens up an audio chat with your buddy so you can have a hands-free discussion about what you're doing on the shared machine.

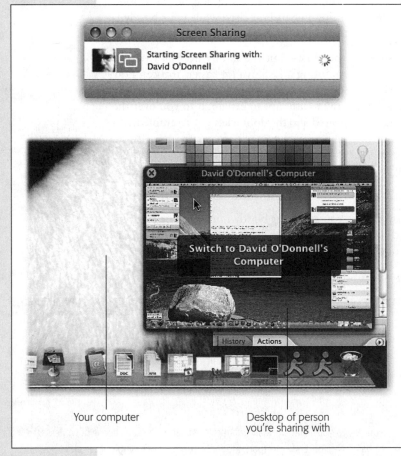

Figure 20-10:
Top: You either send or receive an invitation to start sharing your screen, but make sure you know with whom you're dealing before accepting the offer and starting the sharing process.

Bottom: When you're sharing someone else's screen, you have the option to click back and forth between the two Mac screens.

If you're seeing someone else's screen, you see his Mac desktop in full-screen view, right on your own machine. You also see a small window showing your own Mac; click it to switch back to your own desktop.

Tip: To copy files from Mac to Mac, drag them between the two windows. Files dragged to your Mac wind up in your Downloads folder.

To bail out, press Control-Esc on the Mac's keyboard.

Messages Theater

Talk about the next best thing to being there. The Theater feature lets you make pitches and presentations to people and committees in faraway cities—without standing in a single airport-security line.

That's because Messages Theater turns the chat window into a presentation screen for displaying and narrating your own iPhoto or Keynote slideshows, QuickTime

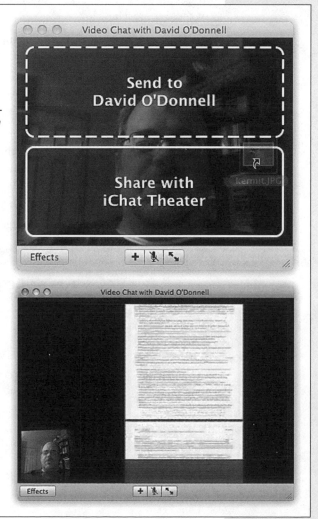

Figure 20-11:
Top: You can start a Messages Theater session by choosing File→Share a File with Messages Theater, or as shown here, by simply dropping the file on an open video chat window and going for the Messages Theater option.

Bottom: Once you've started a Theater show in Messages, the shared file takes center stage so you both can look at it and discuss amongst yourselves.

movie files, and even text documents. Your buddy, on the other end of the Messages line, sees these documents at nearly full size—with you in a little picture-in-picture screen in the corner.

This is all you need:

- **Some stuff to show off.** Messages Theater can display exactly the same kinds of files that Quick Look (Chapter 1) can display: Word, Excel, and PowerPoint documents; photos; text and HTML files; PDF files; audio and movie files; fonts; vCards; Pages; Numbers; Keynote and TextEdit documents, and so on.

- **A zippy broadband Internet connection.** Messages Theater likes 384 kilobits per second or faster; check with your Internet provider if you aren't sure of your connection speed.

To get the show running, start by establishing a video chat. Then, you can take either of these approaches:

- Drag the file(s) you want to share into the video window. As shown in Figure 20-11, top, you're given two targets for your drag. Release the file in the Share with Theater target.

- Click the **+** button below the video image. From the pop-up menu, choose Share a File with Theater. Locate and double-click the file you want to present on your hard drive.

Now the curtain goes up, as shown at the bottom of Figure 20-11. The file you're sharing takes center stage (er, window) and your buddy appears in a little video window off to the side. Click the ◼ button to expand the view to full screen.

Actually, Messages offers several other ways for the two of you to join in harmonious digital unity once a video chat has begun:

POWER USERS' CLINIC

Messages on Autopilot

If you've read this chapter all the way through, then you know that Messages can respond to chat invitations by running an AppleScript. And if you've read Chapter 7, you know that AppleScript is capable of...almost anything.

As a proof of concept, Apple's AppleScript product manager has created a truly evil script that you can choose in the Messages→Preferences→Alerts→Run AppleScript pop-up menu. It's called Messages Autopilot; you can download it from this book's "Missing CD" page at *www.missingmanuals.com*.

In short, this very special script simulates your end of the chat. It carries on a fairly generic conversation, periodically typing perfectly plausible all-purpose utterances, occasionally excusing yourself while you answer the doorbell, and otherwise doing an excellent impersonation of a distracted, preoccupied, but still well-meaning you.

Let it run. Give your buddies the satisfaction of knowing you're there for them. Even though you're really watching TV downstairs.

- **Share a slideshow.** Sharing picture albums is one menu command away: Click the + button below the video image, and choose File→Share iPhoto with Theater. When the Media Browser pops up, pick the album you want to present. The first picture in the selected album appears in the Messages window before iPhoto itself opens, so you can use iPhoto's nice controls for cruising forward (or backward) through your album.

Note: The same thing happens if you're running a Keynote presentation in Theater: The first slide shows up in the chat window while the Keynote program launches to provide you with the proper controls to click through the rest of the slides in the presentation.

- **Share a Web page.** "I'm telling you, Mom, their Web site says they're open until 10! Look, I'll show you!" Click the + button below the video image, and this time choose Share Webpage with Theater. When the little text box appears, paste in (or type in) the Web address you want to share. When you click Share, your chat partner gets to see the Web site in question.

- **Share an application.** You may see another option in the + button's pop-up menu: a weird little thing called "Share an application." If you do, in fact, own any programs that work with this command, they show up here automatically.

 Keynote is one of them, the point being that you can give a little slideshow from Keynote right in your video chat. When you choose the program's name, it opens; start the slideshow as though you're connected to a projector, and narrate away.

When the show is over, move your cursor into the presentation window and click the ✕ to return to your regularly scheduled video chat.

SSH, FTP, VPN & Web Sharing

E mail and Web surfing may be the most popular Internet activities, but the world's most gigantic network has many other uses. The general idea is always the same, though: letting one computer reach out and touch another.

OS X offers a few features that embrace the more literal aspects of that notion. For example, this chapter explores various advanced methods of manipulating your own Mac from the road, including *remote access* technologies like long-distance file sharing, FTP, SSH, and virtual private networking (VPN).

Note: Most of these technologies are designed for full-time Internet connections (cable modem or DSL, for example). If you have a dial-up modem, these features work only when you're actually online. Still, they may occasionally be useful anyway. You could always get online, call up a friend, and say, "Check out my Web site right now—here's the current IP address" or call someone back home to say, "I have to grab a file off my hard drive. Could you make the Mac on my desk go online?"

FTP

FTP (file transfer protocol) sites store pieces of software that can be accessed from the Internet. If you've heard of FTP at all, it was probably under one of two circumstances—either you've downloaded software from an Internet FTP site, or you've created and maintained your own Web site.

Uploading and Downloading from FTP Sites

Hooking into an FTP site generally requires an FTP *client program* that runs on the kind of computer you use (Mac, Windows, or whatever). On OS X, popular FTP client

programs include the shareware programs Transmit, Fetch, Interarchy, and Captain FTP, and the free RBrowser (which is available from the "Missing CD" page at *www. missingmanuals.com*).

Using these programs, Web designers, for example, can view a list of all the text and graphics documents, sitting there on an Internet-connected computer somewhere, that make up their Web pages. The effect is shown in Figure 21-1.

UP TO SPEED

The IP Address Mess: Port Forwarding

There are so many ways to connect to your Mac from another computer. You can use SSH, file sharing, screen sharing, and so on. They're easy to use—when you want to connect across your home or office network.

When you want to connect from across the *Internet*, though, things get complicated fast.

In that case, you need to know your home Mac's *IP address*. (IP stands for Internet Protocol.) An IP address is always made up of four numbers separated by periods, like 192.168.1.104. Every computer on earth that's directly connected to the Internet has its own unique IP address.

Now, if you have only one Mac, and it's connected directly to your broadband modem, no big deal. You can find out its IP address by opening System Preferences, clicking Sharing, and clicking File Sharing.

Unfortunately, your Mac at home probably *isn't* connected directly to the Internet. If you're like most people, it's connected to a router, or maybe an AirPort base station, so that several computers in your house can share the same Internet connection. In this setup, the *router* (or base station) has a unique IP address—not the Macs connected to it.

(The router doles out private IP addresses to each computer in your house or office, usually beginning with 192 or 10. If you check your Mac's IP address in System Preferences, you'll find out only its *private* address—not the public one that's accessible from the Internet. To find out that information, you have to check your router or base station's configuration screen; check the router's manual for instructions.)

All right: How are you supposed to connect to one particular Mac if it's connected to a router and doesn't have a true, "public" IP address?

One solution is Back to My Mac, the remote-access feature described on page 584. It solves the behind-the-router problem for you, but it requires an iCloud account.

Otherwise, your only hope is to turn on a router feature called *port forwarding*. It makes the router pass signals intended for a specific port to one particular computer on the network. For example, you could direct all port-80 communications to the Mac doing Web serving and all port-548 traffic to the Mac doing file sharing.

The point is that, even with port forwarding, you still can't access two different machines using the same port. (For some services, including SSH and Timbuktu, you can work around this limitation by logging into the machine specified for port forwarding, and then from that machine, log into the others on the rest of the network.)

Turning on port forwarding doesn't require a programming degree, but it's not simple by any means. For starters, the steps are different for every router model.

Fortunately, you can find guided tutorials on the Web. You can use Google to search for your particular router model, or check *www.portforward.com*, which offers free step-by-steps for hundreds of router models, including Apple's AirPort base stations. Even so, try to arrange the assistance of someone who knows networking.

In this chapter, the term "your IP address" means your *public* IP address. If you have only one Mac, that's its IP address. If you have a router or wireless network, use *that* device's IP address—as passed along by port forwarding.

When they want to update one of those pages, they add it to this list; to delete a Web page, they remove it from this list.

Figure 21-1:
Top: To access your OS X machine from across the Internet, fire up a program like RBrowser and use the address ftp://111.222.33.4 (or whatever your public IP address is).

Bottom: Once you're looking at an FTP server's contents, you can drag files from your desktop into the list, copy them to your Mac by dragging them out of the list onto your desktop, or open them by double-clicking.

Just Downloading from FTP Sites

If you're just going to *look at* and *download* files (but not upload or delete any), you don't even need a special FTP program. You can get to the files much more directly using one of these two methods:

- Any old Web browser will work. Open Safari, for example, and type *ftp://ftp.apple.com* (or whatever the address is) into the address bar. A dialog box asks for an account name and password, if they're required. Once you're in, you switch to the Finder and see the contents of the FTP site as a window full of standard file icons. (In other browsers, you may see the list of the FTP site right in the browser window.)

- Using the Finder's Go→Connect to Server command, you can mount read-only FTP volumes right on your desktop. In other words, they appear just like any other disk icons.

In the Connect to Server dialog box, just enter the address of the file server you would like to mount—*ftp://ftp.apple.com,* for example. You'll soon see the ftp.apple.com icon appear on your desktop, looking just like your other disks. Open it up and drag out whatever you want to download.

Connecting from the Road

You can also connect to your Mac's regular File Sharing feature (Chapter 14) from over the Internet. This feature is a blessing to anyone who travels, whether with a laptop or to a branch office, because you'll never be up the creek without a paddle if you discover that you left an important file at home.

The easiest way to go about it is to use Back to My Mac, which is one of Apple's iCloud services.

If you'd rather spend time than money, though, you can set up a remote file-sharing system on your own. Start by setting up the home-base Mac for file sharing, as directed in Chapter 14; then figure out your Mac's public IP address, as described in the box on page 774.

Finally, once you're on the road, go online and proceed like this:

1. **Choose Go→Connect to Server.**

 The Connect to Server dialog box appears, as shown in Figure 21-2.

Figure 21-2:
The Connect to Server dialog box lets you type in the IP address for the shared Mac you want to access. (Ensuring that the shared Mac is turned on and connected to the Internet is the network administrator's problem.)

2. **Type in the public IP address of the Mac to which you want to connect, and then click Connect (or press Return).**

 See the box on page 774 for a discussion of public vs. private IP addresses.

3. **Enter your name and password, and then click Connect.**

From here, it's just as though you were connecting to another computer on your office network (Chapter 14), although it's a good bit slower. But when you're in Hong Kong and need a document from your Mac in Minneapolis, you may not care.

Remote Access with SSH

Are you a geek? Take this simple test at home: Do you get excited about OS X's ability to permit SSH access?

If you answered "What's SSH?" or "I'm *already* being quiet," then the following discussion of Unix remote control may not interest you. To be sure, SSH is not a program with a graphic user interface (icons and menus). You operate it from within a program like Terminal by typing commands. (For details on Terminal, see the free downloadable Appendix called "Terminal Crash Course.pdf" on this book's "Missing CD" page at *www.missingmanuals.com.*)

If you're willing to overlook that little peccadillo, though, SSH (Secure Shell) is an extremely powerful tool. It lets you connect to your Mac from anywhere—from across the network or across the Internet. And once you're connected, you can take complete control of it, copying files, running commands, rearranging folders, or even shutting it down, all by remote control.

Getting In

Here's how you go about using SSH:

1. **Set up your Mac by opening the Sharing panel of System Preferences, and then turning on the Remote Login checkbox.**

 You've just told the Mac it's OK for you (or other people with accounts on your machine) to connect from the road. Quit System Preferences.

2. **Go away.**

 You can move to another machine on the network, or another computer on the Internet (if you've dealt with the port-forwarding issue described on page 774). Once you're online with that other machine, you can contact your home-base machine from within a program like Terminal.

Tip: It doesn't have to be Terminal, and it doesn't have to be a Mac. You can get *SSH client* programs for almost any kind of computer.

For pre–OS X Macs, for example, you can try MacSSH or NiftyTelnet SSH, both of which you can download from this book's "Missing CD" page at *www.missingmanuals.com.* For Windows, try Putty (*www.puttyssh.org*).

3. **At the prompt, type *ssh -l chris 111.222.3.44.* Press Return.**

 Instead of *chris,* substitute your short account name (as you're known on the Mac you're tapping into), and replace the phony IP address shown here with your real public address. (If your Mac back home has a domain name unto itself, such as

macmania.com, you can type that instead of the IP address. And if you've turned on port forwarding, use your cable modem/DSL box's IP address.)

If all goes well, the *ssh* command acknowledges your first successful connection by displaying a message like this: "The authenticity of host '111.222.3.44 (111.222.3.44)' can't be established. RSA key fingerprint is d9:f4:11:b0:27:1a:f1: 14:c3:cd:25:85:2b:78:4d:e7. Are you sure you want to continue connecting (yes/no)?" (This message won't appear on subsequent connections.) You're seeing SSH's security features at work.

4. **Type yes and press Return.**

 Now you see one more note: "Warning: Permanently added '111.222.3.44' (RSA) to the list of known hosts." You're then asked for your account password.

5. **Type your account password and press Return.**

 You're in. Issue whatever commands you want. You can now conduct a full Unix Terminal session—but by remote control.

Tip: For a more thorough description of SSH and its options, type *man ssh* at the prompt.

Remote Control Program Killing

One of the most common uses of SSH is quitting a stuck program. Maybe it's a program that doesn't respond to the usual Force Quit commands—maybe even the Finder or Terminal. Or maybe, having just arrived in Accounting on the fifth floor, you realize that you accidentally left your Web browser, open to Dilbert.com, up on your screen in clear view of passersby.

In any case, you'd fire up Terminal and proceed like this (what you type is shown in bold; the Mac's responses are in normal type):

```
home-mac:~ chris$ ssh 172.24.30.182
The authenticity of host '111.222.3.44 (111.222.3.44)' can't be
established. RSA key fingerprint is d9:f4:11:b0:27:1a:f1:14:c3:c
d:25:85:2b:78:4d:e7.
Are you sure you want to continue connecting (yes/no)? yes
Warning: Permanently added '172.24.30.182' (RSA) to the list of
known hosts.
chris@111.222.3.44's password: fisheggs
Last login: Thu Apr 22 17:23:38 2010
Welcome to Darwin!
office-mac:~ chris$ top -u
```

The *top -u* command displays a list of running programs. After a block of memory statistics, you might see a list like this:

```
1156  top         6.6  00:00.27 1/1  0    28   29   1344K+
216K  2052K+ 17M
139   Terminal    2.4  00:34.24 5    1    130- 192- 11M-   28M
```

```
 26M-    51M
 788    bash         0.0  00:00.02 1    0    20    24    656K
 840K   1436K   17M
 787    login        0.0  00:00.04 2    1    34    62    880K
 260K   2144K   49M
 283    Finder       0.0  00:23.02 9    3   247   666   33M    96M
 81M    70M
 426    SystemUIServ 0.0  00:14.24 3    1   290   410   30M    47M
 47M    112M
 151    Dock         0.0  00:05.95 4    2   201   851   22M    36M
 59M    73M
```

As you can see, the Finder is process number 283. If that's the stuck program, then,
you could quit it like so:

```
office-mac:~ chris$ kill 283
```

Or if you're sure of the program's exact name, just use the *killall* command with the
program's name instead of its process ID. To handle a stuck Finder, you would type this:

```
office-mac:~ chris$ killall Finder
```

Either way, the Finder promptly quits (and relaunches in a healthier incarnation, you
hope). You could also, at this point, type *sudo shutdown -h now* to make your Mac,
elsewhere on the network, shut down. (Terminal doesn't type any kind of response.)

If you ended your SSH session by shutting down the other Mac, you can just close the
Terminal window now. Otherwise, type *exit* to complete your SSH session.

Tip: Want a quicker, dirtier method of doing SSH that doesn't even require knowing the other machine's
IP address? OK: Open Terminal. Choose Shell→New Remote Connection. In the list of connection types,
choose ssh/ftp/telnet. Every Bonjour-enabled Mac on your network shows up; click one and then click
Connect to connect!

Virtual Private Networking

After reading the previous pages, you might assume it's a piece of cake for business-
people to connect to their corporate networks across the Internet from wherever they
happen to be: their homes, hotel rooms, or their local Starbucks. But even though
the steps on the preceding pages work fine if you're dialing into your *home* machine,
they'll probably fail miserably when you want to connect to a corporate network.
There's one enormous obstacle in your way: Internet security.

The typical corporate network is guarded by a team of steely-eyed administrators, for
whom Job Number One is preventing access by unauthorized visitors. They perform
this job primarily with the aid of a super-secure firewall that seals off the company's
network from the Internet.

So how can you tap into the network from the road? One solution is to create a hole in the firewall for each authorized user—software that permits incoming Internet traffic only from specified IP addresses like your Mac's. Unfortunately, this setup isn't bulletproof, security-wise. It's also a pain for administrators to manage.

Back in the dial-up modem days, you could dial directly into the corporate network, modem-to-modem. That was plenty secure, but it bypassed the Internet and therefore wound up being expensive. (Want proof? Try this simple test: Make a call from the Tokyo Hilton to the Poughkeepsie Sheet Metal home office. Have a look at your hotel bill when you check out.)

Fortunately, there's a third solution that's both secure and cheap: the *Virtual Private Network,* or *VPN.* Running a VPN allows you to create a super-secure "tunnel" from your Mac, across the Internet, and straight into your corporate network. All data passing through this tunnel is heavily encrypted; to the Internet eavesdropper, it looks like so much undecipherable gobbledygook.

And it's free—whether you're accessing the Internet via your home DSL, a local ISP number from a hotel, or wirelessly from your stool at Starbucks.

Remember, though, that VPN is a corporate tool, run by corporate nerds. You can't use this feature without these pieces in place:

- **A VPN server.** This is a big deal. If your tech department tells you they don't have one, then that's that—no tunneling for you.

 If they do have one, then you'll need to know the type of server it is. OS X's VPN software can connect to VPN servers that speak *PPTP* (Point to Point Tunneling Protocol), *L2TP/IPsec* (Layer 2 Tunneling Protocol over IP Security), or Cisco IPSec. Most corporate VPN servers work with at least one of these protocols.

 You'll also need to know the Internet address of your VPN server (for example, *vpn.ferrets-r-us.com*).

- **An account on the remote network that allows VPN access.** Your remote network can be set up in many different ways, but in every case, you'll still need to confirm with your network administrator that your account on it allows VPN access.

- **All necessary account information.** Make sure you have all the scraps of connection information you'll need to dial in. That would include your **user (account) name,** at the very least. You may also need a **Windows Domain name;** VPN servers are often part of Microsoft Windows Server networks, which won't let you in until you know this domain name.

 Some networks also may require that you type in the currently displayed password on an **RSA SecurID card,** which your administrator will provide. This James Bond-ish, credit card–like thing displays a password that changes every few seconds, making it rather difficult for hackers to learn "the" password. (If your network doesn't require a SecurID card, you'll need a **standard password** instead.)

Finally, if your office offers L2TP connections, you'll need yet another password called a **Shared Secret** to ensure that the server you're connecting to is really the server you intend to connect to.

Setting Up the VPN Connection

If you're lucky, your company's network geek has provided you with a VPN settings file, a little double-clickable icon that automatically opens the Network pane of System Preferences and fills in the blanks for you. If not, you can do all that manually:

Note: OpenVPN is a free, very popular VPN program. If your VPN uses OpenVPN, you'll need to get some connection software from your company's network geeks.

1. **Open System Preferences. Click Network. Click the + button below the list of connections at the left side.**

 The "Select the interface" sheet appears.

Figure 21-3:
You're on your way to joining the corporate network—from thousands of miles away. Virtual private networking is ideal for the paranoid (because it's very secure) and the cheap (because you're using the Internet as a giant wire connecting you to your office).

2. From the pop-up menu, choose VPN.

Now a new pop-up menu appears, called VPN Type; you're supposed to choose either L2TP over IPSec (Layer 2 Tunneling Protocol over IP Security), PPTP (Point to Point Tunneling Protocol), or Cisco IPsec (IP Security). Find out which system your company's network uses.

POWER USERS' CLINIC

Web Sharing—and OS X Server

Until Mountain Lion came along, you could turn your Mac into a Web site (or server), accessible from the Web browsers of people on your office network, the Internet at large, or both. All you had to do was visit the Sharing pane of System Preferences and turn on "Web Sharing."

After you provided your friends and coworkers with your Mac's Web site address, they could view your Web pages, graphics, and documents in their own Web browsers. And whenever your Mac was online, your Web site was also available to anyone on the Internet—but you didn't have to pay a penny to a Web-hosting company.

Web sharing was also an easy and efficient way to share your Mac files with Windows PCs, either those on your office network or those on the Internet. No special software or translation required.

OS X's Web Sharing feature wasn't some feeble junior version, either. Inside was Apache, one of the strongest and most popular Unix Web server programs—precisely the same one that drives over 60 percent of the Internet's commercial Web sites.

The bottom line: If you built it, they didn't necessarily come. But you had the capacity to handle them if they did.

Why the past tense? Because the Web Sharing button is no longer in Mountain Lion.

Weirdly, though, the Apache server is still there. It just lacks a front end so that you can set it up.

Apple cheerfully points out that OS X Server, a $20 add-on for Mountain Lion, offers all the controls you need for hosting Web sites on that Apache software.

So what is OS X Server?

Many of its features are of interest only to people who run servers in a small business or school: calendar server, mail server, file server. For normal non-technical people, iCloud offers these same features for free—so why would you want a server running in your home?

Well, OS X Server's built in file-sharing feature lets you share files over your WiFi network your iPad (a feature called File Sharing for iPad). So you can put files on the server in your home, and you can access them directly from your iPad.

But perhaps the most interesting tool included with Server is Profile Manager. With Profile Manager, you can set up Macs, iPhones, iPads, and iPod Touches—centrally, directly from the Mac running Server. What's more, you can send these configuration changes to those machines wirelessly, by remote control.

These configurations can include almost any setting you can think of: set restrictions on all sorts of things (great for families with young kids): restrict multiplayer gaming, control whether your kid can add friends on game center, and turn on restrictions on TV and movies. You can even remotely configure email accounts, erase a device, or just lock it.

OS X Server gets even more interesting when you combine its features. Want to share an address book with the whole family? Set up the Contacts Server feature, and use Profile Manager to configure all your Macs and iOS devices to use that address book. You can do the same with calendars, too.

OS X Server is aimed at small businesses—and techier ones, at that. But if you want that Web server back, OS X Server is one good way to get it.

Note: OS X can't connect to all Cisco setups; in some cases, you'll still have to use Cisco's own connection software to dial in.

3. **After you choose the type of VPN from the VPN Type pop-up menu, type a name for this connection (it can be anything you want). Click Create.**

 You return to the main Network pane, where the settings boxes for your VPN are waiting (Figure 21-3).

4. **Fill in the server address and account name. Click Authentication Settings to specify your password and other security settings.**

 Here, for example, is where you indicate that you have one of those SecurID cards.

5. **Click OK. Turn on "Show VPN status in menu bar."**

 That checkbox makes the VPN menulet (▦) appear; it's your ticket to getting connected (Figure 21-3, top).

Tip: If you always connect to the same VPN, you can turn on VPN on Demand. It autoconnects you to your corporate VPN every time you direct your Web browser to a Web site, file server, or resource that requires the VPN connection, saving you some steps.

To set this up, click Advanced. (You can see this button in Figure 21-3.) Click VPN on Demand; click **+**. Enter the corporate VPN domain. You're good to go—as long as you've got your network geek's permission. (Some of them get understandably nervous about you storing your network password in your Keychain. It's convenient, yes, but could open up your company's entire network to the evil intentions of whoever walks up to your laptop while you're away from your desk.)

Close System Preferences. You're ready to connect.

Connecting to a VPN

Connect the way you normally do—via cable modem, DSL, office network, modem, AirPort, or whatever. Once you're online, choose your VPN's name from the ▦ menulet. You'll be asked for your credentials: your password, for example, or the code displayed on your SecurID card.

If all goes well, several status messages go by. The last one says, "Connected To" and gives the IP address of the network equipment you've reached out and touched.

At this point, you're connected to the corporate network. You can perform the same network-related tasks you could if you were actually in that office: check your email, view internal corporate Web pages, access internal FTP servers, make printouts on laser printers thousands of miles away, and so on.

Depending on your network, you might even be able to use your Sidebar to view a list of the other computers on the office network, or see a list of networked printers.

If not, to access these services, you must know their IP addresses. For example, to connect to a shared folder on another computer, choose Go→Connect to Server, type its network address, and press Return.

Tip: To connect to a shared folder on a Windows machine, the address looks like this: *smb://111.222.33.4/ sales-docs*. Of course, you'd substitute the correct IP address for the dummy one shown here and insert the actual name of the shared folder. (You can also use its *DNS name* instead of the IP address, if you know it, like this: *smb://big-blue-server.ferret-lan.com/sales-docs.*)

When you're finished accessing the remote network, choose Disconnect from the VPN menulet. (Accessing other Web sites can be slow while you're on a VPN.)

The Fine Points of VPN

For all the wonders of VPN, here are some possible complications:

- If you're using a *router* at home (a little box that shares one cable modem or DSL box with several computers), it might not be able to handle the tunneling protocols, or it might not have that feature turned on. Check the router's manual, or ask its manufacturer for more information. For example, the first-generation (silver) AirPort base stations can't handle VPNs at all.

- If the corporate network doesn't seem to like your name and password, you might need to add your NT domain name and a *backward* slash to the beginning of your account name (like this: *dom01\msmith*) before trying again.

- If you're able to make the connection but experience trouble reaching services by their DNS names (for example, *big-blue-server.com*), your Mac could be having difficulty finding the right DNS server. Working with your network administrator, open the Network pane of System Preferences. Click VPN, then click Advanced, and then DNS; enter the desired DNS server addresses in the DNS Servers box. Click OK, then Apply, and then try the VPN connection again.

- If you're still having problems using the VPN, look at the *logs* (automatically kept technical records) for clues to share with your network administrator. To view these records, open the Console program (in Applications→Utilities). Click Show Log List, expand the */var/log* section, and click *ppp.log*.

Part Six:
Appendixes

6

Installing OS X Mountain Lion

I f your computer came with Mountain Lion already installed on it, you can skip this appendix—for now. But if you're running an earlier version of the Mac OS and want to savor the Mountain Lion experience, this appendix describes how to install the new operating system on your Mac.

As you'll soon discover, the installation process received an enormous, even radical overhaul from Apple this time around. You can't buy Mountain Lion in a box, or on a DVD; you're supposed to download it from the Mac App Store.

There are some very attractive elements to the download-only system. For example, there's no copy protection and no serial numbers to type in. You don't have to pay extra for multiple copies; your one-time $20 covers as many Macs as you own or control. (In other words, there's no Family Plan for Mountain Lion.)

Now there's no disc to hunt down later, when you want to install Mountain Lion again (onto a new Mac, for example). And when you do need a copy again, you'll

POWER USERS' CLINIC

The Partitioning Question

Before you install Mountain Lion, you might want to confront the issue of *partitioning* your Mac's hard drive—dividing its space so that it shows up on your desktop with two different icons and two different names. You can keep Mountain Lion on one and Snow Leopard on the other, for example. Now you can live like a king, enjoying all the advantages of having two separate hard drives.

As a bonus, the Mac even comes with a partitioning program: Disk Utility. And it no longer requires first erasing the drive completely; you can repartition on the fly, without disturbing whatever is already on the drive.

download the latest version—10.8.3 or whatever it is—instead of having to install whatever updates have come out since you got your DVD.

(And what if you don't have a fast Internet connection for downloading Mountain Lion? The world won't come to an end; read on.)

Hardware Requirements

For starters, you need to make sure you and your Mac have what it takes to handle Mountain Lion—specifically:

- **A Mac that's not a geezer.** Mountain Lion can run on the iMac (mid-2007 or newer), aluminum MacBook (late 2008 or newer), plastic MacBook (early 2009 or newer), MacBook Pro (mid-2007 or newer), MacBook Air (late 2008 or newer), Mac mini (early 2009 or newer), or Mac Pro (early 2008 or newer).

- **Snow Leopard or Lion.** Your Mac has to be running Lion or the most recent pre-Lion software version, Mac OS X 10.6.8 (Snow Leopard). (The main reason: You need the App Store to get Mountain Lion, and the App Store debuted in Snow Leopard.) Even if you already have Snow Leopard or Lion, run Software Update to make sure you have the *latest* version.

 If you don't have Snow Leopard, then the cost of Lion just went up. You'll have to buy and install Snow Leopard ($30) and then buy and install Mountain Lion.

- **Free storage space.** You need at least 8 GB free on your hard drive or flash storage to install Mac OS X 10.8.

POWER USERS' CLINIC

Reinstalling: Tricks of the Trade

You can install Mountain Lion on as many Macs as you own, all for the same $20. To install it on a second Mac, for example, open the App Store. Click the Purchases tab at the top. You'll see your previous Mountain Lion purchase listed there; just click Install to start installing Mountain Lion on *that* Mac.

That's what most people will do, anyway. Unfortunately, that means downloading the 4-gigabyte installer again for each Mac. That takes a lot of time and eats up a lot of your monthly Internet data allotment.

There is, fortunately, a trick that saves you the trouble of re-downloading Lion over and over again: Copy the Install OS X Mountain Lion installer program from the *first* Mac to all your other Macs (over the network or on a flash drive, for example). There's also a tricky part to this trick: Ordinarily,

installing Mountain Lion on the first Mac *deletes* that installer program once it's finished, to save you the disk space.

The trick to this trick, then, is to copy the installer to another Mac or drive (or at least take it out of your Applications folder) *before* you install Mountain Lion on the first Mac.

Or you may you want to install Mountain Lion again on the *same* Mac. But if you visit the App Store, you'll discover that you're not allowed to download it again on that machine; the "$19.99" button becomes an unclickable "Installed" button.

To fool the App Store, Option-click the Mountain Lion link in the App Store. Or Option-click the Purchases tab at the top of the screen. Or hold down the Option key as you open the App Store program. One of those three tricks should restore the Buy button for Mountain Lion so you can download it again. (You won't be charged again.)

- **A lot of memory.** Apple recommends at least 2 GB of memory, but OS X absolutely *loves* memory. For the greatest speed, install 4 gigabytes—more if you can afford it. (And these days, you probably can.)

- **The latest firmware.** *Firmware* describes the low-level, underlying software instructions that control the actual circuitry of your Mac. Every now and then, Apple updates it for certain Mac models, and it's very important that your Mac have the absolute latest. If yours doesn't, a message will appear to let you know during the installation. Quit the installer and grab the latest update from *http://support. apple.com/kb/HT1237.*

- **A full backup.** It's a really, *really* good idea to back up your entire Mac before you begin this, or any, upgrade. Even if things go wrong for only, say, 0.01 percent of Mac owners, that's still thousands of people. If you don't have a second hard drive, this is your excuse to buy one; they're dirt cheap these days. You can use Snow Leopard's or Lion's version of Time Machine to make a complete, automatic backup of your Mac as it is now.

Psychological Requirements

Upgrading an operating system is always a traumatic experience for a computer—and, too often, for its owner. If you can rein in your excitement long enough to perform just a few extra steps, you'll be glad you did.

- **Check your hard drive.** Open Disk Utility (page 456), click your main hard drive's name and then click Verify Disk. If the program reports that you have problems, you'll have to start up from a different disk (like the Snow Leopard DVD), run Disk Utility again, and use the Repair Disk button this time.

- **Turn off FileVault, if you're using it.** (You'd remember turning on this Home-folder-encryption feature in Snow Leopard or Lion.)

 Don't complicate matters by asking the installer to translate between the old File-Vault encryption system and the new, Mountain Lion version. Turn off FileVault (and any other company's disk-encryption programs) before you upgrade.

- **Make sure your software will run.** Most modern programs run very smoothly on Mountain Lion. But some older ones won't run—in particular, programs like AppleWorks and Microsoft Office 2004 that relied on the old Rosetta translation technology. Find out for sure by visiting *http://roaringapps.com/apps:table* and looking up the programs you own.

Tip: You can also look up your own programs using the System Profiler program in your Applications→Utilities folder. In the left-side column, click Applications. Click the Kind column heading to sort your programs. The programs listed as *PowerPC* or *Classic* won't run in Mountain Lion.

The Standard Installation

To do the actual installation, open the App Store program on your Mac. If you don't see "OS X Mountain Lion" advertised right there on the home page, you can find it by searching for *mountain lion*. Click the price button, and then click again when it changes to say Install (Figure A-1).

Figure A-1:
Enter your Apple ID and password when you're asked for it, and enjoy a hot mug of your favorite beverage as the download begins. If you have a typical broadband Internet connection, expect to wait about half an hour.

When the download begins, behind the scenes, the App Store puts a 3.8-gigabyte program called *Install OS X Mountain Lion* into your Applications folder.

Tip: If you don't have a fast Internet connection, or if your Internet provider imposes monthly data limits, you might not be thrilled about the prospect of waiting for a 4-gigabyte download.

Your best bet is to take your Mac to an Apple Store and use *its* free, fast WiFi to download Mountain Lion (or a friend's house, a library, a coffee shop…). Alas, Apple no longer sells a flash drive with the installer, as it did for Lion.

You'll know when the downloading is over, because the actual installer opens up automatically and presents you with the proud animal shown in Figure A-2.

The procedure from here:

1. **Click Continue.**

 The installer follows a pattern: Read the instructions, make a couple of choices, and then click Continue to advance to the next screen. As you go, the list on the left side of the screen reveals where you are in the overall procedure.

Figure A-2:
Your installation adventure is about to begin. You've never experienced such a simple operating-system installation. You don't even have to restart the computer before you start. You have far fewer options and decisions to make.

2. **Click Agree to pass the Software License Agreement screen, and then Agree again.**

 The software license agreement requires you to agree with whatever Apple's lawyers say.

3. **Choose the disk or partition where you want to install OS X.**

 The installer proposes the screamingly obvious hard drive: the main one inside your Mac.

 If you have other drives, you can click Show All Disks to see their icons and choose one. Yellow exclamation-mark icons mean, "You can't install here," for one technical reason or another. You can install Mountain Lion only onto a blank hard drive, formatted as a Mac drive (technically, "Mac OS Extended [Journaled]" format), or onto a drive that has Lion or Snow Leopard on it.

4. **Click Install. Enter an administrator's account name and password when you're asked for it.**

Now you're in for a 20- to 30-minute wait as the Installer copies software onto your hard drive. (That's why, if you're using a laptop and it's not plugged in, you'll be encouraged to plug it in.) At one point, it restarts the Mac and carries right on.

OS X 10.8 is now installed on your Mac. That, if you hadn't noticed, was a far less harrowing experience than it was in previous OS X installations. You were never asked what kind of installation you wanted, which language translations or printer drivers you wanted installed, which optional components you wanted, and so on.

Still, you're not quite ready to use Mountain Lion yet. Read on.

The Setup Assistant

What you see depends on whether you installed Mountain Lion onto an older OS X drive or an empty drive.

After Installing Over Snow Leopard or Lion

If you installed onto a drive that already had OS X stuff on it—accounts, files, settings, and so on—then after the Mac restarts, all you have to do is log in as usual. Enjoy the box that warns you about Lion's upside-down scrolling habit (page 11). Click Start Using Mountain Lion, and start using Mountain Lion.

TROUBLESHOOTING MOMENT

Journaling

If you decide to erase your hard drive before installing Mountain Lion, you're offered a choice of several formats for your hard drive. But you should stick with the factory setting, "Mac OS Extended (Journaled)." It turns on a special background feature of OS X known as *file journaling*.

When file journaling is turned on, your Mac keeps a personal diary of everything you do on your hard drive—opening, saving, deleting files, and so on. Journaling offers two benefits: a shorter startup time and safety in the event of a crash.

Here's how it works: When you press the power button, OS X checks to see whether your computer was shut down properly (by choosing →Shut Down, for example, instead of just pulling out the plug).

If you didn't shut down properly, OS X examines your hard drive the next time you start up to see if it needs repair. It has to scan the whole drive—which can take quite a while. Thanks to file journaling, however, Mountain Lion can tell what was happening when your computer shut down—and therefore spend a lot less time checking your hard drive.

There are some downsides to the journaled format, however. First, this procedure doesn't actually recover what you were working on when your Mac shut down; it can only try to keep files you already saved from getting corrupted. Second, file journaling can make it take slightly longer for your programs to save files.

OS X doesn't prevent you from having different hard drives with different formats. You can use the journaled format on your main hard drive, but not on your external FireWire drive—or vice versa. (If you ever want to change the format of one of your disks, use Disk Utility, although you'll have to erase all the information on the disk first.)

If you leave your Mac on all the time (if you run it as a Web server, for example), it's a good idea to use the journaled hard drive format. Keep in mind, too, that blackouts affect your hard drive just as much as pulling the plug. So if you live in Iraq, a solar-powered house, or anywhere else power is inconsistent, journaling can be a lifesaver.

Note: It's possible, at this point, that Mountain Lion will display a message warning you that it found some incompatible software on your Mac during the installation. You'll discover that this outdated software has been summarily tossed into a folder called Incompatible Software in your startup disk's main window.

After Installing onto a Blank Drive

If you installed Mountain Lion onto an empty drive, then the Setup Assistant is a little more involved.

Once again, you're in for a click-through-the-screens experience, this time with the aim of setting up your Mac's various options. After answering the questions on each screen, click Continue.

The number and sequence of information screens you encounter may vary, but here are some of the possibilities:

- **Welcome.** Click the name of the country you're in.

POWER USERS' CLINIC

The Clean Install

In all of OS X's incarnations so far, there were two ways to install it: the *automatic* way and the *clean install*.

The automatic way preserved everything on your Mac. Every program, setting, and file stayed exactly as you had it. In essence, this kind of installation just worked through your System folder, updating each component and disturbing nothing else.

The *clean install* was preferred by power users, especially in times of troubleshooting, because it erased your entire hard drive and *then* installed OS X. Any minor corruptions or ancient software crumbs were swept away, leaving you with a clean, perfect system.

The clean-install option is gone from the Mountain Lion installer; Apple says its automatic installation method is perfect enough that the erase-and-install business is no longer useful.

Sometimes, though, a clean install *is* still useful. For one thing, some people just like the idea of starting fresh. For another, this process lets you install Mountain Lion onto a Mac that's running *Leopard* (Mac OS X 10.5), without having to upgrade it to Snow Leopard first. (This method saves you time, but not money—you'll still need a Mac running Snow

Leopard or Later to *get* the Mountain Lion installer, since you need Snow Leopard to use the App Store to buy Mountain Lion in the first place.)

Anyway, start by making a *complete backup* of the Mac you want to Mountain Lionize. In case you missed it, the clean-install process *erases everything on it.*

Now make a homemade Mountain Lion startup drive, as described on page 796. Use it to start up the Mac you just backed up.

The first thing you'll see is a Utilities screen; you can read more about this Recovery Mode in Appendix B. Click Disk Utility, and then click Continue. In Disk Utility, click the Mac's hard drive name at the left side; click Erase; choose "Mac OS Extended (Journaled)" from the Format pop-up menu; click Erase.

When the erasing is over, quit Disk Utility. You return to the Utilities screen.

Now click Reinstall OS X. Click Continue to trigger the Mountain Lion installation described on these pages. At the end of it, you'll be offered the chance to copy everything from your backup back onto the empty hard drive.

- **Select Your Keyboard.** Different countries require different keyboard layouts. For example, if you choose the Canadian layout, pressing the] key on a U.S. keyboard produces the ç symbol. Click Continue.

- **Select a Network Connection.** This is your chance to introduce the Mac to any networks in the vicinity. Click the name of the WiFi hot spot you want to join, for

GEM IN THE ROUGH

Windows Migration

If, on the Transfer Information screen, you choose From a Windows PC, then you're treated to an unsung hero in Mountain Lion: the Windows Migration tool. It's an automatic tool that copies all your important data from a Windows PC (running Windows XP SP3 or later) to your Mac.

When all is said and done, here's what it accomplishes:

Transfers your email into Mail from Outlook, Outlook Express, Windows Mail, or Windows Live accounts (POP or IMAP). Your messages even show up correctly flagged as having been read, replied to, and flagged (except if they originated in Windows Live).

Transfers your address book into Contacts from Outlook and Outlook Express contacts, and Windows Contacts from the Contact home folder on your PC.

Transfers your calendar into Calendar from Outlook's calendar.

Transfers your iTunes collection from iTunes on Windows into iTunes for the Mac. Everything comes over, including music, photos, videos (but not rentals), and apps and games for iPhone/iPad/iPod Touch.

Transfers everything in your Windows Home folder into the corresponding Mac folders: Music, Pictures, Desktop, Documents, and Downloads.

Transfers your browser bookmarks and preferred home page into Safari from Explorer, Firefox, and Safari for Windows.

Transfers your account settings like language and even your desktop wallpaper.

All of this winds up in a *new* user account on your Mac. The migration program doesn't make any attempt to *merge* your Windows world into your existing account on the Mac.

For this to work, your Windows PC and Mac have to be on the same network; see Chapter 13.

To begin, you'll need the free Windows Migration Assistant program. It's waiting at *www.apple.com/migrate-to-mac.* On your PC, download, install, and then open this program. Click Continue.

The steps now depend on how you arrived at the Transfer Your Information screen on the Mac.

If you're in the process of installing Mountain Lion: Click From a Windows PC (Figure A-3, center) and then click OK. Click your PC's name and then click OK.

If you're doing this later, using the Migration Assistant program in your Mac's Applications→Utilities folder: On the Mac, quit all programs. Click "From another Mac, PC, Time Machine backup, or other disk," and then click Continue. Authenticate yourself, and then click "From another Mac or PC." Click Continue; click the PC's name.

No matter how you got here: When the six-digit passcode appears on the Mac and PC screens, click Continue again.

After a while, the Mac shows you a list of all the stuff it can bring over from the PC (Music, Pictures, Mail Accounts, and so on). Turn on the ones you care about, and then click Continue.

The transferring process may take a *long* time. When you finally start up your Mac again, you'll be asked to provide a name and password for the new account that the Migration Assistant created for your Windows-world-on-the-Mac. (If you didn't *want* your Windows stuff to wind up in a different account, you can always copy it back into your main account using the Users→Shared folder as a tunnel between accounts.)

example. If there's no wireless hotspot at all—hey, it could happen—click Different Network Setup to specify, say, a wired or cellular network hookup.

- **Transfer Information to This Mac.** The Setup Assistant can suck all your old programs, files, folders, and settings from the old Mac to the new one—or even from an old *Windows PC* to your new Mac. Meet the Migration Assistant (Figure A-3).

 Your choices here are **From another Mac** (connect your old Mac to this one over a network, even a wireless one); **From a Windows PC** (ditto); **From Time Machine or other disk** (connect your new Mac to your backup drive); and **Don't Transfer now.**

Tip: You can always perform this sluggish task later. Just open the Migration Assistant program, in your Applications→Utilities folder, when it's a better time. See the facing page for more on migrating from Windows.

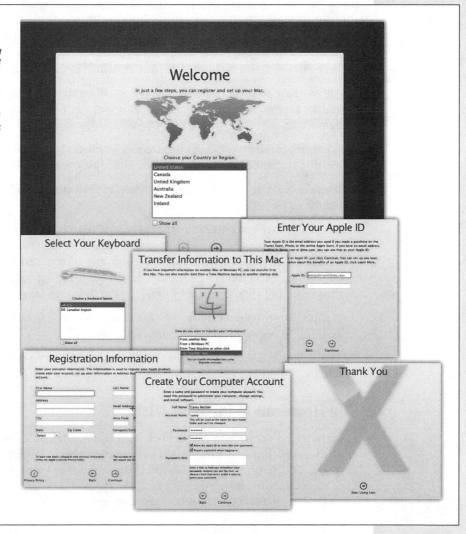

Figure A-3:
The Setup Assistant walks you through the final steps of getting a new Mac (or a clean Mountain Lion installation) ready. It includes the Migration Assistant, which transfers all your files from a backup, an old Mac, or an old Windows PC to your new Mac.

If you choose one of the first options and then click Transfer, the data-copying process begins. It can take a *wicked* long time.

- **Enter Your Apple ID.** Here you're offered the chance to type in an Apple ID (an email address and password for all your Apple dealings), which is more essential in Mountain Lion than ever before. If you don't have one, just click Continue; you can get one and fill it in later.

- **Registration Information.** This is your chance to become a grain of sand on the great beach of the Apple database (and to set up your own "card" in OS X's Contacts program).

Tip: If you're not interested in providing your personal information to Apple, or if you've already done so during a previous installation, press ⌘-Q. A message offers you Skip, Shut Down, and Cancel buttons. If you click Skip, you jump straight ahead to Create Your Computer Account, below.

- **Create Your Computer Account.** Most of the steps up to this point have been pretty inconsequential, but this is a big moment. You're about to create your *account—* your Administrator account, in fact, as described in Chapter 13.

 All you have to do is make up a name, usually a short variation of your name, and a password. Choose carefully, because you can't easily change your account name later.

 What you come up with here is extremely important, especially if several people use this Mac at different times, or if other people connect to it on a network.

 If you're the only one who uses your Mac, it's perfectly OK to leave the password blank empty.

- **Select a Picture For This Account.** If your Mac has a built-in camera (laptops and iMacs do), you can take a photo of yourself to use as your account icon. Just click "Take a video snapshot." You get a 3-second countdown, and then the Mac snaps your photo. (You can always reshoot it.) Adjust the cropping by dragging inside the photo, and adjust the size by dragging the slider beneath it.

 If you're camera-shy, of course, you can choose "Choose from the picture library" and find an Apple-provided icon instead.

- **Thank You.** When you click Start Using Mountain Lion, you wind up at the OS X desktop, just as described in Chapter 1.

The Homemade Installer Disk

Mountain Lion's download-only schtick is revolutionary and, in most cases, incredibly convenient. But sometimes, you'll miss having a physical disk with the Mountain Lion installer on it. You might wish you had one if, for example, you want to install Mountain Lion on a huge array of Macs, like the ones at a school or in a business; downloading that 4-gig installer over and over again would drive you crazy.

You might also wish you had an installation disk when your Mac starts acting up and the tricks described in Appendix B don't seem to work.

As it turns out, you can make a Mountain Lion installation disk fairly easily. All you need is a hard drive, a flash drive, or even a blank DVD. (Hard drives and flash drives are much faster at performing the actual installation.)

Phase 1: Format the Drive

If you're planning to use a flash drive or a hard drive, the first step is to format it so that the Mac will be able to start up from it. To do that, connect or insert the drive. (It needs at least 5 gigabytes of free space. These steps assume that there's nothing else on it.)

Now open Disk Utility (it's in your Applications→Utilities folder). In Disk Utility, click the drive's name in the left-side list (not the partition name beneath it). Then click the Partition tab in the main window.

Under Partition Layout, choose 1 Partition. Then click the actual partition—the big rectangle "map" in the middle of the window—and then click Options beneath it. In the resulting dialog box, click GUID Partition Table; click OK.

Tip: Actually, it's fine to create multiple partitions, so you don't wind up wasting a lot of disk space. Just give the installation partition at least 5 gigabytes so it will have room for the Mountain Lion installer.

Now, back at the Partition window, you can type a name for your drive. From the Format menu, choose "Mac OS Extended (Journaled)." Click Apply. Click Partition in the confirmation window. The process may take a minute or two.

Phase 2: Build Your Installer

Now you'll turn your formatted drive into a Mountain Lion installer.

Start by grabbing the *Install OS X Mountain Lion.app* program that winds up in your Applications folder when you first buy Mountain Lion. (You have to think of this *before* you actually run it, as described in the box on page 788. That box also tells you how you can re-download the Mountain Lion installer app if it's too late for that.)

Control-click (or right-click) the installer's icon. From the shortcut menu, choose Show Package Contents.

In the resulting folder, open Contents, and then open Shared Support. Inside is a disk-image file called *InstallESD.dmg*. Your job is to convert this disk image into an actual disk.

To do that, open Disk Utility again. Drag the *InstallESD.dmg* disk image into the list at the left side of Disk Utility's window. Click *InstallESD.dmg* in the list; then click the Restore tab. Insert the flash drive, or connect the hard drive, that you formatted in Phase 1.

Last steps: Drag your drive's icon out of the left-side list into the Destination box (Figure A-4). Click Restore; enter your administrator name and password when you're asked.

Note: If you want to create a Mountain Lion DVD (instead of a flash drive or a hard drive), here's the only different step. Instead, just click *InstallESD.dmg* in the left-side list, and then click Burn in the toolbar. Insert a blank DVD and then click Burn.

When the "restoring" process is complete, you wind up with an actual Mountain Lion flash drive or disk that you baked all by yourself.

To use it, turn off the Mac. Connect your homemade installer drive. When you turn on the Mac, hold down the Option key so that a choice of startup disks appears. Click your homemade installer to start up from it.

Now you can install Mountain Lion as usual, or use any of the recovery features described in Appendix B.

Figure A-4:
This is what the setup should look like in Disk Utility just before you actually create the installation disk.

Troubleshooting

W hether it's a car engine or an operating system, anything with several thousand parts can develop the occasional technical hiccup. OS X is far more resilient than its predecessors, but it's still a complex system with the potential for occasional glitches.

Most freaky little glitches go away if you just try these two steps, one at a time:

- Quit and restart the wayward program.

- Log out and log back in again.

It's the *other* problems that'll drive you batty.

Minor Eccentric Behavior

All kinds of glitches may befall you, occasionally, in OS X. Your desktop picture doesn't change when you change it in System Preferences. A menulet doesn't open when you click it. A program won't open—it just bounces in the Dock a couple of times and then stops.

When a single program is acting up like this, but quitting and restarting it does no good, try the following steps, in the following sequence.

First Resort: Repair Permissions

An amazing number of mysterious glitches arise because the *permissions* of either that item or something in your System folder—that is, the complex mesh of interconnected Unix permissions described in Chapter 14—have become muddled.

When something doesn't seem to be working right, therefore, open your Applications→ Utilities folder and open Disk Utility. Proceed as shown in Figure B-1.

This is a really, *really* great trick to know.

Figure B-1:
Click your hard drive's name in the left-side list, click the First Aid tab, click Repair Disk Permissions, and then read an article while the Mac checks out your disk. If the program finds anything amiss, you'll see messages like these. Among the text, you may recognize some Unix shorthand for read, write, and execute privileges.

Second Resort: Look for an Update

If a program starts acting up immediately after you've installed OS X 10.8, chances are good that it has some minor incompatibility. Chances are also good that you'll find an updated version on the company's Web site.

Third Resort: Toss the Prefs File

A corrupted preference file can bewilder the program that depends on it.

Before you go on a dumpfest, however, take this simple test: Log in using a *different account* (perhaps a dummy account that you create just for testing purposes). Run the problem program. Is the problem gone? If so, then the glitch exists only when *you* are logged in—which means it's a problem with *your* copy of the program's preferences.

Return to your own account. Open your Home→Library→Preferences folder, where you'll find neatly labeled preference files for all the programs you use. (To open the hidden Library folder, press the Option key as you open the Go menu; choose Library.)

Each preference file ends with the file name suffix *.plist*. For example, *com.apple.finder.plist* is the Finder's preference file, *com.apple.dock.plist* is the Dock's, and so on.

Put the suspect preference file into the Trash, but don't empty it. The next time you run the recalcitrant program, it will build itself a brand-new preference file that, if you're lucky, lacks whatever corruption was causing your problems.

If not, quit the program. You can reinstate its original .plist file from the Trash, if you find that helpful as you pursue your troubleshooting agenda.

Remember, however, that you actually have *two* Preferences folders. In addition to your own Home folder's stash, there's a second one in the Library folder in the main hard drive window (which administrators are allowed to trash; this one contains system-wide preferences, like your network configuration).

In any case, the next time you open the sick program or log in, the Mac creates fresh, virginal preference files.

Fourth Resort: Restart

Sometimes you can give OS X or its programs a swift kick by restarting the Mac. It's an inconvenient step, but not nearly as time-consuming as what comes next. And it can fix problems that cropped up when you started up the computer.

Last Resort: Trash and Reinstall the Program

Sometimes reinstalling the problem program clears up whatever the glitch was.

First, however, throw away all traces of it. Open the Applications folder and drag the program's icon (or its folder) to the Trash. In most cases, the only remaining pieces to discard are its .plist file (or files) in your Home→Library→Preferences folder, and any scraps bearing the program's name in your Library→Application Support folder. (You can do a quick Spotlight search to round up any other pieces.)

Then reinstall the program from its original disc or installer—after first checking the company's Web site to see if there's an updated version, of course.

Frozen Programs (Force Quitting)

The occasional unresponsive application has become such a part of OS X life that, among the Mac cognoscenti online, the dreaded, endless "please wait" cursor has been given its own acronym: SBOD (Spinning Beachball of Death). When the SBOD strikes, no amount of mouse clicking and keyboard pounding will get you out of the recalcitrant program.

Here are the different ways you can go about *force quitting* a stuck program (the equivalent of pressing Ctrl-Alt-Delete in Windows), in increasing order of desperation:

- **Force quit the usual way.** Choose →Force Quit to terminate the stuck program, or use one of the other force-quit methods described on page 170.

- **Force quit the sneaky way.** Some programs, including the Dock, don't show up at all in the usual Force Quit dialog box. Your next attempt, therefore, should be to open the Activity Monitor program (in Applications→Utilities), which shows *everything* that's running. Double-click a program and then, in the resulting dialog box, click Quit to force quit it. (Unix hounds: You can also use the *kill* command in Terminal.)

Tip: If you find yourself having to quit the Dock more than once, here's an easier way: Make yourself a little AppleScript (Chapter 7) consisting of a single line: *tell application "Dock" to quit.* Save it as an application. Whenever you feel that the Dock (or Spaces or Exposé, which technically belong to the Dock) needs a good kick in the rear, double-click your little AppleScript.

- **Force quit remotely.** If the Finder itself has locked up, you can't very well get to Activity Monitor (unless it occurred to you *beforehand* to stash its icon in your Dock—not a bad idea). At this point, you may have to abort the locked program from another computer across the network, if you're on one, by using the *SSH* (secure shell) command. Chapter 21 offers a blow-by-blow description of how you might terminate a program by remote control in this way, either from elsewhere on the office network or even from across the Internet.

Tip: If all of this seems like a lot to remember, you can always force restart the Mac. On most Macs, you do that by holding down the power button for 5 seconds. If that doesn't work, press Control-⌘-power button.

Recovery Mode: Three Emergency Disks

Mountain Lion, as you've probably heard, doesn't come on a DVD. When your Mac won't even start up, there's no DVD to insert as a backup startup disk, as there always was before. That's a scary place to be; if your hard drive is sick, then everything on it may be inaccessible to you. What you need is an emergency drive that can repair the hard drive and get you back in operation.

Apple is way ahead of you on this one. It offers *three* simulated repair disks: three ways to supply disk-repair and system-software repair tools in times of crisis.

The Recovery HD

Here's the sneaky surprise: When you install Mountain Lion, it automatically creates an invisible hidden "hard drive" (a partition of your main drive that has its own icon) called Recovery HD. It's a 650-megabyte "drive" that's generally invisible to you. It's even invisible to Disk Utility, so even if you erase your hard drive, the Recovery HD is still there to help you.

But if you can't seem to start up your Mac properly, or if your hard drive is acting a little flaky, you'll be glad you had this "separate" startup disk. On it, Apple has provided some emergency tools for fixing drive or software glitches, restoring files, browsing the Web, and even reinstalling Mountain Lion.

Note: The Mountain Lion installer creates the Recovery HD partition only if your startup drive is an internal drive. In certain other situations, it won't create the partition—for example, if the disk you're installing Mountain Lion onto is a RAID volume or has a non-standard Boot Camp partition setup.

You can power up your Mac from the Recovery HD in either of two ways:

- **Hold down ⌘-R as the Mac is starting up.** You can let go when you see the Apple logo appear.

- **Hold down the Option key as the Mac is starting up.** When you see the Startup Manager (Figure B-2, top), let go. Click the up-arrow button below the Recovery HD icon.

Figure B-2:
Top: This simple display of disk icons is known as the Startup Manager. It's an easy way to specify which disk you want to start up from.

Bottom: Here's the point of the Recovery HD partition: a screen full of emergency utilities that can fix your Mac's regularly scheduled hard drive. If there's a pop-up menu at the bottom, it's for choosing a WiFi hot spot so that you can access the rest of your network. That might be useful when, for example, you want to access your Time Capsule backups.

Either way, you wind up at the Utilities screen shown in Figure B-2, bottom.

Here, Apple has supplied you with four important tools:

- **Restore From Time Machine Backup.** If your Mac is really hosed, this is the option you want. It restores your *entire* software world—programs, data, settings, OS X itself—from the Time Machine backup you carefully set up as you read Chapter 6.

 This option *completely erases* your existing hard drive, so—you know. Be sure.

 Once you choose this option, click Continue. You're now asked to choose the Time Machine drive, then the time-stamped backup you want to restore from, and, finally, the drive or partition you want to wipe out. You get one more warning that you're about to wipe out the destination drive. When you click Continue, the restoration begins. When it's all over—usually a couple of hours later—the Mac restarts as though nothing ever happened.

- **Reinstall OS X.** You can use this option to install a copy of Mountain Lion onto any hard drive—for example, you could reinstall it on your main internal drive.

Note: This option will download the actual copy of Mountain Lion from the Internet—all 4 gigabytes of it. In other words, it requires an Internet connection and a *lot* of patience.

- **Get Help Online.** This option opens your Safari Web browser, which presents you with some helpful information about using the Recovery Mode that you've fired up. You're actually online at this point, so you can also visit any other Web site you might find helpful.

 Quit Safari when you're finished browsing; you return to the main OS X Utilities window.

- **Disk Utility.** Use this option to open Disk Utility, the Mac's hard drive diagnostics-and-repair program. You can use it to check, fix, erase, or partition any of your hard drives.

 For example, you can repair the main startup disk, which is often the most useful option.

Those four options are the big-ticket items, but don't miss the menu bar. The commands here let you open the Firmware Password Utility (page 522), Network Utility (page 467), and Terminal (page 469).

Mountain Lion Internet Recovery

OK, the Recovery HD concept is clever. And most of the time, it's all you need.

But what if your hard drive is *completely* hosed? What then, smart guy? You can't very well boot up from the Recovery HD if it's sitting on the same dead hard drive.

Or what if you've just installed a brand-new, bigger, or faster hard drive? It doesn't have Mountain Lion on it. It doesn't have Recovery HD on it. How are you supposed to install Mountain Lion?

In those situations, new Mac models—those released after Lion, like the 2011 MacBook Airs and Mac minis—offer an even cleverer option: Internet Recovery. This mode offers the same exact options that the Utilities screen of Recovery HD would have—but you're connecting to that software *online*, over a high-speed Internet connection. You're literally starting up from *Apple's* hard drives, thousands of miles away.

So even if your hard drive is dead as a doornail, you can still repair it, reinstall Mountain Lion, and so on.

To fire up Internet Recovery, make sure your computer is in a WiFi hot spot or connected to an Ethernet network. Then hold down ⌘-R as the computer is starting up. You can let go when you see the screen that asks you to choose a WiFi network. Do that, and then enter the password for the network, if necessary.

Now your Mac downloads a disk image containing just enough software to get you to the Utilities screen described in the previous section.

Note: Once you're up and running, you can re-download the copies of iPhoto, iMovie, and GarageBand that came with your Mac. Just open the App Store program, log in with your Apple ID, click Purchases, and click Accept to download those iLife programs. You won't be charged for them.

Physical Recovery Disks

But what if the hard drive is so sick that you can't start up from the Recovery HD—*and* your Mac isn't new enough to offer the Internet Recovery feature? (Or what if it *does* offer that feature, but you'd rather repair your Mac a quicker way?)

One solution is to build yourself a bootable Mountain Lion flash drive, DVD, or hard drive, as described on page 796c. Not only is it capable of starting up or reinstalling Mountain Lion, but it also has a complete set of recovery tools on board.

But creating a bootable drive takes a lot of steps, and it requires sacrificing an 8-gigabyte (or bigger) flash drive. If you have any flash drive, even a 2-gigabyte one that somebody handed you at a trade show, you can load it up with just the recovery tools, to use in times of trouble. Creating this kind of emergency flash drive is somewhat easier than creating the kind of full-blown reinstallation flash drive described in Appendix A.

Note: To create an emergency "disk," your Mac must have Mountain Lion on it already, including the invisible Recovery HD partition. That's because it *relies* on the data and software on that partition.

Also, you have to format the flash drive correctly, as described on page 797. It's OK if the flash drive is partitioned; just leave at least 2 gigs for the recovery partition.

To get started, download Apple's free Mountain Lion Recovery Disk Assistant. (It's available from this book's "Missing CD" page at *www.missingmanuals.com.*)

Insert your flash drive into the Mac. Open the Mountain Lion Recovery Disk Assistant; click Agree to get through the legalese screen.

Click the name of the flash drive, and then click Continue. You're warned that this process will *erase* the flash drive (or its partition), and you're asked to authenticate yourself with an administrator name and password.

When you click OK, your Mac begins creating the recovery disk. After a minute or so, a message congratulates you, and the newly created drive's icon appears in the Recovery Disk Assistant program, bearing the name Recovery HD.

To use this emergency disk, hold down the Option key as the Mac starts up. You wind up at the Startup Manager screen shown in Figure B-2, top. From the pop-up menu, choose your WiFi hot spot.

Now click the up-arrow button below the Recovery HD icon. (You may even see *two* Recovery HD icons—one of them is the USB flash drive, and the other is the invisible partition on your hard drive.) Your Mac is starting up from the flash drive! After a moment, you wind up at the Utilities screen described earlier in this appendix.

Note: The recovery flash drive you made will work only on the Mac model you used to make it.

Application Won't Open

If a program won't open (if its icon bounces merrily in the Dock for a few seconds, for instance, but then nothing happens), begin by trashing its preference file, as described earlier. If that doesn't solve it, reinstalling the program, or installing the Mountain Lion–compatible update for it, usually does.

Startup Problems

Not every problem you encounter is related to running applications. Sometimes trouble strikes before you even get that far. The following are examples.

Kernel Panic

When you see the cheerful, multilingual dialog box shown in Figure B-3 you've got yourself a *kernel panic*—a Unix nervous breakdown.

(In such situations, *user panic* might be the more applicable term, but that's programmers for you.)

If you experience a kernel panic, it's almost always the result of a *hardware* glitch—most often a bad memory (RAM) board, but possibly an accelerator card, graphics card, or USB hub that OS X doesn't like. A poorly seated AirPort card can bring on a kernel panic, too, and so can a bad USB or FireWire cable.

If simply restarting the machine doesn't help, detach every shred of gear that didn't come from Apple. Restore these components to the Mac one at a time until you find

out which one was causing OS X's bad hair day. If you're able to pinpoint the culprit, seek its manufacturer (or its Web site) on a quest for updated drivers, or at least try to find out for sure whether the add-on is compatible with OS X.

Tip: This advice goes for your Macintosh itself. Apple periodically updates the Mac's *own* "drivers" in the form of a *firmware update.* You download these updates from the Support area of Apple's Web site (if indeed OS X's own Software Update mechanism doesn't alert you to their existence).

There's one other cause for kernel panics, by the way, and that's moving, renaming, or changing the access permissions for OS X's essential system files and folders—the Applications or System folder, for example. (See Chapter 13 for more on permissions.) This cause isn't even worth mentioning, of course, because nobody would be that foolish.

Figure B-3:
A kernel panic is almost always related to some piece of add-on hardware. And look at the bright side: At least you get this handsome dialog box. That's a lot better than the Mac OS X 10.0 and 10.1 effect–random text gibberish superimposing itself on your screen.

You need to restart your computer. Hold down the Power button for several seconds or press the Restart button.

Veuillez redémarrer votre ordinateur. Maintenez la touche de démarrage enfoncée pendant plusieurs secondes ou bien appuyez sur le bouton de réinitialisation.

Sie müssen Ihren Computer neu starten. Halten Sie dazu die Einschalttaste einige Sekunden gedrückt oder drücken Sie die Neustart-Taste.

コンピュータを再起動する必要があります。パワーボタンを数秒間押し続けるか、リセットボタンを押してください。

Safe Mode (Safe Boot)

In times of troubleshooting, Windows fans press an F-key to start up in Safe Mode. That's how you turn off all nonessential system-software nubbins in an effort to get a sick machine at least powered up.

Although not one person in a hundred knows it, OS X offers the same kind of emergency keystroke. It can come in handy when you've just installed some new piece of software and find that you can't even start up the machine, or when one of your fonts is corrupted, or when something you've designated as a login item turns out to be gumming up the works. With this trick, you can at least turn on the computer so that you can uninstall the cranky program.

The trick is to *press the Shift key* as the machine is starting up. Hold it down from the startup chime until you see the words "Safe Boot," in red lettering, on the login screen.

Welcome to Safe Mode.

What have you accomplished?

- **Checked your hard drive.** The Shift-key business makes the startup process seem to take a very long time; as the progress bar suggests, OS X is actually scanning your entire hard drive for problems.

- **Brought up the login screen.** When you do a safe boot, you must click your name and enter your password, even if you normally have Automatic Login turned on.

- **Turned off noncritical kernel extensions (drivers).** All kinds of software nuggets load during the startup process. Some of them you choose yourself, like icons you add to the Login Items list in the System Preferences→Accounts pane. Others are normally hidden, including a large mass of *kernel extensions,* which are chunks of software that add various features to the basic operating system. (Kernel extensions live in your System→Library→Extensions folder.)

 If you're experiencing startup crashes, some non-Apple installer may have given you a kernel extension that doesn't care for OS X 10.8—so in Safe Mode, they're all turned off.

- **Turned off your fonts.** Corrupted fonts are a chronic source of trouble—and because you can't tell by looking, they're darned difficult to diagnose. So just to make sure you can at least get into your computer, Safe Mode turns them all off (except the authorized, Apple-sanctioned ones that it actually needs to run, which are in your System→Library→Fonts folder).

- **Trashed your font cache.** The font cache is a speed trick. OS X stores the visual information for each of your fonts on the hard drive so the system won't have to read every single typeface off your hard drive when you open your Font menus or the Font panel.

 When these files get scrambled, startup crashes can result. That's why a Safe Boot moves all these files into the Trash. (You'll even see them sitting there in the Trash after the startup process is complete, although there's not much you can do with them except walk around holding your nose and pointing.)

- **Turned off your login items.** Safe Mode also prevents any Finder windows from opening *and* prevents your own handpicked startup items from opening—that is, whatever you've asked your Mac to auto-open by adding them to the System Preferences→Accounts→Login Items list.

 This, too, is a troubleshooting tactic. If some login item crashes your Mac every time it opens, you can squelch it just long enough to remove it from your Login Items list.

Tip: If you don't hold down the Shift key until you click the Log In button (after entering your name and password at the login screen), you squelch *only* your login items but *not* the fonts and extensions.

Once you reach the desktop, you'll find a long list of standard features inoperable. You can't use DVD Player, capture video in iMovie, use a wireless network, use cer-

tain microphones and speakers, or use your modem. (The next time you restart, all this goodness will be restored, assuming you're no longer clutching the Shift key in a sweaty panic.)

In any case, the beauty of Safe Mode is that it lets you get your Mac going. You have access to your files, so at least the emergency of crashing-on-startup is over. And you can start picking through your fonts and login items to see if you can spot the problem.

Gray Screen During Startup

Confirm that your Mac has the latest firmware, as described earlier. Detach and test all your non-Apple add-ons. Finally, perform a disk check (see below).

Blue Screen During Startup

Most of the troubleshooting steps for this problem (which is usually accompanied by the Spinning Beachball of Death cursor) are the same as those described under "Kernel Panic" on page 807.

Forgotten Password

If you or one of the other people who use your Mac have forgotten the corresponding account password, no worries: Just read the box on page 524.

Fixing the Disk

The beauty of OS X's design is that the operating system itself is frozen in its perfect, pristine state, impervious to conflicting system extensions, clueless Mac users, and other sources of disaster.

That's the theory, anyway. But what happens if something goes wrong with the complex software that operates the hard drive itself?

Fortunately, OS X comes with its own disk-repair program. In the familiar Mac universe of icons and menus, it takes the form of a program in Applications→Utilities called Disk Utility. In the barren world of Terminal and the command-line interface, there's a utility that works just as well but bears a different name: *fsck* (for file system check).

In any case, running Disk Utility or its alter ego *fsck* is a powerful and useful troubleshooting tool that can cure all kinds of strange ills, including these problems, among others:

- Your Mac freezes during startup, either before or after the login screen.

- The startup process interrupts itself with the appearance of the text-only command line.

- You get the "applications showing up as folders" problem.

Method 1: Disk Utility

The easiest way to check your disk is to use the Disk Utility program. Use this method if your Mac can, indeed, start up. (See Method 2 if you can't even get that far.)

Disk Utility can't fix the disk it's *on* (except for permissions repairs, described at the beginning of this appendix).That's why you have to restart the Mac into Recovery Mode and run Disk Utility from there. The process goes like this:

1. **Start up the Mac from the Recovery HD, or a recovery flash drive.**

 They're both described earlier in this appendix. You wind up, after some time, at the Utilities screen.

2. **Click "Disk Utility: Repair or erase a disk using Disk Utility."**

 After a moment, the Disk Utility screen appears.

3. **Click the disk or disk partition you want to fix, click the First Aid tab, and then click Repair Disk.**

 The Mac whirls into action, checking a list of very technical disk-formatting parameters.

If you see the message, "The volume 'Macintosh HD' appears to be OK," that's meant to be *good* news. Believe it or not, that cautious statement is as definitive an affirmation as Disk Utility is capable of making about the health of your disk.

Disk Utility may also tell you that the disk is damaged but that it can't help you. In that case, you need a more heavy-duty disk-repair program like DiskWarrior (*www. alsoft.com*).

Method 2: fsck at the Console

Techier folk can also boot into the Mac's raw Unix underlayer to perform some diagnostic (and healing) commands.

Specifically, you can run the Unix program *fsck,* for which Disk Utility is little more than a pretty faceplate.

Note: Even so, Apple recommends that you use Disk Utility if at all possible. Use *fsck* only if all else fails.

Like any Unix program, *fsck* runs at the command line. You launch it from the all-text, black Unix screen by typing *fsck* and pressing Return. (You can also use *fsck -f.*)

You can't, however, just run *fsck* in Terminal. You have to run it when the usual arsenal of graphic-interface programs—like the Finder and its invisible suite of accessory programs—isn't running.

Single-user mode (⌘-S at startup)
The Terminal program is the best-known form of OS X's command line, but it's not the only one. In fact, there are several other ways to get there.

In general, you don't hear them mentioned except in the context of troubleshooting, because the Terminal program offers many more convenient features for doing the same thing. And because it's contained in a OS X–style window, Terminal is not as disorienting as the three methods you're about to read.

All these techniques take you into *console mode,* shown in Figure B-4. In console mode, Unix takes over your screen completely, showing white type against black, no windows or icons in sight. Abandon the mouse, all ye who enter here; in console mode, you can't do anything but type commands.

Figure B-4:
In console mode, your entire screen is a com-mand line interface. Unix jockeys can go to town here. Everyone else can timidly type fsck *-y after the localhost:/ root # prompt—see this prompt on the very last line?—and hope for the best.*

```
Found old device 0x0cdea00
IOFireWireDevice,   ROM unchanged 0x0xcdea00
IOFireWireDevice  0x0xcdea00,   ROM generation  zero
Got boot device =
IOService:/Core99PE/pc@f20000000/AppleMacRiscPCI/mac-
io@17/KeyLargo/ata-4@1f000/KeyLargoATA/ATADeviceNube@0/IOA
TABlockStorageDriver/IOATABlockStorageDevice/IOBlockStorageDr
iver/QUANTUM  FIREBALL  CX13.6A
Media/IOApplePartitionScheme/Untitled
@9
BSD root: disk0s9, major  14, minor  9
Rereading  ROM up to 25 quads
devfs on /dev
USB:    4.947: AppleUSBKeyboard[0xDOE80014::start    USB  Generic
Keyboard @ 3 (0x18110000)
Mon Nov 19 23:18:53 EST 2001
Singleuser boot -- fsck not done
Root device is mounted read-only
If you want to make modifications  to files,
run '/sbin/fsck  -y' first and then '/sbin/mount  -uw/'
localhost#
```

To get there in times of startup troubleshooting, press ⌘-S while the Mac is starting up. (If you're stuck at the frozen remnants of a previous startup attempt, you may first have to force restart your Mac; hold down the ⏻ button for 5 seconds.)

Instead of arriving at the usual desktop, you see technical-looking text scrolling up a black screen as the Mac runs its various startup routines. When it finally stops at the *localhost#* prompt, you're ready to type commands. You're now in what's called *single-user mode,* meaning that the Unix multiple-accounts software has yet to load. You won't be asked to log in.

At the *root#* prompt, type *fsck -y* (note the space before the hyphen) and press Return. (The *y* means "yes," as in "yes, I want you to fix any problems automatically.")

Now the file system check program takes over, running through five sets of tests. When it's complete, you'll see one of two messages:

- **The volume Macintosh HD appears to be OK.** All is well. Type *exit* and press Return to proceed to the usual login screen and desktop.

- **File system was modified.** A good sign, but just a beginning. You need to run the program again. One *fsck* pass often repairs only one layer of problems, leaving another to be patched in the next pass. Type *fsck -fy* a second time, a third time, and so on, until you finally arrive at a "disk appears to be OK" message.

Type *exit* at the prompt and press Return to get back to the familiar world of icons and windows.

Where to Get Troubleshooting Help

If the basic steps described in this appendix haven't helped, the universe is crawling with additional help sources. The Apple's Support Web site is a great resource. But the truth is, you'll find more answers faster using Google than you ever will using individual help sites. That's because Google *includes* all those help sites in its search!

Suppose, for example, that you've just installed the 10.8.2 software update, and it's mysteriously turned all your accounts into Standard ones. You could go to one Web site after another, hunting for a fix, repeating your search—or you could just type *mountain lion 10.8.2 standard accounts* into Google. You'll get your answers after just a few more seconds of clicking and exploring the results.

Help Online

These Web sites contain nothing but troubleshooting discussions, tools, and help:

- **Apple Discussion Groups** (*http://discussions.apple.com*). The volume and quality of question-and-answer activity here dwarfs any other free source. If you're polite and concise, you can post questions to the multitudes here and get more replies from them than you'll know what to do with.

- **Apple's help site** (*www.apple.com/support*). Apple's help site includes downloadable manuals, software updates, frequently asked questions, and many other resources.

 Its search box is your ticket to the Knowledge Base, a collection of 100,000 technical articles that the Apple technicians themselves consult when answering calls for help.

- **MacFixIt** (*www.macfixit.com*). The world's one-stop resource for Mac trouble-shooting advice; alas, you have to pay to access the good stuff.

Help by Telephone

Finally, consider contacting whoever sold you the component that's making your life miserable: the printer company, scanner company, software company, or whatever.

If it's a Mac OS problem, you can call Apple at 800-275-2273 (that's 800-APL-CARE). For the first 90 days after your purchase of OS X, the technicians will answer your questions for free.

After that, unless you've paid for AppleCare for your Mac (a three-year extended warranty program), Apple will charge you to answer your questions. Fortunately, if the problem turns out to be Apple's fault, they won't charge you.

The Windows-to-Mac Dictionary

Maybe you were convinced by the old Apple "Switch" ad campaign. Maybe you like the looks of today's Macs. Or maybe you've just endured one virus, spyware download, or service pack too many. In any case, if you're switching to OS X from Windows, this appendix is for you. It's an alphabetical listing of every common Windows function and where to find it in OS X. After all, an operating system is an operating system. The actual functions are pretty much the same—they're just in different places.

Tip: If this listing only whets your appetite for information about making the switch, read *Switching to the Mac: The Missing Manual,* Mountain Lion Edition. In addition to an expanded version of this appendix, it also contains useful information on moving your files from the PC to the Mac, copying over your email, transferring your contacts to Contacts, and so on.

About [this program]

To find out the version number of the program you're using, don't look in the Help menu. Instead, look in the *application* menu next to the menu—the one that bears the name of the program you're in. That's where you find the About command for Macintosh programs.

Accessibility Options control panel

The special features that let you operate the computer even with impaired vision, hearing, or motor control are called Accessibility in Mountain Lion. They're in System Preferences (see Chapter 9).

Active Desktop

The Mac never displays Web pages directly on the desktop—and knowing Apple, that's probably a point of pride. But Dashboard (Chapter 5) keeps Internet data only a keystroke away.

Add Hardware control panel

The Mac requires no program for installing the driver for a new external gadget. The drivers for most printers, mice, keyboards, cameras, camcorders, and other accessories are preinstalled. If you plug something into the Mac and find that it doesn't work immediately, just install the driver from the included CD (or the manufacturer's Web site).

Add or Remove Programs control panel

Here's another one you just don't need on the Macintosh. Installing a program onto the Mac is described in Chapter 5. Removing a program simply involves dragging its icon to the Trash. (For a clean sweep, inspect your Home→Library→Preferences and Library→Application Support folders to see if any preference files got left behind.)

All Programs

There's no Programs menu built into OS X, like the one on the Windows Start menu. If you'd like one, drag your Applications folder into the end of the Dock. Now its icon is a tidy pop-up menu of every program on your machine.

Alt key

On the Mac, it's the Option key, although the key usually says "Alt" on it, too. (In some countries, it says *only* Alt.) You can substitute Option for Alt in any keystroke in most popular programs. The Option key has a number of secondary features on the Mac, too: It hides the windows of one program when you click into another, and so on.

Automatic Update

The →Software Update command does exactly the same thing.

Backspace key

It's in the same place on the Macintosh keyboard, but it's called the Delete key.

Battery level

The battery-level graph (▭) for your Mac laptop appears in the menu bar, rather than in the system tray. (If you don't see it, open System Preferences→Energy Saver and turn it on.)

BIOS

You'll never have to update or even think about the ROM of your Macintosh (the approximate equivalent of the BIOS on the PC). It's permanent and unchanging. The very similar *firmware* of your Macintosh does occasionally have to be updated in order to work with a new version of the Mac operating system or some dramatic

new feature—once every four years, perhaps. You'll be notified on the screen when the time comes.

Briefcase

The Briefcase is a Windows invention designed to help you keep your files in sync between a laptop and a desktop computer. You can use free services like Dropbox.com and SugarSync.com to achieve exactly the same result with your Mac. Or, if it's your calendar, address book, or mail account that you want to sync, just use iCloud, as described in Chapter 17.

Calculator

The Calculator program in OS X is almost identical to the one in Windows, except that it can also perform conversions (temperature, distance, currency, and so on) and features an editable "paper tape." It sits in your Applications folder and is described in Chapter 11. (There's a simpler Calculator in Dashboard, too; see the end of Chapter 5. And don't forget that you can type quick math equations into the ⌕ Spotlight menu.)

Camera and Scanner Wizard

When you connect a digital camera or scanner to your Mac, iPhoto or Image Capture opens automatically and prepares to download the pictures automatically. Details are in Chapter 11.

CDs and DVDs

To open the CD/DVD drawer, or, if you have a slot-loading drive, to spit out the disc that's in it, hold down the ⏏ key on your Mac keyboard. If it's an older Mac keyboard without a ⏏ key, you can eject a CD (or any other disc) by Control-clicking (or right-clicking) its desktop icon and then choosing Eject from the shortcut menu. There are various other ways to eject a disc, but the point is that you never do so by pushing the Eject button on the disc drive itself.

Character Map

This Windows program helps you find out what keys you need to press to trigger trademark symbols, copyright symbols, and other special characters. The equivalent on the Mac is called the Character Viewer (page 254).

Clean Install

The Mountain Lion installer can give you a fresh copy of the operating system, just as the Windows installer can. Instructions are in Appendix A.

Clipboard

The Mac's Clipboard works much like the one in Windows. In the Finder, you can choose Edit→Show Clipboard to see whatever you most recently copied or cut.

Command line

In OS X, the command line is alive and well—but it speaks Unix, not DOS. You get to it by opening Terminal; see page 469.

Control Panel

The Control Panel in OS X is called System Preferences, and you open it from your menu. As in Windows, you can view these icons either by category or in a simple alphabetical list: Just choose either Organize by Categories or Organize Alphabetically from the View menu.

Copy, Cut, Paste

When you're editing in a word processor or graphics program, the OS X Cut, Copy, and Paste commands work exactly as they do in Windows.

At the desktop, however, there are a few differences. You can indeed copy icons and paste them into a new window using the Copy and Paste commands—but *cutting* them out of a window, as you can in Windows, works slightly differently: After you've copied the icons from the first window, open the destination window. Then press the Option key, open the Edit menu, and choose Move Items Here.

Ctrl key

On the Macintosh, you generally substitute the ⌘ key in keystrokes that would involve the Ctrl key in Windows. In other words, the Save command is now ⌘-S instead of Ctrl-S, Open is ⌘-O instead of Ctrl-O, and so on.

Date and Time

To set your Mac's calendar and clock, open Date & Time in System Preferences.

Delete Key (Forward Delete)

Most desktop Mac keyboards have a forward-delete key (labeled ⌦ or *Del*) exactly like the ones on PCs. On Mac laptops, and on Apple's aluminum keyboards, you trigger the forward-delete function by pressing the Delete key while simultaneously pressing the Fn key.

Desktop

The Macintosh desktop is pretty much the same idea as the Windows desktop, with a few key differences:

- Disk icons show up on the Mac desktop as soon as they are inserted or connected. You don't have to open a window to see their icons.

- You change the desktop picture using the Desktop & Screen Saver panel of System Preferences.

- The Trash is an icon in the Dock, not on the desktop.

Directories

Most people call them *folders* on the Mac.

Disk Defragmenter

There's no such utility included with OS X; the system auto-defragments in the background. (A *defragmenting* program moves around the pieces of files on your hard drive in an effort to optimize their placement and speed of opening.)

Disks

Working with disks is very different on the Mac. Every disk inside, or attached to, a Macintosh can be represented on the screen by an icon. OS X does have something like the Computer or My Computer window (choose Go→Computer), but the icons there reflect only the disks currently inserted in your Mac. You'll never see an icon for an empty drive, as you do on Windows, and there's no such thing as drive letters (because the Mac refers to *disks,* not to *drives*—and calls them by name).

Mountain Lion doesn't display icons for disks on the desktop, as earlier OS X versions did—but you can bring them back by choosing Finder→Preferences→General and turning on the checkboxes for different kinds of disks.

Display control panel

The functions of the Windows Display control panel lurk in the OS X System Preferences program—just not all in one place. You set up your desktop picture and screen saver using the Desktop & Screen Saver pane and adjust your monitor settings using the Displays pane. (OS X offers no equivalent to the Appearance tab in Windows, for changing the system-wide look of your computer.)

DLL files

The Macintosh equivalent of DLL files—shared libraries of programming code—are invisible and off limits. As a result, no Macintosh user ever experiences DLL conflicts or out-of-date DLL files.

DOS prompt

There's a command line in OS X, but it's Unix, not DOS. For details, see 496.

Drivers

See "Add or Remove Programs."

End Task dialog box

If some Macintosh program is hung or frozen, you escape it pretty much the same way you would in Windows: by forcing it to quit. To bring up the Force Quit dialog box, you press Option-⌘-Esc or choose →Force Quit.

Exiting programs

You can quit a program either by choosing Quit from the menu bearing its name (next to the menu), or by right-clicking (or Control-clicking) its Dock icon and then choosing Quit from the pop-up menu.

Explorer

The Mac has its own "tree" view of the files and folders on your hard drive: list view. By expanding the "flippy triangles" of your folders, you build a hierarchy that shows you as much or as little detail as you like.

If you prefer the Explorer effect of clicking a folder in *one* pane to see its contents in the next, try column view instead. Both views are described in Chapter 1.

Favorites

In OS X, there isn't one single Favorites menu that lists both favorite Web sites and favorite icons. The Bookmarks menu of Safari, the Web browser, lists only Web sites, and the Sidebar at the desktop (page 19) lists only favorite files, folders, disks, and other icons.

Faxing

Faxing is no longer built into OS X, but you can always buy a non-Apple fax modem and use the software that comes with it.

File Sharing

See Chapter 14 for an in-depth look at the Macintosh networking and file-sharing system.

Floppy disks

Floppy drives on Macs disappeared in about 1998. It's much more efficient to transfer files between machines using an Ethernet cable or improvised wireless network (Chapter 14), a CD or DVD that you burned (Chapter 12), or email (Chapter 18).

Folder Options

The Folder Options control panel in Windows is a collection of unrelated settings that boil down to this:

- **General tab.** Exactly as in Windows, it's up to you whether or not double-clicking a folder opens up a second window—or just changes what's in the first one. On the Mac, you make these changes using the Finder→Preferences command. There you'll find the option called "Always open folders in a new window."

- **View tab.** Most of the options here don't exist on the Mac. For example, system files are *always* hidden on the Mac; you can't opt to make them visible (at least not with the built-in controls). You can, however, choose whether you want to see the file name extensions in your desktop windows (like .doc and .html). Choose Finder→Preferences→Advanced, and turn "Show all file extensions" on or off.

- **File Types tab.** Just as in Windows, you can reassign certain document types so that double-clicking opens them up in the program of your choice. But on the Mac, you can reassign either a whole class of files at once, as in Windows, *or* one file at a time. To do it, you use the Get Info window, as described on page 95.

- **Offline files.** There's no equivalent feature on the Mac.

Fonts

The Mac and Windows PCs both use TrueType, PostScript, and OpenType fonts. (In fact, your Mac can even use the exact font files you had in Windows.) On the Mac, however, there are actually three different folders that can contain them. A complete discussion is in Chapter 15.

Help and Support

At the desktop, choose Help→Mac Help. In other programs, the Help command is generally at the right end of your menus, exactly as in Windows.

Hibernation

The Mac can't hibernate at all, as modern PCs do, cutting all power but remembering what programs and documents you had open for a faster restart later. Sleep mode is the closest it gets; see "Standby mode."

Internet Explorer

Microsoft has abandoned the Mac version of Internet Explorer. Apple would prefer, of course, that you try Safari, its own Web browser, but many a power user prefers Firefox or Chrome, which are nearly identical to the Windows version.

Internet Options

On the Mac, you find the options for your Web browser by choosing Safari→ Preferences.

IRQs

They don't exist on the Mac.

Java

This interpreter of tiny Web page programs is alive and well in OS X. Java programs run fine in all Mac Web browsers.

Keyboard control panel

You can make exactly the same kinds of settings—and more—on the Keyboard & Mouse pane of System Preferences.

Logging in

The multiple-accounts feature of OS X is extremely similar to that of Windows 2000, XP, Vista, and 7. In each case, you can, if you wish, create a requirement to log in with a name and password before using the computer. This arrangement keeps separate the documents, email, and settings of each person who uses the computer. (Chapter 13 tells all.)

Mail control panel

OS X comes with its own email program (described in Chapter 18); all of its settings are contained within the program.

Maximize button

On the Mac, clicking the Zoom button (the green button in the upper-left corner of a window) does something like the Maximize button in Windows: It makes your window larger. On the Mac, however, clicking the zoom button never makes the window expand to fill the entire screen. Instead, the window grows—or *shrinks*—precisely enough to enclose its contents.

Of course, if you see the ⬈ button in the upper-right corner of your window, you can do even better: You can take that program into *full-screen mode,* where every last pixel of screen space is put to work displaying your document.

Menus

On the Macintosh, there's only one menu bar, always at the very top of the screen. The menus change depending on the program and the window you're using, but the point is that the menu bar is no longer inside each window you open.

Tip: Just because you don't see the little underlines in the menus doesn't mean you can't operate all the menus from the keyboard, as in Windows. See page 210 for details.

Minimize button

You can minimize a OS X window to the Dock, just the way you would minimize a Windows window to the taskbar. You do so by double-clicking its title bar, pressing ⌘-M, choosing Window→Minimize Window, or clicking the yellow Minimize button at the top left of a window. (Restore the window by clicking its icon in the Dock.)

Mouse control panel

The equivalent settings can be found in the Mouse panel of System Preferences.

(My) Computer

The Mac's Computer window is very similar (choose Go→Computer), in that it shows the icons of all disks (hard drive, CD, and so on). On the other hand, it shows *only* the disks that are actually inserted or connected. (See "Disks.")

(My) Documents, (My) Pictures, (My) Music

The equivalent buckets for your everyday documents, music files, and pictures are the Documents, Pictures, and Music folders in your Home folder.

(My) Network Places

On the Mac, the "network neighborhood" is almost always on the screen: It's the Sidebar, the panel at the left side of every Finder window. All the Macs and PCs on your network are always listed here, in the Shared category (unless you turned this feature off in Finder→Preferences, of course).

Network Neighborhood

See the previous entry.

Notepad

Chapter 10 documents the new Notes app, which is far more powerful than the Notepad of old.

Personal Web Server

To find out how to turn your Mac into a state-of-the-art Web server, see page 782.

Phone and Modem Options control panel

To find the modem settings for your Mac, see page 648.

Power Options

To control when your Mac goes to sleep and (if it's a laptop) how much power it uses, use the Energy Saver pane of System Preferences (Chapter 9).

Printer Sharing

To share a USB inkjet printer with other Macs on the network, open the Sharing pane of System Preferences on the Mac with the printer. Turn on Printer Sharing.

To use the shared printer from across the network, open the document you want to print, choose File→Print, and choose the name of the shared printer from the first pop-up menu.

Printers and Faxes

For a list of your printers, open the Print & Scan pane of System Preferences (Chapter 15). Faxing is no longer built into OS X.

PrntScrn key

You capture pictures of your Mac screen by pressing Shift-⌘-3 (for a full-screen grab) or Shift-⌘-4 (to grab a selected portion of the screen). There are many options available; see the end of Chapter 15.

Program Files folder

The Applications folder (Go→Applications) is like the Program Files folder in Windows—except that you're not discouraged from opening it and double-clicking things. On the Macintosh, every program bears its true name; Microsoft Word, for example, is called Microsoft Word, not WINWORD.EXE.

Properties dialog box

You can call up something very similar for any *icon* (file, folder, program, disk, printer) by highlighting its icon and then choosing File→Get Info. But objects in Macintosh *programs* generally don't contain Properties dialog boxes.

Recycle Bin

OS X has a Trash icon at the end of the Dock. In general, it works exactly like the Windows Recycle Bin—and why not, since the Macintosh Trash was Microsoft's inspiration?—but there are a couple of differences. The Macintosh never automatically

empties it, for example. That job is up to you: The simplest way is to Control-click it, or right-click it, and then choose Empty Trash from the shortcut menu.

The Mac never bothers you with an "Are you sure?" message when you throw something into the Trash, either. The Mac interrupts you for permission only when you choose File→Empty Trash. And you can even turn that confirmation off, if you like (in Finder→Preferences).

To put icons into the Trash, drag them there, or highlight them and then press ⌘-Delete.

Regional and Language Options control panel

The closest equivalent is the Language & Text panel of System Preferences.

Registry

There is no registry. Let the celebration begin!

Run command

The Mac's command line is Terminal (page 469).

Safe Mode

You can press the Shift key during startup to suppress the loading of certain software libraries, but OS X's "safe mode" isn't quite as massively stripped down as Windows' Safe Mode.

ScanDisk

Just like Windows, the Mac automatically scans and, if necessary, repairs its hard drive every time your machine starts up. To run such a check on command, open Disk Utility (located in the Applications→Utilities folder), click the name of your hard drive, and then click the First Aid tab.

Scheduled Tasks

To schedule a task to take place unattended, use the *launchd* Unix command in Terminal (page 469), or one of the scheduling programs listed at *www.versiontracker.com.*

Scrap files

On the Mac, they're called *clipping files,* and they're even more widely compatible. You create them the same way: Drag some highlighted text, or a graphic, out of a program's window and onto the desktop. There it becomes an independent clipping file that you can drag back in—to the same window or a different one.

Screen saver

The Mac's screen savers are impressive. Open System Preferences and click the Desktop & Screen Saver icon.

Search

In OS X, you have the ultimate file-searching tool: Spotlight (Chapter 3). Get psyched!

To find Web sites, use the Google search box at the top of the Safari browser.

Shortcut menus

They work exactly the same as they do in Windows. You produce a shortcut menu by Control-clicking things like icons, list items, and so on. (If you have a two-button mouse, feel free to right-click instead of using the Control key.)

Shortcuts

On the Mac, they're known as *aliases*. See page 88.

Sounds and Audio Devices

Open System Preferences; click the Sound icon. You may also want to explore the Audio MIDI Setup program in Applications→Utilities.

Speech control panel

The Mac's center for speech recognition and text-to-speech is the Dictation & Speech panel of System Preferences. As Chapter 16 makes clear, the Mac can read aloud any text in any program, and in Mountain Lion, it lets you speak to type.

Standby mode

On the Mac, it's called Sleep, but it's the same idea. You make a Mac laptop sleep by closing the lid. You make a Mac desktop sleep by choosing →Sleep, or just walking away; the Mac goes to sleep on its own, according to the settings in the Energy Saver pane of System Preferences.

Start menu

There's no Start menu in OS X. Instead, you stash the icons of the programs, documents, and folders you use frequently onto the Dock at the edge of the screen, or into the Places section of the Sidebar at the left edge of every Finder window.

Exactly as with the Start menu, you can rearrange these icons (drag them horizontally) or remove the ones you don't use often (drag them away from the Dock and then release). To add new icons of your own, just drag them into place (applications go to the left of the Dock's divider line, documents and folders to the right).

StartUp folder

To make programs launch automatically at startup, include them in the list of Login Items in the System Preferences→Accounts pane.

System control panel

The Mac has no central equivalent of the System window on a Windows PC. But its functions have analogs here:

- **General tab.** To find out your OS X version number and the amount of memory on your Mac, choose →About This Mac.

- **Computer Name tab.** Open System Preferences, click Sharing, and edit your computer's network name here.

- **Hardware tab.** The closest thing the Mac has to the Device Manager is System Profiler (in your Applications→Utilities folder).

- **Advanced tab.** In OS X, you can't easily adjust your virtual memory, processor scheduling, or user profile information.

- **System Restore tab.** OS X's Time Machine feature is like System Restore on steroids; see Chapter 6.

- **Automatic Updates tab.** Choose →Software Updates.

- **Remote tab.** OS X offers remote control in the form of Screen Sharing, described in Chapter 14.

System Tray

The OS X equivalent of the system tray (also called the notification area) is the row of *menulets* at the upper-right corner of your screen.

Taskbar

OS X doesn't have a taskbar, but it does have something very close: the Dock (Chapter 4). Open programs are indicated by a small, shiny dot beneath their icons in the Dock. If you hold down your cursor on one of these icons (or Control-click it, or right-click it), you get a pop-up list of the open windows in that program, exactly as in Windows XP, Vista, and 7.

On the other hand, some conventions never die. Much as in Windows, you cycle through the various open Mac programs by holding down the ⌘ key and pressing Tab repeatedly.

Taskbar and Start Menu control panel

To configure your Dock (the equivalent of the taskbar and the Start menu), choose →Dock→Dock Preferences, or click the Dock icon in System Preferences.

"Three-fingered salute"

Instead of pressing Ctrl-Alt-Delete to jettison a stuck program on the Mac, you press Option-⌘-Esc. A Force Quit dialog box appears. Click the program you want to toss, click Force Quit, confirm your choice, and then relaunch the program to get on with your day.

ToolTips

Small, yellow identifying balloons pop up on the Mac almost as often as they do in Windows. Just point to a toolbar icon or truncated file name without clicking. (There's no way to turn these labels off.)

Tweak UI

The closest equivalent for this free, downloadable, but unsupported Microsoft utility for tweaking the look of your PC is TinkerTool for OS X.

User Accounts control panel

Like Windows 2000, XP, Vista, and 7, OS X was designed from Square One to be a multiuser operating system, keeping each person's files, mail, and settings separate. You set up and manage these accounts in System Preferences→ Accounts (Chapter 13).

Windows (or WINNT) folder

OS X's operating system resides in a folder simply called System, which sits in your main hard drive window. Exactly as in recent Windows versions, you're forbidden to add, remove, or change anything inside. Also as in Windows, most of it is invisible anyway.

Windows logo key

The Mac has no equivalent for the ⊞ key on most PC keyboards.

Windows Media Player

The Mac comes with individual programs for playing multimedia files:

- **QuickTime Player** (Chapter 16) to play back movies and sounds.

- **iTunes** (Chapter 12) to play CDs, Internet radio, MP3 files, and other audio files. (As a bonus, unlike Windows XP, iTunes can even *create* MP3 files.)

- **DVD Player** (Chapter 12) for playing DVDs. This program is in the Applications folder.

Windows Media Player *is,* however, available in an aging Macintosh version, paradoxical though that may sound. You can download it from *www.microsoft.com/mac.*

Windows Messenger

OS X's instant-messaging, audioconferencing and videoconferencing software is called Messages, and it's described in Chapter 20.

WordPad

The TextEdit program (in the Applications folder) is a word processor along the lines of WordPad. It can even open and save Word files, as WordPad can.

Zip files

Zip files exist on the Mac, too, and you create them almost the same way: Control-click (or right-click) a file or folder and choose Compress from the shortcut menu.

OS X: THE MISSING MANUAL

The Master OS X Secret Keystroke List

Here it is, by popular, frustrated demand: the master list of every secret (or not-so-secret) keystroke in OS X Mountain Lion, including all the keys you can press during startup. Clip and post to your monitor (unless, of course, you got this book from the library).

Note: For the most part, the following list doesn't include the keystrokes already listed in your menus, like ⌘-P for Print, ⌘-S for Save, and so on.

Startup Keystrokes

Keys to Hold Down	Effect
C	Starts up from a CD or DVD
N	Starts up from a network server
R	Resets the laptop screen
⌘-R	Starts Recovery Mode
T	Puts the Mac into FireWire or Thunderbolt Target Disk mode
Option	Shows icons of all startup disks and partitions, so you can choose one for starting up
Shift-Option-⌘-Delete	Starts up from external drive (or CD)
Option-⌘-P-R	Zaps the parameter RAM (PRAM) (hold down until you hear the second chime)
⌘-V	Shows Unix console messages during startup, logout, and shutdown

⌘-S	Starts up in single-user (Unix command-line) mode
Mouse down	Ejects a stuck CD or DVD
6 and 4 keys	Starts up in 64-bit mode
Shift	Just after powering up: Turns off *kernel extensions*
Shift	Just after logging in: Prevents Finder windows and startup items from opening (they'll return the next time you start up)

In the Finder

⌘-space	Highlights Spotlight box
Option-⌘-space	Opens Spotlight window
→, ←	Expands or collapses a selected folder in list view
Option-→	Expands a folder in a list view *and* all folders inside it
Option-←	Collapses a folder *and* all folders inside it
⌘-↑	Opens parent folder
Shift-Option-⌘-↑	Selects the desktop
⌘-↓ (or ⌘-O)	Opens the selected icon
Option-click the flippy triangle	Expands or collapses all folders within that window
Tab	Selects next icon alphabetically
Shift-Tab	Selects previous icon alphabetically
space bar	Opens Quick Look preview of highlighted icon(s)
space bar	During a spring-loaded folder drag, opens the disk or folder under the mouse immediately
Option-click Zoom button	Enlarges the window to full screen
Option-click Close button	Closes all Finder windows
Option-click Minimize button	Minimizes all windows (works in most apps)
⌘-drag an icon	Moves it into, or out of, the System folder (administrator password required)
Option	Changes Quick Look button to Slideshow button
⌘-drag	Rearranges or removes menulets or toolbar icons
⌘-click window title	Opens a pop-up menu showing the folder path

⌘ Menu

Option	Changes "About This Mac" to "System Information"
Shift-⌘-Q	Logs out
Shift-Option-⌘-Q	Logs out without confirmation box

Finder Menu

Option	Eliminates the confirmation box from Empty Trash and Secure Empty Trash
Shift-⌘-Delete	Empties the Trash
Shift-⌘-Delete	Puts back a highlighted icon in the Trash
Shift-Option-⌘-Delete	Empties the Trash without confirmation box
Option-Empty Trash	Empties the Trash without confirmation box
⌘-comma	Opens Preferences
⌘-H	Hide this program
Shift-⌘-H	Hide other programs

File Menu

⌘-N	New Finder window
Shift-⌘-N	New folder
Option-⌘-N	New smart folder
⌘-O or ⌘-↓	Open
Control-⌘-O	Open in new window
Option-click File menu	Changes "Open With" to "Always Open With"
⌘-W	Close window
Option-⌘-W	Close All
⌘-I	Get Info
Option-⌘-I	Show Inspector
Control-⌘-I	Summary Info (of selected icons)
⌘-D	Duplicate
⌘-L	Make Alias
⌘-Y	Quick Look
Option-⌘-Y	Slideshow (of selected icons)
⌘-R	Show Original (of alias)
⌘-T	Add to Sidebar
Shift-⌘-T	Add to Favorites
⌘-Delete	Move to Trash
⌘-E	Eject

⌘-F Find
Shift-⌘-F Find by Name

Edit Menu

⌘-Z Undo
⌘-C, ⌘-X, ⌘-V Copy, Cut, Paste
Shift-⌘-V Move copied icons to this window
⌘-A Select All
Option-⌘-A Deselect All

View Menu

⌘-1, -2, -3, -4 Icon, list, column, Cover Flow views
Control-⌘-1, -2, -3, -4, -5, -6 Arrange by Name, Date Modified, Date Cre-
 ated, Size, Kind, Label

Option Changes "Clean Up Selection" to "Clean Up"
Option Changes "Arrange By" to "Sort By"
Option-⌘-T Show/Hide Toolbar
Option-⌘-S Show/Hide Sidebar
⌘-J Show/Hide View Options palette

Go Menu

⌘-[, ⌘-] Back, Forward
⌘-↑ Enclosing folder
Control-⌘-↑ Enclosing folder in new window
Option-⌘-T Show/Hide Toolbar
Shift-⌘-F All My Files window
Shift-⌘-O Documents window
Shift-⌘-D Desktop window
Option-⌘-L Downloads window
Shift-⌘-H Home window
Option Makes Library command appear
Shift-⌘-C Computer window
Shift-⌘-R AirDrop window
Shift-⌘-K Network window
Shift-⌘-A Applications window
Shift-⌘-G Go to Folder
⌘-K Connect to Server

Window Menu

⌘-M	Minimize
Option-⌘-M	Minimize All
Option	Changes "Bring All to Front" to "Arrange in Front"

Help Menu

Shift-⌘-?	Opens help search box

Power Keys

Control-⏏	Brings up dialog box for Shut Down, Sleep, or Restart
Option-⌘-⏏	Sleep
Control-Option-⌘-⏏	Shut Down
Control-⌘-⏏	Restart

The Dock

Option-click a Dock icon	Switches to new program and hides previous one
Option-⌘-D	Hides/shows the Dock
⌘-click a Dock or Stacks icon	Reveals its actual Finder icon
Option-⌘-click a Dock icon	Switches to this program and hides all others
Control-click a Dock icon	Opens a shortcut menu
Hold mouse down on Dock app icon	Triggers Exposé (shows all windows of that app in miniature)
⌘-drag an icon onto a Dock icon	Prevents Dock icons from moving, so you can drop your icon onto one of them
⌘-drag a Dock icon	Drags the actual item
Option-⌘-drag an icon onto the Dock	Forces a Dock program to open the icon you're dropping on it

Managing Programs

Option-click a Dock icon	Switches to new program and hides the previous one
Option-click in a window	Switches to new program and hides the previous one
⌘-H	Hide this program's windows (works in most apps)
Option-⌘-H	Hide all *other* programs' windows (most apps)
Control-←, →	Previous/next Spaces screen

F9	Exposé: Shrinks and tiles all windows in all programs
Shift-F9	Exposé: Shrinks and tiles all windows in slow motion
F10	Exposé: Shrinks and tiles all windows in front-most program
F11	Exposé: Flings all windows in all programs to edges of screen, revealing desktop
F12	Dashboard widgets
⌘-Tab	Press and release: Switches back and forth between current and previous open program
⌘-Tab	Hold down ⌘: Displays floating icons of open programs. Press Tab repeatedly to cycle through them. (Add Shift to cycle *backward* through open programs on the Dock.)
⌘-~	Switches to next open window in this program. (Add Shift to cycle in the opposite direction.)
Option-⌘-Esc	Opens the Force Quit dialog box (to close a stuck program)
Shift-⌘-3	Captures the screen image as a PNG file on your desktop
Shift-⌘-4	Produces a crosshairs; drag to capture a selected portion of the screen as a PNG graphics file. (Press space to get the "camera" cursor that snips out just a menu, icon, or window.)
⌘-space	Switches keyboard layout (if more than one is installed). (If you use Spotlight, you must choose a different keystroke for this function.)

Dialog Boxes

⌘-comma	Opens Preferences dialog box (any Apple program)
Esc	"Clicks" the Cancel button in a dialog box
Enter or Return	"Clicks" the OK button (or other blue, highlighted button) in a dialog box
Option-⌘-F	Moves the insertion point to the search box in most Apple programs
⌘-D, ⌘-R	"Clicks" the Don't Save or Replace button

Trackpad Gestures

You can change many of these gestures, or turn them on and off, in the Trackpad pane of System Preferences. But here are the factory settings:

Two-finger click	Right-click
Two-finger drag up/down	Scroll up/down
Two-finger swipe left-/right	Move among open Web or document pages
Two-finger swipe from right edge	Open Notification Center
Two-finger pinch or spread	Zoom in or out of a picture, PDF, or Web page
Two-finger rotate	Rotate photo or PDF
Two-finger double-tap (not click)	"Smart zoom" into Safari or Preview page
Three-finger swipe up	Mission Control
Three-finger swipe down	Show all windows in this app (Exposé)
Three-finger swipe left/right	Previous/next Spaces screen or full-screen app
Three-finger drag	Move window
Three-finger tap (not click)	Look up this word in Dictionary
Four-finger pinch	Open Launchpad
Four-finger spread	Reveal desktop (Exposé)

Magic Mouse Gestures

A few important gestures also work on the top surface of the Magic Mouse:

One-finger double-tap (not click)	"Smart zoom" into Safari or Preview page
Two-finger double-tap (not click)	Mission Control
One-finger swipe left-/right	Move between open Web or document
Two-finger swipe left/right	Previous/next Spaces screen or full-screen app

Index

Index

Colophon

This book was written on a 13-inch 2012 MacBook Air that remained attached to David Pogue like an appendage. It was updated from the Lion edition of the same book directly in Adobe InDesign, with substantial assistance from the typing-shortcut program TextExpander *(www.smileonmymac.com)*.

The book's screen illustrations were captured with Ambrosia Software's Snapz Pro X *(www.ambrosiasw.com)*, edited in Adobe Photoshop CS5.5 *(www.adobe.com)*, and overlaid with labels, lines, and circles in Adobe Illustrator.

The book was designed and laid out in Adobe InDesign CS5.5 on a Mac Pro. The fonts include Formata (as the sans-serif family) and Minion (as the serif body face). To provide the symbols (, ⌘, ⏏, and so on), Phil Simpson designed two custom fonts using FontLab Fontographer.

The book was then exported as Adobe Acrobat PDF files for final transmission to the printing plant.

OS X Mountain Lion

THE MISSING CD

There's no CD with this book; you just saved $5.00.

Instead, every single Web address, practice file, and piece of downloadable software mentioned in this book is available at *missingmanuals.com* (click the Missing CD icon). There you'll find a tidy list of links, organized by chapter.

Don't miss a thing!
Sign up for the free Missing Manual email announcement list at missingmanuals.com. We'll let you know when we release new titles, make free sample chapters available, and update the features and articles on the Missing Manual website.